Advanced Level Accounting

3rd Edition

Harold Randall

FCA FCCA ACMA ATII MICM

Letts Educational
The Chiswick Centre
414 Chiswick High Road
Chiswick
London
W4 5TF

020 8996 3333

Acknowledgements

The author would like to express thanks to the following for giving permission to reproduce past examination questions.

The Associated Examining Board (AEB)
University of Cambridge Local Examinations Syndicate (Cambridge)
University of London Examinations and Assessment Council (London)
University of Oxford Delegacy of Local Examinations (Oxford)
Northern Examinations and Assessment Board (JMB)
Welsh Joint Education Committee (WJEC)
Northern Ireland Schools Examination and Assessment Council (NI)

Each question used is cross referenced to the appropriate examination board and the title of the paper. The examination boards accept no responsibility whatsoever for the accuracy or method of working in any of the answers to questions given.

A CIP catalogue record for this book is available from the British Library

ISBN 1 85805 162 2

Copyright © Harold Randall 1996

First edition 1990
Reprinted 1991
Second edition 1993
Reprinted 1994, 1995
Third edition 1996
20 19 18 17 16 15 14 13

Printed and bound in Great Britain by
Ashford Colour Press Ltd, Gosport, Hampshire

Pageset by
Philippa Jarvis, Suffolk.

Letts Educational Ltd, a division of Granada
Learning Ltd. Part of Granada plc.

Preface

Aim

Advanced Level Accounting aims to provide all the support needed for the successful pursuit of studies leading to Advanced Level Accounting examinations. In one volume it encompasses the financial, management and social accounting aspects of the subject that are included in the syllabuses for single subject accounting at Advanced Level.

The book assumes that the principles of the subject have been taught and contains a resumé of those principles in the explanatory text which is, however, sufficient also to be used as a course text book.

Need

Teachers, lecturers and students studying Advanced Level accounting have long been aware of the dearth of texts prepared specifically for their requirements. All Advanced Level syllabuses embrace financial, cost and management accounting. An awareness of social accounting is also expected by some of the examining Boards. Accounting text books abound but none has been prepared with all these requirements adequately met within the covers of a single volume; all of which invariably means that two text books must be selected from those that have been written with other syllabuses and needs in mind.

The principles of double entry bookkeeping and accounting remain the same regardless of the differences of approach by examiners; but it is those differences of approach that often put a particular gloss, some would even say a peculiar gloss on occasions, on Advanced Level accounting questions.

Hence the need for a text prepared specifically for these examinations.

Advanced Level Accounting embraces some parts of the topics which are not treated adequately, or at all, in most of the other standard texts. Indeed, in the author's experience as an examiner, it is evident that many students taking Advanced Levels are ill prepared both in the substance of topics and in the techniques required for attempting them in examinations.

The author hopes and believes that *Advanced Level Accounting* will meet the perceived needs for a specially written text for Advanced Levels.

Approach

Each chapter begins with an introduction to the topic or topics to be considered. Aspects of each topic are then explained in sections of manageable length.

The text leads the student step by step through the stages of each topic from what would be the known to the unknown had the subject not already been taught. It serves the dual purpose of reminding students of what they should already have been taught and, hopefully, helping to clarify areas of study in which they have not already a good understanding.

Each principle is clearly demonstrated by an example and followed by one of the many self-test exercises to which answers are given at the back of the book. The text is rounded off on a positive note with 'Key Points to Remember' including examination hints and a brief mention of errors commonly committed in examination scripts.

Finally, each chapter concludes with additional exercises drawn from all the Advanced Level examining bodies in the U.K.

Answers to the Advanced Level examining body questions/exercises are provided free of charge by the publishers to lecturers using the book as a course text (applications by lecturers should be on departmental headed notepaper).

Preface To Second Edition

I have taken the opportunity in preparing this edition to introduce new material covering departmental and branch accounts, leasing and hire purchase, value added statements, job, contract and process costing and inflation accounting.

I have developed the treatment of overheads in Chapter 18 and replaced the chapter on statements of source of application of funds with one on cash flow statements. I have also amplified the text in places to explain various points more fully. Up-to-date practice examination questions at the end of chapters have been included, while older questions which are **current** (reflecting typical examination requirements) have been retained. Out-of-date questions have been removed. In order to help students to know exactly what they should aim at in the examination room, a new chapter (29) has been included which shows typical examination questions with fully worked answers and tutorial notes.

I would like to thank all those who have shown an interest in *Advanced Level Accounting* and made useful suggestions for this edition. In particular, I would wish to thank my colleague at Southgate College, Don Payne, and Mr A. Alpay of Waltham Forest College for checking my manuscript.

Preface to the third edition

In the short time since I prepared the second edition there have been a number of developments which now call for a new edition of *Advanced Level Accounting*. Further Financial Reporting Standards (FRS) have been published and some of those have already been introduced into A Level syllabuses or will no doubt be included before long. There have also been revisions of syllabuses by examining bodies.

I have completely re-written Chapter 9 to give students a simple but comprehensive introduction to companies and company accounts with emphasis on aspects of the topic which constantly feature in examinations. New material has been added to other chapters to aid better understanding of the topics treated in them. Some multi-choice questions have been added to certain chapters to test students' understanding of topics. M-CQs are also useful preparation for the Cambridge new syllabus which includes a Multi-Choice Question paper as a means of testing candidates across the syllabus. It is my belief that this form of testing will be adopted increasingly by other examining bodies.

Many otherwise good students manage to grasp theory but experience difficulty in applying it to examination questions. I have therefore included some fully worked past examination questions with tutorial notes in some chapters to ease the transition from the 'learning' stage to the 'doing' stage.

I have removed the Practice Examination Papers which formed Appendix 1 in the first two editions of the book. They were not past papers set by the examining boards. They will now be found in the Lecturers' Supplement where they may be photocopied for classroom use if required.

HJR
July 1996

Contents

Study and Examination Hints

Study

1. Accounting at Advanced Level is by no means easy; some would say it can be difficult at times. It certainly makes demands upon those who would study it. You will achieve success only if you are diligent in your studies throughout the duration of your course. Given the right determination to succeed, you will find Advanced Level Accounting fully supportive of your efforts.

2. Set aside regular periods of study. Allow nothing and nobody to interfere with these periods.

3. Plan a programme of work which will include regular revision sessions and ensure that you complete the syllabus in ample time before the examination.

4. When concentration begins to wane during your study period, take a short break and then return to your study refreshed. Time spent when concentration has gone is wasted time.

5. Master each part of a topic before moving on to the next part. Work through all examples; make sure you understand them. Tick each figure to show you have understood where it has come from, how it is calculated and how it is being used.

6. Use the examination questions at the ends of chapters for additional practice and for revision. It is always helpful to try questions set by other Boards as well as those of the Board for which you are studying. Reworking the same question more than once at intervals can be helpful. The results will show you whether or not you have mastered the solution to that question and other similar ones; it will also help you to become more familiar with the examiner's style.

7. Attempt some questions under simulated examination conditions and time yourself. It takes discipline to adhere to a time constraint and that discipline must be developed as part of the exercises you do in your studies.

In The Examination

1. Make sure you have all your equipment, pens, calculator etc. ready and in good order on the day before your examination.

   ❑ Do not use coloured inks; continually changing pens for headings, underlinings etc. wastes time which is very precious in the examination room. You are sitting an examination in accounting, not in art! The examiner marks the papers in red and may be irritated by the confusion caused by your use of the same colour.

   ❑ Do not use correcting fluids; not only do they also waste time but they should not be permissible in accounting work anyway. Correct an error by deleting it with a single horizontal stroke and rewriting the correct amount in full above the deletion.

   ❑ Do not write your answers in pencil. It may be difficult to read and examiners are not expected to mark scripts which are too difficult to read.

2. Arrive at the centre in good time. Arriving late and flustered is no way to sit an examination.

3. Familiarise yourself with the rubrics (instructions) on the front of the examination paper.

4. Read all questions through before starting to write. Begin with the question you can do best and do the others in the order of your preference. You do not have to do the questions in numerical order, but you should assemble them in that order if you have answered the questions on loose sheets as opposed to an answer booklet.

5. Read the questions carefully and make sure you understand them and know what you are required to do. There is no point in wasting time giving the examiner something he has not asked for; it will not gain any marks.

6. Calculate the amount of time you should allocate to each question. It is a good idea to write on the question paper the time you should quit a question even if it is unfinished – and keep to it.

7. Submit all workings. You should not waste any valuable time in jotting down your workings but they should be Legible (the examiner should be able to read them) Logical (the steps should follow in order; do not omit any.) Labelled (indicate briefly what each figure is.) Lucid (the examiner should be able to follow them easily.)

1 Revision of basic principles, concepts and techniques

Chapter objectives

Students at this level should already have a good grasp of the basic principles, concepts and techniques of accounting. This chapter is intended as a brief summary of these as they are important for a proper understanding of the chapters that follow. They are:

- classification of ledger accounts; understanding the significance of debit and credit entries and balances
- trial balances; their uses and limitations
- trading and profit and loss accounts
- balance sheets
- provision accounts
- books of prime entry
- concepts to be applied in accounting.

Since a sound grasp of these topics is essential to the successful study of advanced level accounting this chapter is intended as a brief revision of them.

1.1 The double entry model

A ledger account is the history of a particular type of transaction or of the dealings of a business with a particular person.

The 'giving' of a benefit is credited to the account of the 'giver'; the corresponding 'receipt' appears as a debit in the account 'receiving' the benefit.

Entries in ledger accounts represent:

ACCOUNT

Debit side	Credit side
Cash, goods or services received	Cash, goods or services given
Assets	Liabilities
Expenses	Revenue, income
Losses	Profits

See cash posting decision chart on the following page.

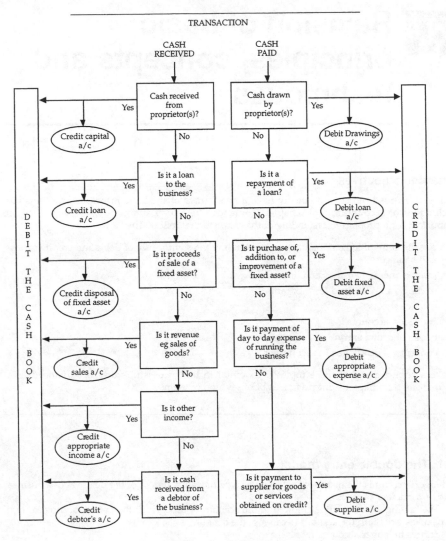

Cash posting decision chart

Classification of ledger accounts

See the diagram on page 3 opposite and memorise it to help you remember:

1. which accounts normally have credit balances and which debit;
2. in which financial statement balances on these accounts are expected to appear.

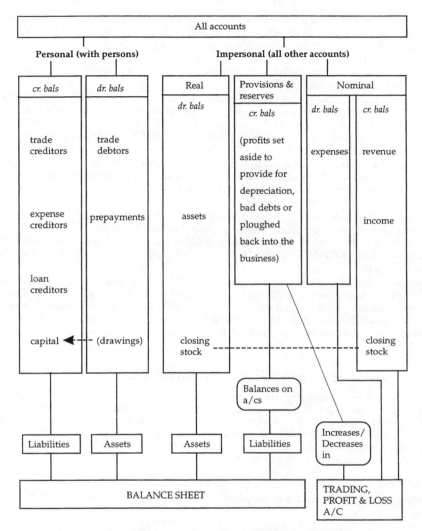

DIAGRAMMATIC REPRESENTATION OF ACCOUNTS CLASSIFICATION

Diagrammatic representation of accounts classification

1.2 Trial balance

A trial balance is a list of all balances existing on ledger accounts at a given date. Always describe it as a 'trial balance at (date)'.

The trial balance distinguishes between those accounts with debit balances and those with credit balances. If the total of the debit balances equals the total of the credit balances, the ledger accounts are, on the face of it, arithmetically correct.

Errors not disclosed by trial balances

1. **Errors of omission.** Transactions omitted completely from the books of account, e.g. if a purchase of stationery for £400 is omitted from the cash book it will not have been posted

from the cash book to the debit of the Postage and Stationery account. The debit side of the Postage account and the credit side of the cash book will both be understated by £400.

2. **Errors of commission.** These occur when a posting is made to a wrong account, but to one of the correct type, e.g. if car insurance, £200, has been posted to Property Insurance account, the debit balance on Property Insurance account will be overstated. and the Motor Expenses account will be understated, by £200.

3. **Errors of principle.** These arise when a posting is made to an account which is not only the wrong account, but one of the wrong type, e.g. an item of capital expenditure (acquisition of, or improvement to, a fixed asset) should be posted to a real (asset) account. If it is posted to a nominal (expense) account in error, it will have been treated wrongly in principle. This would occur if the cost of purchasing a motor van were posted to Motor Expenses account.

4. **Complete reversal of entries.** If a cheque drawn for cash, £300, is debited in the bank account and credited in the cash account, the bank account balance will be overstated by £600 and the cash account understated by the same amount. An amount posted to the wrong side of an account causes an error twice its own size.

5. **An error of original entry.** A transaction recorded in the accounts totally in the wrong amount will not affect the trial balance. e.g. if purchases for £1,200 are credited in the cash book and debited in the Purchases account as £2,100 the cash book debit balance will be understated by £900 but the debit balance on Purchases account will be overstated by the same amount.

6. **Compensating errors** are errors which cancel each other out. As their name implies, they do not affect the trial balance. If purchases, £3,980, are posted to the Purchases account as £3,890, the debit balance on that account will be £90 too little. If the balance on the Fixtures & Fittings account £4,450, has been copied onto the trial balance as £4,540, the addition of £90 to that balance will cancel out the error on the Purchases account, i.e. the errors will 'compensate' each other.

1.3 Conversion of list of balances into trial balance

Examination questions frequently require students to prepare trial balances from lists of ledger balances or to correct trial balances which have been incorrectly prepared in the question paper. It tests a candidate's ability to recognise which accounts should be in credit and which in debit.

In any case, where final accounts have to be prepared from a list of balances, the best plan is to convert the list into a trial balance at once. This can be done quickly and easily by deleting the credit balances and re-writing them in another column to the right of the original.

1.3.1 Example

The following list of balances was extracted from Quincey's ledger at 31 December 19–2

	£
Sales	36,000
Purchases	25,000
Returns inwards	820
Returns outwards	400
Stock at 1.1.-9	2,500
Wages	4,000
Rent and rates	1,600
Carriage inwards	750
Carriage outwards	925
Interest receivable	600
Premises	20,000
Provision for depreciation of premises	2,000
Motor vehicles	8,000
Provision for depreciation of motor vehicles	4,000
Trade debtors	4,500
Trade creditors	1,250
Provision for doubtful debts	200
Balance at bank	1,225
Capital	30,750
Drawings	5,880

Required

Prepare a trial balance for Quincey's business as at 31 December 19-2.

(Note to student: Draft the answer by converting the list of balances into a trial balance on the question paper. The answer may then be quickly 'fair-copied' onto the answer sheet.)

Answer

Quincey: trial balance as at 31 December 19-2

	Dr. £	Cr. £
Sales	~~36,000~~	36,000
Purchases	25,000	
Returns inwards	820	
Returns outwards	~~400~~	400
Stock at 1.1.–9	2,500	
Wages	4,000	
Rent and rates	1,600	
Carriage inwards	750	
Carriage outwards	925	
Interest receivable	~~600~~	600
Premises	20,000	
Provision for depreciation of premises	~~2,000~~	2,000
Motor vehicles	8,000	
Provision for depreciation of motor vehicles	~~4,000~~	4,000
Trade Debtors	4,500	
Trade Creditors	~~1,250~~	1,250
Provision for doubtful debts	~~200~~	200
Balance at bank	1,225	
Drawings	5,880	
Capital	~~30,750~~	30,750
	75,200	75,200

1.3.2 Exercise: correcting a trial balance

Colombo is an inexperienced accounts assistant and has prepared the following trial balance at 31.12.19-9:

	Dr. £	Cr. £
Premises	80,000	
Plant and machinery	65,000	
Office furniture	15,000	
Provision for depreciation: plant and machinery	35,000	
Provision for depreciation: office furniture	10,000	
Stock at 1.1.-9	6,000	
Stock at 31.12.-9		7,200
Debtors	5,500	
Creditors		2,700
Purchases	47,000	
Carriage inwards	1,200	
Carriage outwards		2,100
Sales		90,000
Returns inwards		2,600
Returns outwards	1,400	
Provision for doubtful debts	500	
Selling and distribution expenses	20,800	
Administration expenses	15,400	
Discounts received	2,000	
Discounts allowed	1,800	
Drawings		12,600
Capital		133,400
	306,600	250,600

Required

Prepare a corrected trial balance for Colombo as at 31 December 19-9.

1.4 Depreciation

Depreciation is the difference between the cost of an asset and its sale or scrap proceeds on disposal.

Depreciation is spread over the useful life of an asset by one of the following methods in order to match the cost of the use of that asset to the revenue earned by it.

Main methods of calculating annual depreciation charges:

1. **Straight line.** The depreciation is a fixed charge every year calculated as a percentage of the original cost, as follows:

$$\frac{\text{Cost of asset less estimated residual value at end of useful life}}{\text{estimated useful life (in years)}}$$

2. **Reducing balance.** Depreciation is calculated as a fixed percentage of the written down value of the asset at the beginning of the year. The percentage is calculated as follows:

$$1 - \sqrt[n]{\frac{R}{C}}$$

     where   n = number of years of estimated useful life
                  R = estimated residual value of asset
                  C = cost of asset.

3. **Depletion unit.** Used for mines, quarries, oil wells etc. The annual charge is calculated as follows:

$$\text{Cost of asset} \times \frac{\text{quantity of material extracted}}{\text{estimated total resources of asset}}$$

4. **Machine hour.** For machinery, aircraft, ships etc. It is calculated as follows:

$$\text{Cost of machine} \times \frac{\text{no. of hours used in year}}{\text{estimated total hours of use during useful life}}$$

5. **Revaluation.** Used for assets for which detailed records cannot conveniently be maintained, e.g. loose tools and other small items of equipment. It is calculated as follows:

    Value of asset at beginning of year plus additions during the year
    less value of asset at end of year.

6. **Sum of the digits.** For various assets. Calculated as in the following example:

Cost of asset: £30,000. Estimated useful life 5 years.

		Depreciation
	£	£
Year 1	£30,000 × $5/15$	10,000
2	£30,000 × $4/15$	8,000
3	£30,000 × $3/15$	6,000
4	£30,000 × $2/15$	4,000
5	£30,000 × $1/15$	2,000
	$15/15$	30,000

Accounting entries to record provision for depreciation:

    Debit Profit & Loss account
    Credit Provision for Depreciation of (asset) account
    With the annual charge for depreciation

The annual charge for depreciation is an attempt to match a proportion of the cost of an asset to revenue earned by it in a year. It is a bookkeeping entry. It does not involve any payment of the money; it is a non-monetary item in the Profit and Loss account.

In the balance sheet, deduct the balances on the Provisions for depreciation accounts from the relevant assets in order to show the net book (or written down) values of the fixed assets. See 1.7 for a preferred layout of fixed assets in a balance sheet.

The net book value of an asset, as shown in a balance sheet, is the balance of the original cost not yet written off against revenue; it is the amount being carried forward at the date of the balance sheet to be written off against future revenue from that asset. It is not intended to represent what the asset is worth; still less is it a statement of what the asset will fetch if sold.

Profits and losses on disposal of fixed assets frequently have to be calculated in examination questions.

Calculation:

Proceeds of disposal – (original cost – aggregate depreciation to date of disposal)

i.e. Proceeds of disposal – written down value at date of sale

= profit/(loss)

1.5 Provisions for doubtful debts and discounts

Provisions for doubtful debts

The provisions may be:

specific – against identified debts
or general – based on a percentage of debtors
or a combination of both methods.

Accounting entries

Increase in existing provision:

Debit Profit & Loss account
Credit Provision for Doubtful Debts

Decrease in existing provision:

Debit Provision for Doubtful Debts
Credit Profit & Loss account

Provisions for discounts allowed

Calculate as percentage of those debts which have not become overdue, after deducting any part of the provision for doubtful debts based on those debtors.

In the balance sheet, deduct the provisions for doubtful debts and discounts allowed from the trade debtors.

Discounts receivable on outstanding creditors should be ignored in order not to anticipate profits (prudence.)

1.6 Trading and profit and loss accounts

Give every financial statement you prepare a proper heading; without it the statement will be meaningless. Trading and profit and loss account headings should be as follows:

Name
Trading and profit and loss account
Period covered by the account

For example:

John Brown
Trading and profit and loss account for the year ended 31 December 19-9

Within the trading account, the form in which 'cost of sales' is presented should recognise the correct calculation of the amount of purchases for the period. This figure should include the cost of the goods, less goods returned, plus the cost of getting the goods to their present location (carriage inwards).

Recommended presentation of a trading account where all the above elements are present:

	£	£	£
Sales			25,000
less cost of sales:			
Opening stock		5,000	
Purchases	12,000		
less returns outwards	900		
	11,100		
add carriage inwards	400	11,500	
		16,500	
less closing stock		4,000	12,500
Gross profit			12,500

1.7 Balance sheets

A balance sheet heading should recognise that it is the 'position' statement of a business at a particular point in time. For example:

John Brown
Balance sheet as at 31 December 19-9

Fixed assets

Within a balance sheet, the order in which fixed assets are shown is important. Start with the most permanent assets, progressing to the less permanent ones, e.g.:

Freehold property
Leasehold property
Plant and machinery
Motor vehicles
Office furniture, machinery, etc.

Fixed assets should be displayed where possible to show the total 'cost' and total 'depreciation' as well as the total of 'net book values' where the information is available.

Recommended lay-out of the 'fixed asset' section of a balance sheet

	Cost	Depn	Net
	£	£	£
Fixed assets			
Premises	50,000	20,000	30,000
Plant and machinery	35,000	25,000	10,000
Office furniture	4,000	3,000	1,000
	89,000	48,000	41,000

Current assets

Current assets should be shown in inverse order of liquidity. The most liquid form of current asset is cash; the least liquid form is stock. The usual order items is:

Stock
Debtors
Prepayments
Bank balance
Cash in hand

(The published accounts of limited companies must be considered separately; see Chapter 10.)

1.8 Provisions and reserves

Provisions are amounts set aside out of profits to provide for:

(i) depreciation of fixed assets;
(ii) possible losses caused by bad debts;
(iii) liabilities, the amounts of which cannot be estimated with substantial accuracy when a balance sheet is being prepared.

All other amounts set aside out of profits are reserves. Provisions and reserves are always represented by credit balances.

In a balance sheet, provisions for depreciation should always be deducted from the fixed assets to which they refer, and provisions for bad debts should be deducted from debtors.

1.9 Books of prime entry

You must have a thorough understanding of the purposes of the books of prime entry, and the manner in which the items in them are posted to the books of double entry.

The books of prime entry with which you should be familiar are:

Cash book (and petty cash book where one is kept)
Purchase day book (Purchases journal)
Purchases returns book (Goods Outwards book)
Sales day book (Sales journal)
Sales returns book (Goods Inwards book)
Journal

The cash book is the only book of prime entry which is also a ledger account, and therefore part of the double entry system. The other books are memoranda books only and both aspects of every transaction in them must be posted to the appropriate ledger accounts.

Never prepare a journal entry showing a posting to be made to a book of prime entry; such books are not ledger accounts or, indeed, part of the double entry system at all.

The functions of the books of prime entry are to:

(i)   collect together all transactions of a similar nature in order.

(ii) facilitate reference back to original documents (invoices, etc.)

(iii) control the completeness of all information posted to the accounts.

(iv) reduce the volume of entries made in nominal ledger accounts as only daily (weekly, or monthly) totals need be posted to the sales, purchases etc. accounts.

The purposes of, and the postings made from, the books of prime entry, other than the cash book and journal are:

Book of prime entry	Individual items posted to	Period totals posted to
Purchases day book (purchases on credit)	Credit of suppliers' accounts	Debit of Purchases account
Purchases Returns book (goods returned to suppliers)	Debit of suppliers' accounts	Credit of Purchases Returns/Goods outwards
Sales day book (sales on credit)	Debit of customers' accounts	Credit of Sales account
Sales returns (goods returned by customers)	Credit of customers' accounts	Debit of Sales Returns /Goods Inwards

The journal is used as a book of prime entry for:

(i)   correction of errors;
(ii) transfers between ledger accounts;
(iii) purchases and sales of fixed assets;
(iv) opening entries in new set of ledgers;
(v) any other transaction for which there is no other book of prime entry.

1.10 Bank reconciliation statements

The three steps in preparing a bank reconciliation statement are:

Step 1:   Compare the bank columns of the cash book with the bank statements. Tick all those receipts and payments which can be found in both the cash book and the statements. When this has been done, there may be some unticked items in the cash book and some unticked items in the bank statements.

Step 2:   Bring the cash book up to date by entering the unticked bank statement items into the cash book and calculate the new balance.

Step 3:   Enter the unticked cash book items into the bank reconciliation statement.

Reasons for preparing bank reconciliation statements

1.   To discover items not entered and errors in the cash book.

2. To ensure that the cash book entries are complete. Items missing from the cash book will not have been recorded in other ledger accounts and the business records will be unreliable.

3. To discover bank errors.

4. To discover dishonoured cheques.

5. To monitor 'stale' cheques (those which have not been banked by the payees within six months).

6. To check on fraud and embezzlement.

1.11 The application of concepts in the preparation of final accounts

The historical cost convention

The reason for using the convention

Assets and expenses are recorded in ledger accounts at the actual amounts expended on these items because this has the virtue of being objective, that is, beyond dispute. In most cases, the actual cost of goods or services is ascertainable from invoices, contracts and in some instances, by a firm's costing records if its own workforce has been used to build or install its plant or machinery.

An alternative to recording assets and expenses at cost is to record them at a valuation. This introduces subjectivity into the accounting records as it is likely that no two people may agree on the value of the assets or services.

Some disadvantages of the convention

It fails to allow for the changing value of money (see Chapter 28)

The application of the historic cost convention also means that assets and services having no cost cannot be recorded in ledger accounts.

The concept of money measurement

Only transactions which can be expressed in money terms are recorded in ledger accounts.

Some of the benefits enjoyed by a firm may arise from expenditure which it has incurred but may be incapable of being evaluated in money terms.

Example

A firm may incur expenditure in providing safe and pleasant working conditions for its staff and generally looking after their welfare. The management treat the staff well and pay for them to be properly trained; they consult them on many matters to do with the running of the firm. As a result, it has a loyal, highly motivated staff, but it is not possible to express staff morale and motivation in money terms and record it in financial accounts.

Other items which cannot be measured in monetary units are:

the competence of management;

the skill of the workforce;

the existence of a full or growing order book;

the attitude of local residents to the existence of a factory in the neighbourhood (it provides employment for local people, or it pollutes the atmosphere, etc).

The concept of realisation

Revenue should not be recorded in the accounts before it has been realised. A sale is deemed to take place when the goods which are the subject of the sale have been replaced by cash or a debtor for the sale.

Revenue should not be overstated by sales which have not been realised. A promise by a potential customer to purchase goods at a future date does not amount to a sale. Goods sent on sale or return remain the property of the seller until the consignee intimates, or does some act to imply, that he has accepted the goods.

The matching concept

The purpose of this concept is to ensure that revenue, other income and expenses are recognised in the financial period in which they accrue or are incurred. This is necessary if the financial statements are to state fairly the profit or loss for a given period and the state of the business at the period end.

Revenue should be recognised in the period in which it arises. Sales which have not been realised in a period should not be credited in the trading account of that period. Sales which have been realised should be credited in the trading account even if cash has not been received in respect of the sales. As the recognition of sales is not restricted to those made on a cash basis, trade debtors at the period end are shown on the balance sheet.

Expenses must be accounted for in the profit and loss account as incurred and not on the basis only of payments made in the period. Expenses which have been incurred but not paid must be accrued, and the accrual shown on the balance sheet. Expenses which have been paid but which relate to a later period should not be debited in the profit and loss account covering the period in which the payment was made but should be shown as prepayments on the balance sheet.

Capital expenditure is matched against annual revenue earned by the assets concerned by annual charges for depreciation of fixed assets. The charges for depreciation in the profit and loss account are intended to allocate the original costs of the fixed assets against revenue in an equitable manner over the useful lives of the assets.

Accounting which does not apply the matching concept is said to be on a cash basis and, by its very nature, is unable to show a reliable profit or loss for a period or the position of the business at any stated date.

The concept of materiality

This concept permits the normally accepted treatment of transactions of any particular kind to be disregarded if the amount (or substance) involved is insignificant in the context of the business as a whole.

The concept does require that all items which are sufficiently material to affect evaluations or decisions should be disclosed.

Two factors to be considered in deciding on materiality are:

(a) Will the cost of adhering strictly to form be greater than the benefit obtained? If it is going to cost an additional £10,000 in staff salaries to ensure that the year end stock figure is £50,000 and not £48,000, it is clearly not worth the cost.

(b) Will disclosure or non-disclosure of the item in financial statements influence the evaluations or decisions of persons reading the statements?

The consistency concept

The purpose of this concept is to enable sensible comparisons to be made of the results of a business and its financial position from one year to another. To this end, all items of a similar nature should be treated in a similar manner both within the same accounting period and from one period to the next.

The methods of depreciating fixed assets should be applied consistently from one year to the next. If the straight line method is selected for a type of asset when it is first acquired, the basis should be used for that asset in all future years; it would not be acceptable to change to the reducing balance method in a subsequent year in order to manipulate profit. (A change of method would only be permissible if it could be shown that the new method will give a fairer presentation of the results and of the financial position of the business.)

The basis of valuing stock should be used consistently from one period to the next.

The prudence concept

The prudence concept is concerned with ensuring that the capital of a business is not depleted by overstatement of profit. If an owner's drawings exceed his profits, the capital of the business is depleted. If the process is carried too far, the point will be reached when the business is seriously undercapitalised to the extent that insufficient funds are available to pay creditors or to replace worn out assets. Unless new capital can be introduced, the business is finished.

Prudence is about

(i) profits not being overstated;
(ii) losses being provided for as soon as they are recognised.

The application of this concept requires that:

(a) revenue is not anticipated before it has been realised;

(b) all costs of earning revenue brought to account in the period are charged against that revenue

Prudence is an overriding concept; if, in a given situation, the application of another concept would conflict with prudence, prudence takes precedence over that other concept.

The going concern concept

The going concern concept is concerned with the amounts at which assets are shown in the balance sheet. It requires that business accounts shall be prepared on the assumption that a business is a going concern. If there is any intention to discontinue the business, or to substantially curtail its scope of operations in the foreseeable future, the effect of any such action should be reflected in the balance sheet.

If a business is a going concern, its fixed assets will normally be shown in the balance sheet at cost less aggregate depreciation to date, i.e. at net book value. Stock should be shown at cost or net realisable value, whichever is the less. If a business is not a going concern, the assets should be shown in the balance sheet at the amount they may be expected to realise when sold, bearing in mind that, in an enforced sale, the proceeds may be lower than expected. The effect of writing assets down in this way will increase the amounts charged normally for depreciation in the profit and loss account.

Key points to remember

1. A good understanding of your first-year studies in book-keeping and accounting is essential as you approach advanced level accounting. If you find difficulty with any of the topics in this chapter, revise your first-year studies thoroughly before you proceed any further.

2. Many advanced level accounting questions are concerned to test your understanding of basic concepts: entity, duality, money measurement, realisation, matching, prudence, consistency and going concern.

3. The application of the accounting equation is an essential technique in solving many questions, especially those concerned with incomplete records.

4. Make sure you fully understand the principles of double entry book-keeping, in particular, which account should be debited and which credited to record any transaction. Learn to think in terms of 'double-entry'.

5. You should be able to distinguish readily between those accounts which normally have debit balances and those which have credit balances.

6. Many examination marking schemes reserve marks for the following points, which you should learn and practise in all your exercises.

   (a) When required to write up ledger accounts, take trouble to write them up properly. Each account should be appropriately headed, each transaction dated and the name of the other account in which the corresponding debit or credit entry will be found should be entered as part of each posted amount. Keep to the normal 'T' account format.

   (b) If an account has a balance to be carried down, show the balance also as brought down on the following day to complete the double entry.

   (c) Trading and profit and loss accounts and balance sheets should be headed correctly as in 1.6 and 1.7 above.

   (d) Whenever appropriate, set trading accounts out as shown in 1.6 above.

   (e) Whenever appropriate, set fixed assets out in balance sheets as shown in 1.7 above. Marks may be awarded for total cost and total depreciation figures.

7. Present all your answers neatly; give them suitable headings which accurately describe them. If you make a mistake, cross the whole amount in question out and re-write the correct amount above it. You will not lose marks for crossings out.

Questions

The following draft balance sheet as at 31 March 19-7 of David Sparks, retail trader, was prepared quickly after the year end.

	£	£
Fixed assets:		
Freehold property – at cost	24,000	
– provision for depreciation	4,800	19,200
Motor vehicles – at cost	18,000	
– provision for depreciation	9,000	9,000
		28,200
Current assets:		
Stock	13,000	
Debtors	9,000	
Balance at bank	1,600	
	23,600	
Less: Current liabilities – creditors and accruals	3,800	19,800
		48,000
Represented by:		
Capital – at 1 April 19-6		50,000
Add net profit for the year ended 31 March 19-7		10,000
		60,000
Less drawings		12,000
		48,000

After the draft balance sheet had been prepared, the following discoveries were made:

(a) A quantity of goods sent to T. Beal on a sale or return basis remained unsold on 31 March 19-7. These goods had cost David Sparks £600 and were expected to sell for £1,000. In preparing the draft accounts for the year ended 31 March 19-7, it was assumed that all the goods had been sold, on credit, by T. Beal as planned. T. Beal is to be paid a commission of 2% on the gross proceeds of all sales made for David Sparks.

(b) Debtors include £200 due from K. Peacock who has now been declared bankrupt. It is unlikely that any money will be received for this debt.

(c) A provision for doubtful debts at 31 March 19-7 of 2% of debtors at that date is to be created.

(d) Provision is to be made for electricity charges of £700 accrued due at 31 March 19-7.

(e) On 1 October 19-6, David Sparks hired (leased) a motor van for one year from Hire Vehicles Limited; the hire charge of £3,000 was paid in advance. However, in preparing the above draft accounts, it was assumed that the motor van had been purchased for £3,000.

Additional information:

The depreciation policy applied in the accounts of David Sparks is as follows:

Freehold property: 10% per annum on cost;
Motor vehicles: 25% per annum on cost.

Required

A corrected balance sheet as at 31 March 19-7

(25 marks)
(CAMBRIDGE)

Note

Questions requiring adjustments to balance sheets are common. A sound method of working is all important if errors are to be avoided. The following is a recommended method. Copy the draft balance sheet out in columnar form, placing the credit balances in brackets. Use a separate column for each 'discovery' making sure that credit adjustments are placed in brackets. Ensure that you preserve the double-entry principle by checking that each column adds up to zero. Tick each adjustment on the question paper as you make it so that you do not miss one. Before you cross-add each row for the amended balance sheet column, make sure that all the discoveries on the question paper have been ticked.

13

Working

	Draft bal. sheet £	(a)	(b)	(c)	(d)	(e)	Corrected bal. sheet £
Freehold Ppty.	24,000						24,000
Prov.depn.	(4,800)						(4,800)
Motor vehicles	18,000					(3,000)	15,000
Prov.depn.	(9,000)					375	(8,625)
Stock	13,000	600					13,600
Debtors	9,000	(1,000)	(200)	(156)			7,644
Prepayments						1,500	1,500
Bank	1,600						1,600
Creditors	(3,800)	20			(700)		(4,480)
Capital	(50,000)						(50,000)
Profit	(10,000)	(20)	200	156	700	(375)	
		400				1,500	(7,439)
Drawings	12,000						12,000
Total	0	0	0	0	0	0	0

Answer

David Sparks
Corrected balance sheet as at 31 March 19-7

	Cost £	Depn. £	Net £
Fixed assets			
Freehold property	24,000	4,800	19,200
Motor vehicles	15,000	8,625	6,375
	39,000	13,425	25,575
Current assets			
Stock		13,600	
Debtors		7,644	
Prepayments		1,500	
Balance at bank		1,600	
		24,344	
Less Current liabilities			
Creditors and accruals		4,480	19,864
			45,439
Capital at 1 April 19-6			50,000
Add net profit for the year			7,439
			57,439
Less drawings			12,000
			45,439

Multiple choice questions

1 A debit balance on a ledger account may represent
   A cash or goods or services given, or liabilities, or revenue, or a loss
   B cash or goods or services given, or liabilities, or revenue, or a profit
   C cash or goods or services received, or assets, or expenses, or a loss
   D cash or goods or services received, or assets, or expenses, or a profit

2 Clarkson received a cheque for £600 from P. Green. He credited the £600 to the account of P. Grey in error. He had made
   A a compensating error
   B an error of commission
   C an error involving the complete reversal of entries
   D an error of principle

3 Paula received a cheque for £384 from a customer, M. Banks. She debited the cheque in error as £348 to the account of another customer, M. Darke. The difference between the two sides of the trial balance will be

A   £36

B   £696

C   £732

D   £768

4   A trial balance will not agree if an invoice from Ace Servicing Co in the sum of £5,000 is

A   entered in the Purchase Day Book as £500

B   entered in the Sales Day Book

C   entered on the credit side of Ace Servicing Co's account in the Purchase ledger without being entered in the Purchase Day Book

D   omitted from the Purchase Day Book

5   A trial balance will not agree if

A   a payment to Machine Sales Ltd for a machine purchased on credit is entered in the Machinery Repairs account in error

B   a refund of an insurance premium is credited to Rent Payable account

C   a sales invoice for £196 is entered into the Sales Day Book as £169

D   the total of the Discounts Received column in the cash book is debited to Discounts Allowed account.

6   Buchan Ltd purchases a motor lorry on 1 July 1992 for £15,000. The company depreciates its motor vehicles at the rate of 20% per annum. on cost. It sold the motor lorry on 31 March 1996 for £3,000. In the year to 31 December 1996 Buchan Ltd will

A   credit profit and loss account with a profit on sale of motor lorry, £2,250

B   credit profit and loss account with a profit on sale of motor lorry, £3,000 and debit profit and loss account with depreciation of motor lorry, £1,500

C   debit profit and loss account with depreciation of motor lorry £750 and loss on sale of motor lorry £750

D   debit profit and loss account with a loss on sale of motor lorry, £1,500

7   Scott plc purchased a machine for £40,000 on 1 May 1992. It sold the machine on 30 September 1995 for £18,000. The company depreciates all machinery owned at 31 December each year at the rate of 25% using the reducing balance method. In the year to 31 December 1995, Scott plc will

A   credit profit and loss account with a profit on disposal of £1,125

B   debit profit and loss account with a loss on disposal of £1,125

C   credit profit and loss account with a profit on disposal of £5,344

D   debit profit and loss account with a loss on disposal of £5,344

8   Thomas Ltd provides annually for depreciation of its fixed assets at the rate of 20% on cost. At 31 December 1995, the provision provided to date on one of its fixed assets amounted to £8,000. The asset had cost £12,000. The asset was sold on 30 April 1996 for £2,200. In the profit and loss account for the year to 31 December 1996, the entries in respect of the asset will be

A   provision for depreciation nil; profit on sale £1,800

B   provision for depreciation £800; loss on sale £1,000

C   provision for depreciation £800; profit on sale £1,000

D   provision for depreciation £2,400; profit on sale £600

9   Alpha Ltd makes a provision for bad debts equal to 4% of its debtors at the year end. Debtors at 31 December 1995 amounted to £39,000. Debtors at 31 December 1996 amounted to £42,620 of which £1,570 were known to be bad. The debit to profit and loss account for the year ended 31 December 1996 for the provision for bad debts will be

A   £82

B   £144.80

C   £1,642

D   £1,704.80

10 Beta Ltd had the following information recorded in its books at 31 December 1996.

	£
Credit sales invoiced to customers during the year	120,600
Goods sent on sale or return to customers during December (customers had not indicated their acceptance of the goods by 31 December)	25,800
Goods despatched to customers on 31 December but not invoiced to them until 2 January 1997)	17,420
	163,820

Beta Ltd should credit its trading account for the year to 31 December 1996 with

A £120,600

B £138,020

C £146,400

D £163,820

11 Jones' financial year ended on 30 June 1995. His stock at that date was valued at cost at £17,000. He adds a mark-up of $\frac{1}{3}$ to all goods. On 29 June 1995 Smith had told Jones that he would buy goods for £900 on July 1. Jones sales for the year, ignoring Smith's intended purchase, amounted to £183,450. In his accounts for the year ended 30 June 1995

Jones should record

A sales of £183,450 and stock at £16,700

B sales of £183,450 and stock at £17,000

C sales of £184,350 and stock 1t £16,700

D sales of £184,350 and stock at £16,775

12 On 1 January 1995 Pettit paid an insurance premium of £1,250 for the 15 months to 31 March 1996. when he prepared his profit and loss account for the year to 31 December 1995, Pettit debited only £1,000 of the insurance premium to the account and carried the balance of £250 forward to 1996.

This was an example of the concept of

A going concern

B matching

C prudence

D realisation

Further examination questions

1 The following trial balance has been extracted from the books of Idyia Evans.

	£	£
Stocks at 1 May, 19-7	25,187	
Personal drawings	18,500	
Trade debtors and creditors	22,776	10,238
Rent and rates	12,800	
Advertising and promotion	1,750	
Insurance premiums	1,900	
Purchases and sales	99,817	182,208
Bad debts written off	218	
Development agency loan		50,000
Repairs and modifications to plant	1,581	
Vehicle operating expenditure	2,575	
Wages and salaries	45,012	
Loan interest at 15%	3,750	
Provision for doubtful debts		500
Heating and lighting	7,500	
Carried forward	243,366	242,946

	£	£
Brought forward	243,366	242,946
Plant and machinery – cost	63,260	
– provision for depreciation		18,925
Office expenses	5,817	
Owner's capital account at 1 May, 19-7		53,000
Motor vehicles – cost	21,557	
– provision for depreciation		11,317
Bank overdraft		7,812
	334,000	334,000

Additional information is to be taken account of as follows:

(i) Stock at 30 April, 19-8 was valued at £27,515.

(ii) Loan interest for the six months ended 30 April, 19-8 is outstanding. Reconciliation of the bank account with statements received from the bank indicate that interest of £851 and charges of £1,025 have been entered by the bank. These amounts had not been included in the cash book at 30 April, 19-8.

(iii) Rent paid in advance at 30 April, 19-8 amounts to £870. Rates assessed as due but not yet paid are to be included at £1,200.

(iv) Of the repairs and modifications to plant, £1,000 was expended on safety equipment as required by government health and safety regulations.

(v) Depreciation of plant is to be provided for at 10% of cost and of motor vehicles at 20% of their written-down values.

(vi) Advertising costs of £250 and wages and salaries due of £415 are to be allowed for.

Required

Trading and profit and loss accounts for the year ended 30 April, 19-8 and the balance sheet as at that date. (28 marks)

(WJEC)

2 You are required to explain to a friend with no accounting knowledge why revenues and expenses recorded in a profit and loss account do not necessarily represent receipts and payments made during the period which the profit and loss account covers. Use **three** examples to illustrate your explanation, and finally respond to your friend's query as to why the complications involved in your explanation are felt to be necessary. (16 marks)

(JMB)

3 Ms Price set up a business on 1 January 19-6 with a loan of £10,000 from a friend and £10,000 of her own. With this cash she purchased a machine for manufacturing a new board game called 'Chairmanship'. She submits the following account for her first year's trading.

	£
Cash received from sale of games (2,000 @ £20 each)	40,000
Less cash paid:	
Wages	14,000
Rent	4,000
Raw materials	6,800
General expenses	2,400
Part repayment of loan	3,000
Net income	9,800

Ms Price is somewhat doubtful whether the above statement is very reliable and asks you to prepare a Trading and Profit and Loss Account and Balance Sheet. In addition to the above information you discover:

(i) Ms Price has sold a further 300 units at £20 each for which she has not yet been paid;

(ii) she owes £1,800 for materials already received;

(iii) the machine has a ten year life and no anticipated scrap value;

(iv) Ms Price owes her secretary £400 for working overtime;

(v) there are raw materials at cost £800 left in stock but no work in progress or finished goods;

(vi) the rent payment covers the period from 1 January 19-6 to 31 March 19-7;

(vii) the wages include £8,000 withdrawn by Ms. Price for her own use;

(viii) she has incurred further general expenses of £200 which she has not yet paid.

You are required to:

(a) prepare a revised Trading and Profit and Loss Account for the year ended 31 December 19-6 and a Balance Sheet as at that date; (18 marks)

(b) explain to Ms Price the accounting conventions you have adopted which are primarily responsible for the difference between the original account and your revised Trading and Profit and Loss Account and why such conventions are considered necessary. (7 marks)

(JMB)

4   A company has recently acquired a new machine at a cost of £30,000. The machine has an estimated useful life of three years and an anticipated disposal value of £3,000. Details of units produced by the machine and repair and maintenance costs are as follows.

	Units	Repair and maintenance £
Year to 31 December 19-7 (actual)	14,000	600
Year to 31 December 19-8 (estimate)	16,000	1,400
Year to 31 December 19-9 (estimate)	10,000	2,000

(a) You are required to calculate the annual depreciation charge for each of the three years using the following methods:
   (i)   straight line;
   (ii) reducing balance using the rate of 54%;
   (iii) units produced. (6 marks)

(b) Draft a report to the directors on the merits and problems associated with each of the above methods. (11 marks)

(JMB)

5   Rapid Deliveries Ltd is a small parcels delivery company. In order to ensure a high level of efficiency the vans used are regularly replaced by the latest models. It is company policy not to retain any van for more than four years. The depreciation applied relates to this policy. The company uses the straight line method and calculates the annual depreciation charge on the cost of the vans held at the year end. It assumes no residual value.

Details of the vans appearing in the balance sheet as at 31 December 1990 were:

	£
Vans at cost (5 vans)	81,000
Less depreciation to date	38,750
	42,250

During 1991 two vans of the fleet were sold and three were purchased. The following details relate to these transactions:

Sales:

Date sold	Van reference	Year bought	Cost (£)	Sale proceeds (£)
1 April 1991	1	1988	14,000	4,000
1 July 1991	2	1988	15,000	3,350

Purchases:

Date purchased	Van reference		Cost (£)
1 April 1991	6		19,000
1 August 1991	7		20,000
1 November 1991	8		21,000

Van 3 was bought in 1989 at a cost of £16,000 and vans 4 and 5 were purchased in 1990 at the same price each.

Required

(a) The ledger accounts for the year ended 31 December 1991:
   (i)   vans at cost account;
   (ii) vans provision for depreciation account;
   (iii) vans disposal account. (9 marks)

(b) Explain why it is important to provide for depreciation.   (5 marks)

(c) State clearly what are the merits of the straight line method of depreciation.   (3)
(AEB)

6   Chefs and Co operate a small private catering business for domestic and other social occasions. The company commenced business on 1 March 1990 when it purchased a specially designed food delivery van (G11ABC) for £12,000. A depreciation rate of 25% using the reducing balance method is applied.

As trade expanded it was agreed to replace the existing delivery van by an improved model and in addition, a smaller ordinary van was to be purchased. On 1 March 1992 a quotation for a nearly new improved model (J22CBC) was received. The details were as follows:

	£
Basic cost	19,782
Number plates	12
Comprehensive insurance	238
10 gallons of diesel fuel	26
Delivery charge	56
Road fund licence	200
Specially fitted food containers for the van	1,200
Service and parts	110
Sign-writing on van	150
	21,774
Trade-in allowance for G11ABC	6,200

The other small van (J33CBC) was quoted at an 'on the road' price of £9,620. This figure, apart from the basic cost, only included the road fund licence of £120.

Both quotations were accepted and the vehicles concerned were purchased on 1 March 1992.

Required

(a) The following ledger accounts for the period 1 March 1990 until 28 February 1993:
    (i) vehicles at cost account;
    (ii) depreciation provision on vehicles account;
    (iii) disposal of vehicles account.   (20 marks)

(b) The relevant extracts in the profit and loss account for the year ended 28 February 1993 showing the effects of all the transactions involved.   (6 marks)

(c) The relevant extract in the balance sheet as at 28 February 1993 relating to the vehicles.   (4 marks)

(d) Explain what is meant by the term 'depreciation' and why it is necessary to provide for it   (18 marks)
(AEB)

7   The chief accountant of Warton Ltd has balanced the cash book of the company at the year end, which was 31 March 1994. At that date the cash book showed a credit balance of £4,560 as opposed to a debit balance on the same date in the previous year. The company had made a profit for the year ended 31 March 1994. When the monthly bank statement for March was received it did not agree with the balance in the cash book so an investigation was carried out to establish the reasons for the difference.

The following matters were revealed.

(1) A cheque paid for advertising on 10 March 1994 for £2,148 had been entered in the cash book as £2,184.

(2) On 20 March 1994 a debtor had informed the company that a direct transfer of £1,330 had been remitted to Warton Ltd's bank account. This was in settlement of a sales invoice for £1,400. The entry made in the cash book was £1,400.

(3) A standing order to a trade association for £480 had been paid by the bank on 2 March 1994 but no entry appeared in the cash book.

(4) Cheques amounting to £12,444 had been sent to suppliers and entered in the cash book during March 1994 but had not yet been presented to the bank.

(5) Cheques received from customers amounting to £20,160 had been received by branches of the company, paid into local branches of the bank on 31 March 1994 and entered in the cash book. The bank had not credited these on the March statement.

Required

(a) Adjust the cash book of Warton Ltd and bring down the corrected balance as at 31 March 1994. (10 marks)

(b) Prepare a bank reconciliation statement as on 31 March 1994 which clearly shows the original balance on the March bank statement. (8 marks)

(c) Explain why it is important to prepare a bank reconciliation statement. (6 marks)

(d) Explain why a bank balance may be reduced during a year in spite of a company having made a profit. (10 marks)

(AEB)

2 Control or total accounts

Chapter objectives

For this topic you should be able to:

☐ state the uses of control accounts

☐ recognise the sources of the entries in control accounts

☐ prepare control accounts from given information

☐ correct errors in control accounts and purchases and sales ledgers when the control account balances disagree with the ledgers they are controlling

2.1 Control accounts

The nature and uses of control accounts

A control account is so called because it controls a section of the ledger. By control is meant that the balance on the control account should equal the total of the balances in the section of the ledger it is controlling. A sales ledger control account controls the sales ledger; a purchase ledger control account controls the purchase ledger. If there is a difference on the trial balance, the control accounts will show whether or not any of the difference is in the sales or purchase ledger accounts. If the control accounts agree with the balances on the sales and purchase ledgers, the difference must lie in the nominal or general ledger.

If the customer accounts are numerous, there may be more than one sales ledger; or separate sales ledgers may be kept for customers in different geographical regions. A separate control account will be required for each sales ledger. The same applies if there is more than one purchase ledger.

Control accounts are kept in the general or nominal ledger, not in the ledgers they are controlling. The reason for this is given in 4. below.

Purposes of control accounts

1. To act as independent checks on the arithmetical accuracy of the aggregates of the balances in the sales and purchase ledgers.
2. To provide totals of debtors and creditors quickly when a trial balance is being prepared.
3. To identify the ledger or ledgers in which errors have been made when there is a difference on a trial balance.
4. To act as an independent internal check on the work of the sales and purchase ledger clerks, to detect errors and deter fraud. Duties should be so divided between staff that the sales and purchase ledger clerks have no access to the control accounts, and the person who maintains the control accounts has no access to the sales and purchase ledger accounts. For this purpose, it is important that the control accounts should be kept in the nominal ledger and not in the purchases and sales ledgers.

Form of control accounts

Control accounts contain in total form all transactions which have been posted as individual items to the sales and purchase ledgers. They are often known as Total accounts.

The periodic totals of each type of transaction are obtained from the books of prime entry.

The following example shows very simply how the principle works for a sales ledger control account.

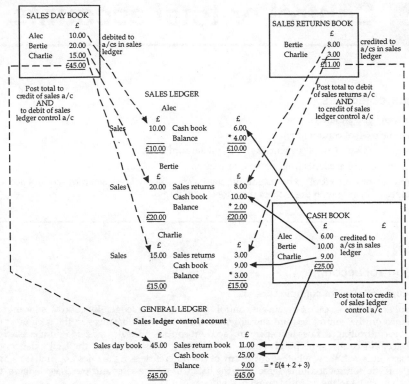

A purchase ledger control account works on a similar principle. See the diagram on the following page.

The usual contents of the ledger control accounts are as follows with the sources of the entries shown in brackets.

Sales ledger control account

Debit side	Credit side
Total of sales ledger debit balances brought forward from previous period	Total of sales ledger credit balances brought forward from previous period
Credit sales for period (total of sales day book)	Sales returns for period (total of sales returns book)
Refunds to customers (cash book)	Cash received from debtors (cash book)
Dishonoured cheques (cash book)	Cash discounts allowed (discount column of cash book)
Interest charged to customers on overdue accounts (journal)	Bad debts written off (journal)
Bad debts previously written off now recovered (journal)	Cash received in respect of bad debts previously written off (cash book)
	Sales ledger balances offset against balances in purchase ledger (journal)
Total of any sales ledger credit balances at end of period carried forward	Total of sales ledger debit balances at end of period carried forward

Notes

1. Cash sales are not recorded in the sales ledger control account.

2. Provisions for doubtful debts do not feature in sales ledger control accounts because the provision accounts are kept in the general ledger, not the sales ledger.

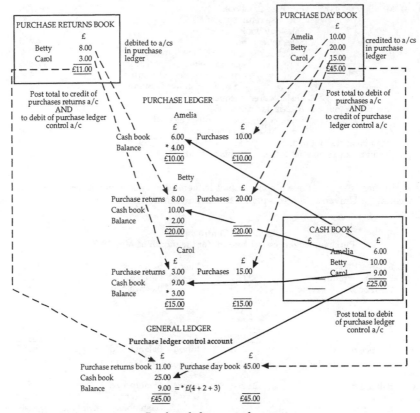

Purchase ledger control account

Debit side	Credit side
Total of purchase ledger debit balances (if any) brought forward from previous period	Total of purchase ledger credit balances brought forward from previous period
Total of goods returned to suppliers (purchase returns book)	Total credit purchases (purchase day book)
Total of cash paid to suppliers (cash book)	Refunds from suppliers (cash book)
Cash discounts received (discount column of cash book)	
Purchase ledger balances offset against balances in sales ledger (journal)	Interest charged by suppliers on overdue invoices (purchase day book or journal)
Total of credit balances at end of period carried forward	Total of debit balances, if any, at end of period carried forward

Note: purchases made for cash do not feature in the purchase ledger control account.

Double entry book-keeping requires that either the sales and purchase ledger accounts are treated as part of the double-entry system and the control accounts are regarded as memoranda accounts only; or the control accounts are treated as part of the double entry and the sales and purchase ledger accounts are regarded as memoranda accounts.

2.1.1 Example

The following data has been extracted from the books of Universal Controls plc for the month of May 19-9:

			£
May 1	Purchase ledger balances brought forward	– dr	405
		– cr	6,210
	Sales ledger balances brought forward	– dr	21,566
		– cr	975

May 31	Monthly totals of:	Purchase day book	44,220
		Purchase returns book	2,630
		Sales day book	86,920
		Sales returns book	4,220
		Cash book – cash paid to suppliers	38,900
		– cash received from debtors	77,840
		– discounts received column	1,400
		– discounts allowed column	3,120
		Dishonoured cheques	784
	Analysis of journal:	Bad debts written off	1,260
		Sales ledger balances offset against purchase ledger balances	2,640
	Debit balances on purchase ledger accounts at 31 May 19-9		600
	Credit balances on sales ledger accounts at 31 May 19-9		800

Required

From the information given above prepare a sales ledger control account and a purchase ledger control account for Universal Controls plc for the month of May 19-9.

Answer

Universal Controls plc
Purchase ledger control account for the month of May 19-9

19–9		£	19–9		£
May 1	Balance b/d	405	May 1	Balance b/d	6,210
May 31	Purchases returns	2,630	May 31	Purchases	44,220
	Cash book – payments	38,900		Balance c/d	600
	– discounts	1,400			
	Contra – sales ledger	2,640			
	Balance c/d	5,055			
		51,030			51,030
June 1	Balance b/d	600	June 1	Balance b/d	5,055

Sales ledger control account for the month of May 19–9

19–9		£	19–9		£
May 1	Balance b/d	21,566	May 1	Balance b/d	975
May 31	Sales	86,920	May 31	Sales returns	4,220
	Dishonoured cheques	784		Cash book – receipts	77,840
	Balance c/d	800		– discounts	3,120
				Bad debts written off	1,260
				Contra – purchase ledger	2,640
				Balance c/d	20,015
		110,070			110,070
June 1	Balance b/d	20,015	June 1	Balance b/d	800

2.1.2 Exercise: practice in preparing control accounts

The following information has been extracted from the books of Total Controls Ltd for the month of September 19-0.

		£
Sales ledger balances at 1 September 19-0	– Dr	5,000
	– Cr	76
Purchase ledger balances at 1 September 19-0	– Dr	124
	– Cr	3,600
Sales for September	– cash	2,400
	– credit	21,790
Purchases for September	– cash	1,020
	– credit	14,500
Goods returned by credit customers		1,760
Goods returned to suppliers (originally bought on credit)		440
Cash received from debtors		20,450
Cash paid to creditors		11,120
Discounts allowed		580
Discounts received		276
Bad debts written off		424

	£
Cash received in respect of a bad debt previously written off	70
Debtors' cheques returned by bank unpaid	826
Interest debited to accounts of overdue debtors	36
Balances in sales ledger offset against purchases ledger accounts	1,200
Balance on Provision for Doubtful Debts account at 1 September 19-0	200
Sales ledger credit balances at 30 September 19-0	150
Purchase ledger debit balances at 30 September 19-0	80

The directors of Total Controls Ltd have decided that the Provision for Doubtful Debts should be adjusted to 5% of debtors at 30 September 19-0.

Required

The Sales Ledger Control account and the Purchase Ledger Control account for the month of September 19-0 for Total Controls Ltd.

Tutorial note

Not all of the information in this question is required for your answer.

2.2 Control accounts and trade discounts

Trade discount is not recorded in double entry book-keeping. Examiners may introduce trade discount into control account questions: the entries in the control accounts should be net of trade discount. Do not credit the purchase ledger control account with the full list price of purchases, with a 'contra' entry for the trade discount on the debit side; this will not be acceptable to the examiner.

Cash discount, which is a discount for prompt payment, is, of course, recorded in the ledger accounts, including the control accounts.

2.2.1 Example

P. Witte is a retailer of goods and he obtains his supplies from various sources, all of which allow him 10% discount off list prices.

Witte's records show the following information for the month of October, 19-4

		£
Purchase ledger balances at 1. 10.-4	– Cr	16,420
	– Dr	1,724
Purchases at list prices		210,000
Purchase returns at list prices		4,640
Cheques sent to suppliers		189,500
Cash discounts received		4,700
Purchase ledger balances at 31.10.-4	– Dr	1,360
	– Cr	?

Required

P. Witte's Purchase ledger control account for the month of October 19-4.

Answer

P.Witte
Purchase ledger control account for the month of October 19-4

19-4		£	19-4		£
Oct 1	Balance b/d	1,724	Oct 1	Balance b/d	16,420
Oct 31	Purchases returns	4,176	Oct 31	Purchases	189,000
	Cheques	189,500		Balance c/d	1,360
	Discounts	4,700			
	Balance c/d	6,680			
		206,780			206,780
Nov 1	Balance b/d	1,360	Nov 1	Balance b/d	6,680

Workings

	List price	less 10%	Net
	£	£	£
Purchases	210,000	21,000	189,000
Purchases returns	4,640	464	4,176

2.2.2 Exercise: practice in treatment of trade discount in control accounts

Dodgson deals in specialised electronic equipment. The following information is extracted from his records for the three months ended 30 June 19-3.

		April £	May £	June £
Balances on purchase ledger at 1 April	dr	625		
	cr	32,000		
Purchases at retail prices		150,000	200,000	180,000
Purchases returns at retail prices		4,000	6,000	5,000
Cheques sent to creditors		100,200	148,000	130,000
Discounts received		2,500	3,800	2,700
Debit balances at month end		410	570	220

Dodgson buys his goods at 20% less than the retail price.

Required

Dodgson's purchase ledger control account for each of the three months for the period in question.

2.3 Correction of errors

These questions are favourites with examiners. It is not possible to frame a concise set of rules to deal with this sort of problem. The best approach is to ask the following questions.

About the book-keeping errors:

1. What entries, if any, have been made in the accounting records?

2. What entries should have been made?

3. What entries are required to correct the errors?

About the records affected:

4. Has the error affected the sales/purchase ledger accounts?

5. Has the error affected the control account?

It is worth remembering the following points:

(i) a transaction omitted from a book of prime entry will be omitted from the personal account in the ledger *and* from the control account.

(ii) a transaction entered incorrectly in a book of prime entry will result in the error being repeated in the personal account in the ledger *and* in the control account.

(iii) a transaction copied incorrectly from a book of prime entry to a personal account will **not** affect the control account.

(iv) an error in the addition of a book of prime entry affects the control account but *not* the personal account.

2.3.1 Example

Tortelier has extracted the balances from his sales ledger as at 31 July 19-1 and they total £17,200, which total Tortelier has inserted as trade debtors in his trial balance. The trial balance does not agree, neither does the schedule of debtors with the balance on the sales ledger control account.

An examination of the records reveals the following errors:

1. The discount allowed column in the cash book has been overcast by £200.

2. An invoice for a sale to Jones has been completely omitted from the books. The invoice is for £84.

3. Goods returned by Smithson, which had been invoiced to him in the sum of £160, had been correctly entered in the sales returns book, but debited to his account as £106.

4. Goods with a selling price of £1,000 had been sent on 'Sale or Return' to Gregson. Although Gregson has not yet indicated his intention to purchase the goods, the transaction has been entered in the sales day book.

5. A bad debt of £50 has been written off in the sales ledger but this item was not entered in the journal.

Required

(a) The sales ledger control account, showing clearly the original balance on the account at 31 July 19-1, and the entries required to adjust the account for the above items.

(b) A calculation of Tortelier's corrected trade debtors figure at 31 July 19-1.

Answer

Tutorial notes:

Error 1 Sales ledger accounts not affected but the total of discounts allowed in the control account is £200 too much. Correct control account by debiting it with £200.

Error 2 Invoice £84 omitted entirely from books. Correct by debiting Jones' account in sales ledger, and the control account, with £84. (Credit sales account: £84).

Error 3 Returns from Smithson: his account in the sales ledger, only, affected. Credit his account with £106 to cancel erroneous debit plus £160 to record the return of goods.

Error 4 Goods on sale or return should not be treated as sales until the consignee has indicated his intention to purchase the goods. The sale should be eliminated from both Gregson's account in the sales ledger and the control account by credit entries in both. Sales account should be debited with the amount.

Error 5 The sales ledger account is correct, only the control account is affected. Credit the £50 written off to control account.

(a)

Tortelier Sales Ledger Control Account

19-1		£	19-1		£
July 31	Balance b/d		July 31	Adjustment of goods on	
	(balancing figure)	16,784		sale or return	1,000
	Adjustment of discounts	200		Bad debt w/o	50
	Adjustment of omission				
	of Jones' invoice	84		Balance c/d [see part (b)]	16,018
		17,068			17,068
Aug 1	Balance b/d	16,018			

(b)

Calculation of revised trade debtors balance at 31 July 19-1

		£	£
Total of schedule of trade debtors before adjustment			17,200
Add: further debit – Jones			84
			17,284
Deduct: credit	– to cancel wrong debit to Smithson	106	
	– to record goods returned by Smithson	160	
		266	
	– to cancel goods wrongly debited to Gregson	1,000	1,266
			16,018

2.3.2 Exercise: practice in correcting errors in the purchase ledger and its control account

Datchett extracted the balances from his purchase ledger on 31 January 19-9 and the totals of the lists were: credit balances £15,240; debit balances £540 (made up of W. Lynne £300; P. Francis £240).

When these balances were inserted in the trial balance, there was a difference on the trial balance. Furthermore, the purchase ledger balances did not agree with the position shown by the purchase ledger control account.

Subsequently, Datchett discovered the following errors which had been made in January 19-9.

1. One page of the purchase day book had not been included in the monthly total of that book; the total of the missing page was £1,250.

2. Goods returned to Sawyer, supplier, amounting to £300 had been entered in the purchase returns book, but had been credited to Sawyer's account in error.

3. A credit note for £400 received from L. Wynne, supplier, had been debited to W. Lynne's account in error. (There is at present a credit balance of £800 on L. Wynne's account.)

4. A contra entry between James' account in the purchase ledger and his account in the sales ledger had been entered in the journal and posted to the sales ledger account correctly but the corresponding entry had not been made in the purchase ledger. The amount concerned was £380. The transfer had been recorded in the relevant control accounts.

5. The total of cheques sent to trade creditors in the month was £13,575. This had been posted to the purchase ledger control account as £15,375.

6. The total of the discounts allowed column in the cash book, £1,321, had been credited to the sales ledger control account, but had also been posted to the debit of the purchase ledger control account as discounts received. The total of the discounts received column in cash book was £1,026.

Required

(a) The purchase ledger control account for the month of January 19-9 showing clearly the balances brought forward and carried forward, and the correcting entries.

(b) A calculation of the correct totals of the debit and credit balances in the purchase ledger.

Key points to remember

1. Control accounts enable trial balances to be prepared sooner than if the purchases and sales ledger balances had to be extracted first.

2. Control accounts help to identify the ledgers in which there are errors contributing to a trial balance difference.

3. Entries in control accounts consist of periodic totals of the books of prime entry.

4. When an examination question gives a list of 'list' prices of purchases and the amount of trade discount, show the purchases 'net' in the control account.

Common errors

1. Items posted to wrong sides of control accounts.

2. Purchases/sales not posted to control accounts net of trade discount.

3. Contra entries between the sales and purchases ledgers entered in one control account only.

4. Failure to identify the purchases and sales ledgers or the control accounts as memoranda records only when correcting errors.

5. Bad debts recovered not posted to both sides of the sales ledger control account.

Questions

Fully worked examination question

(a) List the advantages of using an account to control the debtors' ledger.   (6 marks)

(b) Prepare such an account from the following:

	£
Total debtors' balances at 1 May 19-6	22,000
Cash sales for the month of May	142,000
Credit sales for May	86,000
Credit sales returned during May	420
Cash received from debtors	87,210

	£
Discounts allowed to debtors	1,415
Bad debts written off	250
Doubtful debts provision created	220
Customer's cheque returned by bank marked 'return to drawer'. The customer assures us that the cheque will be settled in June. The customer was allowed a cash discount of £16.	144
A customer has an account in the creditors ledger and it is decided to settle the two by a transfer.	85

(6 marks)

(c) State where the information for each entry in your account would be recorded before being entered in the ledger.

(6 marks)

(OXFORD)

Answer

(a) Advantages of a Debtors' Ledger Control account:

1. It provides the total of debtors quickly and easily when a trial balance is prepared.

2. It acts as an independent check on the arithmetical accuracy of the balances in the Debtors' ledger.

3. It will confirm whether or not a difference on a trial balance is caused by an error in the debtors' ledger or the control account.

4. It acts as a form of internal check to discover errors and deter fraud.

(b)

Debtors' ledger control account

19-6		£	19-6		£
May 1	Balance b/d	22,000	May 31	Sales returns	420
May 31	Credit sales	86,000		Bank	87,210
	Bank – returned cheque	144		Discounts allowed	1,415
	Discount allowed	16		Bad debts w/o	250
				Purchase ledger	85
				Balance c/d	18,780
		108,160			108,160
June 1	Balance b/d	18,780			

(c) *Entry*

Entry	*Book of Prime Entry*
Credit sales	Sales Day Book
Sales returns	Sales Returns Book
Cash received	Cash Book
Discounts	Cash Book – Discounts Allowed column
Returned cheques	Cash Book
Bad debts written off	Journal
Contras to Purchase Ledger	Journal

Multiple choice questions

1 On July 1 the debit balance on a sales ledger control account was £5,600. During the month sales invoices sent to customers totalled £16,000, and £17,200 was received from debtors. In addition, £102 was received in respect of a debt which had been written off as bad in the previous March.

The balance on the sales ledger control account at July 31 was:

A £4,298

B £4,400

C £4,502

D £6,800

2 On March 1 the debit balance on a sales ledger control account was £17,240. During the month, sales invoices sent to customers totalled £52,300. £51,760 was received from debtors.

Discounts for the month amounted to £1,455 and returns were £900. It was decided to make a provision for bad debts in the sum of £600.

The balance on the sales ledger control account at March 31 was:

A £14,825

B £14,885

C £15,425

D £17,225

3 The balance on a purchase ledger control account at May 1 was £4,270. Purchases made during the month were: credit £16,000; cash £2,150. Payments made to creditors were: cheques £17,610; cash £820.

The balance on the purchase ledger control account at May 31 was:

A £1,840

B £2,660

C £3,990

D £4,810

Further examination questions

1 The following figures appeared in the purchase ledger control account of Hudson and Co Ltd on 31 March 19-7.

	£
Creditor balances 1 April 19-6	36,846
Debtor balances 1 April 19-6	328
Discount received	1,957
Purchases	276,220
Payments to creditors	258,972
Purchase returns	3,116
Cash refunded from creditors	262
Bills payable	1,118
Debtor balances 31 March 19-7	419
Contras: sales ledger	784

The control account creditor balance at 31 March 19-7 failed to agree with the total of the list of balances of creditors extracted from the purchase ledger. Subsequent examination revealed the following errors.

(i) A credit balance of £176 on the account of a creditor had been omitted from the list of creditors balances.

(ii) Discount received of £28 had been entered in the cash book and discount received account but not in the creditor's account in the ledger.

(iii) The purchase day book had been undercast by £200.

(iv) An item of £186 in the purchase day book had been posted to the creditor's account as £168.

(v) Discount received for the month of £137 had been posted to the debit instead of the credit side of the discount received account.

(vi) Goods returned to a supplier valued at £82 had been correctly entered in the creditor's account but entered in the purchase returns account as £182.

Required

(i) Show how the control account would appear in the ledger before making any corrections.

(ii) Prepare a statement showing the adjustment of the balance in the control account in (i) above to the correct balance, giving details of the errors.

(iii) Prepare a statement reconciling the corrected balance with the totals as shown by the list of balances before the errors were found, giving details of the relevant errors. (18 marks)
(WJEC)

2   Asktrad was in the process of balancing his sales ledger at his accounting year end. The following balances were extracted from his books:

Sales ledger control account balance	£14,400 debit
Sales ledger balances	£13,650 debit
	£480 credit.

Subsequently the following items requiring adjustment were discovered:

(1) A trade debtor, A Gale, paid £660 on account. This amount was correctly entered in the cash book, but was debited to Gale's account as £600.

(2) Goods sold on credit for £2,000 to John Sparkes were correctly charged to his account but omitted from the sales day book.

(3) Goods returned by a customer for £89 had been correctly entered in the debtor's account, but entered in the returns outward book as £98.

(4) The balance of a trade debtor's account, £4,500 debit, had been set off against a balance in the purchases ledger. No adjustment had been made for this in the sales ledger control account.

(5) The total of the discounts allowed column in the cash book had been overcast by £99.

Required

(a) The sales ledger control account showing clearly the adjustments to the original balance.
                                                                          (3 marks)

(b) The total of the sales ledger balances after the adjustments for the above errors have been made.   (2 marks)

(c) Journal entries for the items (1) to (3) above. Narratives are required.   (8 marks)
                                                                             (AEB)

3   The sales ledger control account of Jack Hill for the year ended 31 December 19-5 had a closing balance of £15,380, made up as follows:

	£
W. Hopper Limited	12,340
Other debtors	3,610
	15,950
Credit balances	570
	15,380

A summarised list of entries in W. Hopper Limited's sales ledger account in the books of Hill, for the year ended 31 December 19-6, is shown in the following table:

	£
Opening balance	12,340
Invoices	6,930
Cheque returned due to insufficient funds being available	150
Journal entry (1)	260
Cheques paid to Jack Hill	5,100
Goods returned	75
Journal entry (2)	1,405

Notes:

Journal entry (1) related to the correction of an error, whereby a cheque received from a creditor in repayment of a duplicated payment made by Hill had been posted incorrectly to Hopper's account.

Journal entry (2) was made to record the transfer of a balance on Hill's purchases ledger for goods purchased from Hopper.

Other information relevant to the personal ledgers of Hill for the year ended 31 December 19-6 is:

	£
Opening creditors	16,330
Purchases	128,400
Sales (other than to W. Hopper Limited)	214,960
Cheques to creditors	97,450
Cheques from debtors (including those from W. Hopper Limited)	179,910

Jack Hill decided that half of the balance on W. Hopper Limited's sales ledger account should be provided for as a doubtful debt on 31 December 19-6. There were no other doubtful debts.

You are required to prepare

(a) the Sales Ledger Control Account in Hill's books for the year to 31 December 19-6.

(13 marks)

(b) Purchase Ledger Control account in Hill's books for the year to 31 December 19-6.

(8 marks)

(c) the entry relating to debtors appearing in Hill's balance sheet as at 31 December 19-6.

(4 marks)

(LONDON)

4   At the end of the financial year of Extra Ltd. the debit balance of £8,792 on the sales ledger control account did not agree with the total of balances extracted from the sales ledger; the latter being included in the trial balance. The following errors have subsequently been discovered.

(1) The total of the discount allowed account in the cash book had been overcast by £190.

(2) No entry had been made in the accounts relating to the writing off as irrecoverable a balance of £650 owed by James.

(3) The return of goods value £210 from Jackson, a customer, had been debited to the returns inward account but had not been posted to Jackson's account.

(4) Goods value £460 sent to a customer on a sale or return basis have been included in the sales day book. The customer has not indicated whether or not he will purchase the items.

(5) The receipt of £1,450 cash from S. Austin had been treated as a payment from S.J. Austin, a customer. The amount received related to the cash sale of a delivery van which was surplus to requirements.

Required

(a) A sales ledger control account showing clearly all the amendments to the original balance.   (8 marks)

(b) The journal entries to correct items (1), (3) and (5) above. Narratives are required.

(4 marks)

(AEB)

5   Sellabrick, a firm trading as builders' merchants, purchases stock on credit from a large number of suppliers. The company maintains a purchase ledger control account as an integral part of its double entry book-keeping system and in addition maintains supplier accounts on a memoranda basis in a purchase ledger. At the end of the financial year ended 31 May 19-7 the balance of £25,450 on the purchase ledger control account failed to agree with the total of balances from the purchase ledger. The following errors have subsequently been discovered.

(1) Goods which cost £350 and which were purchased on credit from Green, a supplier, had been entered in the purchase day book at their retail price of £600.

(2) An amount of £1,500 paid to Hunt, a supplier, had been correctly entered in the cash book but had been entered in Jackson's Account as £1,550.

(3) The return of goods purchased on credit and costing £800 had been completely omitted from the books.

(4) The purchase day book had been undercast by £2,220.

Required

(a) A purchase ledger control account showing clearly all of the amendments to the original balance.   (7 marks)

(b) A calculation showing the total of the balances in the purchase ledger before the corrections were made.   (6 marks)

(AEB)

6   Ahmed Rashid, retailer, whose accounting year end is 31 October, suffered a burglary on 23 October 1991 when a large quantity of stock was stolen along with most of the stock records. However, the following information has been obtained from the accounting records:

As at 31 October 1990 –		£
Trading stock, at cost		32,100
Sales ledger –	debit balances	24,300
	credit balances	710
Purchase ledger –	debit balances	1,100
	credit balances	33,900
Year ended 31 October 1991 –		
Purchases, at list prices		384,000
Purchases returns, at list prices		26,000
Sales		312,000
Sales returns		14,600
Bad debts written off (sales ledger)		970
Discounts allowed		1,090
Cash paid to suppliers		343,200
Discounts received		2,910
Cash received from customers		287,090
General administrative overheads		45,100
As at 31 October 1991 –		
Trading stock, at cost		38,200
Sales ledger –	debit balances	to be determined
	credit balances	530
Purchases ledger –	debit balances	390
	credit balances	to be determined

Additional information:

(i) All purchases are obtained at 10% off list prices.

(ii) Normally all sales produce a gross profit of 25% of turnover. However, during the year ended 31 October 1991, goods costing Ahmed Rashid £9,000 were sold at half normal retail price.

(iii) It can be assumed that Ahmed Rashid will receive from his insurers the cost price of the goods stolen.

(iv) All purchases and sales are on a credit basis.

Required

The following accounts for the year ended 31 October 1991:

(a) The sales ledger control account; (8 marks)

(b) The purchases ledger control account; (8 marks)

(c) The trading and profit and loss account. (9 marks)

(CAMBRIDGE)

7 Aurora Limited prepares control accounts at the end of each month. For May 1995, balances and transactions were as follows:

	£
Opening creditors	7,660
Opening debit balances on creditors' ledger	100
Opening debtors	17,100
Opening credit balances on debtors' ledger	100
Transactions for the month:	
Credit Sales	42,100
Discounts received	960
Sales returns	890
Discount allowed	700
Cheques from customers dishonoured	470
Payments to creditors	23,750
Credit purchases	33,650
Cheques from credit customers	29,420
Cash refund to customer	270
Bad debts written off	1,100
Amounts settled by contra	3,500
Closing credit balances on debtors' ledger	140
Closing debit balances on creditors' ledger	80

(a) Prepare debtors and creditors control accounts for Aurora Limited for May 1995, inserting closing balances for debtors' and creditors' balances. (16 marks)

(b) A control account will not reveal errors of omission, errors of commission or errors of original entry. Give an example of each of these types of error. (9 marks)

(LONDON)

3 Suspense accounts

Chapter objectives

For this topic you should be able to:

☐ distinguish between errors which affect the trial balance and those which do not

☐ draft suitable journal entries to correct errors

☐ write up suspense accounts, from journal entries

☐ revise the net profit or loss per draft accounts to take account of the correction of errors

3.1 Suspense accounts

When a difference exists on a trial balance and immediate checks do not disclose the cause of the difference, a suspense account may be opened in the nominal ledger. It is debited or credited with the trial balance difference. The suspense account balance is then inserted into the trial balance to make it agree, and work on production of final accounts may then proceed.

The causes of the trial balance difference must be investigated at the earliest opportunity and corrected.

A small balance remaining on the suspense account may defeat all reasonable attempts to find the difference. It may cost more in time and effort to continue to check the records than it is worth. The difference may then be written off to profit and loss account. The possibility that the difference, though small, may be concealing two or more large errors should not be overlooked.

An error will require to be corrected through the suspense account unless it is one of the six types of error that do not affect the trial balance. These are:

1. errors of omission
2. errors of commission
3. errors of principle
4. errors of original entry
5. complete reversal of entries
6. compensating errors

These types of error have been described in Chapter 1 §1.2 and a good understanding of them is essential for a proper study of suspense accounts and correction of errors.

3.2 Correction of errors

The best approach is to ask the following questions:

About the nature of the error:

(i) Is it one of the six types of error which do not affect the trial balance? If it is, do not adjust it through the suspense account. (In the rest of this chapter we shall refer to such errors as the 'six types of error').

About the correcting entries required:

(ii) What entries, if any, have already been made in the accounts?

(iii) What entries should have been made?

(iv) What entries are required to correct the error?

3.2.1 Example

Kay Singh extracted a trial balance from the books of her business as at 31 December 19-2. The trial balance totals were: £11,942 (debit) and £12,428 (credit).

Kay debited the difference of £486 to a suspense account so that she could prepare draft accounts, and the draft profit and loss account showed a provisional net profit of £4,200.

Subsequently, Kay found the following errors:

1. The debit side of the Wages account had been overcast by £100.
2. Discounts received, £45, had been posted to the suppliers' accounts but not to the Discounts Received account.
3. A sale of goods on credit to Paul Song for £120 had not been entered in the books at all.
4. A cheque received from a debtor, Ken Toon, £62, had been posted to the debit of his account.
5. The refund of an insurance premium, £30, had been debited in the cash book but no other entry had been made.
6. The purchase of some office equipment for £590 had been debited to office expenses.
7. Rent paid, £400, had been credited to Rent Receivable account.
8. Goods returned to Fast Sales Ltd, a supplier, had been credited to Fast Sales Ltd's account and debited to Purchases Returns account. The goods had originally cost £200.
9. A credit balance in the purchase ledger, £15, had been omitted from the list of balances extracted from that ledger. The total of the list had been included in the trial balance as trade creditors.
10. A purchase of office stationery, £110, had been debited to Telephones and Postages account in error.

Required

(a) The journal entries to correct the foregoing errors (narratives are not required.)

(b) The suspense account showing the correcting entries.

(c) A revised profit figure for the year ended 31 December 19-2.

Answer

(a) **Error 1**

Tutorial note: the debit balance on Wages a/c is overstated by £100. Reduce this by a credit to the account of the same amount. Not one of the 'six errors'; adjust through suspense a/c.

Journal

	Dr. £	Cr. £
Suspense	100	
Wages		100

Error 2

Tutorial note: Discounts Received a/c is short by £45 (credit). Credit that amount to the a/c. Not one of the 'six errors'; adjust through suspense a/c.

Journal

	Dr. £	Cr. £
Suspense	45	
Discounts Received		45

Error 3

Tutorial note: Paul Song £120. This is error of omission, one of the 'six types'; do not adjust through suspense a/c.

Journal

	Dr. £	Cr. £
Paul Song	120	
Sales		120

Error 4

Tutorial note: £62 posted to wrong side of Toon's a/c; item posted to wrong side of a/c produces error twice its own size. Not one of 'six types'; adjust through suspense a/c.

Journal

	Dr.	Cr.
	£	£
Suspense	124	
Ken Toon		124

Error 5

Tutorial note: omission of credit to Insurance a/c has resulted in debit balance on this a/c being overstated by £30. Credit £30 to insurance a/c. Not one of 'six types'; adjust through suspense a/c.

Journal

	Dr.	Cr.
	£	£
Suspense	30	
Insurance		30

Error 6

Tutorial note: purchase of office equipment treated as revenue expense instead of as capital expenditure; error of principle, one of 'six types'. Do not adjust through suspense a/c.

Journal

	Dr.	Cr.
	£	£
Office equipment	590	
Office expenses		590

Error 7

Tutorial note: rent paid posted not only to wrong a/c, but to wrong side of wrong account. Error is £800 (2x£400). Not one of 'six types'; adjust through suspense a/c.

Journal

	Dr.	Cr.
	£	£
Rent Receivable	400	
Rent Payable	400	
Suspense		800

Error 8

Tutorial note: Fast Sales Ltd. This is an example of complete reversal of entries and one of the 'six types'; do not adjust through suspense a/c. Reverse the original entries, using twice the cost of the goods.

Journal

	Dr.	Cr.
	£	£
Fast Sales Ltd	400	
Purchase returns		400

Error 9

Tutorial note: Balance omitted from list extracted from ledger not an error in the double entry. Correct by adding balance to list and amending item of trade creditors in trial balance. Adjust through suspense a/c by 'one sided' journal entry.

Journal

	Dr.	Cr.
	£	£
Suspense	15	

Error 10

Tutorial note: Purchase of office stationery debited to wrong expense a/c.; error of commission, one of the 'six errors'. Do not adjust through suspense a/c.

Journal

	Dr.	Cr.
	£	£
Office stationery	110	
Telephone and postages		110

(b) *Tutorial note:* In this part of the question, open the Suspense account with the trial balance difference and post from your journal entries from part (a).

Kay Singh
Suspense account

19-2		£	19-2		£
Dec 31	Difference on trial		Dec 31	Rent payable	400
	balance	486		Rent receivable	400
	Wages	100			
	Discounts received	45			
	K. Toon	124			
	Insurance	30			
	Increase in trade				
	creditors	15			
		800			800

(c) *Tutorial note:* You must now select those journal entries which affect the profit and loss account i.e. adjustments to nominal accounts. Ignore corrections which affect personal accounts or real accounts only.

Kay Singh
Calculation of corrected net profit for the year to 31 December 19-2

	Decrease (Dr)	Increase (Cr)	
	£	£	£
Net profit per draft accounts			4,200
(1) Reduction in wages		100	
(2) Increase in discounts received		45	
(3) Increase in sales		120	
(5) Reduction in insurance premiums		30	
(6) Reduction in office expenses		590	
(7) Reduction in rent receivable	400		
Increase in rent payable	400		
(8) Increase in purchases returns		400	
	800	1,285	
		800	485
Revised net profit			4,685

Items (4) and (9) do not affect profit.

Tutorial note: Adopt the above lay-out for 'revision of net profit' type questions. Untidy, 'straggly' answers without a logical lay-out do not commend themselves to examiners.

3.2.2 Exercise: correcting accounting errors and calculating a revised profit figure

G. Sobers extracted the balances from his ledgers on 30 June 19-3 and prepared a trial balance as at that date. The trial balance failed to agree and Sobers opened a suspense account to enable him to proceed with the preparation of draft final accounts.

Subsequently, Sobers discovered the following errors:

(1) A cheque received from C.Lloyd, a debtor, had been correctly entered in the cash book as £105, but had been credited to Lloyd's account as £150.

(2) An improvement to a machine at a cost of £750 had been debited to Machinery Repairs instead of to the Machinery (asset) account. (Assets are depreciated on the straight line basis at 10% of cost; a full year's depreciation is calculated in the year of purchase.)

(3) The total of the sales day book for February,19-3, was £10,860; this had been posted to the Sales account as £10,680.

(4) An invoice for the purchase of goods from F.Engineer on 1 June 19-3 had been entirely omitted from the books. The invoice amounted to £300.

(5) A debt of £100 in the sales ledger had proved to be bad and had been written off in the sales ledger, but the appropriate entry had not been made in the Bad Debts account.

Required

(a) Prepare the suspense account in Sober's ledger showing clearly the difference on the trial balance at 30 June 19-3 and the entries made to adjust the above mentioned errors.

(b) Journal entries for errors 2 and 4 above (narratives not required.)

(c) A calculation of the corrected net profit for the year to 30 June 19-3. Sober's first draft of the profit and loss account had disclosed a net profit of £7,550.

Tutorial note: The trial balance difference in the Suspense account will be the figure required to make that account balance after the adjustments have been posted to it.

3.2.3 Exercise: more difficult

P.Hendrie's trial balance at 31 March 19-2 had a difference of £4,510, the total of the debit side being larger by that amount.

Hendrie opened a suspense account until such time as the error(s) could be found. Meanwhile, he prepared final accounts for the business which showed a net loss of £2,300 for the year.

Subsequently, Hendrie found the following errors:

(1) Major repair work to a damaged motor car, in the sum of £2,780, had been debited in error to the motor cars (asset) account as £2,870.

(2) An invoice for the sale on credit to Boon of goods with a selling price of £500 had been debited to Boon's account but had not been entered in the sales day book.

(3) The figure of stock at 1 April 19-1 had been entered into the trial balance as £14,000 instead of £10,400 as shown in the Stock account.

(4) A stock sheet totalling £1,300 had been inadvertently omitted from the closing stock summary at 31 March 19-2.

(5) A credit balance of £160 in the sales ledger had been extracted as a debit balance.

Required

(a) The journal entries required to correct the above mentioned errors in Hendrie's books.

(b) The suspense account showing the entries for the original difference and the correction of errors.

(c) A calculation of the revised profit or loss of P.Hendrie's business for year ended 31 March 19-2.

Key points to remember

1. Journal entries should always be prepared in proper form with the accounts to be debited shown before those to be credited. Include concise narratives unless the question states that narratives are not required.

2. Identify those errors which do not affect the trial balance and will not therefore be adjusted through the suspense account; the remaining errors must be adjusted through the suspense account.

3. When calculating revised profit identify those errors which have affected the profit and loss account. Present your calculation in the form used in this chapter.

Common errors

1. Failure to differentiate between errors which must be adjusted through the suspense account and other errors.

2. Failure to identify the proper entries required to correct errors.

3. Making journal entries to other books of prime entry.

4. Failure to identify errors that affect the profit and loss account and those that do not.

5. Increasing profit when it should be reduced and vice versa.

Questions

In each of the following cases, a trial balance has failed to agree and the difference has been entered into a Suspense account.

1 A credit balance in the sum of £93 has been omitted from the list of balances extracted from the Sales Ledger. The trial balance will not agree because

A the credit side total is £93 short

B the credit side total is £93 too much

C the debit side total is £93 short

D the debit side total is £93 too much.

2 A credit note for £46 sent to A. Moses has been debited to A. Mason's account in the sales ledger. On the trial balance there will be

A no difference

B £46 too little on the credit side and £46 too much on the debit side

C £92 too little on the credit side

D £92 too much on the debit side.

3 The total of the Sales Day Book for one month is £9,160. It has been entered in the Sales account as £9,610. The error must be corrected by:

A debiting the Sales account and crediting the Sales Day Book with £450

B debiting the Sales Day Book and crediting Sales account with £450

C debiting Sales account and crediting Suspense account with £450

D debiting Suspense account and crediting Sales account with £450.

4 An invoice for repairs to machinery, £500, has been entered in the Machinery account. The error must be corrected by:

A debiting Machinery account and crediting Repairs to Machinery account with £500

B debiting Repairs to Machinery account and crediting Machinery account with £500

C debiting Repairs to Machinery account and crediting Suspense account with £500

D debiting Suspense account and crediting Machinery account with £500

5 A trial balance will fail to agree if

A a sales invoice is omitted from the Sales Day Book

B a sales invoice for £415 is entered in the Sales Day Book as £451

C a sales invoice for £600 entered in the Sales Day Book has not been included in the monthly total

D a credit note has been entered in the Sales Day Book

1 At the completion of the financial year ended 30 April 19-4 the trial balance of Rock Ltd. failed to agree and the difference was recorded in a suspense account.

The company does not maintain control accounts.

The following information has been subsequently discovered prior to the preparation of the final accounts.

(1) The purchase of a secondhand delivery van costing £1,500 has been debited to the motor vehicle expenses account.

(2) No entry has been made in the accounts to record the theft of £250 cash from the business by a dishonest former employee. The cash will not be recovered.

(3) The total of the discount allowed column in the cash book has been overcast by £187.

(4) The receipt of £289 from Hand, a customer, has been correctly entered in the cash book but has been debited to Hand's account in the sales ledger as £298.

(5) Although the return of goods, sold for £45, from Brown, a customer, has been correctly entered in the returns inwards account no entry has been made in Brown's account in the sales ledger.

Required

(a) Journal entries correcting each of the five errors given above. Narratives are not required.

(5 marks)

(b) A suspense account showing clearly the original discrepancy on the trial balance.

(5 marks)

(AEB)

2 Mrs Beatrice Morgan has prepared the following trial balance at 31 December 19-6 for the business of her husband:

	£	£
Capital 1 January 19-6		53,780
Purchases and sales	9,000	18,400
Returns Inward	100	
Returns Outward		250
Depreciation for year written off	890	
Wages	4,300	
Discounts allowed		450
Discounts received	270	
Debtors and Creditors	1,250	2,750
Premises	45,000	
Fixtures and fittings	8,900	
Bank Overdraft	1,200	
Cash	150	
Carriage Inwards	370	
Stock 1 January 19-6	2,500	
Carriage Outwards		140
Sundry Expenses	1,420	
Provision for Doubtful Debts	420	–
	75,770	75,770

Although the trial balance balances, Mrs Morgan is sure that something is on the wrong side, but before she can check it she is rushed into hospital for an operation. Mr Morgan asks you to check it for him.

(a) **You are required** to rewrite the trial balance correctly entering the difference (if any) as a suspense account balance.

(b) Mr Morgan asks you to check the books to see if there are any errors and you find the following:
(i) A page of the purchases day book has been undercast by £3,000.
(ii) A total in the sales book has been carried forward as £1,000, instead of £1,600.
(iii) The sale of some old fixtures for cash for £300 has been credited to the sales account.
(iv) Returns inward of £100 have been posted to the returns outward account.

Prepare Journal entries to correct the above errors. (Narrations are not required.)

(c) Write up the suspense account, starting with the balance from your trial balance.

(Total 18 marks)

(OXFORD)

3 At the end of the financial year of Green plc the totals of the trial balance failed to agree and a suspense account was opened. In addition the total of the balances extracted from the purchases ledger, which had been included as the creditors figure in the trial balance, failed to agree with the credit balance of £3,422 on the purchases ledger control account.

The following errors were subsequently discovered:

(1) The total of the discount received column in the cash book had been overcast by £230.

(2) The return of goods value £450 from Smith, a customer, had been credited in Smith's account and debited in the purchases account.

(3) The return of goods, value £150 to Jones, a supplier, had been completely omitted from the accounts.

(4) No entry had been made in the accounts to record the receipt of a cheque for £60 from White, a supplier. The cheque was a refund relating to a previous overpayment for goods supplied.

(5) The payment of £315 to Ash, a supplier, had been correctly entered in the cash book but had been debited to the general expenses account in the nominal ledger as £351.

Required

(a) The journal entries to correct the items above. Narratives are not required.
(10 marks)

(b) An extract of the purchases ledger control account showing clearly the amendments to the original balance of £3,422. (7 marks)
(AEB)

4   In order not to delay the completion of its monthly management financial statements quoting a profit of £25,000, Paste Cymraeg Arall c.c. opened a suspense account, as it was not possible to establish why there were errors in its trial balance. Further investigation has resulted in discovery of the following:

(i) A sales ledger account in the name of Heini Jones had been credited with £73.50, whereas the remittance entered in the company's bank account was only £37.50.

(ii) Another sales ledger account R. Wyddfa had been debited with £235.67, whereas the entry was in respect of a payment made by Paste Cymraeg Arall c.c. to R. Snowden, a supplier of fresh cream.

(iii) £89.67 collected from the canteen pay phone was credited to rents receivable instead of postage and telephones.

(iv) Although F. Squeezer had been allowed a discount of £37.54 and this amount had been properly entered in the cash book, no discounts allowed account is recorded in the trial balance.

(v) Following pressure from S. Rambo for the payment of his account for security services, a cheque for £543.26 was paid by one of the company's directors personally. The directors' fees account was debited with this amount.

Required

(a) Journal entries necessary to allow the discrepancies to be corrected.   (10 marks)

(b) A statement showing the revised profit figure after taking into account the above adjustments. (5 marks)

(c) An explanation of how any balance remaining in a suspense account, which is not sufficiently material to warrant any delay in the publishing of a company's financial statements, should be dealt with in its books of account. (3 marks)
(WJEC)

5   Owing to a shortage of qualified staff locally, Alison Dorset has had to employ an inexperienced book-keeper during the past three months of her financial year ended 30 April 1990. Consequently, when the accountant prepares a trial balance at 30 April 1990, the total of the debit side exceeds the total of the credit side. A suspense account has therefore been opened, and subsequently the following items are discovered:

(i) On 1 April Cumbria Ltd owed Alison Dorset £200. On 28 April a cheque for £195 was received, Cumbria Ltd having deducted discount. The entries made were: total amount credited to J. Cambridge's account, cheque debited in the bank account and discount credited to the discount received account.

(ii) An adjustment has not been made to the provision for bad debts account. The trial balance shows an amount of £1,050. The provision is to be maintained at 2% of debtors.

The trial balance figure for debtors is £48,000. On 10 April, Huntingdon, a customer owing £850, was declared bankrupt, and his creditors received, on 25 April, £0.30 for every pound owing to them. No entries for this have yet been made in Alison's books.

(iii) The book-keeper has decided to record an amount for goodwill in the books, believing that a value should be shown for customer loyalty and the quality of the management and workforce. He has therefore opened a goodwill account with a debit of £50,000, but no corresponding credit.

(iv) He has also written down the value of a piece of specialised equipment from its book value of £18,000 to £450, which a friend has informed him is all that the equipment would be worth if Dorset's were to cease trading immediately. The only entry he made was to credit the equipment account.

(v) The book-keeper has double entered an amount of £1,500 by debiting legal expenses and crediting Rutland, Solicitors, for fees which he is sure will become due in June 1990 as a result of a court case which may be brought against Dorset's.

(vi) An amount of £15,340 paid for plant and machinery has been debited to the purchases account as £14,530, although it has been correctly entered in the bank account.

(vii) An amount of £360 for a refund on an insurance premium has been credited to the bank account and debited to the insurance account.

Alison is interested to know how Statements of Standard Accounting Practice would have affected her accounts if her business had been a limited company.

Required

(a) A suspense account to correct those errors affecting the balancing of the trial balance, showing clearly the original difference in the trial balance totals at 30 April 1990.

(8 marks)

(b) Journal entries, with narratives, for any items that should not appear in the suspense account.

(6 marks)

(c) An explanation of the accounting concepts involved in items (ii) and (iv). (5 marks)

(d) An explanation of the application of Statements of Standard Accounting Practice to items (iii) and (v).

(4 marks)

(OXFORD)

6 G. Carpenter runs a small engineering company, and has prepared the following Trial Balance at 31 March 1992:

	£	£
Capital		50,000
Motor vehicles	8,000	
Equipment and fittings	10,300	
Stock 1 April 1991	11,810	
Purchases	169,400	
Sales		264,030
Premises	65,000	
Debtors	28,045	
Creditors		31,040
Discount allowed	600	
Discount received		1,250
Wages and salaries	38,000	
Sales returns	130	
Purchase returns		210
Drawings	640	
Insurance	720	
General expenses	2,760	
Bank	11,205	
Suspense		80
	346,610	346,610

Mr Carpenter was unable to agree the Trial Balance and has entered the difference in a Suspense Account. He asks you to check the accounts for him, and you find the following errors:

(i) Equipment and fittings bought during the year for £7,000 have been debited to the Purchases account. The company does not provide for depreciation in the year of purchase of fixed assets.

(ii) Discount allowed of £40 has been posted to the credit of Discount received.

(iii) A cheque for £155 from a debtor has been dishonoured, but no record has been made of this in the accounts. There is no reason to believe that payment will not be made in April.

(iv) Purchase returns of £50 have been posted to the debit of Sales returns.

(v) During March 1992, Mr Carpenter remembered that of the insurance already paid, £60 related to a private insurance premium. In an attempt to correct the accounts, he made another debit entry of £60 in the Insurance account, with no other entry being made.

Required

(a) Journal Entries and a Suspense Account to cover the errors (narratives are not required).

(12 marks)

(b) A corrected Trial Balance. (4 marks)

(c) A statement showing the effect of each error on net profit. (5 marks)

(d) If the errors had not been discovered prior to the preparation of the final accounts, how might the Suspense Account balance have been dealt with? (2 marks)

(OXFORD)

4 Incomplete records

Chapter objectives

You should be able to:

☐ calculate net profit or loss for a period using statements of affairs

☐ prepare receipts and payments accounts

☐ prepare trading and profit and loss accounts using total accounts, and ratios of gross profit to turnover or cost of sales

☐ prepare balance sheets

☐ calculate value of stock lost in fire or by theft

'Incomplete records' is a term which is used to describe situations where only single entry bookkeeping is employed (e.g. only a cash book or only personal accounts for debtors and creditors), or where no records are kept at all. As a result, transactions are not recorded in their two-fold aspects, the concept of duality is ignored and final accounts of the business cannot be prepared in the usual way.

Where sufficient information is available from such records as have been kept, including bank statements, bank paying-in book counterfoils, cheque counterfoils, copies of invoices, etc, trading and profit and loss accounts may be prepared. In the absence of such sources of information, the profit or loss may be ascertained by preparing statements of affairs.

4.1 Statements of affairs

A statement of affairs lists the assets and liabilities of a business at a given date. The difference between the assets and liabilities represents capital. (Accounting equation;: assets less liabilities = capital.)

Comparison of capital at different dates to ascertain profit or loss: profit increases capital; a loss decreases capital. Therefore, capital at end of period less capital at start of period = profit or loss for the period. Capital introduced during the period and capital withdrawn during the period (drawings) must be taken into account.

4.1.1 Example

Ms Perfect, hair stylist, has been in business for some years but has never kept records of her takings or expenditure. She has now received an estimated assessment for income tax from H.M. Inspector of Taxes and wishes to check the business profit shown in her assessment. Ms Perfect provides the following information as at the 6 April 19-1 and 5 April 19-2.

	6 April 19-1 £	5 April 19-2 £
Equipment	1,000	1,200
Stocks of hair styling sundries	70	45
Amounts owing from clients	60	72
Rent paid in advance	100	80
Balance at bank	265	180
Creditors for supplies	40	22
Electricity owing	20	35

Ms Perfect has drawn £100 per week from the business.

Answer

Ms Perfect
Calculation of profit for the year to 5 April 19-2
Statements of affairs as at

		6 April 19-1		5 April 19-2
	£	£	£	£
Equipment		1,000		1,200
Stocks of hair styling sundries		70		45
Amounts owing from clients		60		72
Rent paid in advance		100		80
Balance at bank		265		180
		1,495		1,577
less creditors for supplies	40		22	
electricity owing	20	60	35	57
Net assets (= capital)		1,435		1,520
deduct capital at 6 April 19-1				1,435
				85
add drawings for year (52 × £100)				5,200
Profit for year				5,285

4.1.2 Exercise: calculation of profit using statements of affairs

Mr Blower has carried on business as a plumber for some years. He has arranged a visit to his bank manager to arrange overdraft facilities, but he has never kept any proper records and wishes to provide his bank manager with the results of his business for the past year. The only information he has been able to produce is a schedule of his assets and liabilities as at 1 July 19-2 and 30 June 19-3. They are as follows:

	as at 1 July 19-2	as at 30 June 19-3
	£	£
Premises at cost	5,000	5,000
Motor van at cost	4,000	4,000
Motor car at valuation	–	5,500
Plant and equipment	900	1,000
Stock of materials	100	175
Debtors for work done	1,250	640
Balance at bank	2,400	120
Owing to suppliers	975	1,800
Rates owing	–	400
Telephone owing	15	40
Loan from father	–	2,000

The premises were purchased some years ago and were valued at £8,000 on 1 July 19-2; the valuation has not changed since then. The value of the motor van at 30 June 19-3 was £3,200. During the year, Mr Blower brought his private car into the business at the valuation shown above.

Mr Blower has drawn £80 per week from the business.

Required

A calculation of Mr Blower's profit or loss for the year to 30 June 19-3.

Tutorial note: The valuation of assets rather than their cost should be used to calculate capital as the valuation represents the true worth of the owner's investment in the business.

4.2 Trading and profit and loss accounts

If sufficient information is available, trading and profit and loss accounts may be prepared from incomplete records. Two techniques are useful for this purpose: total accounts, and the use of the mark-up, margin and the relationship between them.

Total accounts

These may be used to calculate purchases and sales for a period.

4.2.1 Example

The following information is available from Taylor's business records:

	At 1 Jan 19-4	At 31 Dec 19-4
	£	£
Trade debtors	2,220	2,600
Trade creditors	1,760	2,240

For the year to 31 December 19-4	£
Cash sales	5,600
Cash received from trade debtors	25,800
Cash paid to trade creditors	12,220

Required

Calculate Taylor's purchases and sales for the year to 31 December 19-4

Taylor
Purchases total account

19-4		£	19-4		£
Dec 31	Cash paid to creditors	12,220	Jan 1	Creditors b/d	1,760
Dec 31	Creditors c/d	2,240	Dec 31	Purchases – trading a/c	
				(balancing figure)	12,700
		14,460			14,460

Purchases to be debited in trading account: £12,700

Sales total account

19-4		£	19-4		£
Jan 1	Debtors b/d	2,220	Dec 31	Cash received from debtors	25,800
Dec 31	Sales (balancing figure)	26,180		Debtors c/d	2,600
		28,400			28,400

	£
Credit sales	26,180
Cash sales	5,600
Sales for the year	31,780

Tutorial note: Do not include cash sales in the total account.

4.2.2 Exercise: using total accounts to calculate purchases and sales

The following information is extracted from the records of A. Smith:

	At 1 April 19-3	At 31 March 19-4
	£	£
Trade creditors	14,640	16,100
Trade debtors	19,730	21,150

Other information for the year to 31 March 19-4:

	£
Cheques sent to suppliers	168,000
Discounts received	6,400
Cash received from debtors	199,700
Discounts allowed	4,820

Required

A calculation of Smith's purchases and sales for the year ended 31 March 19-4.

4.3 Mark-up and margin

Mark-up is gross profit expressed as a percentage or fraction of cost of sales.

Example

	£
Cost price of goods	100
Selling price	125
Gross profit	25

$$\frac{\text{Gross profit}}{\text{Cost price}} \times 100 = \frac{25}{100} \times 100 = 25\% \text{ or } \tfrac{1}{4}$$

Margin is gross profit expressed as a percentage or fraction of selling price.

Example (using the data given above)

$$\frac{\text{Gross profit}}{\text{Selling price}} \times 100 = \frac{25}{125} \times 100 = 20\% \text{ or } \tfrac{1}{5}$$

(relationship between mark-up and margin – example as above)

$$\text{Mark-up} = \tfrac{1}{4} \text{ or } \frac{1}{5-1}$$

$$\text{Margin} = \tfrac{1}{5} \text{ or } \frac{1}{4+1}$$

Therefore, in general terms:

when mark-up is $\dfrac{a}{b}$, margin is $\dfrac{a}{b+a}$

and when margin is $\dfrac{a}{b}$, mark-up is $\dfrac{a}{b-a}$

thus:

$$\text{mark-up} = \tfrac{1}{3}, \text{ margin} = \frac{1}{3+1} \text{ or } \tfrac{1}{4}$$

$$\text{mark-up} = \tfrac{2}{5}, \text{ margin} = \frac{2}{5+2} \text{ or } \tfrac{2}{7}$$

$$\text{margin} = \tfrac{1}{6}, \text{ mark-up} = \frac{1}{6-1} \text{ or } \tfrac{1}{5}$$

$$\text{margin} = \tfrac{2}{5}, \text{ mark-up} = \frac{2}{5-2} \text{ or } \tfrac{2}{3}$$

4.3.1 Examples

(i) Mr Wedge's books showed the following information for the year to 31 December 19-2:

	£
Stock at 1 Jan 19-2	5,000
Purchases for year	25,000
Stock at 31 December 19-2	8,000

Mr Wedge adds 25% to his cost of sales to arrive at the selling price. What were his sales for the year to 31 December 19-2?

Answer

	£	
Stock at 1.1.-2	5,000	
Purchases	25,000	
	30,000	
less stock at 31.12.-2	8,000	
Cost of sales	22,000	
add gross profit (25% of £22,000)	5,500	(20% of £27,500)
Sales for the year	27,500	

(ii) Miss Hodges' records showed the following:

	£
Stock at 1 July 19-3	12,000
Stock at 30 June 19-4	15,000
Sales for year to 30 June 19-4	180,000

Miss Hodges sells her goods so as to produce a gross margin of $33\tfrac{1}{3}\%$.

Prepare Miss Hodges, trading account for the year to 30 June 19-4, showing the amount of goods purchased.

Answer

Miss Hodges'
Trading account for the year to 30 June 19-4

	£	£
Sales		180,000
Stock at 1 July -3	12,000	
Purchases (balancing figure 3)	123,000	
(balancing figure 2)	135,000	
less stock at 30 June -4	15,000	
Cost of sales (balancing figure 1)		120,000
Gross profit (33⅓% of £180,000)		60,000

Tutorial note: The 'missing' figures in this answer are 'balancing' figures found by working back from cost of sales to purchases.

4.3.2 Exercise: using the relationship between mark-up and margin

Mr Peters' business records show the following information for the year to 30 September 19-5:

	£
Sales for the year	260,000
Stock at 1 October 19-4	11,000
Stock at 30 September 19-5	14,000

Mr Peters adds 25% to his cost of sales to arrive at his selling prices.

Required

Prepare Mr Peters' trading account for the year to 30 September 19-5, showing the amount of purchases for the year.

4.4 Receipts and payments accounts

Receipts and payments accounts are, in effect, cash books in summarised form

- they show the opening and closing bank or cash balances.
- they record all receipts and payments irrespective of whether they are capital or revenue in nature.
- they record all amounts received or paid in the period irrespective of the periods of time to which they relate.

It will be necessary to prepare a receipts and payments account when one is not already included in an incomplete records question. Prepare separate accounts for bank and cash. Make sure that the cash paid into the bank is the same figure in both accounts.

Treat any expenditure which is not accounted for in the question as drawings in a receipts and payments account.

4.5 Preparation of final accounts from incomplete records

Two methods of approach are given for the preparation of accounts from incomplete records:

1. Using simulated ledger accounts as workings
2. Using a worksheet in the form of an extended trial balance.

Method 2 is the preferred one, but the student should try both and then select the method he or she finds easier to handle. It is the end result that matters. If method 1 is mastered first, method 2 should not be too difficult to grasp.

Method 1

Proceed as follows, taking each step in order. (Steps 1 to 6 can be done as 'rough' workings unless a statement of affairs and a receipts and payments account are required as part of the answer, when care should taken over their presentation.)

1. Prepare statement of affairs at beginning of period to calculate opening capital.

2. Prepare receipts and payments account.

3. Calculate sales and purchases using total accounts, mark-up and margin as appropriate.

4. Open 'T' accounts from opening statement of affairs and complete double entry from receipts and payments accounts.

5. Adjust 'T' accounts for accruals and prepayments at end of period.

6. Make provisions for depreciation and bad debts as required by question.

7. Copy out trading and profit and loss account and balance sheet.

4.5.1 Example

T. Harman, a general dealer, has been in business for some years and has never kept proper records. He now wishes you to prepare accounts for his business for the year to 31 December 19-2. Harman supplies you with the following information:

	1 Jan 19-2	31 Dec 19-2
	£	£
Premises	20,000	20,000
Motor van	7,000	7,000
Equipment	4,000	4,600
Stock	3,000	5,000
Cash at bank	2,700	3,400
Cash in hand	100	80
Trade debtors	1,900	2,480
Trade creditors	1,100	700
Rates in advance	350	425
Insurance in advance	60	75
Garage rent owing	100	125
Electricity owing	230	480
Loan from brother		1,000

In addition the following information for the year is available:

		£
Receipts:	Takings from cash sales	11,450
	Receipts from debtors	15,225
	Loan from brother	1,000
	Interest received on personal holding of savings bonds	700
	Refund of insurance premium	100
Payments:	Trade creditors	11,000
	Purchase of equipment	1,200
	Rates	2,100
	Insurance	500
	Garage rent	475
	Electricity	1,300
	Drawings	5,000

Harman informs you that with the exception of takings from cash sales, all the above receipts and payments passed directly through the bank account. The cash sales money was used to pay wages of £100 per week and to purchase sundry small items totalling £700; the balance of the cash takings were then banked. The loan from Harman's brother was received on 1 July 19-2 and interest is payable on it at the rate of 10% per annum.

You are to provide for depreciation on the motor van at the rate of 20%, and make a provision for bad debts of 5% of debtors at 31 December 19-2.

Required

A trading and profit and loss account for T. Harman's business for the year to 31 December 19-2 and a balance sheet as at that date.

Answer

Step 1   **Statement of affairs at 1 January 19-2**

		£	£
Premises			20,000
Motor van			7,000
Equipment			4,000
Stock			3,000
Cash at bank			2,700
Cash in hand			100
Trade debtors			1,900
Prepayments	– rates		350
	– insurance		60
			39,110
less	Trade creditors	1,100	
	garage rent owing	100	
	electricity owing	230	1,430
Capital at 1 January 19-2			37,680

Step 2   **Receipts and payments account (bank)**

19-2		£	19-2		£
Jan 1	Balance b/f	2,700	Dec 31	Trade creditors	11,000
Jul 1	Loan from brother	1,000		Purchase of equipment	1,200
Dec 31	Takings – cash sales			Rates	2,100
	(balancing figure)	5,250		Insurance	500
	Receipts from debtors	15,225		Garage rent	475
	Interest on savings bonds	700		Electricity	1,300
	Refund of insurance	100		Drawings	5,000
				Balance c/f	3,400
		24,975			24,975

Receipts and payments account (cash)

19-2		£	19-2		£
Jan 1	Balance b/f	100	Dec 31	Wages	5,200
Dec 31	Cash sales	11,450		Sundries	700
				Banked	5,250
				Drawings (bal. fig.)	320
				Balance c/f	80
		11,550			11,550

Step 3   **Purchases total account**

19-2		£	19-2		£
Dec 31	Cheques to suppliers	11,000	Jan 1	Creditors b/f	1,100
	Creditors c/f	700	Dec 31	Purchases (bal.fig.)	10,600
		11,700			11,700

Sales total account

19-2		£	19-2		£
Jan 1	Debtors b/f	1,900	Dec 31	Receipts from debtors	15,225
Dec 31	Credit sales (bal.fig.)	15,805		Debtors c/f	2,480
		17,705			17,705

		£
Total Sales:	credit	15,805
	cash	11,450
		27,255

Steps 4 and 5   **Loan from brother**

19-2		£
Jul 1	Bank	1,000

Capital

19-2		£
Jan 1	Balance b/f	37,680

Equipment

19-2		£	19-2		£
Jan 1	Balance b/d	4,000	Dec 31	P&L – depreciation	600
Dec 31	Bank	1,200		Balance c/d	4,600
		5,200			5,200

Rates

19-2		£	19-2		£
Jan 1	Balance b/f	350	Dec 31	P&L	2,025
Dec 31	Cheques	2,100		Balance c/f	425
		2,450			2,450

Insurance

19-2		£	19-2		£
Jan 1	Prepayment b/d	60	Dec 31	Refund	100
Dec 31	Cheques	500		P&L	385
				Prepayment c/f	75
		560			560

Garage rent

19-2		£	19-2		£
Dec 31	Cheques	475	Jan 1	Accrual b/f	100
	Accrual c/f	125	Dec 31	P&L	500
		600			600

Electricity

19-2		£	19-2		£
Dec 31	Cheques	1,300	Jan 1	Accrual b/f	230
	Accrual c/f	480	Dec 31	P&L	1,550
		1,780			1,780

Wages

19-2		£	19-2		£
Dec 31	Cash	5,200	Dec 31	P&L	5,200

Sundries

19-2		£	19-2		£
Dec 31	Cash	700	Dec 31	P&L	700

Drawings

19-2		£	19-2		£
Dec 31	Cheques	5,000	Dec 31	Interest on savings bonds	700
	Cash	320	Dec 31	Balance	4,620
		5,320			5,320

Step 6

Provision for depreciation of motor van

			19-2		£
			Dec 31	P&L (20% of £7,000)	1,400

Provision for bad debts

			19-2		£
			Dec 31	P&L (5% of £2,480)	124

Interest on loan from brother

19-2		£	19-2		£
Dec 31	Accrual c/f (10% of £1,000 × $\frac{6}{12}$)	50	Dec 31	P&L	50

Step 7

T. Harman
Trading and profit and loss account for the year ended 31 December 19-2

		£	£
Sales			27,255
less	Stock at Jan 1	3,000	
	Purchases	10,600	
		13,600	
	deduct stock at Dec 31	5,000	8,600
Gross profit (carried forward)			18,655

			£	£
Gross profit (brought forward)				18,655
less	Wages		5,200	
	Rates		2,025	
	Insurance		385	
	Garage rent		500	
	Electricity		1,550	
	Sundries		700	
	Interest on loan		50	
	Provision for depreciation	– motor van	1,400	
		– equipment	600	
	Provision for bad debts		124	12,534
Net profit				6,121

Balance sheet as at 31 December 19-2

		£	£	£
Fixed assets				
Premises				20,000
Motor van (7,000 – 1,400)				5,600
Equipment (4,000 + 1,200 – 600)				4,600
				30,200
Current assets				
Stock			5,000	
Debtors (2,480 - 124)			2,356	
Prepayments	– rates	425		
	– insurance	75	500	
Cash	– at bank		3,400	
	– in hand		80	
			11,336	
less Current liabilities				
Creditors		700		
Accrued expenses – garage rent		125		
electricity		480		
loan interest		50	1,355	9,981
				40,181
Deduct loan from brother				1,000
				39,181
Represented by				
Capital at 1 January 19-2				37,680
Add profit for year				6,121
				43,801
Deduct drawings				4,620
				39,181

Tutorial notes:

1. Interest on brother's loan must be provided for the six months to 31 December 19-2.

2. Interest on savings bonds is not business income. Reduce Harman's drawings by this amount.

3. Cash takings banked will be amount required to make the bank balance; be sure to credit the same figure in the cash account.

4. Drawings shown in cash receipts and payments account is the amount required to make the account balance.

5. Depreciation of equipment. This is the difference between the opening balance of equipment at the beginning of the year, plus the additions, less the valuation of the equipment at the end of the year. (Revaluation method: see 1.4).

Method 2

This approach is an alternative to method 1. Prepare a worksheet in the form of an extended trial balance as shown below.

	(1) Statement of affairs 1.1.-2	(2) Receipts & payments Bank	(3) Receipts & payments Cash	(4) Cash banked	(5) Accruals & prepayments	(6) Depreciation	(7) Other adjustments	(8) Trading a/c	(9) Profit & loss a/c	(10) Balance sheet
	£	£	£	£	£	£	£	£	£	£
Premises	20,000									20,000
Motor van	7,000					(1,400)				5,600
Equipment	4,000	1,200				(600)				4,600
Stock at 1.1.-2	3,000							3,000		
Cash at bank	2,700	17,025*								
		(21,575)**		5,250						3,400
Cash in hand	100		11,450#							
			(5,900)##	(5,250)			(320)†			80
Trade debtors	1,900	(15,225)					15,805			2,480
Trade creditors	(1,100)	11,000					(10,600)			(700)
Rates	350	2,100			(425)				2,025	
Insurance	60	500								
		(100)			(75)				385	
Garage rent	(100)	475			125				500	
Electricity	(230)	1,300			480				1,550	
Loan - brother		(1,000)								(1,000)
Sales			(11,450)				(15,805)	(27,255)		
Purchases							10,600	10,600		
Capital (bal. fig.)	(37,680)									(37,680)
Drawings		5,000								
		(700)					320†			4,620
Wages			5,200						5,200	
Sundries			700						700	
Depn. motor van						1,400			1,400	
equipment						600			600	
Prov. for bad debts							124		124	
							(124)			(124)
Interest on loan							50		50	
Prepayments					500					500
Accruals					(605)		(50)			(655)
Stock at 31.12.-2							5,000	(5,000)		
							(5,000)			5,000
Gross profit								18,655	(18,655)	
Net profit									6,121	(6,121)
	–	–	–	–	–	–	–	–	–	–

Place credits in brackets to distinguish them from debits. Understanding why and how the entries are made in the worksheet should be easy if they are compared with the postings made to the 'ledger' accounts in method 1. It is important to make sure that the total of each column is zero. If it is not zero, you have not completed the double entry correctly and the error must be corrected before proceeding further.

Column:

(1) Statement of affairs as at beginning of period. List assets and liabilities at this date; enter difference between assets and liabilities as capital.

(2) Receipts and payments (bank). Enter total of receipts (other than bankings of cash), *£17,025, and total of cheques paid **£21,575 in the row for cash at bank. Complete double entry in this column for the individual items of receipts and payments, adding additional rows as required for the purpose.

(3) Receipts and payments (cash). Where a receipts and payments account is required for cash, it is better to provide a separate column for this to avoid confusion with bank transactions. Complete in similar manner as for the bank column, entering total of cash received (#£11,450) and total of cash payments (##£5,900) and completing the double entry. Ignore the credit for cash banked until the next step.

It is not always necessary to prepare two receipts and payments accounts. This will depend upon the question.

(4) Cash banked. The difference between the cross cast of the cash at bank row and the known closing bank balance is the amount of cash banked in the period. Enter this in column 4 as a debit to bank and a credit to cash. The row for cash at bank should now cross cast to the closing bank balance.

Next, check that the cash in hand row cross casts to the closing cash balance; any difference on the cash in hand should be adjusted through drawings a/c as an unexplained difference in the other adjustments column (7).

(5) Accruals and prepayments, and depreciation are straight forward adjustments.

(6) Other adjustments. The figures required to make the trade debtor and trade creditor rows cross cast to the closing debtors and creditors are the amounts of credit sales and credit purchases respectively. These are the 'missing' figures as calculated in step 3 in method 1.

(7) †£320. This is the amount of the cash deficiency and is required to make the cash cross cast to the final cash balance. It is adjusted through drawings account.

Columns 8–10 for the trading account, profit and loss account and balance sheet are completed by cross-casting the other columns.

This has been a fairly difficult example. It is possible to reduce the number of columns in the worksheet if fewer adjustments are required and when greater facility in working this method has been gained.

4.5.2 Exercise: preparing final accounts from incomplete records

J.T.Forster has a small building and decorating business but has not kept proper records.

The following information is available for Forster's business:

	1.1.-3	31.12.-3
	£	£
Premises	45,000	45,000
Motor lorry CWT100R	8,000	–
Motor lorry HHH999X	–	10,000
Plant and equipment	10,000	11,000
Stock of materials	2,600	3,500
Debtors	3,000	6,000
Creditors for supplies	2,700	4,250
Prepayments – rates	400	500
– advertising	120	340
Cash at bank	1,276	3,540
Cash in hand	300	450
Motor expenses owing	900	–
Electricity owing	200	280

Bank paying-in slip and cheque counterfoils showed that the following amounts had been paid into or paid out of the bank during the year.

		£
Receipts:	takings banked	36,764
	proceeds of sale of motor lorry CWT100R	5,000
	wife's premium bond prize money	2,500
Payments:	creditors for supplies	9,000
	purchase of motor lorry HHH999X	10,000
	purchase of plant and equipment	2,400
	rates	1,000
	advertising	700
	motor lorry running expenses	2,100
	electricity	800
	drawings	10,000
	wages	6,000

In addition, the following amounts were passed through the cash account:

	£
receipts from clients	40,764
purchase of materials	2,000
wages	1,800

Motor lorry CWT100R was sold on 30 June 19-3; motor lorry HHH999X was purchased on 1 July 19-3. Motor lorries are to be depreciated at 20%p.a.

Required

A profit and loss account for the year ended 31 December 19-3 and a balance sheet as at that date.

Tutorial note: A trading account is not appropriate in this case as J.T.Forster is not buying and selling any commodity, i.e. he is not a trader. Credit his revenue for the period to the profit and loss account and show the cost of materials either as a deduction from receipts for work done, or as a debit in the profit and loss account.

4.6 Stock lost in fire or by theft

When goods have been lost in a fire or by theft, the value of such loss must be calculated for:

(a) the loss to be reflected in the trading account at the year- end as a reduction of the cost of sales,

(b) a claim for compensation to be prepared for insurance compensation

(c) tax purposes.

If detailed stock records have not been kept or not survived the incident, the value of stock lost must be calculated using the incomplete records technique of finding a missing closing stock figure in a trading account. Any difference between the quantity of stock so calculated and actual stock remaining after the incident is the value of stock lost.

4.6.1 Example

Mr Georgiou's warehouse was burgled on 10th April 19-4. The thieves stole most of the stock, but left goods worth £1,250. Mr Georgiou has to submit an insurance claim and provides the following information:

Extracted from his balance sheet at 31st December 19-3:

	£
Stock	15,000
Debtors	20,000
Creditors	10,000

Cash book summary 1st January to 10 April 19-4:

	£
Receipts from debtors	88,000
Payments to creditors	60,000

Other information:

	£
Sales invoices outstanding at 10 April 19-4	12,000
Suppliers' invoices unpaid at 10 April 19-4	13,000

Mr Georgiou sells his goods at a mark-up of 25%.

Required

A calculation of the cost of the goods stolen.

Mr Georgiou
Proforma trading account for the period 1 January - 10 April 19-4

		£	£
Sales (W1)			80,000
Cost of sales:	Stock at 1.1.19-4	15,000	
	Purchases (W2)	63,000	
		78,000	
	Stock at 10.4.19-4 (missing figure)	14,000	64,000
Gross profit (£80,000 × 20%)			16,000

Tutorial note: Since mark-up is 25%, margin is 20%.

	£
Calculated stock at 10 April 19-4	14,000
Stock not stolen	1,250
Stock stolen (at cost)	12,750

Workings

1. Sales:

	£
Receipts from debtors	88,000
less debtors at 1.1.-4	20,000
	68,000
add debtors at 10.4.-4	12,000
	80,000

2. Purchases

	£
Payments to creditors	60,000
less creditors at 1.1.-4	10,000
	50,000
add creditors at 10.4.-4	13,000
	63,000

4.6.2 Exercise: calculation of cost of goods lost in fire

On the night of 5 November 19-1, the warehouse of Conn, Flagge, Raye & Son was burned down and most of the stock destroyed. The stock salvaged was valued at cost in the sum of £6,000. The firm claimed for compensation from its insurance company.

Required

Using the following information, calculate the amount of the claim.

Balance sheet as at 30 June 19-1 (extracts):

	£
Stock	23,750
Debtors	16,000
Creditors	11,520

Further information for period 1.7.-1 to 5.11.-1:

		£
Receipts from debtors		61,000
Cash sales		17,220
Payments to creditors		59,630
At 5 November 19-1:	Debtors	18,780
	Creditors	14,210

The firm achieves a margin of $33\frac{1}{3}\%$ on all sales.

Key points to remember

1. When required to calculate profit or loss for a period, and insufficient information is available to prepare a trading and profit and loss account, use statements of affairs to calculate the increase or decrease in capital during the period after allowing for any new capital introduced and drawings during the period.

2. If sufficient information is available, prepare a trading and profit and loss account.

3. Mark-up and margin are useful for calculating sales or cost of sales when it is not possible to prepare a sales or purchases total account.

4. Follow the 7 steps in preparing a trading and profit and loss account from incomplete records; if the question also requires a balance sheet, this will be prepared as part of step 7.

5. Steps 1–6 will generally be workings in support of the answer. If a question requires the preparation of an opening statement of affairs and/or a receipts and payments account, steps 1–2 will become part of the answer.

6. If steps 1–6 appear to be a formidable amount of work to do before you actually begin to write your answer, remember that examination regulations require all workings to be shown anyway.

7. Do not waste time on making your workings as neat as your answer to the question provided they are legible and clearly headed. 'T' accounts may be ruled free-hand, or not ruled at all provided the two sides are made distinct and all amounts shown in them are briefly described. An examiner is not bound to accept figures without descriptions as these may be meaningless.

8. One approach to step 7 is to prepare drafts of the trading and profit and loss account and balance sheet at an early stage so that figures may be inserted as they are calculated. In this way, you will start to accumulate marks at an early stage. Leave room to insert additional items which you may have overlooked.

9. Alternatively, step 7 may be left until all workings have been completed. Trading and profit and loss accounts and balance sheets can be fair-copied quite quickly, especially if you have had plenty of practice before the examination.

Common errors

1. No adjustments to cash receipts and payments for opening and closing debtors and creditors when calculating sales and purchases.

2. Failure to give effect to all the instructions in the question for the preparation of a profit and loss account and balance sheet.

3. No statement of affairs prepared as at beginning of period. It is unwise to insert a balancing figure in the balance sheet for the opening capital; even if it happens to be the correct figure, the method of arriving at it may not be acceptable to the examiner.

Questions

Fully worked examination question

Jim Hastings commenced in business on 1 May 19-7 trading as 'Orbit Records', a retail outlet dealing in records, cassettes and hi-fi accessories. When he commenced business he brought in £6,500 cash, which was banked immediately. He also brought in his car at the start of the business which was valued at £4,100. On 1 August 19-7, the business borrowed £5,300 from a finance institution at an interest rate of 16% per annum. This loan was lodged in the business bank account 1 August 19-7 and is not repayable until 19-5. Jim maintains the minimum of accounting records, but does keep details of all cash and bank transactions. Summary details of cash and bank transactions for the year ended 30 April 19-8 are listed below.

Transaction	Cash £	Bank £
Lease payments for premises		4,800
Wages to staff	3,200	7,050
Redecoration of premises		1,235
General operating expenses	320	1,375
Purchases of goods for resale		105,950
Lighting and heating	95	965
Fixtures and fittings		4,895
Interest payments on loan		424
Accountancy fees		355
Car expenses	155	1,050

Additional information:

(1) The lease agreement, which was entered into at the start of the business, detailed the cost as £960 per quarter payable in advance.

(2) Asset and liability balances at 30 April 19-8:

	£
Cash	125
Cash at bank	8,150
Car	3,150
Fixtures and fittings	4,200
Stocks	14,500
Creditors for purchases	10,950

(There have been no sales of fixed assets during the year to 30 April 19-8)

(3) All sales were made on a cash basis and after meeting cash payments the net amount was banked daily.

(4) Jim Hastings took £100 per week from the cash till for personal purposes and withdrew goods for personal use during the year valued at £335 in cost terms.

(5) Included within general operating expenses was the payment of a personal life assurance premium which amounted to £215.

(6) It has been estimated that one-fifth of the costs relating to the car are for private purposes.

Required

(a) Prepare a cash account and a bank account for the year to 30 April 19-8. (6 marks)

(b) Prepare a trading and profit and loss account for the year ended 30 April 19-8 and a balance sheet as at that date. (16 marks)

(AEB)

Tutorial note: You should preferably prepare your answer to Part (a) in the form of a two-column cash book.

Answer

(a)

Jim Hastings

Cash and bank accounts for the year to 30 April 19-8

19-7		Cash £	Bank £	19-8		Cash £	Bank £
May 1	Capital		6,500	Apr 1	Lease – premises		4,800
Aug 1	Loan		5,300		Wages	3,200	7,050
					Redecoration		
19-8					– premises		1,235
Apr 30	Cash sales	133,544			General operating		
	Cash banked		124,449		expenses	320	1,375
					Purchases of goods		105,950
					Lighting and		
					heating	95	965
					Fixtures and		
					fittings		4,895
					Loan interest		424
					Accountancy fees		355
					Car expenses	155	1,050
					Drawings	5,200	
					Cash banked	124,449	
					Balances c/d	125	8,150
		133,544	136,249			133,544	136,249

(b)
Trading and profit and loss account
for the year ended 30 April 19-8

	£	£
Sales		133,544
Less cost of sales		
Purchases	116,900	
less private use	(335)	
	116,565	
Closing stock	(14,500)	102,065
Gross profit		31,479
Wages	10,250	
Lease of premises	3,840	
Lighting and heating	1,060	
Redecoration of premises	1,235	
General operating expenses	1,480	
Loan interest	636	
Accountancy fees	355	
Car expenses	964	
Depreciation: car	760	
f & f	695	21,275
Net profit		10,204

(c)
Balance sheet as at 30 April 19-8

	£	£	£
Fixed assets			
Motor car at valuation at 1 May 19-7		4,100	
Less depreciation		950	3,150
Fixtures and fittings at cost		4,895	
Less depreciation		695	4,200
			7,350
Current assets			
Stock		14,500	
Rent prepaid		960	
Cash at bank		8,150	
Cash in hand		125	
		23,735	
Current liablities			
Creditors	10,950		
Loan interest	212	11,162	12,573
			19,923
Long-term liability: Loan repayable 19-5			5,300
			14,623
Capital			
Introduced on 1 May 19-5			10,600
Add profit for the year			10,204
			20,804
Deduct drawings (see note below)			6,181
			14,623

Note

	£
Drawings	
Bank	5,200
Goods	335
Car	241
– depn	190
Insurance premium	215
	6,181

Multiple choice questions

1 Jackson commenced business with £10,000 he had received as a gift from his aunt and £8,000 he had received as a loan from his father. He used some of this money to purchase a machine for £15,000. He obtained a mortgage for £20,000 to purchase a workshop. Jackson's capital was:

   A £3,000
   B £10,000
   C £18,000
   D £38,000

2 At 1 January 1996 Robert's business assets were valued at £36,000 and his liabilites amounted to £2,400. At 31 December 1996, Robert's assets amounted to £57,000 and included his private car which he had brought into the business on 1 November when it was valued at £9,000. His creditors at 31 December totalled £17,000 and his drawings during the year were £27,000. Robert's profit for the year to 31 December 1996 was:

   A £6,400
   B £24,400
   C £33,400
   D £58,000

3 At 1 April 1996, Tonkin's business assets were: Motor van valued at £5,000 (cost £8,000), tools £1,600, stock £700, debtors £168, cash £400. His creditors totalled £1,120.

   At 31 March 1997 his assets were: Workshop which had cost £20,000 and on which a mortgage of £16,000 was still outstanding, motor van £4,000, tools £1,900, stock £1,000, debtors £240 (of which £70 were known to be bad), cash £500. His creditors amounted to £800. During the year Tonkin's drawings amounted to £5,200. His profit for the year was:

   A £6,222
   B £6,292
   C £9,222
   D £9,292

4 At 1 March 1996 Allen's debtors amounted to £12,100. In the year to 28 February 1997 he received £63,500 from debtors and allowed them settlement discounts of £3,426. At 28 February 1997 his debtors totalled £14,625.

   Allen's sales for the year were:

   A £62,599
   B £64,401
   C £66,125
   D £69,451

5 At 1 October 1996 Maria's debtors amounted to £7,440. In the year to 30 September 1997 she received £61,080 from debtors. She had to write £384 off as a bad debt. Her debtors at 30 September 1997 were £8,163. Maria's sales for the year were:

   A £60,741
   B £61,419
   C £61,803
   D £62,187

6 All of Grayson's stock was stolen when his business was burgled on 4 March 1996. His stock at 31 December 1995 was £23,000. From 1 January to 4 March sales totalled £42,000 and purchases were £38,000. Grayson's mark up on goods is $33\frac{1}{3}\%$ to arrive at selling price. The cost of the stolen stock was:

   A £28,000
   B £29,500
   C £33,000
   D £40,000

1   Adrover, a retailer, who does not keep proper books of account, provided the following information to his accountant:

Balances as at	30 April 1989	30 April 1990
	£	£
Land and buildings at cost	120,000	140,000
Fixtures and fittings	15,000	18,000
Motor vehicles	12,000	9,000
Trade creditors	17,550	16,900
Trade debtors	26,400	31,200
Rent owing	1,500	–
Wages and salaries owing	5,600	3,800
Stock	28,000	32,000

A summary of his bank account transactions for the year ended 30 April 1990 was as follows:

1989		£	1990		£
May 1	Balance	54,000	Apr 30	Payments to trade creditors	195,600
1990				Rent	6,000
Apr 30	Receipts from trade debtors	120,800		Wages and salaries	14,500
	Receipts from cash sales	150,000		General expenses	7,800
	Sales of fixed assets	1,150		Purchases of fixed assets	29,000

Additional information:

(1) Each week the total receipts from cash sales were banked except that Adrover retained £300 per week for his own private expenses. During the year ended 30 April 1990 he had also taken £2,500 worth of goods for his own use.

(2) Adrover normally valued his stock-in-trade at cost but on the advice of a friend he decided to value his stock at 30 April 1990 at selling price. His normal mark-up on stock was 25%.

(3) Adrover had borrowed £50,000 from his brother on a long term basis on 1 May 1988. Since it was a family transaction he had not bothered to formally record the transaction. They had agreed an interest rate of 10% per annum, but to date no interest had been provided for or paid.

(4) During the financial year ended 30 April 1990 the following fixed asset transactions had taken place:

	Cash paid
Purchases	£
Freehold land	20,000
Motor vehicles	3,000
Fixtures and fittings	6,000

	Cash received	Net book value as at 30 April 1989
Sales	£	£
Motor vehicles	1,000	2,500
Fixtures and fittings	150	1,000

Required

(a) A trading and profit and loss account for the year ended 30 April 1990.

(12 marks)

(b) A balance sheet as at 30 April 1990. (9 marks)

(c) By referring to generally accepted accounting principles, comment on the suggestion made by Adrover's friend that stock should be valued at selling price.

(4 marks)

(AEB)

2   John White commenced business as a retailer on 1 January 1991 with a capital of £40,000 which was used entirely to open a business bank account through which all business receipts and payments are to pass. The following is a summary of receipts and payments during the period January to May 1991:

	January £	February £	March £	April £	May £
Receipts:					
Credit sales	29,000	67,000	54,000	39,000	43,000
Cash sales	25,000	40,000	15,000	26,000	37,000
Payments:					
Purchases	–	65,000	105,000	50,000	63,000
Overheads – Fixed	5,760	15,700	3,600	5,300	6,200
– Variable	22,700	26,300	21,100	11,300	19,600
Purchase of delivery					
vehicle (1 January)	16,000	–	–	–	–
Drawings	1,500	1,500	1,500	1,500	1,500

Additional information:

(1) One quarter of the turnover for the three months ended 31 March 1991 arose from cash sales.

(2) On 31 March 1991, John White decided that a debt of £900 due from a customer, Charles Dawe, was irrecoverable.

(3) A gross profit of 40% of sales has been obtained throughout the three months ended 31 March 1991.

(4) Except where otherwise stated, all receipts and payments occur on the last day of the relevant month.

(5) All purchases are obtained on a monthly credit basis.

(6) Variable overheads for the three months ended 31 March 1991 amounted to 24% of sales. No variable overheads were prepaid at 31 March 1991.

(7) Fixed overheads incurred during the three months ended 31 March 1991 amounted to £18,800; no fixed overheads were accrued due at 31 March 1991.

(8) It is estimated that the delivery vehicle will have a useful life in the business of four years with an estimated nil residual value; the straight line method for depreciation is to be used.

(9) The variable overheads mentioned in (vi) above and the fixed overheads in vii) above do not include bad debts written off or depreciation.

Required

John White's trading and profit and loss account for the three months ended 31 March 1991 and a balance sheet as at that date.

NOTE: Answers should be in as much detail as possible with attention being given to presentation in good style. (25 marks)

(CAMBRIDGE)

3   Ron Watts commenced business on 1 June 1989 importing a new product and selling it through mail order and market trading. Recently he had received a demand from the Inland Revenue for details of the profits he had earned from his business for the period 1 June 1989 to 31 May 1991.

    Watts had not kept complete accounting records but he was able to supply the following financial information to an accountant who had agreed to prepare profit estimates for him.

Summarised financial information as at

	1 June 1989 £	31 May 1990 £	31 May 1991 £
Cash	40,000	28,760	24,910
Balance at bank	–	145,000	136,000
Motor vans at valuation	20,000	35,000	51,000
Stock of goods at cost	50,000	65,000	82,500
Long term loan from Watts' sister	25,000	25,000	25,000
Business premises	–	100,000	100,000
Trade debtors	–	28,000	38,000
Trade creditors	–	70,000	74,900
General expenses in arrears	–	2,850	–
General expenses in advance	–	–	4,500

Additional information:

(1) Watts had kept records of the payments made to trade creditors for goods for re-sale.

During the year ended 31 May 1991, the total of such payments to trade creditors was £412,600.

(2) Watts had not kept accurate records of his receipts from sales, but he was able to supply his accountant with the following:

(i) His profit mark up was 30% on cost.

(ii) He used money from his sales receipts to finance his household expenditure of £500 per week. This weekly expenditure was constant throughout the two years.

(iii) On 1 May 1990 he bought a Mercedes for private use for £30,000. This was paid for from sales receipts.

(iv) During the year ended 31 May 1991 he remembered that he had taken various other amounts of cash out of sales receipts for private use, but he could not remember exactly how much.

(3) The business premises were bought on 1 January 1990. Watts paid £50,000 out of his own private resources and the remainder was financed by a bank mortgage at 15% interest per annum. The interest is paid annually on 1 January.

(4) Watts' sister had agreed that her loan would be provided at an interest rate of 5% per annum. She agreed to waive the first year's interest.

No interest had been paid for the year ended 31 May 1991.

(5) During the year ended 31 May 1991 new motor vans were bought which cost £30,000.

(6) General expenses of £30,000 were paid during the year ended 31 May 1991.

Required

(a) An estimate of the net profit for the year ended 31 May 1990. (9 marks)

(b) A detailed trading and profit and loss account for the year ended 31 May 1991. (8 marks)

(c) A balance sheet as at 31 May 1991. (8 marks)

(AEB)

4 Dorothy has been trading as the 'Smash Hit' music shop for several years but has never kept full accounting records. A summary of the business bank account for the year ended 31 October 19-6 is given below.

	£		£
Opening balance	700	Paid to suppliers	23,600
Cash banked (see note 1)	42,900	Rent and rates	1,500
Closing balance	1,400	Light and heat	2,200
		Advertising	950
		Wages of assistants	5,530
		Drawings	10,300
		Sundry expenses	920
	45,000		45,000

Details of assets and liabilities (other than the bank balance) at the start and end of financial year are as follows:

	1 Nov 19-5	31 Oct 19-6
	£	£
Debtors	218	(see note 2)
Creditors	3,750	4,950
Advertising prepaid	–	600
Advertising accrued	250	–
Stocks at cost	6,120	(see note 3)
Shop fixtures	10,620	(see note 4)

Notes:

1. All takings were banked, with the exception of £830 which had been used to purchase new furniture for Dorothy's house.

2. Closing debtors were equivalent to one week's sales. A quarter of this total is considered 'doubtful' and should be provided for. Assume that the shop was open for fifty weeks in the year.

3. Closing stock valued at selling price was £10,395. Average mark-up on cost price was 75%.

4. Shop fixtures are to be depreciated by the 'straight line' method over a five-year period. By 31 October 19-6, the fixtures had been owned for exactly two years.

Prepare appropriate financial statements for Dorothy's business for the year ended 31 October 19-6.

(25 marks)

(LONDON)

5 Susan owns a health food shop, trading mainly on cash terms. She does not operate a full accounting system, but does have the following records:

(i) Current assets and liabilities:

	31 Dec 1989	31 Dec 1990
	£	£
Debtors	110	195
Creditors	1,320	1,380
Stock	410	540
Prepaid business rate	50	65
Accrued rent	110	100
Accrued electricity	40	45
Bank (asset)	1,430	1,200
Cash	120	110

(ii) The 1989 balance sheet shows fixed assets as follows:

	£
Delivery van	600
Fixtures	900

There were no disposals during the year. Depreciation is charged on the reducing balance method:
Delivery van 25%
Fixtures 10%

(iii) An analysis of bank and cash movements for the year shows:

	Bank	Cash
Receipts	£	£
Shop takings	–	17,200
Received from credit customers	2,410	30
Legacy from cousin	5,000	–
Cash paid into bank	15,600	–
	23,010	17,230
Payments		
Investment	2,000	–
Part-time staff	2,400	1,000
Private drawings	3,000	420
Suppliers	11,100	–
Rent and rates	1,210	–
General expenses	–	220
Fixtures	3,000	–
Telephone	110	–
Heat and light	420	–
Cash paid into bank	–	15,600
	23,240	17,240

The investment was in shares of 'Veggy Foods Ltd', a major supplier.

(iv) During the year Susan took £500 of goods (at selling price) for her own use.

(v) A debtor of £15 is regarded as unlikely to pay.

(a) Prepare Susan's profit and loss account for the year ended 31 December 1990 and balance sheet as at 31 December 1990.

(24 marks)

(b) Explain the main disadvantages of an 'incomplete records' accounting system.

(12 marks)

(c) Explain, with reasons, which treatment you feel is appropriate for Susan's investment in 'Veggy Foods Ltd', bearing in mind that an investment in another business may be either a fixed asset or a current asset. (4 marks)

(JMB)

6   Portia received a legacy of £50,000 from her grandmother so she was able to fulfil a long standing desire to open a fashion boutique. On 1 January 1992 she opened a business bank account with the full amount of the legacy. She was so determined to get the business started that she paid little attention to establishing a full set of accounting records. Only very basic records were kept.

Also on 1 January 1992 she rented premises at a rental of £750 per month payable quarterly in advance. The first payment was made on 3 January 1992.

At 31 December 1992 a summary of Portia's bank transactions revealed the following:

Receipts	£	Payments	£
Legacy	50,000	Rent	6,750
Cash banked	269,000	Fixtures/equipment	21,670
		Business rates	2,400
		Electricity	4,670
		Telephone	690
		Purchases	265,770
		Holiday in the Bahamas	3,400

All Portia's takings were banked after the following cash expenses were paid and personal drawings taken. These were:

wages £410 per week (50 weeks);
sundry expenses £15 per week (50 weeks);
cash purchases £2980 for the year.

Portia always retained a cash float of £250 in the till.

Additional information:

(1) Due to an oversight the last quarter's rent due on 1 October 1992 was not paid until January 1993.

(2) Selling prices were fixed by marking up the goods by 40% on cost price.

(3) Business rates of £1000 had been paid on 5 October 1992 to cover the period 1 October 1992 until 31 March 1993.

(4) It was estimated that Portia owed £1800 for electricity and an accountant's fee of £220 at 31 December 1992.

(5) It was decided to depreciate the fixtures and equipment by £6670.

(6) Creditors for purchases were £6250 at 31 December 1992.

(7) Trade debtors amounted to £38 000 at the year ended 31 December 1992 and a provision for doubtful debts of 5% was to be established at that date.

(8) Closing stock was valued at cost at £15 000.

After preparing Portia's final accounts for the year ended 31 December 1992 the accountant suggested she should consider converting her business into a private limited liability company.

Required

(a) A trading and profit and loss account for the year ended 31 December 1992. (14 marks)

(b) A statement showing the calculation of Portia's drawings. (4 marks)

(c) A balance sheet as at 31 December 1992. (14 marks)

(d) A report from the accountant in response to Portia's request about the advantages and disadvantages of converting her business to a private limited liability company.

(16 marks)

(AEB)

7   Bhupesh Chaughan runs a small retail shop selling costume jewellery. He does not keep a full set of accounting records, but he is able to give the following information about the financial position of the business at 1 May 1994 and 30 April 1995.

The business assets and liabilities were:

	1 May 1994	30 April 1995
	£	£
Fixtures and fittings (cost £10,000)	9,000	8,100
Van(E742 XBA)	7,000	–
Van(M217 PFQ)	–	6,750
Stock	6,000	7,000
Debtors	1,750	1,160
Creditors	850	700
Insurance prepaid	340	400
Rent accrued due	250	200
Balance at bank	1,480	–
Bank overdraft	–	9,170
Cash in hand	140	160

He has also provided the following summary of the business bank account for the year ended 30 April 1995.

	£		£
Balance 1 May 1994	1,480	Purchases	35,670
Receipts from debtors for sales	6,170	Rent and rates	4,170
Proceeds from sale of van		Lighting and heating	2,140
(E742 XBA)	4,500	Advertising	850
Cash banked	41,120	Insurance	1,200
Balance 30 April 1995	9,170	Motor expenses	2,110
		General expenses	3,180
		Van (M217 PFQ)	9,000
		Payments to creditors for	
		purchases	4,120
	62,440		62,440

All the takings from cash sales were banked after the following payments were made:

	£
Purchases	1,360
Wages	15,240
Drawings	14,150

Bhupesh now knows that a part-time assistant who left his employment in October 1994 was systematically stealing cash from the shop; he is uncertain of the exact amount. He was not insured against this loss.

The shop normally earns a uniform gross profit on sales of 50%.

Required

(a) A computation showing how much cash has been stolen from Bhupesh Chaughan's shop. (8 marks)

(b) A trading and profit and loss account for the year ended 30 April 1995 and a balance sheet as at that date. (32 marks)

(c) A memorandum addressed to Bhupesh indicating the measures that he could take to prevent cash being stolen in future. Include advice on how Bhupesh could improve his financial record keeping. (10 marks)

(AEB)

8 Conrad Watts owns a retail business dealing in electrical goods. As he is extremely busy he has not given very much attention to his accounting records. The main sources of information in respect of business transactions are bank statements, a rough cash book and a number of invoices. Conrad, however, recognises that if the performance of the business is to be measured effectively, then details of assets and liabilities are crucial.

Details of all business assets and liabilities are as follows:

	At 31 May 1994	At 31 May 1995
	£	£
Shop premises (at cost)	42,000	42,000
Fixtures and equipment (original cost £25,000)	15,000	19,000
Cash at bank	28,780	1,230
Trade creditors	16,040	15,760

	£	£
Accrued rent	450	–
Prepaid rent	–	500
Prepaid insurance	240	–
Accrued insurance	–	160
Debtors	6,100	2,140
Stock	25,810	26,230
Van (original cost £7,000)	1,200	–
Capital	102,640	?
New van	–	9,000

A summary of the bank statements for the year produced the following details.

Receipts	£	Payments	£
Cheques from debtors	31,700	Cheques to creditors	156,300
Proceeds from sale of old van	800	Purchase of new van	9,000
Net cash takings banked	141,860	Rent	5,600
		Advertising	730
		Insurance	540
		Light and heat	1,630
		Business rates	1,900
		New fixtures and equipment	4,000
		Drawings	22,210
	174,360		201,910

It was found that prior to banking the cash takings the following items were paid:

	£
Staff wages	23,500
Purchase of goods for resale	7,100
Sundry shop expenses	4,950

Additional information:

(1) Conrad Watts took goods amounting to £1050 at cost for his own use.

(2) The bank drawings figure includes £50 per week paid to Conrad's wife for work done by her for the business (50 weeks).

(3) Conrad has been advised that the fixtures and equipment, and vans, should continue to be depreciated by 10% on cost at the end of each year.

Conrad Watts finds that keeping accounting records is tedious and is considering the introduction of a computer which he feels will make things easier for him.

Required

(a) A trading and profit and loss account for the year ended 31 May 1995.
(22 marks)

(b) A balance sheet for the business as at 31 May 1995. (12 marks)

(c) A brief report outlining the problems facing Conrad Watts, suggesting ways in which they may be overcome. (8 marks)

(d) State the advantages and problems of introducing a computerised system of accounting into a small business. (8 marks)
(AEB)

5 Accounts of non-profit making organisations

Chapter objectives

You should be able to prepare:

- ❑ receipts and payments accounts;
- ❑ income and expenditure accounts;
- ❑ trading accounts;
- ❑ balance sheets (for clubs, societies etc).

Most clubs, societies etc do not employ trained bookkeepers as their Honorary Treasurers. Their accounting records are invariably incomplete and the techniques already learned in Chapter 4 are required for the preparation of their annual accounts.

5.1 Main features of non-profit making organisations

(a) An Income and Expenditure account replaces the Profit and Loss account.

(b) A trading account is only prepared for a subsidiary activity which is in the nature of trading and carried on to supplement the income of the club or to provide a service to members, e.g. bar sales.

(c) In the Income and Expenditure account, 'Surplus of income over expenditure' replaces the 'net profit' of a profit and loss account, and 'Excess of expenditure over income' replaces 'net loss'.

(d) In the balance sheet, 'Accumulated fund' replaces the 'capital' account found in the accounts of a sole trader.

Members' subscriptions

The total of subscriptions credited to the Income and expenditure account should equal the annual subscription per member multiplied by the number of members. If this information is not given, prepare a total subscriptions account.

Subscriptions in arrears

Clubs can hardly take legal action against members to recover subscriptions in arrears. The policy of the club committee will determine how arrears of subscriptions will be dealt with in the accounts. Unfortunately, examiners do not always disclose the policy of the committee, which may be one of the following:

(i) To omit unpaid subscriptions from the Income and Expenditure account and the balance sheet. If the subscriptions are paid at a later date, they will be credited to the Income and Expenditure account in the year in which received.

(ii) To credit all subscriptions due for the year to the Income and Expenditure account whether received or not, and to show subscriptions in arrears in the balance sheet as current assets. Insofar as the arrears are not received in the following year, to write them off in that following year.

Course (i) above is the more prudent of the two as it tends to understate income and assets rather than overstate them. On the other hand, the second course has the merits of matching income to the period concerned and of highlighting the amounts of subscriptions in arrears and those that are subsequently written off. The normal method is to treat subscriptions as in (ii) above unless the question indicates that it is the club's policy to adopt a different treatment.

Life subscriptions and entry fees

These are lump sums paid by members and should be dealt with in accordance with the matching concept; they should be credited when received to Deferred Income account and credited to Income and expenditure account in equal annual instalments over such period as determined by the committee.

Donations made to the club

The treatment of donations, legacies etc. made to a club will depend upon the purpose for which they are made. If the donation is simply intended to add to the club funds, it may be credited to the Income and Expenditure account. If the donation is given for a special purpose, such as the provision of a new club house or to coach young members to become better footballers, the wishes of the donor should be respected. They should be recognised by crediting the donation to a special fund and shown in the balance sheet, but not as part of the accumulated fund. The donation should not be used for any other purpose.

5.2 Ancillary activities

Clubs often engage in activities which are ancillary to their main object in order to supplement their subscription income; these may include sales to members of equipment, publications, or bar facilities, which are in the form of trading. Other non-trading activities include the provision of refreshments and raffles. For any activity which constitutes trading, a separate trading account should be prepared and the balance on that account transferred to the Income and expenditure account. For non-trading activities, the income and expenditure should be 'netted' in that account; e.g.

	£	£
Sale of raffle tickets	90	
less cost of prizes and tickets	55	35

5.2.1 Example

The Penny Black Philatelic Society offers its members the opportunity to attend weekly meetings, to hear talks on postage stamps, attend exhibitions and auctions of stamps and to buy and sell stamps and equipment through the society. Its financial year ends on 30 April.

The secretary of the society has supplied the following information:

	Balances at	
	1 May 19-1	30 April 19-2
	£	£
Fixed assets: Display cases	1,000	1,000
Equipment	1,600	1,840
Stock of stamps at cost	2,200	3,120
Debtors for stamp sales	200	110
Subscriptions in arrears	100	80
Subscriptions in advance	40	55
Cash at bank	416	to be found
Rent of hall in advance	100	70
Electricity owing	60	80
Printing expenses outstanding	15	40

Receipts in the year to 30 April 19-2: Subscriptions £1,100; sales of stamps £5,140; sales of raffle tickets £300; refreshments £440.

Payments in the year to 30 April 19-2: Purchase of stamps £3,000; purchase of equipment for use by the society £400; rent £900; electricity £230; printing £60; raffle prizes £100; secretary's expenses £35; refreshments £240.

Display cases are to be depreciated by 10% on book value.

Required

The income and expenditure account of the Penny Black Philatelic Society for the year to 30 April 19-2, and a balance sheet as at that date.

(The profit or loss on sale of stamps should be calculated separately, and the net income from other activities should be shown in the income and expenditure account.)

Workings

1.

Accumulated fund at 1 May 19-1

	£	£
Fixed assets: display cases		1,000
equipment		1,600
Stock of stamps		2,200
Debtors for stamps		200
Subscriptions in arrears		100
Cash at bank		416
Rent in advance		100
		5,616
less Subscriptions in advance	40	
Electricity	60	
Printing	15	115
Accumulated fund at 1.5.19-1		5,501

2.

Receipts and payments account for year to 30 April 19-2

	£		£
Balance at 1.5.19-1	416	Purchase of stamps	3,000
Subscriptions	1,100	Equipment	400
Sales of stamps	5,140	Rent	900
Sale of raffle tickets	300	Electricity	230
Refreshments	440	Printing	60
		Raffle prizes	100
		Secretary's expenses	35
		Refreshments	240
		Balance c/d	2,431
	7,396		7,396

3.

Sale of stamps

	£		£
Debtors at 1.5.19-1	200	Cash received	5,140
Stamp trading account	5,050	Debtors at 30.4.19-2	110
	5,250		5,250

Subscriptions

	£		£
Arrears b/f	100	In advance b/f	40
In advance c/f	55	Bank	1,100
I & E a/c	1,065	Arrears c/f	80
	1,220		1,220

Rent of hall

	£		£
Prepayment b/f	100	I & E a/c	930
Bank	900	Prepayment c/f	70
	1,000		1,000

Electricity

	£		£
Bank	230	Accrual b/f	60
Accrual c/f	80	I & E a/c	250
	310		310

Printing

	£		£
Bank	60	Accrual b/f	15
Accrual c/f	40	I & E a/c	85
	100		100

Equipment

	£		£
Bal b/f	1,600	I & E a/c	160
Additions	400	Balance c/f	1,840
	2,000		2,000

Answer

The Penny Black Philatelic Society
Stamp trading account for the year to 30 April 19-2

	£	£
Sales of stamps		5,050
less cost of stamps sold: Stock at 1.5.-1	2,200	
Purchases	3,000	
	5,200	
Stock at 30.4.-2	3,120	2,080
Profit on sale of stamps		2,970

Income and expenditure account for the year to 30 April 19-2

	£	£
Income:		
Subscriptions		1,065
Profit on sale of stamps		2,970
Raffles – sale of tickets	300	
– less cost of prizes	100	200
Refreshments	440	
less cost of food	240	200
		4,435
Expenditure:		
Rent	930	
Electricity	250	
Printing	85	
Secretary's expenses	35	
Depreciation – display cases	100	
– equipment	160	1,560
Surplus of income over expenditure		2,875

Balance sheet as at 30 April 19-2

	£	£	£
Fixed assets:			
Display cases (1,000 – 100)			900
Equipment (1,600 + 400 – 160)			1,840
			2,740
Current assets:			
Stock of stamps		3,120	
Debtors for stamps		110	
Subscriptions in arrears		80	
Rent in advance		70	
Balance at bank		2,431	
		5,811	
less Current liabilities:			
Subscriptions in advance	55		
Electricity	80		
Printing	40	175	5,636
			8,376
Represented by:			
Accumulated fund at 1 May 19-1			5,501
Surplus of income over expenditure			2,875
			8,376

Note: A worksheet (see Chapter 4 §5) could have been prepared for this question in place of the simulated ledger accounts.

5.2.2 Exercise: preparing club accounts

The Diplock, Pibworth and Parkland Sports and Social Club's financial year ends on 31 December.

The assets and liabilities of the club at the dates stated were as follows:

	At 31 Dec 19-0	At 31 Dec 19-1
	£	£
Equipment	2,500	2,800
Subscriptions in arrears	200	180
Subscriptions in advance	130	110
Creditors for bar stocks	350	430
Bar stocks	800	600
Rent owing	150	100
Electricity owing	105	140
Bank balance (favourable)	723	1,300

In the year to 31 December 19-1, the cash receipts were:

	£
Subscriptions (including £60 of arrears from previous year)	2,100
Bar takings	4,100
Annual dinner/dance, sale of tickets	2,400
Sale of raffle tickets	180

In the same period the following payments have been made:

	£
Affiliation fees	100
Purchase of equipment	800
Bar stocks	2,050
Barman's wages	750
Catering (dinner/dance)	1,440
Hire of band (dinner/dance)	300
Raffle prizes	60
Rent of hall	1,500
Printing and postage	200
Electricity	581
Hon. secretary's expenses	122
Repairs to equipment	300

Required

Diplock, Pibworth and Parkland Sports and Social Club's Income and expenditure account for the year to 31 December 19-1 and the balance sheet as at that date.

Key points to remember

1. Follow the seven steps demonstrated in Chapter 4 (incomplete records) to prepare accounts of non-profit making organisations.

2. Non-profit making organisations have: Income and expenditure accounts (instead of profit and loss accounts); Surplus of income over expenditure (instead of profits); Excess of expenditure over income (instead of losses); Accumulated funds (instead of capital accounts).

3. Prepare a trading account for any trading activity used to raise funds, e.g. a bar, and carry the profit or loss only to the Income and expenditure account.

4. 'Net' expenditure against income in the Income and expenditure account for fund raising activities which do not constitute trading e.g. dinner/dances, raffles.

Common errors

1. Failure to prepare trading accounts, or to show 'net' results in the Income and Expenditure account for activities for which trading accounts are not appropriate.

2. Preparation of profit and loss account instead of an income and expenditure account and the use of incorrect terminology (see 5.1 above).

3. Entrance fees, life membership subscriptions, gifts and legacies credited to Income and expenditure account as received.

4. Subscriptions in arrears treated incorrectly.

5. Accruals and prepayments of expenses, depreciation, ignored or treated incorrectly.

Questions

Fully worked examination question

Members of the Wenbury Choral Society rehearse for, and perform in, three choral concerts per year, and also attend several concerts together in the nearest major town. The Society is dependent upon grants and donations. The size of the grant for each year depends upon the costs and revenues of the concerts given in the previous year, being 80% of the difference. However, the programme has to be decided upon at least one season in advance, so that soloists and orchestras may be booked. For the 1990-91 season, the Society will perform one concert which will require a particularly large orchestra and additional soloists. The grant for 1989-90 was £5,200.

The Treasurer of the Society resigned in December 1989, and a committee member has been trying to keep the records ever since. He has provided the following information:

(i) The Society purchases choral scores which it sells to members at cost plus 10%, and also hires scores for those members who prefer to borrow and return them. The hire charge to the society is 90% of the charge made to members. In the year ended 30 April 1990 the Society bought 170 scores, all of which were sold to members for £5.50 each. It paid hire charges for scores of £360.

(ii) The Society had 96 singing members in 1988-89 and 109 in 1989-90. Husbands and wives who are both members are given a discount of 10% on their total subscription. Over 60's obtain a reduction of 20%. In the year ended 30 April 1990 the normal subscription rate was £25. During the year ended 30 April 1990 there were five husbands and their wives who were both singing members, and ten over 60's, all of whom paid their subscriptions on time, while four ordinary members had failed to pay their subscriptions by the end of the year, although they were still singing with the Society.

(iii) To encourage ticket sales, those sold more than four weeks before a concert are reduced in price by £0.50. The Society sells tickets for its concerts at two prices, £4.50 and £3.50. For the 1989-90 season the numbers of tickets sold were 816 at £4.50 and 362 at £3.50, of which 358 and 210 respectively were at the reduced rate for early payment.

(iv) Printing of tickets and concert programmes for the 1989-90 season cost £415, and the sale of programmes at the concerts realised £595.

(v) Other concert expenses for the season were: hire of concert hall £750, soloists' fees £2,120, orchestral fees £8,360, conductor's fees £270.

(vi) Rehearsal expenses for the year ended 30 April 1990 were: accompanist's fees £840, conductor's fees £1,310, hire of rehearsal hall £1,250.

(vii) Donations from patrons or former Society members were £740.

(viii) The Society has an arrangement with a local coach firm to transport members to four concerts each year. The coach hire for a 40-seater coach is £120. Members pay £4 each. In the year ended 30 April 1990 142 coach seats were filled.

Required

A Prepare the Society's Income and Expenditure account for the year ended 30 April 1990, and from your figures calculate the grant the Society should receive for the following season, not including items i) and vi) in your calculations. State whether or not you think the Society can budget effectively for the future on the basis of the grants it can expect to receive.

(15 marks)

B What financial records do you suggest the Society should keep?   (3 marks)

C What differences would you expect to find between the records of a club or society and those of a small limited company?   (5 marks)

(OXFORD)

Answer

A

Wenbury Choral Society
Income and expenditure account for the year to 30 April 1990

	£	£	£	£
Subscriptions				4,675
Sales and hire of scores		1,335		
Less cost of scores		1,210		125
Donations				740
Grant for the year to 30 April 1990				
(80% of £6,665)				5,332
				10,872
Concert expenses				
Orchestral fees		8,360		
Soloists		2,120		
Conductors' fees		270		
Hire of hall		750		
Printing of programmes and tickets		415		
		11,915		
Less Sale of tickets	4,655			
Sale of programmes	595	5,250	6,665	
Rehearsal expenses				
Accompanist's fees		840		
Conductor's fees		1,310		
Hire of rehearsal hall		1,250	3,400	
Coach hire		480		
Less receipts		568	(88)	9,977
Surplus of income over expenditure				895

Workings

Subscriptions:	10 × £25 × 90%	225	
	10 × £25 × 80%	200	
	170 × £25	4,250	
	190	4,675	

		Cost	Sales
		£	£
Sale of scores			
170 × £5.50			935
Cost (£935 × 100/110)		850	
Hire of scores (10/9 × £360)			400
Cost		360	
		1,210	1,335

Ticket sales		£
Reduced price	358 × £4	1,432
	210 × £3	630
Full price	458 × £4.50	2,061
	152 × £3.50	532
		4,655

The effectiveness of budgeting depends upon the degree of uncertainty or risk connected with the elements of revenue and costs. The costs of concerts may be budgeted with reasonable certainty, and the grant appears to be settled at 80% of losses made. Uncertainty exists regarding the revenue to be received from sale of tickets and programmes. Interest in the concerts depends upon the popular appeal of the programmes and the weather on the days of the performances.

B   The society should maintain records of the receipt and payment of cash (a cash book); a register of members in which to record subscriptions due and paid; a nominal ledger in which to record revenue and expense accounts (and any assets the Society may acquire). These records should be adequate as far as can be ascertained from the question.

C   A small limited company, to comply with the requirements of the Companies Act 1985, should maintain, in addition to the records maintained by a club, sales and purchase ledgers and records of stock. Non financial records that must be maintained by a limited company, apart from the registar of members, must include books in which to record the minutes of meetings of directors and shareholders.

Multiple choice questions

1   In the balance sheet of All Seasons Sports and Social Club at 31 December 1995 the accumulated Fund represents:

A   the assets of the club less its liabilities at 31.12.95

B   the surplus of income over expenditure for the year

C   the surplus of receipts over payments for the year

D   the total assets of the club at 31.12.95.

2   A club's surplus of income over expenditure for a year is represented by:

A   the balance on its Accumulated Fund at the end of the year

B   the increase in the balance on its Receipts and Payments account over the year

C   the increase in its net assets over the year

D   the increase in its total assets over the year

3   A donation to a sports club to help it build a new pavilion will be shown as

A   an addition to the Accumulated Fund

B   an asset in the balance sheet

C   a special fund in the balance sheet

D   income in the club's income and expenditure account

4   Clubs should treat life membership subscriptions as:

A   additions to the accumulated fund

B   deferred income

C   income of the year in which they are received

D   loans to the club

Further examination questions

1   The treasurer of the Comet Kite Club reported the following receipts and payments for the year ended 31 August 1990. The club not only provides kite competitions and social events for members, but also manufactures and sells kites.

	£		£
Members' subscriptions	44,650	Material for kite manufacture	10,000
Sales of kites to the general public	14,700	Payments: casual labour assisting kite manufacture	6,000
Receipts from social events	20,500	Competition entry fees	1,500

	£		£
Trade donation to sponsor 'Europe		Grants to members: subsistence	
1992' special competition	5,000	and travel	12,500
		Social events' expenses	9,800
		Purchase of power tools	900
		Vehicle repairs	1,750
		Power used in kite manufacture	380
		Rates and insurance	470
		Heating costs: club premises	800

Additional information:

(1) Balances as at 1 September 1989:

	£
Club premises	80,000
Balance at bank	25,000
Motor vehicles	14,000
Stock of kite materials	2,000
Members' subscriptions owing for 1988/89	1,100
Club competition kites	15,000
Power tools	2,500

Fixed assets are recorded at net book value.

(2) One quarter of all kites manufactured were children's special kites for selling to hospitals at reduced prices. The sales value of this 1989/90 output was £2,500, but no money had yet been received.

One half of all kites manufactured were sold to the general public.

The remainder of the kites were retained for club members to be used in competitions.

(3) There were no opening or closing stocks of finished kites.

(4) Closing stock of kite materials at 31 August 1990, £3,500.

(5) Amounts owing to the club as at 31 August 1990:

	£
Debtors for kites sold to the general public	900
Members' subscriptions for 1989/90	1,850

(6) Members' subscriptions received for 1990/91 £760

(7) A bill was outstanding for the club's heating costs at 31 August 1990 £250

(8) The club's fixed assets were to be depreciated annually as follows:

	%
Club kites	30
Power tools	20
Vehicles	20

All depreciation is on net book value of assets held at the financial year end.

The power tools were used exclusively for the manufacture of kites.

(9) A condition had been attached to the trade donations for 'Europe 1992' Special Competition. The money is to be placed in a bank deposit account marked 'Europe 1992 Fund'.

Required

(a) For the year ended 31 August 1990
  (i) A manufacturing statement showing the profit or loss on kites.   (6 marks)
  (ii) An income and expenditure account.   (8 marks)

(b) A balance sheet as at 31 August 1990.   (7 marks)

(c) Advise the treasurer of the club as to how the club's liquid assets could be deployed to raise further income.   (4 marks)

(AEB)

2 The Baldac Engineering Co has a social club which provides social and leisure activities for all employees. The club is assisted by the company, but is run as a separate entity with its own officers and committee. Any employee and his immediate family may join by paying an annual fee of

(i) £5 for the employee

(ii) £8 for the employee's husband/wife

(iii) £3 for each child up to the age of 18 years.

Members joining after 31 December in any year are charged half a year's subscription.

Every year the company donates to the club a sum equal to 50% of the total membership fees due from employees, this sum to be calculated on the membership at 31 May each year, and paid in the following July.

The club is able to purchase certain goods through the company's Central Purchasing department at a discount. Some of these are sold to members at cost to the club plus 25%.

The company's monthly magazine 'Baldac Review' is distributed to employees through the social club; the company makes a contribution of two pence for each magazine distributed and the club pays members five pence for every magazine that they are able to distribute to employees who are not members of the social club.

The club's accounting year ends on 31 May each year, and for the year ended 31 May 19-7 the following information concerning the club activities is available.

Receipts		£
Subscriptions received from members:	Employees	3,180
	Husband/wife	2,800
	Under 18	1,800
Receipts from social functions:	Horticultural Show	8,750
	Christmas Dinner and Dance	13,450
	Old time Music Halls	4,700
	Prize draws held at social functions	5,420
	Gala and Sports Day	4,750
	Other social functions	5,350
Receipts from refreshments at social functions		1,400
Receipts from the Company:	Distribution costs 'Baldac Review'	480
	Donations based on membership	1,500
Receipts from sales of goods to members (note 6)		45,375
Receipts from sales in the bar		84,100

Payments		£
Lighting and heating of Club premises		8,830
Telephone and postage		1,625
Insurance		1,415
Repairs and maintenance of premises and equipment		3,630
Costs of functions held:	Horticultural Show	450
	Dinner/Dance	7,640
	Old Time Music Halls	1,140
	Gala and Sports Day	1,285
	Other functions	2,100
Prizes:	Horticultural Show	2,480
	Gala and Sports Day	1,760
	Prize Draws	820
Purchases through the company's Central Purchasing		42,800
Purchases of bar stocks		71,750
Purchase of refreshments		14,800
Payments for distributing 'Baldac Review'		216
Purchase of equipment for club house		12,000
Club Stewards' wages		12,460

Notes

1. The club owns its own premises which at 1 June 19-6 were valued at £242,000.

2. Equipment owned by the club at 1 June 19-6 had a book value of £41,000 (cost £74,000). It is club policy to depreciate equipment at 15% per annum on cost on 31 May. The club also has trophies valued at £54,000 at 1 June 19-6.

3. At 1 June 19-6 £60 was owing by members for subscriptions for the year to 31 May 19-6.

4. The club has the following membership:

	31 Dec 19-6	31 May 19-7
Employees	500	800
Husbands/wives	300	400
Under 18	400	800

No members had left during the year, and at 31 December 19-6 all membership fees had been paid.

5. Cost of refreshments is to be apportioned between the Horticultural show, Christmas Dinner/Dance, Old Time Music Hall, Gala and Sports Day and other social functions in proportion to receipts from these functions, (excluding receipts from refreshments at social functions).

6. Of the goods purchased through the company's Central Purchasing department:
£6,450 were used in the bar
£1,400 were used in the prize draw
£450 were used at other social functions. The remainder apart from the closing stock, was sold to members on a strictly cash basis.The stock of goods unsold at cost at 31 May 19-6 was £3,800.

At 31 May 19-6 the club had £4,750 in the bank, and at 31 May 19-7 bar stocks had increased by £100 to £4,750. One quarter of the stewards' wages is paid to the barman.

You are required to prepare:

(a) A Revenue account (Income and Expenditure) for the year ended 31 May 19-7, showing the profits made by the various club activities as far as can be ascertained.   (21 marks)

(b) A Balance Sheet at 31 May 19-7.   (19 marks)
(OXFORD)

3   The Slemish Common Room is constituted as a private club for members of staff of the North Ulster College of Further Education. It is funded partly from members' subscriptions (£10 per head) and partly from profits from the bar which sells drinks and refreshments.

The following was its balance sheet at 31 August 1990.

	£	£
Fixed assets:		
Bar fixtures and equipment at cost	2,650	
Less depreciation	875	1,775
Net current assets		
Stocks	1,050	
Cash at bank	1,600	
Cash in hand	30	
	2,680	
Less Creditors	(505)	
Rent accrual	(550)	1,625
		3,400
Accumulated fund		3,400

The cash taken over the bar for the year ended 31 August 1991 was accounted for as follows:

	£	£
Opening balance		30
Cash takings for year		20,000
		20,030
Less Cash payments:		
Purchases	5,500	
Wages	6,450	
Cleaning	51	
New bar equipment	100	
Xmas disco expenses	85	
Paid into bank	7,814	20,000
Closing balance		30

The treasurer collected members' subscriptions amounting to £2,500; these were paid directly into the bank.

Stock was not taken at the end of August 1991 but is tightly controlled and may be calculated by reference to the gross profit percentage which is 40% of sales.

The purchases (not including cash purchases) amounted to £7,050.

The following analysis was made of the cheque payments:

	£
Suppliers for purchases	6,775
Cleaning	130
New display cabinets	750
General overheads	1,900
Rent	550

Provision is required to be made for rent due to the North Ulster College which is based on $1\frac{1}{2}$% of turnover and for depreciation on the bar fixtures and equipment at the rate of 20% on cost.

You are required to prepare:

(a) the income and expenditure account of the Slemish Common Room for the year ended 31 August 1991. (13 marks)

(b) balance sheet at 31 August 1991 (7 marks)

(NI)

4   The Baylandsea Sailing Club is an association for sailing enthusiasts and it provides members with a number of activities:

(i) a clubhouse with a bar for drinks and other social functions;

(ii) yacht racing competitions

(iii) hire of boats for members. Non members are charged an extra 20% for boat hire;

(iv) a sailing training school for all age groups.

(1) The following financial information is available as at 1 June 1992:

	£	
Paint and trim shop	50,000	⎫
Freehold premises	400,000	all at net
Boatyard and launch facilities	80,000	book value
Fixtures and fittings	30,000	
Club-owned boats and yachts	350,000	⎭
Members' subscriptions:		
in arrears	4,000	
in advance	5,600	
Balance at bank	110,700	
Bar stocks	31,000	
Bar creditors	5,000	

(2) The following financial information is available for the year ended 31 May 1993:

Receipts	£	Payments	£
Receipts from training school	20,500	Purchase of 2 new club yachts	50,000
Boat hire charges:		Repairs to yachts and boats	19,200
For members	9,000	Purchase of bar stocks	50,100
For non-members	19,600	Bar and social functions' wages	12,600
Members' subscriptions	200,900	Outgoings on yacht racing	
Bar and social functions'		competitions	18,700
takings	80,000	Wages for training school	
Fees and charges from yacht		staff and boat hire	15,000
racing competitions	30,800	General expenses	22,000
Salvage receipt from sunk			
boat	2,000		

Additional information:

(i) At 31 May 1993 there were members' subscriptions in arrears of £3500 and members' subscriptions in advance for 1993/94 of £7900.

(ii) During the year a club boat was involved in a collision whilst at sea. The boat was sunk and is recoverable only as salvage. Net book value of the boat was £20,000.

(iii) The club depreciates its fixed assets as follows:

Freehold premises
Boatyard and launch facilities } 5% per annum of net book value
Club boats and yachts

Fixtures and fittings
Paint and trim shop } 10% per annum of net book value

(iv) As at 31 May 1993 there were outstanding creditors for the following:

	£
Bar purchases	6100
Bar wages	350
Repairs to yachts and boats	3200

(v) The bar's stock valuation was £28,500 at cost on 31 May 1993.

(vi) A retired club member had recently died and in his will left the club two boats. The boats were valued at £30,000 and were formally acquired on 1 May 1993.

(vii) Of the 20% extra charge on the annual receipts from boat hire to non-members, 25% of the charge was donated to a local charity. This donation has not yet been paid.

Required

(a) An income and expenditure account for the year ended 31 May 1993, showing profits/losses on relevant activities. (26 marks)

(b) A balance sheet as at 31 May 1993. (18 marks)

(c) Comment on the club's liquidity. (6 marks)

(AEB)

5 The Chaucer Theatre Club performs a number of plays every year in the premises which they own in Austenville. In addition to these plays the Club organises a variety of other arts functions, which means that their premises are actively used throughout the year.

The Club's membership is composed of individuals and business organisations. Several of the businesses give additional funds to sponsor productions.

The honorary treasurer of the Club has prepared the following receipts and payments account for the year ended 31 March 1994.

	£		£
Rents charged	3,900	Balance brought forward	880
Sponsorship	12,500	Light and heat	3,960
Subscriptions		Insurances	1,820
Individual	4,000	Club advertising	1,560
Business	1,700	Copyright costs	1,504
Programme advertising	320	Caretaker's wages	8,016
Ticket sales from plays	52,880	Printing and stationery	1,575
		Postages and telephone	610
		General expenses	6,772
		Play performance costs	27,800
		Repairs and maintenance	6,318
		Equipment and costume hire	3,725
		Balance carried forward	10,760
	75,300		75,300

The following information is available:

(1) The premises were purchased on 1 April 1984 for £85,000 and are being depreciated at a rate of 4% per annum on cost. The Club also owns a variety of fixtures which originally cost £16,000 and upon which depreciation of £6,200 up to 1 April 1993 has been charged. The rate of depreciation on fixtures is 10% per annum using the reducing balance method.

(2) A cash float of £100 has been maintained but it was decided during the year to increase this to £150. The additional £50 was taken from ticket sales before the takings were banked.

(3) Individual members pay annual subscriptions of £20 each and business organisations pay £100 per annum. At 31 March 1993 four individual members were in arrears but

three businesses had paid in advance. On 31 March 1994 seven individual members had not paid but six had paid for the year 1994/95. Those individual members who had been in arrears at 31 March 1993 have subsequently paid up.

(4) At 31 March 1993 the following amounts had been outstanding – printing £320 and repairs £170, whilst at that date insurances of £120 had been pre-paid.

(5) At 31 March 1994 a telephone bill of £85 and one for electricity of £510 were unpaid but copyright expenses of £125 had been prepaid.

(6) The Club committee agreed to grant an honorarium of £100 each to the secretary and treasurer for the year ended 31 March 1994.

Required

(a) A statement showing the calculation of the accumulated fund of the Chaucer Theatre Club as at 31 March 1993   (10 marks)

(b) Prepare an income and expenditure account for the Club for the year ended 31 March 1994.   (19 marks)

(c) Prepare the balance sheet of the Club as at 31 March 1994.   (13 marks)

(d) Discuss the benefits and drawbacks of sponsorship from the point of view of:
    (i) the business sponsors;   (6 marks)
    (ii) the Club.   (6 marks)
        (AEB)

6   The Warwick Road Tennis and Bowling Club is a private club which has been in existence for a number of years. Its financial year end is 31 October.

The club has two classes of membership:

(i) full members who each pay a subscription of £21 per year;

(ii) bowling-only members who each pay a subscription of £8 per year.

The club buys and supplies tennis balls for use of the members and sells the used balls to local play groups for a nominal sum. There is also a bar which is staffed voluntarily by club members on a rota basis.

The following information has been provided by the club treasurer.

Receipts and Payments Account for the year ended 31 October 1995

	£		£
Balance 1 November 1994	160	Payments to bar creditors	27,683
Bar takings	34,320	Heating and lighting	688
Sales of tennis balls	20	Insurance	526
Bowls' hire	160	Repairs	420
Bowling members' subscriptions	400	General expenses	162
Full members' subscriptions	1,995	Cleaning	308
Dinner dance receipts	1,200	Committee expenses	117
		New lawnmower	460
		Printing – dinner dance tickets	16
		– general	181
		Dinner dance expenses	1,483
		Groundsman's wages	5,720
		Payment to Sports World plc for	
		tennis balls	370
		Balance 31 October 1995	121
	38,255		38,255

Additional information:

(1) Six full members had owed subscriptions at 31 October 1994. Three of them paid their subscriptions in November 1994. The committee has decided to write the remainder off as bad debts.

(2) At 31 October 1994 the club's lawnmower had a book value of £180. During the year ended 31 October 1995 a new lawnmower costing £540 was purchased. The old lawnmower was traded in against this for £80, the balance being paid in cash. It is club policy to depreciate machinery by 10% per annum using the reducing balance method.

The assets and liabilities of the club other than the cash balance were as follows:

	at 31 Oct 1994	at 31 Oct 1995
	£	£
Bar creditors	392	409
Sports World plc – creditor for tennis balls	130	62
Stock of tennis balls	87	79
Full members' subscriptions in advance	42	21
Full members' subscriptions in arrears		
(Note (1) above)	126	–
Fixtures and fittings	4,650	4,250
Lawnmower (Note (2) above)	180	?
Heating and lighting owing	69	123
Insurance in advance	46	57
Bar stocks	2,600	1,750

Required

(a) Prepare the bar trading account and the income and expenditure account for the year ended 31 October 1995   (30 marks)

(b) Prepare a balance sheet as at 31 October 1995   (8 marks)

(c) Draft a report to the club committee indicating **three** possible ways of improving the profitability of Warwick Road Tennis and Bowling Club. Explain why it is necessary for the club to make a surplus.   (12 marks)

                    (AEB)

6 Partnership accounting

Chapter objectives

Questions on this topic test a wide range of knowledge and abilities:

☐ appreciation of the differences between sole traders and partnerships

☐ knowledge of partnership law and accounting

☐ application of accounting concepts

☐ preparation of trading and profit and loss accounts and balance sheets, including the ability to prepare these as forecast statements

☐ correction of errors

☐ preparation of partnership accounts from incomplete records

6.1 Partnership

The Partnership Act of 1890 defines a partnership as 'the relationship which subsists between persons carrying on business in common with a view of profit'. People may form partnerships for a variety of reasons, the most common of which are:

(a) A partnership is usually able to raise more capital than a sole trader.

(b) Partners may contribute a diversity of knowledge, experience and expertise in management of the business.

(c) Partners can 'cover' for each other during holidays and sickness

The possible disadvantages of partnership are:

(a) Partners are not able to act as independently as sole traders.

(b) A partner's plans for the direction and development of the firm may be frustrated by the other partners.

(c) The number of partners is limited to 20 except for certain professional partnerships such as firms of accountants, solicitors etc.

Every partnership should be based upon an agreement which should be in writing to reduce the possibility of disputes about their rights and duties as partners. Agreements may, however, be verbal; but in the case of a dispute which leads to litigation, the Court may assume an implied agreement based on the past practice of the partners.

A partnership agreement should include reference to the following matters amongst others:

(1) Amount of capital to be subscribed by each partner.

(2) Rate of interest, if any, on partners' loans to firm.

(3) Rate of interest, if any, to be allowed on partners' capitals.

(4) Rate of interest, if any, to be charged on partners' drawings.

(5) Amounts of partners' salaries, if any.

(6) Ratio in which profits and losses are to be shared between the partners.

Partnership Act 1890

The following provisions apply only insofar as they are not covered in the partnership agreement:

(1) All partners may contribute equally to the capital of the partnership.

(2) Partners not entitled to:
    (a) interest on capital;
    (b) salaries.

(3) Partners not to be charged interest on drawings.

(4) Partners to share balance of profits and losses equally.

(5) Partners entitled to interest at 5% p.a. on loans made to firm in excess of their agreed capitals.

Tutorial notes:

1. Questions include, as part of the data, such of the above items as are contained in the partnership agreement. If the question is silent on any point, it implies that the point is not covered in the agreement and that the Partnership Act 1890 applies.

2. You are expected to know the provisions of the Act and to apply them when appropriate.

3. Read every partnership question carefully and avoid making invalid assumptions about partners' rights.

Partners' salaries and interest on capitals are methods of regulating the division of profits amongst partners to reward them for extra responsibilities or their relative contributions of capital to the firm.

6.2 Special features of partnership accounts

The following are required :

    A profit and loss appropriation account.

    For each partner: Capital account
                       Drawings account
                       Current account

Treat the balances on partners' capital accounts as fixed. Unless a question specifically requires it, do not post interest, salaries or profit shares to the capital accounts.

    Debit interest on partners' loans to Profit and Loss account; it is an expense of the firm, not an appropriation of profit and should not be debited in the Appropriation account. When a question gives the net profit before charging such interest, the interest must be deducted to arrive at the profit brought down to the Appropriation account.

Accounting entries	Debit	Credit
Interest on partners' loans to firm	Profit & Loss a/c	Partners' Current a/cs
Interest on drawings	Partners' Current a/cs	Appropriation a/c
Interest on capitals	} Appropriation a/c	Partners' Current a/cs
Partners' salaries		
Shares of profit		
Shares of loss	Partners' Current a/cs	Appropriation a/c
Partners' drawings	Partners' Current a/cs	Partners' Drawings a/cs

6.2.1 Example 1: partnership agreement provides for sharing of profits and losses

Abel and Baker make up their accounts annually to 31 December and have been in partnership for some years. Interest is charged on drawings at the rate of 10% p.a. and is allowed on capitals also at 10% p.a. Baker receives a salary of £4,000 p.a. The balance of profits or losses is to be shared: Abel 2/3, Baker 1/3.

At 1 January 19-1, the following balances appeared in the firm's books:

		£
Capital accounts:	Abel	10,000
	Baker	6,000
Current accounts:	Abel	5,000 (Cr)
	Baker	3,000 (Cr)

The net profit for the year to 31 December 19-1 amounted to £15,000 and at that date the balances on the partners' Drawings accounts were: Abel £6,000; Baker £5,000.

Required

(a) The profit and loss appropriation account of the partnership for the year to 31 December 19-1.

(b) The partners' current accounts as at 31 December 19-1.

(c) A balance sheet extract as at 31 December 19-1 showing the partners' capital and current account balances.

Answer

(a)

Abel and Baker

Profit and loss appropriation account for the year ended 31 December 19-1

	£	£		£
Current accounts:			Net profit b/d	15,000
Interest on capitals – Abel	1,000		Current accounts:	
– Baker	600	1,600	Interest on drawings – Abel	600
Salary – Baker		4,000	– Baker	500
		5,600		
Share of profit – Abel ($\frac{2}{3}$)	7,000			
– Baker ($\frac{1}{3}$)	3,500	10,500		
		16,100		16,100

(b)

Partners' current accounts as at 31 December 19-1

		Abel	Baker			Abel	Baker
19-1		£	£	19-1		£	£ £
Dec 31	Interest on			Jan 1	Bal b/d	5,000	3,000
	drawings	600	500	Dec 31	Interest on capitals	1,000	600
	Drawings	6,000	5,000		Salary		4,000
	Balances c/d	6,400	5,600		Share of profit	7,000	3,500
		13,000	11,100			13,000	11,100
				19-2			
				Jan 1	Bal. b/d	6,400	5,600

(c)

Balance sheet (extract) as at 31 December 19-1

	Abel	Baker	
	£	£	£
Capital accounts	10,000	6,000	16,000
Current accounts	6,400	5,600	12,000
	16,400	11,600	28,000

Tutorial note: When a question requires the current accounts to be shown as in (b) above, it is only necessary to show the closing balances on the current accounts in the balance sheet as in (c) above. If the question does not require the current accounts to be shown separately, you should show the details in the balance sheet as in the next example.

Example 2: partnership agreement does not state how profits are to be shared – the provisions of the Partnership Act 1890 are applied

The facts are as stated as in Example 1 except that the agreement makes no mention of interest on drawings or capital or of partners' salaries or profit sharing ratio.

Required

(a) Profit and loss appropriation account for the year to 31 December 19-1; and

(b) balance sheet extract as at 31 December 19-1 showing the partners' capital and current accounts.

Answer

(a)

Abel and Baker

Profit and Loss Appropriation Account for the year to 31 December 19-1

	£	£
Net profit brought down		15,000
Current accounts – share of profits		
Abel ($\frac{1}{2}$)	7,500	
Baker ($\frac{1}{2}$)	7,500	15,000

(The account has been shown this time in vertical format – the form of final accounts preferred by examiners.)

(b) **Balance sheet (extract) as at 31 December 19-1**

		£	£	£
Capital accounts:	Abel		10,000	
	Baker		6,000	16,000
Current accounts		**Abel**	**Baker**	
Balances at 1.1.-1		5,000	3,000	
Profit for year		7,500	7,500	
		12,500	10,500	
less drawings		6,000	5,000	
		6,500	5,500	12,000
				28,000

Example 3: preparing of a forecast trading and profit and loss account and recognising the differences between sole trader and partnership entities

Addison carries on business as a sole trader selling office equipment, and his trading and profit and loss account for the year to 31 December 19-1 was as follows:

	£	£
Sales		100,000
less cost of sales		58,000
Gross profit		42,000
Salaries and wages	20,000	
Rent, rates and insurance	3,800	
Heating and lighting	2,320	
Advertising	4,000	
Delivery expenses	2,000	
Sundry expenses	2,200	34,320
Net profit		7,680

Addison's net profits for the previous two years were:

19-9	£12,000
19-0	£9,600

The forecast for the foreseeable future is not good and profits seem set to decline at the same rate as for the past three years.

Addison has not followed the latest trends in information technology and has confined his trading to older, conventional types of equipment which has steadily become more obsolete every year.

Addison has employed Steele as manager since January 19-9 at a salary of £8,000 per annum. Steele previously worked for a high technology firm and has acquired considerable knowledge and experience in selling micro-computers and word processors.

In order to arrest the decline in his profits, Addison is now considering taking Steele into partnership and making Steele responsible for marketing micro-computers and word processors as a new line of business.

Steele would introduce £20,000 into the business as capital and would continue to receive his present salary in addition to $\frac{1}{3}$ share of the balance of profits. Both partners would be entitled to interest on capital at the rate of 10% p.a. Addison's Capital account balance at 31 December 19-1 was £50,000.

If Steele is admitted as a partner, to manage the new line of business whilst Addison continues to manage the existing business, the following results are forecast.

	Existing business	New business
	£	£
Sales	80,000	100,000
Gross profit	46,400	20,420

In addition, it will be necessary to engage a new sales assistant at an annual salary of £6,000. Insurance premium will increase by £500 p.a. Advertising and delivery expenses will each increase by 50%.

Required

(a) A forecast trading and profit and loss account for the year to 31 December 19-2 assuming Addison takes Steele into partnership.

(b) State whether, in your opinion, Addison should admit Steele as a partner, with reasons.

(c) Give your views on the proposed profit sharing arrangements and, in particular, whether or not you think Steele would be justified in accepting only one third share of the balance of profits.

Answer

(a)

Addison and Steele
Forecast trading and profit and loss account for the year to 31 December 19-2

		£	£
Sales (80,000 + 100,000)			180,000
less: Cost of sales (balancing figure)			113,180
Gross profit (46,400 + 20,420)			66,820
Salaries and wages (20,000 – 8,000 + 6,000)		18,000	
Rent, rates and insurance (3,800 + 500)		4,300	
Heating and lighting		2,320	
Advertising (4,000 + 2,000)		6,000	
Delivery expenses (2,000 + 1,000)		3,000	
Sundry expenses		2,200	35,820
Net profit			31,000
Steele – salary		8,000	
Interest on capitals:	Addison	5,000	
	Steele	2,000	15,000
			16,000
Share of profit:	Addison ($\frac{2}{3}$)	10,667	
	Steele ($\frac{1}{3}$)	5,333	16,000

(b) Outline answer:

1. Addison should take Steele into partnership. As a sole trader he could expect his net profit in 19-2 to be about £6,144. (His profits have been falling by 20% year on year.) As a partner, he can expect to receive £15,667.

2. Steele's expertise can be used more fully, increasing his motivation at the same time as the business benefits.

3. A new lease of life is injected into the business by the introduction of a new line in technology.

4. The introduction of new capital by Steele will increase the liquidity of the firm; but the new line of business will result in an increase in stock, debtors and creditors.

(c) 1. Interest on capital rewards partners proportionately to their unequal capitals.

2. Addison's $\frac{2}{3}$ share of profits maintains his position of seniority.

3. Steele's salary guarantees him a minimum share of profits; he will receive it even if no profits are available. (It could actually increase a loss.)

Example 4: guaranteed shares of profit

Donald, Peter and Paul are in partnership sharing profits in the ratio of 3:2:1. Paul is guaranteed a minimum share of profits of £8,000.

		£
Profit for the year to:	31 December 19-0	60,000
	31 December 19-1	40,000

Required

Show the share of profit due to each partner for each of the years 19-0 and 19-1.

Appropriation account for the year to 31 December 19-0

	£	£
Net profit b/d		60,000
Shares of profit: Donald $\frac{3}{6}$	30,000	
Peter $\frac{2}{6}$	20,000	
Paul $\frac{1}{6}$	10,000	60,000

Appropriation account for the year to 31 December 19-1

	£	£
Net profit b/d		40,000
Shares of profit: Donald ($\frac{3}{5}$ of £32,000)	19,200	
Peter ($\frac{2}{5}$ of £32,000)	12,800	
Paul (guaranteed)	8,000	40,000

Tutorial notes:

1. As Paul is entitled to a minimum share of £8,000, Donald and Peter share the balance of £32,000.

2. The profit sharing ratio between Donald and Peter is 3:2, or 3/5 and 2/5; not 3/6 and 2/6

6.2.2 Exercise 1: preparing a partnership appropriation account applying the provisions of the Partnership Act 1890

Gray and Green have been carrying on business in partnership for a few years but have never prepared a partnership agreement. At 1 April 19-9, the following balances appeared in their books:

		£	
Capital accounts:	Gray	20,000	
	Green	14,000	
Current accounts:	Gray	7,000	(Cr.)
	Green	2,000	(Cr.)
Loan account:	Gray	10,000	

In the year ended 31 March 19-0, the partnership made a profit of £8,000 before interest on Gray's loan.

At 31 March 19-0 the balances on the partners' Drawing accounts were: Gray £4,000; Green £3,000.

Required

Prepare the partnership appropriation account for the year ended 31 March 19-0 and a balance sheet extract as at that date showing the partners' capital accounts, and their current accounts in detail.

Exercise 2: application of terms of partnership agreement and adjustments for accruals and prepayments

Palmer and Green have been in partnership for some years. The terms of their agreement provide for interest at 10 per cent per annum on partners' loans to the firm. It also allows for interest at 10 per cent per annum on capitals and drawings. Green receives a salary of £8,000 per annum and the balance of profits are to be shared: Palmer 3/5 , Green 2/5 .

The following balances had been extracted from the books at 31 December 19-0 after the trading account for the year had been prepared:

		£			£
Capitals: Palmer		35,000	Premises at cost		100,000
Green		20,000	Provision for depreciation of		
Loan by Palmer		8,000	premises		25,000
Current accounts:	Palmer	4,000 (Cr)	Motor cars		16,000
	Green	3,000 (Dr)	Provision for depreciation of		
Drawings:	Palmer	7,000	motor cars		8,000
	Green	8,000	Stock at 31.12.-0		12,000
Gross profit for year		80,000	Debtors		36,000
Selling and distribution expenses		23,500	Creditors		8,300
Administration expenses		16,400	Bank loan (repayable 1.1.-2)		30,000
Bank overdraft		3,600			

The following adjustments are to be made in the preparation of the profit and loss account:

1. Selling and distribution expenses accrued at 31 December 19-0: £1,500
2. Administration expenses prepaid at 31 December 19-0 £800
3. Depreciation is to be provided for the year as follows: Premises: 4% on cost Motor cars: 20% on cost

Required

(a) The partnership profit and loss and appropriation accounts for the year to 31 December 19-0
(b) The current accounts of the partners as at 31 December 19-0
(c) The balance sheet as at 31 December 19-0

Exercise 3: a partner has a guaranteed share of profit

Doyle, Lee and Carter are in partnership sharing profits and losses in the ratio of 5:3:2. Carter, however, is guaranteed a minimum share of £5,000. At 31 December, 19-2, the partners' capital account balances were as follows: Doyle £25,000, Lee £17,000, Carter £6,000. By the partnership agreement, they are entitled to interest on capital at 10% per annum.

In the year to 31 December, 19-3, the net profit of the firm was £7,000.

Required

The appropriation account of the partnership for the year ended 31 December, 19-3.

Exercise 4: forecast trading and profit and loss account and balance sheet of partnership; choice between (a) continuing to trade as a sole trader and (b) forming a partnership

Bath has been in business as a sole trader for some years and at 31 December 19-0 the final accounts of his business were as follows:

Trading and profit and loss account for the year to 31 December 19-0

	£	£
Sales		70,000
Cost of sales		42,000
Gross profit		28,000
Salaries and wages	10,000	
Rent and rates	3,600	
Insurance	800	
Entertainment expenses	500	
Car expenses	2,600	
Bank overdraft interest	240	
Advertising	1,500	
Sundry expenses	660	
Depreciation: Motor car	1,000	
Fixtures and fittings	750	21,650
Net profit		6,350

Balance sheet as at 31 December 19-0

	£	£	£
Fixed assets: Motor car		4,000	
less depreciation		1,000	3,000
Fixtures and fittings		3,750	
less depreciation		750	3,000
			6,000
Current assets: Stock		2,200	
Debtors		3,000	
		5,200	
less Current liabilities: Bank overdraft	2,500		
Creditors	1,900	4,400	800
			6,800
Capital account			6,800

Profit has remained static in recent years and the liquidity of the business is beginning to cause Bath some concern.

Wells is a friend of Bath, and has engaged in his spare time in a business which could successfully be combined with Bath's. Wells, however, lacks suitable business premises and there would be room in Bath's premises for both businesses. Bath sees that his own liquidity position could be improved by the additional capital which Wells would introduce if they went into partnership.

Wells would enter into partnership on 1 January 19-1 on the following terms: Wells to pay into the firm £5,000 in addition to bringing in his car at a valuation of £5,000; Bath's capital to remain unchanged; both capital accounts to be regarded as fixed; interest to be allowed on capitals at 10% per annum, and Wells to be entitled to a salary of £8,000 per annum. Balance of profits to be shared: Bath $\frac{3}{5}$, Wells $\frac{2}{5}$.

Bath estimates that the partnership would result in the following:

Bath's business: Sales would increase by £10,000 and the gross profit percentage would remain unchanged.

Well's business: Sales would be £120,000 on which the margin would be 30%.

Salaries and wages would increase by £4,000. Entertainment expenses and car expenses would double. Advertising costs would increase by £1,800. Sundry expenses would be £1,000.

Motor cars would be depreciated at the rate of 25% on the reducing balance. Fixtures and fittings would be depreciated at the rate of 20%, also on the reducing balance.

Bath's stock would remain constant and Well's stock at 31 December 19-1 would be £8,000.

Debtors would increase by 200% whilst creditors would increase by 100%.

Required

(a) A forecast trading and profit and loss account for the year to 31 December 19-1 and a forecast balance sheet as at that date on the assumption that Bath admits Wells as a partner on the terms shown above.

(b) Whether in your opinion Bath should go into partnership with Wells, giving your reasons.

Tutorial note: The item 'Bank' in your balance sheet will be the figure required to make your balance sheet balance.

Key points to remember

1. Advantages of partnership:
   (a) Provision of capital.
   (b) Diversity of knowledge, experience and expertise.
   (c) 'Cover' for partners during sickness and holidays.
   Disadvantages:
   All partners must agree on policy etc. Sole trader is free agent to run his own business.

2. Partnership Act 1890:
   (a) All partners entitled to contribute equally to capital of firm.
   (b) NO interest on capitals or drawings.
   (c) NO partners' salaries.
   (d) Interest on partners' loans to firm 5% p.a.
   These provisions only apply where not covered by partnership agreement.

3. Partnership accounts:
   (a) Appropriation account for division of profits including interest on capital and drawings (but not on loans).
   (b) For each partner: capital account, current account, drawings account.

4. Always debit interest on partners' loan to firm in profit and loss account, not in appropriation account.

5. Unless question requires otherwise, treat partners' capitals as fixed and complete double entry from appropriation account to their current accounts.

   Interest on loans will also be credited to the current accounts.

   For accounting entries see 6.2.

6. Always transfer balances on partners' Drawings accounts to their current accounts at the year end.

7. Partnership questions are not difficult for examinees who think about what they are doing and apply all the information in the questions. Avoid omitting to give effect to all the data and requirements, by ticking each item on the question paper as you give effect to it.

   Check that everything has been ticked before you complete your answer.

Common errors

1. Interest on partners' loans shown in appropriation account;
2. Interest on capitals, loans, drawings, omitted although stated by question to be included in the partnership agreement;
3. Appropriations of profit posted to capital accounts when capitals are fixed;
4. Failure to transfer balances on drawings accounts to current accounts at year end.

Questions

Fully worked examination question

Misfit and Wartz are in partnership. At 31 December 19-4 they agree that their assets are worth:

	£
Premises	200,000
Fixtures	80,000
Motor Vehicles	60,000
Stock	20,000
Debtors	8,200
Bank	1,200
Cash	300
At the same date they have creditors of	5,700

During the year ended 31 December 19-5 the following transactions took place:

1. On 1 July 19-5 Misfit loaned the partnership £20,000 for ten years.
2. At the same date, Wartz increased his capital by £36,000 to make it equal to Misfit's.
3. Cash sales for the year were £300,000.
4. £490,200 was paid into the bank during the year.
5. Expenses paid in cash during the year were £2,400.
6. Expenses paid by cheque during the year were:
   (i) Wages £56,000
   (ii) Lighting and heating and rates £9,700
   (iii) Motor vehicle expenses £18,300
   (iv) Carriage on purchases £3,400
   (v) Other expenses £18,800.
7. Some small items of goods for resale were purchased and paid for out of the cash £10,000.

8. Goods which cost £1,200 had been returned to credit suppliers.

9. £288,720 was paid to creditors during the year. 10% cash discount had been deducted from all payments.

10. No discounts were allowed to debtors, but £200 had been written off as bad.

11. One of the vehicles is used occasionally by Misfit's wife. The cost of this usage (included in the Motor vehicle expenses) is estimated to be £3,400; this is to be charged to Misfit.

12. Both partners had taken goods from the business during the year valued at cost. These were estimated at:

Misfit £2,800   Wartz £1,900

13. At 31 December 19-5, Fixtures and Motor vehicles were valued at £72,000 and £60,341 respectively, stocks were valued at £22,500. Debtors owed £5,500 and creditors were owed £6,400.

14. A small amount of cash is kept in the business from cash sales for paying expenses and at 31 December19-5 there is £500 not paid into the bank.

15. On 1 June 19-5 a small van with a book value of £750 was sold for £900 and replaced by a new one at a cost of £7,800. The difference was paid by cheque.

16. During the year the partners had withdrawn from the bank for their own use: Misfit £3,840: Wartz £18,200.

17. Watkinson is the general manager for the partnership and apart from his wages he is entitled to a bonus of 10% of the net profit of the business calculated after charging this bonus. The bonus will be paid on 1 February 19-6.

18. Interest is allowed on partnership capitals of 5% per annum and Wartz is allowed a salary of £15,000 per annum. Interest is charged on drawings, but apart from these no other agreements have been made.

19. The interest on drawings for the year has been calculated at Misfit £300 and Wartz £550.

You are required to prepare

(a) the Trading and Profit and Loss account of the partnership for the year ended 31 December 19-5,

(b) the partners' current accounts and

(c) the balance sheet at 31 December 19-5.   (Total 40 marks)
                                                              (OXFORD)

Answer

(a)   **Misfit and Wartz**
        Trading and profit and loss account for the year to 31 December 19-5

	£	£	£
Sales			444,300
Cost of sales			
Stock at 1 Jan 19-5		20,000	
Purchases	328,000		
less returns	1,200		
	326,800		
Carriage inwards	3,400	330,200	
		350,200	
Stock at 31 Dec 19-5		22,500	327,700
Gross profit			116,600
Discounts received			32,080
Profit on disposal of fixed asset			150
			148,830
Wages		56,000	
Light, heating and rates		9,700	
Motor vehicle expenses		14,900	
Other expenses		21,200	
Carried forward		101,800	148,830

		£	£	£
Brought forward			101,800	148,830
Bad debt written off			200	
Depreciation: Fixtures			8,000	
Motor vehicles			6,709	
Loan interest			500	
Manager's commission (31,621/11)			2,875	120,084
Net profit				28,746
Interest on drawings	Misfit		300	
	Wartz		550	850
				29,596
Interest on capital	Misfit		10,000	
	Wartz		9,100	
			19,100	
Salary	Wartz		15,000	34,100
				(4,504)
Share of loss	Misfit		(2,252)	
	Wartz		(2,252)	(4,504)

(b)

Partners' current accounts

19-5		Misfit £	Wartz £	19-5		Misfit £	Wartz £
Dec 31	Drawings: cash	3,840	18,200	Dec 31	Interest on cap.	10,000	9,100
	goods	2,800	1,900		Salary		15,000
	veh.exp	3,400			Interest on loan	500	
	Int. on drawings	300	550		Balance c/d	2,092	
	Share of loss	2,252	2,252				
	Balance c/d		1,198				
		12,592	24,100			12,592	24,100
19-6				19-6			
Jan 1	Balance b/d	2,092		Jan 1	Balance b/d		1,198

(c)

Balance sheet as at 31 December 19-5

		£	£	£
Fixed assets				
Premises				200,000
Fixtures				72,000
Motor vehicles				60,341
				332,341
Current assets				
Stock			22,500	
Debtors			5,500	
Bank			67,540	
Cash			500	
			96,040	
Current liabilities				
Creditors		6,400		
Manager's commission		2,875	9,275	86,765
				419,106
Long-term loan – Misfit				(20,000)
				399,106
Capital accounts:	Misfit		200,000	
	Wartz		200,000	400,000
Current accounts:	Misfit		(2,092)	
	Wartz		1,198	(894)
				399,106

Multiple choice questions

1 A partnership Profit and Loss Appropriation account may show

   A interest on capitals, partners' salaries, partners' drawings and profit shares.

   B interest on capitals, interest on partners' loans, interest on drawings and profit shares

   C partners' salaries, interest on capitals, interest on drawings and profit shares

   D partners' salaries, interest on capitals, interest on drawings, goods taken by partners for own use and profit shares

2 Amos and Bead are in partnership. Their capitals are fixed by agreement and current accounts are maintained for them in the partnership books. They are allowed interest on capitals and charged interest on their drawings. At the end of the financial year, the following journal entries will be made:

   A credit appropriation account and debit partners' current accounts with interest on capitals and drawings

   B credit appropriation account with interest on drawings and debit it with interest on capitals; credit interest on capitals to partners' capital accounts and debit interest on drawings to their current accounts

   C credit appropriation account with interest on drawings and debit it with interest on capitals; credit interest on capitals and debit interest on drawings to their current accounts

   D debit appropriation account and credit partners' current accounts with interest on capital and drawings

3 Chato and Dominic are in partnership sharing profits in the ratio 3:2. For one year the net profit is £30,000. Other information for that year is as follows:

	Chato £	Dominic £
Interest on drawings	300	400
Interest on capitals	1,200	800
Salary	–	4,000

The balance of profit will be shared:

   A Chato £14,400 Dominic £9,600

   B Chato £14,820 Dominic £9,880

   C Chato £15,660 Dominic £10,440

   D Chato £16,380 Dominic £10,920

4 Elif and Fahdi, partners in a firm, share profits in the ratio 2:1. For one year the net profit is £63,000. Additional data is as follows:

	Elif £	Fahdi £
Interest on loan to firm	900	–
Interest on capitals	2,000	1,500
Salary		10,000

The balance of profit will be shared:

   A Elif £16,500 Fahdi £33,000

   B Elif £33,000 Fahdi £16,500

   C Elif £37,066 Fahdi £18,534

   D Elif £37,617 Fahdi £18,833

5 Leo, Mac and Nick are in partnership sharing profits in the ratio 3:2:1. Leo is entitled to interest of £1,200 on a loan to the firm. Nick is guaranteed a minimum profit share of £8,000. When the profit is £47,000, the profit shares will be:

   A Leo £18,900 Mac £12,600 Nick £8,000

   B Leo £19,500 Mac £13,000 Nick £8,000

   C Leo £22,680 Mac £15,120 Nick £8,000

   D Leo £23,400 Mac £15,600 Nick £8,000

1   The following draft balance sheet as at 31 May 19-7 of the partnership of X and Y has been produced following the completion of the revenue accounts for the year ended 31 May 19-7. X and Y share profits and losses equally.

	Cost	Aggregate depreciation	
	£	£	£
Fixed assets: Plant and machinery	50,000	24,000	26,000
Motor vehicles	40,000	13,000	27,000
	90,000	37,000	53,000
Current assets: Stock at cost	28,000		
Debtors	14,000		
Balance at bank	10,000	52,000	
less Current liabilities			
Creditors		12,000	40,000
			93,000
Capital accounts X		30,000	
Y		50,000	80,000
Current accounts X		18,000	
Y		(5,000)	13,000
			93,000

After the preparation of the draft final accounts the following information became available.

(1) Included in the stock figure of £28,000 was an item valued at cost of £4,000. The item is now in short supply and would cost £9,000 to replace. The recommended selling price of the item is £15,000.

(2) No entry has been made in the accounts to record the sale on credit to J. Smith of an item of plant and machinery for £5,000 on 25 April 19-7. The machinery was purchased on June 1 19-3 for £15,000. It is company policy to depreciate plant and machinery by 10% per annum based on the cost of assets shown in the books at the end of the financial year.

(3) Included in the figure for debtors is a debt of £3,000 which was owed by Green, a long established customer. Green, in partial payment of the debt, had given X some materials for his house extension which had a value of £2,000. No entry has been made in the accounts to record that transaction nor the fact that Green is unable to pay the balance of his debt.

(4) On 29 May 19-7 the firm formally agreed to purchase on credit items of stock at a cost of £8,000 and accepted the invoice dated that day. The stock has not been received by 31 May but it has been despatched by the supplier. No entry has been made in the accounts to record the transaction.

Required

(a) The journal entries to record transaction (2) above. Narratives are not required.
(6 marks)

(b) A statement showing the effect, if any, of each of the four items above on the Current Account balances of X and Y. (8 marks)

(c) A redrafted balance sheet as at 31 May 19-7 of X and Y after the items above had been taken into consideration. (5 marks)
(AEB)

2   Franklin, Michael and Longman are trading in partnership. The following information has been extracted from the partnership agreement and books of account for the year ended 31 October 19-8:

(1) Partners are to be credited with interest on capital account balances at the rate of 9% per annum. Interest is to be charged on cash drawings only, at the rate of 10% per annum.

(2) The partnership net trading profit for the year per the draft accounts amounted to £72,190 and the profit is to be appropriated in the following ratios:

Franklin 1: Michael 2: Longman 2.

(3) Cash drawings during the year amounted to:

	£
Franklin	5,500
Michael	6,200
Longman	4,900

It should be assumed that all cash drawings took place on 30 April 19-8

(4) The balances on the partners' capital and current accounts at 1 November 19-7 were:

	Capital a/c	Current a/c
	£	£
Franklin	18,000	Cr. 9,310
Michael	40,000	Cr. 4,650
Longman	33,000	Cr. 2,170

(5) Each partner had taken goods for his own use during the year at cost as follows:

Franklin £3,200, Michael £1,900 and Longman £2,500. No entries had been made in the books of account to record these transactions.

(6) The partnership disposed of a motor vehicle on 25 October 19-8 for £4,200 and the proceeds of sale were recorded as income in arriving at the profit for the year. The vehicle had a book value of £6,100 at the time of sale and this amount had been transferred to a suspense account at 31 October 19-8.

(7) An insurance premium of £230 relating to Michael's home was paid by the partnership and charged to the profit and loss account.

Required

(a) A statement of the corrected net trading profit for the partnership for the year ended 31 October 19-8. (6 marks)

(b) The profit and loss appropriation account for the year ended 31 October 19-8 (6 marks)

(c) The capital and current accounts of Franklin, Michael and Longman as they would appear in the balance sheet at 31 October 19-8. (6 marks)

(AEB)

3   Patel and Phipp are trading in partnership with a number of retail shops. Their partnership agreement provides for interest on capital of 11% per annum, a salary of £15,000 per annum for Phipp and the balance of any remaining profits or losses to be shared equally.

The following summarised profit statement had been prepared for the year ended 31 May 1991.

	£	£
Sales		850,400
Less cost of goods sold		
Opening stock	48,500	
Purchases	560,900	
	609,400	
Less closing stock	59,200	550,200
Gross profit		300,200
Variable expenses	149,700	
Fixed expenses	61,000	210,700
Net profit		89,500

Subsequent to the preparation of the summarised profit statement it was determined that the following adjustments were necessary.

(1) A sale of goods on credit for £1,500 had been entered in the purchases day book and not in the sales day book.

(2) Staff are paid an annual bonus related to sales. The bonus is calculated as 3% of all sales turnover except for the first £750,000 of turnover.

No provision had been made for this bonus in the accounts.

(3) During the year both partners had taken goods from stock (at cost) for their own personal use. The amount of stock taken for the year was:

	£
Patel	1,560
Phipp	2,100

No entries had been made in the accounts.

(4) Repairs to motor vehicles for the year of £5,250 included an amount for the provision of a new engine, cost £1,500. It was now agreed that this latter amount should be capitalised, but no depreciation on this amount is to be provided for the year ended 31 May 1991.

(5) During the year one of the partnership's shops was re-fitted.

The fittings of this shop were included in the partners' accounts, as at 31 May 1990, as follows:

	£
Fixtures and fittings. At cost	20,000
Depreciation to date	7,800

All these fixtures have been sold to the shopfitter for £6,000 except for some items sold to staff for £950.

The estimated cost of the new fixtures and fittings was £30,000 and half of this amount had been paid on account. The work was completed on 31 March 1991 and the final invoice on completion was for £16,090. No depreciation has been provided on these new fixtures and it is the firm's policy to depreciate for a full year on all assets held at each accounting year end. Fixtures and fittings are depreciated at 15% per annum, on cost.

(6) When preparing the profit statement a trial balance difference had occurred. The respective totals were:

DR	CR
£901,750	£904,540

A suspense account had been opened for the difference. It was discovered that a trade debtor for £4,130 had been listed in the trial balance as £1,340 debit. This has not yet been corrected.

Additional information:

The following balances existed as at 31 May 1990.

Fixed capital accounts	£	Current accounts	£
Patel	100,000	Patel	75,400 CR
Phipp	50,000	Phipp	54,900 CR
Cash drawings made during the year were:			
Patel	£40,000	Phipp	£26,400

Required

(a) A detailed statement showing the effect of the items 1) to 6) on the net profit for the year ended 31 May 1991. (11 marks)

(b) Using the absolute figures produced in a) above, prepare a profit and loss appropriation account for the year ended 31 May 1991. (3 marks)

(c) The partners' current accounts for the year ended 31 May 1991. (7 marks)

(AEB)

4 Clarkson and Philpott were in partnership as retailers. Their accounts clerk, having calculated a net trading profit for the year ended 31 December 1992, had just completed the following schedule of information before drawing up the formal appropriation account:

Interest on capital: Clarkson £7500, Philpott £5000

Share of profit: Clarkson £31,500, Philpott £31 500

The partners having seen the schedule advised the clerk that although his calculations were numerically correct, he had used the old partnership agreement, and that the partners had agreed a revised partnership deed with effect from 1 January 1992. The deed provided for:

salaries: Clarkson £15,000 per annum; Philpott £20 000 per annum

Interest on fixed capitals at 9% per annum whereas it had previously been 10% per annum.

Share of profits: Clarkson $\frac{3}{5}$; Philpott $\frac{2}{5}$

The partners also listed the following items which had not been taken into account when the clerk had calculated the net profit for the year:

(1) Clarkson had taken goods for his own use during the year of £2500;

(2) A motor vehicle which cost £20 000 and with accumulated depreciation as at 31 December 1992 of £12 000, had been taken by Philpott for his wife's use at a valuation of £4500;

(3) Clarkson provided the partnership with a loan of £30 000 on 1 January 1992. Interest was to be paid at 9% per annum;

(4) An amount of £3500 due from K. Henry had been written off in the financial year ended 31 December 1991. Fortunately, Henry is now in a position to pay and has sent a cheque for £3500 to the partnership on 1 December 1992.

Additional information.

(i) Cash drawings for the year ended 31 December 1992:

Clarkson	£31,500
Philpott	£28,750

(ii) The partners' accounts as at 1 January 1992:

Capital accounts		Current accounts	
Clarkson	£75,000	Clarkson	£23,700 CR
Philpott	£50,000	Philpott	£31,100 CR

(iii) Other balances as at 31 December 1992:

	£	
Freehold land and premises	50,000	
Motor vehicles	41,500	all at net book value
Fixtures and fittings	16,700	
Trade creditors	18,400	
Expenses owing	9,000	
Stock	41,600	
Trade debtors	21,700	
Expenses paid in advance	8,000	
Cash in hand	3,900	
Balance at bank	69,050	

None of these balances had been adjusted for the items (1) to (4) above, except where Clarkson brought in the relevant amount of cash in respect of the loan.

Required

(a) A corrected profit and loss statement for the year ended 31 December 1992.
(12 marks)

(b) An appropriation account for the partnership for the year ended 31 December 1992 on the basis of the new agreement. (8 marks)

(c) The partners' current accounts for the year ended 31 December 1992 as they appear in the ledger. (14 marks)

(d) A balance sheet as at 31 December 1992. (10 marks)

(e) Comment on the partnership's liquidity. (6 marks)
(AEB)

7 Partnership changes

Chapter objectives

This aspect of partnership accounting entails:

❏ preparation of separate profit and loss accounts for the periods before, and after, the change.

❏ revaluation of partnership assets on partnership change

❏ goodwill

7.1 Accounting for changes

The admission of a new partner, or the retirement or death of an existing partner, constitute the termination of one partnership and the commencement of a new one.

Separate accounts should be prepared for the old partnership and the new one.

Examination questions on this topic invariably pose situations where no new entries are made in the partnership books to reflect changes as they occur, and require the separate accounts for the two firms to be produced at the end of the financial year.

Prepare the profit and loss accounts for the two firms in columnar form, one for the period to the date of change, the other for the period following the change.

Split the expenses in the profit and loss accounts in the manner indicated in the question. Expenses which vary with turnover should be split in proportion to turnover, e.g salesmen's commission on sales; those which are related to time, e.g. rent, rates, should be split on a time basis. Other items may be split on some other basis stated in the question, e.g. provisions for doubtful debts which will depend upon the debtors outstanding at the date of change in the partnership, and those outstanding at the year end.

Any expenses applicable only to the old partnership, or to the new one only, will not be split but entered in the appropriate period. In this connection, take care to calculate partners' salaries and interest on their loans, capitals and drawings on a time basis when these are expressed in the question on an annual basis.

7.1.1 Example

East and New are in partnership as general traders, sharing profits and losses equally after allowing East a salary of £4,000 p.a. At 1 January 19-1, their capital accounts were: East £10,000, New £8,000. Their current account balances were East £3,000 (Cr.), New £2,000 (Cr.)

On 1 July 19-1, they admitted Barnet as a partner. From that date profits were to be shared between East, New and Barnet in the ratio 2:2:1. Barnet is to receive a salary of £3,000 p.a.

It was agreed that from 1 July 19-1 East would transfer £2,000 from his capital account to a loan account on which interest would be paid at 10% p.a.

Barnet brought his private car into the firm at a valuation of £5,000.

No entries to reflect the foregoing matters were made in the books before the end of the financial year on 31 December 19-1.

The following information is available for the year to 31 December 19-1:

	£
Sales (spread evenly throughout the year)	80,000
Cost of sales	35,000
Rent and rates	10,000
Wages	14,000
General expenses	6,000

The car is to be depreciated over 4 years on the straight line basis; it is assumed it will have a nil residual value.

Of the General expenses, £2,000 was incurred in the six months to 30 June 19-1.

All sales produce a uniform rate of gross profit.

Required

(1) The trading and profit and loss and appropriation accounts of the partnership for the year to 31 December 19-1.

(2) The partners' current accounts as at 31 December 19-1.

Answer

(a)

East, New and Barnet
Trading and profit and loss account for the year to 31 December 19-1

						£
Sales						80,000
less cost of sales						35,000
Gross profit						45,000

		6 months to 30 Jun		6 months to 31 Dec		Total
	£	£	£	£	£	£
Gross profit b/d		22,500		22,500		45,000
Rent and rates	5,000		5,000		10,000	
Wages	7,000		7,000		14,000	
General expenses	2,000		4,000		6,000	
Interest on loan	–		100		100	
Depreciation – car	–	14,000	625	16,725	625	30,725
Net profit		8,500		5,775		14,275
Salary – East	2,000				2,000	
Salary – Barnet			1,500		1,500	
Share of profit						
East $(\frac{1}{2})$	3,250		$(\frac{2}{5})$ 1,710		4,960	
New $(\frac{1}{2})$	3,250		$(\frac{2}{5})$ 1,710		4,960	
Barnet	–		$(\frac{1}{5})$ 855		855	
		8,500		5,775		14,275

Tutorial note: When a partnership change involves only a change in the profit sharing ratios of existing partners without affecting profit and loss account items, it is necessary to split the appropriation account only.

7.1.2 Exercise 1: involving a change in the profit sharing ratios only

Toll, Puddle and Martyn have been in partnership for some years sharing profits in the ratio 3:2:1.

The following data for the year ended 31 December 19-2 has been extracted from the partnership books:

	£
Sales for the year	74,000
Cost of sales	38,000
Wages	8,000
General expenses	3,000
Depreciation of fixed assets	1,000

The partners have agreed that from 1 July 19-2, Toll shall be entitled to a salary of £3,000 p.a. and the balance of the profits shall be shared equally. Sales have taken place evenly throughout the year and all sales earned a uniform rate of gross profit. No entries to reflect the change in profit sharing ratio have been made in the books before the year end.

Required

The trading and profit and loss and appropriation accounts of the firm for the year to 31 December 19-2.

Exercise 2: introduction of a new partner during financial year

Crook and Shank were in partnership in a firm of general dealers, sharing profits in the ratio of 3:2. They made up their accounts annually to 31 March. On 1 October 19-1, they admitted Spindle as a partner. Spindle paid £20,000 into the firm's bank account on that date as capital.

The new partnership agreement allowed interest on cash introduced as capital at 10% p.a. Spindle would receive a salary of £4,000 p.a. and the balance of profit would be divided as follows: Crook 2/5, Shank 2/5, Spindle 1/5.

Information extracted from the books of the firm for the year to 31 March 19-2 was as follows:

	£
Sales	190,000
Cost of sales	100,000
Salaries and wages	21,000
Rent and rates	8,500
Lighting and heating	3,200
General expenses	2,400
Loan made to firm by Crook on 1 October 19-1 with interest at 12% p.a.	10,000
Motor cars at cost 1 April 19-1	20,000
Motor car brought into partnership on 1 October 19-1 by Spindle at valuation	8,000
Provision for doubtful debts at 1 April 19-1	500
Debtors at 30 September 19-1	12,000
Debtors at 31 March 19-2	14,000
Capital accounts at 1 April 19-1: Crook	40,000
Shank	30,000

The following further information is also available:

1. Rent and rates prepaid at 31 March 19-2: £2,500.
2. Heating and lighting owing at 31 March 19-2: £800.
3. General expenses incurred to 30 September 19-1: £1,100.
4. Motor cars are to be depreciated at the rate of 20% on cost or valuation as appropriate.
5. The provision for doubtful debts to be maintained at the rate of 4% of debtors.
6. Owing to the seasonal nature of the business, one third of the sales occurred in the first six months of the financial year.
7. All sales produced a uniform rate of gross profit.

Required

The trading and profit and loss and appropriation accounts of the partnership for the year to 31 March 19-2.

7.2 Revaluation of assets

On a change in the profit sharing arrangements in a partnership, which obviously includes the admission or retirement of a partner, the partners' capital accounts should show their true interests in the firm.

Partners' capitals equal the net worth of their business. The real net worth of a business depends upon the realistic valuation of the assets and liabilities. Therefore it is usual to review the values of these items on a partnership change.

A revaluation account must be opened in the general ledger.

Accounting entries	Account to be debited	Account to be credited
Increases in values of assets	Asset	Revaluation
Decreases in values of assets	Revaluation	Asset
Provisions for depreciation on revalued assets	Provision for depreciation	Revaluation
Profit on revaluation	Revaluation	Capitals*
Loss on revaluation	Capitals*	Revaluation

* In the proportion in which partners shared profits and losses before the change.

Tutorial note: Profits and losses on revaluation of assets affect the partners' investment in the firm: the profits or losses are unrealised profits or losses of a capital nature unlike trading profits and losses. Therefore they must be adjusted through the capital accounts. If they were entered in the partners' current accounts, that would imply that any profits were realised profits which could be drawn out by the partners, and that would deplete the long term capital of the firm, perhaps with serious results.

7.2.1 Example

Daisy and Pansy are in partnership sharing profits and losses in the ratio 3:2. They decide to admit Poppy as a partner on 1 May 19-2 when the profit sharing ratio will become: Daisy $\frac{1}{2}$, Pansy $\frac{1}{3}$ and Poppy $\frac{1}{6}$.

The balance sheet of Daisy and Pansy on 30 April 19-2 was:

		£	£
Fixed assets:	Motor car		6,000
	Office furniture		4,000
			10,000
Current assets:	Stock	2,000	
	Debtors	1,200	
	Bank	2,500	
		5,700	
less Current liabilities:	Creditors	300	5,400
			15,400
Capital accounts:	Daisy	9,000	
	Pansy	6,000	15,000
Current accounts	Daisy	800	
	Pansy	(400)	400
			15,400

It is agreed that the assets shall be revalued as follows: motor car £4,000; office furniture (some of which has been found to be genuinely antique) £7,000; stock which originally cost £200 is damaged and is considered to be of no value. No provision has been made for doubtful debts and it is agreed that a provision of 10% of debtors should be created.

The adjustments are made in the books at 30 April 19-2 and Poppy is admitted as a partner on the following day, paying £2,500 into the firm's bank account as capital.

Required

(a) Journal entries to show the entries in the books of the firm on 30 April 19-2 to give effect to the above adjustments. (Narratives are not required.)

(b) The revaluation account.

(c) The capital accounts of Daisy and Pansy at 30 April 19-2.

(d) The opening balance sheet of the firm of Daisy, Pansy and Poppy as at 1 May 19-2.

Answer

(a)

Daisy and Pansy
Journal

	Dr £	Cr £
Revaluation	2,000	
Motor car		2,000
Office furniture	3,000	
Revaluation		3,000
Revaluation	200	
Stock		200
Revaluation	120	
Provision for doubtful debts		120

(b)

Revaluation account

19-2		£	19-2		£
Apr 30	Motor car	2,000	Apr 30	Office furniture	3,000
	Stock	200			
	Provision for doubtful debts	120			
	Capitals: Daisy	408			
	Pansy	272			
		3,000			3,000

(c)

Partners' Capital accounts (old firm)

		Daisy £	Pansy £			Daisy £	Pansy £
19-2				19-2			
Apr 30	Balance c/d	9,408	6,272	Apr 30	Balance b/d	9,000	6,000
					Revaluation	408	272
		9,408	6,272			9,408	6,272
				May 1	Balance b/d	9,408	6,272

(d)

Daisy, Pansy and Poppy
Opening balance sheet as at 1 May 19-2

		£	£	£
Fixed assets:	Motor car			4,000
	Office furniture			7,000
				11,000
Current assets:	Stock		1,800	
	Debtors	1,200		
	less provision	120	1,080	
	Bank		5,000	
			7,880	
less Current liabilities:	Creditors		300	7,580
				18,580
Capitals:	Daisy	9,408		
	Pansy	6,272		
	Poppy	2,500		18,180
Current accounts:	Daisy	800		
	Pansy	(400)		400
				18,580

Tutorial note: Had the profit on realisation been credited to the current accounts of Daisy and Pansy, that would have implied that they could withdraw the profits. However, the profits have not been realised and must go to their capital accounts with the clear implication that if the partners withdraw those profits they will reduce their permanent capitals in the business, which would be imprudent.

7.2.2 Exercise: revaluation of assets on admission of new partner

Legge and Spinner were in partnership sharing profits equally. At 31 December 19-2, their balance sheet was as follows:

		£	£
Fixed assets:	Freehold premises		40,000
	Plant and machinery		15,000
	Motor vans		16,000
			71,000
Current assets:	Stock	14,000	
	Debtors	12,000	
	Balance at bank	7,500	
		33,500	
less Current liabilities:	Creditors	7,500	26,000
			97,000
Capital accounts:	Legge	40,000	
	Spinner	40,000	80,000
Current accounts:	Legge	9,000	
	Spinner	8,000	17,000
			97,000

Legge and Spinner agreed to admit Bowler as a partner on 1 January 19-3 when the assets were revalued as follows:

	£
Freehold premises	70,000
Plant and machinery	10,000
Motor vans	8,000

It was also agreed that stock which had cost £7,000 was now worth £3,000, and further stock which had cost £2,000 now had nil value.

Debtors at 31 December 19-2 included bad debts of £2,000; no provision for doubtful debts had been made in the past but a provision equal to 4% of debtors as at 31 December 19-2 should be created.

The adjustments for the foregoing matters were made in the books as at 31 December 19-2 and Bowler was duly admitted as a partner on 1 January 19-3 and subscribed £25,000 as capital.

Required

(a) Journal entries to adjust for the revaluation of assets referred to above. (Narratives are not required.)

(b) The revaluation account at 31 December 19-2.

(c) The capital accounts of Legge and Spinner as at 31 December 19-2.

(d) The opening balance sheet of the partnership of Legge, Spinner and Bowler as at 1 January 19-3.

7.3 Revaluation of fixed assets which have been subject to provisions for depreciation

In addition to adjusting the 'fixed asset at cost' accounts for increases or decreases in values on revaluation, transfer any provisions for depreciation on those assets at the date of revaluation to the Revaluation account. If this is not done, the assets will be recorded in the books at the new valuation less the amount of a depreciation provision which is now redundant.

7.3.1 Example

The following is an extract from the balance sheet of Dandy and Pixie at 28 February 19-1; they share profits and losses equally.

	Cost £	Depn £	Net £
Fixed assets			
Freehold property	80,000	30,000	50,000
Plant and machinery	45,000	25,000	20,000
Motor vehicles	38,000	23,000	15,000
	163,000	78,000	85,000
Current assets			
Debtors	24,000		
less provision for doubtful debts	1,200	22,800	

Dandy and Pixie agreed to admit Puck as a partner on 1 March 19-1, on which date the assets were valued as follows:

	£
Freehold property	100,000
Plant and machinery	15,000
Motor vehicles	12,000

It was also agreed that the provision for doubtful debts should be adjusted to $2\frac{1}{2}$% of debtors.

Required

Journal entries to give effect to the revaluation of the partnership assets at 28 February 19-1. (The answer should include the transfers to the partners' capital accounts from the Revaluation account.)

Answer

	Dr	Cr
	£	£
Freehold property	20,000	
Provision for depreciation of freehold property	30,000	
Revaluation account		50,000
Revaluation account	5,000	
Provision for depreciation of plant and machinery	25,000	
Plant and Machinery		30,000
Revaluation account	3,000	
Provision for depreciation of motor vehicles	23,000	
Motor vehicles		26,000
Provision for doubtful debts	600	
Revaluation account		600
Revaluation account	42,600	
Capital accounts: Dandy		21,300
Pixie		21,300

(Transfer of profit on revaluation of assets to partners' capital accounts)

Notes

(1) Provision for doubtful debts:

	£
Balance at 28.2.19-1	1,200
Provision required ($2\frac{1}{2}$ % of £24,000)	600
Balance transferred to Revaluation account	600

(2)   Profit on revaluation: £(50,000 + 600 − 5,000 − 3,000) = £42,600

7.3.2 Exercise: preparation of revaluation account involving provisions for depreciation of fixed assets

Carey and Street are in partnership sharing profits in the ratio 3:2. They propose to admit Court as a partner on 1 July 19-2. The following is an extract of Carey and Street's balance sheet at 30 June 19-2.

	£	£
Fixed assets		
Plant and equipment at cost	14,000	
less provision for depreciation	9,000	5,000
Motor vans	11,000	
less provision for depreciation	8,300	2,700
Office machinery	5,000	
less provision for depreciation	2,800	2,200
		9,900
Current assets		
Debtors	6,000	
less provision for doubtful debts	120	5,880

It is agreed that the partnership assets should be revalued as follows:

	£
Plant and equipment	4,000
Motor vans	2,000
Office machinery	4,000

On 1 July, the partners learned that a debtor owing £800 had become bankrupt. They also decided to increase the provision for doubtful debts to 5% of debtors.

Required

(a) Journal entries to give effect to the above mentioned adjustments. Narratives should be included.

(b) Show all the relevant ledger accounts concerned after the necessary postings have been made.

7.4 Goodwill

'The goodwill of a business is the advantage ... which a person gets by continuing to carry on ... a business which has been carried on for some time previously'. (The words of a judge in 1905.)

Goodwill may be regarded as that which enables a business to earn greater profits than the return normally expected on the net tangible assets of a business because of the reputation or special advantages which the business enjoys with the rest of the world.

In accounting, goodwill is an intangible asset and is only recorded as an asset in the accounts if it has a monetary value, i.e. the price paid for it. Sole traders and partnerships do not usually record goodwill in their books unless they have actually paid for it on purchasing a ready-made business because of the difficulty of placing a value on it, or even of proving that goodwill actually exists. Even if it is recorded in the books, prudence requires that it should be written off to the profit and loss account within a reasonable period as 'purchased goodwill' will progressively be replaced by the goodwill created by the new owner of the business.

Statement of Standard Accounting Practice (SSAP) 22 defines goodwill as the difference between the value of a business as a whole and the aggregate of the fair value of its separable net assets. For the purpose of this topic, therefore, goodwill will be regarded as the difference between the price paid for a business and the net asset value acquired by the purchaser. (If the price paid is less than the net asset value, the difference is 'negative goodwill', not 'badwill'.)

Since a change in the constitution of a partnership amounts to the dissolution of one partnership and the commencement of another, the new partnership acquires the business of the old. The old partners are entitled to, and should, agree a figure of goodwill with the new partners, who will benefit from this. It makes no difference that the partners in the old firm may well continue as partners in the new firm.

7.4.1 Example

Sweeney and Todd's balance sheet at 31 December 19-3 was as follows:

		£	£
Fixed assets:	Plant and equipment		3,000
	Motor van		4,000
	Office equipment		1,500
			8,500
Current assets:	Stock	800	
	Debtors	300	
	Bank	1,000	
		2,100	
less: Current liabilities:	Creditors	450	1,650
			10,150
Capital accounts:	Sweeney	5,100	
	Todd	5,050	10,150

On 1 January 19-4 Sweeney and Todd sold their business to Barber and Leech who took over the fixed assets, stock and debtors at the following valuations: plant and equipment £2,500; motor van £3,000; office equipment £1,200 and stock £1,000. Barber and Leech paid £10,000 for the fixed assets, stock and debtors, and agreed to pay the creditors.

Required

A calculation of the price paid for goodwill by Barber and Leech.

Answer

	£
Net value of assets taken over:	
Plant and equipment	2,500
Motor van	3,000
Office equipment	1,200
Stock	1,000
Debtors	300
	8,000
less creditors	450
Net asset value	7,550
Price paid for business	10,000
Goodwill	2,450

Tutorial note: Assets may not be taken over at their balance sheet values; the values to be taken in calculating goodwill are those which the purchaser is prepared to pay for the assets.

7.5 Treatment of goodwill on a change in a partnership

Goodwill should be valued and the following accounting entries made in the partnership books before the change:

	Account to be debited	**Account to be credited**
A. If goodwill is to be retained in the books	Goodwill	Capital accounts of partners in old firm (in old profit sharing ratios)
B. If goodwill is not to be retained in the books	(i) Goodwill	Capital accounts of partners in old firm (in old profit sharing ratios)
	(ii) Capital accounts of partners in new firm (in new profit sharing ratio)	Goodwill (to close goodwill account again.)

An alternative method to B above, and the one to be preferred when goodwill is not to be recorded in the books, is to credit or debit each partner's capital account in the old and new partnerships with the net amount of any change in his share of goodwill after the change.

7.5.1 Example

Datchett and Petworth are partners in a firm and share profits equally. Their capitals are: Datchett £50,000, Petworth £30,000. On 1 January 19-2 they admit Polbrook as a partner when the profit sharing ratio will be Datchett $\frac{2}{5}$, Petworth $\frac{2}{5}$, Polbrook $\frac{1}{5}$. Goodwill is valued at £12,000 but is not to be recorded in the firm's books.

Polbrook pays £30,000 into the firm's bank account as capital.

Required

Show the entries in the partners' Capital accounts to adjust for goodwill.

Answer

		(a) Old firm (in old profit sharing ratios) £	**(b)** New firm (in new profit sharing ratios) £	**(c)** Entries in capital accounts [col(a)-col(b)]. + = credit; – = debit. £
Datchett	($\frac{1}{2}$)	6,000	($\frac{2}{5}$) 4,800	+1,200 (Cr.)
Petworth	($\frac{1}{2}$)	6,000	($\frac{2}{5}$) 4,800	+1,200 (Cr.)
Polbrook	–	–	($\frac{1}{5}$) 2,400	–2,400 (Dr.)
		12,000	12,000	–

Partners' capital accounts

19-1	Datchett £	Petworth £	Polbrook £	19-1	Datchett £	Petworth £	Polbrook £
Jan 1 Goodwill			2,400	Jan 1 Balance b/d	50,000	30,000	
Balance c/d	51,200	31,200	27,600	Bank			30,000
				Goodwill	1,200	1,200	
	51,200	31,200	30,000		51,200	31,200	30,000
				Balance b/d	51,200	31,200	27,600

7.5.2 Exercise: adjustment of capital accounts on admission of new partner

Parchment and Deedes, partners in a firm of solicitors, share profits and losses equally. At 31 December 19-3 their balance sheet was as follows:

		£	£
Fixed assets:	Freehold premises		100,000
	Motor cars		40,000
	Office furniture and equipment		6,000
			146,000
Current assets:	Estimated undelivered costs	20,000	
	Unpaid delivered costs	48,000	
	Balance at bank	12,000	
		80,000	
less:			
Current liabilities:	Creditors	8,000	72,000
			218,000
Capital accounts:	Parchment	100,000	
	Deedes	100,000	200,000
Current accounts:	Parchment	12,000	
	Deedes	6,000	18,000
			218,000

Parchment and Deedes admitted Tape, their senior clerk, as a partner on 1 January 19-4 and he introduced £50,000 as capital plus his private car which was valued at £12,000 on the same day. It was agreed that the freehold premises should be revalued at £130,000, the motor cars of the old firm at £35,000, and the office furniture and equipment at £1,000. The partners agreed that a provision of 5% of unpaid delivered costs should be created.

The new profit-sharing ratio was to be Parchment $\frac{2}{5}$ Deedes $\frac{2}{5}$, Tape $\frac{1}{5}$.

Goodwill was valued at £50,000 but was not to be recorded in the books.

Required

(a) Journal entries to record the entries in the accounts of the partnership on the admission of Tape as a partner.

(b) The partners' capital accounts as at 1 January 19-4.

(c) The opening balance sheet of the firm of Parchment, Deedes and Tape, Solicitors, as at 1 January 19-4.

Tutorial note: Estimated undelivered costs are solicitors' equivalent of work in progress; unpaid delivered costs are debtors for work done.

7.6.1 Example: illustrating all the aspects of partnership changes covered in this chapter

Dragge and Pullen have been in partnership for some years and their partnership agreement provided as follows:

1. Accounts to be prepared annually to 31 December.
2. Interest on capital to be allowed at 10% p.a.
3. Pullen to be entitled to a salary of £12,000 p.a.
4. Profits and losses to be shared in the ratio 2:1.

At 31 December 19-0 the balance sheet of Dragge and Pullen was as follows:

	Cost £	Depn. £	Net £
Fixed assets			
Freehold premises	87,000	17,000	70,000
Plant and machinery	45,000	31,000	14,000
Motor cars	36,000	27,000	9,000
Office equipment	12,000	8,000	4,000
	180,000	83,000	97,000
Current assets			
Stock		13,000	
Debtors	11,800		
less provision for bad debts	600	11,200	
Carried forward		24,200	97,000

	£	£	£
Brought forward		24,200	97,000
Current liabilities			
Trade creditors	7,400		
Bank overdraft	4,800	12,200	12,000
			109,000
less: Long term liability: Loan from Shover			
(Carrying interest at 15% p.a.)			25,000
			84,000

Represented by:

	Capitals	Current Accounts	
	£	£	£
Dragge	50,000	2,600	52,600
Pullen	30,000	1,400	31,400
	80,000	4,000	84,000

Note to accounts: Depreciation has been calculated on the fixed assets at cost as follows: freehold premises 4%; plant and machinery 20%; motor cars 25%; office equipment 10%.

On 1 September 19-1, Dragge and Pullen admitted their manager, Pushkin, as a partner. Pushkin had been receiving a salary of £15,000 p.a. as manager.

Under the revised partnership agreement Pullen's salary would be increased to £18,000 p.a.; interest would continue to be allowed at the rate of 10% p.a. on capital; profits and losses would be divided equally.

The partners agreed that the assets should be revalued at 31 August 19-1 as follows:

	£
Freehold premises	120,000
Plant and machinery	12,000
Motor cars	6,000
Office equipment	3,000

Stock costing £2,000 was to be written off.

Goodwill was valued at £30,000, but no goodwill account was to be opened in the firm's books.

Fixed assets would be depreciated at the same rates as hitherto, but calculated on their revalued amounts.

No additions to, or sales of, fixed assets had taken place between 31 December 19-0 and 31 August 19-1.

On the 1 September, 19-1, Pushkin paid £30,000 into the firm's bank account as capital and also brought his private car, valued at £10,000, into the business.

On the same day, the loan to Shover was repaid together with the accrued interest, and Dragge transferred £20,000 from his capital account to a loan account on which interest would be paid at 10% p.a.

The following data was available from the partnership books for the year to 31 December 19-1:

	£
Receipts from debtors	299,800
Payments to suppliers	159,400
Wages and salaries	52,000
Rent rates and insurance	20,000
Heating and lighting	2,500
Sundry expenses	4,000
Shover: repayment of loan with accrued interest	27,500

Notes

1. Sales were spread evenly throughout the year and a uniform rate of gross profit was earned on all sales.
2. Stock at 31 December 19-1 was valued at cost, £15,000
3. Accrued expenses at 31 December 19-1: Rent £5,000 Heating and lighting £200
4. Prepaid expenses at 31 December 19-1: Rates £3,000, Insurance £1,000
5. Trade debtors at 31 August 19-1 £9,000; at 31 December 19-1 £12,000
6. Trade creditors at 31 December 19-1 £8,000

7. The provision for doubtful debts is to be adjusted to 6 % of trade debtors
8. Drawings in year to 31 December 19-1: Dragge £15,000; Pullen £20,000; Pushkin £3,000
9. Sundry expenses: £3,000 of these related to the eight months to 31 August 19-1

Required

(a) The trading and profit and loss and appropriation accounts of the firm of Dragge and Pullen for the eight months to 31 August 19-1.

(b) The trading and profit and loss and appropriation accounts of the firm of Dragge, Pullen and Pushkin for the four months ended 31 December 19-1.

(c) The balance sheets of the firm of Dragge, Pullen and Pushkin as at 31 December 19-1.

(d) The capital accounts and current accounts of Dragge, Pullen and Pushkin for the year to 31 December 19-1.

Answer

(a) and (b)   **Dragge, Pullen and Pushkin**
        Trading and profit and loss account for the year to 31 December 19-1

				£
Sales				300,000
less cost of sales				156,000
Gross profit carried down				144,000

		8 months to 31 Aug	4 months to 31 Dec	Total
		£	£	£
Gross profit b/d		96,000	48,000	144,000
less:	Wages and salaries	38,000	14,000	52,000
	Rent, rates & insurance	14,000	7,000	21,000
	Heating and lighting	1,800	900	2,700
	Sundry expenses	3,000	1,000	4,000
Interest on loans – Shover		2,500		2,500
– Dragge			667	667
Provision for doubtful debts		(60)	180	120
Provision for depreciation:				
Freehold premises		2,320	1,600	3,920
Plant & machinery		6,000	800	6,800
Motor cars		6,000	1,333	7,333
Office equipment		800	100	900
		74,360	27,580	101,940
Net profit		21,640	20,420	42,060
less:				
Salary – Pullen		8,000	6,000	14,000
Interest on capital –	Dragge	3,333	2,602	5,935
	Pullen	2,000	1,634	3,634
	Pushkin	–	1,000	1,000
		13,333	11,236	24,569
		8,307	9,184	17,491
Shares of profit –	Dragge	5,538	3,061	8,599
	Pullen	2,769	3,061	5,830
	Pushkin	–	3,062	3,062
		8,307	9,184	17,491

(c)

Balance sheet as at 31 December 19-1

	At valuation £	Depreciation £	Net £
Fixed assets			
Freehold premises	120,000	1,600	118,400
Plant and machinery	12,000	800	11,200
Motor cars	16,000	1,333	14,667
Office equipment	3,000	100	2,900
	151,000	3,833	147,167
Current assets			
Stock		15,000	
Trade debtors	12,000		
less provision	720	11,280	
Prepayments		4,000	
Bank		21,600	
		51,880	
less Current liabilities			
Trade creditors	8,000		
Expense creditors	5,200	13,200	38,680
			185,847
Long-term liability: Loan from Dragge			20,000
			165,847

	Capitals £	Current Accounts £	£
Dragge	78,080	2,801	80,881
Pullen	49,040	4,864	53,904
Pushkin	30,000	1,062	31,062
	157,120	8,727	165,847

(d)

Capital accounts for the year to 31 December 19-1

19-1		Dragge £	Pullen £	Pushkin £	19-1		Dragge £	Pullen £	Pushkin £
Sep 1	Goodwill			10,000	Jan 1	Balance b/f	50,000	30,000	
	Loan a/c	20,000			Aug 31	Reval. a/c	38,080	19,040	
Dec 31	Bals. c/d	78,080	49,040	30,000	Sep 1	Goodwill	10,000		
						Bank			30,000
						Motor car			10,000
		98,080	49,040	40,000			98,080	49,040	40,000
					19-2				
					Jan 1	Bal. b/d	78,080	49,040	30,000

Current accounts for the year to 31 December 19-1

19-1		Dragge £	Pullen £	Pushkin £	19-1		Dragge £	Pullen £	Pushkin £
Dec 31	Drawings	15,000	20,000	3,000	Jan 1	Balance b/f	2,600	1,400	
	Bals. c/d	2,801	4,864	1,062	Dec 31	Salary		14,000	
						Int. on loan	667		
						Int. on capital	5,935	3,634	1,000
						Share of profit	8,599	5,830	3,062
		17,801	24,864	4,062			17,801	24,864	4,062
					19-2				
					Jan 1	Balance b/d	2,801	4,864	1,062

Workings

1.

Revaluation account

	£		£
Plant and machinery	33,000	Freehold premises	33,000
Motor cars	30,000	Provisions for depn:	
Office equipment	9,000	Freehold premises*	19,320
Stock	2,000	Plant & machinery*	37,000
Capital accounts:		Motor cars*	33,000
Dragge (²/₃)	38,080	Office equipment*	8,800
Pullen (¹/₃)	19,040		
	131,120		131,120

*Depreciation is made up of the balances on the provisions for depreciation as at 31 December 19-0 (per the balance sheet) plus the additional depreciation for the eight months to 31 August 19-1 (per the profit and loss account).

2.

Goodwill

	Old firm £	New firm £	Adjustment £	
Dragge	($\frac{2}{3}$) 20,000	($\frac{1}{3}$) 10,000	10,000	(Cr)
Pullen	($\frac{1}{3}$) 10,000	($\frac{1}{3}$) 10,000	–	
Pushkin		($\frac{1}{3}$) 10,000	10,000	(Dr)
	30,000	30,000		

3.

Bank account

	£		£
Sales	299,800	Balance b/f	4,800
Pushkin – capital	30,000	Purchases	159,400
		Wages and salaries	52,000
		Rent, rates and insurance	20,000
		Heating & lighting	2,500
		Sundry expenses	4,000
		Shover – interest	2,500
		repayment of loan	25,000
		Drawings Dragge	15,000
		Pullen	20,000
		Pushkin	3,000
		Balance c/d	21,600
	329,800		329,800

7.6.2 Exercise: a comprehensive exercise to test overall grasp of topic

Johanne, Sebastian and Bach were in partnership, making up their accounts annually to 30 June. At 30 June 19-2 their balance sheet was as follows:

	Cost £	Depn. £	Net £
Fixed assets			
Freehold premises	40,000	10,000	30,000
Motor cars	20,000	12,000	8,000
Office machinery	18,000	8,000	10,000
	78,000	30,000	48,000
Current assets			
Stock		8,000	
Debtors		3,000	
Bank		9,000	
		20,000	
less Current liabilities: Creditors		6,000	14,000
			62,000

	Capitals	Current a/cs	
	£	£	£
Johanne	30,000	5,000	35,000
Sebastian	15,000	3,000	18,000
Bach	15,000	(6,000)	9,000
	60,000	2,000	62,000

The partners' policy was to provide for depreciation on fixed assets on cost as follows: freehold premises $2\frac{1}{2}$%; motor cars 20%; office machinery 25%.

Johanne received a salary of £10,000 p.a. and the partners were allowed interest on capitals at 10% p.a. and were charged with interest at the same rate on drawings. Profits and losses were shared: Johanne $\frac{1}{2}$, Sebastian $\frac{1}{4}$ Bach $\frac{1}{4}$.

Johanne retired on 31 December 19-2 and the partners agreed the following:

1. Johanne should take over one of the firm's cars at a valuation of £4,000. The car had been purchased for £8,000 on 1 July 19-1. Of the amount due to Johanne on his retirement, £30,000 should be transferred from his capital account to a loan account carrying interest at 10% p.a. The balance of his capital account was paid to him on 31 December 19-2.

2. The fixed assets should be revalued as follows at 31 December 19-2: Freehold premises £60,000; motor cars (other than the one taken by Johanne) £6,000; office machinery £4,000.

3. Goodwill to be valued at £20,000, but not to be recorded in the books.

4. Sebastian and Bach would continue as partners after Johanne's retirement on the following terms:

    (i) The balances on their current accounts at 31 December 19-2 should be transferred to their capital accounts as at that date. They would adjust the balances on their capital accounts as at 31 December 19-2 (after the transfers from their current accounts) to £25,000 by payments into or withdrawals from the firm's bank account.

    (ii) Sebastian and Bach would share Johannes' duties between them, for which Sebastian would receive a salary of £7,000 p.a. and Bach a salary of £3,000 p.a.

    (iii) The balance of profits and losses would be shared equally.

    (iv) Depreciation of fixed assets would be charged at the same rates as before, but calculated on the new valuations.

The following details were extracted from the books of the partnership for the year to 30 June 19-3:

			£
Receipts:	Cash sales		60,000
	Cash received from debtors		34,000
Payments:	Purchases		28,000
	Selling expenses		6,000
	Distribution expenses		4,000
	Wages and salaries		20,000
	General expenses		3,000
	Drawings:		
	(to 31.12. 19-2)	Johanne	4,000
		Sebastian	6,000
		Bach	5,000
	(1 Jan – 30 June 19-3):	Sebastian	4,000
		Bach	5,000
Trade debtors at 30 June 19-3			5,000
Trade creditors at 30 June 19-3			7,000

The following were owing at 30 June 19-3: selling expenses £1,200; distribution expenses £800; general expenses £200.

Stock at 30 June was £4,000.

Sales occurred evenly throughout the year and a uniform profit margin was earned on all sales.

Required

(a) The trading and profit and loss and appropriation accounts of the firm of Johanne, Sebastian and Bach for the six months to 31 December 19-2.

(b) The trading and profit and loss and appropriation accounts of the firm of Sebastian and Bach for the six months to 30 June 19-3.

(c) The balance sheet of Sebastian and Bach as at 30 June 19-3.

(d) The partners' capital and current accounts for the year to 30 June 19-3.

Key points to remember

1. A partnership change constitutes the termination of one partnership and the commencement of a new one.

2. Separate accounts should be prepared for the old and new partnership. Do this by preparing the profit and loss and appropriation accounts for the two firms in columnar form.

3. Apportion revenue and expenses as directed by the question and perform the arithmetical calculations very carefully.

4. Accruals and prepayments of expenses must be treated with care; adjust for these before apportioning the revenue and expenses in the profit and loss accounts.

5. Remember that partners' salaries, interest on capitals and drawings, although stated in questions on an annual basis, must be calculated on a time basis before and after the partnership change.

6. Revaluation of fixed assets. Adjust the fixed asset accounts for revaluation using a Revaluation account to complete the double entry. Credit increases in values to the Revaluation account and debit that account with decreases in values. Transfer all provisions for depreciation on those assets up to the date of the revaluation to the credit of the Revaluation account.

7. Profits or losses on revaluation of fixed assets. Transfer the balance on the Revaluation account to the old partners' capital accounts in their old profit sharing ratios.

8. Goodwill. Note carefully whether or not goodwill is to be recorded in the ledger for inclusion in future balance sheets. Do not leave the goodwill in the books if the question states that a goodwill account is not to be opened or that goodwill account is not to be shown in the balance sheet in future. Make the goodwill adjustments in the partners' capital accounts. The old partners' accounts must be credited with their shares of goodwill in their old profit sharing ratios; the capital accounts of the partners in the new firm must be debited with goodwill in their new profit sharing ratios. Follow the method shown in 7.5.1 above.

9. Outgoing partners. Transfer the balance on an outgoing partner's Drawings account to his Current account and, after the Current account has been adjusted for the partner's share of profit to the date of retirement, close the Current account off to his Capital account. Note carefully how the question requires the final balance on the outgoing partner's Capital account to be treated, i.e. repaid to him, or transferred to a loan account.

10. Read the question very carefully two or three times before commencing your answer. Tick every figure and instruction in the question as you deal with it in your answer to make sure you do not miss anything.

Common errors

1. Failure to apportion the gross profit correctly between the periods before and after a change.

2. Failure to prepare separate profit and loss accounts for the periods before and after a partnership change.

3. Arithmetic errors in calculating the apportionment of revenue and expenses.

4. Failure to apportion annual salaries to partners or annual rates of interest on capitals and drawings on a time basis.

5. Failure to transfer the depreciation provisions on revalued assets up to the date of revaluation to the Revaluation account.

6. Failure to deal with the revaluation of fixed assets altogether.

7. Showing revalued assets in subsequent balance sheets as 'at cost' instead of 'as at valuation'.

8. Failure to deal correctly, or at all, with goodwill.

Questions

Fully worked examination question

Winston, Nancy and Maurice are in partnership, sharing profits and losses in the ratio 2:2:1. Interest is charged on drawings at 5% per annum, and interest is credited on capital at 6% per annum. On 31 May 19-8, the balance sheet of the partnership was as follows:

		£	£	£
Fixed Assets:	Freehold Land and Buildings			180,000
	Machinery			60,000
	Office Equipment			15,000
	Motor Vehicles			35,000
				290,000
Current Assets:	Stock		34,000	
	Debtors		41,000	
			75,000	
Current Liabilities:	Creditors	45,000		
	Bank	10,000	55,000	20,000
				310,000
Capital Accounts:	Winston		140,000	
	Nancy		100,000	
	Maurice		70,000	310,000

The partners have now realised that their capital account balances do not reflect the following matters:

(i) Interest had not been charged on the following drawings:

Date	Winston	Nancy	Maurice
19-7	£	£	£
1 June	6,000	15,000	10,000
1 December	9,000	–	5,000

(ii) Interest on partners' capital at 6% per annum has not been credited.

Partners' capital, *for the purpose of interest calculations*, is taken as:

	£
Winston	70,000
Nancy	50,000
Maurice	30,000

These amounts were unchanged throughout the year.

Maurice decided to retire on 1 June 19-8, on the following terms:

(1) He will receive £8,000 payable by cheque immediately.

(2) The freehold land and buildings are to be revalued at £250,000.

(3) Goodwill is to be valued at £100,000.

(4) Maurice will take ownership of a partnership vehicle at its balance sheet value of £9,000.

(5) The balance of Maurice's capital will be left on loan with the partnership.

It was decided to open a goodwill account in the partnership books.

You are required to

(a) prepare the capital accounts of the three partners, showing in detail all the adjustments necessary, and the revised balances both at (i) 31 May 19-8 and (ii) after Maurice's retirement on 1 June 19-8. (14 marks)

(b) prepare the balance sheet of the partnership of Winston and Nancy as at 1 June 19-8. (6 marks)

(c) to give two reasons why the partnership should charge interest at only 5% per annum on partners' drawings when it is having to pay 14% per annum to the partnership's bank in respect of its overdraft. (5 marks)

(LONDON)

Answer

(a) (i)

Partnership capital accounts at 31 May 19-8

19-8	Winston £	Nancy £	Morris £	19-7		Winston £	Nancy £	Morris £
May 31 Int. on				Jun 1	Bal. b/f	140,000	100,000	70,000
drawings	525	750	625	19-8				
Adj. of profit				May 31 Int. on				
share	2,840	2,840	1,420		capitals	4,200	3,000	1,800
Bal. c/d	140,835	99,410	69,755					
	144,200	103,000	71,800			144,200	103,000	71,800

(ii)

Partnership capital accounts after Maurice's retirement

19-8	Winston £	Nancy £	Morris £	19-8		Winston £	Nancy £	Morris £
May 31 Bank			8,000	May 31	Bal. b/d	140,835	99,410	69,755
Motor vehicle			9,000		Reval. land			
Transfer: loan			86,755		& buildings	28,000	28,000	14,000
Bal. c/d	208,835	167,410			Goodwill	40,000	40,000	20,000
	208,835	167,410	103,755			208,835	167,410	103,755
				Jun 1	Bal. b/d	208,835	167,410	

(b)

Winston and Nancy – balance sheet as at 1 June 19-8

		£	£	£
Fixed assets:	Goodwill		100,000	
	Freehold property		250,000	
	Machinery		60,000	
	Office equipment		15,000	
	Motor vehicles		26,000	
			451,000	
Current assets:	Stock	34,000		
	Debtors	41,000		
		75,000		
Current liabilities:	Creditors	45,000		
	Bank	18,000	63,000	12,000
				463,000
Long-term liability:	Loan, Maurice			86,755
				376,245
Capitals:	Winston	208,835		
	Nancy	167,410		376,245

(c) Reasons for partnership charging interest at only 5% on partners' drawings when it has to pay 14% per annum on the bank overdraft:

1. The partnership agreement was probably prepared when bank interest rates were lower.

2. The difference between the rate charged to partners on drawings (5%) and the rate paid on the bank overdraft (14%) will affect the net profit of the firm and be borne by the partners in their profit sharing ratios, anyway.

Multiple choice questions

1   Green and Haricot have been in partnership for some years. The firms financial year ends on December 31. On 31 March 1996 they admitted Bean as a partner. In addition to introducing cash into the firm as capital, Bean brought his private car (cost when new £16,000) into the business at a valuation of £10,000.

   The firm depreciates its fixed assets at 20% on cost each year. The depreciation provided in respect of Bean's car for the year to 31 December 1996 is

   A   £1,500

   B   £2,000

   C   £2,400

   D   £3,200

2   Holly and Ivy have been in partnership for some years sharing profits and losses equally. They admit Berry as a partner and adjust the profit sharing ratio to Holly $\frac{2}{5}$, Ivy $\frac{2}{5}$, Berry $\frac{1}{5}$. Goodwill is valued at £36,000 but no goodwill account is to be kept in the books. Adjustment for goodwill in the firm's books will be

   A   credit the capital accounts of Holly and Ivy with £3,600 each and debit Berry's capital acount with £7,200

   B   credit Berry's capital acount with £7,200 and debit the capital accounts of Holly and Ivy with £3,600 each

   C   debit Berry's current acount with £7,200 and credit the current accounts of Holly and Ivy with £3,600 each

   D   debit the current accounts of Holly and Ivy with £3,600 each and credit Berry's current acount with £7,200

3   Archer Belloc and Conrad were in partnership sharing profits and losses in the ratio of 3:2:1. Conrad retired and Archer and Belloc remained partners sharing profits equally. The entries in the firm's books to record the adjusatment for goodwill will be:

   A   credit the capital accounts of Archer and Belloc with £2,500 each and debit Conrad's capital account with £5,000

   B   credit the capital accounts of Archer and Belloc with £5,000 each and debit Conrad's capital account with £5,000

   C   debit Belloc's capital account with £5,000 and credit Conrad's capital account with £5,000.

   D   debit Conrad's capital account with £5,000 and credit Belloc's capital account with £5,000

4   Dickens and Chaucer are in partnership sharing profits and losses equally. They admit Swift as a partner. A revaluation of the firm's net assets at the same date shows a loss on revaluation of £52,000. The new profit/loss sharing ratio is Dickens 2/5, Chaucer 2/5, Swift 1/5. The revaluation of the assets will be recorded in the books as:

   A   increases in the balances on Dickens' and Chaucer's capital accounts

   B   reductions in the balances on Dickens' and Chaucer's capital accounts

   C   increases in the balances on Dickens' and Chaucer's capital accounts and a reduction Swift's capital

   D   reductions in the balances on Dickens' and Chaucer's capital accounts and an increase in Swift's capital.

Further examination questions

1   Gupta, Richards and Jones are in partnership sharing profits and losses in the ratio 5:4:3. On 1 January 1990 Richards retired from the partnership and it was agreed that Singh should join the partnership, paying a sum of £30,000. From this date, profits are to be shared equally between the three partners and, in view of this, Jones agrees to pay a further £10,000 into the partnership as capital.

The Balance Sheet at 31 December 1989 showed:

		£	£
Fixed Assets:	Property		60,000
	Fixtures		30,000
			90,000
Current Assets:	Stock	30,000	
	Debtors	15,000	
	Bank	5,000	
		50,000	
Creditors		10,000	40,000
			130,000
Capital Accounts:	Gupta	60,000	
	Richards	40,000	
	Jones	25,000	
			125,000
Current Accounts:	Gupta	1,000	
	Richards	2,500	
	Jones	1,500	5,000
			130,000

It was agreed that in preparing a revised opening balance sheet of the partnership on 1 January 1990 the following adjustments should be made:

(i) Property is to be revalued at £70,000 and fixtures are to be revalued at £32,000.

(ii) Stock is considered to be shown at a fair value in the accounts. A provision for doubtful debts of £1,200 is required.

(iii) Professional fees of £600 relating to the change in partnership structure are to be regarded as an expense of the year to 31 December 1989, but were not included in the profit and loss account of that year. They are expected to be paid in March 1990.

(iv) Goodwill of the partnership as at 31 December 1989 is estimated at £30,000. No account for goodwill is to be entered in the books, but appropriate adjustments are to be made in the partners' capital accounts.

(v) On retirement Richards is to be paid a sum of £40,000. The balance owing to him will be recorded in a loan account carrying interest of 12%, to be repaid in full after two years.

(vi) All balances on current accounts are to be transferred to capital accounts. All balances on capital accounts in excess of £20,000 after this transfer are to be transferred to loan accounts carrying interest at 12%.

You are required to

(a) compute the balances on the loan accounts of Richards and the new partners on 1 January 1990, following completion of these arrangements. (12 marks)

(b) prepare an opening balance sheet for the partnership on 1 January 1990, following completion of these arrangements. (8 marks)

(c) explain briefly *three* factors to be taken into account when establishing profit-sharing arrangements between partners. (8 marks)

(d) explain briefly any *four* factors to be taken into account when deciding whether or not to convert a partnership into a limited company. (12 marks)

(JMB)

2 Patel and Robinson are in partnership and share profits in the ratio 2:1 respectively. Interest is paid on capital at 10 per cent per annum.

On 1 January 1991, Tann was admitted as a partner, bringing in £14,726 cash, part of which was payment for goodwill and the balance, capital. Goodwill was to be calculated as three quarters of the average profits, after interest on capital, for 1989 and 1990. Profits in those two years before interest were £14,803 and £18,605 respectively. No goodwill account was to be opened.

Under the new partnership Patel, Robinson and Tann will share profits in the ratio 3:2:1 respectively; interest on capital will no longer be paid.

The partners' balances at 1 January 1991 were:

	Capital	Current
Patel	£16,300 Cr	£4,500 Cr
Robinson	£12,700 Cr	£900 Dr

The capital balances had remained unchanged for several years.

The net profit for the year ended 31 December 1991 was £19,470. Drawings were:

	£
Patel	15,000
Robinson	6,000
Tann	3,000

(a) Show the partners' current accounts and capital accounts for the year ended 31 December 1991. (12 marks)

(b) Give one reason why a partner's current account might show a debit balance at any time during a financial year. (3 marks)

(LONDON)

3 Page, Dickson and Saville are in partnership and own a sports business which manufactures sports clothing and retails sports goods and equipment. The latest available partnership balance sheet as at 29 February 19-8 revealed the following:

	£	£	£
Fixed assets, at net book value			116,325
Current assets			
Stocks		73,500	
Debtors		51,900	
		125,400	
Creditors, less than one year			
Bank overdraft	11,900		
Creditors	63,000	(74,900)	50,500
			166,825
Capital accounts			
Page		40,000	
Dickson		35,000	
Saville		50,000	125,000
Current accounts			
Page		16,325	
Dickson		12,100	
Saville		13,400	41,825
			166,825

Additional information:

(1) Page and Dickson wish to expand the retail base of the business and to raise the necessary capital they have agreed to transfer the manufacturing activities to Saville.

(2) After settlement of his capital and current account balances Saville has agreed to pay cash for the net assets of the manufacturing business transferred to him.

(3) The net assets to be transferred to Saville were as follows:

	Values in the balance sheet of Page, Dickson and Saville	Agreed transfer value to Saville
	£	£
Fixed assets	64,950	76,500
Stocks	41,500	39,200
Debtors	43,200	41,450
Creditors	39,000	39,000

(4) Any profit or loss on transfer of net assets to Saville is to be shared equally by the remaining two partners and debited/credited to their capital accounts.

(5) Page and Dickson have agreed the following terms and details for their new partnership:
  (i) Each partner would bring in additional capital of £15,000 on 1 March 19-8.
  (ii) Each partner would be entitled to interest on capital at 8% per annum for the year ending 28 February 19-9 and the balance of profits and losses would be shared equally.

(iii) Partnership salaries have been agreed at: Page £9,000 and Dickson £7,000 p.a.

(iv) The new partnership estimate that profits from the retail business before interest on capital and partners' salaries will be £65,000 for the year to 28 February 19-9.

Required

(a) Prepare a balance sheet for the partnership of Page and Dickson on 1 March 19-8, assuming that Saville takes over the manufacturing business on the terms agreed.

(12 marks)

(b) Prepare a forecast profit and loss appropriation account for the new partnership of Page and Dickson on the basis of the above information for the year ending 28 February 19-9.

(7 marks)

(c) Briefly discuss the advantages and disadvantages to Page and Dickson of selling the sports clothing manufacturing business to Saville. (4 marks)

(AEB)

4   Redfern and Froggatt are partners in a wholesale trading company and their partnership agreement provides for the following:

Interest on fixed capitals at 10% per annum and the balance of profits and losses to be shared equally.

Their bookkeeper, an inexperienced accounting clerk had prepared a provisional set of final accounts which showed that the business had made a net profit (before appropriation) of £90,580 for the financial year ended 31 December 1990.

Subsequently the following errors were discovered:

(1) During stock taking *all* stock had been incorrectly valued by 10% owing to the use of out-of-date cost prices. The correct value was 110% of the value included in the provisional final accounts.

In addition, an amount of damaged stock had been overlooked. This damaged stock had cost £1,500, but was expected to fetch only £600 on the open market.

Note: the value of the total closing stock included in the provisional final accounts had been £40,800.

(2) Redfern frequently made private trips in his business car. It was estimated that the cost of fuel and servicing attributable to these private trips was £1,500. These private expenses had been included in the motor vehicle expenses.

(3) Goods sold to a customer, Nigel Smith, on credit for £4,500 had been correctly recorded in the accounts. However, Smith returned the goods as unsatisfactory. No entry was made in the returns inward book but an entry was made in the sales day book treating the return as a further sale of goods on credit.

(4) No entry had been made in the accounts for staff wages still owing at 31 December 1990 of £3,000.

(5) The total of the discounts received column (£3,170) from the cash book had been transferred to the final accounts as revenue expenditure.

(6) The partners sub-let part of their premises to a retailer at an annual rent of £15,000. The sub-let commenced on 1 January 1990 with half the rent due on that date and the other half on the 1 July, but owing to a mis-understanding no rent was received until 31 December 1990 when a cheque for £25,000 was received. No entries had been made in the accounts for the rent due or the receipt of this cheque.

(7) No entry had been made in respect of a debt of £2,500 incurred by R. Gee. The debt was irrecoverable.

Additional information:

(i)   Redfern and Froggatt do not maintain total debtors accounts or total creditors accounts.

(ii) Balances on the partners' accounts as at 1 January 1990 were:

Capital accounts	£	Current accounts	£
Redfern	240,000	Redfern	10,000 CR
Froggatt	235,000	Froggatt	15,000 CR

It should be assumed that no changes to these balances occurred during the year.

(iii) Froggatt worked full time in the business, but during 1990 Redfern worked only infrequently and usually only to be consulted on policy.

Required

(a) Journal entries for the items 1) to 7) above. (Narratives not required.) (9 marks)

(b) A detailed statement of the corrected net profit. (9 marks)

(c) A partnership appropriation account for the year ended 31 December 1990. (2 marks)

(d) For each partner calculate suitable figures showing the return on his own capital invested as at the 1 January 1990. Comment on the results. (5 marks)

(AEB)

5 Swift, Rook and Dove are designers who operate in a partnership. Their written agreement states that they share the profits or losses of the business in the ratio 2:2:1. The day to day management of the business is under the control of Crowe with a salary of £15,000 per annum, together with a commission of 6% of the net profit after charging such commission.

On January 1991 Swift, Rook and Dove invited Crowe to join them in partnership. At that date the partnership's goodwill was valued at £41,600 and it was agreed that the value of the fixed assets should be raised by £8,400 and that a goodwill account should not be retained in the new partnership.

Crowe brought into the partnership £50,000 as his capital and no other payments took place.

The four partners agreed that the new arrangement for sharing profits or losses would be in the following ratio:

Swift 4: Rook 3; Dove 2: Crowe 1.

As it was realised that Crowe's share of any profits would only be modest, it was decided to make a special arrangement to cover this situation. This stated that if in any year Crowe's share of the profit fell below what he would have received from salary and commission when he managed the business, then Swift would contribute the difference to Crowe from his own share of the profit.

The net profit for the year ended 31 December 1991 amounted to £190,000; the partners agreed that £16,000 of this excellent result should be paid to the staff as a bonus.

Required

(a) The journal entries, including those relating to cash, to give effect to the introduction of Crowe's capital, the arrangements relating to the goodwill and the revaluation of the fixed assets. Narratives are required. (8 marks)

(b) A statement to show how the profit for 1991 is distributed among the partners before and after the special arrangement is taken into consideration. (7 marks)

(c) A list of provisions of the Partnership Act 1890 regarding profit sharing that apply when no agreement exists between the partners. (3 marks)

(AEB)

6 Smith and Khan operate an international travel agency; their partnership agreement states that they share profits and losses in the ratio 4:3 respectively.

On 1 December 1992 Chow joined the partnership and paid into the partnership accounts £35 000 as his capital.

The terms relating to the distribution of profit of the new partnership which came into being on 1 December 1992 were:

Partner's annual salaries – Smith £9000, Kahn £6600 and Chow £4900;

Interest to be allowed on capital at 2% per annum;

The balance of profits or losses to be shared between Smith, Kahn and Chow in the ratio 4:3:2 respectively.

The trial balance of the partnership which relates to the year which ended at 31 May 1993 was:

		DR £	CR £
Bank			1,960
Commission on holiday bookings			70,420
Commission on holiday insurances sold			8,820
Loss on tours operated by the firm		22,600	
Debtors and creditors		16,400	28,800
Salaries (staff)		31,000	
Postage and telephone		3,850	
Printing and stationery		4,220	
Sundry expenses		2,100	
Freehold premises at cost		160,000	
Office furniture and equipment (cost £40,000) at 1 June 1992)		18,000	
Cars (cost £30 000) at 1 June 1992		21,000	
Business rates		2,800	
Fixed capital accounts	– Smith at 1 June 1992		100,000
	– Kahn at 1 June 1992		55,000
	– Chow at 1 December 1992		35,000
Current accounts	– Smith	8,000	
	– Kahn	5,500	
	– Chow	3,700	
Bad debts written off		830	
		300,000	300,000

The following information is available at the year end 31 May 1993.

(1) Profits or losses are assumed to accrue evenly throughout the year.

(2) Business rates £600 and printing £520 were outstanding at 31 May 1993.

(3) The telephone rental of £150 was paid in advance on 25 May 1993 to cover the period 1 June to 31 August 1993.

(4) Depreciation is charged annually on cost at the following rates:

Office furniture and equipment 10%
Cars 25%.

Required

(a) Prepare the profit and loss and appropriation accounts of the partnership for the year ended 31 May 1993. (20 marks)

(b) Prepare a balance sheet as at 31 May 1993. (14 marks)

(c) Prepare the partners' current accounts for the year ended 31 May 1993. (8 marks)

(d) Identify any action that the partners may take to improve the financial position of the business. (8 marks)

(Total 50 marks)
(AEB)

7 Cole and Rich are in partnership operating a retail business selling musical instruments and products. They share profits and losses in the ratio 2:1 respectively. The only other agreed item between the partners was to allow interest of 6% per annum to be calculated on the opening balance of their capital accounts. The annual accounting date of the partnership is 31 May. Due to the need to meet increasing demand the partners had invited Goodman to join the partnership from 1 December 1994. Goodwill was valued at £60 000. Goodman introduced £45 000 into the business on that date. However, £5000 of this was transferred to his current account.

The terms of the partnership provided that:

(1) no goodwill account would appear in the books;

(2) interest of 5% per annum to be allowed on opening capital account balances;

(3) the balance of profits and losses to be shared between Cole, Rich and Goodman in the ratio of 3:2:1 respectively.

On 31 May 1995 the following trial balance was prepared for the partnership.

	£	£
Capital accounts at 1 June 1994		
Cole		90,000
Rich		60,000
Current accounts at 1 June 1994		
Cole		24,000
Rich		18,000
Cash contributed by Goodman on 1 December 1994		45,000
Gross profit		280,000
Stock on 31 May 1995	76,000	
Freehold premises acquired 1 June 1994	100,000	
Fixtures at cost	16,000	
Vehicles at cost	51,000	
Wages and salaries	106,750	
Provision for depreciation at 1 June 1994		
Fixtures		6,000
Vehicles		18,000
Debtors and creditors	43,500	57,000
Business rates	10,800	
Repairs incurred in July 1994	2,000	
Light and heat	14,100	
General expenses	38,000	
Bank	100,050	
Drawings accounts at 31 May 1995		
Cole	17,800	
Rich	14,600	
Goodman	7,400	
	598,000	598,000

Additional information:

(1) Any apportionment of gross profit was to be on the basis of sales; and, unless otherwise indicated, expenses were to to be apportioned on a time basis. (Sales for the period 1 June 1994 to 30 November 1994 were £225,000 out of a total sales figure for the year of £525,000.)

(2) The wages and salaries figure includes an amount of £4750 which relates entirely to the period 1 December 1994 to 31 May 1995.

(3) At 31 May 1995 business rates paid in advance amounted to £3800 whilst £900 was accrued at that date for light and heat.

(4) Provision for depreciation was to be made on the following basis.

Fixtures – 5% per annum on cost

Vehicles – 20% per annum on cost

(5) Goodman owns a warehouse which he leased to the partnership at £8000 per annum from 1 December 1994. No rent had yet been paid or credited to him for this.

Required

(a) Profit and loss, and appropriation accounts for the partnerships. (24 marks)

(b) Write up the partners' capital and current accounts for the year ended 31 May 1995.

(12 marks)

(c) What factors could contribute to the establishment of goodwill in a business? (8 marks)

(d) Outline some recommendations to the partners about ways in which they could develop their business. (6 marks)

Total 50 marks

(AEB)

8 Afghan, Berber and Chinoise were partners, sharing profits in the ratio of 3:2:1. On 31 December 1995, Berber retired, and Durry was admitted to the partnership, bringing in an amount of capital equal to a third of the new partnership's net assets.

The balance sheet of Afghan, Berber and Chinoise at 31 December 1995 was as follows:

	£	£	£
Fixed Assets(Building)			840,000
Current Assets			
Stock		1,500,000	
Debtors	600,000		
Less Provision for Doubtful Debts ,	60,000		
		540,000	
Bank		420,000	
		2,460,000	
Less: *Creditors due for payment within one year*:			
Creditors		1,050,000	
			1,410,000
			2,250,000
Capital Accounts			
Afghan		1,125,000	
Berber		750,000	
Chinoise		375,000	
			2,250,000

The terms of the changes to the partnership were as follows:

1. Goodwill was valued at £1 020 000.

2. Stock was written down by £60 000.

3. The provision for doubtful debts was reduced to 5% of outstanding debtors.

4. Durry brought into the partnership equipment worth £345 000 and the balance of his contribution was paid by cheque.

5. The balance on Berber's account was paid to him by cheque.

(a) Show the revaluation account, the bank account and the capital accounts of Afghan, Berber and Chinoise, including all entries necessary to reflect the changes in the partnership. (10 marks)

(b) Prepare a balance sheet of the partnership of Afghan, Chinoise and Durry after all relevant entries have been completed in the partnership's books. (5 marks)

Total 15 marks
(LONDON)

8 Partnership amalgamations; dissolution; sale of partnerships to limited companies

Chapter objectives

Questions on these topics
- ❐ require application of principles already learned in Chapter 7
- ❐ test understanding of entries required to close partnership books

8.1 Partnership amalgamations

Sometimes two or more partnerships amalgamate. Be prepared to suggest reasons for such amalgamations:

(a) the firms have worked together well in the past.

(b) the businesses are similar and amalgamation will enable them to achieve economies of scale e.g. they may be able to purchase goods more cheaply by taking advantage of bulk discount; or they may be able to share the same premises.

(c) the businesses are complementary e.g. car sales and car servicing.

(d) a variety of skills, expertise and experience may be concentrated in one firm.

(e) the enlarged firm may be in a position to fulfil larger, more profitable contracts or act for more prestigious clients. e.g. firms of accountants amalgamate to enable them to act for larger, more profitable clients.

(f) the geographical area of operations may be enlarged where the firms are situated in different parts of the country or of the world.

Accounting procedure

Basically, the procedure for answering questions of this type is to add the balance sheets of the firms together after making any adjustments necessary to the separate balance sheets to ensure that the partners' capital accounts realistically reflect their true interests in their respective firms. The procedure involved in adjusting the balance sheets are those already covered in Chapter 7:

For each firm

1. Adjust the partners' capital accounts for goodwill and profits or losses on revalued assets.

2. Deal with any assets not being transferred to the new firm. Assets taken over by partners should be debited to their capital accounts at the agreed values. Assets sold should be dealt with as normal disposals and profit or loss on disposal transferred to the capital accounts in the partners' old profit sharing ratios.

3. Give effect to any other requirements of the question such as transfers of current account balances to capital accounts, or adjustment of capital account balances to be included in the new firm by the introduction or withdrawal of cash.

4. The adjusted balance sheets may now be combined.

8.1.1 Example. Joyner & Co.

John and George are partners in the firm of John & Co., sharing profits and losses equally. Nerissa and Sally are partners in the firm of Nerissa & Co. and share profits and losses in the ratio of 3/5 and 2/5 respectively.

The partners in each of the firms agree to amalgamate under the name of Joyner & Co. as from 1 October 19-9. The profits and losses in the new firm will be shared as follows:

John	25%
George	30%
Nerissa	25%
Sally	20%

The balance sheets of the separate partnerships at 30 September 19-9 are:

		John & Co.	Nerissa & Co.
		£	£
Fixed assets		12,000	16,000
Stocks		8,400	24,000
Cash		9,600	4,000
		30,000	44,000
Capital accounts:	John	10,000	
	George	20,000	
	Nerissa		20,000
	Sally		24,000
		30,000	44,000

For the purpose of the amalgamation the assets are to be valued at the following amounts:

	John & Co.	Nerissa & Co.
	£	£
Fixed assets	18,000	20,000
Stocks	11,200	17,600
Goodwill	8,000	32,000

The new partnership does not intend to show goodwill in its balance sheet.

The capitals of the partners in the new firm are to be:

	£
John	10,000
George	15,000
Nerissa	30,000
Sally	25,000

Required

(a) The capital accounts of the partners showing the entries required as a result of the amalgamation.

(b) The opening balance sheet of Joyner & Co. as at 1 October 19-9.

Answer

(a)

Capital accounts

19-9		John £	George £	Nerissa £	Sally £	19-9		John £	George £	Nerissa £	Sally £
Sep 30	Revaluation			1,440	960	Sep 30	Balances b/f	10,000	20,000	20,000	24,000
Oct 1	Goodwill	6,000	8,000				Revaluation	4,400	4,400		
	Bank		1,400		2,840	Oct 1	Goodwill			9,200	4,800
	Balance c/d	10,000	15,000	30,000	25,000		Bank	1,600		2,240	
		16,000	24,400	31,440	28,800			16,000	24,400	31,440	28,800
						Oct 1	Balance b/d	10,000	15,000	30,000	25,000

(b)

Joyner & Co.
Balance sheet as at 1 October 19-9

	£	£
Fixed assets (18,000 + 20,000)		38,000
Stocks (11,200 + 17,600)	28,800	
Cash (13,600 +1,600 + 2,240 - 1,400 - 2,840)	13,200	42,000
		80,000

Capital accounts:			
	John	10,000	
	George	15,000	
	Nerissa	30,000	
	Sally	25,000	80,000

Working   **Revaluation accounts**

	John & Co £	Nerissa & Co £		John & Co £	Nerissa & Co £
Reduction in stock		6,400	Increase in fixed assets	6,000	4,000
Capital accounts			Increase in stock	2,800	
John ($\frac{1}{2}$)	4,400		Capital accounts		
George ($\frac{1}{2}$)	4,400		Nerissa ($\frac{3}{5}$)		1,440
			Sally ($\frac{2}{5}$)		960
	£8,800	£6,400		£8,800	£6,400

Goodwill

	Old firms £	New firm £	Adjustment £
John & Co £8,000			
John ($^1/2$)	4,000	(25%) 10,000	6,000 (dr.)
George ($^1/2$)	4,000	(30%) 12,000	8,000 (dr.)
Nerissa & Co £32,000			
Nerissa $^3/5$	19,200	(25%) 10,000	9,200 (cr.)
Sally $^2/5$	12,800	(20%) 8,000	4,800 (cr.)
	40,000	40,000	

8.1.2 Exercise (for practice in partnership amalgamation)

Fortnum, Marks & Co.

Chas. Fortnum and Tony Mason are carrying on business in partnership; Stan Marks and Mike Spencer are also in partnership and carrying on a similar type of business to that of Fortnum and Mason. The two firms agree to amalgamate as from 1 September 19-1 as Fortnum, Marks & Co.

Fortnum and Mason have shared profits and losses in the ratio of 8:7; Marks and Spencer have shared profits and losses in the ratio 3:2. The balance sheets of the two firms on 31 August 19-1 are as follows:

		Fortnum & Mason £	Marks & Spencer £
Freehold property		15,000	10,000
Fixtures		3,600	2,800
Vehicles		5,000	3,400
Stock		11,800	13,400
Debtors		14,200	13,000
Investments		3,000	
Balance at bank		8,400	6,200
		61,000	48,800
Capital accounts:	Fortnum	24,000	
	Mason	21,000	
	Marks		22,000
	Spencer		15,600
Current accounts:	Fortnum	2,000	
	Mason	1,200	
Creditors		12,800	11,200
		61,000	48,800

The partners agree that the following provisions should be made effective on the amalgamation:

1. The freehold property and fixtures of Marks and Spencer are to be sold and this is done on 1 September 19-1. The proceeds of sale amount to £20,000.

2. Fortnum, Marks & Co. are to take over the assets of the old partnerships at the following values:

	Fortnum & Mason £	Marks & Spencer £
Stock	11,400	12,400
Vehicles	4,600	3,000
Fixtures	4,000	
Freehold property	19,000	

3. Provision is to be made for doubtful debts in the sums of £800 by Fortnum and Mason, and £1,000 by Marks and Spencer; both firms are to allow for discounts of $2\frac{1}{2}$% to be received from their creditors.

4. Fortnum is to take over his firm's investments at £2,400.

5. Fortnum and Mason's goodwill is valued at £15,000 and that of Marks and Spencer at £10,000. Fortnum, Marks and Co. will not show goodwill in its balance sheet.

6. As from 1 September 19-1 the profit sharing ratios are to be:

Fortnum	30%
Mason	25%
Marks	25%
Spencer	20%

7. Fortnum, Marks & Co. will have a capital of £100,000 which will be provided by the partners in the same ratios as they share profits and losses; any adjustments necessary for this purpose will be made by the partners paying cash to or withdrawing cash from the firm's bank account.

Required

For the old firms:

(a) the revaluation accounts

(b) the partners' capital accounts;

For Fortnum, Marks & Co.

(c) the partners' capital accounts

(d) the cash account

(e) the opening balance sheet as at the start of business on 1 September 19-1.

8.2 Dissolution of Partnerships

Partnership assets are sold; profits or losses on realisation are apportioned to the partners' capital accounts in their profit sharing ratio; the balance of cash is used to pay creditors and expenses of dissolution and, finally, to repay the balances on their capital accounts to the partners.

Note: Unrecorded goodwill and asset revaluation are not relevant in this topic.

Accounting:

Transfer the balances on the partners' current accounts to their capital accounts; the current accounts are now no longer required.

Open a Realisation account to record the sale of assets and proceed to make the accounting entries in the following order:

		Debit	Credit
1	Assets at net book value	Realisation a/c	Asset a/cs
2	Proceeds of sale of assets	Bank (cash)	Realisation a/c
3	Assets taken over by partners (at valuation)	Capital a/c of partner concerned	Realisation a/c
4	Costs of dissolution	Realisation a/c	Bank (cash)

		Debit	Credit
5	Payment of creditors	Creditors' a/cs	Bank (cash)
6	Discounts received from creditors	Creditors' a/cs	Realisation a/c
7	Cash received from debtors	Bank (cash)	Debtors' a/cs
8	Bad debts and discounts allowed	Realisation a/c	Debtors' a/cs
9	Credit balance on Realisation a/c (profit on realisation)	Realisation a/c	Partners' capital a/cs
or	Debit balance on Realisation) a/c (loss on realisation)	Partners' capital a/cs	Realisation a/c
	(in profit/loss sharing ratio)		
10	Repayment of partner's loan to firm	Partner's loan a/c	Bank
11	Repayment of partners' capitals	Partners' capital a/cs	Bank
	Debit balance on partner's capital account	Bank	Partner's capital a/c

All accounts should now be closed.

8.2.1 Example

Lilley, Dilley and Willey have been carrying on business in partnership for some years sharing profits in the ratio 3:2:1. On 31 December 19-3 they decided to dissolve the partnership. On that date the firm's balance sheet was as follows:

		Cost £	Depn £	Net £
Fixed assets:	Plant and equipment	25,000	13,000	12,000
	Motor vehicles	18,000	15,000	3,000
	Office machinery	3,000	2,400	600
		46,000	30,400	15,600
Current assets:				
Stock			21,000	
Debtors			6,400	
Bank			3,800	
			31,200	
less Current liabilities: Creditors			2,700	28,500
				44,100
less Loan from Lilley				5,000
				39,100
Capitals:	Lilley		20,000	
	Dilley		10,000	
	Willey		2,000	32,000
Current accounts:	Lilley		4,000	
	Dilley		5,000	
	Willey		(1,900)	7,100
				39,100

Willey was allowed to retain his car which was valued at £4,000. The remaining assets realised the following amounts on the 1 January 19-4.

	£
Plant and equipment	10,000
Motor cars	5,000
Office machinery	400
Stock	24,000
Debtors	6,200

All creditors were paid and discounts received amounted to £74.

The expenses of dissolution amounted to £800.

Required

Show the following accounts with the entries in them to record the dissolution of the partnership:

(i) Realisation account

(ii) the partners' capital accounts in columnar form

(iii) the firm's bank account.

Answer

Workings　　　　　**Journal entries to close asset accounts:**

	Dr. £	Cr. £
Realisation account	12,000	
Provision for depreciation of plant and equipment	13,000	
Plant and equipment at cost		25,000
Realisation account	3,000	
Provision for depreciation of motor vehicles	15,000	
Motor vehicles at cost		18,000
Realisation account	600	
Provision for depreciation of office machinery	2,400	
Office machinery at cost		3,000
Realisation account	21,000	
Stock		21,000
Capital account – Willey	4,000	
Realisation account		4,000
Realisation account	200	
Sundry debtors		200
Sundry creditors	74	
Realisation account		74

(i)

Realisation account

	£		£
Plant and equipment	12,000	Capital - Willey	4,000
Motor vehicles	3,000	Bank	39,400
Office machinery	600	Sundry creditors	74
Stock	21,000		
Sundry debtors	200		
Bank – dissolution expenses	800		
Capitals – Lillee ($\frac{3}{6}$) 2,937			
Dilley ($\frac{2}{6}$) 1,958			
Willey ($\frac{1}{6}$) 979	5,874		
	43,474		43,474

(ii)

Capital accounts

	Lilley £	Dilley £	Willey £		Lilley £	Dilley £	Willey £
Current account			1,900	Balances b/f	20,000	10,000	2,000
Realisation a/c – car			4,000	Current a/cs	4,000	5,000	
Bank	26,937	16,958		Realisation a/c	2,937	1,958	979
				Bank			2,921
	26,937	16,958	5,900		26,937	16,958	5,900

(iii)

Bank

	£		£
Balance b/f	3,800	Sundry creditors	2,626
Realisation a/c	39,400	Realisation a/c costs	800
Sundry debtors	6,200	Lillee - loan account	5,000
Capital – Willey	2,921	Capitals – Lillee	26,937
		– Dilley	16,958
	52,321		52,321

8.2.2 Exercise: for practice in closing partnership books on dissolution of firm

Penn, Punch and Staple, partners in an office supplies business, made up their accounts to 30 June 19-0. The following was their balance sheet at that date:

Fixed assets		Cost £	Depn. £	Net £
Leasehold premises		21,000	16,000	5,000
Delivery vans		7,000	5,000	2,000
Fixtures and fittings		3,000	1,000	2,000
		31,000	22,000	9,000
Current assets:	Stocks		12,000	
	Debtors		3,400	
			15,400	
less Current liabilities:				
Trade creditors		3,900		
Bank overdraft		900	4,800	10,600
				19,600
Less: Loan from Quire				3,000
				16,600
Capitals:	Penn	5,000		
	Punch	2,000		
	Staple	2,000		9,000
Current accounts:	Penn	3,400		
	Punch	2,500		
	Staple	1,700		7,600
				16,600

Penn, Punch and Staple have always shared profits and losses in the ratio 2:2:1.

On 30 June 19-0, the partners agreed to terminate the partnership; Penn took over one of the delivery vans, which had a net book value of £1,000, at a valuation of £2,500. Staple took over, at a valuation of £6,000, stock which had cost £6,500.

A ready buyer was found for the leasehold premises, the remaining delivery vans, fixtures and fittings, and the balance of the stock, at an agreed price of £11,500. Debtors realised the sum of £3,225.

After the creditors had been paid in full, the partners received the monies due to them on capital account or paid what was due to the firm from them.

Required

The entries to record the above events in

(i)   the Realisation account

(ii) the firm's bank account, and

(iii) the partners' capital accounts.

8.3 Insolvent Partners (Garner v. Murray)

It may happen that a partner is insolvent and unable to clear a debit balance on his capital account on the dissolution of the firm. The debit balance on his capital account must be shared by the other partners in the ratio of the last agreed balances on their capital accounts; in practice, this means the balances shown on their latest balance sheet. This follows the decision in a case known as Garner v. Murray. It must only be applied when the partner concerned is insolvent, and this is clearly stated or implied in an examination question.

8.3.1 Example

Hall, Cotton, and Loss were in partnership sharing profits and losses equally. On 1 April 19-2, the partners decided to dissolve the partnership. After realising all the assets, the balance sheet appeared as follows:

		£
Cash at bank		27,000
Capital accounts:	Hall	18,000
	Cotton	12,000
	Loss	(3,000)
		27,000

Loss was unable to pay the amount of the balance due from him to the firm.

Required

The partners' capital accounts showing the entries required to close the books.

Answer

Partners' capital accounts

19-2		£ H	£ C	£ L	19-2		£ H	£ C	£ L
Apr 1	Bal b/f			3,000	Apr 1	Bal b/f	18,000	12,000	
	L-Cap.					Cap.a/cs			
	(18:12)	1,800	1,200			L & C			3,000
	Bank	16,200	10,800						
		18,000	12,000	3,000			18,000	12,000	3,000

Note: The debit balance on Loss's capital account is NOT shared by Hall and Cotton in their profit/loss sharing ratios.

8.3.2 Exercise: on the application of Garner v. Murray

Bent, Bold and Broke have been in partnership for some years sharing profits and losses in ratio 3:2:1.

At 31 December 19-1, their summarised balance sheet was as follows:

			£	£
Fixed assets				22,000
Current assets	Stock		18,000	
	Debtors		5,000	
	Bank		3,000	
			26,000	
less Current liabilities				
	Trade creditors		6,000	20,000
				42,000

	Capitals £	Current accounts £	
Bent	20,000	2,000	
Bold	20,000	(2,000)	
Broke	5,000	(3,000)	
	45,000	(3,000)	42,000

On 1 January 19-2 the firm was dissolved and only £20,000 was obtained from the sale of the fixed assets and stock. Debtors realised £4,000. The creditors were paid in full.

Broke proved to be insolvent and therefore unable to contribute cash to meet the debit balance on his capital account.

Required

The Realisation account, the bank account and the partners' capital accounts, showing the entries required to close the books of the partnership.

8.4 Sale of partnership to limited company

A partnership may be sold to an existing limited company, or the partners may form a limited company and sell the partnership business to it in order to obtain the benefits of limited liability. In either case, it makes no difference to the entries required in the partnership books.

The limited company may pay for the partnership business in cash, or by issuing shares and possibly debentures to the partners; or by a combination of cash, shares and debentures.

Accounting entries. Steps 1-9 for the dissolution of a partnership still apply (see 8.2) but the procedure which follows step 9 is modified as follows:

	Dr.	**Cr.**
Purchase consideration	Account opened for — Ltd.	Realisation a/c
Payment in cash	Bank	— Ltd.
Payment in preference shares	Preference shares in — Ltd,	— Ltd.
Payment in ordinary shares	Ordinary shares in — Ltd.	— Ltd.
Payment in debentures	Debentures in — Ltd.	— Ltd.
Closure of partners' capital accounts	Partners' capital accounts	Bank, preference, ordinary shares, debentures, in— Ltd. co. a/cs.

Follow the distribution of shares, debentures and cash to the partners as directed in the question. In the absence of any directions in the question, where the partners are to continue as directors of the limited company, receiving salaries and shares of profits as hitherto, use the following procedure:

Partners' salaries

Award the partners directors' salaries equal to their partnership salaries.

Partners' loans to the partnership

Allocate debentures to any partner who has made to the partnership a loan which will be transferred to the limited company. Where the rate of interest on the debentures is different from that paid on the loan, the amount of the debentures allocated to the partner must be such as will give him the same amount of interest each year as he received from the partnership.

Partnership shares of profit

Preserve the partners' profit sharing ratio by allocating ordinary shares in their respective capital/profit sharing ratio, so that the balance on the capital account of the partner with the lowest capital/profit sharing ratio is satisfied in full by his allocation of ordinary shares.

Satisfy any balances remaining on partners' capital accounts with preference shares (or cash).

8.4.1 Example: sale of a partnership to a limited company

Arthur, Bill and Charles had been in partnership for some years sharing profits in the ratio 2:2:1. At 30 June 19-4 their summarised balance sheet was as follows:

		£	£
Fixed assets (at net book value)			140,000
Current assets:	Stock	40,000	
	Debtors	28,000	
	Bank	9,000	
		77,000	
less Current liabilities		17,000	60,000
			200,000
less Loan from Arthur (carrying interest at 10% p.a.)			20,000
			180,000
Capitals	Arthur		80,000
	Bill		60,000
	Charles		40,000
			180,000

On 1 July 19-4, the partners decided to form a limited company, ABC Ltd. to take over the business of Arthur, Bill and Charles.The purchase consideration was satisfied by the issue to the partners of 180,000 ordinary shares of £1 each, 25,000 12% Preference shares of £1 each and sufficient 8% debenture stock to give Arthur the same return on his loan as he had received from the partnership.

Required

The entries to close the partnership books in:

(a) Realisation account

(b) ABC Ltd. account

(c) Accounts for the purchase consideration

(d) Partners' Capital accounts.

Answer

Working: Allocation of 8% debenture stock:

In partnership, Arthur received annual interest on his loan of £20,000 × 10% = £2,000. Amount of 8% debenture stock which will give Arthur £2,000 p.a. on loan of £20,000 = £20,000 × 10/8 = £25,000

	£
Total purchase consideration will be:	
180,000 ordinary shares of £1 each	180,000
25,000 preference share of £1 each	25,000
£25,000 8 % debenture stock	25,000
	230,000

(a)

Realisation account

		£		£
Fixed assets		140,000	Creditors	17,000
Stock		40,000	ABC Ltd.	230,000
Debtors		28,000		
Bank		9,000		
Capitals: Arthur	12,000			
Bill	12,000			
Charles	6,000	30,000		
		247,000		247,000

(b)

ABC Ltd.

	£		£
Realisation account	230,000	8% debenture stock	25,000
		12% Preference shares	25,000
		Ordinary shares	180,000
	230,000		230,000

8% Debenture stock in ABC Ltd.

	£		£
ABC Ltd.	25,000	Arthur capital account	25,000

12% Preference shares in ABC Ltd.

	£		£
ABC Ltd.	25,000	Capital accounts:	
		Arthur	15,000
		Charles	10,000
	25,000		25,000

Ordinary shares of £1 in ABC Ltd.

	£		£
ABC Ltd.	180,000	Capital accounts	
		Arthur	72,000
		Bill	72,000
		Charles	36,000
	180,000		180,000

Arthur – Loan account

	£		£
Capital account	20,000	Balance b/f	20,000

Capital accounts

	A £	B £	C £		A £	B £	C £
Ordinary shares	72,000	72,000	36,000	Bal b/f	80,000	60,000	40,000
12% Pref. shares	15,000		10,000	Realisation	12,000	12,000	6,000
8% debenture stock	25,000			Loan	20,000		
	112,000	72,000	46,000		112,000	72,000	46,000

Note: Allocation of ordinary shares:

Capital/profit sharing ratios:

	Arthur	Bill	Charles
Capitals	80,000	60,000	40,000
Profit shares	2	2	1
=	40,000	30,000	40,000

Bill has the least Capital/profit sharing ratio, so will receive whole balance on his capital account in ordinary shares; the allocation of ordinary shares will therefore be:

	Profit sharing ratio	Ordinary share allocation
Arthur	2	72,000
Bill	2	72,000
Charles	1	36,000
		180,000

8.4.2 Exercise: for practice in closing partnership books when firm is sold to a limited company

Dee, Emma and Fay are in partnership sharing profits equally. At 31 March 19-5, the following was the summarised balance sheet of the firm:

		£
Fixed and current assets		75,000
less loan from Dee (carrying interest at 8% p.a.)		5,000
		70,000
Capitals:	Dee	30,000
	Emma	25,000
	Fay	15,000
		70,000

On the same date, Dee, Emma and Fay decided to accept an offer of £90,000 from Enterprise Ltd., an old established company, for their business. The offer consisted of sufficient 10% debenture stock in Enterprise Ltd. to guarantee Dee the same interest annually as she had received on her loan to the partnership, 60,000 ordinary shares of £1 each and the balance in cash.

Required

(a) The realisation account of the partnership.

(b) The accounts necessary to record the purchase consideration paid by Enterprise Ltd.

(c) The partners' capital accounts.

8.5 Key points to remember

Amalgamation of partnerships.

1. Before amalgamating the businesses, adjust the balance sheets of the individual firms to reflect revised values of assets, asset disposals, or assets taken over by partners, using Revaluation accounts. The resulting balances on the partners' capital accounts will more truly reflect their real investments in the firms being merged.

2. Add the revised balance sheets together. Give effect to any further capital adjustments to be made by the partners in cash.

Dissolution of partnerships.

3. Open a Realisation account. Debit the Realisation account with the net book values of assets being disposed of and the costs of dissolution. Credit the Realisation account with the proceeds of the sale of assets. Transfer any balance on the Realisation account, profit or loss, to the Partners' capital accounts.

4. Repay creditors, then loans by partners and, last of all, settle the balances on the partners' capital accounts.

Debit balance on partner's capital account.

5. Normally settle this by showing a payment by the partner, of the amount required to clear the balance, into the firm's bank account.

6. If, and only if, the question indicates that the partner in question is insolvent, apply the rule in Garner v. Murray. Transfer the debit balance on the insolvent partners' capital account to the other partners in proportion to their last agreed capitals (i.e. capitals shown on their latest balance sheet.)

Sale of partnership to limited company.

7. Open a Realisation account, and accounts for the limited company and for each constituent item of the purchase consideration.

8. Debentures may be allocated to partners who have made loans to the partnership.

9. Where the partners' former profit sharing ratios are to be preserved, allocate the ordinary shares to all partners in profit sharing ratio so that the balance on the capital account of the partner with the lowest capital/profit sharing ratio will be satisfied in full.

10. Close the remaining partners' capital accounts by allocations of preference shares, cash.

Common Errors

1. failure to adjust partners' capital accounts correctly before amalgamation of balance sheets.

2. failure to transfer net book values of assets being sold to Realisation account. (Confusion with Revaluation account to which only increases/decreases in asset values are transferred.)

3. application of Garner v. Murray when question does not state that partner is insolvent.

4. apportioning debit balance on insolvent partner's capital account to other partners' capital accounts in profit/loss sharing ratios.

5. inability to choose appropriate method of allocating shares to partners when partnership is sold to a limited company.

Questions

Fully worked examination question

Beryl and Gordon, who shared profits and losses in the ratio 5:3 respectively, decided to dissolve their partnership on 1 January 19-7. The partnership's balance sheet at that date was as follows:

		£	£
Fixed Assets:			
Tangible	Premises		45,000
	Vehicle		15,000
Intangible	Goodwill		5,000
			65,000
Current Assets:			
	Stock	7,500	
	Debtors	14,000	
	Bank	12,000	
Carried forward		33,500	65,000

	£	£
Brought forward	33,500	65,000
Current liabilities		
Creditors	12,500	
		21,000
		86,000
Capital accounts		
Beryl	50,000	
Gordon	36,000	
		86,000

The premises were sold for £48,000 and Gordon took over the car at an agreed valuation of £8,000. The stock was sold for £6,000, the debtors realised £13,500, and the creditors were paid in full. Expenses of realisation amounted to £600.

(a) Prepare the realisation account, the bank account and the partners' capital accounts to record the above information. (11 marks)

(b) Part of the 'expenses of realisation' was a fee of £150 from the accountant who 'closed' off the business books. The partners sent a letter to the accountant asking him to explain why it was considered necessary to make closing entries. They argue that 'no-one is interested in a business which is no longer in existence'. State, with reasons one of the justifications for making the closing entries. (4 marks)

(Total 15 marks)
(LONDON)

Answer

(a)

Realisation account

19-7		£	19-7			£
Jan 1	Premises	45,000	Jan 1	Gordon-cap.a/c		8,000
	Vehicle	15,000		Bank – premises		48,000
	Goodwill w/o	5,000		– stock		6,000
	Stock	7,500		Capitals:		
	Debtors w/o	500		Beryl	7,250	
	Realisation exps	600		Gordon	4,350	11,600
		73,600				73,600

Bank

19-7		£	19-7		£
Jan 1	Balance b/f	12,000	Jan 1	Sundry creditors	12,500
	Sundry debtors	13,500		Realisation exps	600
	Realisation –			Capital accounts	
	Premises	48,000		Beryl	42,750
	Stock	6,000		Gordon	23,650
		79,500			79,500

Capital accounts

		Beryl £	Gordon £			Beryl £	Gordon £
19-7				19-7			
Jan 1	Realisation			Jan 1	Balance b/f	50,000	36,000
	– vehicle		8,000				
	– loss	7,250	4,350				
	Bank	42,750	23,650				
		50,000	36,000			50,000	36,000

(b) Reasons for making closing entries:

1. Disposal of assets must be recorded and profits or losses on disposal calculated in order to adjust the partners' capitals.

2. To ensure that all debts are collected.

3. To ensure that all creditors are paid.

4. Until steps 1–3 above have been completed, the amounts due to or from partners on their capital accounts cannot be ascertained.

Examination Questions

1 The partnership of Allegro, Lento and Largo, sharing profits/losses in the ratio 4:3:2, has been in business for many years. Recently, the firm's market share has been declining, and thus, when Largo decides to retire on 31 May19-8, the partnership is dissolved. The final balance sheet of the partnership is:

		£	£	£
Fixed assets (net)				
Premises				103,500
Motor vehicles				20,360
Office equipment				26,000
				149,860
Current assets				
Stock			12,628	
Debtors			14,734	
Bank			5,282	
			32,644	
Current liabilities				
Creditors		13,260		
Accruals – loan interest		2,250		
			15,510	
				17,134
				166,994
Long term liability				
15% Bank loan				50,000
				116,994
Capital:	Allegro	50,000		
	Lento	20,000		
	Largo	40,000		
			110,000	
Current a/cs:	Allegro	10,358		
	Lento	(12,341)		
	Largo	8,977		
			6,994	
				116,994

Allegro feels that he could run a similar business successfully on a smaller scale from his own home, and therefore elects to take some of the partnership's assets at agreed valuations as follows:

Motor vehicle	£5,200
Office equipment	£7,850

The premises realise £120,000, the remaining vehicles and office equipment £2,080 and £3,160 respectively, and the stock is sold for £2,810. Debtors settle for £11,455, and dissolution costs amount to £1,277. Creditors accept £12,750 in full settlement.

Lento is unable to meet his final obligation to the partnership.

You are required to provide

(i) The realisation account, bank account and partners' capital accounts, showing the closing entries of the business.   (13 marks)

(ii) A comment on the advantages and disadvantages faced by Allegro in running a similar business as a sole trader instead of being a member of a partnership.   (4 marks)

(iii) An indication of the problems that would have faced Allegro and Lento if they had decided to form a new partnership on Largo's retirement.   (3 marks)

(Total 20 marks)

(OXFORD)

2   James and Dance were in partnership sharing profits and losses in the ratio 3:1. The Balance Sheet for the partnership at 31 March 19-7 was as follows:

Balance Sheet as at 31 March 19-7

	£	£		£	£
Capital accounts			Fixed Assets		
James	30,000		Plant		37,000
Dance	21,000	51,000	Cars		6,500
Current accounts			Current Assets		
James	4,500		Stock	18,600	
Dance	300		Debtors	9,300	
		4,800	Bank	2,400	
Loan: James		6,000			30,300
Creditors		12,000			
		73,800			73,800

The partners agreed to dissolve the partnership on 31 March19-7. The loan was repaid, the creditors were paid £11,700 in full and final settlement. Dance took over one car for £1,000 and the remaining assets realised the following amounts:

	£
Plant	46,000
Cars	3,500
Stock	17,100
Debtors	8,700

You are required to prepare the following ledger accounts for the dissolution of the partnership:

(a) the Realisation account   (9 marks)

(b) the Bank account   (5 marks)

(c) the Partners' Capital accounts.   (4 marks)

                                                     (Total 18 marks)

                                                                (JMB)

3   Penny and Victor are in partnership, sharing profits and losses in the ratio 3:2. On 31 May 1990, the balance sheet of the partnership was as follows:

		£
Fixed Assets:		
Freehold Land and Buildings		52,000
Machinery		60,000
Fixtures		9,000
Motor Vehicles		22,000
Computers		13,000
		156,000
Current Assets:		
Stocks	9,000	
Debtors	12,000	
Bank and Cash	3,000	
	24,000	
Current Liabilities:		
Creditors	7,000	
Loan from Connie	4,000	
	11,000	
		13,000
		169,000
Capital Accounts:		
Penny	102,000	
Victor	67,000	
		169,000

On 1 June 1990, the partnership was dissolved, and a Company, PVC Limited was formed to take over the business. The following values were agreed:

	£
Goodwill	20,000
Freehold Land and Buildings	70,000
Machinery	40,000

	£
Fixtures	6,000
Motor Vehicles (see note 1)	7,000
Computers	12,000
Stock	9,000
Debtors	10,000
Bank and Cash	3,000
Creditors	7,000
Loan from Connie (see note 2)	4,000

Notes

1. Penny acquired one of the vehicles, which had a book value of £11,000, for her private use, at an agreed valuation of £10,000.

2. Connie's loan was not taken over by the new company. Instead, the debt to Connie was settled by an issue of shares shown below:

   The authorised capital of the company was in the form of ordinary shares of £1 each, and they were issued at a premium of 70p each. The shares were allocated as follows:
   (i) To Connie: the exact number of shares necessary for her to own $\frac{1}{40}$th of the new company.
   (ii) To the partners: in the same proportion as the closing balances on their capital accounts.

3. No current accounts are maintained.

   Required

   (a) The capital accounts of Penny and Victor, showing the entries required to close off the books of the partnership. (12 marks)
   (b) The balance sheet of PVC Limited on 1 June 1990. (4 marks)
   (c) A breakdown of the shareholdings of Penny, Victor and Connie. (4 marks)
   (d) An explanation of the permissible treatments of goodwill in the limited company's accounts, according to standard accounting practice. (5 marks)

   (Total 25 marks)
   (LONDON)

4   Philip and Simon have been in partnership for many years as bottlers and canners of non-alcoholic drinks. Their partnership profit sharing agreement provided for:

(i)   interest on capital at 6% per annum

(ii) interest charged on drawings at 8% per annum calculated from the date of withdrawal to the end of the year

(iii) balance of profits shared between Philip and Simon in the proportions 3:2

(iv) balance on current accounts to be transferred to capital accounts after the closing entries for every year have been made.

The trial balance of the firm at 31 December 1990 after the net profit for 1990 had been calculated but before its appropriation was as follows:

			£000	£000
Plant and equipment at cost			90,000	
Provision for depreciation of plant and equipment to 31 December 1990				27,500
Stocks at 31 December 1990			100,500	
Debtors			80,000	
Creditors				65,000
Bank overdraft				29,500
Drawings,	Philip	30 June	14,000	
		31 December	13,500	
	Simon	31 March	8,500	
		30 September	9,000	
Capital accounts at 1 January 1990,				
Philip				96,700
Simon				53,300
Net profit for 1990				43,500
			315,500	315,500

The factory from where the firm carried on its operations was owned by Philip who leased it to the firm. Before the profit was appropriated to the partners adjustment was required for the annual rent of £3,500 which was due to Philip.

Changing lifestyles indicate a considerable increase in the market for non-alcoholic beers which will present Philip and Simon with an opportunity to increase their profits in the future. They have been advised to incorporate their business into a company. Accordingly Philip and Simon (Bottlers) Ltd took over the business on 1 January 1991.

Philip who is well endowed with private resources agreed to take over the creditors, but all the other assets and liabilities were taken over by the company. The purchase consideration for the transfer was agreed at £220,000 which was satisfied by the issue of 100,000 shares of £1 (to be allocated equally between Philip and Simon) and the balance in 10% loan stock.

You are required to

(a) show the ledger accounts necessary to close the books of the partnership, viz.
  (i)   profit and loss appropriation account for 1990;
  (ii) partners' current accounts for 1990;
  (iii) realisation account; and
  (iv) partners' capital accounts to include the allocation of the purchase consideration.
  (16 marks)

(b) explain how the profit or loss on realisation should be accounted for in the books of Philip and Simon (Bottlers) Ltd. (4 marks)

(Total 20 marks)
(NI)

5   At the close of business on 31 May 1992, Mixers, a partnership, had the following balances on its capital and current accounts:

Capital Accounts	£
Mark Solo	21,000
Lara Todd	10,000
Norma Unison	6,000
Current Accounts	£
Mark Solo	14,000
Lara Todd	6,000
Norma Unison	3,000 (Debit)

At 31 May 1992, the goodwill of the partnership was agreed at £28,000, but no goodwill account existed in the partnership books. Mark, Lara and Norma shared partnership profits and losses in the ratio 5:5:4 respectively.

On 1 June 1992, the partners decided to convert their partnership into a limited company, Shakers Limited, and the following decisions were made.

1.   The company should have an issued and fully paid up share capital of 90,000 ordinary shares of £1 each, to be issued amongst the partners of Mixers in *equal* proportions.

2.   Norma should acquire a computer owned by the partnership at a valuation of £750, which was £140 less than its book value. All other assets and liabilities will be transferred to the company.

3.   Any balances remaining on partners' current accounts after the above decisions have been implemented should be transferred to partners' capital accounts. The balances on the capital accounts should then be settled by the partners paying in cash to or drawing out cash from the partnership bank account. Assume that there is sufficient cash available for this purpose.
  (a) Show the entries in the partners' capital and current accounts required to close off the partnership books. (8 marks)
  (b) Show the opening balance sheet of Shakers Limited as at 1 June 1992. (3 marks)
  (c) Explain why a limited company must make public certain information about its financial affairs, whereas a partnership is not required to publish accounting information. (4 marks)

(Total 15 marks)
(LONDON)

6   Markham, Norman and Osaki have been in partnership for a number of years sharing profits and losses in the ratio 3:2:1 respectively. The summarised balance sheet of the partnership as at 28 February 1994 was as follows:

Fixed Assets	£	£	Capital Accounts	£	£
Premises		56,000	Markham		50,000
Machinery		18,000	Norman		30,000
Vehicles		27,000	Osaki		18,000
		101,000			98,000
Current Assets			Current Accounts		
Stock	11,000		Markham	3,100	
Debtors	18,500	29,500	Norman	1,900	
			Osaki	(1,000)	4,000
			Loan Account		
			Norman		5,000
			Current Liabilities		
			Creditors	14,000	
			Bank overdraft	9,500	23,500
		130,500			130,500

The partners have accepted an offer of £105,000 from Holly Ltd to buy all the assets of the business except for debtors and three of the vehicles which have been used by the partners over the last year.

The agreed purchase consideration was settled by Holly Ltd by the issue of 75,000 ordinary shares of 50p each and the payment to the partnership of £60,000 cash. The shares were divided equally between the partners. The final balances on the partners' capital accounts were settled in cash.

Each partner agreed to take over personally the vehicle which he had been using during the year. Details of these vehicles were:

	Book value of vehicle	Agreed take-over prices
	£	£
Markham	5,000	6,000
Norman	5,000	5,000
Osaki	7,000	8,000

Cash collected from debtors amounted to £17 900 and the partners paid £12 500 to creditors in full settlement of the amounts due to them.

The costs of the dissolution of the partnership amounted to £4500 and were paid by the partnership.

Required

(a) A calculation of the profit or loss on the dissolution and sale of the partnership.
(14 marks)

(b) Write up the capital accounts of the partners recording the dissolution and sale.
(20 marks)

(c) Calculate the agreed value of an ordinary share in Holly Ltd and explain why it may be different from the nominal value.
(6 marks)

(d) Explain why the partners may have accepted shares in Holly Ltd rather than insisting on a full cash settlement.
(10 marks)
(AEB)

7   Lilly and Vic had been trading as a partnership for several years, sharing profits and losses in the ratio 3:2 respectively. Their balance sheet as at 31 May 1995 was as follows:

		£	£
Fixed assets (net book value)			54,000
Current Assets			
Stock		22,500	
Debtors		13,500	
Bank		3,000	
		39,000	
Less: Creditors		2,250	
			36,750
			90,750
Capital Accounts:	Lilly	36,000	
	Vic	48,000	
			84,000
Current Accounts:	Lilly	300	
	Vic	450	
			750
			84,750
Loan from Vic			6,000
			90,750

Notes:

1. On 1 June 1995, Lilly and Vic transferred their business to a new limited company, Petowker Limited. The agreed valuation of the partnership was £105,000, to be satisfied by the issue of 10,500 ordinary shares of £1 each, fully paid, and 42,000 4% preference shares of £1 each, fully paid.

2. The issued and authorised share capital of Petowker Limited is £52,500. The preference shares, issued at par, were distributed between the partners in proportion to their capital accounts at 31 May 1995. The ordinary shares were allocated in their partnership profit and loss sharing proportions.

3. All the partnership assets were transferred to Petowker Limited, with the exception of debtors and the bank balance. The loan from Vic and the creditors were repaid in full on 1 June 1995, and the debtors paid £13,000 in full settlement on the same date.

4. The partners paid in or withdrew cash to close their capital accounts.

    (a) Prepare the partnership realisation account, showing the entries needed to reflect the transfer of the business to Petowker Limited.   (8 marks)

    (b) Prepare the capital accounts of the partners, showing the entries required to close off the partnership books.   (12 marks)

    (c) Show the opening balance sheet (including any goodwill arising) of Petowker Limited.   (5 marks)

Total 25 marks
(LONDON)

9 Accounts of limited companies

Chapter objectives

(In this chapter we are concerned only with accounts produced for internal use by the directors and management. The form of accounts for publication and distribution to shareholders and other interested parties is dealt with in Chapter 10.)

Examination questions on this topic cover the following:

❑ differences between partnerships and limited companies;

❑ distinction between public and private limited companies;

❑ types of share capital;

❑ distinction between shares and debentures;

❑ accounting for issues of shares and debentures;

❑ reserves and provisions;

❑ dividend policy;

9.1 Limited companies

Limited companies owe their origin to the need to raise large amounts of capital to finance businesses. During the nineteenth century, the industrial revolution saw the decline of cottage industries and the move towards construction of factories which had to be equipped with costly machinery. Many providers of capital did not take part in the management of the businesses they were financing but entrusted the running of them to managers, or directors, who became stewards of the money invested. The companies were regulated by a series of Acts of Parliament which limited the liability of the members of a company for its debts.

At present, companies are regulated by the Companies Act 1985 as amended by the Companies Act 1989.

Two of the reasons for forming a limited company are, therefore, to facilitate the raising of capital and to protect the members with limited liability.

A limited company is a separate legal entity; i.e. it is regarded in law for all purposes as having a separate existence from that of its members. This is not to be confused with the accounting concept of entity, which treats all businesses as having separate existences from their owners for accounting purposes only and has no legal consequences.

The members, or shareholders, of a limited company are not liable for the debts of the company beyond the amounts they have agreed to pay on their shares, except in certain unfortunate circumstances which are outside the scope of this study.

Much of the legislation concerning limited companies is for the protection of creditors as a result of the shareholders enjoying limited liability. Much is also concerned with the interests of the shareholders to ensure, as far as possible, that the directors give a proper account of their stewardship.

A limited company is formed by the registration of certain documents with the Registrar of Companies, compliance with certain legal requirements and the payment of stamp duties and fees.

The Memorandum and Articles of Association are two of the documents which have to be filed. The Memorandum defines the relationship of the company to the outside world; the Articles are the internal rules governing the rights of members and the running of the company.

9.2 Limited companies and partnerships compared

Limited companies	Partnerships
(i) Not less than two members	Not less than two partners
(ii) Maximum number of members determined by number of shares.	Not more than 20 partners (except in certain professional firms.)
(iii) Liability of members for debts of company is limited to amounts they have agreed to pay on their shares	Liability of partners for debts of firm is not limited (except in limited partnerships);their private assets may be seized to pay the creditors.
(iv) Amount of capital limited only by authorised capital stated in Memorandum of Association, but this may be increased.	Capital as determined in partnership agreement and limited by personal resources of partners.
(v) Profits are distributed by way of dividend. (Amount dependant upon shareholding.) Some profits may be retained in . the company	All profits are credited, losses debited, to the partners' current accounts in accordance with partnership agreement.
(vi) Companies are liable to pay Corporation Tax on their Profits.	Partnerships are not assessed to income tax on profits; income tax is assessed upon the partners on their shares of profit.
(vii) Shareholders not entitled to take part in the management of the company. Directors are appointed for this purpose.	Normally, all partners entitled to take part in running of the firm.

9.3 Limited companies – public and private

Public company

The company registers as a public company and describes itself as such in its Memorandum;. The name of the company must end with 'Public limited company' or the abbreviation 'plc'. If it is a Welsh company, the name will end with the Welsh for public limited company (cwmni cyfyngedig cyhoeddus'). The authorised capital must be at least £50,000 of which at least one quarter of the nominal amount and the whole of any premium must have been paid.

A public company may offer its shares to the public and its shares will be traded on the Stock Exchange.

Private company

The company does not describe itself as a public company and its name will end with 'Limited' or 'Ltd.' The authorised capital may be less than £50,000.

A private company may not offer its shares to the public; they will not, therefore be traded on the Stock Exchange.

9.4 The accounts of a limited company

A company must publish its accounts annually in a form which meets the requirements of the Companies Act. This form is explained in chapter 10. This chapter is concerned with accounts which are prepared for use internally in the company by the directors and management. They need more detailed profit and loss accounts and balance sheets than those prepared for publication to help them manage the company. These more detailed accounts are usually prepared in a form which can easily be converted into the form for publication.

The General Trading Company PLC's accounts have been prepared for internal use and may look like the accounts of a sole trader at first sight. Closer inspection reveals some differences which are explained in the notes following the accounts.

9.5 Trading and profit and loss account

The General Trading Company PLC

Trading and profit and loss account
for the year ended 31 December 1996

Notes		£m	£m	£m
	Sales			100.0
	Less Cost of Sales			54.0
	Gross profit			46.0
	Selling and distribution			
	Salespersons' salaries		(2.1)	
	Warehouse expenses		(1.9)	
	Depreciation: warehouse machinery		(0.5)	
	delivery vans		(0.8)	(5.3)
	Administration			
	Administrative salaries		(14.6)	
	Property expenses		(16.0)	
	Depreciation: Fixtures and fittings		(0.7)	
	Office machinery		(0.2)	(31.5)
A	Financial charges: Interest on debentures			(0.4)
B	Profit before tax			8.8
C	Taxation			(2.5)
	Profit after tax			6.3
D	Transfer to general reserve		(2.0)	
E	Dividends paid and proposed:			
F	Preference – paid	(0.4)		
	proposed	(0.4)		
G	Ordinary – paid	(0.6)		
	proposed	(1.2)	(2.6)	(4.6)
H	Retained profit for the year			1.7
	Retained profit brought forward			1.5
	Retained profit carried forward			3.2

The trading and profit and loss account looks very similar to that of any sole trader or partnership down to the line 'Profit before tax', except perhaps for the fact that the amounts are stated in millions of pounds. The overheads have been grouped under the headings 'Selling and distribution', 'Administration expenses' and 'Finance charges'. This is partly because those are sensible groupings, but also this grouping enables the accounts used for internal purposes by the directors to be redrafted easily for the purpose of publication in accordance with the Companies Act requirements.

A **A debenture** is a loan made to a company or, more strictly, the document which is evidence of such a loan. Debentures carry the right to fixed rate of interest which is debited as an expense in the Profit and Loss account. Debentures are explained more fully in 9.16

B **Profit before tax**. This item really marks the end of the profit and loss account and the beginning of a profit and loss appropriation account because all the items that follow show how the profit is 'appropriated' to particular purposes.

C **Taxation**. Companies are liable to pay Corporation Tax on their profits. The tax charge is shown as a charge in the profit and loss appropriation account. This is in contrast to the accounts of a sole trader or a partnership where the business entity is not subject to Income Tax. Sole traders and partners are liable to pay tax on the profits of their businesses, and if they pay the tax out of business funds, the payment is treated as drawings.

D **Transfer to General Reserve**. Revenue reserves are created to strengthen the financing of a company by ploughing profits back into the business. They are created for various purposes and will be explained more fully in the context of the balance sheet in 9.11 . Renenue reserves are created or increased by debiting the profit and loss appropriation account and crediting the amount to a Reserve account.

E **Dividends**. Shareholders are rewarded for investing in a company by being paid dividends on their shares. The dividends are debited in the Profit and Loss account as appropriations of profit and credited to a Dividends account. When the dividends are paid, the cash paid is debited to the Dividends account.

F **Preference dividend**. The holders of Preference shares are entitled to a fixed rate of dividend on their shares. The dividend is calculated as a percentage of the nominal value of the shares. The balance sheet shows that the nominal value of each share is £1 and that the holders of the shares are entitled to receive a dividend of 8% on the nominal value, i.e. 8p for every share held. The balance sheet also shows that the total of the issued Preference shares is £10m.; the dividend to be paid to the Preference shareholders each year, therefore, is £0.8m. Half the dividend, £0.4m. has already been paid and the directors now 'propose' to pay the other half as shown in the appropriation account.

G **Ordinary dividend**. The ordinary shareholders are not entitled to a fixed rate of dividend on their shares. The directors may pay an interim dividend to shareholders during the year and may propose at the end of the year to pay a final ordinary dividend. The topic of dividend policy is considered in more detail in 9.17 .

H **Retained profit**. The balance on the profit and loss appropriation account after transfers to reserves and dividends is the retained profit for the year. It is added to retained profit brought forward from the previous year to provide the retained profit carried forward to the next year.

9.6 Balance sheet

Balance sheet as at 31 December 1996

Notes		£m	£m	£m
	Fixed assets			
I	Intangible assets			10.0
J	Tangible fixed assets			87.0
K	Investments			5.0
				102.0
	Current assets			
	Stock		4.0	
	Debtors		16.8	
	Bank		17.4	
			38.2	
L	Creditors: amounts falling due within one year			
	Creditors	26.4		
M	Taxation	2.5		
N	Dividends – proposed	1.6	30.5	7.7
				109.7
O	Creditors: amounts falling due after more than one year			
P	10% Debentures 2003/2005			4.0
				105.7
	Share capital and reserves			
Q	Authorised share capital			
	60,000 Ordinary shares of £1 each		60.0	
	20,000 8% Preference shares of £1 each		20.0	
			80.0	
R	Issued and fully paid			
	Ordinary shares of £1 each			45.0
	8% Preference shares of £1 each			10.0
S	Share premium account			22.5
T	Revaluation reserve			20.0
U	General reserve			5.0
V	Profit and loss account			3.2
				105.7

I **Intangible fixed assets** are those which cannot be seen or touched. Goodwill is an example of an intangible fixed asset; other examples are patents and trade marks.

J   **Tangible fixed assets** are those which have a physical existence and can be touched and felt e.g. property, plant and machinery and office furniture.

K   **Fixed asset investments** are investments, usually shares in other companies, which are held for the long term. A company will buy shares in another company in order to have some say in the way that other company is run, or to gain some other benefit. Thus it may buy shares in a company which supplies it with goods or materials, or in a company which is an outlet for its own products. It may buy shares in a company which is in the same line of business, perhaps a competitor.

     If one company owns more than 50 per cent of the voting shares in another company it has gained control of that other company which becomes its 'subsidiary'. The company owning the shares is the 'parent' company

L   **Creditors: amounts falling due within one year**. This is the term used by the Companies Act 1985 for **current liabilities**.

M   **Taxation**. Corporation Tax on a company's profit is not due for payment until 9 months after the end of the company's financial period. The General Trading Company Plc's tax of £2.5m. is therefore not due to be paid until 9 months after 31 December 1996, i.e. 1 October 1997 and is a liability at the 31 December 1996.

N   **Dividends.** Dividends proposed by the directors at the year end will not be paid by the balance sheet date and must therefore be shown in the balance sheet as a liabilty. The liability in this case is made up of:

	£
Proposed preference dividend	0.4
Proposed ordinary dividend	1.2
	1.6

O   **Creditors: amounts falling due after more than one year**. This is the term used in the Companies Act for long term liabilities.

P   **Debentures** are long term liabilities unless they are due to be redeemed within twelve months of the date of the balance sheet. See 9.16.

Q   **Authorised share capital** The authorised share capital is the maximum amount of share capital which a company may issue as stated in its Memorandum of Association. This amount must not be exceeded; but the company may comply with certain formalities required by law to increase the amount of authorised capital.

     A company must either show its called up capital in its balance sheet, or disclose it by way of a note to the balance sheet.

R   **Issued share capital** is the amount of share capital which has actually been issued to shareholders or members. The share capital is divided into shares having a particular face value known as their nominal (or par) value. They may have a nominal value per share of £1, 50p, 25p, 20p, or even 5p. On the other hand the nominal value per share may be more than £1. Share capital is considered in more detail in 9.7 and shares are more fully described in 9.8

S to U   The items denoted with these items in The General Trading Company Plc's balance sheet are reserves and are explained in 9.11.

9.7 Terms used to describe share capital

Called-Up Capital A company may not require all the money due on its issued shares to be paid by the shareholders immediately. It may 'call up' only sufficient for its immediate requirements. The 'called-up' capital may therefore be less than the issued capital.

Uncalled Capital is that part of the share capital which has not yet been called up. If a company gets into financial difficulties, the liability of the shareholders for its debts is limited to the amount unpaid on their shares. The shareholders can be required to pay the balance due on their shares, but their liability ends there.

Paid-Up capital is that part of the called-up share capital for which the company has actually received cash from the shareholders.

Calls in advance represent money received from shareholders in advance of calls made by the company

Calls in arrear are calls on share capital made by a company for which money has not yet been received from shareholders.

Forfeited shares are shares which have been forfeited in accordance with the Articles of Association by the holders when they have not paid arrears of money due on the shares.

9.8 Types of shares

Preference shares. Preference shareholders are entitled to receive a fixed rate of dividend in priority to any dividend payable to ordinary shareholders. The dividend entitlement is expressed as a percentage of the nominal value of the shares and forms part of the description of the shares. Preference shareholders are also entitled to receive the return of their capital before the ordinary shareholders when a company is 'wound up' or liquidated (the terms used for terminating the existence of a company.)

Non-cumulative preference shares. If the profits of a company are insufficient in any year to meet the dividend on preference shares, and the shares are non-cumulative, the holders of these shares will lose all or part of their dividend for that year.

Cumulative preference shares. Holders of cumulative preference shares are entitled to have any arrears of dividend made good in future years when sufficient profits are available.

9.8.1 Example to show the difference between non-cumulative and cumulative preference shares and their effect upon dividends available for ordinary shareholders.

Ebbanflow Ltd. was formed with 10,000 ordinary shares of £1 each and 5,000 8% Non-cumulative Preference shares of £1 each.

The profits available for dividend were as follows:

19-1 £1,100; 19-2 £500; 19-3 £200; 19-4 £600; 19-5 £300; 19-6 £800.

Year	19-1	19-2	19-3	19-4	19-5	19-6
	£	£	£	£	£	£
Profit	1,100	500	200	600	300	800
Pref.div.	400	400	200*	400	300*	400
Ord.div.	700	100	-	200	-	400
do. %	7	1	-	2	-	4

* The preference shareholders lose the balance of their dividends in these years.

If the Preference shares had been 8% Cumulative Preference shares, the dividends would have been as follows:

Year	19-1	19-2	19-3	19-4	19-5	19-6
	£	£	£	£	£	£
Profit	1,100	500	200	600	300	800
Pref.div.	400	400	200	600*	300	500*
Ord.div.	700	100	-	-	-	300
do. %	7	1	-	-	-	3

* In these years the preference shareholders receive arrears of dividends.

9.8.2 Exercise: to test understanding of the effect on preference and ordinary dividends of fluctuating profits

Chance Ltd. had the following share capital: 80,000 10% Preference shares of £1 each, and 120,000 Ordinary shares of £1 each. Profits of the company were as follows:

19-1 £22,000; 19-2 £6,000; 19-3 £11,000; 19-4 £7,000 19-5 £10,000.

Required

Tables showing the dividends on the Preference and Ordinary shares if the Preference shares are (i) non- cumulative, and (ii) cumulative.

Participating preference shares. These give the holders the right to participate in the distribution of profit beyond the stated rate of dividend payable on the shares if the profit is more than adequate for the ordinary shareholders' dividend.

Ordinary shares (the equity). The holders of ordinary shares must wait until the preference shareholders, if any, have been allocated their dividend before they can receive any share of the profits. In the liquidation of a company, the ordinary shareholders must wait until the preference shareholders have had their capital repaid before they can receive the return of their own capital. In a company which is being run successfully, the ordinary shareholders' share of profits may be very good and, if the company is wound up, they may stand to receive repayment in excess of their original capital outlay. On the other hand, if a company becomes insolvent and has to be wound up, the ordinary shareholders may get little or none of their capital repaid.

Shares issued at a premium. The directors of a company may consider that shares to be issued are worth more than their nominal (or par) value. In that case, they may issue them at a premium. For instance, ordinary shares of £1 each may be issued at £1.20 i.e. at a premium of 20p.

Redeemable shares. Under certain circumstances, a company may redeem its shares provided the shares were described as 'redeemable' when they were issued. This topic is covered in more detail in chapter 12.

9.9 Issue of shares

Companies do not 'sell' their shares; they are said to issue them.

Like other contracts, the issue of shares involves offer, acceptance and consideration.

The application by a person to subscribe for shares consitutes an offer to the company.

The allotment of shares by the company to applicants constitutes acceptance of the offer.

The consideration is the money paid by the shareholders for their shares.

The sequence of events is as follows:

1. The company issues an invitation (prospectus) for applications for shares in the company
2. Investors (the applicants) apply for shares; with their applications they send the cash due on application.
3. The company allots shares to the applicants who are now known as the allottees. At the same time, application money is returned to unsuccessful applicants.
4. The allottees send the money due on allotment to the company
5. Any further calls are made and the shareholders pay the calls as and when due.

Accounting entries

Issue of prospectus:	No entries are made in the books.
Receipt of applications with money due on application	• Debit Bank • Credit Application and Allotment account with money received on application.
Allotment of shares	• Debit Application and Allotment account • Credit Share capital account with money due on application and allotment
Receipt of money due on allotment	• Debit Bank • Credit Application and Allotment account with money received on allotment.
Making of call	• Debit Call account • Credit Share capital account with money due on call

Receipt of call money
- Debit Bank
- Credit Call account

with money received on call.

Share premium

The premium must not be credited to the share capital account. The accounting entries will be:

When premium becomes due
(often on application)
- Debit Application and Allotment account
  (or call account)
- Credit Share Premium account

9.9.1 Example

New Venture Plc was formed with an authorised share capital of 100,000 ordinary shares of £1 each. These shares were offered to the public on the following terms: On application: 45p per share (including 20p premium). On allotment: 25p per share. First and final call: the balance of 50p per share. Applications were received for 141,000 shares. The directors rejected applications for 21,000 shares and allotted shares to the remaining applicants on the basis of 5 shares for every 6 applied for.

Answer

New Venture Plc
Ordinary share capital

	£		£
Balance c/d	100,000	Application & allotment	50,000
		First & final call	50,000
	100,000		100,000
		Balance b/d	100,000

Share Premium

			£
		Application & allotment	20,000

Bank

	£		£
Application & allotment	63,450	Application & allotment	9,450
Application & allotment	16,000	Balance c/d	120,000
Call	50,000		
	129,450		129,450
Balance b/d	120,000		

Application and allotment account

	£		£
Ordinary Share capital	50,000	Bank (application money)	63,450
Share premium	20,000	Bank (bal. on allotment)	16,000
Bank (refunds)	9,450		
	79,450		79,450

First and final call

	£		£
Share capital	50,000	Bank	50,000

9.9.2 Exercise: practice in recording an issue of shares

The Goodbuy Co. plc. has invited applications for its new issue of 300,000 Ordinary shares of £1 each at £1.25p per share. The terms of the issue are: Payable on application: 50p; on allotment: 50p. (including the premium); on call three months after allotment: 25p.

Applications for 373,500 shares were received and the directors decided not to allot shares to applicants for 23,500 shares and to allot shares to the other applicants on the basis of 6 shares for every 7 applied for. Application monies were returned to the unsuccessful applicants and all monies due on allotment and call were received on the due dates.

Required

The accounting entries to record the issue of the shares by The Goodbuy Co.plc.

9.10 Forfeiture and re-issue of shares

A company's Articles of Association usually provide that where a shareholder fails to pay the call money on shares, the directors may, if they are unable to recover the money, make the shareholder forfeit the shares. The directors may then re- issue the shares to some other person.

The accounting entries are as follows:

When shares are forfeited

- Debit:
  Investments: Own Shares account
  with the amount of the unpaid call
- Credit
  Call account

When the shares are re-issued

- Debit
  Bank account
- Credit
  Investments: Own Shares account

with the consideration received from the new shareholder

- Debit
  Investments: Own Shares account
- Credit
  Share premium account

with the balance on the Investments: Own Shares account, being the premium received on the re-issue.

9.10.1 Example

Lost Horizons plc invited applications for 500,000 ordinary shares of £1 each at £1.30, payable as to 40p on application, 70p (including 30p premium) on allotment, and 20p on first and final call 4 months after allotment. Applications for all the shares were received and the shares duly allotted. All the allotment money was received but the holder of 1,000 shares failed to meet the call and forfeited his shares in accordance with the Articles of the company.

All the forfeited shares were subsequently reissued as fully paid shares at 80p each.

Answer

Lost Horizons plc
Ordinary Share Capital

	£		£
Balance c/d	500,000	Application and Allotment	400,000
		Call	100,000
	500,000		500,000
		Balance b/d	500,000

Share Premium

	£		£
Balance c/d	150,600	Application and Allotment	150,000
		Investment: Own Shares	600
	150,600		150,600
		Balance b/d	150,600

Bank

	£		£
Application & Allotment	200,000	Balance c/d	650,600
Application & Allotment	350,000		
Call	99,800		
Investment: Own Shares	800		
	650,600		650,600
Balance b/d	650,600		

Application and Allotment

	£		£
Ordinary share capital	400,000	Bank	200,000
Share premium	150,000	Bank	350,000
	550,000		550,000

Call

	£		£
Ordinary share capital	100,000	Bank	99,800
		Investment: Own Shares	200
	100,000		100,000

Investment: Own Shares

	£		£
Call	200	Bank	800
Share premium	600		
	800		800

9.10.2 Exercise: practice in accounting for forfeiture and reissue of shares

Jollysticks Ltd. issued 60,000 ordinary shares of 50p each at a premium of 7p. The terms of the issue were that 30p was payable on application and the balance, including the premium, was payable on allotment.

Applications were received for 71,000 shares. The directors allotted 60,000 shares to successful applicants and returned application money to the unsuccessful applicants.

The money due on allotment was received from allottees of 58,900 shares; the remaining shares were forfeited and later reissued to another applicant as fully paid on payment of 40p per share.

Required

Prepare the ledger accounts necessary to record the foregoing transactions.

9.11 Types of reserves

It is important to remember that all the reserves of a company belong to the ordinary share-holders. They represent profits which have been ploughed back into the business from the profit and loss account, or other amounts which have been placed to reserve in accordance with the requirements of the Companies Act. There are, therefore, two main types of reserves: revenue and capital.

Revenue reserves

Revenue reserves are profits which have been ploughed back into the company by debiting Profit and Loss Appropriation account and crediting the appropriate reserve account. They may be either specific or general.

Specific reserves are revenue reserves which have been set aside for some specific purpose such as replacement of fixed assets or in anticipation of an expansion of the business.

General reserves are other revenue reserves considered desirable or necessary to reinforce the financial position of the company.

Setting profits aside as revenue reserves reduces the amount available for dividends at least for the time being. If at some future date the revenue reserves are found to be unnecessary or excessive, they may be credited back to the profit and loss account and made available for the payment of dividends.

Capital reserves

Capital reserves are not created by setting aside amounts out of operating profits; they are created in other particular circumstances. Because of this, the Companies Act prohibits the transfer of capital reserves to the Profit and Loss account and they may not, therefore, be used to pay cash dividends to shareholders. If they are distributed they will be distributed in the form of bonus shares which are explained in 9.13 and chapter 12. Examples of capital reserves are the Share Premium account, Revaluation Reserves and Capital Redemption Reserves.

Share premium account

The creation of the share premium account has already been dealt with in 9.9 above. The Companies Act provides that a share premium account may be applied:

1. In paying up unissued shares as fully paid bonus shares.
2. To write off:
   (i) preliminary expenses (expenses incurred in forming the company)
   (ii) expenses of, or the commission paid on, any issue of shares or debentures
3. To provide any premium payable on the redemption of shares or debentures.

Revaluation reserve

A Revaluation Reserve is created when an asset is revalued to reflect an increase in value. The bookkeeping entries are:

Debit: Asset account

Provision for depreciation of asset account

Credit: Asset Revaluation Reserve

with the difference beteen the asset's net book value before revaluation and its revalued amount.

Capital Redemption Reserve

If a company redeems or buys back any of its own shares otherwise than out of the proceeds of a new issue of shares, it must protect the creditors by replacing the shares so redeemed or purchased, with profits that would otherwise be available for distribution as dividends. The Capital Redemption Reserve created in this way may be used to issue unissued shares as fully paid bonus shares.

When a company uses reserves to issue fully paid up bonus shares to its shareholders, the reserves are transferred to the credit of the share capital account. Revenue reserves capitalised in this way no longer become available for distribution as dividends. The shares are called 'bonus' shares because the shareholders do not have to pay for them; the reserves were theirs anyway. (This topic is dealt with more fully in chapter 12) Distinguish between a bonus issue, and a rights issue in which the shareholder buys the shares for cash (see 9.14).

9.11.1 The valuation of shares using balance sheet values.

The summarised balance sheet of Jack Ltd. is as follows:

	£	£
Fixed assets		8,000
Current assets	10,000	
less creditors	3,000	7,000
		15,000
Capital and reserves		
Share capital		
12,000 ordinary shares of £1 each		12,000
Revenue reserve		2,500
Retained profit		500
		15,000

Required

Assuming the fixed and current assets are shown in the balance sheet at realistic values, calculate the value of one ordinary share.

Answer

Total net assets: £15,000

No. of shares: 12,000

Each share is therefore worth £15,000/12,000 = £1.25p (based on balance sheet values.)

[The net assets of the company are equal to the share capital plus the reserves. If the assets are not shown in the balance sheet at their realisable values, these must be substituted for their balance sheet values. The creditors must be paid before any money which would be returnable to the shareholders; the money due to the creditors must therefore be deducted from the total assets to arrive at the value of the share capital.]

9.8.2 Exercise: in the valuation of shares

Jill Ltd.'s summarised balance sheet is as follows:

	£	£
Fixed assets		102,000
Current assets	54,000	
less creditors	9,000	45,000
		147,000
Share capital and reserves		
75,000 Ordinary shares of £1 each		75,000
25,000 8% Preference shares of £1 each		25,000
Share Premium		15,000
Asset Replacement Reserve		20,000
Retained profit		12,000
		147,000

A realistic valuation of the assets shows that the fixed assets would realise £86,000 and the current assets have a realisable value of £48,000.

Required

Calculation of the value of one ordinary share based on: (i) balance sheet values and (ii) the realisable values of the assets.

9.12 The distinctions between reserves, provisions and liabilities

The distinctions between reserves, provisions and liabilities are of the utmost importance and must be learned.

Provisions are:

amounts written off or retained by way of providing for depreciation, renewals or diminution in the value of assets,

or, retained by way of providing for any known liability of which the amount cannot be determined with substantial accuracy.

Increases and decreases in provisions are debited or credited in the Profit and Loss account and credited to a Provision account.

Reserves are:

any other amounts set aside out of profits by debiting Profit and Loss Appropriation account and crediting the relevant provision accounts,

and amounts placed to capital reserve in accordance with the Companies Act, such as share premium, unrealised surpluses on the revaluation of fixed assets, and amounts set aside out of distributable reserves to maintain capital when shares are redeemed.

Liabilities are amounts owing which can be determined with substantial accuracy.

9.13 Bonus shares

It has already been stated that a company's reserves belong to the ordinary shareholders. If the directors of a company consider that the balance on the Ordinary Share Capital account does not adequately reflect the long term capital of the company, they may transfer, with the agreement of the shareholders, some of the balances on the reserves to the Ordinary Share Capital account. The directors will then issue to the ordinary shareholders additional share certificates equal to the amount of the reserves transferred in proportion to the shares they already hold. These new shares are known as bonus shares because the shareholders do not pay any additional cash for them. However, the description is misleading in so far as the directors are not giving the shareholders anything they did not already have, i.e. the reserves.

An issue of bonus shares is often referred to as a **'scrip issue'**.

9.14 Rights issues

The preliminary formalities involved in issuing shares to the general public can be a very expensive matter. A private company may not make such an offer in any case. The directors may therefore decide to raise additional capital by a 'rights' issue, for which the formalities are less demanding.

A rights issue is one in which the shares are offered to existing shareholders, not to the general public. The right is one to apply for a specified number of shares at a stated price, and the number is based upon the shareholder's present holding. The offer price of the shares is usually an advantageous one to the shareholder and the company is saved the expense and inconvenience of preparing a full prospectus as for a public issue. If a shareholder does not wish to exercise his right, he may sell the right to another person.

An additional advantage of a rights issue is that control of the company remains with the existing shareholders, which would almost certainly not be the case if the shares were offered to the public generally.

9.15 Underwritten issues

A company may have its issue of shares underwritten by one or more financial houses to ensure that the share issue is successful. The underwriters guarantee to subscribe for any shares which are not taken up by the public.

9.16 Debentures

A debenture is a document containing details of a loan made to a company. The loan may be secured on the assets of the company, when it is known as a *mortgage debenture*. If the security for the loan is on certain specified assets of the company, the debenture is said to be secured by a *fixed charge* on the assets. If the assets are not specified, but the security is on the assets as they may exist from time to time, it is known as a *floating charge* on the assets. An unsecured debenture is known as a *simple* or *naked debenture*.

Debentures carry the right to a fixed rate of interest which forms part of the description of the debentures. The General Trading Company Plc's debentures (9.6) carry the right to interest at 10% per annum. The interest must be paid whether or not the company makes a profit. This is one of the distinctions between debentures, and shares on which dividends may only be paid if profits are available. Debenture interest is debited as an expense in the Profit and Loss account to arrive at the profit before tax.

Debentures are usually redeemable on or before a specified date which is shown as part of their description. The debentures of The General Trading Company Plc (9.6) are redeemable between 2003 and 2005.

Debenture holders are not members of the company in the same way as shareholders are, and debentures must not be confused with the share capital and reserves in the balance sheet. Debentures should always be shown as long term liabilities (amounts falling due after more than one year) unless they are to be redeemed within one year from the date of the balance sheet, when they are shown as current liabilities (amounts falling due within one year).

One of the attractions to a company of raising capital by an issue of debentures is that debenture interest is an allowable expense for tax purposes, whereas dividends on shares are appropriations of profit and not allowable for tax.

Convertible loan stock gives the holders the opportunity at a future date to convert the loan into shares of the company at a predetermined price. If, when the time arrives for the stock holders to exercise their option, the market value of the shares is higher than the predetermined price, the debenture holders could find the exchange attractive. On the other hand, if the share value is below the predetermined price, they would be unlikely to exercise their option. Advantages of exercising the option are:

1. the debenture holders continue to have an interest in the company and will be entitled to attend and vote at company meetings.
2. dividends on the shares may be likely to exceed the interest on the debentures.
3. There is also the possibility that while holders of debentures usually see their capital invested diminished over time by inflation, the value of shares should increase in a healthy company.

9.17 Dividend policy

Distributable profits are accumulated realised profits less accumulated realised losses. Realised profits(in general) = the credit balance on Profit and Loss account + the revenue reserves.

In recommending a dividend the directors of a company will have regard to the following:

1. The availability of distributable profits.
2. The availability of liquid funds to pay the dividend. (A cash forecast statement is essential.)
3. Whether the revenue reserves are adequate or need to be increased by further profits ploughed back into the business.
4. A balance between dividend growth and capital growth.
5. The effect of the dividend policy on the market price of the shares.
6. The liability to advance corporation tax which arises from the payment of a dividend.

Directors may pay interim dividends providing they are satisfied that profits for the purpose have been realised and that the liquid resources and requirements of the company will permit the payment of the dividend.

Directors, however, may only recommend payment of Final Dividends. The necessary resolution to pay the dividend must be passed by the members at the Annual General Meeting. Therefore, proposed final dividends will appear in the balance sheet as current assets. (Creditors: amounts falling due within one year.)

9.17.1 Example

The following is an extract from the balance sheet of Box and Cox plc.:

	£
Share capital and reserves	
100,000 Ordinary shares of £1 each	100,000
Share Premium	25,000
Property Revaluation Reserve	70,000
Asset Replacement Reserve	45,000
General Reserve	20,000
Retained profit	10,000
	270,000

A major shareholder has written to the chairman of the company expressing the view that since the reserves of the company total £170,000 and belong to the shareholders, they should be used to pay a good dividend to the shareholders, especially as the dividends paid for some years past have been low.

Required

Prepare a report to the chairman of Box and Cox plc. suggesting points that he should bear in mind in his reply to the shareholder.

Answer

To the Chairman,

Box and Cox plc

Profits available for dividend to ordinary shareholders.

You have received a request from a shareholder that the reserves of the company, totalling £170,000, should be used to increase the dividend payable to the shareholders to compensate for allegedly low dividends in past years.

1. The shareholder is quite correct in stating that all the reserves of the company belong to the ordinary shareholders. However, not all the reserves are available for distribution in cash as dividends.
2. The Share Premium and the Property Revaluation Reserve are capital reserves which, by the Companies Act 1985, may not be used to pay cash dividends to shareholders.
3. On the face of the balance sheet the only profits which are available for dividend are the Retained Profit £10,000 which could be used to pay a dividend of 10% (10p per share)
4. The Asset Replacement Reserve and the General Reserve are revenue reserves which could, in theory, be used to pay a dividend.

5. Unless the directors are of the opinion that the Asset Replacement Reserve is no longer needed because of a change in policy or that it is excessive, it should not be used to pay a dividend.

6. General reserves are normally created in order to conserve or increase working capital as a shield against inflation or to provide additional working capital for business expansion. The General Reserve may be used to pay dividends only to the extent that the directors consider the reserve to be excessive to requirements.

7. Any proposal to pay a dividend must be covered by available cash, and the directors will need to consider the cash budget of the company to see if the payment of any dividend now will cause liquidity problems later. They must take into their reckoning the liability to pay advance corporation tax.

8. The directors will also bear in mind the rates of dividends being paid by other companies of similar size and in the same line of business.

(Signed)

(Date)

[*Tutorial note:* The question has asked for a report; the answer must be drafted in report form, addressed to the appropriate person, mentioning the subject of the report, signed and dated.]

9.17.2 Exercise: a calculation of the maximum dividend payable on ordinary shares

The following is the summarised draft balance sheet of Splendiferous plc as at 31 March 19-2 before any interest payable has been charged in the profit and loss account or any appropriations made for dividends.

	£
Net assets (other than cash at bank)	30,000
Cash at bank	8,000
	38,000
12% debentures	(5,000)
	33,000
Share capital and reserves	
10,000 Ordinary shares of £1 each	10,000
2,000 8% Preference shares of £1 each	2,000
Share premium	1,000
General reserve	10,000
Retained profit	10,000
	33,000

Required

A calculation of the maximum amount that can be paid to the ordinary shareholders as dividend for the year to 31 March 19-2.

9.18 Investment opportunities

A person may invest in a company by buying ordinary shares, preference shares, debentures or convertible loan stock, depending upon which of these is available in the company concerned.

Debentures

Advantages

Debentures are a relatively 'safe' investment because they are generally secured on the assets of the company (mortgage debentures). This means that if the company gets into difficulties, the assets on which the debentures are secured may be sold and the proceeds applied in paying to the debenture holders the amounts due to them. Short-dated debentures are 'safer' than long-dated ones because their exposure to risk of default by the company is less. Interest is payable at a fixed rate whether the company makes a profit or not.

Disadvantages

The rate of interest on debentures is fixed. If interest rates, generally, rise, the reward for debenture holders becomes relatively less attractive. Of course, the opposite is also true and if other interest rates fall, the debentures become relatively more attractive. If the debentures are held until they are redeemed, the debenture holders will receive back only what they originally invested, unless the debentures are redeemable at a premium or were issued at a discount. In real terms, the repayment to the debenture holders may be worth a lot less than they invested if money has lost some of its purchasing power in the meantime.

Convertible loan stock

This form of investment is similar to investment in debentures but it has the added advantage of offering investors the option to convert the loan stock into shares in the company at a future date at a predetermined price. The option will be attractive if that price is less than the market price of the shares at the date at which the option can be exercised.

Preference shares

Advantages

Preference shareholders are entitled to receive dividends and repayment of capital in priority to ordinary shareholders. Dividends are at a fixed rate and, in the case of cumulative shares, arrears of dividends may be made good out of profits in a later year.

Disadvantages

The rate of dividend paid will not increase if profits increase. If the company is liquidated (wound up), there is no guarantee that the assets will be sufficient to repay the capital due to the preference shareholders after the debenture holders and creditors have been repaid. The amount received on redemption of the shares may be worth less than the amount originally invested if inflation has occurred in the meantime. If the shares are sold, the benefit to the seller will depend upon the state of the market.

Ordinary shares

Advantages

Ordinary shareholders are entitled to be paid dividends out of the profits that remain after payment of preference dividends. If profits increase, ordinary dividends stand a chance of increasing as well. Much depends upon the company's dividend policy. All the company's reserves belong to the ordinary shareholders. There is opportunity for capital, as well as dividend, growth. In a liquidation, the ordinary shareholders may fare very well if the realised net assets are considerably in excess of the amount required to satisfy the debenture holders and preference shareholders.

Disadvantages

The fortunes of the ordinary shareholders depend upon the company's profitability as dividends may only be paid out of available realised profits. Additionally, the profits available for ordinary shareholders can be affected by the gearing of the company, or the relationship between fixed cost capital and the equity of the company. (See chapter 24). In a liquidation, there may be nothing left for the ordinary shareholders after creditors, debenture holders and preference shareholders have been satisfied. The shareholders are dependent upon the state of the market when they wish to sell their shares.

9.19 Methods by which shares may be acquired

Shares may be acquired in two ways:

1. By subscribing to an issue of shares made by a company.
2. By purchasing shares from another shareholder, probably on the Stock Exchange.

When a company issues shares, the issue price will be determined by reference to the perceived value of the shares and, if applicable, to the price at which the shares of the company are presently being traded on the Stock Exchange. The shares may therefore be issued at a premium. Companies are prohibited by the Companies Act from issuing shares at a discount. Cash received from subscribers is debited in the company's cash book and the nominal amount of the shares issued is credited to the share capital account. Any share premium is credited to the share premium account. The share issue therefore has an effect upon the balance sheet of the issuing company.

In addition, the names of the shareholders are recorded in the company's Register of Members.

When shares are purchased by somebody from another shareholder, the transaction usually involves the services of a stockbroker. The consideration for the shares in a quoted public company will be determined by the Stock Exchange price ruling at the time. The price is determined by the market's view of the company's prospects taking into account economic, political, sociological and evironmental conditions. The price may therefore be above or below the nominal value of the shares.The money is kept by the person selling the shares; none of it goes to the company and no entries are made by the company in its accounts. The transaction has no effect on the company's balance sheet. The only action the company will take is to replace the former shareholder's name with that of the new shareholder in the Register of Members.

Key points to remember

1. A company is a separate legal entity.
2. The liability of members is limited to the amount they have paid, or have agreed to pay, on their shares.
3. A company can raise more capital than a partnership.
4. Public companies may issue shares to the general public; private companies must include a restriction on the issue of shares in their Articles of Association.
5. The differences between limited companies and partnerships (9.2).
6. The differences between non-cumulative preference shares, cumulative preference shares, ordinary shares and debentures.
7. The definitions of capital reserves, revenue reserves, provisions and liabilities.
8. All reserves form part of the ordinary shareholders' interest in the company.
9. Factors affecting dividend policy.

Common errors

1. showing debentures as part of the company's share capital and reserves
2. failure to ensure that a full year's interest on debentures is debited in the Profit and Loss account
3. omission of outstanding debenture interest from the balance sheet as a liability.
4. failure to include interim dividends paid during the year in the Profit and Loss Appropriation account.
5. omission of the final dividend for the year from the balance sheet as a liability.

Questions

Fully worked Examination question

Bandana Ltd. has an authorised share capital of 75,000 £1 ordinary shares. On 31 March 19-8 the following balances were extracted from its books.

	£
Ordinary shares, fully paid	50,000
Other reserves	70,000
Leasehold Land & Buildings, at cost	65,500
Motor vehicles, at cost	10,650

	£
Plant and machinery, at cost	54,400
Creditors	39,400
Cash and bank	98,410
Stock at 1 April 19-7	10,640
Sales	280,520
Purchases	182,530
Wages	19,546
Selling expenses	16,428
Administrative expenses	22,392
Profit and Loss Account at 1 April 19-7	29,246
Debtors	56,750
Interim dividend, paid	2,500
Provision for depreciation	
Leasehold land & building	32,750
Motor vehicles	6,420
Plant and machinery	30,290
Provision for bad debts	1,030

The following information is relevant:

(i) Stock on hand at 31 March 19-8 amounted to £11,450

(ii) Provision for bad debts is to be adjusted to 2% of the outstanding debtors as on 31 Marech 19-8

(iii) Provision is to be made for:

    (a) Audit fee £1,000

    (b) Depreciation on leasehold land and buildings at 5% on cost, and motor vehicles at 20% on cost.

(iv) The directors wish to transfer £10,000 to general reserve and recommend a final dividend of 10%

(v) administrative expenses include insurance payments of £2,000 which cover a 15 month period to 30 June 19-8.

(vi) The company is being sued for £19,000 in respect of costs arising from the expiration of a lease on a property formerly occupied by the company. The company's legal advisers are of the opinion that the company will not be held liable for this amount.

Required

(a) prepare, not necessarily in a form for publication, a Trading and Profit and Loss Account for the year ending 31 March 19-8 and a Balance Sheet as at that date: (22 marks)

(b) explain and justify your treatment of the claim against the company in respect to the expiration of the lease. (3 marks)

(Total 25 marks)

(JMB)

Answer

(a)
Bandana Ltd.
Trading and profit and loss account
for the year ended 31 March 19-8

	£	£
Sales		280,520
Cost of sales: Stock at 1.4.-7	10,640	
Purchases	182,530	
	193,170	
Stock at 31.3.-7	11,450	181,720
Gross profit		98,800
Selling expenses	16,428	
Administrative expenses (note)	53,398	69,826
Operating profit		28,974
Transfer to general reserve	10,000	
Dividends paid and proposed	7,500	17,500
Retained profit for the year		11,474
Retained profit brought forward		29,246
Retained profit carried forward		40,720

Balance sheet as at 31 March 19-8

Fixed assets	Cost £	Depn £	£
Leashold land and buildings	65,500	36,025	29,475
Plant and machinery	54,400	35,730	18,670
Motor vehicles	10,650	8,550	2,100
	130,550	80,305	50,245

Current assets	Stock	11,450	
	Debtors	55,615	
	Prepayment	400	
	Cash and bank	98,410	
		165,875	

Current liabilities			
Creditors	39,400		
Accruals	1,000		
Proposed dividends	5,000	45,400	120,475
			£170,720

Share capital and reserves		
Authorised capital:		
75,000 £1 ordinary shares		75,000
Issued:		
50,000 £1 ordinary shares, fully paid		50,000
Reserves		80,000
Retained profit		40,720
		£170,720

Note: Admin. expenses. T.B £22,392 + wages £19,456

(b) The result of the claim against the company is a contingent liability. It is a remote liability according to legal advice received and therefore does not have to be provided for or disclosed.

This is a topic covered in chapter 11 (SSAP 18)

Multiple choice questions

1　A public limited company must have a minimum authorised capital of

   A　£5,000

   B　£12,500

   C　£25,000

   D　£50,000

2　A private limited company may not

   A　issue bonus shares

   B　issue debentures

   C　make a rights issue

   D　offer its shares to the public

3　A company has an authorised share capital of £100,000 ordinary shares of 50p. It has issued 60,000 of the shares. The directors propose to pay a dividend of 8%. The total dividend will amount to

   A　£2,400

   B　£4,000

   C　£4,800

   D　£8,000

4   A company has an authorised capital of 100,000 ordinary shares of 25p each. It has issued 80,000 of the shares. A dividend of 10% has been proposed. The dividend payable will be

    A   £2,000

    B   £2,500

    C   £8,000

    D   £10,000

5   On 31 March 1997 a company pays a final dividend of £7,000 in respect of its financial year ended 31 December 1996. On 1 July 1997 it pays an interim dividend of £4,000. Its balance sheet at 31 December 1997 includes an amount of £9,000 for dividend payable. The dividends debited in the profit and loss account for the year ended 31 December 1997 amount to

    A   £9,000

    B   £11,000

    C   £13,000

    D   £20,000

6   The following is an extract from the balance sheet of a company:

Share capital and reserves	£m
1,000,000 ordinary shares of £1 each	1.0
200,000 8% preference shares of £1 each	0.2
Share premium account	0.4
Propery revaluation reserve	0.8
General reserve	0.7
Profit and loss account	0.5
	3.6

The company also has issued 10% debentures amounting to £1m. Each ordinary share will be valued on a balance sheet basis at

    A   £2.40

    B   £2.60

    C   £3.40

    D   £3.60

7   The order of priority which a company must give to payment of interest and dividends is

    A   debenture interest, ordinary dividends, preference dividends

    B   debenture interest, preference dividends, ordinary dividends

    C   preference dividends, debenture interest, ordinary dividends

    D   preference dividends, ordinary dividends, debenture interest

8   Convertible loan stock is the term used for

    A   a loan which can be converted into cash at any time

    B   a loan which may be exchanged for shares at a future date on predetermined terms

    C   goods lent to the company for selling

    D   preference shares which may be converted into ordinary shares

9   The following is an extract from the balance sheet of a company:

Share capital and reserves	£
200,000 ordinary shares of 50p.	100,000
50,000 6% preference shares of £1	50,000
Share premium account	20,000
General reserve	35,000
Profit and loss acocunt	15,000
	220,000

The balance sheet includes a fixed asset of Land and Buildings with a net book value of £80,000. It has now been ascertained from a professional valuation that at the date of the balance sheet the fair value of the land and buildings was £120,000.

The fair valuation of each ordinary share is

A   85p

B   £1.05

C   £1.70

D   £2.10

10   A company may improve its bank balance by

A   issuing bonus shares

B   making a rights issue

C   transferring money from the share premium account

D   redeeming its debentures

11   Andy holds 1,000 ordinary shares of £1 each in Busted Ltd. He has paid in full all the calls made amounting to 80p. on each share. If the company runs into financial difficulty, Andy will be liable at most for

A   £200

B   £800

C   £1,000

D   jointly with all the other shareholders for all the debts of the company.

12   During the year to 31 December 1996 a company paid the final dividend for the year ended 31 December 1995 in the sum of £800,000. It also paid interim dividends on account of the year to 31 December 1996 amounting to £300,000. The directors propose paying a final dividend for the year of £1m. The entry in the profit and loss account for the year ended 31 December 1996 for dividends will be

A   £300,000

B   £800,000

C   £1,300,000

D   £2,100,000

13   The following information is available for Jilly Ltd. regarding dividends paid and proposed:

	Paid £	Proposed £
For the year ended 31.12.95		
Final preference dividend	8,000	
Final ordinary dividend	25,000	
For the year ended 31.12.96		
Interim preference dividend	8,000	
Interim ordinary dividend	15,000	
Proposed final preference dividend		8,000
Proposed final ordinary dividend		30,000

The balance sheet at 31 December 1996 will show

A   no current liabilty for dividends

B   a current liability for divedends of £8,000

C   a current liability for dividends of £38,000

D   a current liability for dividends of £61,000

14   The safest form of investment in a limited company is in

A   long dated debentures

B   ordinary shares

C   preference shares

D   short dated debentures

Further examination questions

1   The agenda for the Annual General Meeting of a public limited company contains the following resolution:

'The final dividend for the year ended 31 May 19-8 shall be 0.7p per share.'

An extract from the company's profit and loss account for the year ended 31 May 19-8 is given below:

	£'000
Net profit after taxation	2,370
Proposed dividend	280
Retained profit for the year	2,090
Retained profit brought forward	7,560
Retained profit carried forward	9,650

The company chairman has received a letter from a shareholder who is unhappy about the size of the proposed dividend. The shareholder wants to see the dividend significantly increased to 10p per share.

(a) Advise the chairman regarding the options which are available to directors when deciding upon the appropriation of profits.   (12 marks)

(b) Prepare a reasoned reply from the chairman to the shareholder in defence of the company's dividend policy.   (8 marks)

(Total 20 marks)
(LONDON)

2   The balance sheet of De Vere Carter plc included the following information at 31 May 1992:

	£
Issued Share Capital:	
Ordinary shares of £1 each, fully paid	240,000
10% Preference shares of £1 each, fully paid	90,000
Reserves:	
Share premium account	65,000
Capital redemption reserves	40,000
Revaluation reserve	120,000
Profit and loss account	56,000

On 1 June 1992, the company is planning to increase its ordinary share capital in the following ways:

(i) An issue of bonus shares to existing members, with one bonus share being issued for every three ordinary shares held. The directors wished to retain the maximum flexibility regarding future dividend payments, so an appropriate choice of reserves was to be made for the purpose of the bonus issue.

(ii) A rights issue, whereby existing shareholders (both of ordinary and preference shares) may subscribe for five ordinary shares at £1.90 each for every three shares of either class held (excluding bonus shares). £1 is payable on application (by 30 June 1992), and 90p on allotment (by 31 July 1992).

(iii) A public issue of 100,000 ordinary shares to be made at £2.50 each, with £1.10 payable on application (by 30 June 1992) and the balance on allotment (by 31 July 1992). Existing shareholders are to be given priority, as their applications will be accepted before those of the general public.

Applications were received as follows:

1. 90% of the rights issue was taken up, and paid for by the due dates.

2. Existing shareholders applied for, and were allotted, 60,000 of the share issue. Other applications totalled 90,000 shares, and these were scaled down on a pro-rata basis, with excess application money being refunded on 10 July 1992. All application and allotment monies were paid by the due date, with the exception of £3,000 allotment money due from existing shareholders.

(a) Show the company's application and allotment account, and ordinary share capital account for the period 1 June 1992 to 31 July 1992.   (12 marks)

(b) Calculate the final number of shares held by a shareholder with an initial holding of 900 ordinary shares, who applied for the rights issue and 500 shares in the new share issue.

(3 marks)

(c) Explain two advantages and two disadvantages to a company of raising funds by a share issue, and suggest three alternative ways of raising funds that the company could have considered.

(10 marks)

(Total 25 marks)

(LONDON)

3   The trial balance of Oscar Limited at 31 December 1992 appeared as follows:

	£	£
Ordinary shares of £1 each, fully paid		100,000
Purchases	440,000	
Retained profit		60,000
Freehold land at cost	160,000	
Fixtures, at cost	30,000	
Depreciation on fixtures		18,000
Business rates	6,000	
Motor vehicles, cost	56,000	
Depreciation on vehicles		28,000
Insurance	4,000	
Stock at 1 January 1992	80,000	
Debtors	60,000	
Trade creditors		48,000
Sales		620,000
Bank	24,200	
12% Debentures (issued in 1989)		80,000
Debenture interest	4,800	
Wages and salaries	68,000	
Heat and light	8,200	
Professional fees	7,800	
General expenses	2,400	
Motor expenses	4,000	
Provision for bad debts		2,000
Bad debts	600	
	956,000	956,000

Notes

1.   Stock at 31 December 1992 was £90,000.

2.   Depreciation for 1992 has yet to be provided on the following bases:

Fixtures   10% straight line
Motor vehicles   20% straight line

3.   Account was to be taken of an adjusting post balance sheet event on 21 January 1993, when a customer, who owed £15,000 to Oscar Limited on 31 December 1992, was declared bankrupt. The debt had been considered as good at the year end. The provision for bad debts (a general provision of 3% of debtors), was to be adjusted and carried forward.

4.   Insurance of £600 had been prepaid at the year end, and wages of £6,000 were to be accrued.

5.   The directors propose a dividend of £15,000 for the year.

6.   Taxation of £5,450 is to be provided.

(a) Prepare a profit and loss account and balance sheet based on the above information (not necessarily in a form suitable for publication).

(18 marks)

(b) Explain why the company has retained profits carried forward at the end of its financial year, and why it does not distribute all these profits to its shareholders.

(7 marks)

(Total 25 marks)

(LONDON)

4   Outlaws plc, a company which manufactures bottled drinks, arrived at a draft net profit before taxation of £327,000 for the year ended 31 October 1992. In January 1993, on reviewing the accounts, the auditors queried the following items:

1.   An amount of £10,000 paid to the company's legal advisors as a fee for negotiating the sale of leasehold property during the year has been shown as part of 'Professional Fees' in the Profit and Loss Account. The property, which had an amortised value of £400,000 at the date of sale, was sold for £435,000. The 'profit' of £35,000 has been credited to a suspense account, which has been included in the balance sheet at 31 October 1992.

2.   A motor lorry which cost £40,000 during the year has been written off in the profit and loss account, although the normal depreciation policy is to write off such assets over four years.

3.   Stock valued at £7,000 at 31 October 1992 has been included at its retail price, which is 40% higher than its cost.

4.   A customer, whose debt of £20,000 was considered bad and was written off in the year to 31 October 1992, paid the debt in full in December 1992.

(a) Re-calculate the company's net profit before taxation after making any adjustments necessary for items 1-4 above.   (7 marks)

(b) Explain your treatment of each of the items 1-4 above.   (8 marks)
                                                                         (Total 15 marks)
                                                                              (LONDON)

5   Expansion p.l.c. is to issue shares to the public at the same time as a rights issue is made to its existing members. Bonus shares will also be issued.

The company's most recent balance sheet provides the following information:

		£
Paid up share capital -		
100,000 preference shares at £1		100,000
500,000 ordinary shares at 50p		250,000
Reserves -		
Share premium account		100,000
Capital redemption reserve		75,000
Revaluation reserve		100,000
General reserve		200,000
Asset replacement reserve		50,000
Profit and loss account		75,000
		950,000

Authority to increase the company's capital has been obtained.

An extraordinary meeting of members has resolved the following:

(i)   One bonus share is to be issued for each five ordinary shares held.

(ii) Both preference and ordinary shareholders will be allowed to subscribe for ten ordinary shares for every ten shares (excluding bonus shares) of either class held: 10p per share is payable on application and 80p on allotment.

(iii) Additional shares may be applied for both by existing shareholders and the public. Applications from existing shareholders are to be accepted in full before any allotments are made to the public: 25p per share is payable on application and £1.50 on allotment.

When the application lists closed it was found that:

(i)   The rights issue was entirely taken up and no shareholder at the time held less than 10 shares. No shareholders held any fraction of 5 shares.

(ii) Existing shareholders applied for and were allotted 50,000 shares.

(iii) Members of the public sent in application monies for a further 75,000 shares, of which only 50,000 were allotted. The directors allotted two shares for every three applied for. No fractional adjustments were required.

Required

(a) An extract from the company's balance sheet showing the shares and reserves after the allotments have taken place but before amounts due on allotment have been paid.
                                                                              (10 marks)

(b) A statement of the entries to be included in the bank account. (4 marks)

(c) An explanation of why shares are sometimes issued at a premium. (4 marks)

(Total 18 marks)

(WJEC)

6 The following trial balance was extracted from the books of Togo Ltd on 31 December 1991.

	£	£
Share capital (ordinary shares of £1)		800,000
Share premium		400,000
Revenue reserve		92,800
Freehold premises – cost	650,000	
Plant – cost	600,000	
Plant – depreciation		208,000
Purchases	2,017,000	
Sales		3,178,900
Wages	312,000	
Salaries	231,200	
Rent and rates	43,000	
Light and heat	15,500	
General expenses	316,900	
Bad debts	7,500	
Bad debt provision		8,600
Debtors	217,800	
Stock	256,900	
Creditors		175,200
Bank	173,700	
Suspense	22,000	
	4,863,500	4,863,500

You are given the following additional information.

(i) In preparing the trial balance two errors were made:

debtor balances were undercast by £20,000;

an item of plant purchased for £1,000 had been correctly credited to the bank account but had been credited instead of debited to the plant account.

(ii) A review of debtors has revealed balances of £5,300 that are irrecoverable and £7,900 that are doubtful.

(iii) Closing stock amounted to £313,200.

(iv) Plant costing £20,000 with accumulated depreciation of £18,000 at 1 January 1991 was sold for £3,000. The only accounting entry made so far for this transaction has been to debit bank and credit the sale proceeds to the sales account.

(v) The company's policy is to depreciate plant by the straight line method at 10%. The company provides a full year's depreciation in the year of acquisition and no depreciation in the year of disposal.

(vi) Payments due at the end of the year were:

	£
Wages	5,800
Light and heat	1,900

(vii) Rates paid in advance at the end of the year were £3,200.

(viii) A final dividend of £100,000 is proposed for the year.

(a) **You are required** to prepare a profit and loss account for the year ended 31 December 1991 and a balance sheet as at 31 December 1991. (24 marks)

(b) The Chairman of Togo Ltd says "I have read that a company's most important asset is the skill and dedication of its employees. Why is this not shown in the balance sheet?" **Discuss** this question. (8 marks)

(c) **Discuss** the extent to which company accounts do, and can, report the full costs of pollution. (8 marks)

(Total 40 marks)

(JMB)

7   The following financial data is available for two companies for the year ended 30 June 1993.

(1)

	Boda plc	Ventura plc
	£000	£000
Net trading profit for year	13,500	6,000
Retained earnings as at 1 July 1992	26,000	7,000
The directors have decided to transfer to General Reserve	10,000	2,550

(2)

Ordinary dividends for the year:

Interim paid	6p per share	4p per share
Proposed final	30p per share	12p per share
Preference dividends paid for year	11%	–

(3) Balances as at 30 June 1993:

	Boda plc	Ventura plc
	£000	£000
Issued share capital		
£1 ordinary shares, fully paid	30,000	5,500
£1 preference shares, fully paid	5,000	–
Share premium	10,000	8,650
12% debentures 2000-2005	8,000	–
Current assets	39,000	8,180
Fixed assets	73,150	24,860
Current liabilities (excluding dividends)	14,000	2,500

(4) Balances as at 1 July 1992:

	Boda plc	Ventura plc
	£000	£000
General reserve	8,000	3,610

Additional information:

(i)   The Board of Directors of Boda plc are currently considering whether to invest funds in Ventura plc.

(ii) Included in Ventura plc's fixed assets are freehold land and buildings at a cost valuation of £8m. However the current market valuation is only £3.5m due to property prices having fallen in recent months.

(iii) Owing to a recession within the economy several of Ventura's trade debts had become bad. These debts amounted to £500 000 but had not yet been written off. Consideration was also being given to the creation of a provision for doubtful debts covering an additional £1m of trade debtors.

(iv) The directors of Ventura plc were concerned about the future of the company and were considering the possibility of making a rights issue in the next financial year. The most favoured option is to issue one new ordinary share for every two shares currently held. The issue price would be £1.20 a share.

Required

(a) Profit and loss appropriation accounts for each of the companies for the year ended 30 June 1993 presented in columnar form.   (14 marks)

(b) A balance sheet for Ventura plc as at 30 June 1993.   (10 marks)

(c) Explain why one company may wish to invest in another company   (12 marks)

(d) Write a brief report for the Board of Boda plc on the prospects of Ventura plc as an investment. Your report should consider both adjusted and unadjusted figures

(14 marks)

(Total 50 marks)

(AEB)

10 Limited companies: published accounts

Chapter objectives

Questions on published accounts of limited companies test ability to:

☐ prepare profit and loss accounts and balance sheets from given information in forms prescribed by the fourth schedule of the Companies Act 1985

☐ prepare notes to the balance sheet and profit and loss account to provide information required to be disclosed by the Companies Act 1985.

☐ discuss or explain the purpose of the requirements to disclose certain information in the accounts

The published accounts of limited companies are used by:

- shareholders
- prospective investors
- debenture holders
- creditors
- financial analysts
- the financial Press.

Statutory regulations governing the requirements of published accounts of limited companies have existed for a very long time. The Companies Act 1981 sought to bring the presentation of accounts of U.K. companies into line with those of the rest of the European Common Market;.

The requirements are now embodied in the Companies Act 1985 as amended by the Companies Act 1989, which provides in Section 227 that

'In the case of every company, the directors shall in respect of every accounting reference period of the company prepare a profit and loss account for the financial year... ...and shall prepare a balance sheet as at the last day of the period.'

Section 228 of the Act provides that 'A company's accounts prepared under section 227 shall comply with the requirements of Schedule 4 (so far as applicable) with respect to the form and content of the balance sheet and profit and loss account and any additional information to be provided by way of notes to the accounts.

Schedule 4 of the Act gives two balance sheet formats and four profit and loss account formats together with a statement of accounting principles and rules and notes to be appended to the accounts.

Schedule 5 deals with miscellaneous matters to be disclosed in the notes to the accounts.

Section 239 states that a company's accounts for a financial year are to be taken as comprising:

(a) the company's profit and loss account and balance sheet

(b) the directors' report

(c) the auditors' report;, and

(d) group accounts where applicable.

Section 240 requires every company to send a copy of the company's accounts, not less than 21 days before the Annual General Meeting, to the following persons:

(a) every shareholder

(b) every debenture holder

(c) all other persons entitled to receive copies (e.g. the auditors.)

The directors of a company may adopt any format they wish for accounts produced for internal use within the company, but will probably adopt a form close to that required for the published accounts as that will facilitate the production of the published accounts. The accounts for internal use will be much more detailed than the published ones as the directors will not wish to include any information in the latter which will be of use to competitors. Nevertheless, published accounts often include more information than is required by law, the additional matter being calculated to improve the information given to the public and to improve the image of the company.

When answering questions on published accounts, adhere strictly to the requirements of the Companies Act; any departure, giving more or less information than legally required, will be interpreted as a display of an inadequate knowledge of the topic.

10.1 Profit and loss account format 1

1. Turnover
2. Cost of sales *
3. Gross profit or loss
4. Distribution costs *
5. Administrative expenses *
6. Other operating income
7. Income from shares in group companies
8. Income from shares in related companies
9. Income from other fixed asset investments **
10. Other interest receivable and similar income **
11. Amounts written off investments
12. Interest payable and similar charges ***
13. Tax on profit or loss on ordinary activities
14. Profit or loss on ordinary activities after taxation
15. Extraordinary income
16. Extraordinary charges
17. Extraordinary profit or loss
18. Tax on extraordinary profit or loss
19. Other taxes not shown under the above items
20. Profit or loss for the financial year.

* Items 2,4 and 5. These items shall be stated after taking into account any necessary provisions for depreciation or diminution in value of assets.

** Items 9 and 10. Income and interest derived from group companies shall be shown separately from income and interest derived from other sources.

*** Item 12. The amount payable to group companies shall be shown separately.

10.2 Balance sheet format 1

A. Called up share capital not paid *

B. Fixed assets

    I   Intangible assets

        1. Development costs

        2. Concessions, patents, licenses, trade marks and similar rights and assets

        3. Goodwill #

        4. Payments on account

  II Tangible assets
    1. Land and buildings
    2. Plant and machinery
    3. Fixtures, fittings, tools and equipment
    4. Payments on account and assets in course of construction

  III Investments
    1. Shares in group companies
    2. Loans to group companies
    3. Shares in related companies
    4. Loans to related companies
    5. Other investments other than loans
    6. Other loans
    7. Own shares

C. Current assets

  I Stocks
    1. Raw materials and consumable stores.
    2. Work in progress
    3. Finished goods and goods for resale
    4. Payments on account

  II Debtors
    1. Trade debtors
    2. Amounts owed by group companies
    3. Amounts owed by related companies
    4. Other debtors
    5. Called up share capital not paid *
    6. Prepayments and accrued income **

  III Investments
    1. Shares in group companies
    2. Own shares
    3. Other investments

  IV Cash at bank and in hand

D. Prepayments and accrued income **

E. Creditors: amounts falling due within one year
    1. Debenture loans
    2. Bank loans and overdrafts
    3. Payments received on account ##
    4. Trade creditors
    5. Bills of exchange payable
    6. Amounts owed to group companies
    7. Amounts owed to related companies
    8. Other creditors including taxation and social security
    9. Accruals and deferred income ***

F. Net current assets (liabilities) ###

G. Total assets less current liabilities

H. Creditors: amounts falling due after more than one year
    1. Debenture loans
    2. Bank loans and overdrafts
    3. Payments received on account ##
    4. Trade creditors
    5. Bills of exchange payable
    6. Amounts owed to group companies
    7. Amounts owed to related companies
    8. Other creditors including taxation and social security
    9. Accruals and deferred income ***

I.   Provisions for liabilities and charges
    1. Pensions and similar obligations
    2. Taxation including deferred taxation
    3. Other provisions

J.   Accruals and deferred income ***

K.   Capital and reserves
    I   Called up share capital
    II Share premium account
    III Revaluation reserve
    IV Other reserves
        1. Capital redemption reserve
        2. Reserve for own shares
        3. Reserves provided for by the articles of association
        4. Other reserves
    V Profit and loss account.

*   Called up share capital not paid. This item may be shown in either of the two positions given.

**   Prepayments and accrued income. This item may be shown in either of the two positions given.

*** Accruals and deferred income. The two positions given for this item at E.9 and H.9 are an alternative to the position at J, but if the item is not shown in a position corresponding to that at J it may be shown in either or both of the other two positions (as the case may require).

\#   Goodwill. Amounts representing goodwill shall only be included to the extent that goodwill was acquired for valuable consideration.

\#\#   Payments received on account. Payments received on account of orders shall be shown for each of these items in so far as they are not shown as deductions from stocks.

\#\#\# Net current assets(liabilities). In determining the amount to be shown for this item any amounts shown under 'Prepayments and accrued income' shall be taken into account wherever shown.

10.3 Accounting principles

The amounts to be included in respect of all items shown in a company's accounts shall be determined in accordance with the following principles:

1.   The company shall be presumed to be carrying on business as a going concern.

2.   Accounting policies shall be applied consistently from one financial year to the next.

3.   The amount of any item shall be determined on a prudent basis:

    (a) only profits realised at the balance sheet date shall be included in the profit and loss account; and

    (b) all liabilities and losses which have arisen or are likely to arise in respect of the financial year to which the accounts relate or a previous financial year shall be taken into account.

4.   All income and charges relating to the financial year to which the accounts relate shall be taken into account, without regard to the date of receipt or payment.

5   In determining the aggregate amount of any item the amount of each individual asset or liability that falls to be taken into account shall be determined separately.

Departure from the accounting principles

If it appears to the directors of a company that there are special reasons for departing from any of the principles stated above in preparing the company's accounts in respect of any financial year they may do so, but particulars of the departure, the reasons for it and its effect shall be given in a note to the accounts.

Tutorial note: The accounting principles 1–4 stated above are the concepts of going concern, consistency, prudence and accruals with which the student should already be familiar. See Chapter 1.

10.4 Notes to the accounts

The following information, if not given in the company's accounts, must be shown by way of notes to the accounts:

Disclosure of Accounting Policies

The accounting policies adopted by the company in determining the amounts to be included in respect of items shown in the balance sheet and in determining the profit or loss of the company shall be stated. (This includes such policies as those relating to the depreciation and diminution in value of assets.)

Notes relating to the profit and loss account

Turnover

Turnover means the amounts derived from the provision of goods and services falling within the company's ordinary activities, after deduction of:

(a) trade discounts

(b) value added tax, and

(c) any other taxes based on the amounts so derived

Where, during a financial year, the business of a company has consisted of two or more classes that differ substantially from each other, a note to the accounts shall state the amount of the turnover attributable to each class and the amount of profit or loss before taxation attributable to that class.

If a company has supplied substantially different geographical markets, the amount of turnover attributable to each market shall be shown by way of note.

Example

Profit and loss account: Turnover £99m

Note to profit and loss account:

	Turnover £m	Profit before tax £m
Food	36	2.1
Furniture	54	16.0
Travel & tourism	9	0.9
	99	19.0

	Turnover £m
United Kingdom	54
Europe	30
North and South America	15
	99

The following items shall be shown by way of note to supplement the information given in the profit and loss account:

Interest

The amount of interest on or any similar charges in respect of:

(a) bank loans and overdrafts, loans made to the company (except bank loans and overdrafts) which:

  (i) are repayable otherwise than by instalments and fall due for repayment within five years of the date to which the accounts are made up; or

  (ii) are repayable by instalments the last of which falls due for payment before the end of that period; and

(b) loans of any other kind made to the company.

Income

The amount of income from investments listed on a recognised stock exchange.

Rent from Land

The net amount to be shown if it forms a substantial part of the company's revenue for the year.

Hire of Plant and Machinery

The amount charged in the profit and loss account in respect of sums payable for the hire of plant and machinery.

Auditors' Remuneration

The amount shown must include the amount of auditors' expenses paid by the company.

Taxation

Details should be given of the charge in the accounts showing:

(a) UK corporation tax and the basis upon which it has been computed.

(b) UK income tax and the basis upon which it has been computed.

(c) irrecoverable advance corporation tax.

(d) tax attributable to dividends received from other UK companies (known as franked investment income.)

Particulars of Staff

(a) The average number of persons employed by the company in the financial year;

(b) The average number of persons so employed within each category of persons employed by the company. (e.g. manufacturing, clerical etc.)

(c) (i) wages and salaries paid or payable in the year

(ii) social security costs incurred by the company on their behalf

(iii) other pension costs

(d) The number of employees earning over £30,000 within each band of £5,000 over that amount. e.g.

Emoluments	Number of employees
£30,001 – £35,000	6
£35,001 – £40,000	2
£40,001 – £45,000	1
	9

Particulars of Directors' Emoluments

(a) (i) Total emoluments including pension contributions and benefits in kind (e.g.company car), distinguishing between fees as director and other emoluments.

(ii) Total of pensions paid to past directors

(iii) Total of compensation for loss of office.

(b) Where the total of the directors' emoluments exceeds £60,000, the following must be shown:

(i) The emoluments of the chairman.

(ii) The emoluments of the highest paid director if he is not the chairman,

(iii) The number of directors whose emoluments fall within the range £0 – £5,000, and of each higher band of £5,000. e.g.

Directors emoluments:	£'000
Total emoluments paid to directors	185
Chairman's emoluments	40
Emoluments of highest paid director	52
Number of directors not included above receiving	
£5,001 – £10,000	2
£10,001 – £15,000	4
£15,001 – £20,000	1

Earnings per Share

Statement of Standard Accounting Practice 3 requires listed companies (i.e. those dealt with on a stock exchange) to show the earnings per share.

Notes relating to the balance sheet

Share Capital

Note should show:

(a) authorised share capital

(b) number and aggregate nominal value of each class of shares allotted.

(c) with regard to any redeemable shares:

  (i) the earliest and latest dates on which the company has power to redeem the shares

  (ii) whether shares are redeemable in any event, or at option of the company or of shareholder

  (iii) amount of any premium payable on redemption

Fixed Assets

The various classes of fixed assets should be shown at cost, or revaluation where appropriate, at beginning of the year. Additions during the year at cost, and the original cost or revaluation amounts of assets disposed of during the year should be shown.

The provisions for depreciation of fixed assets at the beginning of the year, together with such provisions on assets disposed of during the year and the charges for depreciation for the year for each class of asset should be shown.

Example

Note to balance sheet:

Fixed assets	Freehold property £'000	Plant & machinery £'000	Motor vehicles £'000
At cost at beginning of year (see note 1)	1,600	852	660
Additions during year	–	280	206
Disposals	–	(97)	(147)
	1,600	1,035	719
Depreciation			
At beginning of year	280	568	410
Charge for the year	28	207	180
On disposals	–	(83)	(122)
	308	692	468
Net book value at end of year	1,292	343	251

Note 1. Freehold property: freehold land £200,000; buildings £1,400,000

(Statement of Standard Accounting Practice 12 requires that the following should also be disclosed:

1. Method of depreciation used

2. Economic life or depreciation rate in use.)

Revaluation of Fixed Assets

Revaluation of fixed assets is accounted for in a revaluation reserve. The directors must reduce the reserve if in their opinion any part of it is no longer necessary; the adjustment may only be made through the profit and loss account if the amount in question was originally charged to the profit and loss account, or it represents a realised profit.

Losses on the revaluation of certain fixed assets, or classes of assets, are realised losses (unless they offset an unrealised surplus previously recorded for the same asset); individual surpluses should be treated as unrealised profits.

If all the fixed assets are revalued, individual deficits should be regarded as unrealised losses.

In the year of revaluation of a fixed asset, a note to the balance sheet must state the names of the valuers or their qualifications, and the method of valuation used.

The annual depreciation charge on a revalued asset should be based on the revalued amount and the estimated remaining useful life of the asset.

10.4.1 Example: disclosure requirements relating to fixed assets

Snook, Erdwell, Potter, Black and Co. plc had the following fixed assets at 31 December 19-1:

	Cost £'000	Provision for depreciation to date £'000
*Freehold land and buildings	1,200	400
Plant and machinery	640	210
Motor vehicles	275	135

* (Land cost £200,000; buildings cost £1,000,000)

The depreciation policy of the company is to provide for depreciation as follows:

Freehold buildings	2% p.a. straight line
Plant and machinery	15% p.a. straight line
Motor vehicles	20% p.a. straight line

During the year to 31 December 19-2, the following events occurred:

1. On 1 January 19-2, the freehold property was professionally revalued by Billyard and Billyard, chartered surveyors, at £1,800,000, of which £400,000 was attributable to the land. The buildings were estimated to have a further useful life of 25 years.

2. Plant and machinery: original cost £140,000, scrap value £5,000 and written down value £40,000.

3. New plant and machinery was acquired at a cost of £240,000 on 1 April 19-2.

4. Motor vehicles which had cost £35,000 were sold for £15,000, making a profit on disposal of £5,000.

5. New motor vehicles were purchased on 1 July 19-2 at a cost of £80,000.

At a meeting of the directors on 1 December, 19-2, the sales director suggested that as freehold property tended to appreciate in value, no depreciation need be provided in future years on that property. The personnel director suggested that it would be more prudent to continue with the depreciation policy followed hitherto for freehold property. After a lengthy discussion, the directors agreed that the freehold property should be depreciated on generally accepted accounting principles.

Required

(a) A note, prepared in suitable form, for inclusion in the published accounts of the company, showing the information required to be disclosed in relation to tangible fixed assets.

(b) Your comments on the discussion that took place at the directors' meeting on 1 December 19-2 regarding the depreciation policy as it affected freehold property.

Answer

(a) Note to balance sheet

Tangible fixed assets

	Freehold land & buildings £'000	Plant & machinery £'000	Motor vehicles £'000
Balance at 31 December 19–1	1,200	640	275
Increase on revaluation	600		
Additions at cost		240	80
Disposals at cost		(140)	(35)
	1,800	740	320
Depreciation			
Provisions at 31 December 19–1	400	210	135
Transfer to Revaluation Reserve	(400)		
Provisions on disposals		(100)	(25)
Charge for the year	56	102	56
	56	212	166
Balance sheet	1,744	528	154

Note to be included under 'Principal accounting policies'

Tangible Fixed Assets

Depreciation is calculated so as to write off the cost of the fixed assets on a straight line basis over the expected useful economic lives of the assets concerned.

The annual rates used for this year are:

Freehold buildings	4%
Plant and machinery	15%
Motor vehicles	20%

The rates shown above for the plant and machinery and motor vehicles are consistent with those used in the previous year.

The rate used for freehold buildings, consequent upon revaluation, is 4%, based upon the revalued amount and the expected remaining useful economic life of 25 years. The additional annual charge for depreciation for freehold buildings resulting from the revaluation amounts to £36,000.

Freehold land is not depreciated.

(b) The sales director overlooked the fact that although freehold property may appreciate in value, buildings do not have an infinite life and must be replaced at some time in the future.

The personnel director recognised that buildings have finite lives, but overlooked the fact that the previous depreciation policy, at 2% p.a., would write the buildings off over 50 years, whereas the estimated remaining useful economic life is 25 years.

The policy adopted by the Board is to write off the revalued amount of the buildings over 25 years; this conforms with the requirements of SSAP 12.

10.4.2 Exercise: based on the disclosure requirements for tangible fixed assets

The Wooden Box Co. Ltd. had the following balances in its books at 30 June 19-2:

	£
Freehold land and buildings which cost £250,000 in 1964, and had been revalued in 1971 at	400,000
Plant and machinery purchased on 1 July 19-0 at a cost of	240,000
Plant and machinery purchased on 1 July 19-1 at a cost of	156,000
Motor vehicles purchased on 1 January 19-1 at a cost of	80,000
Motor vehicles purchased on 1 July 19-1 at a cost of	50,000

The annual rates of depreciation, based on cost with estimated nil residual values, and which have always been consistently used are:

Freehold land and buildings	not depreciated
Plant and machinery	20% straight line
Motor vehicles	25% straight line

When the freehold land and buildings were purchased in 1964, the cost was allocated as follows: land £50,000; buildings £200,000. The revalued amount for this asset in 1971 was allocated as follows: land £100,000; buildings £300,000.

In the year to 30 June 19-3, the following events took place:

1. Freehold land and buildings were again revalued by Coffyn, Paul, Bayer and Stone, chartered surveyors, on 1 July 19-2 at £1,000,000, of which £200,000 related to the land. The freehold buildings were estimated to have a residual life of 20 years.

2. The following sales took place:

   1 January 19-3 Plant and machinery which had been purchased on 1 July 19-0 at a cost of £100,000
   1 April 19-3 Plant and machinery which had been purchased on 1 July 19-1 at a cost of £6,000
   1 April 19-3 Motor vehicles which had been purchased on 1 January 19-1 at a cost of £20,000

3. The following purchases were made:

   1 July 19-2 A lease on property for 20 years for £100,000
   1 October 19-2 Motor vehicles for £32,000
   1 January 19-3 Plant and machinery for £110,000

The directors decided to depreciate freehold property and to amortise the lease as from 1 July 19-2 in accordance with accepted accounting practice. The depreciation policy for the other fixed assets was continued consistently with previous years.

Required

Prepare a note or notes for inclusion in the published accounts of The Wooden Box Company Ltd. to show the information that should be disclosed concerning the tangible fixed assets in the balance sheet at 30 June 19-3.

10.5 The directors report is required by the Companies' Act 1985 to contain the following matters:

1. Review of the business during the year and of its position at the end of the year. Principal activities of company during year and significant changes in those activities

2. Particulars of significant changes in fixed assets during the financial year. Where the market value of land differs substantially from the value shown in the balance sheet, and that difference is significant, an indication of that difference as precisely as is practicable.

3. Particulars of important events affecting the company since the end of the financial year.

4. An indication of likely future developments in business of company.

5. An indication of the company's activities in research and development.

6. Amounts of any recommended dividends and proposed transfers to reserves.

7. Names of persons who were directors of company at any time during the year. Their interests in shares or debentures of the company.

8. If money given for political or charitable purposes exceeds £200 in the financial year, a disclosure of the total given for each purpose. If the amount given to a political party exceeds £200, disclosure of the identity of the party and the amount given.

9. Information regarding the arrangements in force for securing the health, safety and welfare at work of the employees.

10. If the average number of employees exceeds 250, a statement of the company's policy regarding the employment of disabled persons.

10.6 Modified accounts for small and medium-sized companies

Small and medium-sized companies are permitted to file modified final accounts with the Registrar of Companies, although they are still required to distribute full accounts to their shareholders. To qualify for this concession they must satisfy at least two of the following criteria:

	Small Companies	Medium Companies
Turnover	Not more than £2,800,000	Not more than £11,200,000
Balance sheet total	Not more than £1,400,000	Not more than £5,600,000
Average number of employees	Not exceeding 50	Not exceeding 250

Small companies need not file a profit and loss account or directors' report. They may file a modified balance sheet showing only those items to which a letter or a Roman number is assigned in the format (see 10.2)

Medium sized companies must file a profit and loss account in which items 1,2,3 and 6 (turnover, cost of sales, other operating income) in Format 1 may be combined under the heading 'gross profit or loss', which will be the first item in that financial statement. Analyses of turnover and profit are not required. The balance sheet must be prepared in full and the directors' report filed with the accounts.

10.7 Auditor's report

The auditors report to the shareholders, not to the directors.

They must satisfy themselves that the company has kept proper accounting records and that the balance sheet and profit and loss account are in agreement with those records. They must state whether in their opinion

(a) the balance sheet and the profit and loss account have been prepared in accordance with the requirements of the Companies Act; and

(b) the balance sheet gives a true and fair view of the company's affairs at the end of the financial year, and the profit and loss account gives a true and fair view of the company's profit or loss for the financial year.

Key points to remember

1. Memorise the order of items within the formats of the Profit and Loss account and the balance sheet. As far as possible try to keep to the wording prescribed by the Companies' Act.

2. Make yourself familiar with the notes that should be appended to the profit and loss account and the balance sheet, including the forms in which such notes should be prepared as shown in this chapter.

3. Although information required for a note may not be given in a question, you should make reference in your answer to the requirement for the note and its content.

4. When required to prepare accounts in a form suitable for publication, you may be penalised just as severely for disclosing too much information as for disclosing too little; either way, you show that you are unfamiliar with the statutory requirements.

5. In most cases, it is best to treat discounts receivable as a reduction of administrative expenses in published accounts.

Common errors

1. failure to observe the order of headings within the prescribed format.

2. inclusion of items within the wrong headings.

3. notes to the accounts omitted as a result of ignorance, oversight; no reference to note because requisite information is not given in question.

Questions

Fully worked examination question

1   Sagunto Ltd has an authorised capital of 1.5 million £1 ordinary shares, of which 1 million have been issued as fully paid.

The following information was extracted from the accounts for the year ended 30 September 19-6.

	£	£		£
Freehold premises at cost		250,000	Purchases	430,000
Carriage inwards		13,500	Returns inward	18,000
Sales		750,000	Returns outward	25,000
Stock 1 Oct 19-5		80,000	Directors' remuneration	20,000
Wages & salaries:			Auditors' fees	2,500
Administration	20,000		General administrative expenses	9,000
Distribution	40,000	60,000	Discounts allowed	2,500
Motor vehicle running costs		11,000	Retained earnings	260,000
			(Cr. Bal. 1 Oct 19-5)	

Additional information:

(1) The closing stock was valued at £90,000 cost.

(2) The ordinary share dividends for the year were:

Interim   3% Already paid.

Final   8% Proposed.

(3) The directors decided to transfer £100,000 to General Reserve

(4) Expenses in arrear at 30 September 19-6 were:

	£
Motor vehicle running costs	1,100
Salaries and wages: distribution staff	3,000

(5) Expenses paid in advance at 30 September 19-6 were:

	£
General administrative expenses	1,500

(6) The liability for corporation tax for the year ended 30 September 19-6 had been agreed at £95,000

(7) The company depreciated freehold premises at 4% per annum on cost. Aggregate depreciation to 30 September 19-5 was £40,000.

(8) On 1 October 19-5 the company's assets included:

	£
Motor vehicles at cost	40,000
Depreciation to date	16,000

Depreciation is provided at 20% per annum on a reducing balance basis.

The above figures include a motor vehicle which cost £8,000, and which had been in company ownership for exactly two years. It was sold for £2,500 on 1 October 19-5. There were no other purchases or sales of vehicles during the year.

(9) The company's motor vehicles were used by staff as follows

Distribution staff 30,000 miles per annum
Administration staff 10,000 miles per annum

Required

(a) The trading and profit and loss account for the year ended 30 September 19-6

(13 marks)

(b) The appropriation account for the year ended 30 September 19-6 (4 marks)

(c) From your answer to (a) above, list those items which the company would be required to include in its published accounts under the Companies' Acts 1948-81. (8 marks)

(Total 25 marks)
(AEB)

[*Tutorial note*: The requirements of the Companies' Acts 1948-81, in so far as they relate to this question, were consolidated in the Companies Act 1985]

Answer

(a)

Sagunto Ltd   **Tutorial Notes**

Trading and Profit and Loss Account for the year ended 30 September 19-6

	£	£	£	Tutorial Notes
Turnover			732,000	2.
Less cost of sales:				
Stock at 1 October 19-5		80,000		
Purchases	405,000			3.
Carriage inwards	13,500	418,500		4.
		498,500		
Stock at 30 September 19-6		90,000	408,500	
Gross profit			323,500	5.
Distribution costs				
Wages and salaries	43,000			
Motor vehicle running costs	9,075			
Loss on disposal of vehicle	1,965			6.
Depreciation: motor vehicles	2,832	56,872		
Administrative costs				
Wages and salaries	20,000			
Directors' remuneration	20,000			
Motor vehicle running costs	3,025			
Auditors' fees	2,500			
General expenses	7,500			
Carried forward	53,025	56,872	323,500	

Tutorial Notes: 1.

	£	£	£
Brought forward	53,025	56,872	323,500
Discounts allowed	2,500		
Loss on disposal of vehicle	655		
Depreciation: motor vehicles	944		
freehold premises	10,000	67,124	123,996
Profit on ordinary operations			199,504

(b)

	£	£	
Profit on ordinary activities before taxation		199,504	7.
Tax on profit on ordinary activities		95,000	
Profit on ordinary activities after taxation		104,504	
Retained profit at 1 Oct 19-5		260,000	
		364,504	
Transfer to general reserve	100,000		
Ordinary dividend – interim	30,000		
proposed	80,000	210,000	
Retained profit carried forward		154,504	

(c) Sagunto Ltd must include the following items in its published accounts:

	£	
Turnover	732,000	8.
Cost of sales	(408,500)	
Gross profit	323,500	
Distribution costs	(56,872)	
Administration costs	(67,124)	
Profit on ordinary activities before taxation	199,504	

Notes to the accounts

1. Accounting policies.   9.
   (i) Accounting basis. The accounts have been prepared under the historic cost convention
   (ii) Depreciation of fixed assets has been provided on the following bases:
   Freehold premises: straight-line basis on 4% of cost.
   Motor vehicles: reducing balance method using rate of 20%

2. Net profit is stated after charging the following:

	£
Directors' remuneration	20,000
Auditors' remuneration	2,500
Depreciation of freehold premises	10,000
Depreciation of motor vehicles	3,776

Tutorial Notes

1. The trading and profit and loss accounts must be headed properly

2. Sales £750,000 less returns £18,000

3. Purchases £430,000 less returns £25,000

4. It is important to get the model for cost of sales correct; it must include carriage inwards.

5. Significant totals and balances e.g. cost of sales, gross profit and net profit must be recognised with descriptions.

6. Non-statutory accounts are usually prepared in such a form that the statutory accounts can easily be prepared from them. Distribution costs and administration costs are grouped accordingly in the non-statutory accounts. Reconciliation of the two sets of accounts is facilitated.

7. The headings prescribed by the Companies Act are suitable for the non-statutory accounts.

8. The list of items may well be shown in the form in which they would appear in the statutory accounts, as here. Note: only the items included in Part (a) are required.

9. These notes are required by the Companies Act. They disclose certain information not shown in the published profit and loss account, but required to be disclosed by the Act.

Examination questions

1   The following data is a summary of some of the financial information relating to Somerset plc for the year ended 30 April 1990.

   (i)   Tangible fixed assets at cost on 1 May 1989 were:

	£	
Land and buildings	450,000	(land £240,000)
Plant and machinery	370,000	
Equipment	120,000	

   Depreciation at 1 May 1989:

	£
Land and buildings	90,000
Plant and machinery	187,700
Equipment	48,000

   (ii) Land was revalued at £490,000 on 1 January 1990.

   (iii) New machinery was bought on 1 September 1989 for £88,000.

   (iv) Some equipment originally purchased on 1 August 1986 for £24,000 was sold on 1 October 1989 for £12,500.

   (v) Depreciation policy: 2% p.a. on the cost of buildings
                                 30% p.a. on the reducing balance of plant and machinery
                                 10% p.a. on the cost of equipment

   Depreciation is provided from the date the asset is bought until the date it is sold.

   (vi) Audit fees relating to the year ended 30 April 1990: paid £1,300, accrued £850.

   (vii)

	£
Manufacturing wages were	210,110
Selling and administrative wages were	97,460
Employer's national insurance costs	31,000
Employer's pension costs	25,500

   (viii) Stocks:

	Cost £	Net realisable value £
Raw materials	36,850	35,200
Work in progress	13,260	20,910
Finished goods	28,315	29,500
	78,425	85,610

   (ix) The company has issued two classes of debentures:
        12% debentures 1993-95, issued at par in 1986 for £400,000
        11% debentures 1998-99, issued at par on 1 September 1989 for £300,000.

Required

   (a) Prepare notes to the published accounts of Somerset plc for the year ended 30 April 1990, including a schedule of fixed assets, from the information available.   (15 marks)

   (b) Published accounts are available for the benefit of different categories of user. What information do you consider that management, shareholders, potential shareholders and creditors would find useful from the notes you have prepared and any others required to be published with the accounts of limited companies?   (8 marks)

(Total 23 marks)
(OXFORD)

2   The following Trial Balance was extracted from the books of Jade plc, on 31 May 1991.

	£	£
£1 Ordinary Shares		500,000
General Reserve		21,200
Profit and loss balance		22,560
Stock 1 June 1990	97,555	
Purchases	531,461	
Sales		1,085,529
Premises at cost	480,000	
Carried forward	1,109,016	1,629,289

	£	£
Brought forward	1,109,016	1,629,289
Provision for depreciation on premises		96,000
Office equipment, at cost	62,000	
Provision for depreciation on office equipment		— 34,000
Delivery vehicles at cost	31,000	
Provision for depreciation on delivery vehicles		12,000
Provision for bad debts		5,120
Creditors		85,685
Debtors	193,666	
Discounts received		16,145
Bad debts	7,200	
General administration expenses	266,267	
Bank		17,800
General distribution costs	226,190	
Loss on dale of delivery vehicle	700	
	1,896,039	1,896,039

Additional information:

1. The Authorised Capital is £800,000 in ordinary shares of £1 each.

2. Depreciation is to be provided as follows:
    (i)   delivery vehicles 20% p.a. on cost;
    (ii) office equipment 10% p.a. on cost;
    (iii) premises $2\frac{1}{2}$% p.a. on cost.

It is company policy to charge a full year's depreciation on all assets held at the year end.

Office equipment costing £6,000 was bought during the year. A delivery vehicle bought during the year ended 31 May 1989 for £7,000 was sold for £3,500 on 1 January 1991, these transactions have already been correctly dealt with in the accounts.

The premises are divided between distribution and administration in the ratio of 3:2.

3. At 31 May 1991 stock was valued as follows
    At net realisable value   £99,420
    At cost to the company   £95,200

4. Provision for bad debts is to be provided as £586 for a specific debt plus $2\frac{1}{2}$% on the remainder of debtors. This item is to be treated as an administration expense.

5. £160 is owing for general distribution costs, and the general administration expenses include a prepayment of £920.

6. The directors recommend a transfer to general reserve of £10,000, and an ordinary share dividend of 6%.

7. Corporation Tax for the year on the profit from ordinary activities is estimated at £17,400.

Required

A   A profit and loss account for the year ended 31 May 1991, and a balance sheet as at that date. These to be in accordance with the minimum required by the Companies Act 1985. (Notes to the accounts are not required.)   (18 marks)

B   A schedule of fixed assets as it would appear in the notes to the accounts of Jade plc.
                                                                                  (7 marks)

C   Using illustrations from the question, briefly explain the following:
    a)   authorised capital and issued capital;
    b)   revenue reserves and provisions;
    c)   the closing stock valuation used in final accounts.   (6 marks)

                                                                    (Total 31 marks)
                                                                          OXFORD

3   Borsetshire Limited's trial balance at 31 May 19-8 was as follows:

	£	£
Advertising	10,500	
Bad debts	587	
Bank interest	2,030	
Bank overdraft		17,750
Cash in hand	370	
Creditors		31,272
Delivery expenses	15,103	
Debtors	107,810	
Debenture interest	1,300	
Directors' salaries	33,600	
Fixtures and fittings (cost £35,000)	17,900	
General reserve		70,000
Insurance	1,900	
Issued share capital:		
100,000 Ordinary shares of £1 each		100,000
43,750 8% Preference shares of £1 each		43,750
Leasehold premises (cost £280,000)	245,000	
Motor Vehicles (cost £56,200)	53,550	
Profit and Loss account		34,895
Provision for bad debts		2,400
Purchases	268,464	
Rent and rates	11,550	
Sales (exclusive of VAT)		468,570
Share premium account		35,250
Stock	20,280	
Sundry expenses	8,268	
Wages and salaries	31,675	
10% debenture 19-0/-5		26,000
	829,887	829,887

Notes

(1) Stock at 31 May 19-8 was valued at £37,100.

(2) The delivery expenses were the only distribution costs during the year.

(3) Authorised share capital is as follows:

200,000 Ordinary shares of £1 each.

50,000 8% Preference shares of £1 each.

(4) The remainder of the debenture interest is to be accrued.

(5) Depreciation is to be provided as follows:

Leasehold premises at 4% p.a. on cost

Motor vehicles at 20% p.a. on cost

Fixtures and fittings at 40% on reducing balance

(6) A dividend of 5% is proposed on the ordinary shares, and the full year's preference dividend is to be provided for.

(7) £4,200 is owing for wages and salaries, and £200 has been prepaid for rent at 31 May 19-8

(8) Corporation Tax for the year is to be provided for in the sum of £19,000

(9) The provision for bad debts is to be increased to £2,900

(10) No fixed assets were bought or sold in the year

You are required to prepare

Borsetshire Limited's profit and loss account for the year ended 31 May 19-8 and a balance sheet as at that date, in a form suitable for publication and complying, in so far as the information permits, with the disclosure requirements of the Companies Act 1985.   (25 marks)
(LONDON)

4 (a) You are required to arrange the following balances in a format that would be acceptable for publication in the audited accounts of Sigma Signs plc. The balances relate to the year ended 31 December 19-5

	Dr. £'000s	Cr. £'000s
Interest receivable		1,200
Cost of Sales	12,362	
Distributive Costs	893	
Administrative Expenses	1,121	
Interest payable	960	
Turnover		18,326
Taxation on Profit on Ordinary Activities	870	
Extraordinary Loss (net of Taxation)	738	
Proposed Ordinary Dividend	1,200	

(12 marks)

(b) Explain the logic of the presentation that you have used in presenting the accounts of Sigma Signs plc.

(6 marks)

(Total 18 marks)

(JMB)

5 The following balances have been extracted from the ledger of Greengrove plc on 31 March 1992.

	£000	£000
Purchases	500	
Sales		1,200
Stock at 1 April 1991	55	
General expenses – administration	10	
– distribution	15	
Salaries – administration	50	
– distribution	65	
Debenture interest paid	30	
Income from fixed asset investments		10
Interim dividend paid	20	
Depreciation written off		
– property (an administrative overhead)	20	
– equipment (an administrative overhead)	10	
– motor vehicles (a distributive overhead)	10	
Retained profits at 1 April 1991		900

The following information is related to the accounts of Greengrove plc for the year ended 31 March 1992.

(i)   Stocks at 31 March 1992 were £65,000.

(ii) Corporation tax on the 1991/92 profits is estimated at £175,000.

(iii) A final dividend of £40,000 is proposed.

(iv) Salaries include the following emoluments in respect of directors:

	£
S Black (sales director)	35,000
R White (finance director)	25,000
W Green (chairman)	14,000

(v) Provision is to be made for the following costs which were unpaid at 31 March 1992.

	£
Audit fee	5,000
Hire of Plant	2,500

(vi) The debentures are repayable in the year 2002.

(vii)   The called up share capital is 800,000 ordinary shares of £1 each.

Requirement

You are required to prepare the profit and loss and appropriation account for publication (including relevant notes) of Greengrove plc for the year ended 31 March 1992 in accordance with the minimum requirements of the Companies Acts and related statements of standard accounting practice. (20 marks)

(N.I)

6 The following trial balance was extracted from the books of Bardon Trading PLC on 31 March 19-7:

	£	£
Called-up capital:		
1,760,000 Ordinary shares of 25p each		440,000
200,000 10% Preference shares of £1 each,75p called		150,000
Delivery vehicles, at cost	51,000	
Provision for depreciation of delivery vehicles		21,000
Bank loan		60,000
Sales		1,321,000
Cost of sales	1,025,005	
Fixtures and fittings at cost	43,100	
Provision for depreciation of fixtures and fittings		19,040
Stock at 31 March 19-7	278,122	
Freehold premises, at cost	390,000	
13% Loan stock 1997, unsecured		200,000
Profit and loss account balance	62,550	
Trade debtors	322,160	
Trade creditors		181,200
General reserve		50,000
Management expenses	62,600	
Calls on Preference shares unpaid	500	
Interest on loan stock	13,000	
Insurances	3,000	
Directors' fees	33,300	
Interest on bank loan	4,100	
Cash at bank and in hand	52,703	
Wages and salaries	101,100	
	2,442,240	2,442,240

The following matters have to be taken into consideration in preparing the final accounts:

(i) A half year's interest is due on the 13% loan stock

(ii) Depreciation is to be provided as follows:

Fixtures and fittings at the rate of 10 % per annum on cost.

Delivery vehicles at the rate of 20% per annum on cost. They include a new delivery vehicle which was purchased at a cost of £8,000 on 1 October 19-6.

(iii) Authorised capital is as follows:

Ordinary shares of 25p each	£500,000
Preference shares of £1 each	£200,000

(iv) The following apportionments are made between administration expenses and selling and distribution expenses:

	Administration	Selling & distribution
Wages and salaries	75%	25%
Directors' Fees	100%	
Insurance	two-thirds	one-third
Management	80%	20%

(v) Wages and salaries owing amount to £900 and insurance prepaid amounts to £300.

(vi) One year's dividend is to be provided for on the nominal value of the preference shares.

(vii) One quarter of the bank loan is repayable during the year ended 31 March, 19-8 and the remainder after that date.

Required

Prepare a Profit and Loss Account for the year ended 31 March 19-7 and a Balance Sheet as at that date, drawn up in vertical form incorporating all the information provided, for internal use and for publication, in so far as possible from the information provided.

(28 marks)
(WJEC)

7   The main purpose of a company's annual published statements is to give information about the results of trading activities and also the financial position of the business.

Legal requirements influence the contents of such statements with companies frequently being faced with demands by a variety of users for greater and wider levels of disclosure.

Companies generally seek to improve the quality and effectiveness of the statements which they prepare to satisfy these requests.

Required

(a) State clearly the purposes of published financial statements.   (8 marks)

(b) Describe the problems that public companies must consider when preparing annual financial statements for publication.   (8 marks)

(c) Outline what you consider are the basic characteristics (e.g. clarity) needed to produce effective financial statements.   (8 marks)

Total 24 marks
(AEB)

11 Accounting standards

Chapter objectives

Statements of Standard Accounting Practice (SSAPs) and Financial Reporting Standards (FRSs) are a very important topic at Advanced Level and are specifically included in the syllabi; they may be examined either

❑ directly in questions requiring explanations or discussion of the principles involved in one or more specified Standards

❑ directly in questions requiring an explanation of the correct accounting treatment of certain transactions or situations according to Standards not specified in the question

❑ indirectly in accounting questions where the correct treatment of transactions or situations will only result from an application of an appropriate Standard

11.1 About SSAPs and FRSs

1. An unsatisfactory situation existed in company reporting up to the end of the 1960's.

2. Treatment by companies of certain kinds of transactions and the way they reported certain situations was not necessarily incorrect, but relied upon opinions of directors and accountants.

3. As result of 2. above, the objectivity upon which company reporting should be based suffered, and so did public confidence in the accounting profession.

4. To remedy the situation, the major professional accountancy bodies established the Consultative Committee of Accountancy Bodies (CCAB) to coordinate future policies and pronouncements regarding recommended practices.

5. The Accounting Standards Committee (ASC) was a sub-committee of the CCAB and its purpose was to set standards, the objects of which were:

   1. To narrow the areas of difference and variety in accounting;
   2. To recommend disclosure of accounting bases;
   3. To require disclosure of departure from standards;
   4. To introduce a system for wide consultation on standard setting;
   5. To seek improvements in existing disclosure requirements of company law and the Stock Exchange.

6. In 1990, The Financial Reporting Council was established. It is independent of the accountancy profession and guides the standard setting process.

7. The Accounting Standards Board (ASB) has replaced the Accounting Standards Committee and issues Financial Reporting Standards (FRS) without having to obtain the prior agreement of the CCAB.

8. In 1991, an Urgent Issues Task Force (UITF) was formed to tackle urgent matters not covered by existing standards, and for which, given the urgency, the normal standard setting process would not be practicable. The Force makes Consensus Pronouncements

9. All members of the professional accountancy bodies comprising the CCAB are expected to comply with standards currently in use. All auditors of limited companies belong to one of four of the bodies as do many company directors and company accountants.

10. Any significant departure from any of the standards must be disclosed in the accounts unless it would be impracticable or misleading to do so in the context of giving a true and fair view.

11. Deliberate failure to comply with the standards can result in the appropriate professional body taking disciplinary action against the offending member or members.

11.2 Summaries of the statements of standard accounting practice and financial reporting standards

SSAP 1 Accounting for associated companies

Tutorial note: We have already met the term 'Related company' in the balance sheet format in Chapter 10. The Companies Act 1985 defines 'Related company' slightly differently from the definition given to 'Associated company' in this SSAP. Advanced level students may take the two terms as being synonymous.

The relevance of this SSAP lies in the fact that an increasing number of companies have extended their operations by acquiring trade investments, entering into joint ventures or forming consortia (plural of consortium: a temporary arrangement for companies to co-operate to achieve an objective). Such arrangements do not amount to the creation of a holding company/subsidiary company relationship.

Associated company: A company in which the interest of the group (or company) is for the long term investing and is substantial and having regard to the disposition of the other shareholdings, the investing group (or company) is in a position to exercise a significant influence over the company in which the investment is made.

Significant influence over a company means participation in, but not necessarily control over, the financial and operating policy decisions of that company, including the dividend policy.

Where the interest of the investing group or company amounts to 20 per cent or more of the equity voting rights of a company, it should be presumed that the investing group or company has the ability to exercise significant influence over that company unless it can clearly be demonstrated otherwise. When considering the amount of investment in a company, the aggregate of all the shares held in it by all the companies in a group must be taken into account.

An associated company is not a subsidiary of the investing company.

Standard accounting practice

Investing company's own financial statements:

An investing company must show in its own financial statements dividends received and receivable from associated companies.

An investing company's interest in an associated company will be shown in the balance sheet at cost less amounts written off, unless it is shown at a valuation.

Consolidated financial statements

An investing group's consolidated profit and loss account must show the group's share of the before-tax profit of the associated company and separate disclosure of the tax attributable to that share of profit.

The names of the principal associated companies should be disclosed in the financial statements of the investing company with details, for each of the companies, of the proportion of the number of the issued shares of each class held and an indication of the nature of its business.

SSAP 2 Disclosure of accounting policies

Tutorial note: This SSAP is an important examination topic and students should be familiar with its contents.

The relevance of this SSAP lies in the fact that prior to its introduction in 1971, some companies abused or made arbitrary use of accounting principles. The publicity given in the Press in the 1960s to some unfortunate events in corporate accounting began to undermine the accountancy profession's credibility.

The SSAP is intended to allow less flexibility in the observance of accounting principles and to compel directors to select and adhere to specific accounting policies which should be disclosed by way of note to the accounts.

The SSAP defines three terms:

Fundamental Accounting Concepts

Broad basic assumptions which underlie the periodic financial accounts of business enterprises.

The SSAP mentions four concepts in particular: going concern; accruals; consistency; prudence.

Accounting Bases

The methods which have been developed for expressing or applying fundamental accounting concepts to financial transactions and items.

The SSAP mentions a number of matters for which different accounting bases are recognised: depreciation of fixed assets; (e.g straight line, reducing balance, etc.) treatment and amortisation of intangibles (such as research and development expenditure, patents and trade marks); stocks and work in progress (e.g. FIFO, LIFO AVCO, etc.); long term contracts etc.

Accounting Policies

The specific accounting bases judged by business enterprises to be most appropriate to their circumstances, and adopted by them for the purpose of preparing their financial accounts.

The SSAP defines the four concepts mentioned above.

(a) **The Going Concern Concept**: the enterprise will continue in operational existence for the foreseeable future. This means in particular that the profit and loss account and the balance sheet assume no intention or necessity to liquidate or curtail significantly the scale of operation.

(b) **The Accruals Concept**: revenue and costs are accrued (that is, recognised as they are earned or incurred, not as money is received or paid), matched with one another so far as their relationship can be established or justifiably assumed, and dealt with in the profit and loss account of the period to which they relate; but if the accruals concept conflicts with the concept of prudence in any particular circumstance, the latter prevails.

(c) **The Consistency Concept**: there is consistency of accounting treatment of like items within each accounting period and from one period to the next.

(d) **The Prudence Concept**: revenue and profits are not anticipated, but are recognised by inclusion in the profit and loss account only when realised in the form either of cash or of other assets the ultimate cash realisation of which can be assessed with reasonable certainty: provision is made for all known liabilities (expenses and losses) whether the amount of these is known with certainty or is a best estimate in the light of the information available.

Requirements of SSAP

If accounts are prepared using different concepts from the four mentioned above, that fact must be disclosed. In the absence of a clear statement to the contrary, there is a presumption that the four fundamental concepts have been observed.

The accounting policies followed for dealing with items which are judged to be material or critical in determining profit or loss for the year and in stating the financial position should be disclosed by way of a note to the accounts.

Tutorial note: The Companies Act 1985 includes all four of the above concepts as the accounting principles stated in schedule 4 of the Act.

SSAP 3 Earnings per share

This SSAP applies only to companies listed on a recognised stock exchange; such companies are required by this SSAP to show the earnings per share on the face of the profit and loss account.

Earnings per share is important as it forms the basis for calculating Price/Earnings ratios which are universal indicators of companies' performances

Definitions

Earnings: The profit in pence attributable to each equity share, based on the profit of the period after tax and extraordinary items and after deducting preference dividends and other appropriations in respect of preference shares. In the case of a group, the relevant profit is the consolidated profit; the profit attributable to minority interests must be deducted.

Earnings per share: Earnings as defined above divided by the number of equity shares in issue and ranking for dividend in respect of the period

SSAP 4 Accounting for government grants

Under certain circumstances, businesses may obtain government grants towards expenditure incurred. The grants may be towards revenue expenditure (for example, wages in an area having high unemployment), or capital expenditure.

Revenue-based grants should be credited to revenue in the same period in which the revenue expenditure to which they relate is charged.

Grants relating to fixed assets should be credited to revenue over the expected useful life of the asset by:

(a) crediting the amount of the grant to the fixed asset account; or

(b) crediting the amount to a defered income account, and transferring a portion of the amount to revenue annually.

This SSAP was issued in 1974. As the Companies Act 1985 requires fixed assets to be shown at purchase price, method (a) above is now considered to be unacceptable.

SSAP 5 Accounting for value added tax

In the case of businesses registered for VAT purposes, sales should be credited to the Sales account net of VAT and the VAT credited to 'H.M.Customs and Excise' account. Similarly, purchases should be debited net of VAT to Purchases account, and the VAT debited to 'H.M.Customs and Excise' account. Any credit balance on 'H.M.Customs and Excise' account is an amount due to them; a debit balance represents the amount of refund due from H.M.Customs and Excise.

In the following cases, VAT is not recoverable on purchases:

(a) businesses not registered for VAT

(b) businesses carrying on exempted activities, such as banks and insurance companies

(c) 'non-deductible inputs', VAT on private motor cars and entertainment of UK customers. In these cases, the gross amount of expenditure (including VAT) will be debited to the accounts concerned.

In all other cases, sales, purchases and expenses will be shown 'net' in the accounts.

SSAP 8 The treatment of taxation under the imputation system in the accounts of companies

Tutorial note: Companies are subject to Corporation tax on their profits, the tax being payable 9 months after the end of the financial year. When a company pays a dividend, it must make an advance payment of part of the corporation tax due on the profit of the year on which the dividend is paid. This payment of Advance Corporation Tax (ACT) is 'imputed' to the recipients of the dividend, who receive the dividend and a tax credit (a 'certificate') equal to their 'share' of the ACT. 'Franked Investment Income' is a dividend received by one company from another UK company. Companies deduct ACT paid during a year from the Corporation Tax liability on the profit for the year to arrive at the Mainstream Corporation Tax which is payable nine months after the end of their financial year.

The SSAP requires the following:

Companies must show:

• Franked Investment Income in their profit and loss account gross; ie the amount of cash received plus the tax credit.

• Dividends paid or proposed in their profit and loss account net ie only the amount of cash paid or payable.

• Corporation tax must be shown in the appropriate place in the profit and loss account format.

Taxation liabilities are shown in the balance sheet under the heading 'Creditors: amounts falling due within one year, other creditors including taxation and social security'. The liability includes the amount due for corporation tax on the profits for the period less any ACT recoverable from the payment (= mainstream corporation tax). ACT payable on the proposed dividend must be included as a liability under this heading. ACT recoverable on the proposed dividend will be deducted from the balance on the Deferred Tax account under the heading of 'Provisions for liabilities and charges: Taxation including deferred taxation.' If there is no Deferred Tax account, ACT recoverable will be shown as a deferred current asset.

SSAP 9 Stocks and work in progress

Tutorial note: This is probably the SSAP which forms the basis of examination questions more than any other. It is one with which the student must be properly acquainted because of the considerable impact which the valuation of stocks and work in progress can have on profit and the working capital of a business. The topic is dealt with further in Chapter 17.

Definitions:

Stocks and work in progress include:

(a) goods or other assets purchased for resale

(b) consumable stores

(c) raw materials and components purchased for incorporation into products for sale

(d) products and services in intermediate stages of completion

(e) finished goods

Cost: expenditure which has been incurred in the normal course of business in bringing the product or service to its present location and condition.

Cost of conversion comprises:

(a) costs which are specifically attributable to units of production,i.e.direct labour, direct expenses and sub-contracted work;

(b) production overheads (see below);

(c) other overheads, if applicable.

Production overheads: overheads incurred in respect of materials, labour or services for production, based on the normal level of activity, taking one year with another.

Net realisable value: the actual or estimated selling price

less:

(a) all further costs to completion; and

(b) all costs to be incurred in marketing, selling and distributing.

FIFO (first in, first out): the calculation of the cost of stocks and work in progress on the basis that the quantities in hand represent the latest purchases or production.

LIFO (last in, first out): the calculation of the cost of stocks and work in progress on the basis that the quantities in hand represent the earliest purchases or production.

Long term contract: a contract entered into for manufacture or building of a single substantial entity or the provision of a service where the time taken to manufacture, build or provide is such that a substantial proportion of all such contract work will extend for a period exceeding one year.

Requirements of SSAP

Stocks and Work in Progress (other than long term contract work in progress) should be stated at the total of the lower of cost and net realisable value of the separate items of stock and work in progress or of groups of similar items.

To compare the total realisable value of stocks with the total cost could result in an unacceptable setting off of foreseeable losses against unrealised profit.

Acceptable bases of valuation at cost:

FIFO (see Chapter 17)

AVCO (see Chapter 17)

Standard cost (provided it bears a reasonable relationship to actual costs obtaining during the period)

(see Chapter 22)

Not acceptable:

LIFO (see Chapter 17) (LIFO often results in stock being stated in the balance sheet at amounts that bear little relationship to recent cost levels.)

Base stock (As for LIFO)

Replacement cost (Unless it provides best measure of net realisable value, and net realisable value is less than cost.)

Manufactured Goods and Work in Progress should be valued at total cost of production and not prime cost even though some of the production overheads may accrue on a time basis.

Tutorial note: This will result in some overheads being carried forward to a future period in the closing stock instead of being borne in the period in which they were incurred. This seems to conflict with the concept of prudence; but the SSAP takes the view that the recommended practice matches costs to revenue and gives a true and fair view of profit.

Long Term Contracts These should be valued at cost plus any attributable profit, less any foreseeable losses and progress payments received and receivable. If anticipated losses on individual contracts exceed cost incurred to date less progress payments received and receivable, such excesses should be shown separately as provisions. (Attributable profit is that part of the total profit currently estimated to arise over the duration of the contract which fairly reflects the profit attributable to that part of the work performed at the accounting date.)

SSAP 12 Accounting for depreciation

Tutorial note: This is another important examination topic; students should familiarise themselves thoroughly with the requirements of this SSAP.

Depreciation is the measure of the wearing out, consumption or other loss of value of a fixed asset whether arising from use, effluxion of time or obsolescence through technology and market changes. (as defined by SSAP 12).

Accounting treatment

Provision for depreciation of fixed assets having a finite useful life should be made by allocating the cost (or revalued amount) less estimated residual values of the assets as fairly as possible to the periods expected to benefit from their use.

Where there is a revision of the estimated useful life of an asset, the unamortised cost should be charged over the revised remaining useful life.

If at any time the unamortised cost of an asset is seen to be irrecoverable in full, it should be written down immediately to the estimated recoverable amount which should be charged over the remaining useful life.

A change from one method of providing depreciation to another is permissible only on the grounds that the new method will give a fairer presentation of the results and of the financial position.

Where there is a change from one method of depreciation to another, the unamortised cost of the asset should be written off over the remaining useful life on the new basis commencing with the period in which the change is made. The effect should be disclosed in the year of change, if material.

Where assets are revalued in the financial statements, the provision for depreciation should be based upon the revalued amount and current estimate of remaining useful life, with disclosure in the year of change, of the effect of the revaluation, if material.

It is not appropriate to omit charging depreciation of a fixed asset on the grounds that its market value is greater than its net book value.

Freehold land, unless subject to depletion by, for example, the extraction of minerals or to reduction in value due to other circumstances, will not normally require a provision for depreciation. However, the value of freehold land may be adversely affected by considerations such as the desirability of its location either socially or in relation to available sources of materials, labour or sales and in these circumstances it should be written down.

Buildings have a limited life which may be materially affected by technological and environmental changes and they should be depreciated using the same criteria as in the case of other fixed assets.

An increase in the value of land and buildings does not remove the necessity for charging depreciation on the buildings.

This SSAP does not apply to investment properties, see SSAP19.

The following should be disclosed in the financial statements for each major class of depreciable asset:

(a) the depreciation methods used;

(b) the useful lives or the depreciation rates used;

(c) total depreciation allocated for the period;

(d) the gross amount of depreciable assets and the related accumulated depreciation.

SSAP 13 Accounting for research and development

Definitions:

Pure research

Original investigation undertaken in order to gain new scientific or technical knowledge and understanding; not primarily directed towards any specific practical aim or objective.

Applied research

Original investigation undertaken in order to gain new scientific or technical knowledge and directed towards a specific practical aim or objective.

Development

The use of scientific or technical knowledge in order to produce new or substantially improved materials, devices, products, processes, systems or services prior to the commencement of commercial production.

Accounting treatment

The cost of **fixed assets** acquired or constructed to provide facilities for research and development activities over a number of accounting periods should be capitalised and written off over their useful life.

Tutorial note: In other words, treated like any other fixed asset.

Other expenditure on **pure and applied research** should be written off in the year of expenditure

Development expenditure should be written off in the year of expenditure except in the following circumstances when it may be deferred to future periods:

(a) there is a **clearly defined project**

(b) the related expenditure is **separately identifiable**

(c) The outcome of such a project has been assessed with reasonable certainty as to

    (i) its **technical feasibility**

    (ii) its ultimate **commercial viability**

(d) If further development costs are to be incurred on the same project the **aggregate of such costs** are reasonably expected to be **more than covered** by related future revenues.

(e) **Adequate resources** exist, or are reasonably expected to be available, to enable the project to be completed and to provide any consequential increases in working capital.

Development costs deferred to future periods should be amortised. Amortisation should commence with the commercial production or application of the product, and should be allocated on a systematic basis to each accounting period by reference to either (i) the sale or use of the product, or (ii) the period over which it is expected to be sold or used.

Disclosure requirements

The accounting policy on research and development expenditure should be stated and explained.

The total amount of research and development expenditure charged in the profit and loss account should be disclosed. It should be analysed between current year expenditure and amounts amortised from deferred expenditure.

SSAP 15 Accounting for deferred tax

The liability to tax is calculated on a different profit figure from that appearing in the profit and loss account of a company. That is because some items of expense not deductible for tax purposes have been deducted in the profit and loss account, whilst other items, not subject to corporation tax have been credited in the profit and loss account.

There are other items which are taxable, or allowable as deductions for tax purposes, but not in the same period as they appear in the profit and loss account; they are recognised for tax purposes in a later period. Income accrued but not received will be credited in the profit and loss account in the year in which it is receivable, but will not be taxed until it is actually received in a later period. A general provision for bad debts will not be allowed for tax purposes, but the debts will be allowed if they actually become bad in a later period. These are examples of timing differences. Depreciation is another such item.

The SSAP states that provision should be made for tax on items which are the subject of timing differences and sets out the accounting treatment for the provision for 'deferred tax'.

In the profit and loss account:

Deferred tax relating to the ordinary activities of the company should be shown separately as a part of the tax on profit or loss on ordinary activities, either on the face of the profit and loss account or in a note.

In the balance sheet

The deferred tax balance, and its major components, should be disclosed in the balance sheet or in a note.

Transfers to or from deferred tax should be disclosed in a note.

Advance corporation tax which is available for offset against deferred tax liabilities (ACT recoverable on a proposed dividend) should be deducted from the balance on the deferred tax account.

SSAP 17 Accounting for post balance sheet events

Events arising after the balance sheet date need to be reflected in the financial statements of a company if they provide additional evidence of conditions that existed at the balance sheet date and materially affect the amounts to be included.

Definitions:

Post balance sheet events are those events, both favourable and unfavourable, which occur between the balance sheet date and the date on which the financial statements are approved by the board of directors.

Adjusting events are post balance sheet events which provide additional evidence of conditions existing at the balance sheet date. e.g. fixed assets may have been purchased or sold before the balance sheet date, but the purchase or selling price, as the case may be, was not determined until after the balance sheet date. The valuation of property after the balance sheet date may provide evidence of the value of that property at the balance sheet date. Adjusting events require changes in amounts to be included in the financial statements.

Non-adjusting events are post balance sheet events which concern conditions which did not exist at the balance sheet date; e.g. losses of fixed assets or stocks after the balance sheet date as a result of a catastrophe such as fire or flood; closing a significant part of the trading activities after the balance sheet date if this was not anticipated at the year end.

A material post balance sheet event requires **changes** in the amounts to be included in the financial statements where:

(a) it is an adjusting event; or

(b) it indicates that application of the going concern concept to the whole or a material part of the company is not appropriate.

A material post balance sheet event should be **disclosed** where:

(a) it is a non-adjusting event of such materiality that its non-disclosure would affect the ability of the users of the financial statements to reach a proper understanding of the financial position; or

(b) it is the reversal or maturity after the end of the year end of a transaction entered into before the year end, the substance of which was primarily to alter the appearance of the company's balance sheet.

In this case, the following information should be stated by way of notes in the financial statements:

(a) the nature of the event; and

(b) an estimate of the financial effect, or a statement that it is not practicable to make such an estimate.

SSAP 18 Accounting for contingencies

Definition: A contingency is a condition which exists at the balance sheet date, where the outcome will be confirmed only on the occurrence or non-occurrence of one or more uncertain future events.

Accounting practice: A material contingent material loss should be accrued in the financial statements where it is **probable** that a future event will confirm a loss which can be estimated with reasonable accuracy at the date on which the financial statements are approved by the board of directors.

A material contingent loss not accrued should be disclosed except where the possibility of loss is **remote**.

Contingent gains should not be accrued in the financial statements. A material contingent gain should be disclosed in financial statements only if it is probable that the gain will be realised.

The treatment of contingent losses and gains may easily be memorised from the following summary:

	Contingent losses	Contingent gains
Probable	Accrue in accounts	Disclose
Possible	Do not accrue but disclose	Not disclosed
Remote	No need to disclose	Not disclosed

The following information should be stated by way of notes in respect of each contingency which is required to be disclosed:

(a) the nature of the contingency

(b) the uncertainties which are expected to affect the ultimate outcome; and

(c) a prudent estimate of the financial effect, or a statement that it is not practicable to make such an estimate.

SSAP 19 Accounting for investment properties

Investment properties should not be subject to periodic charges for depreciation on the basis set out in SSAP 12, except for properties held on lease which should be depreciated on the basis set out in SSAP 12 at least over the period when the unexpired term is 20 years or less.

Investment properties should be included in the balance sheet at their open market value.

Changes in the value of investment properties should not be taken to the profit and loss account but should be disclosed as a movement on an investment revaluation reserve;. There should never be a debit balance on the investment revaluation reserve; any deficit should be charged in the profit and loss account in the period in which it arises.

SSAP 20 Foreign currency translation

Individual companies

Each asset, liability, revenue or cost arising from a transaction denominated in a foreign currency should be translated into the local currency at the exchange rate in operation on the date on which the transaction occurred. An average rate may be used as an approximation if the rates do not fluctuate significantly. Where a trading transaction is to be settled at a contracted rate, that rate should be used.

At each balance sheet date, monetary assets and liabilities should be translated by using the closing rate.

All exchange gains or losses on settled transactions should be reported as part of the profit or loss for the year from ordinary activities.

The methods used in the translation of the financial statements of foreign enterprises and the treatment afforded to exchange differences should be disclosed in the financial statements. The net movement on reserves arising from exchange differences should also be disclosed.

The statement deals separately with foreign currency translation in group accounts.

SSAP 21 Accounting for lease and hire purchase contracts

Definitions

A finance lease is a lease that transfers substantially all the risks and rewards of ownership of an asset to the lessee.

An operating lease is a lease other than a finance lease.

A hire purchase contract is a contract for the hire of an asset which contains a provision giving the hirer an option to acquire legal title to the asset upon the fulfilment of certain conditions stated in the contract.

A finance charge is the amount borne by the lessee over the lease term, representing the difference between the total of the lease payments and the amount at which he records the leased asset at the inception of the lease. Hire purchase contracts which are of a financing nature should be accounted for on a basis similar to that set out below for finance leases.

Accounting by lessees

A finance lease should be recorded in the balance sheet of the lessee as an asset and as an oblig- ation to pay future rentals at the present value of the minimum lease payments. The fair value of the asset will often be a sufficiently close approximation to the present value of the minimum lease payments and may be substituted for it. (This treatment recognises that the substance of the transaction is more relevant for accounting purposes than its legal form.)

Rentals payable should be apportioned between the finance charge and repayment of the capital sum. The total finance charge under a finance lease should be allocated to accounting periods during the lease term so as to produce a constant periodic rate of charge on the remaining balance of the obligation for each accounting period.

An asset leased under a finance lease should be depreciated over the shorter of the lease term and its useful life. An asset being acquired under a hire purchase contract should be depreciated over its useful life. Rentals payable under an operating lease should be charged on a straight line basis over the lease term, even if the payments are not made on such a basis.

Accounting by lessors

Lessors should show amounts due from lessees under finance leases as debtors in the balance sheet; the assets will not be recorded as fixed assets. On the other hand, assets held for use in operating leases by a lessor should be recorded as fixed assets in the lessor's balance sheet and depreciated over their useful lives.

The total gross earnings (finance income) under a finance lease should normally be allocated to accounting periods to give a constant periodic rate of return on the lessor's net cash investment in the lease in each period

Disclosure by lessees

Lessees must disclose the gross amounts of assets which are held under finance leases (or hire purchase contracts) together with the related accumulated depreciation. Disclosure must be for each major class of asset. The total depreciation allocated for a period in respect of assets held under finance leases should be disclosed by each major class of asset.

Lessees must show the amounts of obligations related to finance leases (net of finance charges allocated to future periods) separately from other obligations and liabilities. The obligations should be analysed between amounts payable in the next year, amounts payable in the second to fifth years inclusive from the balance sheet date, and the aggregate amounts payable there- after.

The aggregate finance charges allocated for the period in respect of finance leases (or hire purchase contracts) must be disclosed.

Disclosure by lessors

Lessors must show the net investment in (i) finance leases and (ii) hire purchase contracts at each balance sheet date. They must also disclose the gross amounts of assets held for use in operating leases, and the related accumulated depreciation charges.

Lessors must disclose the policy adopted for accounting for operating leases, finance leases and hire purchase contracts. They must also disclose the aggregate rentals receivable in respect of an accounting period.

SSAP 22 Accounting for goodwill

Definitions

Goodwill is the difference between the value of a business as a whole and the aggregate of the fair values of its separable net assets.

Purchased goodwill is goodwill which is established as a result of the purchase of a business accounted for as an acquisition.

Non-purchased goodwill is any goodwill other than purchased goodwill.

Negative goodwill arises when the aggregate of the fair values of the separable net assets exceeds the value of the business as a whole.

Accounting practice

Non-purchased goodwill should not be shown in the balance sheet.

The amount to be attributed to goodwill should be the difference between the fair value of the consideration given and the aggregate of the fair values of the separable net assets acquired.

The amount attributed to purchased goodwill should not include any value for separable intangibles. The amount of these, if material, should be included under the appropriate heading within intangible fixed assets in the balance sheet.

Purchased goodwill should not be carried in the balance sheet of a company as a permanent item.

Purchased goodwill (other than negative goodwill) should normally be eliminated from the accounts immediately on acquisition against reserves, or may be amortised through the profit and loss account in arriving at profit or loss on ordinary activities on a systematic basis over its useful life.

Purchased goodwill should not be revalued. A permanent diminution in the value of purchased goodwill should be written down immediately through the profit and loss account to its estimated recoverable value.

Negative goodwill should be credited directly to reserve.

The accounting policy followed in respect of goodwill should be explained in the notes to the accounts.

While this text was being typeset, the ASB issued a discussion document (Exposure Draft) of which students should be aware. It contains a proposal to withdraw from companies the option of writing goodwill off against reserves. This will make it impossible for directors to 'hide' the amount that they have paid for goodwill on acquisitions. Although companies have to disclose all movements on reserves, not all shareholders have the ability to understand the significance of amounts written off to reserves. Hiding items in reserves (or 'reserve accounting') is a method by which directors could conceal from shareholders information (in this case, the amount paid for goodwill) which should really be shown in the balance sheet.

Another objection to writing goodwill off against reserves is the immediate effect that this has on the net worth of the acquiring company.

The principle recommendations of the Exposure Draft are:

1. *Goodwill should be shown in the balance sheet ('capitalised') and not written off to reserves on acquisition.*

2. *The life expectancy and value of goodwill should be reviewed annually.*

3. *Goodwill need not be written down if its value is expected to be maintained indefinitely.*

4. *If the goodwill is expected to have a limited life, it should be amortised through the profit and loss account on a systematic basis over a period not exceeding 20 years unless there are good reasons for taking a longer period. In the latter event, such reasons must be disclosed in the company's accounts.*

5. *Companies will be permitted to 'write back' goodwill which has already been written off to reserves and to show it in the balance sheet. This is not expected to be made compulsory.*

To overcome the problem of equity depletion, some companies have apportioned amounts paid for goodwill to such intangible fixed assets as 'brands' acquired with the purchased undertaking. These intangible fixed assets are then shown in the balance sheet and the payment for 'goodwill' has been correspondingly reduced.

The Exposure Draft will permit these intangible fixed assets to be shown separately in the balance sheet if they could be reliably valued at the time of acquisition and disposed of separately from the goodwill. Intangible assets shown this way on the balance sheet must be treated in the same way as capitalised goodwill.

A new standard to replace SSAP 22 will have to be introduced if effect is to be given to these proposals.

SSAP 24 Accounting for pension costs

Importance of pension costs

The provision of a pension is part of the remuneration package of many employees. Pension costs form a significant proportion of total payroll costs and they give rise to special problems of estimation and of allocation between accounting periods. Accordingly, it is important that standard accounting practice exists concerning the recognition of such costs in the employers' financial statements. This statement deals with the accounting for, and the disclosure of, pension costs and commitments in the financial statements of enterprises that have pension arrangements for the provision of retirement benefits for their employees.

A defined contribution scheme is one in which the benefits are directly determined by the value of contributions paid in respect of each member; the benefits are not guaranteed. The cost to the employer is easily determined.

A defined benefit scheme is a pension scheme in which the rules specify the benefits to be paid and the scheme is financed accordingly. Contributions to the fund are expected to be sufficient to enable the benefits to be paid. An employer may have to make good any deficiencies, and to that extent, the cost to the company is uncertain.

Defined benefit schemes rely upon periodical actuarial valuations to determine the cost of pensions to be charged to the company each year.

Standard accounting practice

Defined contribution schemes

The charge against profits should be the amount of contributions payable to the fund in the year.

Defined benefit schemes

The pension cost should be calculated using actuarial valuation methods. The method of providing for expected pension costs over the service lives of employees should be such that the regular pension cost is a substantially level percentage of the current and expected future pensionable payroll in the light of the current actuarial assumptions.

Variations in the regular cost should be allocated over the expected remaining service lives of current employees in the scheme.

Prudence may require that a material deficit be recognised over a period shorter than the expected remaining service lives of employees.

SSAP 25 Segmental reporting

Many entities carry on several classes of business or operate in several geographical areas, with different rates of profitability, different opportunities for growth and different degrees of risk. Users of financial statements may wish to form opinions about such matters as the nature of the activities of an entity, the contribution that each activity makes to the overall result of the entity and the future prospects of the activities. The purpose of segmental reporting is to provide information to assist users of financial statements to form a better appreciation of the results and financial position of an entity by permitting a better understanding of its past performance. This helps users to form a better assessment of its future performance and to be aware of the impact that changes in significant components of the entity may have on the business as a whole.

The standard is intended to ensure as far as possible that the segmental information is disclosed on a consistent basis, year by year.

The standard applies to any entity that

(a) is a public limited company or has a public limited company as a subsidiary; or

(b) is a banking or insurance company or group; or

(c) exceeds the criteria, multiplied in each case by 10, for defining a medium-sized company under Section 248 of the Companies Act 1985, as amended from time to time by statutory instrument. (See Chapter 10 §6)

A separate class of business is a distinguishable component of an entity that provides a separate product or service or a separate group of related products or services.

A geographical segment is a geographical area comprising an individual country or a group of countries in which an entity operates, or to which it supplies its products or services.

Standard accounting practice

The classes of business and geographical segments should be defined. For each, the following information should be given:

(a) turnover, distinguishing between turnover from external customers and turnover derived from other segments.

(b) result, before accounting for taxation and minority interests, and

(c) net assets.

FRS 1 Cash flow statements

The FRS applies to all financial statements intended to give a true and fair view of the financial position and profit or loss except those of entities that are: companies entitled to the exemptions for small companies (see Chapter 10 §6), and wholly owned subsidiaries of a parent company which prepares a consolidated cash flow statement dealing with the cash flows of the group.

Definitions

Cash: Cash in hand and deposits repayable on demand with any bank or other financial institution. Cash includes cash in hand and deposits denominated in foreign currencies.

Cash equivalents: Short-term, highly liquid investments which are readily convertible into known amounts of cash without notice and which were within three months of maturity when acquired; less advances from banks repayable within three months from the date of advance. Investments and advances denominated in foreign currencies are included provided that they fulfil the foregoing criteria.

Cash flow: An increase or decrease in an amount of cash or cash equivalent resulting from a transaction.

Inflows and outflows of cash and cash equivalents for a period should be reported under the following standard headings:

> operating activities
> returns on investments and servicing of finance
> taxation
> investing activities; and
> financing

in that order and showing a total for each standard heading and a total of the net cash inflow or outflow before financing.

A reconciliation between the operating profit reported in the profit and loss account and the net cash flow from operating activities should be given as a note to the cash flow statement. The reconciliation should disclose separately the movements in stocks, debtors and creditors related to operating activities and other differences between cash flows and profits.

A reconciliation of the amounts shown in the balance sheet in respect of items reported in the financing section of the cash flow statement with the equivalent figures in the previous year's balance sheet. See also Chapter 14 Cash Flow Statements.

FRS 2 Accounting for subsidiary companies

The FRS refers to 'undertakings' rather than 'companies' because it encompasses unincorporated bodies.

The FRS states that its objective is to require parent undertakings to provide financial information about the economic activities of their groups by preparing consolidated financial statements. These statements are intended to present financial information about a parent undertaking and its subsidiary undertakings as a single economic entity to show the economic resources controlled by the group, obligations of the group and the results the group achieves with its resources.

Minority interests in total should be reported separately in the consolidated balance sheet and profit and loss account. When an entity becomes a subsidiary undertaking the assets and liabilities attributable to its minority interest should be included on the same basis as those attributable to the interest held by the parent and other subsidiary undertakings. No goodwill should be attributed to the minority interest.

Profits or losses resulting from intra-group transactions and included in the book value of assets must be eliminated in full in the consolidation.

Uniform group accounting policies should be used in preparing the consolidated financial statements; in exceptional cases different policies may be used with disclosure.

The financial statements of all subsidiary undertakings to be used in preparing consolidated financial statements should have the same financial year end and be for the same accounting period as those of the parent undertaking of the group.

When a subsidiary undertaking is acquired, its identifiable assets and liabilities are to be brought into the consolidation at their fair values at the date that undertaking becomes a subsidiary undertaking. Goodwill should be calculated by reference to that fair value.

The FRS recognises that the aggregation and adjustments required to consolidate financial information for the parent undertaking and its subsidiary undertakings may obscure information about the separate undertakings and activities. It encourages parent undertakings to consider how the information may be provided by segmental reporting.

FRS 3 Reporting financial performance

The purpose of FRS 3 is to help users of financial statements to understand the performance achieved by the company or group and to assist them in forming an opinion of its future results and cash flows.

The FRS modifies the formats for the profit and loss account given in the Companies Act 1985; they should be changed when necessary to meet the following requirements:

(a) The analysis between continuing operations, acquisitions and discontinued operations should be disclosed to the level of operating profit. The analysis of turnover and operating profit is the minimum disclosure required in this respect on the face of the profit and loss account.

(b) All exceptional items, other than those in (c) below, should be included under the statutory headings to which they relate. They should be separately disclosed by way of note or, on the face of the profit and loss account.

(c) The following items should be shown separately on the face of the profit and loss account after operating profit and before interest:
   - profits or losses on sale or termination of an operation
   - costs of a fundamental reorganisation or restructuring
   - profits or losses on the disposal of fixed assets

(d) Extraordinary items. These are defined as material items possessing a high degree of abnormality which arise from events or transactions that fall outside the ordinary activities of the reporting entity and which are not expected to recur. They do not include exceptional items nor do they include prior year items merely because they relate to a prior period. Tax on an extraordinary profit or loss should be shown separately.

(Most extraordinary items concerned costs of fundamental reorganisation or restructuring of a business. Such costs are now considered to be an on-going part of any business and are to be treated as exceptional items as in (c) above.)

In the case of an entity that has revalued its assets, a note of the historic cost profit or loss should be presented. (Depreciation charges based on historic costs will be different from those based on a revaluation of assets.) The note should contain a reconciliation of the reported profit on ordinary activities before taxation to the equivalent historic cost amount.

A note should be presented reconciling the opening and closing totals of shareholders' funds of the period.

The following example of a profit and loss account is given by way of illustration; it is not taken from the FRS.

Profit and loss account for the year to 31 December 1993

	£m	£m
Turnover		
Continuing operations	480	
Acquisitions	72	
	552	
Discontinued operations	224	776
Cost of sales		(483)
Gross profit		293
Net operating expenses		(128)

	£m	£m
Operating profit		
Continuing operations	140	
Acquisitions	41	
	181	
Discontinued operations	(16)	
		165
Loss on disposal of discontinued operations		(24)
Profit on ordinary activities before interest		141
Interest payable		(23)
Profit on ordinary activities before taxation		118
Tax on profit on ordinary activities		(21)
Profit on ordinary activities after taxation		97
Dividends		(40)
Retained profit for the year		57

FRS 4 Capital instruments

A capital instrument is any instrument (a document containing contractual terms) issued by a company to raise finance. The definition includes shares, debentures, convertible loan stock, loans, and options or warrants which entitle the holder to subscribe for or obtain capital instruments.

The purpose of the FRS is to ensure that companies treat capital instruments in a 'clear, coherent and consistent' manner in 'all financial statements which are intended to give a true and fair view of a company's financial position and profit or loss for a period' (in other words, in its balance sheet and profit and loss account).

The need for this standard may be understood if one imagines a company which shows a loan as a long term liability when it should be shown as a short term one. This misrepresentation may conceal a liquidity problem.

The FRS does not apply to instruments which are

1. warrants issued to employees under an employee share scheme. (The warrants are instruments which require the company to issue shares to the employees.)

2. leases, which are covered by SSAP 21.

3. equity shares issued as part of a business merger.

Instruments covered by this FRS must be shown under one of the following headings as appropriate:

– liabilities

– shareholders' funds

– minority interests (in the case of a consolidated balance sheet).

Liabilities

Capital instruments should be shown under this heading if they contain an obligation to transfer economic benefits. Economic benefits may be cash payments (interest) or transfers of property of any kind. Debentures, bonds and loans are included under this heading. Payments of interest on these is obligatory. The treatment applies even if the obligation is only contingent, that is, it will arise only on the happening of a future event; therefore convertible debt instruments (convertible loan stock) must be shown as liabilities. Conversion should not be anticipated by showing convertible debt as shareholders' funds before conversion has taken place. No profit or loss is to be shown on conversion.

The finance costs of the debt must be spread over the periods of the debt at a constant rate on the carrying amount and charged to profit an loss account. Finance costs are defined as 'the difference between the net proceeds of an instrument and the total amount of the payments (or other transfers of economic benefits) that the issuer may be required to make in respect of the instrument'.

Analysis of liabilities

The debt must be analysed between convertible debt and non- convertible debt.
Maturity. Debts must be further analysed by reference to the earliest date on which the lender can require repayment:

(a) in one year or less, or on demand

(b) between one and two years

(c) between two and five years; and

(d) in five years or more

Shareholders' funds

The balance sheet should show the total amount of shareholders' funds. These funds must be analysed between equity and non- equity interests.

The finance costs for non-equity shares should be calculated on the same basis as the finance costs for debt (as explained above).

All dividends should be accounted for in the profit and loss account as appropriations of profit.

The following should be disclosed:

(a) the rights to dividends;

(b) the dates at which the shares are redeemable and the amounts payable in respect of redemption;

(c) their priority and the amounts receivable on a winding up;

(d) their voting rights.

These disclosures are not required for equity shares provided they have all the following features:

(a) no right to dividends other than those that may be recommended by the directors

(b) no rights of redemption

(c) unlimited right to share in the surplus remaining on a winding up after all liabilities and participation rights of other classes of shares have been satisfied

(d) one vote per share

Minority interests

The amount of profit due to minority interests in a consolidated profit and loss account should be analysed between equity and non-equity minority interests.

FRS 5 Reporting the substance of transactions

Off balance sheet finance and creative accounting

Some transactions result in the legal title resulting from a transaction being vested in some person other than the person who enjoys the economic benefits and bears the risks. An example of this has already been seen above in SSAP 21 (page 197). A legal title to an asset being acquired on hire purchase belongs to the seller but the purchaser enjoys the use and benefits of the asset and bears the risks. If the asset were not shown on the balance sheet because the legal title belonged to another person, this would be an example of 'off balance sheet financing', or the undisclosed provision of a resource. The result would be the absence of provision for depreciation in the profit and loss account and a distortion of operating results and accounting ratios.

Some companies used off balance sheet financing as 'window dressing' in their balance sheets, a practice that earned the name 'creative accounting'.

The aim of FRS 5 is to require companies to observe the principle of 'substance over form'; that is, they should disclose the real effect of a transaction and not just its outward (or formal) appearance. An asset being acquired on hire purchase should be shown in the balance sheet with the other assets of the company together with the outstanding liability under the hire purchase agreement.

The application of FRS 5 to transactions in which legal title and beneficial possession are vested in different persons has already been illustrated. Other situations to which the FRS may apply are

1. a transaction which forms part of a series of transactions and the single transaction can only be fully understood if considered in the context of all the others, and

2. a transaction which includes options and it is likely that the company will exercise one of the options.

FRS 6 Acquisitions and mergers

An acquisition takes place when one company acquires the shares in another company, usually by paying cash to the shareholders of that other company.

A merger takes place when one company issues its shares to the shareholders of another company in exchange for the shares in that other company. Alternatively, a new company may be formed to issue new shares to the shareholders of both the old companies. In neither case has cash passed; the companies have merged. All the shareholders at the time of merger remain shareholders after the merger.

One difference between acqustion accounting and merger accounting concerns pre-acquisition profits. In acquisition accounting, the profits are not available for distribution as dividends, but they remain distributable if merger accounting is used. Merger accounting was therefore attractive even when an acquisition and not a merger had taken place.

FRS 6 provides that acquisition accounting is to be used when one company has acquired another. Merger accounting should only be used when it is not prohibited by legislation and the following five criteria are met:

1. neither party is portrayed as acquirer or acquired

2. all parties take part in establishing the management structure and this is done by consensus rather than by the relative voting rights

3. the relative sizes are not so different that one party dominates the other party by virtue of size

4. any consideration in the form of non-equity shares is immaterial when compared to the total consideration

5. no equity shareholder of either of the old companies keeps a material interest in the future performance of only part of the combined entity.

FRS 7 Fair values in acquisition accounting

This FRS concerns the acquisition method of accounting for the combination of businesses.

1. Assets and liabilities of the acquired company should be recognised only if they existed at the acquisition date.

2. Non-monetary assets should be valued at replacement cost or the recoverable amount, whichever is less.

3. Intangible assets should be valued at their replacement cost.

4. Monetary amounts should be valued at the amounts expected to be received or paid. They should be discounted to present values, if appropriate.

Key points to remember

1. Try to understand the concepts that underlie each standard. This will help you to remember the requirements of each one more easily and accurately than if you try to learn them parrot-fashion.

2. You should be able to explain and discuss the requirements of the standards clearly and concisely in your own words to show that you understand them. Illustrate your answers with simple but apt examples where appropriate.

3. Look for occasions in the production of financial statements where you will be expected to demonstrate your knowledge of and ability to apply, standards.

Common errors

1. insufficient attention paid in the preparation for examinations to the contents and requirements of standards

> 2. failure to recognise the application of standards in the preparation of financial statements, especially those requiring the statements to be prepared in a form suitable for publication.

Questions

Examination questions

1   An article on Accounting Standards which appeared in a leading professional accountancy magazine included the following comments:

"We do not belong to a tradition which regards mere compliance with rules as satisfactory. Instead, we make life difficult by asking whether the rules lead to a result which accurately portrays economic reality, and then argue incessantly among ourselves about what the rules ought to say. In the last resort, we leave it to directors' and auditors' private judgement to decide what, in the particular circumstances of the particular company, gives a true and fair view. We regard it as essential that this principle should override all other accounting rules."

(a) Give two examples of areas in a balance sheet where it may be said that accounting results prepared under conventional accounting principles might not 'portray economic reality'. (10 marks)

(b) Explain why it may be unwise to leave decisions over the 'truth and fairness' of accounting reports to the 'private judgement' of directors and auditors. (10 marks)

(Total 20 marks)
(LONDON)

2   With reference to **Statement of Standard Accounting Practice** (SSAP) 18 – Accounting for contingencies, *you are required to*:

(a) define a 'contingency'; (4 marks)

(b) explain how material contingent losses should be treated in the published accounts, and what disclosure is required; (10 marks)

(c) explain how material contingent gains should be treated in the published accounts. (6 marks)

(Total 20 marks)
(JMB)

3   The auditors' report to the shareholders of a public limited company included the following two paragraphs:

'The accounts have been prepared on a going concern basis and the validity of this depends on the company's bankers continuing their support by providing adequate overdraft facilities'.

'Because of the materiality of the matters referred to in a previous paragraph we are unable to form an opinion as to whether the accounts give a true and fair view of the state of affairs of the company.'

Required

Explain the following terms:

(a) Going concern basis

(b) Materiality. (10 marks)
(LONDON)

4   The auditor's report on the accounts of a public limited company included the following two paragraphs:

'As explained in the note on accounting policies, it is the Company's policy to capitalise costs incurred on the research and development of the Company's inventions. The costs capitalised during the year have been quantified by the Directors and represent their allocation and apportionment of expenditure incurred for these purposes. We have been unable to determine whether the amounts capitalised of £3,600,000 have been properly quantified or whether it is appropriate to carry forward these amounts in the balance sheet.'

'The Accounts have been prepared on a going concern basis, and the validity of this depends on the Company's bankers continuing their support by providing adequate overdraft facilities.'

(a) In relation to the first paragraph, discuss the circumstances where it *might* be appropriate for a company to carry forward these amounts in the balance sheet.   (9 marks)

(b) In relation to the second paragraph, explain the meaning 'going concern basis' and discuss the possible changes to a balance sheet which had *not* been prepared on such a basis.   (6 marks)

(Total 15 marks)
(LONDON)

5   Prado plc has prepared accounts for the year to 31 December 1991 showing a profit before tax of £3,700,000. On reviewing the accounts, the directors have decided to seek advice on the following matters.

(i) During 1991 a government grant of £220,000 was received and credited to the profit and loss account. This grant was made as a contribution to the cost of purchasing a machine for £1,100,000. The machine is being depreciated by the straight line method over a period of five years.

(ii) On 1 January 1991 a business was acquired by the company. Goodwill of £300,000 arising on the acquisition was written off immediately in the profit and loss account, on the grounds that the goodwill has an estimated economic life of only three years.

(iii) Plant costing £360,000 on 1 January 1990 was initially estimated to have a five year life with no residual value, and was depreciated accordingly. During 1991 experience has shown that an estimate of a total ten year life would be more appropriate, so that £36,000 depreciation has been charged on this item.

(iv) On January 1991 an item of plant with a fair value of £55,404 was leased from a finance company. During the year payments on the lease have been £18,616. In practice the company expects to have the use of the asset for a total of four years, and the implicit finance charge for 1991 is £5,283. The company has accounted for this as an operating lease, but now accepts that finance lease treatment would be more appropriate.

You are required to advise on the best treatment of **each** of the above items, quoting relevant Statements of Standard Accounting Practice (SSAPs) and computing any necessary adjustments to the profit figure.

(20 marks)
(JMB)

6   The ledgers of Gamma plc have been closed for the year ending 31 March 19-6, and the following items have been referred to the directors by the company accountant and all are considered to be of material significance.

(i) A Government grant of £265,000 for a new factory has been approved and, although the funds have not been received, the project was completed during the financial year. The new factory is to be depreciated over 15 years.

(ii) Theta Limited, which owes Gamma plc £138,000 at 31 March 19-6, has gone into receivership and it is forecast that the unsecured creditors of Theta Limited are likely, in due course, to receive approximately 25 pence in the pound.

(iii) During the stocktaking it was found that, of the total stock of £835,000, approximately £93,000 of stock was missing and had been misappropriated. A further £50,000 of stock was estimated to be obsolete, with very little likelihood of resale.

(iv) The directors have received a professional valuation of the company's properties valuing them at £2,850,000 as against the cost of £1,935,000 which is recorded in the accounts.

(v) Due to unusual market conditions, Gamma plc has managed to negotiate the sale of an existing contract with Sigma Limited to Alpha plc for £385,000, with no costs to be borne by Gamma plc.

You are required to

(a) advise the directors how each item should be treated in the company's audited accounts;
(13 marks)

(b) explain any alternative treatments and refer to Statements of Standard Accounting Practice where appropriate.
(12 marks)
(Total 25 marks)
(JMB)

7 (a) The Accounting Standards Committee has produced its Statement of Standard Accounting Practice Number 18, Accounting for Contingencies.
  (i) What is a contingency? (2 marks)
  (ii) What are the alternative accounting treatments for contingencies? (3 marks)
  (iii) Explain how the alternative accounting treatments are determined. (3 marks)

(b) The Delta Company manufactures and sells a fluorescent thermostat. The financial year end was 31 March 19-6. How should the following items be dealt with in the accounts for the year ended 31 March 19-6?
  (i) A competitor has started producing a similar product which, it is believed, is in breach of a patent owned by Delta. On 25 February 1 19-6 the company commenced legal proceedings. These are progressing slowly, but the company's lawyers believe that there is a 70 per cent chance that within twelve months the company could receive damages in the region of £250,000. (5 marks)
  (ii) A customer has also commenced legal proceedings against Delta for damages based on a claim that the thermostat has caused ill health due to radiation. The company's lawyers believe that the £500,000 claim for damages has only a 30 per cent chance of success. At 31 March 19-6 correspondence between the two parties was at a preliminary stage. (5 marks)
(Total 18 marks)
(JMB)

8 Explain what is meant by **each** of the following terms in Statement of Standard Accounting Practice (SSAP) 9 ('Stocks and work in progress').
  (a) cost (4 marks)
  (b) net realisable value (4 marks)
  (c) long-term contract (4 marks)
  (d) attributable profit (4 marks)
  (e) foreseeable losses (4 marks)
(Total 20 marks)
(JMB)

9 (a) Define goodwill and explain how it arises in a company's accounts. (5 marks)

(b) Outline the alternative treatments of goodwill that are permitted by Statement of Standard Accounting Practice Number 22, Accounting for Goodwill. (4 marks)

(c) Explain the principles underlying the treatments permitted by the Standard. (8 marks)
(Total 17 marks)
(JMB)

10 The following is a list of unrelated transactions of different companies and shows the proposed treatment of these transactions in the accounts of the company concerned.
  (i) Buildings which originally cost £240,000 have been professionally revalued at £450,000. It is proposed to state these buildings at their current market value in the balance sheet and credit the surplus to the profit and loss account. In addition, it is proposed to continue to depreciate the buildings on their historic cost.

(ii) £420,000 was spent during the year on research into the creation of a vaccine to prevent the spread of a newly discovered virus. In previous years similar expenditure has been charged to the profit and loss account. It is proposed to treat this expenditure as an asset in the balance sheet at the year end.

(iii) A specialised piece of equipment with an estimated useful life of six years was purchased during the year. It is proposed that the total cost of this equipment be charged against the current year's revenue on the grounds that if the company were to go into liquidation it would have no resale value.

(iv) Stocks which cost £20,000 can now be replaced for £14,000. The estimated net realisable value of this stock is £17,000. It is proposed that the stock should be written down to £17,000.

(v) As a result of a declining order book the directors have decided to cut back production. They estimate that this will result in the loss of two hundred production employees and thirty administrative employees early in the firm's next financial year. It is estimated that redundancy costs will be £900,000. It is proposed to create a provision for these costs in the current year by charging them as an extraordinary item in the profit and loss account.

You are required to state, giving your reasons, which accounting principles or conventions are followed or violated in each of the above proposals and how you think each transaction should be treated in the accounts. Make reference where appropriate to any relevant Statement of Standard Accounting Practice. (25 marks)

(JMB)

11 Given below are five unconnected transactions made by five different businesses together with the proposed treatment of each transaction in the final accounts of the business concerned.

(1) Perry Ltd commenced trading in the early 1980s. Since then company sales have increased by 400% and the number of customers has doubled. The company has an extremely good name in the trade. As a result the directors propose to introduce £80,000 goodwill into the balance sheet as a fixed asset.

(2) Fishwick Ltd bought new premises in 1988. The market value of these premises fell between 1988 and 1992. Consequently the premises were depreciated until 1992. Since 1992 property prices have started to rise again so the directors are proposing to discontinue the practice of providing for depreciation on premises.

(3) Patel values his business stock at cost. He is proposing to value his closing stock of clothing at £90,000. Included in this figure is a batch of damaged sweatshirts which cost £800. After undertaking repairs costing £100 they could be sold for £850. The cost of replacing the damaged sweatshirts would be £700.

(4) Glynn Ltd commenced business in January 1990. In the first two years losses were incurred. Since 1992 the company has started to make profits. For the year ended 31 December 1993 debenture interest paid amounted to £18,000. Bank overdraft interest was £1,500. The directors would like to declare a dividend of £20,000. They propose to show an entry in the profit and loss account - interest and dividends £39 500.

(5) Nelson plc had written off a bad debt of £23,000 owed by Saunders & Co in the year ended 30 April 1991. In the current year Nelson plc has received a payment of £23,000 from the receivers of Saunders & Co. The directors are proposing to credit the £23,000 to retained earnings as the amount recovered refers to a previous year.

Required

Explain, giving reasons, how each proposal should have been treated and explain which generally accepted accounting conventions and principles should have been applied.

(50 marks)

(AEB)

**Companies:
capital reconstruction
and redemption of shares
and debentures**

Chapter objectives

This chapter is concerned with:

❑ how companies are permitted by the Companies Act 1985 to alter their share capital
❑ the issue of bonus shares
❑ capital reduction schemes
❑ redemption of shares

A company's memorandum of association contains details of its authorised share capital. The Companies Act 1985 section 121 provides that a company may –

(a) increase its share capital by new shares of such amount as it thinks expedient;

(b) consolidate and divide all or any of its shares into shares of larger amount than its existing shares;

Tutorial note: i.e. if it has a share capital of 1,000 ordinary shares £1 each it may consolidate them into 200 shares of £5 each, or shares of any other denomination.

(c) convert all or any of its paid-up shares into stock, and re-convert that stock into paid-up shares of any denomination;

Tutorial note: stock consists of 'bundles of shares'. Shares may only be bought and sold in discrete amounts, i.e. £1 shares may only change hands in multiples of £1, £5 shares in multiples of £5 and so on. Stock may be traded in fractional amounts.

(d) sub-divide its shares, or any of them, into shares of smaller amount than is fixed by the memorandum;

Tutorial note: share capital of, say, 1,000 ordinary shares of £1 may be converted into 4,000 shares of 25p, or 5,000 shares of 20p or 10,000 shares of 10p or 20,000 shares of 5p, etc. This may happen when, for instance, the market price of £1 shares has risen permanently to such an extent that dealings are hindered by the large sums of money required to purchase a reasonable number of £1 shares.

(e) cancel shares which, at date of the passing of the resolution to cancel them, have not been taken or agreed to be taken by any person, and diminish the amount of the company's share capital by the amount of the shares so cancelled.

12.1 Increase of issued share capital – bonus shares (scrip issue)

Issued share capital may be increased, subject to the maximum imposed by the authorised capital of the company stated in its Memorandum of Association, by the issue of additional shares. Normally, the issue of shares results in an increase in the assets of the company. If the shares are issued for cash, the asset of cash is increased. Shares may also be issued for a consideration other than cash, e.g. in payment for the acquisition of the assets of another business. This will result in an increase in the assets of the acquiring company.

When a company issues bonus shares to its shareholders the assets of the company are not increased. They are not issued in consideration for cash or other assets. The procedure involves the capitalisation of reserves. As all reserves belong to the ordinary shareholders, the directors are not really giving the shareholders anything they did not own before the issue.

The reasons why directors may propose a bonus issue are:

1. The reserves are considerable and must be considered as part of the long term capital of the company. If they are retained in the balance sheet as reserves, the real capital employed in the business is obscured.

2. The reserves may be capital reserves which cannot be distributed to the shareholders as cash dividends.

3. It may not be financially prudent to distribute the revenue reserves as cash dividends; the liquidity position of the company may not permit this sort of distribution anyway.

An issue of bonus shares is also known as a scrip issue.

Example 12.1.1

Balance sheet (summarised)

	£	£
Fixed assets		80,000
Current assets	7,000	
less Current liabilities	3,000	
		4,000
		84,000
Share capital and reserves		
20,000 ordinary shares of £1		20,000
Share premium account		4,000
Profit and loss account		60,000
		84,000

In a typical examination question a shareholder complains that the directors are withholding profits from the shareholders and wants the profits distributed as a cash dividend. The objections to such a distribution, as exemplified above, are:

1. Obviously, the cash resources of the company will not allow such a distribution to be made.

2. Only £20,000 of the fixed assets are financed by share capital; the balance of £60,000 is financed by the reserves. The reserves could only be distributed by selling the fixed assets.

3. A distribution of £60,000 would amount to a dividend of 300% on the shares, which would be unpopular with the workers who never have pay rises of such proportions, and with the company's customers, who would infer that they are being grossly overcharged for the company's products.

All reserves belong to the ordinary shareholders, a point of which the shareholder in the question was aware, but one that is not usually recognised by workers or customers.

The solution is to distribute the reserves as bonus shares. This is one of the purposes for which the share premium account may be used; otherwise, as a capital reserve, its uses are rather restricted.

The directors could decide to issue to the shareholders 3 bonus shares for every share presently held by them, using the share premium account and as much of the profit and loss account balance as is required to make up the difference. The balance sheet would therefore appear as follows after this had been done.

	£	£
Fixed assets		80,000
Current assets	7,000	
less current liabilities	3,000	4,000
		84,000
Capital and reserves		
80,000 ordinary shares of £1		80,000
Profit and loss account		4,000
		84,000

The journal entries to show the accounting entries involved are:

	Dr	Cr
	£	£
Share premium	4,000	
Profit and loss	56,000	
Bonus account		60,000
Bonus account	60,000	
Ordinary share capital		60,000

12.1.2 Example

Birchwood plc's balance sheet at 15 May 19-2 was as follows:

	£	£
Fixed assets		300,000
Current assets	65,000	
less Current liabilities	42,000	23,000
		323,000

	£	£
Share capital and reserves		
100,000 shares of £1 each		100,000
Share premium account		25,000
Asset revaluation reserve		80,000
Retained profits		118,000
		323,000

The directors proposed to issue bonus shares on the basis of two bonus shares for every share already held, using reserves for the purpose in such a way as to leave the remaining reserves in the most flexible form after the issue of the shares. The directors further proposed that following the bonus share issue there would be a rights issue on a one for three basis. These proposals were approved by the company and the shares duly issued.

Required

The balance sheet of the company after the rights issue has been made.

Answer

Balance sheet

	£	£
Fixed assets		300,000
Current assets	165,000	
Less Current liabilities	42,000	123,000
		423,000
Share capital and reserves		
400,000 ordinary shares of £1		400,000
Retained profits		23,000
		423,000

Tutorial note: The current assets are increased by the cash received from the rights issue. The bonus issue has been made out of the share premium, £25,000, asset revaluation reserve, £80,000 and retained profits, £95,000.

12.1.3 Exercise (involving a bonus issue followed by a consolidation of the share capital and a rights issue)

Pinewood plc's balance sheet at 31 January 19-3 was as follows:

	£	£
Fixed assets		852,000
Current assets	377,000	
less Current liabilities	191,000	186,000
		1,038,000
Share capital and reserves		
1,000,000 ordinary shares of 20p		200,000
Share premium account		53,000
General reserve		600,000
Profit and loss account		185,000
		1,038,000

On 1 February 19-3 the following following events took place in the order shown:

(i) A bonus issue of 3,500,000 ordinary shares was made so as to leave the remaining reserves in the most flexible form.

(ii) The ordinary shares were then consolidated into shares of £1.

(iii) A rights issue, at a premium of 10p per share, was offered and fully taken up on the basis of one share for every three already held.

Required

The balance sheet of Pinewood plc after the above events had taken place.

12.2 Capital reduction

Debit balances on profit and loss accounts may lead to an erosion of capital and it may be necessary to recognise the fact by a capital reduction scheme. A Capital Reduction account is used for the purpose.

12.2.1 Example

The following is the balance sheet of Oakwood Ltd. at 31 December 19-0:

	£	£
Fixed assets		50,000
Current assets	36,000	
less Current liabilities	24,000	12,000
		62,000
Capital and reserves		
100,000 ordinary shares of £1		100,000
Profit and loss account		(38,000)
		62,000

No provision has been made for depreciation of the fixed assets which, at the date of the balance sheet, were estimated to be worth £42,000, and it has been discovered that a major customer, owing £4,000 has become bankrupt.

However, the directors are of the opinion that the company will begin to make a profit of £5,000 per annum from now on.

Required

A scheme of capital reduction and the balance sheet as it will appear after the scheme has been put into effect.

Answer

The shares are worth 62p (£62,000/100,000) on balance sheet values, but it is necessary to substitute the estimated realisable values of the assets to find the real value of the shares. They are really worth £(42,000 + 8,000)/100,000 = 50p. Furthermore the shareholders will have to wait 8 years before the future profits will have eliminated the debit balance on the profit and loss account and they can look forward to a dividend.

This situation may be resolved in a number of ways, one of which would be to reduce the nominal value of the shares to 50p. Each £1 share could be cancelled and replaced by one new share of 50p.

The accounting entries will require the use of a Capital Reduction account:

	Dr	Cr
	£	£
Ordinary share capital	50,000	
Capital reduction account		50,000
Capital reduction account	50,000	
Fixed assets		8,000
Debtor (personal account)		4,000
Profit and loss		38,000

The resulting balance sheet will then be as follows:

	£	£
Fixed assets		42,000
Current assets	32,000	
less Current liabilities	24,000	8,000
		50,000

	£	£
Capital and reserves		
100,000 ordinary shares of 50p		50,000

Tutorial notes

1. The shareholders have not lost anything as a result of the reconstruction of the capital of the company as their shares had already lost 50p of their value; the reconstruction merely recognises this fact.

2. The debit balance has been eliminated from the profit and loss account. If the profit of £5,000 is achieved, it will be equivalent to a dividend of 10% payable to the shareholders immediately; they will not have to wait 8 years for a dividend.

12.2.2 Exercise: to record a scheme of reconstruction to reduce share capital

The balance sheet of Pinewood Ltd. is as follows:

	£	£	£
Fixed assets at cost			45,000
Current assets		28,000	
Less Current liabilities:			
Creditors	12,000		
Bank overdraft	5,000	17,000	11,000
			56,000
Share capital and reserves			
100,000 ordinary shares of £1			100,000
Less Profit and loss account			(44,000)
			56,000

The directors consider that the fixed assets should be depreciated by £5,000 and a provision of £1,000 should be created for bad debts. It is decided to reduce the nominal value of the ordinary shares to 50p, to eliminate the debit balance on profit and loss account and to create provisions for depreciation of the fixed assets and for bad debts.

Required

(a) Prepare the Capital Reduction account showing the entries to record the above scheme of reconstruction;

(b) Redraft the balance sheet as it will appear immediately after the reduction of the share capital.

12.3 Redemption and purchase of own shares by a company

A company is permitted by the Companies Act 1985, to issue redeemable shares.

A company may issue redeemable shares because

(i) They may be redeemed when there is a surplus of capital and the surplus funds cannot be put to profitable use.

(ii) Capital may be needed in the medium term for a project, but the project may be expected to generate sufficient funds in due course to enable the capital to be repaid.

(iii) Private companies may have difficulty in raising share capital as their shares are not traded on the Stock Exchange. A potential investor who may be wary of putting money into shares which cannot be sold easily may be encouraged to invest if the shares are redeemable by the company.

(iv) If a shareholder in a 'family' company dies, his personal representatives may require money as a matter of some urgency to pay taxes.

The Act is concerned to protect the creditors of any company which decides to redeem shares; otherwise cash which should be used to pay the creditors could be paid instead to shareholders.

Companies are permitted to redeem their own shares either:

1. Out of the proceeds of a new issue of shares.
2. By capitalising profits that would otherwise be distributable to the shareholders, or
3. By a combination of both methods.

Method 2. requires the creation of a Capital Redemption Reserve;.

Shares may be redeemed at a premium; the premium on redemption may be charged to share premium account only if:

1. The shares to be redeemed were originally issued at a premium, and
2. The shares are to be redeemed out of the proceeds of a new issue of shares.

The amount of the premium which may be debited to share premium account is limited to

(i) the premium on the shares when they were issued, and
(ii) the balance presently standing to the credit of the share premium account (i.e. the share premium account must not end up with a debit balance)

Note

(i) Private limited companies may use capital reserves to create the Capital Redemption Reserve, but only to the extent that their distributable reserves are insufficient for this purpose.
(ii) If a private limited company's revenue and capital reserves together are insufficient to fill the 'gap' created by the redemption of shares, the Companies Act allows for a shortfall in the Capital Redemption Reserve.

Neither of the provisions mentioned in this note applies to public limited companies.

12.3.1 Example 1

The balance sheet of Pelican Foods plc is as follows:

	£'000	£'000
Fixed assets		540
Current assets	284	
Less Current liabilities	177	107
		647
Share capital and reserves		
300,000 ordinary shares of £1		300
100,000 10% redeemable preference shares of £1		100
Share premium		60
Retained profits		187
		647

It has been decided to redeem the 10% redeemable preference shares at a premium of 10p per share. There will be a further issue of 50,000 ordinary shares at a premium of £1 to provide funds for the redemption of the preference shares. The preference shares were originally issued at a premium of 15p per share.

Required

Show the balance sheet as it will appear immediately after the above events have been complete.

Answer **Pelican Foods plc**

	£'000	£'000
Fixed Assets		540
Current assets (284+100–110)	274	
Less Current liabilities	177	97
		637
Capital and reserves		
350,000 ordinary shares of £1		350
Share premium (60+50–10)		100
Retained profits		187
		637

Example 2

The balance sheet for Pelican Foods Ltd. as in Example 1.

The company decides to redeem the preference shares at a premium of 10p. No new shares are to be issued.

Required

Show the balance sheet as it will appear immediately after the redemption of the preference shares.

Answer

Pelican Foods plc

	£'000	£'000
Fixed assets		540
Current assets (284–110)	174	
Less current liabilities	(177)	(3)
		537
Capital and reserves		
300,000 ordinary shares of £1		300
Share premium		60
Capital Redemption Reserve		100
Retained profits (187–100–10)		77
		537

Tutorial note: £100,000 of the distributable profit has been used to create the Capital Redemption Reserve; a further £10,000 has been used to write off the premium on the redemption of the preference shares.

12.3.2 Exercise 1

The balance sheet of Penguin Beakers Ltd. is as follows:

	£'000
Net assets	101
Capital and reserves	
75,000 ordinary shares of £1	75
10,000 8% redeemable preference shares of £1	10
Share premium account	6
Retained profits	10
	101

The directors intend to redeem the preference shares at a premium of 20p; the preference shares were originally issued at a premium of 10p. The redemption is to be financed out of the proceeds of a new issue of 10,000 £1 ordinary shares at a premium of 25p.

Required

The balance sheet of Penguin Beakers Ltd. after the new ordinary shares have been issued and the preference shares have been redeemed.

Exercise 2

The following is the balance sheet of Flamingo plc:

	£'000
Net assets	1,250
Capital and reserves	
750,000 ordinary shares of £1	750
100,000 10% preference shares of £1	100
Share premium account	40
Revenue reserves	360
	1,250

The preference shares are to be redeemed at a premium of 10p each; no new shares are to be issued.

Required

The balance sheet of Flamingo plc after the preference shares have been redeemed.

Exercise 3

At 30 September 19-2 the balance sheet of Ostrich Ltd. a private limited company was as follows:

	£
Net assets	13,000
Capital and reserves	
6,000 ordinary shares of £1	6,000
4,000 10% preference shares of £1	4,000
Share premium account	1,000
Retained profits	2,000
	13,000

It has been decided to redeem the preference shares at par (nominal value) without the issue of any new shares.

Required

The balance sheet of Ostrich Ltd. a private limited company, after the redemption of the preference shares has been completed.

12.4 The purchase by a company of its own shares

Shares which have not been issued as 'redeemable' shares may be purchased from the holders by a company; the accounting entries are similar to those required for the redemption of shares.

12.5 Redemption of debentures

The accounting treatment of the redemption of debentures is similar to that for the repayment of any other loan. There is no legal obligation to replace the debentures with the equivalent of the Capital Redemption Reserve, but it is often considered prudent to recognise the nature of debentures as a source of long term finance by capitalising an equivalent amount of revenue reserves.

Key points to remember

1. Bonus shares are created by transferring reserves to share capital account. No cash is received by the company for the shares.

2. Reduction of share capital requires the use of a Capital Reduction account to which is credited the reduction of share capital. The debit balance on profit and loss account, and reductions in asset accounts are debited to the Capital Reduction account.

3. Shares may be redeemed out of the proceeds of a new issue of shares; otherwise a Capital Redemption Reserve must be created. A premium payable on redemption of shares may only be debited to share premium if certain conditions are fulfilled. (See 12.3)

Common errors

1. confusion of bonus shares with rights issues.

2. failure to adjust a balance sheet correctly after a capital reduction; make sure the double entry is completed properly for each adjustment.

3. failure to observe the basic rules for the redemption of share capital; this often results from a failure to read the question carefully.

Questions

1   Chesterton plc produced a set of draft accounts for the year ended 31 December 19-8. The trial balance at that date included the following balances:

	Dr £	Cr £
Ordinary shares of 25p each, fully paid		260,000
8% Redeemable Preference Shares, of £1 each, fully paid		80,000
Share Premium Account		40,000
Interim Ordinary dividend	13,000	
Preference dividend	3,200	
Net Profit for the year		195,700
Retained Profit 1 January 19-8		156,078
Cash at Bank	24,000	
Debtors and Creditors	45,000	36,000
Stock at 31 December 19-8	129,000	

Note: Authorised share capital is 1.2 million ordinary shares of 25p each, and 80,000 8% Redeemable Preference Shares of £1 each.

The following decisions have been taken which will affect the draft accounts:

1.   The preference shares are to be redeemed at par at the year end. No new shares will be issued in replacement.

2.   Taxation of £30,000 is to be provided on the year's profit.

3.   £10,000 is to be transferred to an Asset Replacement Reserve.

4.   The remaining preference dividend is to be paid, together with a final ordinary dividend of 2 pence per share. Both dividends will be paid in February 19-9.

5.   An adjustment is necessary in respect of directors' salaries due but unpaid at the year end, amounting to £8,000.

(a) You are required to prepare:
   (i)   The profit and loss appropriation account for the year ended 31 December 19-8.
(8 marks)
   (ii) Extracts from the balance sheet at 31 December 19-8 showing current assets, current liabilities, share capital and reserves.
(10 marks)

(b) After the redemption of shares it is usual for a company to maintain the total of its share capital and capital reserves at their pre-redemption level. Explain the reasons for this.
(7 marks)

(Total 25 marks)
(LONDON)

2   A company has an authorised capital of 2,000,000 £1 shares of which 1,500,000 have been issued. At 31 May 19-5 the balance sheet of the company shows the following items:

	£
Premium account	82,000
Profit and Loss account	515,000
£1 Ordinary shares	1,000,000
8% Preference shares (issued at a premium)	500,000
6% Convertible stock	200,000

The following transactions took place during the year ending 31 May 19-6:

June 19-5   A rights issue was made of 200,000 Ordinary shares at £1.50 each. These rights were all taken up and the proceeds received by the end of the month.

July 19-5   The 8% redeemable preference shares were redeemed at a premium of 5%.

Half of the stock holders opted to convert their stock to Ordinary shares at a rate of three shares for each £4 of stock held.

Aug 19-5   The company made a bonus issue of one ordinary share for every five shares held at that date.

Required

Show the journal entries, with narrations, to record the above transactions.   (18 marks)
(OXFORD)

3   The accounts of Coldstream plc showed the following balances on 31 December 19-6.

	£	£
Issued Share Capital:		
1,000,000 Ordinary Shares of £0.50 each, fully paid		500,000
400,000 10% Redeemable Preference Shares of £1.00 each, fully paid		400,000
		900,000
Share Premium	9,000	
General Reserve	340,000	
Profit and Loss	27,800	376,800
		1,276,800

The redeemable preference shares were issued in October 19-4.

In January 19-7, the following transactions were undertaken:

(i)   an issue of 200,000 ordinary shares of £0.50 each as a bonus issue utilising the general reserve;

(ii) the redemption of 140,000 10% redeemable preference shares at a 20% premium.

Required

(a) prepare the appropriate ledger accounts, excluding bank, to record the above transactions:
(12 marks)

(b) prepare the shareholders' funds section of the Balance Sheet immediately after the issue and redemption.
(6 marks)
(Total 18 marks)
(JMB)

4   The accounts of Richmal plc included the following balances on 31 December 1992:

	£	£
Issued Share Capital:		
2m ordinary shares of 25p each, fully paid		500,000
300,000 12% redeemable preference shares of £1 each, fully paid		300,000
		800,000
Share Premium	20,000	
Retained earnings	243,000	
		263,000
		1,063,000

In January 1993, the company made a bonus issue of 300,000 ordinary shares of 25p each, by utilising part of the balance of retained earnings. It also redeemed 100,000 redeemable preference shares at a premium of 10p each. When issued, the redeemable preference shares had been sold at £1.06 each.

(a) Prepare the appropriate ledger accounts (excluding the bank account) necessary to record the above transactions.
(12 marks)

(b) Show the shareholders' funds section of the balance sheet immediately after the bonus issue of ordinary shares and the redemption of preference shares.
(5 marks)

(c) Explain why a company might choose to issue redeemable preference shares. (4 marks)

(d) State the circumstances where a capital redemption reserve is created, and explain why such a reserve is needed.
(4 marks)
(Total 25 marks)
(LONDON)

5 (a) Explain what is meant by a "reserve" and a "provision". (4 marks)

   (b) Why is a reserve for the replacement of fixed assets dealt with in financial statements in a different manner from a provision for depreciation? Explain whether such a reserve may be used for dividend distribution. (8 marks)

   (c) Explain the significance of "share premium accounts" and "capital redemption reserves". (8 marks)

   (Total 20 marks)
   (WJEC)

6 (a) Explain what distinguishes a rights issue from a bonus issue of ordinary shares. (6 marks)

   (b) Outline the advantages available from issuing debentures in preference to the issue of additional share capital. (6 marks)

   (c) Justify the issue of redeemable shares when a company has a positive view of its trading prospects. (6 marks)

   (Total 18 marks)
   (WJEC)

7 The chief accountant of Corchester Ltd had prepared the following balance sheet as at 1 July 1994.

	£000	£000
Fixed assets		
Freehold property		100
Other fixed assets		480
		580
Current assets (including bank)	440	
Less current liabilities	200	240
		820
Financed by		
Issued and paid up share capital		
400 000 ordinary shares of £1 each		400
150 000 8% redeemable preference shares at £1 each		150
		550
Reserves		
Capital redemption reserve	100	
Share premium account	50	
General reserve	45	
Profit and loss account	75	270
		820

The directors had decided to carry out the following transactions during July and August 1994.

(1) 8 July 1994. A rights issue of one ordinary share for every four held was made at £1.20 per share. All shareholders took up their rights.

(2) 1 August 1994. A bonus issue was made of one ordinary share for every ten held, based on the revised ordinary share capital. This was carried out by utilising equal amounts from the revenue reserves.

(3) 5 August 1994. 40 000 preference shares were redeemed at a premium of 5p per share. This was achieved out of profits with the exception of the premium which was covered by the share premium account.

(4) 15 August 1994. The freehold property was revalued at £130 000.

(5) 19 August 1994. Fixed assets costing £10 000 were purchased on credit.

Required

(a) A balance sheet as at 19 August 1994 after the completion of all transactions indicated above. (20 marks)

(b) Describe the features of
   (i)   a rights issue of shares   (5 marks)
   (ii) a bonus issue of shares   (5 marks)
(c) Explain the differences between capital and revenue reserves.   (5 marks)

(Total 35 marks)

(AEB)

8   The balance sheet as at 30 September 1994 of Beamish Ltd is as follows:

	Cost	Aggregate Depreciation	
	£000	£000	£000
Fixed assets			
Property	280	–	280
Equipment	110	50	60
	390	50	340
Current assets			
Stock	80		
Debtors	156		
Bank	34	270	
Less current liabilities			
Creditors	30		
Tax due	20		
Dividend due	10	60	210
			550
Financed by:			
Capital – Issued and paid up			
380,000 ordinary shares of £1 each			380
100,000 10% redeemable preference shares of £1 each			100
			480
Reserves – General		60	
Profit and loss account		10	70
			550

The company has an authorised capital of:
   500 000 ordinary shares of £1 each and
   100 000 10% preference shares of £1 each.

The company makes all its purchases and sales on credit.

During the year ended 30 September 1995:·

(i)   the company paid the tax and dividend shown in the above balance sheet;

(ii) the company redeemed 20,000 preference shares at par out of the proceeds of an issue of 70,000 ordinary shares of £1.10 per share.

(iii) the following aggregate cash transactions occurred:

	£
Payments for expenses	216,000
Payments for equipment	40,000
Payments to creditors	561,000
Receipts from debtors	971,000

At 30 September 1995 the directors made the following decisions.

(1) To provide £30,000 for corporation tax on the profits of the year.

(2) To propose a dividend of 6% on the ordinary share capital at 30 September 1995.

(3) To provide for the preference dividend which was now due.

(4) To revalue the property at £300,000.

(5) To create a provision for doubtful debts of $2\frac{1}{2}$% of the debtors at 30 September 1995.

(6) To continue the policy of providing depreciation at 20% per annum on the cost of equipment held at 30 September 1995.

(7) To transfer £50,000 to general reserve.

Additional information available at the year end.

	£
Closing stock (at cost)	70,000
Due from debtors	160,000
Due to creditors	44,000

There were no accruals or prepayments either at the beginning or at the end of the year.

Required

(a) A trading, profit and loss and appropriation account for the year ended 30 September 1995. (16 marks)

(b) A balance sheet as at 30 September 1995. (16 marks)

(c) Explain the following terms, giving one example of each:
    (i) a provision (3 marks)
    (ii) a reserve (3 marks)

(Total 38 marks)
(AEB)

9   The *"share capital and reserves"* section of Academe plc at 31 December 1995 was as follows:

	£000
Called up share capital (25p shares)	375
Share premium account	125
Profit and loss account	200
	700

The chairman of the company is considering a number of alternative possibilities for reorganising the company:

(1) Use the share premium account to issue bonus shares on a 1 for 3 basis.

(2) Use the share premium account to pay a dividend of £125 000 to the shareholders.

(3) Use the profit and loss account balance to issue bonus shares on a 1 for 3 basis

(4) Use the profit and loss account balance to pay a dividend of £125 000 to the shareholders.

(a) For each of the above alternatives, you are required to comment on the legality of the suggestion. (4 marks)

(b) Redraft the balance sheet extract on the assumption that only alternative (1) is implemented. (4 marks)

(c) Redraft the balance sheet extract on the assumption that only alternative (4) is implemented. (4 marks)

(d) Explain the effect on potential future dividends of a bonus issue paid up from a capital reserve. (4 marks)

(e) Explain the effect on potential future dividends of a bonus issue paid up from a revenue reserve. (4 marks)

(Total 20 marks)
(LONDON)

13 Amalgamations and take-overs; consolidated accounts

Chapter objectives

This chapter is concerned with:

☐ one company acquiring the net assets of another or other companies i.e. an amalgamation of companies

☐ one company acquiring more than 50% of the share capital of another or other companies i.e a take-over

☐ simple consolidations of the profit and loss accounts and balance sheets of a group of companies

---

One company may acquire an interest in another company either by:

1. Purchasing the net assets of that other company or
2. Purchasing shares in that other company

or

3. A third company may be formed to acquire the share capitals of the other two.

13.1 Amalgamations

When two companies amalgamate, one of the companies purchases the net assets of the other company; in other words, the former company purchases the assets of the other company and assumes responsibility for paying its creditors.

The amalgamation is then recorded by combining the assets and liabilities of the companies concerned.

Three points to remember when amalgamating balance sheets:

1. The assets of the 'acquired' company may not be taken over at their balance sheet values. The values at which they are taken over must be substituted for their balance sheet values.
2. Any excess of the purchase price over the value of the net assets being acquired represents a payment for goodwill;.
3. Adjust the 'acquiring' company's balance sheet for the cash it pays and/or the shares it issues as the purchase consideration.

13.1.1 Example 1 (Simple acquisition in exchange for shares and cash)

The balance sheets of Laurel Ltd. and Hardy Ltd. at 31 March 19-0 were as follows:

	Laurel Ltd. £	Laurel Ltd. £	Hardy Ltd. £	Hardy Ltd. £
Fixed assets				
Freehold premises		20,000		–
Plant and equipment		19,000		12,000
Motor vehicles		11,000		8,000
Office computer		–		3,000
Carried forward		50,000		23,000

	Laurel Ltd.		Hardy Ltd.	
	£	£	£	£
Brought forward		50,000		23,000
Current assets				
Stock	4,000		1,200	
Debtors	5,400		900	
Bank	31,700		1,000	
	41,100		3,100	
less Creditors	3,600	37,500	475	2,625
		87,500		25,625
Capital and reserves				
Ordinary shares of £1		75,000		25,000
Profit and loss account		12,500		625
		87,500		25,625

Laurel Ltd. acquires at their book values all the assets of Hardy Ltd except the bank account and assumes responsibility for paying the creditors. The purchase consideration will consist of 20,000 ordinary shares in Laurel Ltd at par, and the balance in cash.

Required

The balance sheet of Laurel Ltd. immediately after the acquisition of the net assets of Hardy Ltd.

Answer

(Working: The value of the net assets acquired is £25,625 – £1,000 (bank account) = £24,625. Purchase consideration will consist of £20,000 in shares and £4,625 in cash);

Laurel Ltd. – Balance sheet at 1 April 19 -0

	£	£
Fixed assets		
Freehold premises		20,000
Plant and equipment (19,000 + 12,000)		31,000
Motor vehicles (11,000 + 8,000)		19,000
Office computer		3,000
		73,000
Current assets		
Stock (4,000 + 1,200)	5,200	
Debtors (5,400 + 900)	6,300	
Bank (31,700 – 4,625)	27,075	
	38,575	
less Creditors (3,600 + 475)	4,075	34,500
		107,500
Share Capital and reserves		
Ordinary shares of £1 (75,000 + 20,000)		95,000
Profit and loss account		12,500
		107,500

Example 2: acquisition of business at fair valuation and payment for goodwill

The balance sheets of Pig Ltd. and Whistle Ltd. at 31 May 19–3 were as follows:

	Pig Ltd.		Whistle Ltd	
	£	£	£	£
Fixed assets				
Freehold property		–		25,000
Plant and machinery		40,000		19,000
Motor vehicles		31,000		27,000
Office equipment		5,000		8,000
		76,000		79,000
Current assets				
Stock	14,000		11,000	
Debtors	9,000		7,600	
Bank	27,000		9,400	
less Creditors	(17,000)	33,000	(14,000)	14,000
		109,000		93,000

	Pig Ltd.		Whistle Ltd	
	£	£	£	£
Share capital and reserves				
Ordinary shares of £1 each		100,000		100,000
Profit and loss account		9,000		(7,000)
		109,000		93,000

Pig Ltd. agreed to take over the assets of Whistle Ltd, except for the bank account, at the following valuations:

	£
Freehold property	30,000
Plant and machinery	16,000
Motor vehicles	24,000
Office equipment	3,000
Stock	10,000
Debtors	7,000

Pig Ltd. also agreed to settle Whistle Ltd.'s creditors.

The purchase price was fixed at £80,000 which was to be settled by the issue to Whistle Ltd's shareholders of 50,000 ordinary shares of £1 each in Pig Ltd. at a premium of 50p each, and the balance in cash.

Required

(a) The balance sheet of Pig Ltd. immediately after the completion of the acquisition of the business of Whistle Ltd.

(b) The balance sheet of Whistle Ltd. immediately following the sale of the business to Pig Ltd.

Answer

(a) Working: Value of net assets acquired:

	£
Total of assets per question	90,000
Less creditors	14,000
	76,000
Consideration:	80,000
Goodwill	4,000
Consideration: Shares: 50,000 × £1.50	75,000
Cash	5,000

Pig Ltd.
Balance sheet at 1 June 19–3

	£	£
Fixed assets		
Intangible assets		
Goodwill		4,000
Tangible assets		
Freehold property	30,000	
Plant and machinery (40,000 + 16,000)	56,000	
Motor vehicles (31,000 + 24,000)	55,000	
Office equipment (5,000 + 3,000)	8,000	149,000
		153,000
Current assets		
Stock (14,000 + 10,000)	24,000	
Debtors (9,000 + 7,000)	16,000	
Bank (27,000 – 5,000)	22,000	
	62,000	
less Creditors (17,000 + 14,000)	31,000	31,000
		184,000
Share capital and reserves		
150,000 shares of £1		150,000
Share premium		25,000
Profit and loss account		9,000
		184,000

(b)

Whistle Ltd.
Balance sheet as at 1 June 19–3

	£	£
Shares in Pig Ltd. at cost		75,000
Bank (9,400 + 5,000)		14,400
		89,400
Share capital and reserves		
Ordinary shares of £1		100,000
Profit and loss account	(7,000)	
add loss on sale of assets		
(*83,600 – 80,000)	(3,600)	(10,600)
		89,400

* Total net assets £93,000 less bank account not taken over £9,400

13.1.2 Exercise: preparation of the balance sheet of a company after it has acquired two other businesses

Gerald Mercer for some years owned two businesses in Uptown: Gerald (Menswear) and Mercer Fashions. Both businesses required additional capital. Gerald's two brothers agreed to supply additional capital provided the two businesses were converted into a limited liability company.

Accordingly, a new company, Merger (19-1) Ltd. was formed on 1 July 19-1 to acquire the net assets of Gerald (Menswear) and Mercer Fashions. Mercer and his two brothers subscribed for a total of 100,000 ordinary shares of £1 each in Merger (19-1) Ltd. and paid the cash for the shares into the company's bank account.

At 1 July, 19-1 the balance sheets of Merger (19-1) Ltd., Gerald Menswear and Mercer Fashions were as follows:

	Merger (19-1) Ltd £'000	Gerald (Menswear) £'000	£'000	Mercer Fashions £'000	£'000
Fixed assets					
Freehold premises	–		40		15
Delivery vans			8		6
Fixtures and fittings			7		11
Office equipment			3		1
			58		33
Current assets					
Stock		40		66	
Debtors		5		17	
Bank	100	–		–	
	100	45		83	
less Current liabilities					
Trade creditors		(32)		(76)	
Bank overdraft		(16)	(3)	(22)	(15)
	100		55		18
Capital					
100,000 ordinary shares of £1	100				
Gerald Mercer– Capital	—		55		18

It was agreed by the brothers that Merger (19-1) Ltd. should take over the assets of the two businesses at their net book values except for the following assets which would be taken over at the values shown.

	Gerald(Menswear) £'000	Mercer Fashions £'000
Freehold premises	75	25
Delivery vans	net book value	5
Fixtures and fittings	4	net book value
Stock	38	55
Debtors	4	60

It was further agreed between the brothers that Merger(19-1) Ltd. would pay:

£100,000   for Gerald (menswear), to be settled by the allotment of 60,000 ordinary shares of £1 each in Merger(19-1) Ltd. and £28,000 in cash;

and   £60,000   for Mercer Fashions, to be settled by the allotment of 40,000 ordinary shares of £1 each in Merger(19-1) Ltd., and £12,000 in cash.

Required

Prepare the balance sheet of Merger (19-1) Ltd. as it would have appeared immediately after the above agreed matters had been implemented.

13.2 Purchase by one company of shares in another company

A company may gain control of another company by purchasing more than 50 per cent of the shares that carry voting rights in that other company; that normally means the ordinary share capital.

The company acquiring the shares is known as the *holding company*; the company whose shares have been acquired is a *subsidiary company* of the holding company. When the holding company owns all the issued shares in its subsidiary, the latter is known as a *wholly-owned* subsidiary. If the holding company owns less than 100% of the issued shares in its subsidiary, the shares which it does not hold are held by *minority interests*. A holding company and its subsidiary company or companies are known as a *group*.

In the balance sheet of the holding company the shareholding(s) will be shown under fixed assets as 'Investment' at cost, subject to the following:

Whilst dividends paid out of post-acquisition profits by the subsidiary company to the holding company may be credited to the holding company's profit and loss account, a dividend paid out of pre-acquistion profits to the holding company should be credited to the Investment account, thus reducing the cost of the asset in the balance sheet. (Pre-acquisition profits = profits made before the holding company acquired the shares; post-acquisition profits = those made after.)

This is the 'Acquisition method' of accounting, and the reason for treating dividends paid out of pre-acquisition profits in this way is because the cash used to pay the dividend formed part of the assets of the business when it was purchased. The payment of the dividend is really a return of purchase money for the shares.

An alternative known as the 'merger method' allows all dividends received by a holding company to be credited to its profit and loss account, whether paid out of pre- or post-acquisition profits. The merger method should only be used in a true merger, not in a takeover. (See chapter 11 FRS 6).

13.3 Consolidated balance sheets

A company having one or more subsidiary companies must prepare group accounts in addition to its own profit and loss account and balance sheet. Group accounts usually take the form of a consolidated balance sheet and consolidated profit and loss account.

Preparation of Consolidated Balance Sheets

A consolidated balance sheet is prepared by adding together the balance sheets of the holding company and its subsidiaries, subject to the following:

(It is assumed for the present that the holding company has acquired the whole of the shares in its subsidiary and that the consideration for those shares is equal to the value of the net assets of the subsidiary company.)

1.   Cancel the item 'Investment in subsidiary' appearing in the holding company's balance sheet against the share capital and reserves in the subsidiary company's balance sheet.

2.   Cancel inter-company indebtedness from the creditors of one company and the debtors of the other company.

3.   Eliminate unrealised profit from the closing stock of a company which has bought that stock from another company in the same group; deduct the unrealised profit from the retained profit of the company which sold the stock within the group.

When the consideration paid for the shares is greater than the net asset value of subsidiary.

Treat the difference between the cost of the investment and the net assets at the date the shares were acquired as goodwill in the consolidated balance sheet.

When the consideration paid for the shares is less than the net asset value of the subsidiary.

Treat the difference between the cost of the investment and the net assets at the date the shares were acquired as a capital reserve in the consolidated balance sheet.

When the holding company acquires less than 100 percent of the shares in the subsidiary (i.e. there are minority interests).

Show the minority interest in the consolidated balance sheet at the amount of its shares plus its proportion of the reserves at the date of the balance sheet.

13.3.1 Example 1: holding company owning whole of share capital in subsidiary

Hotdogs Ltd. acquired the whole of the share capital of Chips Ltd. on 31 December 19-1 when the reserves of the latter amounted to £10,000.

The balance sheets of Hotdogs plc and Chips Ltd. at 31 December 19-2 were as follows:

	£'000	Hotdogs Ltd. £'000	£'000	Chips Ltd. £'000
Tangible fixed assets		300		80
Investment in Chips Ltd. at cost		110		–
Current assets				
Stock	80		25	
Debtors	55		30	
Bank	30		4	
	165		59	
Less creditors	(35)	130	(14)	45
		540		125
Capital and reserves				
Ordinary shares of £1		400		100
Reserves		140		25
		540		125

Further information:

1. At 31 December 19-2, Chips Ltd. owed Hotdogs Ltd. £8,000.
2. Included in the stock of Hotdogs Ltd. are goods which Hotdogs Ltd. has purchased from Chips Ltd. for £10,000. Chips sells goods to Hotdogs Ltd at cost plus 25%.

Required

Prepare the consolidated balance sheet for the group as at 31 December 19-2.

Answer

Workings:

1. Calculation of unrealised profit:
   If mark–up is 25% ($\frac{1}{4}$), margin is 20% ($\frac{1}{5}$)
   Goods in stock cost Hotdogs £10,000; therefore unrealised profit = 20% of £10,000 = £2,000.

Stock	
Reduce stock of Hotdogs by £2,000: £(80,000 – 2,000) =	£78,000
Add stock in Chips balance sheet	£25,000
Stock to be included in consolidated balance sheet	£103,000

2. Inter–company indebtedness:
   In the balance sheet of Chips Ltd.:

reduce creditors by £8,000: £(14,000 – 8,000) =	£6,000
On consolidation creditors will be Hotdogs £35,000 + Chips £6,000 =	£41,000

   In balance sheet of Hotdogs Ltd:

reduce debtors by £8,000: £(55,000–8,000) =	£47,000
On consolidation debtors will be Hotdogs £47,000+ Chips £30,000 =	£77,000

3. Capital and reserves

Chips Ltd.2	Share capital £	Reserves £
Per balance sheet at 31.12. 19–2	100,000	25,000
Cancel against Investment in Hotdogs Ltd. balance sheet	(100,000)	(10,000)
Deduct unrealised profit on goods sold to Hotdogs Ltd.		(2,000)
	–	13,000
Add Hotdogs Ltd. capital and reserves	400,000	140,000
Per consolidated balance sheet	400,000	153,000

Hotdogs Ltd. and subsidiary company
Consolidated balance sheet as at 31 December 19-2

	£'000	£'000
Tangible fixed assets (300,000 + 80,000)		380
Current assets		
Stock (see working 1)	103	
Debtors (see working 2)	77	
Bank (30,000 + 4,000)	34	
	214	
Creditors (see working 2)	41	173
		553
Share capital and reserves		
400,000 ordinary shares of £1 each		400
Reserves (see working 3)		153
		553

Example 2: goodwill on consolidation

Facts as in Example 1 above, except that investment is shown in Hotdogs Ltd.'s balance sheet at £125,000, and Hotdogs Ltd.'s reserves at 31 December 19-2 are £155,000.

Calculation of goodwill:

Cost of acquisition	£125,000
Share capital and reserves of Chips Ltd. 31 December 19–1	£110,000
Goodwill per consolidated balance sheet	£15,000

Hotdogs Ltd. and subsidiary company
Consolidated balance sheet as at 31 December 19–2

	£'000
Intangible fixed asset:	
Goodwill	15
Tangible fixed assets	380
	395
Net working capital (as in example 1 above)	173
	568
Share capital and reserves	
400,000 ordinary shares of £1 each	400
Reserves (155,000 +13,000)	168
	568

Example 3: negative goodwill on consolidation

Facts as in Example 1 above, except that investment is shown in Hotdogs Ltd. balance sheet at £96,000, and Hotdogs Ltd.'s reserves at 31 December 19–2 are £126,000.

Working:	
Cost of acquisition	£96,000
Share capital and reserves of Chips Ltd.at 31 December 19–1	£110,000
Negative goodwill – capital reserve	£14,000

Hotdogs Ltd. and subsidiary company
Consolidated balance sheet as at 31 December 19–2

	£'000
Tangible fixed assets	380
Net working capital (as in example 1)	173
	553
Share capital and reserves	
400,000 ordinary shares of £1	400
Capital reserve	14
Other reserves (126,000 + 13,000)	139
	553

Example 4: involving minority interests

Facts as in Example 1, except that Hotdogs Ltd. acquired 80,000 ordinary shares of £1 each in Chips Ltd. for £110,000.

Working

1 Share capital of Chips Ltd. held as follows:

Hotdogs Ltd.	80%	
Minority interest	20%	

Proportion of net assets at 31 December 19-1 attributable to Hotdogs Ltd.'s

	£
holding = 80% of Chips Ltd.'s share capital and reserves at	
31 December 19-1 = 80% of £110,000 =	88,000
Cost of acquisition =	110,000
Goodwill per consolidated balance sheet =	22,000

2. Reserves:

	£
Reserves per Hotdogs Ltd balance sheet at 31 December 19–2	140,000
80% of Chips Ltd. increase in reserves at 31 December 19–2 (80% of £15,000)	12,000
	152,000
Less unrealised profit (see example 1)	2,000
Per consolidated balance sheet	150,000

3. Minority Interest:

	£
20% of share capital of Chips Ltd.	20,000
20% of reserves at 31 December 19–2 (20% of £25,000)	5,000
	25,000

Hotdogs Ltd. and subsidiary company
Consolidated balance sheet as at 31 December 19-2

	£'000
Intangible fixed asset	
Goodwill (working 1)	22
Tangible fixed assets	380
Net working capital	173
	575
Capital and reserves	
400,000 shares of £1 each	400
Reserves (working 2)	150
	550
Minority interest (working 3)	25
	575

13.3.2 Exercise 1: consolidated balance sheet for holding company and two subsidiaries

The balance sheets at 31 December 19-1 of Doulla Ltd. and its two subsidiary companies, Rosalia Ltd. and Tracey Ltd. were as follows:

	Doulla Ltd		Rosalia Ltd		Tracey Ltd	
	£'000	£'000	£'000	£'000	£'000	£'000
Fixed assets						
Freehold property		100		–		–
Plant and equipment		80		65		40
Motor vehicles		42		35		28
Office machinery		30		15		20
		252		115		88
Investments						
150,000 ordinary shares in Rosalia Ltd.		200				
150,000 ordinary shares in Tracey Ltd.		150				
Current assets						
Stock	74		51		39	
Debtors	52		39		22	
Bank	60		27		30	
	186		117		91	
Less: Creditors	48	138	50	67	22	69
		740		182		157
Capital and reserves						
Ordinary shares of £1		600		150		150
Reserves		140		32		7
		740		182		157

Required

The consolidated balance sheet of Doulla Ltd. and its subsidiary companies as at 31 December 19-1.

Exercise 2: consolidated balance sheet for holding company and two wholly owned subsidiaries where there are inter-company indebtedness and unrealised profit

Mei Yiu Ltd. and Sing Yiu Ltd. became wholly owned subsidiaries of Hon Wai Ltd. on 30 April 19-4. Their balance sheets immediately afterwards were as follows:

	Hon Wai Ltd		Mei Yiu Ltd		Sing Yiu Ltd	
	£'000	£'000	£'000	£'000	£'000	£'000
Fixed assets						
Freehold property		180		–		–
Plant and machinery		75		64		80
Motor vehicles		30		45		28
		285		109		108
Investments						
150,000 ordinary shares in Mei–Yiu Ltd.		195				
120,000 ordinary shares in Sing–Yiu Ltd.		150				
Current assets						
Stock	60		48		45	
Debtors	54		26		19	
Bank	31		13		4	
	145		87		68	
Creditors	36	109	19	68	21	47
		739		177		155
Capital and reserves						
Ordinary shares of £1		700		150		120
Reserves		39		27		35
		739		177		155

Further information:

1. At 30 April 19-4, Mei Yiu Ltd.'s stock included goods which had been purchased from Hon Wai Ltd. for £28,000. The goods had cost Hon Wai Ltd £20,000.
2. At 30 April 19-4 Sing Yiu Ltd. owed £5,000 to Mei Yiu Ltd.

Required

A consolidated balance sheet for Hon Wai Ltd. and its subsidiaries as at 30 April 19-4.

Exercise 3: preparation of a consolidated balance sheet with minority interests

On 1 January 19-0, Buckle Ltd. acquired shares in Lace Ltd. and Pin Ltd. Their respective balance sheets were then as follows:

	Buckle Ltd £'000	Buckle Ltd £'000	Lace Ltd. £'000	Lace Ltd. £'000	Pin Ltd £'000	Pin Ltd £'000
Fixed assets						
Freehold premises		–		40		–
Motor vehicles		70		15		50
Equipment		25		20		30
		95		75		80
Investments						
80,000 ordinary shares in Lace Ltd.	100					
75,000 ordinary shares in Pin Ltd.	70					
		170				
Current assets						
Stock	42		50		14	
Debtors	54		28		10	
Bank	12		7		5	
	108		85		29	
Creditors	27	81	20	65	13	16
		346		140		96
Share capital and reserves						
Ordinary shares of £1		300		100		100
8% Preference shares of £1		–		30		–
Retained profits		46		10		(4)
		346		140		96

Required

Prepare a consolidated balance sheet for Buckle Ltd. and its subsidiary companies as at 1 January 19-0.

Exercise 4: preparation of consolidated balance sheet with minority interests, inter-company indebtedness and unrealised profit

Wader Ltd. acquired shares and debentures in Swan Ltd. and Heron Ltd. on 1 May 19-5, when the respective balance sheets of those companies were as follows:

	Wader Ltd. £'000	Wader Ltd. £'000	Swan Ltd. £'000	Swan Ltd. £'000	Heron Ltd. £'000	Heron Ltd. £'000
Fixed assets						
Freehold property	300		–		84	
Plant and machinery	140		86		51	
Motor vehicles	45	485	28	114	15	150
Investments						
120,000 ordinary shares in Swan Ltd.	180					
20,000 preference shares in Swan Ltd.	20					
100,000 ordinary shares in Heron Ltd.	75					
£20,000 debentures in Heron Ltd.	20	295				
Current assets						
Stock	75		36		29	
Debtors	64		47		23	
Bank	33		35		17	
	172		118		69	
Creditors	45	127	27	91	39	30
		907		205		180
Less Debentures		–		–		60
		907		205		120
Capital and reserves						
Ordinary shares of £1		800		150		150
Preference shares of £1				25		
Retained profits		107		30		(30)
		907		205		120

The following information is relevant:

1. At 1 May 19-5 Heron Ltd. owed Swan Ltd. £7,000.
2. Included in the stock of Heron Ltd. is stock which it had bought from Wader Ltd. for £18,000. The goods had cost Wader Ltd. £12,000.

Required

A consolidated balance sheet for Wader Ltd. and its subsidiaries as at 1 May 19-5.

13.4 Valuation of subsidiary's assets at fair valuation

So far, it has been assumed that the assets and liabilities of the company which has been acquired are represented in its balance sheet at approximately their fair values. This will not necessarily be the case.

FRS 2 (see Chapter 11) requires the identifiable assets and liabilities of a subsidiary to be brought into the consolidated balance sheet on acquisition at their fair values. This may affect the valuation of goodwill on consolidation. See also FRS 7.

Example

In 13.3.1, Example 2, it was assumed that the net assets (represented by share capital and reserves) of Chips Limited were worth £110,000 at the date of acquisition by Hotdogs Ltd, and the cost of the shares in Chips Ltd was £125,000. This valued goodwill on consolidation at £15,000. If the fair values of Chips Ltd's assets and liabilities had been £120,000, they would have had to be brought into the consolidated balance sheet at that amount and goodwill would have been reduced to £5,000. The consolidated balance sheet would then have been as follows:

Hotdogs Ltd and subsidiary company
Consolidate balance sheet as at 31 December 19-2

	£'000
Intangible fixed asset	
Goodwill	5
Tangible fixed assets	390
	395
Net working capital	173
	568
Share capital and reserves	
400,000 ordinary shares of £1	400
Reserves	168
	568

13.5 Consolidated profit and loss accounts

Method of consolidating profit and loss accounts of a group:

1. *When there are no inter-company sales, dividends, unrealised profits in stock, or minority interests:*
    Add profit and loss accounts together.
2. *When there are inter-company sales:*
    Add profit and loss accounts together after deleting inter-company sales at selling price from sales of vending company and from cost of sales (purchases) of purchasing company.
3. *When closing stock includes unrealised profits on stock purchased within the group:*
    Deduct unrealised profit from closing stock (cost of sales) of company concerned. (This adjustment corresponds to the adjustment made to stock in the balance sheet, as demonstrated above.)
4. *Minority interests:*
    Deduct minority interest from 'profit on ordinary activities after taxation.'
5. *Calculation of minority interests:*
    Minority's share of preference dividends (if any) plus Minority's share of balance of profits (after preference dividends, if any).

6. *Extraordinary profit:*
   Aggregate holding company's extraordinary profits/losses with groups' share of subsidiaries' extraordinary profits/losses.

7. *Retained profits from previous year:*
   Add holding company's retained profit to group's share of post-acquisition profits of subsidiaries.

8. *Proposed dividends:*
   Show holding company's dividends only.

9. *Transfers to reserves:*
   Aggregate holding company's transfers to reserves and group's share of subsidiaries' transfers to reserves.

13.5.1 Example

The issued share capital of Circle Ltd. consists of 100,000 £1 ordinary shares and 30,000 10% preference shares of £1 each.

Cone Ltd. holds 80,000 of the ordinary shares and 20,000 preference shares of Circle Ltd. During the year to 31 December 19-2 Cone Ltd. sold goods to Circle Ltd. for £25,000; these goods had cost Cone Ltd. £15,000. One half of these goods were still in Circle Ltd.'s stock at 31 December 19-2.

The profit and loss accounts of the two companies for the year to 31 December 19-2, and the consolidated profit and loss account for that year are as follows:

	Cone Ltd. £'000	Cone Ltd. £'000	Circle Ltd. £'000	Circle Ltd. £'000	Group £'000	Group £'000
Turnover		850		298		(A)1,123
Cost of sales		526		145		(B)(C) 651
Gross profit		324		153		472
Distribution costs	53		20		73	
Administration expenses	67	120	32	52	99	172
Profit on ordinary activities before taxation		204		101		300
Tax on profit on ordinary activities		42		27		69
Profit on ordinary activities after taxation		162		74		231
Minority interest					(D)	47
		162		74		184
Extraordinary profits net of tax		44		15	(E)	56
Profit for the financial year		206		89		240
Retained profits from last year		109		75	(F)	169
		315		164		409
Proposed dividends:						
Preference			3			
Ordinary	100		60		100 (G)	
Transfer to reserves	80	180	30	93	104 (H)	204
Retained profits carried forward to next year		135		71		205

Workings

A less £25,000 goods sold to Circle Ltd. (see 2. above)
B less £25,000 goods bought from Cone Ltd. (see 2. above)
C add £5,000: $\frac{1}{2} \times$ £(25,000 – 15,000) (see 3. above)
D minority interest = $\frac{1}{3}$ of preference dividend   £1,000
   plus $\frac{1}{5}$ of: profit (after tax and after preference dividend):
   $\frac{1}{5} \times$ £(231,000 – 1,000)   £46,000
   (see 4 and 5 above)   £47,000
E £44,000 + $\frac{4}{5}$ of £15,000 (see 6 above)
F £109,000 + $\frac{4}{5}$ of £75,000 (see 7 above)

G   (see 8 above)

H   £80,000 + $\frac{4}{5}$ of £30,000 (see 9 above)

13.5.2 Exercise 1: consolidated profit and loss account of holding company with one wholly owned subsidiary company

Cox Ltd. is the wholly owned subsidiary of Box Ltd. The profit and loss accounts of Box Ltd. and Cox Ltd. for the year to 31 March 19-1 were as follows:

	Box Ltd.		Cox Ltd.	
	£'000	£'000	£'000	£'000
Turnover		100		80
Cost of sales		60		50
Gross profit		40		30
Distribution costs	8		5	
Administration expenses	22	30	13	18
Profit on ordinary activities before taxation		10		12
Taxation on profit on ordinary activities		4		3
Profit on ordinary activities after taxation		6		9
Extraordinary profits net of tax		5		2
Profit for the financial year		11		11
Retained profits from the previous year		13		7
		24		18
Proposed dividend	8		5	
Transfer to reserve	10	18	8	13
Retained profit carried to next year		6		5

Further information:

Cox Ltd. has sold goods to Box Ltd. during the year for £18,000; the goods cost Cox Ltd. £15,000. All these goods were still in stock at Box Ltd. at 31 March 19-1.

Required

A consolidated profit and loss account for Box Ltd. and Cox Ltd. for the year ended 31 March 19-1.

Exercise 2: consolidated profit and loss account for a holding company and its subsidiary in which there are minority interests

Bat plc owns 75 percent of the ordinary shares of Ball Ltd. and 2/3rd of its preference shares. At the 30 September 19-3 the profit and loss accounts of the two companies were as follows:

	Bat plc		Ball Ltd.	
	£'000	£'000	£'000	£'000
Turnover		1,000		750
Cost of sales		684		525
Gross profit		316		225
Distribution costs	36		18	
Administrative expenses	84	120	36	54
Profit on ordinary activities before taxation		196		171
Taxation on profit on ordinary activities		67		50
Profit on ordinary activities after taxation		129		121
Extraordinary profit net of taxation		24		20
Profit for the financial year		153		141
Retained profit from previous year		116		80
		269		221
Proposed dividends				
Preference	–		42	
Ordinary	120		120	
Transfer to reserve	80	200	32	194
Retained profit carried to next year		69		27

Bat Ltd. sold goods for £24,000 to Ball Ltd. on 26 September 19-3; at 30 September 19-3 Bat Ltd. had not paid for these goods, all of which were still in stock. Ball Ltd. sells to Bat Ltd. at a mark-up of 50%.

Required

A consolidated profit and loss account for Bat Ltd. and its subsidiary for the year to 30 September 19-3.

13.6 Consolidated accounts reconsidered

Consolidated accounts are intended to give the shareholders of the parent company, and others, information about the assets and liabilities and the profitability of the group as a whole. The parent company's own profit and loss account only shows dividends received and receivable from other companies in the group; it does not show the profitability or otherwise of the individual subsidiaries. The parent company's balance sheet shows investments in subsidiaries at cost; it does not reveal the underlying assets and liabilities in the subsidiaries, nor the amounts representing goodwill which is revealed on consolidation.

The weakness of consolidated accounts lies in the fact that they give an overall view of the group's resources and profitability; they do not disclose the resources and profitability or otherwise of individual companies. They may be of little help, for instance, to creditors. A creditor can only look to the assets of the debtor company for satisfaction of a debt; he has no claim against the assets of other companies in the group.

FRS 2 recognises that the aggregation and adjustments required to consolidate financial information for the parent undertaking and its subsidiary undertakings may obscure information about the separate undertakings and activities. The FRS encourages parent undertakings to consider how the information may be provided by segmental reporting. Many public companies were providing segmental information before the FRS was introduced.

Key points to remember

1. Accounting for an amalgamation (or merger) requires the net assets acquired to be added to those of the purchasing company. The aggregation should take into account the fair values of the assets acquired if these are different from their net book values.

2. An excess of the purchase price over the aggregate of the fair values of net assets acquired represents the price paid for goodwill. If the price paid for the net assets is less than the aggregate of their fair values, the difference must be recorded as a capital reserve.

3. When one company acquires shares in another company, the investment should be shown in the balance sheet of the acquiring company at cost. Dividends received out of pre-acquisition profits from a subsidiary should be credited to the investment account to reduce the cost of the asset in the balance sheet. A note to the balance sheet should state the current market value of the investments, if quoted. A permanent reduction in value should be written off in the profit and loss account.

4. A take-over involving the acquisition of shares in another company does not give rise to goodwill in the balance sheet of the acquiring company.

5. When consolidating group company balance sheets proceed in the following order:
   (i) Calculate goodwill
   (ii) Calculate the group's share of reserves
   (iii) Calculate minority interests
   (iv) Cancel inter-company indebtedness
   (v) Deduct unrealised profit from stock

6. When consolidating profit and loss accounts,
   (i) Delete inter-company sales from turnover and cost of sales
   (ii) Delete unrealised profit from closing stock (i.e. add to cost of sales)
   (iii) Deduct minority interests from 'net profit after tax on ordinary activities'

(iv) Items which occur after the deduction of minority interests represent the **group's share only** of those items; *except* that **only the holding company's dividends will be shown**.

7. Practise making adjustments in consolidation of profit and loss accounts and balance sheets by attempting as many questions as possible. Students should make up some examples of their own; much can be learned in this way.

8. As with all financial statements, you should head your consolidated accounts with appropriate headings.

Common errors

1. failure to recognise goodwill or negative goodwill when accounting for amalgamations.

2. failure to calculate and adjust for goodwill, inter-company indebtedness, unrealised profit, group reserves, minority interests, in consolidated accounts.

Questions

Further examination questions

1 Magwitch Limited's finance director produced the following forecast break-even chart for the year ending 31 May 1991:

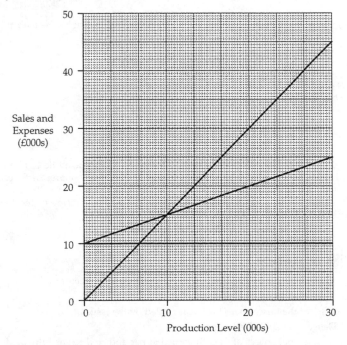

Production Level (000s)

During the year the company produced and sold 20,000 units, and both revenue and expenses were 10% higher than forecast.

Compeyson PLC has made an agreed takeover bid for the company at a value of twelve times the net profit for the year ending 31 May 1991.

Magwitch's assets and liabilities are to be taken over at their balance sheet values, with the exception of fixed assets, which are to be revalued at £40,000.

The summarised balance sheets of Magwitch Limited and Compeyson PLC at the takeover date of 31 May 1991 are as follows:

	Magwitch £000	Compeyson £000
Fixed Assets	32	160
Current Assets	65	340
Short-term Liabilities	(26)	(110)
	71	390
Share Capital (£1 shares)	40	200
Reserves	31	190
	71	390

The terms of the takeover are that Compeyson PLC will give three of its shares (value £1.80 each) for every two shares in Magwitch Limited, plus a cash payment to make up the total agreed takeover price.

Magwitch Limited will cease to trade on 31 May 1991, and its assets and liabilities will be assumed by Compeyson PLC . Any goodwill arising is to be written off immediately against reserves.

(a) Draw up a summarised profit and loss account for Magwitch Limited for the year ended 31 May 1991. (5 marks)

(b) Draw up a balance sheet for Compeyson PLC after the takeover of Magwitch Limited has taken place. (15 marks)

(c) Calculate how many shares and how much cash would be received by a holder of 6,000 shares in Magwitch Limited as a result of the takeover. (5 marks)

(Total 25 marks)
(LONDON)

2 The balance sheet of Elton Presley, a manufacturer, stood as follows at 31 December 1991.

	£
Capital	38,000
Plant and machinery (net book value)	26,000
Fixtures and fittings (net book value)	4,600
Stock	9,000
Debtors	6,200
Bank	1,200
	47,000
Less trade creditors	9,000
	38,000

On 1 January 1992, the business became a limited company called Nashville Limited. It had an authorised share capital of £70,000 divided into 60,000 ordinary shares of £1 each and 10,000 11% preference shares of £1 each.

Nashville Limited took over the assets and liabilities of Elton Presley at the following agreed valuations.

	Agreed Valuation £	
Plant and machinery	17,000	
Fixtures and fittings	5,000	
Trade creditors	8,800	(less £1,200 which was paid out of Presley's bank account)

All other assets were taken over at book value.

The purchase price of the business, £41,000 was settled by the issue of:

£6,000 8% Debentures 2001/2006 at par;

£10,000 11% preference shares of £1 each, issued at par and credited as fully paid;

ordinary shares at a premium of 25% over par value, to be credited as fully paid.

(a) Prepare the journal entries, including narrations, to close the books of Elton Presley.

(10 marks)

(b) Prepare the balance sheet of Nashville Limited at 1 January 1992. (9 marks)

(c) Explain your accounting treatment of the difference between the price paid for Elton Presley';s business, and the net assets of that business. Suggest how this difference might be accounted for in a year's time, when the company has built up revenue reserves.

(6 marks)

(Total 25 marks)

(LONDON)

3   The summarised balance sheets as at 31 October 1992 of Arts Limited and Crafts Limited are as follows:

	Arts Limited	Crafts Limited
	£000	£000
Fixed assets	150	130
Net current assets	100	70
	250	200
Ordinary share capital		
(£1 Ordinary shares fully paid)	180	120
Retained earnings	70	80
	250	200

The companies have been valued at 31 October 1992 as follows:

	£000
Arts Limited	450
Crafts Limited	240

It has been agreed that Arts Limited should acquire all the share capital of Crafts Limited on 1 November 1992 on the basis of the valuations of the companies on 31 October 1992; the purchase consideration being newly issued fully paid ordinary shares in Arts Limited.

Required

(a) A computation showing the number of shares in Arts Limited to be issued to the existing shareholders of Crafts Limited. (9 marks)

(b) The balance sheet as at 1 November 1992 of Arts Limited. (8 marks)

Note: Assume no transactions having taken place other than those mentioned above.

(c) Explain how a share premium account arises. (8 marks)

(Total 25 marks)

(CAMBRIDGE)

4   Mater and Pater each own a small business and they agree to merge their respective businesses into a Company, Family Limited, with effect from 1 October 1990. It was agreed that the issued share capital of Family Limited should be 1,000 shares of £1 each held equally between Mater and Pater, and , on 1 October 1990 they each paid £500 into a newly-opened company bank account.

Except for paying company formation expenses of £200, the company bank account was not used and Mater and Pater continued trading much as before except for using the company's name on all their stationery and letterheads. The accounting reference date for the company is fixed at 31 March. At 31 March 1991, after preparing the profit and loss accounts of the separate businesses, the three trial balances appeared as follows:

	Mater Dr. £	Mater Cr. £	Pater Dr. £	Pater Cr. £	Family Limited Dr. £	Family Limited Cr. £
Share Capital						1,000
Capital, 1 April 1990		80,000				
Capital, 1 July 1990				50,000		
Net profit, 12 months		18,000				
Net profit, 9 months				9,900		
Current assets	67,400		40,600		800	
Current liabilities		33,500		12,100		
Carried forward	67,400	131,500	40,600	72,000	800	1,000

	Mater		Pater		Family Limited	
	Dr.	Cr.	Dr.	Cr.	Dr.	Cr.
	£	£	£	£	£	£
Brought forward	67,400	131,500	40,600	72,000	800	1,000
Fixed assets, cost & depreciation						
1 April 1990	90,000	27,000				
1 July 1990			60,000	30,000		
Depreciation to 31 March 1991						
12 months		9,000				
9 months				4,500		
Paid to Family Limited	500		500			
Formation expenses					200	
Drawings £800 per month	9,600					
£600 per month			5,400			
	167,500	167,500	106,500	106,500	1,000	1,000

Mater and Pater agree that:

1. all assets and liabilities are to be taken over by the Company on 1 October 1990 at book values;

2. goodwill is to be valued as follows: Mater £8,000, Pater £4,000 and is to be written off in four equal annual instalments on the accounting reference date;

3. any necessary apportionments are to be made on a strict time basis;

4. directors' salaries are to be paid with effect from 1 October 1990 at the following annual rates, Mater £12,000, Pater £9,000;

5. the balances due to Mater and Pater at 1 October 1990 following the sale of their businesses are to be treated as loans to the company.

Required

(a) A calculation at 30 September 1990 of the net assets of the business of Mater and that of Pater. (7 marks)

(b) A profit and loss account for the Company, Family Limited, for the six months ended 31 March 1991. (6 marks)

(c) The balance sheet of Family Limited at 31 March 1991. (12 marks)

(Total 25 marks)
(CAMBRIDGE)

5 The following financial information was available on three limited companies:

Balance Sheets as at 31 December 1989

	Atom Ltd	Neutron Ltd	Proton Ltd
	£000	£000	£000
Fixed assets less depreciation	360	140	220
Investments			
15,000 shares in Neutron Ltd at cost	20	–	–
35,000 shares in Proton Ltd at cost	60	–	–
Current assets	250	70	160
	690	210	380
Called-up capital			
£1 Ordinary shares fully paid	–	90	75
50p Ordinary shares fully paid	150	–	–
Share premium	100	–	75
Retained earnings	150	20	–
Retained earnings as at 1 January 1989	–	–	20
Net profit for 1989	–	–	90
General reserve	120	40	60
Current liabilities	170	60	60
	690	210	380

Additional information:

(1) Proton Ltd have not prepared a profit and loss appropriation account for the financial year ended 31 December 1989.

The directors made the following recommendations:

    (i) An ordinary dividend for the year of 10% was declared, to be paid on 20 January 1990.

    (ii) A transfer of £50,000 is to be made to general reserve.

(2) Subsequent to the preparation of a revised balance sheet in good format, Atom Ltd decided that stock of £15,000 (valued at cost) was obsolete. It was sold as scrap on 10 January 1990 for £2,500.

(3) Atom Ltd decided to purchase further shares in the open market as follows:

    10,000 £1 Ordinary shares in Neutron Ltd at £2 per share;
    10,000 £1 Ordinary shares in Proton Ltd at £4.50 per share.

    The transactions were effected and paid for on 31 January 1990.

(4) In order to finance the additional share purchases Atom Ltd sold surplus land and buildings for £200,000. The net book value of the land and buildings on 31 December 1989 was £50,000. The transaction was completed and cash received by 31 January 1990.

(5) There were no other transactions in the month of January 1990.

(6) Ignore taxation.

Required

(a) A profit and loss appropriation account for the year ended 31 December 1989 for Proton Ltd.   (4 marks)

(b) A revised balance sheet for Atom Ltd as at 31 January 1990.   (9 marks)

(c) Define what is meant by the term 'subsidiary company'.   (3 marks)

(d) Using suitable calculations determine whether or not Neutron Ltd and/or Proton Ltd are subsidiary companies of Atom Ltd as at 31 January 1990.   (3 marks)

(e) What investment significance does the following information have for Atom Ltd?

	Neutron Ltd	Proton Ltd
1989 return on capital employed	5%	25%

Note: capital employed is defined as total assets.   (6 marks)

                                                   (Total 25 marks)
                                                        (AEB)

6   The following financial information is available on Spirotax Ltd and Elmet Ltd:

Balance Sheets as at 31 August 1992

	Spirotax Ltd	Elmet Ltd
	£000	£000
Fixed assets less depreciation	500	200
Investments:		
60,000 shares in Elmet Ltd at cost	50	-
Current assets	400	90
	950	290
Called-up capital		
£1 Ordinary shares fully paid	200	–
50p Ordinary shares fully paid	–	50
Share premium	200	50
General reserve	200	25
Retained earnings	250	135
Current liabilities	100	30
	950	290

Additional information:

(1) On 1 September 1992 Spirotax Ltd bought a further 20,000 ordinary shares in Elmet Ltd at a price of £1.50 per share. The shares were bought for cash.

(2) On 2 September 1992 the directors of Elmet Ltd decided to issue bonus shares on a one for one basis. The issue was funded out of retained earnings. All shares qualify for the dividend of 5p per share to be paid in respect of the last year.

(3) On 3 September 1992 Elmet Ltd issued £100,000 11% debentures 2,000-2,005 at par to fund the expansion of a factory in France. The issue was fully subscribed, and the expenses of the issue, £5,000, were written off immediately.

(4) Spirotax Ltd bought some new plant on 4 September 1992 for £80,000. Half of the cost was paid on this date, the remainder being due in two months' time.

(5) Spirotax Ltd provided Elmet Ltd with a long term loan of £150,000 on 5 September 1992. The loan was given in cash.

(6) It was decided that £20,000 of Spirotax's stock at 31 August 1992 was redundant. It was sold on the open market for £5,000 on 6 September 1992.

(7) During the last financial year Spirotax's return on capital employed was 25% per annum.

Required

(a) Balance sheets for Spirotax Ltd and Elmet Ltd as at 6 September 1992.   (11 marks)

(b) (i) Calculate the dividend yield that Spirotax Ltd obtained on its shares in Elmet Ltd for the year ended 31 August 1992.
(ii) Comment on Spirotax's share investment in Elmet Ltd using appropriate financial information to support your views.   (5 marks)

(c) Explain why Spirotax Ltd's share investment in Elmet Ltd is valued at cost in the balance sheet.   (3 marks)

(d) What advantages may accrue to Spirotax Ltd given that Elmet Ltd is a subsidiary company?   (4 marks)

(e) Calculate how many more shares must Spirotax Ltd buy in Elmet Ltd in order to make it a wholly-owned subsidiary.   (2 marks)

(Total 25 marks)
(AEB)

7 The balance sheets of Sun plc and its subsidiary Shine Ltd at 31 December 1991 were as follows.

	Sun plc		Shine Ltd	
	£000	£000	£000	£000
Fixed assets (net book value)		200		250
Investment,				
60,000 shares in Shine Ltd		100		–
Current assets	120		80	
less current liabilities	70	50	50	30
		350		280
Financed by:				
Share capital, £1 shares		150		80
General reserve		40		–
Profit and loss account		160		100
		350		180
18% Debentures 2005/7		–		100
		350		280

Sun plc owns 60,000 shares in Shine Ltd which were acquired when the profit and loss account of Shine Ltd was £40,000.

Requirement

You are required to

(a) prepare the consolidated balance sheet for the Sun plc group at 31 December 1991.
(10 marks)

(b) explain how the accounting treatment of a subsidiary differs from that of an associated company.   (5 marks)

(Total 15 marks)
(NI)

8   The following information is available for three companies, Lander plc, Yelstet plc and Oviedo plc as at 31 December 1992, and after the preparation of the annual accounts.

	Lander plc £000	Yelstet plc £000	Oviedo plc £000
Issued share capital			
£1 ordinary shares, fully paid	1500	700	–
25p ordinary shares, fully paid	–	–	100
£1 11% preference shares, fully paid	400	–	200
Share premium	1100	450	500
General reserve	600	200	150
Retained earnings	750	280	110
9% debentures 2005	–	400	–
Current liabilities	550	350	400
Fixed assets	2300	1510	960
Current assets	1900	870	500
Investment in Yelstet plc			
350 000 £1 ordinary shares at cost	700	–	–

Additional information:

(1) Lander plc had paid the preference share dividend for the year and had also declared a final ordinary dividend for the year of 5p a share.

(2) For the year ended 31 December 1992, the net trading profits for each of the companies were:

	£000
Lander plc	350
Yelstet plc	110
Oviedo plc	90

(3) The directors of Lander plc had made a transfer of £200 000 to general reserve on 31 December 1992.

(4) After the completion of the annual accounts Oviedo plc made a bonus issue of one ordinary share for every two shares held. The issue was funded from the share premium account.

(5) Lander plc wanted to strengthen its market position within the European Community. Thus it decided to acquire the following shares; the terms of issue were agreed by the companies involved.
  (i)   50 000 ordinary £1 shares in Yelstet plc at £2.50 per share. The transaction was settled in cash.
  (ii) 320 000 ordinary 25p shares in Oviedo plc. It was agreed that the shares in Oviedo plc were to be valued at £1 a share. Lander plc issued £250 000 new £1 convertible stock at par with the balance in cash to the ordinary shareholders in Oviedo plc who had accepted the offer.
  This share purchase occurred after Oviedo plc had made the bonus issue.

Required

(a) A profit and loss appropriation account for Lander plc for the year ended 31 December 1992.   (10 marks)

(b) A balance sheet for Lander plc after the acquisition and issue of shares as identified in item (5)   (16 marks)

(c) Explain what is meant by a subsidiary company. By making appropriate calculations determine whether Yelstet plc and Oviedo plc are subsidiaries of Lander plc.

  Your calculations should be made after taking into account items (4) and (5) above.
                                                                                  (14 marks)

(d) Explain why Lander plc believes that after acquiring further shares in Yelstet plc and Oviedo plc it will be able to strengthen its market position. Identify any further advantages that may accrue to Lander plc.   (10 marks)

                                                                          (Total 50 marks)
                                                                                  (AEB)

9   The following draft balance sheet as at 30 September 1995 has been prepared for David
    Goldstein plc.

	Cost £	Depreciation £	Net £
Tangible Fixed Assets			
Land and buildings	420,000	60,000	360,000
Machinery	175,000	105,000	70,000
Vehicles	135,000	40,000	95,000
	730,000	205,000	525,000
Investments at cost			
1 625 000 ordinary shares of 20p each in Zitwak Ltd			325,000
Current Assets			
Stock		46,000	
Debtors		8,400	
Bank		6,200	
Cash		340	
		60,940	
Creditors: amounts falling due within one year			
Trade creditors		3,180	
			57,760
			907,760
Share Capital and Reserves			
600 000 ordinary shares of 50p each fully paid			300,000
250 000 8% preference shares of £1 each fully paid			250,000
Share premium			180,000
Profit and Loss account			177,760
			907,760

Notes

The following information has not yet been included in the draft balance sheet.

(1) Zitwak Ltd was a wholly owned subsidiary of David Goldstein plc. The shares in Zitwak
    Ltd were sold to Drakko Ltd on 7 September 1995, the purchase consideration being
    £275 000. Drakko Ltd issued 2 750 000 ordinary shares of 10p each to David Goldstein plc
    in settlement of the purchase consideration. Drakko Ltd has an authorised and issued
    capital of £1 000 000.

(2) Included in the debtors' figure is an amount of £3140 owed by Shrimpers Ltd. There is
    no chance that this amount will ever be paid and is therefore to be written off.

(3) On 12 September 1995 a vehicle which had cost £30 000 some years earlier was involved
    in an accident. It has had to be written off. This vehicle had been depreciated by £20 000.
    The insurance company has agreed to pay £4000 under the comprehensive insurance
    policy. The cheque is expected in October 1995.

(4) Stock which had cost £2400 was found to be damaged and will only sell for £2000. The
    replacement cost of this stock is £1900.

(5) On 1 September 1995 the company offered for sale to existing shareholders 400 000
    ordinary shares of 50p each at a price of £1.05 on the basis of 2 new shares for every 3
    shares currently held by the shareholder. The offer was fully subscribed and all monies
    were received by 30 September 1995.

(6) The directors have proposed dividends as follows:

    8% on preference shares;
    5p per share on ordinary shares
    Dividends are to be based on shareholdings on 30 September 1995

Required

(a) The journal entries in the books of David Goldstein plc to record the adjustments
    outlined in **notes** (1), (4) and (5). (Narratives are not required.)   (10 marks)

(b) Explain the accounting concepts used when dealing with **notes** (2) and (4)   (4 marks)

(c) Prepare the balance sheet of David Goldstein plc as at 30 September 1995 as it would
    appear after the adjustments in **notes** (1(to (6) have been made.   (20 marks)

(d) Explain why David Goldstein plc might have
  (i)   sold its stake in Zitwak Ltd;   (4 marks)
  (ii) acquired the shares in Drakko Ltd.   (4 marks)

(e) Draft a memorandum to the departmental managers of David Goldstein plc explaining the terms:
  (i)   subsidiary company
  (ii) wholly-owned subsidiary.

Make reference to relevant information from the draft and the amended balance sheets of David Goldstein plc.   (8 marks)

(Total 50 marks)
(AEB)

14 Cash flow statements

Chapter objectives

The preparation of cash flow statements requires ability to

☐ prepare statements in accordance with the requirements of FRS 1

☐ recognise cash inflows and outflows for a period under standard headings

☐ distinguish between cash and non-cash events and transactions

☐ comment upon the liquidity, viability and financial adaptability of a business as disclosed by its cash flow statement

☐ distinguish between profitability and liquidity

This chapter should be studied in conjunction with the section on FRS 1, Cash Flow Statements in Chapter 11.

14.1 The purpose of cash flow statements

Cash flow statements are intended to disclose information that is not available from inspection of profit and loss accounts and balance sheets alone.

A profit and loss account shows the result of carrying on a business over a given period of time. A balance sheet discloses the position of a business at a particular moment in time. Neither of these statements provides information about one of the most important aspects of a business – what cash was received by the business, and how it was spent during the period. Cash is so important that it is often described as being the 'life blood' of a business. Shareholders and others are not only entitled to know, but should be aware of, the way in which the directors of a company have managed its cash. FRS 1 makes cash flow statements mandatory for most limited companies, which must include cash flow statements with their published profit and loss accounts and balance sheets.

Use of cash flow statements for reviewing past events and assessing future cash flows.

FRS 1 states that a cash flow statement in conjunction with a balance sheet provides information on liquidity, viability and financial adaptability of a company at a particular moment in time, i.e. at the balance sheet date. Cash flow statements give an indication of the relationship between profitability and cash generating ability, and thus of the quality of the profit earned.

It goes on to say that some transactions that take place in one period may be expected to result in further cash flows in a future period. An example of this could be a substantial expenditure on plant in one year that can be expected to produce cash flows in the next and subsequent years. FRS 1 says that cash flow statements should normally be used in conjunction with profit and loss accounts and balance sheets when making assessments of future cash flows.

Those businesses which are not required by FRS 1 to produce cash flow statements, i.e. small companies, sole traders and partnerships, will nevertheless find that the statements can provide useful information. Cash flow statements will almost certainly be required when negotiating loans with a bank and other lenders.

Examination questions are often based upon businesses that are experiencing liquidity problems in spite of being profitable. Candidates are required to explain the difference between profitability and liquidity and why an increase in profitability does not necessarily result in a corresponding increase in the bank balance. The explanation will usually be found in a cash flow statement.

14.2 Cash, cash equivalents and cash flow statements

Definitions of cash, cash equivalents and cash flow.

Cash includes cash in hand and deposits repayable on demand with any bank or financial institution.

Cash equivalents are short term, highly liquid investments which are readily convertible into known amounts of cash without notice and which were within three months of maturity when acquired; less advances from banks repayable within three months from the date of the advance.

Cash flow is an increase or decrease in an amount of cash or cash equivalent resulting from a transaction.

Form of cash flow statements

FRS 1 requires cash flows to be reported under the following standard headings in the order shown:

operating activities
returns on investments and servicing of finance
taxation
investing activities
financing

Cash flow statements are required to show the net cash inflow or outflow before financing.

The net total of the cash inflows and outflows under the five main headings represents the increase or decrease in cash and cash equivalents during the period.

Reconciliations with balance sheet figures

It is important that shareholders should be able to link cash flow statements to balance sheets. Therefore FRS 1 requires that the movements in cash and cash equivalents and the items shown in the financing section of cash flow statements must be reconciled to the related items in the balance sheets. Analyses are therefore required for:

changes in cash and cash equivalents during the year
balances of cash and cash equivalents as shown in the balance sheet
changes in financing during the year.

The following is an example of a cash flow statement. The figures are by way of illustration only. Cash outflows are shown in brackets. Explanatory notes follow the example.

Giventake Ltd
Cash flow statement for the year ended 31 December 19-3

	£000	£000	Notes
Net cash inflow from operating activities		987	
Returns on investments and servicing of finance			
Interest received	18		a
Interest paid	(20)		b
Dividends paid	(300)		c
Net cash outflow from returns on investments and servicing finance		(302)	
Taxation			
Corporation tax paid	(280)		d
Tax paid		(280)	
Investing activities			
Purchase of tangible fixed assets	(685)		
Sale of plant and machinery	184		
Net cash outflow from investing activities		(501)	
Net cash outflow before financing		(96)	
Financing			
Issue of ordinary share capital	200		e
Redemption of debentures	(100)		f
Net cash inflow from financing		100	
Increase in cash		4	

1. Reconciliation of operating profit to net cash inflow from operating activities

Operating profit	800	g
Depreciation	205	h
Loss/(profit) on sale of tangible fixed assets	94	i
Decrease/(increase) in stocks	(151)	j
Decrease/(increase) in debtors	(72)	k
Increase/(decrease) in creditors	111	l
Net cash inflow from operating activities	987	

2. Analysis of changes in cash and cash equivalents during the year

	£000
Balance at 1 January 19-3	324
Net cash inflow	4
Balance at 31 December 19-3	328

3. Analysis of the balances of cash and cash equivalents as shown in the balance sheet

	At 31 Dec 19-3	At 31 Dec 19-2	Change in year
	£000	£000	£000
Cash at bank and in hand	248	154	94
Short term investments	80	170	(90)
	328	324	4

4 Analysis of changes in financing during the year

	Share capital	Debenture loan
	£000	£000
Balance at 1 January 19-3	900	250
Cash inflow/(outflow) from financing	200	(100)
Balance at 31 December 19-3	1,100	150

Tutorial notes

a. Interest received must be stated on a cash basis, not on an accruals basis (as in the profit and loss account).

b. Interest paid must be stated on a cash basis.

c. Dividends paid. These will include the final dividend for the previous year and any interim dividends paid in the current year. It will not include the proposed dividend shown as a current liability in the balance sheet as at the end of the current year.

d. Corporation tax will be the tax actually paid in the current year. It may not always be the tax liability shown in the balance sheet as at the end of the previous year.

e. Financing from an issue of share capital will include share premium received.

f. Redemption of shares and debentures. This will include any premium payable on redemption.

g. Profit before interest and tax. Interest and tax payments are accounted for specifically elsewhere in the statement.

h. Depreciation charged in the profit and loss account does not result in a cash outflow. It must be added back to profit

i. Profits and losses on sale of fixed assets, being adjustments of past depreciation charges, must be treated similarly to depreciation in the statement. Losses must be added back to profit, profits deducted.

j. An increase in stock implies an outflow of cash and must be deducted from cash generated by operations. Conversely, a reduction in stock implies a cash inflow and must be added.

k. An increase in debtors implies an outflow of cash; a decrease in debtors implies an inflow.

l. An increase in creditors implies an increase in the cash and is added; a decrease in creditors implies a decrease in cash and must be deducted.

The direct method of calculating cash flow from operating activities

The Accounting Standards Board encourages the adoption of the direct method of reporting cash flows from operating activities where the costs of providing the information do not outweigh the benefits to the users of it. Knowledge of the specific sources of cash receipts and the purposes for which cash payments were made in past periods may be useful in assessing future cash flows.

The direct method of reporting net cash flow from operating activities shows the operating receipts and payments, aggregating to the net cash flow from operating activities. In particular, it shows cash receipts from customers, cash payments to suppliers, cash payments to and on behalf of employees and other cash payments.

The operating activities section of Giventake Ltd's cash flow forecast could possibly have looked as follows if it had been prepared on the direct method:

Operating activities	£'000	£'000
Cash received from customers	19,000	
Cash payments to suppliers	(14,460)	
Cash paid to and on behalf of employees	(3,230)	
Other cash payments	(323)	
Net cash inflow from operating activities		987

Note 1 to the cash flow statement reconciles the net cash flow from operating activities calculated by the direct method with the operating profit.

It is worth pausing at this stage to see what information may be gained from the statement of Giventake Ltd which would not be available from a study of its profit and loss account and balance sheet:

The cash generated by operations was sufficient to meet the cost of servicing the finance and the tax payable on the profit of the previous year. It was not sufficient to finance the heavy expenditure on new plant. In addition to cash received from the sale of fixed assets, it was necessary to increase the ordinary share capital to finance the capital expenditure and to pay for the redemption of some of the debenture stock.

14.3 Preparation of cash flow statements

As a cash flow statement is a link between two balance sheets, the very simplest statement can be produced by deducting one balance sheet from the other.

14.3.1 Example

Georgina's balance sheets for her business at 31 December 19-1 and 19-2 were as follows:

		19-1		19-2
	£	£	£	£
Fixed assets:				
Equipment at cost	6,000		8,000	
less depreciation	2,400	3,600	3,200	4,800
Motor car at cost	4,000		4,000	
less depreciation	3,000	1,000	3,500	500
Office machinery at cost	2,000		–	
less depreciation	1,800	200	–	–
		4,800		5,300
Current assets:				
Stock	2,000		3,500	
Debtors	3,800		3,000	
Bank	2,100		3,250	
	7,900		9,750	
less Current liabilities				
Creditors	1,700	6,200	2,300	7,450
		11,000		12,750
Capital at 1 January		8,000		11,000
Profit for year		10,000		9,000
		18,000		20,000
less Drawings		7,000		9,250
Capital at 31 December		11,000		10,750
Loan from father				2,000
				12,750

There was neither profit nor loss on the sale of the office machinery

The loan from Georgina's father was received on 1 January 19-2 and carries interest at the rate of 10% per annum.

Required

A cash flow statement for the year ended 31 December 19-2.

Answer

GEORGINA
Cash flow statement for the year ended 31 December 19-2

	£	£
Net cash inflow from operating activities		10,400
Returns on investments and servicing of finance		
Interest paid	(200)	
Drawings	(9,250)	
Net cash outflow from returns on investments and servicing of finance		(9,450)
Taxation (not applicable to sole trader)		
Investing activities		
Payments to acquire new equipment	(2,000)	
Receipts from sale of office machinery	200	
Net cash outflow from investing activities		(1,800)
Net cash outflow before financing		(850)
Financing		
Increase in loans	2,000	
Net cash inflow from financing		2,000
Increase in cash		1,150

Reconciliation of operating profit to net cash flow from operating activities		
	£	£
Net profit before interest (9,000 + 200)	9,200	
Depreciation (800 + 500)	1,300	
Increase in stock	(1,500)	
Decrease in debtors	800	
Increase in creditors	600	10,400

Analysis of changes in cash during the year	£
Balance at start of the year	2,100
Net cash inflow	1,150
Balance at end of year	3,250

14.3.2 Exercise: for practice in the preparation of a simple cash flow statement

Mary owns a successful boutique and makes up her accounts to 31 March in each year. She informs you that she made a good profit in the year to 31 March 19-4, but was surprised to find that the bank balance had reduced in spite of the profit and the fact that her drawings from the business were less than usual. She seeks your advice, and shows you the following balance sheets of the business:

Balance sheets as at	31 March 19-3		31 March 19-4	
	£	£	£	£
Fixed assets				
Leasehold property		20,000		18,000
Equipment at cost	8,000		17,000	
less depreciation	3,000	5,000	4,400	12,600
Motor van at cost	6,400		6,400	
less depreciation	3,200	3,200	4,800	1,600
Office equipment at cost	4,000		3,000	
less depreciation	2,800	1,200	2,400	600
Current assets		29,400		32,800
Stock	5,000		8,000	
Debtors	1,800		2,800	
Bank	7,060		4,740	
Cash	100		100	
Carried forward	13,960	29,400	15,640	32,800

	£	£	£	£
Brought forward	13,960	29,400	15,640	32,800
less: Creditors	1,980	11,980	4,560	11,080
		41,380		43,880
Capital at 1 April		31,416		36,380
Profit for the year		20,584		18,940
		52,000		55,320
less Drawings		15,620		14,440
Capital at 31 March		36,380		40,880
Long term liability: loan from father		5,000		3,000
		41,380		43,880

Mary informs you that she is amortising the leasehold property over the remainder of the lease which expires in 9 years.

She has not sold any equipment during the year to 31 March 19-4 but she has sold a word processor which cost £1,000 to a friend at its net book value, £200

During the year to 31 March 19-4, Mary paid £400 loan interest to her father.

Required

(a) Prepare a cash flow statement for the year to 31 March 19-4

(b) Using the information contained in your answer to part (a), draft a letter to Mary explaining to her why the balance at the bank is less than a year ago in spite of the profit made during the year.

14.4 Ascertainment of profit of company

The preparation of cash flow statements for companies follows the same principles as those applied for sole traders, but it may be a little more difficult to extract some of the information from the balance sheets. The difficulties are easily overcome if certain simple procedures are followed.

One such difficulty may be in ascertaining profit before tax and interest.

When an extract of a company's profit and loss account is available, the profit to be included in the cash flow statement is the net profit before tax and interest, not the retained profit:

Extract of profit and loss account:

	£000	£000
Profit before tax (after interest payable, £60,000)		400
Tax		(118)
Profit after tax		282
Transfer to reserve	(100)	
Proposed dividend	(80)	(180)
Retained profit for the year		102
Retained profit b/f		74
Retained profit c/f		176

Profit before tax and interest = £(400k + 60k) = £460k.'

When the profit and loss account is not given in a question the profit before tax must be found from the balance sheet

14.4.1 Example

The following are extracts from the balance sheets of Mario plc as at 31 December 19-1 and 19-2:

	19-1	19-2
	£000	£000
Creditors: amounts due within one year		
Taxation	125	232
Dividends proposed	220	280
Capital and reserves		
Share capital	1,200	1,200
Reserve for replacement of fixed assets	600	800
Retained profit	950	1,132

Calculation of profit before tax for the year to 31 December 19-2:

	£000
Retained profit at 31 December 19-2	1,132
less Retained profit at 31 December 19-1	950
	182
add taxation provision for the year 19-2	232
proposed dividend as at 31 December 19-2	280
transfer to asset replacement reserve (800 – 600)	200
Profit for the year to 31 December 19-2 before tax	894

Proof: reconstruction of profit and loss account for the year to 31 December 19-2

		£000
Profit before tax		894
Tax		(232)
Profit after tax		662
Transfer to reserve for replacement of fixed assets	(200)	
Proposed dividend	(280)	(480)
Retained profit for the year		182
Retained profit brought forward		950
Retained profit carried forward		1,132

14.4.2 Exercise: calculation of a company's profit before tax from its balance sheets

The following are extracts from the balance sheets of Andrew and Demetriou plc as at 31 March 19-3 and 19-4:

	at 31 March 19-3	at 31 March 19-4
	£000	£000
Creditors: amounts due within one year:		
Taxation	700	540
Proposed dividends	340	600
Debenture interest (on £1m. of 10% debentures)	100	100
Share capital and reserves		
Share capital	500	600
Share premium account	50	70
Asset revaluation reserve	–	150
Asset replacement reserve	160	185
General reserve	200	230
Retained profit	110	85

Required

A cash flow statement for the year to 31 March 19-4 is being prepared for Andrew and Demetriou plc and you are to calculate the item 'net profit before interest and tax' to be included in that statement.

14.5 Tangible fixed assets – purchase, sale, depreciation, and profit or loss on disposal

When preparing cash flow statements, take care to account properly for:

(a) funds applied in the purchase of fixed assets

(b) proceeds of sales of fixed assets

(c) depreciation provided in the year

(d) profits/losses on disposals of fixed assets.

Examination questions often do not give all the information about these items and they have to be found by the 'missing figure' technique.

14.5.1 Example

The following are extracts from the balance sheets of Malini, Priya and Co. Ltd as at 30 June 19-2 and 19-3:

	at 30 June19-2		at 30 June 19-3	
	£000	£000	£000	£000
Freehold premises		750		1,000
Plant and machinery at cost	400		430	
less provision for depreciation	220	180	230	200
Motor vehicles at cost	250		281	
less provision for depreciation	175	75	205	76
		1,005		1,276
Capital and reserves				
Asset revaluation reserve		–		250

In the year to 30 June 19-3, plant and machinery which had cost £80,000 and had been written down to £10,000 was sold for £7,000. In addition, motor vehicles which had cost £33,000 were sold for £8,000 at a profit of £2,000.

Required

Calculate the figures to be included in a cash flow statement for the year to 30 June 19-3 to account for the movements in tangible fixed assets.

Answer

[*Tutorial note*: reconstruct the ledger accounts to find the 'missing figures'.]

Plant and machinery at cost

	£000		£000
Balance b/f	400	Plant & machinery sold	80
* Plant purchased (balancing figure)	110	Balance c/f (per question)	430
	510		510

Provision for depreciation of plant and machinery

	£000		£000
Disposal	70	Balance b/f	220
Balance c/f (per question)	230	* Profit and loss (balancing figure)	80
	300		300

Plant & machinery disposal account

	£000		£000
Plant and machinery at cost	80	Provision for depreciation	70
		Sale proceeds	7
		* Loss on sale (P&L a/c)	3
	80		80

Motor vehicles at cost

	£000		£000
Balance b/f	250	Motor vehicles sold	33
*Motor vehicles purchased (balancing figure)	64	Balance c/f (per question)	281
	314		314

Provision for depreciation of motor vehicles

	£000		£000
* Disposal(per Disposal account)	27	Balance b/f	175
Balance c/f (per question)	205	* Profit & loss (balancing figure)	57
	232		232

Motor vehicles disposal account

	£000		
Motor vehicles (at cost)	33	*Provision for depreciation (balancing figure)	27
Profit on sale (P&L a/c)	2	Sale proceeds	8
	35		35

[*Tutorial note*: The items marked * are balancing figures]

Information for cash flow statement

	£000	£000
Operating activities:		
Depreciation for year to be added to profit before tax:		
on plant and machinery	80	
on motor vehicles	57	137
Loss on disposal of tangible fixed assets (3-2)		1

	£000
Investing activities	
Purchases of fixed assets (£110,000+£64,000)	(174)
Proceeds of sales of fixed assets (£7,000+£8,000)	15

[*Tutorial note*: Asset revaluation reserves are created when fixed assets, notably freehold property, are revalued upwards. In the above example, the freehold premises have increased in value by £250,000 between the dates of the two balance sheets. During the same period, a revaluation reserve of the same amount has been created indicating that the increase in freehold property arises from revaluation and not because of further expenditure.]

14.5.2 Exercise: to calculate details regarding tangible fixed assets for a cash flow statement

Pondayne plc's balance sheets for the years to 31 December 19-3 and 19-4 contained the following extracts:

	at 31 Dec 19-3		at 31 Dec 19-4	
	£000	£000	£000	£000
Freehold premises at valuation		900		1,200
Plant and machinery at cost	450		690	
less provision for depreciation	376	74	520	170
Fixtures and fittings at cost	60		40	
less provision for depreciation	54	6	30	10
		980		1,380
Capital and reserves				
Property revaluation reserve		150		450

During the year to 31 December 19-4 plant and machinery which had cost £80,000 and which, at the time of sale, had a written down value of £16,000 was sold for £8,000. Also fixtures and fittings were sold for £5,000; they had originally cost £40,000, and £38,000 had been provided for depreciation on these fixtures and fittings.

Required

Calculate

(a) the non-cash items relating to the tangible fixed asset information given above,

(b) the utilisation of funds during the year for the purchase of tangible fixed assets

14.6 Intangible fixed assets

Intangible fixed assets, such as goodwill, written off in the profit and loss account are non-cash items and should be added back to profit in the same way as depreciation.

14.7 Share capital and debentures

Increases in share capital and debentures *for cash* are sources of funds; shares or debentures issued *for other consideration* will be non-cash items. Bonus shares are non-cash items and must be ignored in the cash flow statement, but they must be shown in the analysis of changes in financing. Do not confuse bonus issues with Rights Issues which are made for cash and must be included in the statement if made in the period.

A premium received on shares issued in the period should be included in the cash inflow from the issue of share capital.

Redemption or purchase by a company of its own shares or debentures is an application of funds; the remarks regarding share premium on issues of shares also apply to redemption.

14.8 Taxation

Taxation shown as a current liability (creditor, payment due within one year) in a balance sheet will be paid in the year before the next annual balance sheet. Taxation shown in the earlier of two balance sheets will therefore be an application of funds in a cash flow statement produced at the date of the second balance sheet.

Taxation shown in a balance sheet is not necessarily the amount which will eventually be agreed as the liability by the Inland Revenue and the actual payment may differ.

To be sure of the tax payment to be included in a cash flow statement, it is often advisable to reconstruct the taxation account on the following lines:

Taxation

Debit	Credit
£	£
Tax liability carried forward (per later balance sheet)	Tax liability brought forward (per earlier balance sheet)
Tax payment during year (balancing figure)	Tax debited in profit and loss account.

14.8.1 Example

The taxation liability shown in Albrind plc's balance sheet at 31 December 19-1 was £345,000. The liability for taxation shown in the balance sheet at 31 December 19-2 was £410,000. In the company's profit and loss account for the year ended 31 December 19-2, the following item appeared:

	£000
Taxation	398

Required

A calculation of the taxation paid in the year to 31 December 19-2.

Answer

Taxation

	£		£
Taxation c/f	410,000	Taxation b/f	345,000
Tax paid during the year (balancing figure)	333,000	Profit and Loss a/c	398,000
	743,000		743,000

[*Tutorial note:* The taxation liability provided for in 19-1 was £12,000 too much; this excess of £12,000 reduces the amount that needs to be debited in the profit and loss account in 19-2 (410,000 − 12,000 = 398,000)]

14.8.2 Exercise (calculation of taxation paid)

The following extracts are taken from the balance sheets of The Vortex Puzzle Co. Ltd:

	As at 30 June 19-5 £000	As at 30 June 19-6 £000
Creditors: amounts falling due within one year		
Taxation	157	201

The following is an extract from the company's profit and loss account for the year to 30 June 19-6:

	£000
Profit before taxation	974
Taxation	(210)
Profit after taxation	764

Required

Calculate the amount of taxation paid by the Vortex Puzzle Company Ltd in the year to 30 June 19-6.

14.9 Dividends

Proposed dividends are shown in company balance sheets. Interim dividends paid during the year are debited in the profit and loss account together with the proposed final dividend for the year If, in examination questions, interim dividends have been paid they must be included in the dividend payments under the heading 'servicing of finance'.

The payment of dividends will therefore represent the payment of the final dividend for the previous year plus interim dividends paid in respect of the year covered by the cash flow statement.

Unless a question states that an interim dividend has been paid during the year and the amount of the dividend, then, where such a dividend has been paid, the question must provide an extract from the profit and loss account for the year. As with taxation, it will probably be as well to reconstruct the dividends account:

Dividends paid and proposed account

£		£
Proposed dividend for current year c/f (per later balance sheet)		Proposed dividend for previous year b/f (per earlier balance sheet)
Dividends paid during current year (balancing figure)		Dividends debited in profit and loss account

14.9.1 Example

The following extracts are taken from the balance sheets of Imitation Bunting Ltd.

	at 30 April 19-0 £000	at 30 April 19-1 £000
Creditors: amounts falling due within one year		
Proposed dividends	75	120

The profit and loss account for the year to 30 April 19-1 contained the following: 'Dividends paid and proposed £170,000'.

Required

Calculate the amount paid as dividends by Imitation Bunting Ltd in the year to 30 April 19-1.

Answer

Dividends

	£000		£000
Proposed dividend c/f	120	Proposed dividend b/f	75
Paid during the year	125	Profit and loss account	170
	245		245

Dividends paid during the year to 30 April 19-1: £125,000 (i.e. final dividend for 19-1 £75,000 plus interim dividend for 19-2 £50,000)

14.9.2 Exercise: calculation of dividends paid

The following extracts are taken from the balance sheets of Portable Grummitts plc.:

	as at 31 May 19-3 £000	as at 31 May 19-4 £000
Dividends proposed	300	250

The company's profit and loss account for the year to 31 May 19-4 contained the following item:

	£000
Dividends paid and proposed	280

Required

A calculation of the amount of dividends paid by Portable Grummitts Plc in the year to 31 May 19-4.

14.10 Worked example and exercise

14.10.1 Example

The Homer Double Glazing Company plc's balance sheets as at 31 December 19-1 and 19-2, and the profit and loss account for the year to 31 December 19-2 are as follows:

	as at 31 December 19-2		as at 31 December 19-1	
	£000	£000	£000	£000
Fixed assets:				
Freehold property at valuation		1,000		850
Plant and machinery at cost	780		695	
less provision for depreciation	320	460	280	415
Motor vehicles at cost	400		332	
less provision for depreciation	185	215	170	162
Office computer equipment at cost	60		55	
less provision for depreciation	30	30	28	27
		1,705		1,454
Current assets:				
Stocks	250		222	
Debtors	102		107	
Short term investments	300		–	
Cash at bank	54		75	
	706		404	
Creditors: amounts due within one year				
Trade creditors	(45)		(68)	
Taxation	(140)		(86)	
Proposed dividends	(120)		(100)	
Net current assets		401		150
Total assets less current liabilities		2,106		1,604
Creditors: amounts falling due after more than one year				
10% Debenture stock		(100)		(150)
		2,006		1,454
Capital and reserves				
Issued share capital		1,000		600
Share premium		30		210
Freehold property revaluation reserve		150		–
Asset replacement reserve		250		200
General reserve		400		300
Retained profit		176		144
		2,006		1,454

Profit and loss account (extract) for the year to 31 December 19-2

	£000	£000
Profit before tax		494
Taxation		(132)
Profit after tax		362
Transfer to asset replacement reserve	(50)	
Transfer to general reserve	(100)	
Dividends paid and proposed	(180)	(330)
Retained profit for the year		32
Retained profit brought forward from 31 December 19-1		144
		176

Notes

1. During the year to 31 December 19-2 the following transactions took place:

    (i) Plant and machinery which cost £120,000 and on which depreciation of £95,000 had been provided, was sold for £22,000

    (ii) Motor vehicles which had cost £85,000 and which had a written down value of £15,000 at the date of sale were sold for £28,000.

(iii) Office computer equipment which had cost £10,000 and on which depreciation of £5,000 had been provided was sold at a loss of £2,000.

2. During the year to 31 December 19-2 a bonus issue of shares was made on the basis of one bonus share for every three shares already held. This was done by using part of the share premium account. The company then made a rights issue on the basis of one share for each four held, the new shares being offered at a premium of 10p on each share.

3 There had been no additions to freehold property during the year to 31 December 19-2.

4. The 10% debenture stock is redeemable at par. The debenture stock redemption took place on 1 January 19-2

5. The short term investments are immediately realisable.

Required

A cash flow statement for the year to 31 December 19-2 for The Homer Double Glazing Company plc.

Answer

The Homer Double Glazing Company plc
Cash flow statement for the year to 31 December 19-2

	£000	£000
Net cash inflow from operating activities		677
Returns on investments and servicing of finance		
Interest paid	(10)	
Dividends paid	(160)	
Net cash outflow from returns on investments and servicing of finance		(170)
Taxation		
Corporation tax paid	(78)	
Tax paid		(78)
Investing activities		
Payments to acquire tangible fixed assets (205+153+15)	(373)	
Receipts from sales of fixed assets (22+28+3)	53	
Net cash outflow from investing activities		(320)
Net cash inflow before financing		109
Financing		
Issue of ordinary share capital, including premium	220	
Repayment of debenture stock	(50)	
Net cash inflow from financing		170
Increase in cash		279
Reconciliation of operating profit to net cash flow from operating activities		
Operating activities		
Net profit before interest and tax (494+10)	504	
Depreciation (135+85+7)	227	
Loss on sale of tangible fixed assets	(8)	
Increase in stock	(28)	
Decrease in debtors	5	
Decrease in creditors	(23)	677

Analysis of cash and cash equivalents

	£'000
Balance at 1 January 19-2	75
Net cash inflow	279
Balance at 31 December 19-2	354

Analysis of cash and cash equivalents as shown in the balance sheet

	19-2 £'000	19-1 £'000	Change in year £'000
Cash at bank	54	75	(21)
Short term investments	300	–	300
	354	75	279

Analysis of changes in financing during the year

	Share capital	Debenture loans
	£'000	£'000
Balance at 1 January 19-2	600	150
Bonus shares issued during year	200	
Cash inflow/(outflow) from financing	200	(50)
Balance at 31 December 19-2	1,000	100

Workings

Fixed assets

	Plant & machinery					Provn for depn.				Disposals		
b/f	695	Disp.	120	Disp	95	b/f	280	P&M	120	Depn	95
*Pchse	205	c/f	780	c/f	320 *	P&L	135			Cash	22
	900		900		415		415			*Loss	3
									120		120

	Motor vehicles					Provn for depn.				Disposals		
b/f	332	Disp.	85	*Disp	70	b/f	170	M.V	85	Depn	70
*Pchse	153	c/f	400	c/f	185 *	P&L	85 *	Prft	13	Cash	28
	485		485		255		255		98		98

	Office computer					Provn for depn				Disposals		
b/f	55	Disp	10	*Disp	5	b/f	28	Comp	10	Depn	5
*Pchse	15	c/f	60	c/f	30	*P&L	7			*Cash	3
	70		70		35		35			Loss	2
									10		10

Purchases = (205+153+15) = 373

Depn for year= (135+85+7) = 227

Proceeds = (22+28+3) = 53

Profit less losses on disposals = (13-3-2) = 8

	Taxation				Dividends		
*Paid	78	b/f	86	*Paid	160	b/f	100
c/f	140	P&L	132	c/f	120	P&L	180
	218		218		280		280

Tutorial notes

1. Items marked * in workings are balancing figures.

2. Revaluation of freehold property is a non-cash item; see increase in freehold property revaluation reserve.

3. Bonus shares issued: $\dfrac{600,000}{3}$ = 200,000 (non cash item; £200,000 transferred from share premium account to share capital account.)

4. Rights issue: $\dfrac{800,000}{4}$ = 200,000 shares issued for cash.

   Addition to share premium account = 10% of £200,000 = £20,000

14.10.2 Exercise: preparation of cash flow statement

The Ovid Egg Products Ltd's balance sheets at 31 December 19-0 and 19-1 were as follows:

	At 31 December 19-1		At 31 December 19-0	
	£000	£000	£000	£000
Tangible fixed assets (note 1)		435		434
Current assets				
Stock	110		70	
Debtors	61		35	
Bank	37		24	
	208		129	
Creditors: amounts due within one year				
Creditors	(25)		(38)	
Taxation	(51)		(45)	
Dividends proposed	(30)	(106)	(35)	(118)
Net current assets		102		11
Total assets less current liabilities		537		445
Creditors: amounts due after one year				
12% Debentures		(80)		(50)
		457		395
Capital and reserves				
Share capital (Ordinary shares of £1 fully paid)		250		200
Share premium		25		15
General reserve		130		80
Retained profits		52		100
		457		395

Notes

1. Tangible fixed assets

	Freehold property	Plant & machinery	Motor vehicles	Office equipment	Total
	£000	£000	£000	£000	£000
At cost					
Balance at 31.12 -0	375	72	111	20	578
Additions		58	50	10	118
Disposals at cost	(49)	(20)	(23)		(92)
At cost at 31.12 -1	326	110	138	30	604
Provisions for depreciation					
Balance at 31.12 -0	–	(60)	(72)	(12)	(144)
Depreciation on disposals		18	20		38
Depreciation for year		(28)	(32)	(3)	(63)
	–	(70)	(84)	(15)	(169)
Net book value at 31 December 19-1	326	40	54	15	435

2. During the year to 31 December 19-1, freehold premises which were surplus to requirements were sold for £37,000; plant was sold for £3,000 and motor vehicles were sold for £5,000.

3. 50,000 shares of £1 each were issued at a premium of 20p each on 1 July 19-1.

4. An interim dividend of 5p per share was paid on 30 June 19-1.

5. Taxation in the sum of £55,000 had been debited in the profit and loss account.

6. The additional debentures had been issued on 1 January 19-1

Required

(a) A cash flow statement for the year ended 31 December 19-1 for Ovid Egg Products Ltd.

(b) A concise report to the shareholders of Ovid Egg Products Ltd on the reasons for the large increase in the working capital of Ovid Egg Products Ltd so far as the information is available from your answer to part (a).

(c) State briefly the uses of cash flow statements.

Key points to remember

1. Memorise the format of cash flow statements and the usual items to be found under each heading.

2. Recognise the usual non-cash items for which 'profit before interest and tax' must be adjusted: depreciation; profits/losses on disposals of fixed assets; goodwill written off.

3. Recognise other non cash items: bonus shares; revaluation of properties.

4. An important examination technique is to start to earn marks as quickly as possible in an answer. A candidate who has adequately practised preparing cash flow statements before the examination should be able to prepare a statement in outline without delay, leaving spaces for additional items which may have to be inserted as the answer proceeds. The figures may then be inserted in the outline as soon as they have been calculated.

5. Prepare 'T' accounts if necessary to calculate fixed asset, depreciation, profit or loss on disposal, taxation and dividend figures.

Common errors

1. inability to calculate 'net profit before interest and tax'.

2. failure to adjust for non cash items.

3. confusing liabilities for tax and proposed dividends in current balance sheet with tax and dividends actually paid in the year.

Questions

Further examination questions

1   Patel Johnstone plc is a company which manufactures kitchen equipment.

The company balance sheet as at 31 May 1995 was as follows:

1994 £		1995 £	£
	Fixed Assets – Note(1)		
220,000	Premises		264,000
100,000	Machinery		72,400
40,000	Vehicles		22,500
360,000			358,900
30,000	**Investments**		30,000
	Current Assets		
19,000	Stock	23,000	
8,000	Debtors	7,000	
4,000	Bank balance	–	
1,000	Cash balance	2,000	
32,000		32,000	
	Creditors – amounts falling due within one year		
6,000	Creditors	9,000	
–	Bank overdraft	15,400	
12,000	Proposed ordinary dividend	–	
5,600	Proposed preference dividend	5,600	
23,600		30,000	
8,400	Net current assets(liabilities)		2,000
398,400	Carried forward		390,900

£		£
398,400	Brought forward	390,900
	Creditors – amounts falling due after more than one year	
100,000	12% debentures 1994 – **Note(2)**	
–	7% debentures 2025 – **Note(2)**	40,000
298,400		350,900
	Capital and Reserves	
150,000	Ordinary share capital	230,000
70,000	8% preference share capital	70,000
30,000	Share premium account	–
34,400	Retained earnings	36,900
14,000	General reserve	14,000
298,400		350,900

Notes to the balance sheet

(1) **Fixed Assets**

		31 May 1994 £	31 May 1995 £
Premises	cost	250,000	
	valuation		300,000
	depreciation	30,000	36,000
	net book value	220,000	264,000
Machinery	cost	180,000	?
	depreciation	80,000	?
	net book value	100,000	72,400
Vehicles	cost	175,000	210,000
	depreciation	135,000	187,500
	net book value	40,000	22,500

(i) During the year ended 31 May 1995 the premises were re-valued at £300,000.

(ii) During the year ended 31 May 1995 a machine which had cost £24,000 6 years ago was sold for £10,000.

(iii) The accumulated depreciation charged on this machine to the year ended 31 May 1994 amounted to £14,500.

(iv) No machinery was acquired during the year.

(v) There were no disposals of premises or vehicles during the year.

(2) The 12% debentures were redeemed at par on 30 November 1994 (no transfer to a capital redemption reserve was made).

On the same date a new issue of 7% debentures was made at par and all were sold.

(3) A bonus issue of shares had been made during the year to 31 May 1995. The revaluation reserve and the share premium account had been utilised for this purpose.

Required

(a) Prepare a cash flow statement for Patel Johnstone plc for the year ended 31 May 1995.

(32 marks)

(b) Explain the reasons for producing a cash flow statement. (12 marks)

(c) Outline **two** measures which may be taken to improve a poor working capital situation.

(6 marks)

(Total 50 marks)

(AEB)

2 The balance sheets of Traddles plc as at 31 May 1993 and 1994 are as follows.

	31.5.93 £000	31.5.93 £000	31.5.94 £000	31.5.94 £000
Fixed assets (net book value)		3,587		3,894
Current assets:				
Stock	420		527	
Debtors	603		643	
Bank	1,755		1,921	
	2,778		3,091	
Creditors due for payment within one year:				
Creditors	530		660	
Taxation	1,607		1,304	
Proposed dividends	1,330		1,600	

	£000	£000		£000	£000
		3,467			3,564
Net current liabilities		(689)			(473)
		2,898			3,421

		31.5.93			31.5.94
	£000	£000		£000	£000
Share Capital:					
Ordinary shares of £1 each		520			620
Share Premium Account		40			53
Retained Earnings		2,338			2,748
		2,898			3,421

The summarised profit and loss accounts for the two years ended 31 May 1994 are as follows:

	1993	1994
	£000	£000
Net profit on Trading (note 1)	3,432	3,296
Interest Received	30	24
Interest Paid	(6)	(6)
Net Profit	3,456	3,314
Taxation	1,607	1,304
Net Profit after tax	1,849	2,010
Dividends	1,330	1,600
Retained Earnings	519	410
Retained Earnings b/f	1,819	2,338
Retained Earnings c/f	2,338	2,748

Notes

1. Net Operating Profit for 1994 is calculated after charging

	£000
Depreciation	490
Loss on sale of assets	3

2. The assets which were disposed of realised £23,000, resulting in a loss on disposal of £3,000 when compared with their book value.

Required

Produce a Cash Flow Statement for Traddles plc for the year ended 31 May 1994, in accordance with the Financial Reporting Standard (FRS)1; Cash Flow Statements.   (25 marks)
(LONDON)

3   The balance sheets of Codger plc as at 31 May 1994 and 1995 are as follows:

		31.5.94			31.5.95
	£000	£000		£000	£000
Fixed assets (net book value)		10,761			11,682
Current assets:					
Stock	1,260			1,581	
Debtors	1,809			1,929	
Bank	5,265			5,763	
	8,334			9,273	
Creditors due for payment within one year:					
Creditors	1,590			1,980	
Taxation	4,821			3,912	
Proposed dividends	3,990			4,800	
	10,401			10,692	
Net Current Liabilities		(2,067)			(1,419)
		8,694			10,263
Share Capital:					
Ordinary Shares of 25p each		1,560			1,860
Share Premium Account		120			159
Retained Earnings		7,014			8,244
		8,694			10,263

The summarised profit and loss accounts for the two years ended 31 May 1995 are as follows.

	1994	1995
	£000	£000
Net Operating Profit (note 1)	10,296	9,888
Interest Received	90	72
Interest Paid	(18)	(18)
Net profit	10,368	9,942
Taxation	4,821	3,912
Net Profit after tax	5,547	6,030
Dividends	3,990	4,800
Retained Earnings	1,557	1,230
Retained Earnings b/f	5,457	7,014
Retained Earnings c/f	7,014	8,244

Notes

1. Net Operating Profit for 1995 is calculated after charging

	£000
Depreciation	1,470
Profit on sale of fixed assets	9

2. The assets which were disposed of realised £69,000, resulting in a profit on disposal of £9,000 when compared with their book value.

Required

(a) Produce a Cash Flow Statement for Codger plc for the year ended 31 May 1995 in accordance with Financial Reporting Standard (FRS)1: Cash Flow Statements.

You should provide notes to the statement showing:
(i)   a reconciliation of operating profit to net cash flow from operating activities;
(ii) analysis of changes in cash and cash equivalents in the year;
(iii) analysis of changes in financing during the year.   (20 marks)

(b) Explain briefly the ways in which a cash flow statement is of use to a potential investor in a company.   (5 marks)

(Total 25 marks)
(LONDON)

4   The summarised balance sheets as at 31 March 19-8 and 19-9 of Alto Limited are as follows:

	19-9		19-8		
	£000	£000	£000	£000	Additional information
Fixed assets; at net book value		245		210	1
Current assets	126		112		2
Creditors, less than one year	(98)	28	(70)	42	
		273		252	
Creditors, more than one year:					
10% Debentures		(42)		(42)	
		231		210	
Capital and reserves					
Ordinary shares of £1 each		126		112	3
8% Redeemable preference shares					
of 50p each		–		42	3
Share premium account		35		28	3
Capital redemption reserve		21		–	
Profit and loss account		49		28	
		231		210	

Additional information:

	Cost £000	Depreciation £000	Net Book Value £000
(1) Fixed assets			
Balance at 31 March 19-8	280	70	210
Additions	84	–	84
Disposals	(56)	(35)	(21)
Depreciation for the year to 31 March 19-9	–	28	(28)
Balance at 31 March 19-9	308	63	245

Fixed assets disposed of during the year were sold for £30,800.

(2) Current assets at 31 March for each of the two years comprise the following:

	19-9 £000	19-8 £000
Stocks	49	38
Debtors	31	39
Bank	34	31
Cash	12	4
	126	112

(3) The preference shares were redeemed during the year ended 31 March 19-9. This redemption was funded by a new issue of ordinary shares at a premium.

(4) A transfer of £21,000 from the profit and loss account was made to the capital redemption reserve.

Required

(a) Prepare a cash flow statement for Alto Limited for the year ended 31 March 19-9, showing clearly the change in the cash and bank balances (15 marks)

(b) Explain the purpose and uses of a cash flow statement. (7 marks)

(Total 22 marks)

5 The following summarised balance sheets have been prepared for Entwistle plc as at 30 September 19-8 and 30 September 19-9.

Balance sheet as at 30 September

19-8 £000	19-8 £000		19-9 £000	19-9 £000	19-9 £000
		Fixed assets			
285		Freehold land and buildings (net book value)			675
180		Plant and machinery (net book value)			292
	465				967
	285	Investments (at cost)			30
	750				997
		Current assets			
180		Stocks		105	
222		Trade debtors		92	
–		Balance at bank		200	
28		Cash		66	
430				463	
		Less current liabilities			
52		Trade creditors	99		
27		Proposed dividend	39		
50		Bank overdraft	–		
129	301		138	325	
	1,051	Carried forward			1,322

19-8					19-9		
£000	£000			£000	£000	£000
	1,051	Brought forward					1,322
		Financed by:					
		Share Capital					
	150	£1 Ordinary shares fully paid					450
		Reserves					
	367	Share premium					292
	–	Land revaluation					150
	398	Retained earnings					294
	915						1,186
		Loan capital					
	136	10% Debentures 1989 – 96					136
	1,051						1,322

Additional information:

(1) Profit and loss appropriation for the year ended 30 September 19-9

	£000
Net profit	10
Less final dividend proposed	39
Transfer to retained earnings	(29)

(2) (i) The freehold land and buildings were revalued on 1 June 19-9 by £150,000
   (ii) On 1 July 19-9 further freehold land and buildings were purchased at a cost of £240,000
   (iii) There were no sales or provision for depreciation of freehold land and buildings.

(3) (i) On 1 July 19-9 a bonus issue was made of 3 shares for every 2 shares held. The issue was financed from the share premium account £150,000, and the balance from retained earnings.
   (ii) On 1 August 19-9 75,000 new £1 ordinary shares were issued at £2 a share.

(4) During the financial year 19-8/-9 investments which cost £255,000 were sold for £300,000.

(5) The depreciation on plant and machinery was £60,000 for the year, and there were no revaluations or sales of plant and machinery.

Required

(a) A cash flow statement for Entwistle plc for the year ended 30 September 19-9. Show the change in the cash and bank balances over the year   (15 marks)

(b) Write a brief report on Entwistle plc explaining:
   (i) How the company is able to finance an expansion in its productive capacity when in the current year profits are extremely poor.
   (ii) Why the company has made an issue of bonus shares.   (8 marks)

(c) For the financial year 19-9/-0 the company has a budget target for return on equity capital employed (as at 30 September 19-9) of 18%

What net profit must the company earn in order to meet its target?   (2 marks)

(Total 25 marks)

6 The following financial information is available from Chico Limited

Balance sheet as at 30 April

	19-8				19-9	
	£000	£000	£000	£000	£000	£000
Fixed Assets						
Land and buildings(at cost)		350			490	
Plant & Equipment						
Cost	238			336		
Less Depreciation	120	118		134	202	
Goodwill		154			77	
			622			769
Current Assets						
Stocks	245			350		
Trade Debtors	133			105		
Expenses Prepaid	30			30		
Bank	152			110		
Cash	14			21		
	574			616		
Current Liabilities						
Trade Creditors	77			119		
Interest Accrued	7			14		
Proposed Dividend	35			28		
	119			161		
Net working capital			455			455
			1,077			1,224
Financed by:			£000			£000
Share Capital £1 ordinary shares						
fully paid			560			560
Share Premium			448			448
General Reserves			28			28
Profit and Loss			41			48
10% Debentures 1998/9			–			140
			1,077			1,224

Additional information:

1. Plant and equipment which originally cost £189,000 was sold for £42,000. At the date of sale, 1 May 19-8, the book value was £105,000.

2. Depreciation of £98,000 was provided against plant and equipment held during the year.

3. The profit and loss appropriation account for the year ended 30 April 19-9 showed:

		£
Net Profit		56,000
Less Net Dividends		
Interim (Paid)	21,000	
Final (Proposed)	28,000	49,000
Retained		£7,000

Required

(a) A cash flow statement for the year ended 30 April 19-9 showing clearly the cash inflows and outflows for the year.   (18 marks)

(b) Comment on the information disclosed by the cash flow statement prepared in (a)
                                                                                (5 marks)

(c) Why are cash flow statements considered as an important part of business accounting information.   (2 marks)

(Total 25 marks)

7 The balance sheets of Magnum Ltd as at 31 December 19-8 and 19-7 are as follows:

31.12 –7		31.12.-8
£		£
45,000	Fixed Assets (net book value)	60,000
	Current Assets:	
25,000	Stock	27,000
10,000	Debtors	12,000
7,000	Bank	–
87,000		99,000
	Share Capital:	
22,000	Ordinary Shares of 25p each	27,000
24,000	Preference Shares of £1 each	7,000
–	Capital Redemption Reserve	17,000
280	Share Premium Account	420
18,460	Retained Earnings	25,060
64,740		76,480
	Current Liabilities:	
13,860	Creditors	8,500
5,600	Taxation	7,000
2,800	Proposed dividends	4,200
–	Bank	2,820
87,000		99,000

Notes

1. A summary of the company's Fixed Assets Account in the general ledger for the year ended 31 December 19-8 is shown below:

		£			£
1 Jan 19-8	Cost b/f	106,400	31 Dec 19-8	Disposal A/c	11,200
31 Dec 19-8	Additions	30,800	31 Dec 19-8	Cost c/f	126,000
		137,200			137,200

The assets were sold for £2,520, which represented a loss of £4,480 compared with their book value.

2. A bonus (scrip) issue of 1,000 shares was made during the year, the shares being paid up from the balance standing to the credit of the Share Premium Account.

3. The preference shares were redeemed at par in November 19-8

Required

(a) Prepare the profit and loss appropriation account for the year ended 31 December 19-8.
(5 marks)

(b) Draw up a cash flow statement for the year ended 31 December 19-8. (15 marks)

(c) Explain the difference between a bonus issue and a rights issue. (5 marks)

(Total 25 marks)

8   The balance sheets at the end of the last two years for Singh plc are shown below:

31 May 19-7				31 May 19-8		
£	£	£	Fixed Assets	£	£	£
62,700		48,975	Goodwill			35,250
120,000		120,000	Premises	300,000	–	300,000
356,078	118,778	237,300	Plant and Machinery	397,500	115,350	282,150
135,000	11,850	123,150	Office Equipment	147,000	33,750	113,250
673,778	130,628			844,500	149,100	
		187,890	Investments			229,125
		717,315				959,775
			Current Assets			
	101,722		Stock		133,335	
81,172			Debtors	90,398		
3,150			less provision for bad debts	3,563		
	78,022				86,835	
	–		Bank		13,815	
	179,744				233,985	
			Current Liabilities			
59,805			Creditors	74,730		
43,125			Corporation Tax	47,250		
27,240			Ordinary Share Dividend	39,000		
8,130			Accruals	3,480		
33,944			Bank overdraft	–		
	172,244				164,460	
		7,500				69,525
		724,815				1,029,300
			Long Term Liability			
		75,000	12% Bank Loan			94,350
		649,815				934,950
			Issued Share Capital			
		375,000	£1 ordinary shares			637,500
		240,000	£1 6% redeemable preference shares 19-7 –9			112,500
		615,000				750,000
			Reserves			
		–	Share Premium		49,500	
		–	Capital Redemption Reserve		45,000	
		18,000	General Reserve		57,000	
		16,815	Profit and Loss		33,450	
		34,815				184,950
		649,815				934,950

During the year ended 31 May 19-8, an interim ordinary dividend of £23,250 was paid. Some of the redeemable preference shares, which had been issued at par, were redeemed at a premium of 2%. Preference dividend was also paid but only on the preference shares still in issue.

Plant and machinery costing £63,000, book value £27,000, was sold for £30,750, and new plant and machinery was purchased for £104,422.

There was a revaluation of the premises and a subsequent bonus issue of £1 ordinary shares to the value of the revaluation reserve.

The increase in the bank loan was made on 1 June 19-7.

Required

(i) A cash flow statement for the year ended 31 May 19-8 for Singh plc.   (30 marks)

(ii) A comment on the performance and policies of the company during the year ended 31 May 19-8 as revealed by your answer to (i)   (10 marks)

(Total 40 marks)

15 Departmental and branch accounts; leasing and hire purchase

Chapter objectives

Questions on these topics test

- ❑ understanding of apportionment of overheads over departments, branches
- ❑ ability to calculate branch contributions to overall profit of business
- ❑ appreciation of factors, financial and non-financial, to be considered in the closure of unprofitable departments and branches
- ❑ ability to record hire purchase and leasing transactions and to apportion finance charges correctly to accounting periods
- ❑ ability to record outstanding obligations under hire purchase and leasing in balance sheets

15.1 Departmental accounts

15.1.1 The purpose of departmental accounts

A business may have two or more departments. In order to reveal the separate results of the departments, it will prepare separate trading and profit and loss accounts for each. The following example will show the need for departmental accounts:

The profit and loss account of the Rainbow Department Store showed that the store made a profit of £110,000 in the year to 31 December 19-4. This seemed to be an acceptable result to the directors until separate results for each department were shown to them. There were five departments and the respective net results for the year were as follows:

Department	Net profit £	Net loss £
Men's wear	45,000	
Ladies' wear	47,000	
Footwear	23,000	
Furniture		20,000
Hardware	15,000	
	130,000	20,000

If it were not for the Furniture department loss, the profit could have been £130,000.

Departmental accounts are necessary to show the contribution that each department is making to the overall result of a business and to indicate departments which need either to improve their performance or face closure.

A departmental manager may be entitled to a commission based upon the profit he earns. If the commission is calculated as a percentage of the profit after charging the commission, the calculation is as follows:

$$\text{Profit before commission} \times \frac{\text{percentage of commission}}{100 + \text{percentage of commission}}$$

15.1.2 Departmental trading accounts

Separate records must be kept of the sales and purchases for each department. The books of prime entry must provide for transactions to be analysed to the separate departments. Unless this is done, it is not possible to prepare separate trading accounts.

Example

Jonas Bros. Ltd is a departmental store with four departments: furnishings, fashion, electrical, and garden. The following is an extract from its purchases day book.

Purchases day book

	Total £	Furnishing £	Fashion £	Electrical £	Garden £
Comfihome Electrical	3,446			3,446	
Velvet Drapes Ltd	1,860	1,860			
Dress Sense Ltd	1,632		1,632		
Gnomes & Gardens	448				448
Four Poster Beds Ltd	4,000	4,000			
Fridge & Freezers Ltd	2,540			2,540	
	13,926	5,860	1,632	5,986	£448
Individual invoices credited to suppliers' accounts in appropriate purchases ledgers		Total debited to Furnishing Purchases a/c and credited to Furnishing Purchases Control a/c	Total debited to Fashion Purchases a/c and credited to Fashion Purchases Control a/c	Total debited to Electrical Purchases a/c and credited to Electrical Purchases Control a/c	Total debited to Garden Purchases a/c and credited to Garden Purchases Control a/c

The sales day book and the returns books must be analysed in a similar fashion and separate stock-taking lists prepared for each department.

15.1.3 Departmental profit and loss accounts

Overheads should be apportioned on equitable bases between the departments. Examples of bases of apportionment are:

Departmental wages, salaries	Actual payroll costs for each department obtained by analysis of the payroll.
Administrative salaries	On basis of number of employees in each department or on respective turnovers
Rent, rates, heating, lighting, property insurance	On relative floor areas of the departments
Depreciation	On cost of fixed assets employed by each department.
Insurance of fixed assets other than property	On replacement values of assets in each department

Example

Wellies the Chemists have separate departments for drugs, cosmetics and photographic equipment. The following balances were extracted from their books for the year to 31 December 19-4.

		£	£
Purchases:	Drugs	57,600	
	Cosmetics	50,600	
	Photographic	26,500	134,700
Sales	Drugs	90,000	
	Cosmetics	120,000	
	Photographic	50,000	260,000

Stock at 1 January 19-4		
Drugs	13,400	
Cosmetics	11,700	
Photographic	16,000	41,100
Salaries and wages		46,500
Sales commission		11,500
Rent and rates		14,000
Heating and lighting		3,750
Advertising		2,400
Delivery expenses		2,100
Depreciation of fixed assets		5,250
Administration and general expenses		12,000

Additional information:

1. Stocks at 31 December 19-4 were as follows:

	£
Drugs	12,500
Cosmetics	13,300
Photographic	13,500

2. Salaries and wages are to be allocated as follows:

	£
Drugs	14,600
Cosmetics	19,400
Photographic	12,500

3. Sales commission is to be apportioned in the ratio of the turnover of each department.

4. Rent and rates, light and heat, are to be apportioned in the ratio of departmental floor areas as follows:

Drugs 30%;　Cosmetics 40%;　Photographic 30%

5. All other expenses are to be apportioned equally between the departments.

WELLIES THE CHEMISTS
Departmental trading and profit and loss accounts for the year ended 31 December 19-4

	Drugs		Cosmetics		Photographic		Total	
	£	£	£	£	£	£	£	£
Sales		90,000		120,000		50,000		260,000
less Cost of sales								
Stock 1 Jan 19-4	13,400		11,700		16,000		41,100	
Purchases	57,600		50,600		26,500		134,700	
	71,000		62,300		42,500		175,800	
Stock 31 Dec 19-4	12,500	58,500	13,300	49,000	13,500	29,000	39,300	136,500
Gross profit		31,500		71,000		21,000		123,500
Salaries and wages	14,600		19,400		12,500		46,500	
Sales commission	3,981		5,308		2,211		11,500	
Rent and rates	4,200		5,600		4,200		14,000	
Heating and lighting	1,125		1,500		1,125		3,750	
Advertising	800		800		800		2,400	
Delivery expenses	700		700		700		2,100	
Depreciation	1,750		1,750		1,750		5,250	
Administration and general expenses	4,000	31,156	4,000	39,058	4,000	27,286	12,000	97,500
Net profit/(loss)		344		31,942		(6,286)		26,000

15.1.4 Exercise: on the preparation of departmental accounts

Harwoods Stores Ltd has two departments: (i) Hardware and (ii) Kitchen Furniture.

The following is an extract from the trial balance at 30 June 19-3:

		£	£
Stock at 1 July 19-2:	Hardware	120,000	
	Kitchen furniture	45,000	
Purchases:	Hardware	350,000	
	Kitchen furniture	250,000	

		£	£
Sales:	Hardware		490,000
	Kitchen furniture		310,000
Wages:	Hardware	25,000	
	Kitchen furniture	20,000	
Carriage outwards		6,000	
Carriage inwards		4,800	
Heating and lighting		2,400	
Rent of premises		30,000	
Discounts allowed		2,400	
Discounts received			12,000
Depreciation of fixtures and fittings		7,500	

Further information:

1. Stocks at 30 June 19-3 were: Hardware £132,000; Kitchen furniture £65,000.

2. The Hardware department occupies two thirds of the premises and the remainder is taken up by the Kitchen Furniture dept.

3. Fixtures and fittings at cost are: Hardware £60,000; Kitchen furniture £15,000

4. Carriage inwards and discounts received are to be apportioned on the basis of departmental purchases. Carriage outwards and discounts allowed are to be apportioned on the basis of departmental sales. Rent and heating and lighting are to be apportioned on the basis of the respective areas of the departments.

Required

Prepare departmental trading and profit and loss accounts for the year to 30 June 19-3 for Harwoods Stores Ltd,

15.1.5 Factors to be considered before closing a department

Before making a decision to close an unprofitable department, all factors should be taken into account. Examples of factors to be considered are:

1. The apportionment of overheads to the department should be fair and reasonable; an otherwise profitable department may appear to be making a loss because the apportionment between the departments is not equitable.

    In the example of Wellies the Chemists in 15.1.3, the administration and general expenses would probably have been more fairly apportioned on the basis of departmental sales; the results would then have been as follows:

	£	
Drugs	190	(profit)
Cosmetics	30,404	(profit)
Photographic	(4,593)	(loss)

    This would seem to show that the photographic department, while still making a loss, was unfairly treated by the division of administration and general expenses equally between the departments.

2. Other departments may suffer if the loss making department is closed. For example:

    (i) the overheads of the business may not be correspondingly reduced, and the other departments may be burdened with larger shares of overheads to the detriment of their profitability

    (ii) the loss-making department may be attracting customers to the profitable ones. For example, many departmental stores have restaurants which are usually situated so that the customers have to pass through the other departments to get to them. The turnover of the other departments may benefit as a result.

Some businesses prepare departmental trading accounts, but only one profit and loss account for the whole business rather than make arbitrary apportionments of overheads between the departments.

Key points to remember

1. Departmental accounts are necessary to disclose the details of the trading of individual departments of a business. The information shows whether departments need to be made more profitable or that they should be closed

2. Departmental accounts may be necessary for particular purposes such as calculating managers' commission or staff bonuses.

3. Overheads should be apportioned on reasonable and fair bases. Appropriate bases must be selected.

4. A department may appear to be unprofitable because it is being charged with an unfair proportion of overheads.

5. Before deciding to close an unprofitable department, management should consider the consequences:

    (i) Closure will probably not result in a commensurate reduction in the overheads of the business. The remaining departments may have to bear a larger share of overheads to the detriment of their profitability.

    (ii) A loss making department may in fact be attracting customers for the other departments.

    (iii) The possibility of using the resources (e.g. space, etc) freed by closure for the benefit of the other departments or for a new department.

    (iv) Costs of closing the department e.g. redundancy payments.

    (v) Closure may have social consequences; the department may be providing an only source of supply or service to the local community

Common errors

1. choice of wrong bases for apportioning overheads to departments

2. arithmetical errors in calculating apportionments

15.2 Branch accounts

A business having a head office and branches may retain all the accounting records for the branches at head office, or allow the branches to maintain their own accounting records.

15.2.1 Branch accounts maintained at head office

Branch accounts will be maintained at head office when the administration of the business is centralised there. The purpose of centralisation is to ensure proper control over branch operations so that all goods and cash are accounted for and losses are not concealed by branches. All purchasing will be carried out at head office to take advantage of bulk discounts.

Goods will be invoiced by head office to branches at selling price or at cost plus a percentage mark up as a means of control over the branches. For example, if goods are invoiced to a branch for £2,000, the branch must at any particular time account for cash or unsold goods to that amount. It sends periodical returns to head office for cash and credit sales, cash remitted to head office, cash and stock in hand.

There are two systems of maintaining branch accounts at head office.

Method 1

1. **The price at which goods are sent to branches is recorded in memorandum form only.**

This method uses the following accounts in the head office books:

    Branch Stock account with memorandum columns to record the invoiced value of goods sent to branch

    Goods Sent to Branch account in which goods sent to branch are recorded at cost

    Branch total debtors account

The Branch Stock account is debited with the goods sent to the branch and credited with goods returned by the branch and cash remitted to head office. Unsold stock is carried down as a balance at the year end and is included at cost in the head office balance sheet. Stock shortages are revealed by discrepancies between the memorandum columns and should be investigated if material.

The Branch Stock account also acts as a branch profit and loss account, the profit or loss being carried to the head office profit and loss account.

Goods Sent to Branch account is used to complete the double entry to record goods sent to, or returned by, the branch. The balance on this account is deducted from cost of sales in the head office trading account since the goods represented by the balance have been sold by the branches and not by head office.

15.2.2 Example

Bough Ltd is situated in Forest Hill and has a branch in Oakwood. Bough Ltd purchases goods for the branch and transfers the goods to the branch at a uniform mark-up of 50%.

The branch sells goods on cash but also has credit customers who are required to settle their accounts direct to the head office in Forest Hill.

The following information is available for the month of October 19X2:

	£
At 1 October 19X2:	
Stock at branch (at cost price)	8,000
Branch debtors	865
During the month to 31 October 19X2:	
Goods sent to branch (at cost)	12,000
Goods returned by branch to head office (at cost)	800
Goods returned by customers to branch (at selling price)	150
Goods returned by customers to head office (at selling price)	240
Branch sales – cash	10,000
– credit	8,642
Cash remitted by customers to head office	8,400
At 31 October 19X2:	
Stock at branch (at cost)	6,662

Required

(a) the accounts in the books of Bough Ltd to record

   (i)   goods sent to branch

   (ii) branch stocks

   (iii) branch debtors

   (iv) cash received

BOUGH LIMITED
Branch Stock

19X2		Memorandum column at selling price £	£	19X2		Memorandum column at selling price £	£
Oct 1	Stock b/d	12,000	8,000	Oct 31	Goods sent to branch – returns	1,200	800
31	Goods sent to branch	18,000	12,000		Sales – cash	10,000	10,000*
	Branch debtors	150	150*		– credit	8,642	8,642*
	Branch debtors - goods returned to HO by customers		80†				
	Profit & loss		5,874		Stock c/d	9,993	6,662
					P & L Stock loss	315§	
		30,150	26,104			30,150	26,104
Nov 1	Balance b/d	9,993	6,662				

*   Sales and sales returns are recorded in both columns at selling price

†   When goods are returned to head office by branch customers, the mark up must be debited to the Branch Stock account to cancel out the profit element included in the sale on the credit side.

§ A difference between the totals of the memorandum columns represents a stock loss at the branch. An entry is made in the memorandum column on the credit side to balance the columns, but no entry is required in the double entry column. The loss is automatically reflected in the profit carried to the profit and loss account.

Goods sent to branch

19X2		£	19X2		£
Oct 31	Branch stock – returns	800	Oct 31	Branch stock	12,000
	Branch debtors – returns	160			
	Trading account	11,040			
		12,000			12,000

Branch debtors

19X2		£	19X2		£	£
Oct 1	Balance b/d	865	Oct 31	Branch stock goods returned to branch		150
	Branch stock	8,642		Goods returned to H O		
				– Goods sent to branch	160	
				– Branch stock	80	240
				Bank		8,400
				Balance c/d		717
		9,507				9,507
Nov 1	Balance b/d	717				

[Proof of profit:		£	£	£
Sales (10,000 + 8,642)				18,642
less returns (150 + 240)				390
				18,252
Cost of sales:	Stock at 1 Oct 19X2		8,000	
	Goods sent to branch	12,000		
	less returns (800 + 160)	960	11,040	
			19,040	
	less stock at 31 Oct 19X2		6,662	12,378
Profit				5,874]

15.2.3 Exercise: to prepare branch accounts

Firtree Limited maintains a head office in London which purchases goods on behalf of its branch in Potters Bar. The head office sends the goods to the branch at selling price which is arrived at by adding a mark-up of $33\frac{1}{3}\%$

The branch sells goods on cash but also has credit customers who are required to settle their accounts direct to the head office in London.

The following information is available for the month of October 1992:

	£
At 1 October 19-2:	
Stock at branch (at cost)	18,000
Branch debtors	1,200
During the month to 31 October 19-2:	
Goods sent to branch (at cost)	54,000
Goods returned by branch to head office (at cost)	600
Goods returned by customers to branch (at selling price)	1,200
Goods returned by customers to head office (at selling price)	800
Branch sales – cash	25,000
– credit	42,000
Cash remitted by customers to head office	39,400
At 31 October 19-2	
Stock at branch (at cost)	21,600

Required

Prepare the following accounts as they will appear in the books of Firtree Ltd at 31 October 19-2:

(i) Branch Stock account

(ii) Goods Sent to Branch account

(iii) Branch Debtors account

15.2.4 Method 2

Branch Stock Adjustment account

This method dispenses with the memorandum columns in the Branch Stock account; this is maintained at selling price only. The mark up on the cost of goods sent to branch is recorded in a Branch Stock Adjustment Account which becomes the branch trading account.

15.2.5 Example

Data as in 15.2.2 for Bough Ltd.

The journal entries for the goods sent to branch, (cost £12,000), and goods returned to head office from the branch,(cost £800), will explain the entries made in the ledger accounts:

	£	£
Branch Stock	18,000	
Goods Sent to Branch		12,000
Branch Stock Adjustment		6,000
Goods sent to Oakwood branch		
Goods sent to Branch	800	
Branch Stock Adjustment	400	
Branch Stock		1,200
Goods returned to H.O by Oakwood branch		

Bough Ltd
Branch stock (at selling price)

19X2		£	19X2		£
Oct 1	Stock b/f	12,000	Oct 31	Goods sent to branch	1,200
31	Goods sent to branch	18,000		Sales – cash	10,000
	Branch debtors	150		– credit	8,642
				Stock c/d	9,993
				Branch Stock Adjustment	315*
		30,150			30,150
Nov 1	Balance b/d	9,993			

* The difference between the two sides represents a shortage of goods or cash which must be written off against profit in the Branch Stock Adjustment account.

Goods sent to branch (at cost price)

19X2		£	19X2		£
Oct 31	Branch stock	800	Oct 31	Branch stock	12,000
	Branch debtors	160			
	Trading account	11,040			
		12,000			12,000

Branch stock adjustment (mark up)

19X2		£	19X2		£
Oct 31	Branch stock	400	Oct 1	Balance b/d	4,000*
	Branch debtors	80	31	Branch stock	6,000
	Balance – unrealised profit				
	c/d	3,436			
	Branch Stock Adjustment				
	stock shortage	210			
	Profit & loss	5,874			
		10,000			10,000
			Nov 1	Balance b/d	3,436

* The balance brought down on the Branch Stock Adjustment account represents the profit element in opening stock.

Branch debtors

19X2		£	19X2		£	£
Oct 1	Balance b/d	865	Oct 31	Branch stock		
	Branch stock	8,642		goods returned to branch		150
				Goods returned to HO		
				– Goods sent to branch	160	
				– Branch stock	80	240
				Bank		8,400
				Balance c/d		717
		9,507				9,507
Nov 1	Balance b/d	717				

15.2.6 Exercise: to record transactions in head office books using a branch stock adjustment account

Data as in Exercise 15.2.3. for Firtree Ltd but a Branch Stock Adjustment account is maintained in the head office books.

Required

Prepare the following accounts as they would appear in the books of Firtree Ltd.

(i)   Branch stock account

(ii) Goods sent to Branch account

(iii) Branch Stock Adjustment account

(iv) Branch Debtors Account

15.2.7 Branches maintaining own accounting records

If branches maintain their own accounting records, there has to be a link between the head office records and those at the branch. This link is between a Branch Current account maintained in the head office books and a Head Office Current account kept in the branch books.

The accounting entries are as follows:

In head office books

Expenditure incurred by head office on behalf of the branch:

Debit	BranchCurrent account	Credit	Bank
		or	Goods sent to branch
		or	other expense account

Goods returned, or cash remitted by branch to head office:

Debit	Bank	Credit	Branch Current account
	or Goods returned by branch		

In branch books

Expenditure incurred by head office on behalf of the branch:

Debit	Bank	Credit	Head office current account
	or Goods from head office		
	or other asset or expense account		

Goods returned, or cash remitted to head office:

Debit Head office current account	Credit	Bank
	or	Goods returned to head office account

15.2.8 Example

Turwin Ltd, a retail hardware company, decides to open a branch in Nottingham. During October, the following transactions take place:

October	1	Turwin Ltd secures leasehold premises in Nottingham for the branch at a cost of £20,000
	4	Goods purchased for cash £10,000 and sent to branch
	6	Turwin Ltd transfers cash to branch to pay wages, £2,000
	7	Turwin Ltd purchases fixtures and fittings for the branch, £7,000

8   The branch returns goods to Turwin Ltd; cost £800

9   Branch sells goods for cash £8,000

10 The branch buys office sundries out of takings, £400

14 The branch pays electricity bill, £131

20 The branch remits cash to Turwin Ltd £6,000

In head office books:

Nottingham branch current account

Oct		£	Oct		£
1	Bank – leasehold premises	20,000	8	Goods returned by branch	800
4	Bank – goods	10,000	20	Bank	6,000
6	Bank – wages	2,000		Balance c/d	32,200
7	Bank – fixtures and fittings	7,000			
		39,000			39,000
21	Balance b/d	32,200			

In Nottingham branch books

Head Office current account

Oct		£	Oct		£
8	Goods returned to head office	800	1	Leasehold premises	20,000
20	Bank	6,000	4	Goods from head office	10,000
	Balance c/d	32,200	6	Wages	2,000
			7	Fixtures and fittings	7,000
		39,000			39,000
			21	Balance b/d	32,200

Bank

Oct		£	Oct		£
9	Sales	8,000	10	Office sundries	400
			14	Electricity	131
			20	Head office current account	6,000
				Balance c/d	1,469
		8,000			8,000
20	Balance b/d	1,469			

Leasehold Premises

Oct		£	Oct		£
1	Head Office current account	20,000			

Goods from head office

Oct		£	Oct		£
4	Head Office current account	10,000			

Wages

Oct		£	Oct		£
6	Head Office current account	2,000			

Fixtures and fittings

Oct		£	Oct		£
7	Head Office current account	7,000			

Goods returned to head office

Oct		£	Oct		£
			8	Head office current account	800

Sales

Oct		£	Oct		£
			9	Bank	8,000

Office sundries

Oct		£	Oct		£
10	Bank	400			

Electricity

Oct		£	Oct		£
14	Bank	131			

The entries in the head office current account in the branch books mirror those in the branch current account in the head office books and they have equal but opposite balances.

The debit balance on the branch current account in the head office books represents Turwin Ltd's investment in the branch. The credit balance on the head office current account in the branch books is effectively the 'owner's' capital account in the branch books.

15.2.9 Exercise

Ofra Ltd, a furniture business in Newcastle, opened a branch shop in Hexham on 1 October 19-3. The branch maintains its own accounting records. The following transactions took place between Ofra Ltd and the branch:

Oct. 1   Ofra Ltd purchased freehold premises in Hexham for £150,000, and fixtures and fittings for the branch, £18,000.

2   Ofra Ltd transferred £5,000 into an account at the Hexham branch of its bank for the branch

3   Ofra Ltd purchased stock on credit from Kopak Ltd. The stock was to be delivered to the Hexham branch and cost £40,000

Ofra Ltd sent goods from its own stock to Hexham branch; cost of goods £10,000

5   The branch purchased more stock and paid cash £3,000

6   The branch paid staff wages from its bank account at Hexham £900

7   The branch sold goods for cash £7,000, and remitted £4,000 to Ofra Ltd.

Required

(a) Enter the above transactions, as they affect Ofra Ltd's head office in the Branch Current account in the head office books.

(b) Enter the above transactions into the ledger accounts of the Hexham branch

15.2.10 Year end procedure

The branch extracts its own trial balance and prepares a branch profit and loss account. The branch profit or loss is passed to head office through the current accounts.

Head office is able to prepare a combined trading and profit and loss account and a balance sheet by aggregating the branch trial balance with its own. The balance on the current account in the branch trial balance will be cancelled out against the balance on the current account in the head office trial balance.

Cash and goods in transit at the year end

It is possible that the balances on the head office and branch current accounts will not agree at the year end. There may be two reasons for this.

Cash which has been remitted to head office but which has not been credited in the head office bank account before the year end will have been debited to head office by the branch but not credited by head office to the branch current account. Goods which have been sent by head office but not received by the branch at the year end will have been debited to the branch by head office but not credited to head office by the branch.

To reconcile the two current accounts, the head office makes adjusting entries in the branch current account in its books by carrying down balances for these items.

Unrealised profit in stock

When goods are transferred by head office to the branch at selling price or including a mark up, and some of these goods remain in stock at the branch, the unrealised profit must be provided for in the head office profit and loss account. The provision is deducted from stock in the balance sheet to reduce it to cost.

15.2.11 Example

Root Limited's head office is in Basildon. The company has a branch in Harrow. Goods purchased by head office are sold to the branch at cost plus 20%. The trial balances extracted from the head office and the branch books at 30 September 19X2 were as follows:

	Head office Debit £	Head office Credit £	Branch Debit £	Branch Credit £
Sales		280,000		172,000
Purchases	180,000		123,200	
Stock at cost or at cost to branch at 1 October 19X1	12,000		7,200	
Goods sent to branch		132,800		
Administrative expenses	108,000		7,200	
Distribution costs	24,000		9,600	
Profit and loss account at 1 October 19X1		22,400		
Provision for unrealised profit on stock held by the branch		1,200		
Fixed assets at net book value	306,400		30,400	
Debtors	12,000		16,000	
Creditors		18,000		4,000
Cash at bank and in hand	15,200		1,600	
Branch current account	36,800			
Head office current account				19,200
Called up share capital (ordinary shares of £1 each)		240,000		
	694,400	694,400	195,200	195,200

Additional information:

1. Stock at 30 September 19X2 was valued as follows:

	£
Head office at cost	16,000
Branch at cost to branch	19,200
Goods in transit to branch at cost to branch	9,600

2. At 30 September 19X2 the branch had transferred £8,000 to the head office's bank account but as at that date no record had been made in the head office's books of account.

Required

(a) The head office, the branch, and combined trading and profit and loss accounts for the year to 30 September 19X2, and

(b) The head office, the branch and combined balance sheets as at that date.

Root Limited
Trading and profit and loss accounts for the year ended 30 September 19X2

	Head office £	Branch £	Combined £	
Sales	280,000	172,000	452,000	
Goods sent to branch	132,800			(note 1)
	412,800	172,000	452,000	
Opening stock (note 2)	12,000	7,200	18,000	
Purchases	180,000	–	180,000	
Goods received from head office		123,200		(note 1)
	192,000	130,400	198,000	
Less closing stock (note 3)	(16,000)	(19,200)	(40,000)	
Cost of sales	176,000	111,200	158,000	
Gross profit	236,800	60,800	294,000	
Increase in provision for unrealised profit (note 4)	(3,600)			
Administrative expenses	(108,000)	(7,200)	(115,200)	
Distribution costs	(24,000)	(9,600)	(33,600)	
Net profit for the year	101,200	44,000	145,200	
Branch profit transferred through current accounts	44,000	(44,000)		
Profit brought forward	22,400		22,400	
Profit carried forward	167,600		167,600	

Root Limited
Balance sheets as at 30 September 19X2

	Head office £	Branch £	Combined £
Fixed assets at net book value	306,400	30,400	336,800
Current assets			
Stocks	16,000	19,200	32,000
Goods in transit	8,000		8,000
Debtors	12,000	16,000	28,000
Branch current account	60,000		
Cash at bank and in hand	15,200	1,600	16,800
Cash in transit	8,000		8,000
	119,200	36,800	92,800
Creditors: amounts falling due within one year			
Creditors	18,000	4,000	22,000
Head office current account		63,200	
	18,000	67,200	22,000
Net current assets	101,200	(30,400)	70,800
Total assets less current liabilities	407,600		407,600
Capital and reserves			
Called up share capital	240,000		240,000
Profit and loss account	167,600		167,600
	407,600		407,600

Notes

1 Transfers between head office and the branch do not affect the overall position of the business

2	Opening stock	£	£
	Head office		12,000
	Branch (at cost to branch)	7,200	
	less unrealised profit (1/6)	1,200	6,000
	Combined		18,000

3	Closing stock	£	£
	Head office		16,000
	Branch	19,200	
	less unrealised profit (1/6)	3,200	16,000
	add goods in transit		
	at cost to branch	9,600	
	less unrealised profit (1/6)	1,600	8,000
	Combined		40,000

4	Provision required for unrealised profit	£
	On goods at branch (W3)	3,200
	On goods in transit (W3)	1,600
		4,800
	less provision brought forward 1.10.91	1,200
	Increase required	3,600

5 Reconciliation of current accounts
(Head office books)

Branch current account

	£		£
Balance b/f	36,800	Goods in transit c/d	9,600
Net profit	44,000	Cash in transit c/d	8,000
		Balance c/d	63,200
	80,800		80,800
Goods in transit b/d	9,600		
Cash in transit b/d	8,000		
Balance b/d	63,200*		

* This must be reduced by the unrealised profit on goods in stock at the branch in the head office balance sheet: £(63,200 – 3,200) = £60,000

(Branch books)

Head office current account

	£			£
Balance c/d	63,200	Balance b/d		19,200
		Net profit		44,000
	63,200			63,200
		Balance b/d		63,200

15.2.12 Exercise

Trunk Limited has its head office in London, and it also has a branch in Lincoln. The branch maintains its own accounting records. The following trial balances have been extracted from the head office and branch books as at 31 October 19X2

	Head Office Debit £	Head Office Credit £	Branch Debit £	Branch Credit £
Called up share capital				
(ordinary shares of £1 each)		420,000		
Plant and machinery (net book value)	536,200		53,200	
Branch current account	64,400			
Head office current account				33,600
Goods sent to branch		232,400		
Debtors	21,000		28,000	
Creditors		31,500		7,000
Cash at bank and in hand	26,600		2,800	
Stock at cost or cost to branch at				
1 November 19X1	21,000		12,600	
12,600				
Sales		490,000		301,000
Purchases	315,000		215,600	
Administration expenses	189,000		12,600	
Distribution expenses	42,000		16,800	
Profit and loss account at 1 November 19X1		39,200		
Provision for unrealised profit on stock		2,100		
	£1,215,200	£1,215,200	£341,600	£341,600

Additional information:

1. Stock at 31 October 19X2 was valued as follows:

	£
Head office at cost	28,000
Branch, at cost to branch	33,600
Goods in transit to branch at cost to branch	16,800

2. Goods purchased by head office and sold to the branch are transferred at cost plus 20%

3. At 31 October 19X2 the branch had transferred £14,000 to the head office's bank account but this had not been entered in the head office's bank account or cash book at that date.

Required

Prepare in adjacent columns:

(a) the head office, the branch, and the combined trading and profit and loss accounts for the year to 31 October 19X2, and

(b) the head office, the branch, and the combined balance sheets as at that date

15.2.13 Head office overheads charged to branches

A head office inevitably performs duties for branches. These duties may include maintenance of branch premises, personnel administration and other functions. Branches are charged for these services by being debited through the current account with a proportion of head office overheads. A number of points emerge from a consideration of this process:

1. The apportionment of the overheads should be fair and reasonable.

2. An unfair apportionment will distort branch results and some branches may appear to be unprofitable when they may, in fact, be profitable. Conversely other branches may appear to be more profitable than they are because their share of head office overheads is understated.

3. If management are unable to make an unprofitable branch profitable, it is likely to be closed. Closure of a branch usually does not mean a corresponding reduction in head office overheads, and the remaining branches may have to bear greater shares of the overheads.

15.2.14 Branch contributions to overall business results

The contribution of a branch to the overall results of a business is measured by the difference between the incremental revenue derived by the branch less the incremental cost to the business of having the branch. The incremental revenue is normally the branch turnover, which would not be gained by the business but for the existence of the branch. Incremental cost is the additional cost to the business arising from the existence of the branch. In calculating incremental cost, exclude from the calculations all head office costs charged to the branch.

15.2.15 Example: of calculating branch contribution

Herewood Ltd has a branch in Manchester; the trading, profit and loss account of the branch for the year to 31 December 19-3 was as follows:

	£	£
Sales		346,000
Cost of sales		211,000
Gross profit		135,000
less Wages	47,000	
Rent	35,000	
Cleaning	3,720	
Sundry	2,340	
Head office overheads	29,000	117,060
Net profit		17,940

Calculation of branch contribution:

	£	£
Sales		346,000
less Cost of sales	211,000	
Branch overheads		
(excluding H.O. overheads)	88,060	299,060
Branch contribution		46,940

The branch contribution is the amount a branch contributes to head office overheads and profit.

15.2.16 Exercise: to calculate branch contribution

Mortlake and Putney, grocers, have branches in Chiswick and Richmond. The following are the summarised profit and loss accounts of the two branches for the year to 30 June 19-4:

	Chiswick		Richmond	
	£	£	£	£
Sales		100,000		60,000
Cost of sales		40,000		24,000
Gross profit		60,000		36,000
Wages	15,000		12,000	
Rent	10,000		8,000	
Electricity	6,000		4,000	
Rates	8,000		6,000	
Head office overheads	7,000	46,000	7,000	37,000
Net profit/(loss)		£14,000		£(1,000)

Required

(a) Calculate the branch contributions towards the overall results of Mortlake and Putney for the year to 30 June 19-4.

(b) Comment on the contributions of the two branches as calculated in (a)

> ## Key points to remember
>
> 1. Head office may exercise control over branches by centralising accounting at head office.
> 2. Goods sent to branches may be recorded in the Branch Stock account at selling price. This will entail the use of memorandum columns to record selling price in that account, or the use of a Branch Stock Adjustment account.
> 3. When a branch maintains its own accounts, the link between those accounts and head office accounts is the current account in each set of books.
> 4. The Branch Current account in the head office books must be adjusted for cash and goods in transit at the year end.
> 5. Transactions between head office and branch (e.g. goods sent to branch) must be eliminated in the trading and profit and loss account for the business as a whole.
> 6. Unrealised 'profit' in the closing stock at branch must be eliminated in cost of sales and the balance sheet in the combined year end accounts.
> 7. Branch contribution to head office overheads and profit is an important factor when branch results are being examined.
> 8. Head office overheads apportioned to branches must be on a fair and reasonable basis.
>
> ## Common errors
>
> 1. failure to deduct unrealised profit from branch stock
> 2. arithmetical errors in calculating profit or mark up
> 3. failure to adjust the Branch Current account in the head office books for cash and goods in transit
> 4. failure to eliminate transactions between head office and branch in the combined accounts

15.3 Hire purchase accounts and leasing

15.3.1 Hire purchase

A business may purchase its assets in several ways:

(1) Paying cash
(2) Buying on credit
(3) Paying by instalments
(4) Hire purchase
(5) Leasing

In the first three methods, the buyer acquires ownership of the assets at the time of sale. If the buyer fails to pay the price, the seller has the right to sue for the amount of the unpaid debt.

In the case of an asset bought on hire purchase, the hire purchaser pays instalments and the ownership of the asset remains with the seller until the last hire purchase instalment is paid. Until then, the hire purchaser has, in law, been hiring the asset. If the hire purchaser fails to pay the instalments when they fall due, the seller may repossess the asset. The hire purchaser may make an additional payment, usually of a nominal amount, with the last instalment to exercise his option to purchase the asset. The property in the asset then passes from the seller to the buyer. This is the legal situation.

From an accounting point of view, a hire purchaser is using the asset being acquired as if he already owns it. In that respect, it is indistinguishable from all the other assets of his business. The only difference is in the way the asset is being acquired. Accountants, therefore, consider that the possession and use of an asset being acquired under hire purchase should be reflected in the balance sheet of the business concerned; this should override the strictly legal form of treating the asset as belonging to the seller. This known as the doctrine of 'substance over form'. The asset is recorded as a fixed asset in the books of the purchaser. This is, in fact, the treatment required by SSAP21.

15.3.2 Leases: financing and operating

Assets may be acquired on lease. SSAP 21 defines a lease as a contract between a lessor and a lessee for the hire of a specific asset. The lessor retains ownership of the asset but conveys the right to the use of the asset to the lessee for an agreed period of time in return for the payment of specified rentals.

Assets may be acquired under finance or operating leases.

A **finance lease** is one in which the lessor transfers substantially all the risks and rewards of ownership of the asset to the lessee. Assets being acquired under a finance lease usually remain with the lessee for the duration of their useful lives and are treated as fixed assets in the books and balance sheet of the lessee in the same way as assets being acquired on hire purchase.

The accounting treatment of hire purchase transactions and finance leases is similar and is explained below.

An **operating lease** is any lease other than a finance lease. The risks of ownership remain with the lessor. Assets which are the subjects of operating leases may remain with a lessee for a short term and then be re-leased by the lessor to another lessee. Rentals payable under operating leases should be charged to revenue on a straight line basis over the term of the lease, even if the payments are not made on such a basis, unless another systematic and rational basis is more appropriate.

15.3.3 Treatment by the purchaser of the financing charge included in the hire purchase price

As the accounting treatment for hire purchase and finance leasing is similar, the treatment described here for hire purchase applies equally to finance leasing.

A hire purchase agreement usually provides for payment by the purchaser of an initial instalment at the time of purchase and a number of further instalments to be made at specified intervals.

The seller of goods on hire purchase, in arriving at the hire purchase charge, adds a finance charge to the cash price of the goods. The finance charge is the interest which the hire purchaser has to pay on the outstanding capital payments under the term of the hire purchase agreement. The interest element in the hire purchase instalments is therefore the difference between the cash price and the hire purchase price.

Example

Cater Ltd acquires a new machine on hire purchase on 1 July 19-3. The cash price of the machine is £70,000. The hire purchase agreement provides for an immediate payment of £18,000, three further instalments of £18,000 to be made on 1 January 19-4, 1 July 19-4, 1 January 19-5 and a final instalment of £18,148 on 1 July 19-5. The finance charge is calculated as follows:

	£
Hire purchase price (4 × £18,000 + 18,148)	90,148
less cash price	70,000
Finance charge	20,148

The purchaser should allocate the total finance charge to accounting periods during the hire purchase term so as to produce a constant periodic rate of charge on the remaining balance of the obligation for each accounting period, or a reasonable approximation thereto. Three methods of allocating the finance charge are: actuarial, sum of the digits and straight line.

Actuarial method. The total finance charge of £20,148 is equivalent to interest at 29% p.a. on the reducing balance calculated at half yearly rests.

		Interest calculated on	Interest for 6 months at rate of 29% (rounded)	Balance at end of next six months
		£	£	£
1.7.-3	Cost	70,000		
	1st payment	(18,000)		
		52,000	7,540	59,540
1.1.-4	b/f	59,540		
	2nd payment	(18,000)		
		41,540	6,023	47,563
1.7.-4	b/f	47,563		
	3rd payment	(18,000)		
		29,563	4,287	33,850
1.1.-5	b/f	33,850		
	4th payment	(18,000)		
		15,850	2,298	18,148
1.7.-5	b/f	18,148		
	5th payment	(18,148)		
	Total finance charge		20,148	

The actuarial method is the only one which allocates the finance charge in the manner required by SSAP 21

Sum of the digits method

Where the number of periods between payments = n and $\sum$ = the sum of the integers 1 to n,

interest allocated to: the first period is $n/\sum \times$ total finance charge

                 the second period is $n\text{-}1/\sum \times$ total finance charge

                 the third period is $n\text{-}2/\sum \times$ total finance charge

                 the final period is $1/\sum \times$ total finance charge

In the example of Cater Ltd, the calculation is:

No. of periods: 4. Sum of the periods = 1 + 2 + 3 + 4 = 10

Six months to: 1 Jan 19-4 £20,148 × 4/10   = £8,059

                    1 Jul 19-4 £20,148 × 3/10   = £6,044

                    1 Jan 19-5 £20,148 × 2/10   = £4,030

                    1 Jul 19-5 £20,148 × 1/10   = £2,015

                                        £20,148

The sum of the digits method does not truly reflect the intentions of SSAP 21, but is a convenient method which is frequently used.

Straight line method

The total finance charge is divided by the number of periods, giving a fixed charge for each period. This does not satisfy the requirements of SSAP 21 as it makes no attempt to match the periodic charge against revenue to the interest on the outstanding balance for the period.

If Cater Ltd used the straight line method, the six monthly hire purchase interest charge would be

$\dfrac{£20,148}{4}$ = £5,037

15.3.4 Accounting entries to record hire purchase transactions in the books of the purchaser

There are two methods of recording the purchase of an asset on hire purchase or under a finance lease in the books of the purchaser:

Method 1 Uses a Hire Purchase Loan account and an Interest Suspense account.

Method 2 Uses a Hire Purchase Loan account and an Interest Payable account.

Method 1

The Hire Purchase Loan account is a personal account for the hire purchase creditor and is credited with the total hire purchase price and debited with the instalments as they are paid. The Interest Suspense account is debited with the total amount of the finance charge and credited with the annual amounts of interest which are debited to the profit and loss account.

15.3.5 Example: using the data given for Cater Ltd in 15.3.3

Journal entry to record purchase

		£	£
1.7.-3	Machinery at cost	70,000	
	Interest Suspense	20,148	
	Hire Purchase Loan		90,148
	Purchase of machine from X on hire purchase.		
	Cash price: £70,000; finance charge £20,148.		
	Hire Purchase Loan	18,000	
	Bank		18,000
	1st payment due this day on hire purchase of machine		
1.1.-4	Hire Purchase Loan	18,000	
	Bank		18,000
	2nd payment due this day on hire purchase of machine		
	Profit and loss account	7,540	
	Interest Suspense		7,540
	Interest on hire purchase of machine included in above payment.*		

* In practice, the transfer to Profit and Loss account would be made annually rather than on the occasion of each payment.

Machinery at cost

19-3		£	19-3		£
Jul 1	H P Creditor	70,000			

Hire Purchase Loan

19-3		£	19-3		£
Jul 1	Bank	18,000	Jul 1	Machinery at cost	70,000
Dec 31	Balance c/d	72,148		Interest Suspense	20,148
		90,148			90,148
19-4			19-4		
Jan 1	Bank	18,000	Jan 1	Balance b/d	72,148
Jun 30	Balance c/d	54,148			
		72,148			72,148
Jul 1	Bank	18,000	Jul 1	Balance b/d	54,148
Dec 31	Balance c/d	36,148			
		54,148			54,148
19-5			19-5		
Jan 1	Bank	18,000	Jan 1	Balance b/d	36,148
Jun 30	Balance c/d	18,148			
		36,148			36,148
Jul 1	Bank	18,148	Jul 1	Balance b/d	18,148

Interest Suspense

19-3		£	19-3		£
Jul 1	Hire Purchase Loan	20,148	Dec 31	Profit & loss	7,540
				Balance c/d	12,608
		20,148			20,148
19-4			19-4		
Jan 1	Balance b/d	12,608	Jun 30	Profit & loss	6,023
				Balance c/d	6,585
		12,608			12,608

19-3		£	19-3		£
Jul 1	Balance b/d	6,585	Dec 31	Profit & loss	4,287
				Balance c/d	2,298
		6,585			6,585
19-5			19-5		
Jan 1	Balance b/d	2,298	Jun 30	Profit & loss	2,298

Note: The amount owing to the H P Creditor at the end of each half year is represented by the balance on Hire Purchase Loan account less the balance on the Interest Suspense account.

Method 2

The accounting entries may be summarised by the following journal entries:

	Dr	Cr
Asset at cost	X	
Hire Purchase Loan		X
with cash price of asset		
Hire Purchase Loan	X	
Bank		X
with instalments		
Interest Payable	X	
Hire Purchase Loan		X
Interest payment included in each instalment		
Profit and Loss	X	
Interest Payable		X
with annual amount of interest		

Hire Purchase Loan

19-3		£	19-3		£
July 1	Bank	18,000	Jul 1	Machinery at cost	70,000
Dec 31	Balance c/d	59,540	Dec 31	Interest payable	7,540
		77,540			77,540
19-4			19-4		
Jan 1	Bank	18,000	Jan 1	Balance b/d	59,540
Jun 30	Balance c/d	47,563	Jun 30	Interest payable	6,023
		65,563			65,563
Jul 1	Bank	18,000	Jul 1	Balance b/d	47,563
Dec 31	Balance c/d	33,850	Dec 31	Interest payable	4,287
		51,850			51,850
19-5			19-5		
Jan 1	Bank	18,000	Jan 1	Balance b/d	33,850
Jun 30	Balance c/d	18,148	Dec 31	Interest payable	2,298
		36,148			36,148
Jul 1	Bank	18,148	Jul 1	Balance b/d	18,148

Interest Payable

19-3		£	19-3		£
Dec 31	Hire Purchase Loan	7,540	Dec 31	Profit and loss	7,540
19-4			19-4		
Jun 1	Hire Purchase Loan	6,023	Jun 30	Profit and loss	6,023
Dec 31	Hire Purchase Loan	4,287	Dec 31	Profit and loss	4,287
19-5			19-5		
Jun 30	Hire Purchase Loan	2,298	Jun 30	Profit and loss	2,298

15.3.6 Depreciation

An asset acquired on hire purchase should be depreciated over its useful life. An asset leased under a finance lease should be depreciated over the shorter of the lease term and its useful life.

15.3.7 Balance sheet presentation

Fixed assets acquired on hire purchase or under a finance lease should be shown in the balance sheet at net book value; the outstanding liability to the seller should be shown as a current liability except for any portion that is not due for payment within 12 months, which should be shown as a long term liability. Interest on the capital sum which has not started to accrue at the balance sheet date must not be included as a liability.

15.3.8 Example

Assuming that Cater Ltd bases its depreciation charges for machinery on a ten year life with no residual value, its balance sheet extracts at 31 December 19-3 and 19-4 would appear as follows:

Cater Ltd
Balance sheet extracts as at 31 December

	19-3 £	19-4 £
Fixed assets		
Tangible fixed assets	70,000	70,000
less depreciation	3,500	10,500
Net book value	66,500	59,500
Creditors: amounts falling due within one year		
Amount due under hire purchase obligation	25,690	33,850
Creditors: amounts falling due after more than one year		
Amount due under hire purchase obligation	33,850	

15.3.9 Exercise

Zeta Limited decided to purchase a new machine the cash price of which was £75,000. The directors entered into a hire purchase agreement whereby the company paid an initial deposit on 1 October 19-2 of £8,000. The balance was to be settled by four equal instalments of £20,000 each, payable on 31 March and the 30 September, in the years 19-3 and 19-4 respectively.

The machine has an estimated useful life of 10 years at the end of which it should have a residual value of £5,000.

The directors decided that interest should be apportioned to the respective accounting periods using the sum of digits method. Zeta Limited's financial year ends on the 31 March.

Required

(a) Write up the following ledger accounts for each of the three years to 31 March 19-3, 19-4 and 19-5 respectively:

    (i) the Hire Purchase Loan account; and

    (ii) the Hire Purchase Interest account; and

(b) show the following balance sheet extracts relating to the machine as at 31 March 19X3, 19X4, 19X5 respectively:

    (i) fixed assets: machine at net book value;

    (ii) creditors: amounts payable within one year – obligation under hire purchase contract; and

    (iii) creditors: amounts falling due after more than one year – obligation under hire purchase contract.

15.3.10 Operating leases

Rentals paid by a lessee under an operating lease will be debited to the *lessee's* profit and loss account on a straight line basis over the lease term even if the payments are not made on such a basis. The *lessor company* shows the assets as fixed assets in its balance sheet less accumulated depreciation.

15.3.11 The essence of hire purchase and leasing transactions summarised

Questions on hire purchase and leasing are based upon the difference between hire purchase and finance leases on the one hand and operating leases on the other. They test understanding of the appropriate treatment of assets being acquired on hire purchase or by leasing. The matching concept is tested by the allocation of interest or financing charges, and depreciation charges, to accounting periods.

Businesses usually acquire assets on hire purchase or by leasing because they have not sufficient cash resources to enable them to purchase the assets outright.

Key points to remember

1. A **finance lease** transfers substantially all the risks and rewards of ownership of an asset to the lessee. Any other lease is an **operating lease**.

2. An asset acquired on hire purchase or under a finance lease is treated as a fixed asset in the balance sheet of the lessee (substance over form). It should be depreciated over the term of its useful life or, in the case of a finance lease, over the lease term if this is shorter than the useful life

3. The total finance charge should be allocated to accounting periods during the term of the lease or hire purchase so as to produce a constant periodic rate of charge on the remaining balance of the obligation for each accounting period.

4. The rental under an operating lease should be charged to profit and loss account on a straight line basis over the lease term.

Common Errors

1. Incorrect treatment of the financing charge when (i) Interest Suspense account, or (ii) Interest payable account, are used.

2. Failure to distinguish between short term and long term obligations under a hire purchase or finance lease in the balance sheet.

3. Inclusion of 'future' interest as an obligation in the balance sheet.

Questions

Further examination questions

1. Perplexed Limited makes and sells furniture. It has a manufacturing division, and a retail division comprising two shops. Its accountants produce a revenue statement at the end of the financial year which gives only an overall summary of the company's trading results, showing total income and expenditure.

   (a) Write a report to the finance director of Perplexed Limited on how more useful information than that currently produced can be given to the management of the company by its accountants. (9 marks)

   (b) Explain, giving examples, two problems which may arise through producing separate profit figures for two or more divisions of a company. (6 marks)

   (Total 15 marks)
   (LONDON)

2. Bettermake Ltd has been selling household goods as a retailer for several years. On 1 January 1990 a decision was taken to open retail shops in Bexville and Amstead, two neighbouring towns.

   The following summarised information is available for the financial year ended 31 December 1990:

Bettermake Ltd

	Head Office Shop		Bexville Shop		Amstead Shop	
		£000		£000		£000
Sales		150		30		55
Cost of goods sold		60		15		23
Gross profit		90		15		32
Variable expenses	15		12		16	
Fixed expenses	28	43	13	25	10	26
Net profit/loss		47		(10)		6

The fixed costs of the two branches consist of the following components:

(i) Head Office has allocated £6,000 of its own fixed expenses to each branch.

(ii) The remaining fixed expenses are wholly attributable to the branches.

Required

(a) Explain what is meant by the accounting term contribution. (5 marks)

(b) Identify the contribution made by each branch to the company for the year ended 31 December 1990. (5 marks)

(c) Prepare a brief report for the Board of Bettermake Ltd providing a financial analysis of the results of the whole business for the year ended 31 December 1990. (7 marks)

(d) Identify the circumstances in which a retail branch shop should be closed. (3 marks)

(Total 20 marks)

(AEB)

3 Spencer Reddaway had been selling goods as a retailer for some years and he decided to expand by opening two branches.

All goods were invoiced to the branches at cost. He expected the branches to show a gross profit/sales ratio in the region of 25% and at least to make some net profit.

The following information is available for the financial year ended 30 June 1991, this being the second year of operation for the branches:

	Branch A	Branch B
	£	£
Sales	800,000	1,200,000
Goods from Head Office sent to branch	660,000	1,035,000
Branch variable expenses	70,000	80,000
Branch fixed expenses		
(Wholly attributable to the branches)	60,000	60,000
Goods returned by branch to Head Office	54,000	38,000
Branch stocks:		
Opening	40,000	65,000
Closing (valued at invoiced price)	73,000	141,900

Additional information:

(1) Both branches were run by managers. Managers receive a commission of 1% of net sales, payable three months after the end of an accounting year.

Managers were also responsible for half of all stock losses at their respective branches.

(2) Year end stock taking revealed redundant and damaged stock as follows:

Branch A	Branch B
£3,000	£1,900

The stock values above as at 30 June 1991 have not been adjusted for these amounts.

(3) Reddaway was aware that both branches benefited from some of the facilities provided by the Head Office and he decided that for the year ended 30 June 1991 he would allocate £190,000 of Head Office expenditure equally between the two branches.

(4) Reddaway had received a report from both branch managers that they were experiencing difficulties in collecting debts from a number of trade debtors. Some of these

debts had been outstanding for 18 months and despite repeated attempts at collection they had failed. The amount of debts involved were:

	Branch A	Branch B
	£12,000	£18,000

The owner has not yet decided to write these debts off as bad.

Required

(a) Columnar revenue accounts for **both** of the branches for the year ended 30 June 1991 clearly showing the gross profit and net profit. (12 marks)

(b) A report to Reddaway advising him on the profitability of his branches.

Your report should consider whether the branches should continue to operate or not. Use appropriate financial analysis to support your reasoning. (8 marks)

(c) As Reddaway's accountant advise him as to how to improve the settlement of debts. Your advice should include a consideration of the effect of poor credit control on:
(i) the cash flow
(ii) the profitability of the branches. (5 marks)

(Total 25 marks)

(AEB)

4 Solna Ltd prepares accounts to 31 December. On 1 July 1990 the company plans to enter into an agreement to pay £1,000 per quarter, in advance, to lease a computer. At the end of the two-year period Solna may extend the agreement indefinitely for a nominal annual payment of £1. The cash price of the computer is £7,230, and the quarterly finance cost implicit in the lease is 3%. The interest charges will amount to £350 in 1990, £391 in 1991, and £29 in 1992. In practice the company expects to retain the computer in use for one year beyond the two-year period. The company uses straight line depreciation, apportioned on a time basis in the years of requisition and disposal.

Required

a) show the amounts that will appear in the accounts relating to this finance lease agreement for the four years from 1990 to 1993; (12 marks)

b) explain what is meant by the term 'finance lease' as used in Statement of Standard Accounting Practice (SSAP) 21. (8 marks)

(Total 20 marks)

(JMB)

5 (a) Explain what is meant by "substance over form" in relation to leasing or hire-purchase contracts. Particular reference should be made to the use of the balance sheet by prospective creditors who need knowledge of outstanding liabilities. (8 marks)

(b) Explain how a hire-purchase contract differs from a leasing contract in the transfer of property rights and whether this should be reflected in a firm's financial statements. (6 marks)

(c) State what contingent liabilities arise if a firm enters into a hire-purchase or leasing contract. (4 marks)

(Total 18 marks)

(WJEC)

6 A note to the balance sheet of Ashley Holdings plc at 31 January 1991 showed the following details relating to fixed assets.

		£000
Freehold property at 1989 valuation		1,650
Plant and equipment at cost		4,780
Provision for depreciation	– freehold property	250
	– plant and equipment	3,820

In 1991 company policy in regard to the financing of fixed asset acquisitions changed: assets were no longer purchased outright but instead were acquired subject to lease. The following lease payments in regard to plant were made in the year ending 31 January 1992.

	£000
Payments under finance leases	750
Payments under operating leases	190

The fair value of assets acquired under finance leases was £2,750,000 and the finance charge (true rate of interest) was $22\frac{1}{2}\%$ of the outstanding obligation. The lease duration under the operating leases is two years and total payments over the two years will be £380,000.

In the year ending 31 January 1992 the following proceeds were received from the sale of fixed assets owned at 31 January 1991.

	£000
Freehold property	
(cost £350,000, 1989 valuation £500,000 depreciation at 31 January 1991 £50,000)	420
Plant and equipment	
(cost £1,150,000 depreciation at 31 January 1991 £85,000)	200

The accounting policy in regard to the depreciation of fixed assets of Ashley Holding plc is

Freehold property	2%	a full year's depreciation is provided for in the
Plant and equipment	15%	year of acquisition.

Required

In regard to the published accounts of Ashley Holdings plc for the year ended 31 January 1992, **you are required to show**

(a) the profit and loss account entries relating to fixed assets, their use and financing.

(7 marks)

(b) the fixed asset schedule which serves as a note to the balance sheet.   (8 marks)

(Total 15 marks)

(NI)

7   Jock Tadd is a sole trader who owns and operates supermarkets in each of three villages near Housanby. He has drafted his own accounts for the year ended 31 May 1994 for each of the branches. They are as follows:

	Ardale		Blencarn		Clifton	
	£	£	£	£	£	£
Sales		690,000		510,000		290,000
Cost of sales		517,500		382,500		217,500
Gross profit		172,500		127,500		72,500
Less expenses:						
Jock Tadd's salary	8,000		8,000		8,000	
Other salaries and wages	108,500		73,500		59,500	
Rent			15,000			
Rates	6,000		4,000		2,000	
Advertising	2,000		2,000		2,000	
Delivery van expenses	4,000		4,000		4,000	
General expenses	8,500		2,500		900	
Telephone	2,000		1,500		1,200	
Wrapping materials	6,000		3,000		2,000	
Depreciation						
Fixtures	6,000		3,000		2,000	
Vehicle	2,000		2,000		2,000	
		153,000		118,500		83,600
Net profit (loss)		19,500		9,000		(11,100)

The figures for the year ended 31 May 1994 follow the pattern of recent years. Because of this Jock Tadd is proposing to close the Clifton supermarket immediately.

Jock Tadd employs twelve full-time and twenty part-time staff. His recruitment policy is based on employing one extra part-time assistant for every £30 000 increase in branch sales.

His staff deployment at the moment is as follows:

	Ardale	Blencarn	Clifton
Full-time staff (including managers)	6	4	2
Part-time staff	8	6	6

Will Fallace, the manager of the Clifton supermarket, asks Jock to give him another year to make the supermarket profitable. Will has calculated that he must cover £95 000 expenses out of his gross profit in the year ended 31 May 1995 in order to move into profitability. His calculations include extra staff costs and all other extra costs.

Additional information:

(1) General advertising for the business as a whole is controlled by Jock Tadd. This costs £3000 per annum. Each manager spends a further £1000 advertising his own supermarket locally.

(2) The delivery vehicle is used for deliveries from the Ardale supermarket only.

(3) Jock Tadd has a central telephone switchboard which costs £1200 rental per annum. Each supermarket is charged for all calls actually made. For the year ended 31 May 1994 these amounted to:

	£
Ardale	1,600
Blencarn	1,100
Clifton	800

Required

(a) A report addressed to Jock Tadd advising him whether to close the Clifton supermarket. Your report should include a detailed financial statement based on the results for the year ended 31 May 1994 relating to the Clifton branch.   (22 marks)

(b) Calculate the increased turnover and extra staff needed if Will's suggestion is implemented.   (12 marks)

(c) Comment on the social implications for the residents of Clifton if
   (i) Jock Tadd closes the supermarket   (10 marks)
   (ii) Will Fallace's recommendation is undertaken   (6 marks)

(Total 50 marks)
(AEB)

8   Hamza Khan owns a retail shop which sells a range of products which are classified under the three headings shown below in the income statements.

He is rather concerned that one section of his shop has made a small loss over each of the past three years.

Hamza is considering the following options.

Option 1 – Close down the tobacco and sweets section and sub-let the area to a hairdresser who will pay an annual rental of £6000 per annum

Option 2 – Build a partition to section off the area now used for the sale of tobacco and sweets. At present Hamza has no plans as to how to utilise this area.

Option 3 – Continue to sell tobacco and sweets

Given below are the income statements for each of the three sections for the year ended 31 October 1995.

	Newspapers and magazines		Tobacco and sweets		Cards and fancy goods	
	£	£	£	£	£	£
Sales		132,000		150,000		80,000
Cost of sales		88,000		127,500		40,000
Gross profit		44,000		22,500		40,000
Wages	13,200		15,000		8,000	
Rent and rates	1,300		1,300		2,600	
Heat and light	925		925		1,850	
Motor expenses	1,400		1,400		1,400	
Stationery and wrapping	240		240		240	
General expenses	1,500		1,500		1,500	
Carried forward	18,565	44,000	20,365	22,500	15,590	40,000

	£	£	£	£	£	£
Brought forward	18,565	44,000	20,365	22,500	15,590	40,000
Insurance	900		900		900	
Depreciation of fixtures	50		200		350	
Advertising	1,200		1,200		1,200	
		20,715		22,665		18,040
Profit (loss)		23,285		(165)		21,960

Notes to the accounts

(1) 10 part-time assistants are employed in the shop. Each assistant is paid £3620 per annum. If the tobacco and sweets section is closed down only 7 assistants would be employed.

(2) Rent and rates have been charged according to the space taken up by each section.

(3) If the tobacco and sweets section is closed a saving of £340 per annum would be made on heating and lighting.

(4) Hamza owns a car. All expenses relating to the car are charged to the business. Hamza uses the car to collect goods from a cash and carry at the beginning of each month. If he closes the tobacco and sweets section it will save him £100 per annum in motor expenses.

(5) Although the stationery and wrapping have been apportioned equally, an accurate split would show that one-eighth of the total cost is used in the selling of sweets and seven-eighths are used for wrapping fancy goods.

(6) The fixtures and fittings were bought 4 years ago at a price of £6000. It is expected that the life of the fixtures and fittings will be 10 years.

(7) If the section is closed the following savings will be made:

	£
general expenses	850
insurance	1,200

(8) Advertising costs will remain the same whichever option is selected.

Required

Using contribution statements, advise Hamza which option he should follow. Your advice should be based on non-financial factors as well as financial factors. (50 marks)

(AEB)

16 Manufacturing accounts

Chapter objectives

This topic tests your ability to:

☐ prepare the manufacturing, trading and profit and loss accounts of a manufacturing enterprise in good form

☐ recognise 'Prime Cost'

☐ distinguish between factory overheads and other overheads

☐ treat work in progress correctly

☐ account for manufacturing profit correctly

☐ provide for unrealised profit included in the valuation of closing stocks of finished goods

☐ disclose stocks of raw materials, work in progress and finished goods correctly in the balance sheet

16.1 Manufacturing, trading and profit and loss accounts

Businesses which manufacture all or some of the goods they sell preface their trading account with a manufacturing account which shows the cost of goods produced. This 'cost of production' is transferred to the trading account to calculate the cost of goods sold.

The manufacturing account comprises two main sections:

1. Prime cost section:
    (a) Direct materials (those contained in the goods made).
    (b) Direct labour (wages of the operatives who actually make the goods).
    (c) Other direct expenses (royalties, licence fees paid on each unit produced; electricity, only if question indicates this is separately ascertainable for powering machinery).

2. Overheads section:

    Debit this with factory overheads;:

    (a) Indirect material (lubricating oil and cotton waste for cleaning machines and other materials not contained in the goods made).
    (b) Indirect labour (wages of supervisors, storemen, cleaners, factory canteen staff etc.).
    (c) Other indirect expenses (factory rent, rates, heating, lighting etc., depreciation of factory buildings, machinery, etc.).

All other overheads of the business which do not relate to the factory must be debited in the profit and loss account.

Stocks of raw materials and work in progress:

Purchases of raw materials must be adjusted by the difference in opening and closing stocks of raw materials to find cost of materials used in the period.

Factory costs for the period must be adjusted by the difference in opening and closing stocks of work in progress to find cost of goods produced in the period. For valuation of work in progress, see 19.4.3.

When apportioning overheads between the manufacturing and profit and loss accounts, and the overheads are subject to accruals and prepayments, adjust for the accruals and pre-payments before making the apportionment.

Outline form of Manufacturing, Trading and Profit and Loss Account

		£
Direct materials		X
Direct Labour		X
Other direct expenses		X
Prime Cost		X
Factory overheads		X
		X
Add: Opening work in progress		X
		X
Deduct: Closing work in progress		X
Cost of goods produced transferred to Trading Account		X
Sales		X
Less Cost of sales		X
Gross Profit		X
Add other income		X
Less: Selling and distribution costs	X	
Administration costs	X	
Finance costs	X	X
Net profit		X

16.1.1. Example

Ross, Wye Limited: extract from trial balance at 31st December 19-8

		Dr. £	Cr. £
Stocks at 1.1.19-8			
Raw material		12,000	
Work in progress		14,200	
Finished goods		22,000	
Purchases:-	raw materials	144,000	
	indirect materials	1,000	
Factory wages	– direct	210,000	
	– indirect	32,500	
Rent and rates	– factory	20,000	
	– offices	12,600	
Heating and lighting	– factory	7,100	
	– offices	3,400	
Carriage inwards		1,360	
Carriage outwards		4,725	
Office salaries	– salesmen	12,000	
	– other	8,800	
Debenture interest		500	
Sales			556,135
Rent receivable			2,000

Other information:

Stocks at 31st December 19-8			£
Raw materials			10,100
Work in progress			15,900
Finished goods			16,000
Rent and rates paid in advance:	factory		3,000
	offices		800
Wages and salaries accrued: factory	– direct		12,000
	– indirect		1,800
	salesmen		2,000
	other		700
Depreciation for the year:	– Machinery		15,000
	– Office equipment		1,000
	– Delivery vans		4,000

Required

(a) Manufacturing, trading and profit & loss account for Ross, Wye Ltd., for year to 31 December 19-8.

(b) A balance sheet extract as at 31 December 19-8 showing stocks on hand at that date.

(a)

ROSS, WYE LIMITED
Manufacturing, Trading and Profit and Loss Account
for the year ended 31st December 19-8

	£	£	£
Raw materials: Stock at 1.1.–8		12,000	
Purchases	144,000		
Carriage inwards	1,360		
	145,360		
less Stock at 31.12.–8	10,100	135,260	147,260
Direct wages (W1)			222,000
PRIME COST			369,260
Add factory overheads:			
Indirect materials		1,000	
Indirect wages (W2)		34,300	
Rent and Rates (W3)		17,000	
Heating and lighting		7,100	
Depreciation – machinery		15,000	74,400
			443,660
Add: Work in progress at 1.1.–8		14,200	
less Work in progress at 31.12.–8		(15,900)	(1,700)
Cost of goods produced transferred to			
Trading Account			441,960
Sales			556,135
Less: Cost of sales			
Stock of finished goods at 1.1.–8		22,000	
Cost of goods produced		441,960	
		463,960	
less stock at 31.12.–8		16,000	447,960
Gross profit			108,175
Add: Rent receivable			2,000
			110,175
Less: Selling and distribution (W4)		22,725	
Administration (W5)		25,700	
Finance costs (Debenture Interest)		500	48,925
Net Profit			61,250

(b)

Balance sheet extract as at 31st December 19–8:

	£
Current assets	
Stocks: Raw materials	10,100
Work in progress	15,900
Finished goods	16,000
	42,000

Workings:

	T.B.	Accrued (Prepaid)	Total
	£	£	£
1. Direct wages	210,000	12,000	222,000
2. Indirect wages	32,500	1,800	34,300
3. Factory rent and rates	20,000	(3,000)	17,000
4. Selling and distribution			
Salesmens' salaries	12,000	2,000	14,000
Carriage outwards			4,725
Depreciation – vans			4,000
			22,725
5. Administration			
Rent and rates – offices	12,600	(800)	11,800
Heating and lighting			3,400
Salaries	8,800	700	9,500
Depreciation – office machinery			1,000
			25,700

16.1.2 Exercises

Exercise 1: THE JOBBITT CO. LTD. – to provide practice in the preparation of manufacturing, trading and profit and loss accounts in good form

The Jobbitt Co. Ltd. commenced as manufacturers of window frames on 1st October 19-7. The following balances were extracted from the company's books at 30th September 19-8:

		Dr.	Cr.
		£	£
Sales			700,000
Raw materials		115,000	
Direct labour		200,000	
Indirect materials		10,000	
Indirect labour		25,000	
Rent and rates	– factory	35,000	
	– offices	15,000	
Electricity	– factory	8,000	
	– offices	2,000	
Salaries	– factory	20,000	
	– offices	40,000	
Sundry expenses	– administration	2,000	

Other information:	
Stocks at 30th September 19-8	£
Raw materials	13,000
Work in progress	9,500
Finished goods	2,800
Provide for depreciation for the year as follows:	£
Factory machinery	12,000
Office equipment	1,000

Required

Manufacturing, trading and profit and loss account for The Jobbitt Co. Ltd. for the year to 30th September 19-8 and an extract from the balance sheet as at that date showing the relevant entries for current assets.

Exercise 2: COLLETTE FABRICATIONS LTD. – to provide practice in the apportionment of overheads when accruals and prepayments are involved

Prepare a manufacturing, trading and profit and loss account for the year to 30th April 19-9 from the following which has been extracted from the books of Collette Fabrications Ltd. at that date.

		£
Sales		800,000
Purchase of raw materials		176,000
Direct Wages		195,000
Indirect Wages		26,000
Rent and rates		60,000
Heating and lighting		56,400
Insurance		4,200
Office Salaries		68,600
Carriage inwards		15,340
Carriage outwards		3,360
Motor van expenses		8,000
Loose tools		9,000
Discounts receivable		4,125
Stocks at 1.5.19-8:	Raw materials	15,000
	Work in progress	24,000
	Finished goods	36,000
	Loose tools	5,000

Other information:

Stocks at 30.4.19-9:	Raw materials	17,500
	Work in progress	21,000
	Finished goods	32,000
	Loose tools	4,000

The following expenses must be accrued at 30th April 19-9:

	£
Rent	5,000
Heating and Lighting	3,600

The following expenses were prepaid at 30th April 19-9:

	£
Rates	14,000
Insurance	1,200

Expenses are to be apportioned as follows:

Rent and rates: Factory 75%; Offices 25%

Heating and lighting: Factory $\frac{2}{3}$, Offices $\frac{1}{3}$

Insurance: Factory $\frac{9}{10}$, Offices $\frac{1}{10}$

Motor van costs: Factory 50%

Provide for depreciation as follows:	£
Factory building	4,000
Machinery	14,000
Office machinery and equipment	5,000
Motor vans	10,000

16.2 Profits/losses on manufacture

Firms producing their own goods usually do so because they can make them more cheaply than they can buy them from outside ('bought-in' goods). The difference between costs of manufacture and cost of 'bought-in' goods is a factory profit, or profit on manufacturing, and increases the profits of the firm. The difference between the 'manufacturing profit' and 'gross profit on trading' is important and the two must be kept separate until they are aggregated in the profit and loss account.

(If the cost of production exceeds the cost of similar 'bought-in' goods, a factory loss results.)

Treatment of profits/losses on manufacture

In manufacturing account:
   Add factory profit to cost of production
   Deduct factory loss from cost of production

In profit and loss account:
   Add factory profit to net profit on trading
   Deduct factory loss from net profit on trading.

Model:	£
Prime cost	X
Factory overheads	X
	X
Work in progress adjustment	X
	X
Add factory profit	A
or Deduct factory loss	(B)
Transfer to Trading account	X
Sales	X
Less cost of sales	(X)
Gross profit	X
Less administration etc. overheads	(X)
Net profit or (loss)on trading	X
Add factory profit	A
or Deduct factory loss	(B)
Overall net profit (or loss)	X

16.2.1 Example

The following data has been extracted from the books of Betta Widgetts Ltd. at 31st December 19-9:

		Dr. £'000	Cr. £'000
Stocks at 1.1.-9:	Raw materials	16	
	Work in progress	24	
	Finished goods	40	
Purchase of raw materials		120	
Sales			650
Direct labour		260	
Rent and rates		80	
Electricity		40	
Office salaries		65	
Stocks at 31.12.-9	Raw materials	20	
	Work in progress	30	
	Finished goods	38	
Depreciation for the year:	Factory	40	
	Office	8	

Rent, rates and electricity are to be apportioned: Factory 75%, Offices 25%

Finished goods are to be transferred to the trading account at a profit of 15% on factory cost.

BETTA WIDGETTS LTD.
Manufacturing, Trading and Profit and loss account for the year ended 31st December 19-9.

		£'000	£'000
Raw materials:	Stock at 1.1.–9	16	
	Purchases	120	
		136	
	less stock at 31.12.–9	20	116
Direct labour			260
Prime cost			376
Add Factory Overheads:			
Rent and rates		60	
Electricity		30	
Depreciation		40	130
			506
Work in progress at 1.1.–9		24	
Work in progress at 31.12.–9		(30)	(6)
Factory cost of goods produced			500
Add factory profit (15% of £500)			75
Transferred to Trading account			575

	£'000	£'000
Sales		650
less Cost of sales:		
Stock of finished goods at 1.1.–9	40	
Cost of goods produced	575	
	615	
less stock at 31.12.–9	38	577
Gross profit		73
less: Salaries	65	
Rent and rates	20	
Electricity	10	
Depreciation	8	103
Net loss on trading		(30)
Add factory profit		75
Overall Net profit		45

16.2.2 Exercises

Exercise 1: BONNIE AND CLYDE – an exercise involving factory profit

Bonnie and Clyde are in partnership, manufacturing kitchenware. The following details are extracted from their trial balance as at 31st March 19-7:

		Dr. £'000	Cr. £'000
Sales			400
Stocks at 1.4..-6:	Raw materials	7	
	Work in progress	8	
	Finished goods	14	
Raw materials		96	
Direct labour		124	
Factory overheads		85	
Rent receivable			20
Office overheads		64	
Stocks at 31st March 19-7 were:		£'000	
	Raw materials	13	
	Work in progress	15	
	Finished goods	24	
Depreciation charges for the year:	Factory	8	
	Offices	2	

Completed production is to be transferred to the warehouse in the sum of £350,000.

Required

A Manufacturing, Trading and Profit and Loss account for Bonnie and Clyde for year to 31 Mar 19-7.

Exercise 2: KONTAKKI LTD. – an exercise involving a factory loss

Kontakki Ltd., manufactures products for the leisure industry. The following information is extracted from the company's books at 30th June 19-8:

		£'000
Stocks at 1.7.-7:	Raw materials	40
	Work in progress	16
	Finished goods	32
Purchases:	Raw materials	110
	Finished goods	60
Direct wages		85
Office salaries		28
Rent and rates		40
Heating and lighting		16
Repairs to property – factory		20
Redecoration of offices		15
Depreciation charges for the year:	Machinery	30
	Salesmen's cars	15
Sales		300

		£'000
Stocks at 30.6.-8:	Raw materials	55
	Work in progress	14
	Finished goods	30

Rent, rates, heating and lighting are to be apportioned on the following basis: Factory 75% Office 25%

Finished goods are to be transferred to the trading account at £250,000.

Required

A Manufacturing, Trading and Profit and Loss Account for Kontakki Ltd., for the year to 30th Jun 19-8.

16.3 Elimination of unrealised manufacturing profit from unsold stocks of finished goods

The Prudence Concept requires that profit shall not be anticipated before it is realised.

If the valuation of closing stocks of finished goods includes an element of factory profit, this unrealised profit must be eliminated in the profit and loss account and balance sheet by making an appropriate provision.

The entries to be made for the annual adjustment to the provision are as follows:

Increase in provision:
    debit profit and loss account;
    credit provision account with the amount of the increase

Decrease in provision:
    debit provision account;
    credit profit and loss account with the amount of the decrease

In balance sheet: deduct provision from stock of finished goods

Example

		£	£
Current assets			
Stocks:	Raw materials		12,000
	Work in progress		20,000
	Finished goods	50,000	
less	provision for unrealised profit	8,000	42,000
			74,000

Note: Adjustment for unrealised profit on stock should only be made if required or implied by the question.

16.3.1 Example

The following information is available after the preparation of the manufacturing and trading accounts of Dickery Dock Ltd.,for the year ended 31st December 19-6.

		Dr.	Cr.
		£	£
Gross profit on trading			38,000
Manufacturing profit			12,000
Selling, distribution and administration		24,000	
Provision for unrealised profit on stock at 1.1.19-6			2,000
Stocks at 31.12.19-6:	Raw materials	4,000	
	Work in progress	5,000	
	Finished goods	8,000	

The stock of finished goods at 31.12.-6 included unrealised profit on manufacture of £2,100.

DICKERY DOCK LTD
Profit and loss account for the year ended 31st December 19-6.

	£	£
Gross profit on trading		38,000
Selling, distribution and administration		24,000
Net profit on trading		14,000
Add Manufacturing profit	12,000	
Less increase in provision for unrealised profit	100	11,900
Overall net profit		25,900

Balance sheet extract as at 31st December 19–6:

	£	£
Current Assets		
Stocks: Raw materials		4,000
Work in progress		5,000
Finished goods	8,000	
less provision for unrealised profit	2,100	5,900
		14,900

16.3.2 Exercises

Exercise 1: DORRITT AND DOMBIE LTD – an exercise involving the treatment of provision for unrealised profit on stock of finished goods

Dorritt and Dombie Ltd. manufactures an electronic unit under licence. At 31st March 19-2, the following balances appeared in the trial balance:

		Dr. £'000	Cr. £'000
Sales (4,500) units			1,800
Purchase	– Raw materials	300	
	– Finished goods (232 units)	58	
Stocks at 1.4.–1	– Raw materials	28	
	– Work in progress	58	
	– Finished goods (132 units)	33	
Wages	– direct	360	
	– indirect	88	
Licence fees		104	
Property expenses		82	
Canteen expenses		36	
Other administration		40	
Selling and distribution		37	
Office salaries		50	
Provision for unrealised profit at 1.4.–8			3

Further information:

Stocks at 31.3.–2	– Raw materials	32
	– Work in progress	54
	– Finished goods (264 units)	66

		£
Depreciation for year:	machinery	36
	canteen equipment	10
	Office machinery	5

The following expenses were owing at 31.3.-2:

	£'000
Property expenses	8
Canteen expenses	4
Other administration	5
Selling and distribution	3

Property and canteen expenses are to be apportioned as follows: Factory 80% Offices 20%.

Production is transferred to the warehouse at a mark-up of 10%.

The provision for unrealised profit on closing stock of finished goods at 31.3.-2 must be increased to £6,000.

Required

(a) A manufacturing, trading and profit and loss account for Dorritt and Dombie Ltd. for the year ended 31st March 19-2.

(b) a balance sheet extract as at 31st March 19-2 showing the item of stocks.

(c) a calculation of the total (absorption) cost of each unit of production completed in the year.

Exercise 2: THE PREMIER MANUFACTURING CO LTD – an exercise involving the calculation of unrealised profit in closing stock of finished goods

The following trial balance has been extracted from the books of The Premier Manufacturing Co. Ltd. at 31st December 19-8:

		Dr. £	Cr. £
Stocks at 1.1.-8:	Raw materials	18,000	
	Work in progress	27,800	
	Finished goods	42,500	
	Loose tools	15,000	
Purchases:	Raw materials	245,500	
Direct wages		345,000	
Indirect wages		21,000	
Rent and rates	– factory	54,000	
	– offices	28,000	
Electricity	– factory	27,000	
	– offices	13,500	
Repairs and maintenance	– factory	10,000	
	– offices	8,200	
Insurance:	– factory	12,000	
	– offices	4,000	
Purchase of loose tools		13,650	
Sales			1,200,000
Motor vehicle expenses		17,600	
Carriage inwards		1,350	
Selling and distribution		52,190	
Administration		74,000	
Discounts		2,140	1,760
Debenture interest		800	
Freehold property (at cost)		240,000	
Provision for depreciation of freehold property			96,000
Plant and machinery (at cost)		215,000	
Provision for depreciation of plant and machinery			125,000
Motor vehicles (at cost)		84,000	
Provision for depreciation of motor vehicles			42,000
Office machinery and equipment (at cost)		26,000	
Provision for depreciation of office equipment			18,000
Debtors and creditors		114,640	23,540
Bank		54,260	
Provision for unrealised profit			4,000
Share capital (150,000 ordinary shares of £1 each)			150,000
8% debentures			20,000
Retained profits			86,830
		1,767,130	1,767,130

Notes

1. Stock at 31.12.-8:

	£
Raw materials	22,000
Work in progress	24,500
Finished goods	67,500
Loose tools	13,400

2. Accrued expenditure at 31.12.-8:

	£
Rent – factory	5,000
– offices	2,800
Direct wages	6,000
Indirect wages	1,900
Selling and distribution	3,000

3. Prepayments

	£
Rates – factory	1,000
– offices	800

	£
Insurance – factory	1,800
– offices	600

4. Depreciation to be provided for the year on straight line basis:

Freehold premises – 4% on cost ($\frac{3}{4}$ factory, $\frac{1}{4}$ administration)
Plant and machinery – 20% on cost
Motor vehicles – 25% on cost
Office machinery – 20% on cost

5. 50% of motor vehicle costs are to be apportioned to the factory.

6. Finished goods were transferred from the factory to the warehouse at £900,000.

7. Provide for unrealised profit on stock of finished goods at 31st December 19-8.

Required

(a) The manufacturing, trading and profit and loss account of The Premier Manufacturing Co. Ltd. for the year to 31st December 19-8 and a balance sheet as at that date.

(b) State how the following concepts are relevant to the financial statements you have prepared for (a) above:

(i) accruals or matching concept

(ii) cost concept

(iii) going concern concept

Key points to remember

1. Head your answers correctly with the name of the business, followed by 'Manufacturing, Trading and Profit and Loss Account for the (period) ended — 19–.' (This heading may need to be adapted to the requirement of the question.) It is best to avoid inserting headings between the manufacturing, trading and profit and loss accounts.

2. Recognize 'Prime Cost', 'Gross profit' and 'Net profit' by writing those descriptions against them.

3. Make sure you add factory overheads to prime cost; some candidates lose marks because they deduct the overheads instead.

4. Distinguish clearly between factory overheads, which appear in the manufacturing account, and the others which appear in the profit and loss account.

5. Make any adjustments to overheads for accruals and prepayments before apportioning them to the manufacturing and profit and loss accounts.

6. Check that you have calculated and treated factory profit and unrealised profit on stocks of finished goods correctly.

7. Distinguish between the manufacturing account and the trading accounts clearly; do not place the item 'Sales' in the manufacturing account.

8. Remember to make appropriate adjustments in the manufacturing account for opening and closing stocks of raw materials and work in progress.

Common errors

1. sales shown in the manufacturing account.

2. prime cost not calculated correctly; not recognised as such in the manufacturing account.

3. factory overheads, especially depreciation of machinery, shown in the profit and loss account instead of in the manufacturing account.

4. opening and closing stocks of raw materials and work in progress not adjusted in manufacturing account.

5. factory overheads deducted from prime cost instead of being added to prime cost.

6. inability to deal with factory profit correctly.

7. cost of finished goods in trading account does not correspond with amount for that item in the manufacturing account.
8. incorrect treatment of the provision for unrealised profit.
9. accruals and prepayments not treated correctly.

Questions

Fully worked examination question

Carter, a sole trader, commenced business on 1 September 19-6 as a manufacturer of three types of products.

The following balances were extracted from his trial balance at 31 August 19-7.

	Dr £	Cr £
Purchases of raw materials	280,000	
Returns	1,000	4,000
Carriage in	2,000	
Selling and distribution costs	20,000	
Rent	15,000	
Royalties	12,000	
Indirect factory labour	24,000	
Direct labour	125,000	
Administrative costs	35,000	
Sales		540,000
General factory expenses	15,000	
Plant and machinery at cost	140,000	
Delivery vans at cost	10,000	

The following information is also available:

(1) Rent was paid until the end of November 19-7 and was to be apportioned between the factory and general administration on the basis of 2:1.

(2) Selling and distribution costs of £8,000 were accrued on 31 August 19-7.

(3) Plant and machinery are depreciated by 20% per annum on cost and delivery vans are to be depreciated by 30% per annum on cost

(4) The stock of raw materials at 31 August 19-7 was valued at £40,000.

(5) Although there was no work in progress at the end of the year there was a stock of finished goods of 3,000 units. Carter is uncertain as to how to value the goods which at present are selling for an average price of £30 per unit. During the year 25,000 units have been produced.

Required

(a) The manufacturing account for the year ended 31 August 19-7 (7 marks)

(b) Using *two* accepted methods of valuing the closing stock of finished goods complete the trading and profit and loss accounts for the year ended 31 August 19-7 (12 marks)

(c) Explain to Carter the difficulties involved in calculating a separate cost of sales figure for each of the three products produced. (6 marks)

(Total 25 marks)

(AEB)

Answer

(a)

Carter
Manufacturing account for the year ended 31 August 19-7

	£	£	Tutorial notes
Raw materials	280,000		1.
less returns out	4,000		
	276,000		
add carriage inwards	2,000		
	278,000		
less stock of raw materials at 31.8.-7	40,000	238,000	
Direct labour		125,000	
Royalties		12,000	
PRIME COST (£15 per unit)		375,000	2.
Add factory overheads			
Indirect labour	24,000		3.
Factory rent	8,000		
General factory expenses	15,000		
Depreciation of plant and machinery	28,000		
		75,000	4.
Factory cost of production		450,000	

(b)   **Trading and profit and loss account for the year ended 31 August 19-7**

Closing stock valued at:

		prime cost	total cost of production		
	£	£	£	£	5.
Sales		540,000		540,000	
less returns		1,000		1,000	
		539,000		539,000	
Cost of goods produced	450,000		450,000		6.
less closing stock					
(3/25 × £375,000)	45,000	405,000			
(3/25 × £450,000)			54,000	396,000	
Gross profit		134,000		143,000	
Rent	4,000		4,000		
Administrative costs	35,000		35,000		
Selling and distribution costs	28,000		28,000		
Depreciation – delivery vans	3,000		3,000		
		70,000		70,000	
Net profit		64,000		73,000	

(c) Difficulties involved in calculating a separate cost of sales figure for each of three products:

(i) Analyses are required of direct expenses (direct materials, direct labour and royalties) for each product. This involves analysing the materials requisitions and payroll records between the separate products.

(ii) Difficulty may be experienced in apportioning factory overheads to each product on an equitable basis. Machine hour or direct labour hour rates should be calculated as a means of apportioning the overheads equitably.

Tutorial notes

1. The correct model for prime cost is important. Carriage inwards must be added to cost of raw materials.

2. The words 'Prime Cost' are an essential part of the answer

3. A common error is to show depreciation of plant and machinery in the P&L a/c

4. Another common error is the *subtraction* of total overheads from prime cost.

5. The two methods of valuing stock referred to in the question are at prime cost and total cost. Prime cost is not an acceptable method for the purpose of SSAP 9.

6. In this type of question, the profit and loss accounts are best presented in columnar form as here.

7. It is important to show the practical difficulties involved in calculating separate costs for each product. This part of the question carries 6 marks only, but that may be enough make a difference of two grades The answer must be both clear and concise.

Multiple choice questions

1 Prime cost includes the
   A   cost of oil to lubricate machinery
   B   carriage inwards
   C   factory heating and lighting
   D   storekeepers' wages

2 In a manufacturing company loose tools will be normally be depreciated using the
   A   straight line method
   B   reducing balance method
   C   revaluation method
   D   machine-hour method.

3 A manufacturing company's cost of production was £100,000. The finished goods were transferred from its factory to the warehouse at £110,000. At the year-end 9% of these goods were still in stock. The stock of finished goods will be shown
   A   in the trading account and in the balance sheet as £9,000
   B   in the trading account as £9,900 and in the balance sheet as £9,000
   C   in the trading account as £9,900 and in the balance sheet as £8,910.
   D   in the trading account and in the balance sheet as £9,900

4 A factory loss is
   A   credited to the manufacturing account and debited in the profit and loss account
   B   debited to the manufacturing account and credited in the profit and loss account
   C   debited in both the manufacturing account and in the profit and loss account.
   D   ignored in the manufacturing account and in the profit and loss account.

5 When a manufacturing company adds factory profit to the cost of goods transferred from its factory to its warehouse, it
   A   has no effect on the gross profit but increases the net profit
   B   increases both the gross profit and the net profit
   C   reduces the gross profit but increases the net profit
   D   reduces both the gross profit and the net profit

6 The profit and loss account of a manufacturing company will not include an annual depreciation charge for the depreciation of
   A   delivery vehicles
   B   factory machinery
   C   office machinery
   D   warehouse

Further examination questions

1 H. Wagner, a manufacturer, provided the following information for the year ended 31 August 1990.

Stocks at 1 September 1989	£		£
Raw materials	25,000	Raw materials returned	7,800
Work in progress	15,900	Factory maintenance wages	19,000
Finished goods	26,600	Administrative expenses	30,000

Raw materials purchased	176,600	Selling and distribution expenses	15,100
Factory general expenses	14,800	Plant and machinery at cost	178,000
Direct wages	86,900	Freehold land and buildings at cost	160,000
Repairs to plant and machinery	9,900	Provision for depreciation on plant	
Factory lighting and heating	20,010	and machinery (at 1 September 1989)	80,000
Carriage inwards	1,910		
Carriage outwards	2,500		
Sales	320,000		

Additional information:

(1) Amounts owing at 31 August 1990.

	£
Direct wages	4,800
Factory heating and lighting	1,500

(2) Depreciation on plant and machinery is to be provided at 10% per annum on cost. There were no sales or purchases of plant and machinery during the year.

(3) Stocks at 31 August 1990.

	£
Raw materials	30,000
Work in progress	17,800
Finished goods	35,090

The raw materials are valued at cost, the work-in-progress at factory cost, whilst the stock of finished goods is valued at the factory transfer price.

(4) All manufactured goods are transferred to the warehouse at factory cost plus 10%.

(5) Other balances at 31 August 1990.

	£
Trade debtors	26,000
Trade creditors	38,000

(6) Wagner was concerned that despite making manufacturing profits in recent years, his business overall had been making losses.

As a result he decided to sell the business to Harold Parma, who agreed to buy the business on the following terms:

All the assets listed above at net book value less 15%, except for land and buildings for which Parma would pay cost price.

Parma would take over all outstanding creditors listed above at their book value.

It was agreed that goodwill would have a nominal value of only £100.

Required

(a) A manufacturing account for the year ended 31 August 1990. (8 marks)

(b) A trading and profit and loss account for the year ended 31 August 1990. (6 marks)

(c) Calculate the purchase price that Parma is prepared to pay for the business. (3 marks)

(d) Comment on Wagner's current year manufacturing profitability. (4 marks)

(e) Parma is determined that his newly acquired business will return to making profits. What financial techniques are available to assist him in this task? (4 marks)

(Total 25 marks)

(AEB)

2   Zacotex Ltd., a manufacturer, produced the following financial information for the year ended 31 March 19-9.

	£		£
Raw material purchases	250,000	Stocks at 1 April 19-8	
Direct labour	100,000	Raw materials	65,000
Direct expenses	80,900	Finished goods	48,000
Indirect factory labour	16,000	Work in progress	52,500
Factory maintenance costs	9,700	Other factory overhead	14,500
Machine repairs	11,500	Factory heating and lighting	19,000
Sales of finished goods during the year	788,100	Factory rates	11,500
		Administration expenses	22,000
		Selling and distribution expenses	36,800

Additional information:

(1) The stocks held at 31 March 19-9 were:

	£
Raw materials	51,400
Finished goods	53,800
Work in progress	41,000

N.B. Raw materials are valued at cost; finished goods at factory cost; work in progress at factory cost.

Of the raw materials held in stock at 31 March 19-9, £15,000 had suffered flood damage and it was estimated that they could only be sold for £2,500.

The remaining raw material stock could only be sold on the open market at cost less 10%.

(2) One quarter of the administration expenses are to be allocated to the factory.

(3) The raw materials purchases figure for the year includes a charge for carriage inwards. On 31 March 19-9 a credit note for £1,550 was received in respect of a carriage inwards overcharge. No adjustment had been made for this amount.

(4) Expenses in arrears at 31 March 19-9 were:

	£
Direct labour	6,600
Machine repairs	1,700
Selling and distribution expenses	4,900

(5) Plant and machinery at 1 April 19-8:

	£
at cost	250,000
aggregate depreciation	75,000

During the year an obsolete machine (cost £30,000, depreciation to date £8,000) was sold as scrap for £5,000.

On 1 October 19-8 new machinery was purchased for £70,000 with an installation charge of £8,000.

The company depreciates its plant and machinery at 10% per annum on cost, on all items in company ownership at the end of the accounting year. Items purchased during the year are allocated a full year's depreciation charge.

(6) An analysis of the sales of finished goods revealed the following:

	£
Goods sold for cash	105,000
Goods sold on credit	623,100
Goods sold on sale or return: returned	25,000
Goods sold on sale or return: retained and invoice confirmed	35,000
	788,100

(7) On 1 April 19-8 the company arranged a long term loan of £250,000 at a fixed rate of interest of 11% per annum. No provision had been made for the payment of the interest.

(8) The factory works manager felt that the preparation each year of a manufacturing account on an historical basis was inadequate for the control of costs. Thus he decided to seek the advice of an independent accountant on how to control his most important costs – direct labour and direct materials.

Required

(a) For the year ended 31 March 19-9:
  (i) a manufacturing account showing prime cost and factory cost of goods produced.

(12 marks)

  (ii) a trading and profit and loss account (6 marks)

(b) As the independent accountant prepare a brief report advising the factory works manager what financial techniques are available to control direct labour and material costs. Give suitable numerical examples. (7 marks)

(Total 25 marks)

(AEB)

3 The following balances refer to the workshops of the Cantalupe Engineering Company for the half year ended 31 December 19-6.

	£
Stocks at 1 July, 19-6:	
Raw materials	7,566
Work-in-progress	11,884
Finished goods	12,716
Direct factory wages	39,212
Indirect factory wages	26,076
Licence fees paid to patent holder	15,440
Heating and lighting	4,506
General factory expenses	12,710
Insurance of plant	5,274
Rates on factory premises	3,244
Purchases of raw materials	135,556
Raw materials returned to suppliers	1,652
Plant at cost	65,280
Depreciation provision: plant	26,112
Stocks at 31 December, 19-6	
Raw materials	6,354
Finished goods	10,034
Market value of goods completed	350,162

Notes

1. Licence fees are to be treated as a direct expense.

2. Expenses owing at 31 December, 19-6 were: Direct wages £580; indirect wages £666; general expenses £223.

3. Expenses prepaid at 31 December, 19-6 were: Insurance £422; rates £274; heating and lighting £156.

4. Plant is to be depreciated at the rate of 5 per cent on cost for the period.

Required

(a) Show the manufacturing account for the six months ended 31 December 19-6, assuming that the closing work-in-progress is valued at 5 per cent of full factory cost inclusive of work-in-progress. (15 marks)

(b) State the manufacturing profit if closing work-in-progress is calculated at 5 per cent of prime cost. (4 marks)

(c) Explain the meaning of the term 'equivalent production;' and show how equivalence is used in the valuation of work-in-progress. (6 marks)

(Total 25 marks)
(LONDON)

4 The following list of balances as at 31 March 1991 has been extracted from the books of Excel Enterprises Limited:

	£
Ordinary share capital – Ordinary shares of 50p each fully paid	40,000
Share premium account	4,000
General reserve	7,000
Retained earnings	4,400
Prime cost of goods manufactured	32,000
Raw materials stocks at cost at 31 March 1991	2,100
Factory overheads – fixed	19,100
– variable	13,700
Trading stock of tables at wholesale prices at 1 April 1990	5,000
Administrative expenditure	18,700
Sales and distribution expenditure	26,300
Sales	138,000
Plant and machinery – bought 1 April 1990	49,600
Debtors	7,500
Creditors	3,100
Balance at bank	12,500
Investment in Central Material Suppliers Limited, Ordinary shares of £1.00 each, at cost	10,000

Prior to 1 April 1990, Excel Enterprises Limited was engaged exclusively in the retail sale of the Excel Super Oak dining room tables which were bought at the wholesale price of £1,000 each. Since 1 April 1990, the company has manufactured and sold the tables; tables manufactured are transferred from the manufacturing account to the trading account at the wholesale price of £1,000 per table.

Additional information:

(i) 90 tables were manufactured during the year ended 31 March 1991, 92 tables were sold during the year.

(ii) One table was stolen from the company's warehouse during the year ended 31 March 1991; since the warehouse was not properly locked, the insurance company rejected the claim for compensation.

(iii) There was no work in progress on 31 March 1991.

(iv) The plant and machinery has an estimated useful life in the business of 8 years and a nil estimated residual value. It is proposed to use the straight line method of depreciation.

(v) Administrative expenditure prepaid at 31 March 1991 amounted to £2,300.

(vi) It is now proposed to transfer £5,000 to the general reserve and recommend a dividend on the ordinary shares of 15p per share.

(vii) Effect has not been given in the accounts to the bonus issue of one ordinary share of 50p for every eight ordinary shares held on 31 March 1991. The bonus shares issued will not rank for dividends until 1 January 1992. If possible, the retained earnings account should not be affected by this matter.

Required

(a) A manufacturing, trading and profit and loss account for the year ended 31 March 1991.
(12 marks)

(b) A balance sheet as at 31 March 1991. (7 marks)

(c) What are general reserves and why are they created? (6 marks)

(Total 25 marks)
(CAMBRIDGE)

5 On 31 March 1992 the following balances were extracted from the books of Slater Manufacturing Co Ltd.

	£	£
Stocks 1 April 1991		
Raw materials	30,600	
Work in progress	53,119	
Finished goods	59,565	
Purchases: Raw materials	973,350	
Direct wages	289,320	
Indirect wages	51,915	
Sales		1,608,525
Debtors	171,400	
Creditors		155,735
Debenture interest	1,000	
Rates and Insurance	6,080	
General office expenses	53,200	
Rent receivable		3,200
Premises at cost	230,000	
Provision for depreciation of premises		23,000
Plant and machinery at cost	170,000	
Provision for depreciation of plant and machinery		38,750
Provision for unrealised profit on goods manufactured		5,415
Provision for bad debts		3,100
Bank	80,536	
10% Debentures 1994		20,000
General Reserve		70,000
Ordinary Share Capital (£1 ordinary shares)		250,000
Profit and Loss account balance	7,640	
	2,177,725	2,177,725

Additional information:

(i)   Stock as at 31 March 1992:

Raw materials	£26,300
Work in progress	£41,340

The company transfers finished goods from the factory to the Trading Account at a cost of £627 per unit, this being factory cost plus 10% manufacturing profit. This price has been unchanged for the past two years.

Provision is to be made for unrealised profit on stock of finished goods at 31 March 1992.

(ii)   Sales have been at a constant price throughout the year, with 2,383 units sold.

(iii)   Rates and Insurance are apportioned between the Factory and General Administration on the basis 70:30, and include a prepayment of £100.

(iv)   Provision for bad debts is to be provided at 2% of debtors.

(v)   Rent receivable of £300 is outstanding for the year.

(vi)   Provision is to be made for depreciation as follows:

Premises:	2% p.a. on cost to be apportioned 70:30 between the Factory and General Administration.
Plant and machinery:	10% p.a. on cost (exclusive to the factory). The balance includes new machinery purchased for £15,000 on 1 October 1991. No disposals took place during the year.

(vii)   The directors recommend an ordinary share dividend of 10 pence per share, and a transfer to the General Reserve of £50,000.

(viii)   The debentures were issued in 1989, and are repayable after five years.

(ix)   Corporation tax for the year is estimated at £67,140.

Required

(a)   A Manufacturing Trading and Profit and Loss Account for the year ended 31 March 1992, and a Balance Sheet as at that date (for internal use only, not for publication).(23 marks)

(b)   The company is planning an expansion of fixed assets in 1992/93. Whilst in the past all plant and equipment has been purchased outright, it is now considering finance leasing as an alternative. Explain how such leasing would be dealt with in Slater's final accounts. Outline what you consider to be the main benefits to a company of leasing fixed assets.

(8 marks)

(Total 31 marks)
(OXFORD)

6   During the three months ended 31 May 1992, the Toft Processing Co Ltd completed 8,000 tonnes of product, with a further 300 tonnes partially completed. The partially completed product was 90 per cent complete as far as materials were concerned, 70 per cent completed for labour, and 60 per cent completed by way of overheads.

The following balances refer to the activities of the company for the three months ended 31 May 1992.

	£
Raw materials:	
Stocks at 1 March 1992	5,576
Stocks at 31 May 1992	6,400
Direct factory wages	58,042
Indirect factory wages	40,573
Heating and lighting	11,803
General factory expenses	10,839
Insurance of plant	6,664
Rates on factory premises	15,151
Purchases of raw materials	76,110
Raw materials returned to suppliers	2,510
Output at market price	271,000

Notes

(i) £3,450 direct factory wages paid during the period referred to the previous three months. At 31 May 1992, £4,520 was owing for the current period.

(ii) £1,860 of the lighting and heating was for the period ended 28 February 1992. £1,320 was still owing for the period ended 31 May 1992.

(iii) £810 general factory expenses were prepaid and £760 were owing at 31 May 1992.

(iv) £1,490 insurance was prepaid and rates were prepaid £4,012 at 31 May 1992.

(v) Indirect wages were accrued £5,490 at 31 May 1992.

(vi) Factory plant is depreciated at 10 per cent *per annum* based on the 1990 valuation of £254,800.

(vii) There had been no product in course of manufacture at 1 March 1992 because of a major breakdown during February 1992.

Required

(a) Calculate the value of semi finished product using the method of equivalent production.
(6 marks)

(b) Prepare the manufacturing account of Toft Processing for the three months ended 31 May 1992, showing clearly the prime cost, the total cost of product manufactured, and the manufacturing profit.
(14 marks)

(c) Explain the purposes of preparing a manufacturing account.
(5 marks)

(Total 25 marks)
(LONDON)

7   Due to the absence because of illness of the accountant of Protheus Ltd. a very junior accounts assistant was asked to draft the annual financial statements. The outcome of this attempt was the following:

Balance sheet for the year ended 31 March 1993

	£000	£000
Assets		
Premises	977	
Machinery	860	
Vehicles	240	
Investment (cost £90) – market value	102	
Stocks	297	
Debtors	350	
Balance at bank	51	
	2,877	
less **Provisions** as at 31 March 1993		
Depreciation – machinery	180	
vehicles	54	
Doubtful debts	6	
Discounts receivable	3	
Discounts allowable	2	
Dividends due	120	
Corporation tax due	110	
	475	2,402
Financed by:-		
Issued capital 1.8 million ordinary shares of £1 each		1,800
less Unissued capital 0.2 million ordinary shares of £1 each		200
		1,600
less Share premium		90
		1,510
Current liabilities		
Creditors	92	
Accruals less prepayments	3	
Debentures (10%)	80	175
Carried forward		1,685

	£000	£000
Brought forward		1,685
Reserves		
General	150	
Revaluation	40	
Profit and loss	191	381
		2,066
Difference in books		336
		2,402

Profit and loss account as at 31 March 1993 (all figures £000)

	£000	£000	£000
Sales £3,600 *less* purchases of raw materials £1,900			1,700
Returns inwards £52 *less* returns outwards £40			12
Closing stock raw materials £189 *less* opening stock £158			31
Closing stock work in progress £55 *less* opening stock £38			17
Opening stock finished goods £63 *less* closing stock £53			10
			1,770
less Production overheads (including direct wages £120)		900	
Administration overheads (less accruals £4)		66	966
Gross profit			804
less Carriage inwards		50	
Selling overheads (plus prepayments £1)		94	
Financial overheads		8	
Legal costs re purchase of property		3	
Depreciation – machinery	120		
– vehicles	18	138	
Debenture interest paid		4	
Dividend paid		60	
Corporation tax due		110	467
Net profit			337
less Transfer to reserves		106	
Dividend due		120	226
Undistributed profit			111
Balance b/f			80
Balance c/f			191

Required

(a) Prepare a corrected manufacturing, trading and profit and loss account for the year ended 31 March 1993 for Protheus Ltd.   (30 marks)

(b) Prepare the balance sheet as at 31 March 1993 for Protheus Ltd.   (20 marks)

(Total 50 marks)
(AEB)

8   Bowburn Products Ltd is a company operating in the chemical industry. The annual accounts are prepared at 31 December each year.

At 31 December 1993 the accountant produced the following trial balance:

		£000	£000
Authorised and Issued Capital			
200 000 ordinary shares of £10 each fully paid			2,000
400 000 8% redeemable preference shares of £1 each			400
Revenue reserve			300
Profit and loss account balance 1 January 1993			176
10% debenture stock			500
Tangible assets (at cost):	freehold property	1,492	
	plant	692	
	vehicles	240	
Provisions for depreciation at 1 January 1993:	plant		360
	vehicles		110
Trade debtors and creditors		740	420
Bank and cash balances		474	
Purchases of raw materials		3,334	
Customs duties on imported raw materials		26	
Carried forward		6,998	4,266

	£000	£000
Brought forward	6,998	4,266
Manufacturing wages	1,550	
Manufacturing expenses	640	
General expenses (see note 3)	910	
Salaries	654	
Debenture interest paid	50	
Provision for doubtful debts at 1 January 1993		30
Sales		7,550
Stocks at 1 January 1993: raw materials	440	
work in progress	30	
finished goods	574	
	11,846	11,846

The following information is available:

(1) The stocks on hand at cost at 31 December 1993 were:

	£
Raw materials	720,000
Work in progress	31,000
Finished goods	640,000

(2) The following expenses were accrued at 31 December 1993.

	£
Manufacturing wages	40,000
Audit fee	3,000
Carriage outwards	2,000

(3) The general expenses comprise:

	£
Administration expenses	410,000
Selling and distribution costs	500,000

The salaries are apportioned equally between manufacturing, selling and distribution costs, and administration expenses

(4) Plant costing £28,000 has been bought during the year and charged in error to manufacturing expenses.

(5) Depreciation on the tangible assets is calculated using the straight line method on the cost of such assets at the year end. The rates are:

Plant 12.5% (All manufacturing)

Vehicles 20% (Apportioned between selling and distribution costs and administration expenses in the proportion 2:1)

It is company policy not to depreciate freehold property.

(6) The provision for doubtful debts is to be maintained at 5% of all debtors. This is considered to be an administrative expense.

(7) The directors have made the following decisions.
  (i) To provide for corporation tax of £70,000 on the profits of the year.
  (ii) To provide for the preference share dividend due.
  (iii) To recommend that a dividend of 30p per share be provided for the ordinary shareholders.

Required

(a) Prepare the manufacturing, trading, profit and loss and appropriation account of the company for the year ended 31 December 1993   (30 marks)

(b) Prepare a balance sheet of the company as at 31 December 1993   (12 marks)

(c) Explain the following terms:
  (i) ordinary shares and preference shares;   (4 marks)
  (ii) reserves and provisions.   (4 marks)

(Total 50 marks)
(AEB)

17 Remuneration of labour; valuation of stock and work in progress

Chapter objectives

Questions on these topics cover:-

☐ the objectives to be met in setting a wages system
☐ the employee relationship aspects to be considered in setting a wages system
☐ methods of calculating remuneration; time rates, piece rates, incentive bonus schemes
☐ accounting for labour
☐ the financial considerations involved in stock valuation
☐ different methods of valuing stock; their advantages and disadvantages

17.1 Remuneration of labour

Objectives:

1. Main objective of business is usually to obtain best return on capital employed; this involves maximising profits.
2. Subsidiary objectives usually aimed at helping to achieve main objective; e.g. maintaining good relations with the public, showing consideration for social and environmental factors etc.; but, very importantly, maintaining good staff relationships and motivating the staff. (Good conditions of employment including satisfactory level of remuneration.)

   Low staff morale leads to low productivity, spoilt work, industrial disputes, strike action etc.
3. Main objective will require 'cost of sales' to be minimised. This implies giving production staff incentive to improve productivity i.e. to produce more goods of an acceptable quality in less time.

Various methods of remuneration are aimed at achieving this.

Methods of Remuneration

Time Rates

Workers are paid an hourly or weekly rate.

Advantages:

1. Workers are guaranteed a fixed wage each week provided they work the agreed hours.
2. The method is uncomplicated and easy for the workers to understand.
3. The wages are easy to calculate.
4. The method can be applied to all workers.
5. Quality of work is not sacrificed as a consequence of attempts to increase earnings.

Disadvantages:

1. All workers are paid the same regardless of whether they work well or not.
2. There is no incentive for them to make any extra effort.
3. Workers may slack during normal hours in order to work overtime at enhanced rates of pay.
4. It may be necessary to instal rigid systems of control to ensure adequate productivity.

Straight Piece Rates

Workers are paid an agreed amount for every completed unit of production, e.g. If they complete one unit, they are paid £1; if they complete 5 units, they are paid £5 and so on.

Advantages:

1. Wages paid are proportionate to production.
2. Wages are easy to calculate.
3. The system encourages greater efficiency.
4. The work is completed more quickly and time wasting is discouraged.

Disadvantages:

1. May not be suitable for all workers; only suitable when a standard item is being produced or the work is of a repetitive nature.
2. Workers are unfairly penalised when production is halted because of shortage of materials, machinery breakdown, etc.
3. Unless careful control is exercised, workers will be tempted to rush the work in order to increase wages; this will lead to substandard work, spoilt production and unacceptable wastage of materials.
4. More rigid quality control may be needed.
5. Increased cost of supervision occasioned by need to check amount of each worker's output.
6. Unions may be contentious over fixing of piece rates.

High Day Rates

A higher than normal wage rate is offered for a continuously higher than normal performance.

Advantages:

1. Wage calculations are simple.
2. The firm benefits from high performance through lower unit costs.
3. Employment with such a firm is usually well sought after.
4. The firm is in a position to choose a better class of worker.

Disadvantage:

Standards must be continuously and closely monitored.

Time/Piece Rates

Workers are paid on a piece rate basis, but guaranteed a minimum weekly wage.

Advantage:

Some degree of uncertainty about the wage to be received at the end of the week is removed for the workers.

Disadvantages:

Most of those already mentioned above.

Bonus schemes

Various schemes allow for rewarding individual workers whose efficiency is above that normally expected. The amount of the bonus increases with increased efficiency. Strict control must be exercised over production to ensure that the quality of the work does not suffer in an attempt to increase the bonus.

Installation of Bonus Systems

Management should consult trade unions and/or staff. The scheme must be explained clearly to the workforce and satisfactory terms need to be agreed. A scheme imposed upon the workforce may be counter productive and lead to a withdrawal of labour.

Accounting for labour

Basic records

- clock cards for time rate workers. Clocking-in and out should be controlled to prevent 'clocking on' for late or absent workers.
- job cards or piece work cards for piece workers. These should be initialled by a foreman or manager as verification that the entries for work satisfactorily completed are correct.

Summaries

- details from the basic records should be copied onto summary sheets and the gross wages calculated and independently checked.

Pay roll sheets

- the gross wages should be copied onto the payroll sheets and the deductions for tax etc. and net pay calculated. The calculations should be independently checked.

Computerised payrolls

- The information will be input to the computer from the summary sheets. A print out of that information will then be obtained and checked by an independent, responsible official.

  Cheque signatories for the pay roll should see that the payroll has been signed by the compiler and the checker, authorised by a senior manager, and that all appears to be in order.

  Payment of wages should be witnessed by an independent person, or some other system of check should be installed to ensure that the wage packets are paid to bona fide employees.

17.2 The valuation of stock

This section should be read in conjunction with SSAP 9 (Chapter 11)

Importance of stock valuation

Value of closing stock determines cost of sales and, therefore, gross profit. It also affects net working capital, of which it is a constituent item, in the balance sheet.

Stock should be valued at the lower of cost and net realisable value.

Net Realisable Value

Proceeds of sale less any further costs to be incurred in putting goods into saleable condition and conveying them to the place of sale.e.g. Goods cost £1,000; if sold, they will fetch £1,300. Before they can be sold, some work is required to put them into a saleable condition at a cost of £275. The cost of transporting the goods to the place of sale will be £65. Net realisable value is: £[1,300 -(275+65)] = £960. As this is less than cost, the goods should be valued at £960.

Cost

Where it is not possible or practicable to identify the cost of individual items of stock, cost is ascertained by making an assumption about the items in stock.

It may be assumed

- that stock has been used or sold in the order in which it has been received (First In, First Out – FIFO)
- that the most recently received stock has been used or sold before older stock (Last In, First Out – LIFO)

OR

- stock may be valued at weighted average cost (AVCO;)

  The use of a particular method of valuing stock does not mean that stock is actually used in that particular order; e.g. stock may be valued using the FIFO method, but actually sold in LIFO order or in random order.
- standard cost (see chapter 22)

Perpetual and Periodic Inventories

A perpetual inventory is one in which a running balance is maintained of stock remaining after every receipt and issue of stock.

A periodic inventory is one in which only the totals of receipts and issues are recorded at the end of each accounting period and a new balance calculated at the period end only.

17.2.1 Example: showing the effect of valuing stock on various bases

During the month of March the following were the purchases and sales of Igoxi:

		Receipts		Sales	
		Quantity kilos	Price per kilo £	Quantity kilos	Price per kilo £
March	1	100	2		
	5			60	5
	8	80	2.50		
	12	40	3		
	14			80	5
	21	50	3.50		
	25			100	6
	28	100	4		
	31			100	6

Required

Trading accounts for the month of March showing the gross profit if closing stock is valued on each of the following bases:

(a) FIFO

(b) LIFO

(c) AVCO

Answer

Workings

FIFO	March		1	8	12	21	28
		Price	£2	£2.50	£3	£3.50	£4
		Received	100	80	40	50	100
Issues	5		(60)				
			40				
	14		(40)	(40)			
			–	40			
	25			(40)	(40)	(20)	
				–	–	30	
	31					(30)	(70)
						–	30

Closing stock: 30 kilos × £4 = £120

LIFO	March		1	8	12	21	28
		Price	£2	£2.50	£3	£3.50	£4
		Received	100	80	40	50	100
Issues	5		(60)				
			40				
	14			(40)	(40)		
				40	–		
	25		(10)	(40)		(50)	
			30	–		–	
	31						(100)
							–

Closing stock: 30 kilos × £2 = £60

AVCO	Received (kilos)	£	Sales (kilos)	Balance (kilos)	Average £	Balance £
March 1	100	2		100	2	200
5			60	(60)		120
				40	2	80
8	80	2.50		80		200
				120	2.3333	280
12	40	3		40		120
(carried forward)				160	2.50	400

AVCO	Received (kilos)	£	Sales (kilos)	Balance (kilos)	Average £	Balance £
(brought forward)				160	2.50	400
March 14			80	(80)		200
				80	2.50	200
21	50	3.50		50		175
				130	2.8846	375
25			100	(100)		288
				30		87
28	100	4		100		400
				130	3.7462	487
31			100	(100)		(374)
				30	3.7462	113

Closing stock: 30 kilos: £113

Trading account for the month of March

	FIFO £	FIFO £	LIFO £	LIFO £	AVCO £	AVCO £
Sales (140 × £5 + 200 × £6)		1,900		1,900		1,900
Purchases	1,095		1,095		1,095	
less Closing stock	(120)	975	(60)	1,035	(113)	982
Gross profit		925		865		918

17.2.2 Exercise: preparation of manufacturing accounts using different methods of valuing stock

On 1 March 19-2 The Beta Manufacturing Co. Ltd. commenced to manufacture Betabits and took delivery of Stibateb, a material used in the manufacture of Betabits, as follows:

		Kilos	Price per kilo (£)
March	1	300	4
	17	200	4.50
April	5	400	5
	22	300	5.50
May	8	300	6
	24	400	6.50

Issues of Stibateb to production took place as follows:

		Kilos
March	8	240
	20	240
April	10	360
	28	300
May	12	240
	28	180

The other costs of production for the three months to 31 May 19-2 were as follows:

	£
Direct wages	16,500
Variable overheads	4,000
Depreciation	3,180
Other fixed overheads	11,200

There was no work in progress at 31 May 19-2

Required

Manufacturing accounts for the Beta Manufacturing Co. Ltd for the three months to 31 May 19-2 showing factory cost if closing stock is valued on the following bases:

(a) FIFO

(b) LIFO

(c) AVCO

17.3 Advantages and disadvantages of FIFO, LIFO, AVCO and standard cost

FIFO

Advantages

1. It is realistic because it is based on the assumption that issues from stock are made in the order in which the goods are received.
2. Stock values are easy to calculate.
3. Values are based upon prices actually paid for stock.
4. Closing stock valuation is based upon most recent prices paid.
5. FIFO is acceptable for the purposes of the Companies Act 1985 and SSAP 9 (see Chapter 11)
6. FIFO is acceptable to the Inland Revenue for tax purposes.

Disadvantages

1. In a manufacturing business, the prices at which raw materials are issued to production may not be the most recent prices, a fact to be borne in mind in fixing the selling price of the product.
2. Identical items of stock may be issued to production/jobs at different prices simply because they are deemed to be made out of different batches of purchases.
3. If prices of commodities are rising, FIFO values stock at the latest (high) prices. This is hardly in conformity with the principle of prudence insofar as it gives a lower cost of sales figure than other methods and thereby increases profit.

LIFO

Advantages

1. The value of closing stock is easy to calculate.
2. The valuation is based on prices actually paid for stock.
3. Raw materials and components are issued to production at the most recent prices.

Disadvantages

1. It is usually unrealistic because it is based on the assumption that the most recently acquired stock is used or sold before older stock.
2. Identical items of stock may be issued to production/jobs at different prices simply because they are deemed to be made out of different batches of purchases.
3. Closing stock is not valued at the most recent prices.
4. LIFO is not acceptable for the purposes of SSAP 9,see chapter 11, (although it is acceptable for the Companies Act 1985.)
5. LIFO is not acceptable to the Inland Revenue for taxation purposes.

AVCO

Advantages

1. As prices paid for identical items purchased at different times are averaged, AVCO recognises that all such items have equal value.
2. Variations in the pricing of materials to different jobs, simply because the materials are deemed to be issued from batches bought at different times, are minimised.
3. Averaging has the effect of 'smoothing out' cost of production and cost of sales so that profits of different periods may be more realistically compared.
4. The valuation of closing stock will usually be fairly close to the latest prices paid.
5. AVCO is acceptable for the purposes of SSAP9 and the Companies Act 1985.

Disadvantages

1. A new average must be calculated with every purchase of stock.
2. The calculated average does not represent any price actually paid for stock.

STANDARD COST

Advantages

1. Once a standard has been set, calculations of prices for receipts, issues and balances are simple.
2. Monetary values may be omitted from the stores ledger cards if desired. The calculations are easily made on an 'ad hoc' basis if and when required.
3. Less clerical work is entailed in maintaining the stores ledger.
4. It enables the efficiency of the purchasing function to be measured.
5. Fluctuations in the value of material issued to production are eliminated
6. It is an essential component of a full standard costing system.
7. It is acceptable for the purposes of the Companies Act 1985 and SSAP 9 and the Inland Revenue provided the standard is reviewed regularly and approximates to actual cost. (See chapter 11).

Disadvantages

1. It requires a predetermined standard to be set which involves a degree of subjectivity.
2. Profits or losses arise as a result of differences between standard and actual prices. This will not be a disadvantage if a full standard cost accounting system is in operation.
3. The standard may seldom, if ever, correspond with any price actually paid for stock.
4. Actual price trends are ignored.
5. The standard must be regularly reviewed.

17.4 Valuation of separable items of stock or of groups of similar items

Separable items of stock or groups of similar items should be valued separately to arrive at cost and net realisable value in order to prevent losses on some items from being hidden by the valuations on other items of stock. This is required by the Companies Act 1985.

Example

A company sells six different grades of cloth for soft furnishings. The costs and net realisable values of the stocks of the six grades are as follows:

	Cost	NRV	Value to used for stock valuation
	£	£	£
Grade 1	11,000	15,000	11,000
Grade 2	13,000	12,000	12,000
Grade 3	21,000	19,000	19,000
Grade 4	8,000	11,000	8,000
Grade 5	14,000	17,000	14,000
Grade 6	15,000	18,000	15,000
	82,000	92,000	79,000

If the stock were valued as a whole, it would be valued at cost, £82,000 as this is less than NRV. However, the Companies Act 1985 requires the grades to be treated separately for valuation purposes; the total value of the stock will be taken as £79,000. The losses on grades 2 and 3 must not be concealed by the values placed upon the other grades.

17.5 The effect of stock valuation on profit

Profit over the total life of a business is unaffected by the method used for valuing stock. The somewhat artificial custom of dividing the life of a business into periods, usually years, to measure profit results in the reported periodical profits varying with the method adopted for valuing stock. Compare the annual and overall results of a business which uses (i) FIFO, (ii) LIFO to value its stock. Sales and purchases are the same in both cases.

FIFO

Year	1	2	3	4
	£	£	£	£
Sales	10,000	20,000	25,000	20,000
Opening stock	–	3,000	4,000	5,000
Purchases	8,000	10,000	12,000	8,000
Closing stock	(3,000)	(4,000)	(5,000)	–
Cost of sales	5,000	9,000	11,000	13,000
Gross profit	5,000	11,000	14,000	7,000

Total profit: £37,000

LIFO

Year	1	2	3	4
	£	£	£	£
Sales	10,000	20,000	25,000	20,000
Opening stock	–	2,000	3,200	4,350
Purchases	8,000	10,000	12,000	8,000
Closing stock	(2,000)	(3,200)	(4,350)	–
Cost of sales	6,000	8,800	10,850	12,350
Gross profit	4,000	11,200	14,150	7,650

Total profit: £37,000

17.6 SSAP 2 and stock valuation

The application of the four concepts of SSAP 2 are explained as follows:

Going concern. Stock must be valued at the lower of cost or net realisable value. If a business is not a going concern, net realisable value may be lower than normal if the stock must be disposed of in an enforced sale.

Matching. Valuing stock at net realisable value instead of at cost matches loss to the period in which it was incurred, i.e. the year in which the purchase of stock was less than prudent.

Prudence. A loss in the value of stock is provided for as soon as it is recognised by valuing the stock at net realisable value.

Consistency. The policy adopted for the valuation of stock, FIFO, LIFO, AVCO, etc. must be applied consistently from one period to the next.

17.7 Work in progress (WIP)

Work in progress is a component of the stock of a business which produces its own stock in trade; it is partly completed production.

Prime cost is made up of direct materials (those materials which form part of the finished product), plus direct labour (the wages of the operatives who actually make the finished product) and other direct expenses (those directly attributable to each unit of production e.g. a royalty paid on each item produced to the owner of a patent.)

Total cost of production consists of prime cost plus production overheads. (See Manufacturing accounts Chapter 16)

Work in progress may be valued either at prime cost or at total cost of production. It involves expressing partly completed units of production in terms of completed units. For example, if work in progress at a particular date consists of 200 units 50% complete plus 100 units 75% complete, it is equivalent to (50% of 200) + (75% of 100) units = 175 complete units.

It is possible to value work in progress either at prime cost or at total cost. The difference between the two methods, and the effect of each, may be seen from the following examples:

	(a) WIP valued at prime cost £	(b) WIP valued at total cost of production £
10,000 units produced including 1,000 equivalent units of work in progress)		
Prime cost	50,000	50,000
Total production overheads	150,000	150,000
Total cost of production	200,000	200,000
less Work in progress		
$(\frac{1,000}{10,000}) \times 50,000)$	(5,000)	
$(\frac{1,000}{10,000} \times 200,000)$		(20,000)
Cost of finished goods	195,000	180,000

In (a), all the overheads of the period covered by the account have been charged to that period; in (b), a proportion of the overheads have been included in the work in progress and carried forward as part of the stock valuation to the next period. (a) observes the concept of prudence by treating overheads as expenses to be charged in the period in which they were incurred. (b) observes the concept of matching by carrying forward all the expenses of production of work in progress to the period in which the revenue from the sale of those goods will be realised. SSAP 9 recommends that a proper proportion of overheads should be included in the valuation of work in progress. This is an instance where the matching concept would appear to override that of prudence, but the Accounting Standards Committee, which produced SSAP 9, considered that the standard would result in a fairer statement of profits as between one accounting period and another.

Key points to remember

1. Questions on remuneration of labour and valuation of stock generally require arithmetical calculations which should be done accurately.
2. Apart from being able to calculate stock values on FIFO, LIFO and AVCO bases, be prepared to discuss the advantages and disadvantages of each method.
3. Learn the requirements of SSAP 9 and be ready to state and discuss them if required to do so.
4. Read questions carefully to ascertain whether they refer to the prices of stock issues or the value of stock on hand. It is most important to answer questions exactly as set.

Common error

1. to confuse the assumptions on which FIFO and LIFO are based with the actual way in which stock is issued.

Questions

Multiple choice questions

1 A company should value its stocks at the lower of

   A   cost and net realisable value

   B   cost and replacement cost

   C   net realisable value and replacement cost

   D   selling price and net realisable value

2   A company purchased 100 kilos of raw material for £400 on March 1, another 40 kilos for £180 on March 15 and a further 70 kilos for £350 on March 26. 20 kilos were used on March 13 and another 60 kilos on March 25. The stock of raw materials at the end of the month, valued on the LIFO basis, was

A   £590

B   £610

C   £630

D   £650

3   A company's closing stock of goods is valued on the FIFO basis at £5,000. On LIFO it would have been valued at £4,800. If LIFO had been used instead of FIFO the company's

A   gross and net profits would have been increased by £200

B   gross profit would have been increased by £200 but the net profit not affected.

C   gross and net profits would have been reduced by £200

D   gross profit would have been reduced by £200 but the net profit not affected

4   A method of valuing stock which is not generally acceptable is

A   cost

B   net realisable value

C   replacement cost

D   standard cost

Further examination questions

1   Avon Ltd, a firm of wholesalers, has an accounting year ended 30 April 1990. At the end of April each year the storekeeper carries out stocktaking to ascertain the closing stock figures for the final accounts. However, this year he was suddenly taken ill, and there was no-one else available who could understand the stock records. Eventually stock is counted on 14 May 1990, and is valued at £98,370.

The following information concerning stock movements is available:

(i)   (a) The accounts department confirms that, during the period 1-14 May 1990, invoices totalling £40,698 have been sent to customers. This figure includes carriage on sales at 5%; £13,860 of goods were despatched before 1 May.

(b) It is also known that credit notes have been issued to customers who returned goods selling price £1,250 of which £960 relates to the period 1-14 May. The firm's mark-up is $33\frac{1}{3}$%.

(ii) (a) The purchases department confirms that orders already sent to suppliers for delivery during 1-14 May were for goods totalling £22,890. However, this includes goods list price £3,750 on which a trade discount of 20% is given, and orders for £5,840 of goods which have not yet been received.

(b) It was noticed on 4 May that one consignment of goods was of a different grade from that ordered, and these goods, invoiced by the supplier at £2,400, were returned on 6 May. Other returns of £740 were made from the goods delivered between 1 and 14 May.

(iii) The sales department "borrowed" stock selling price £6,400 on 28 April for display at an exhibition in which the firm is taking part. This has already helped to attract orders of £12,500 for the firm's products, although none of these goods have yet been sent out or invoiced.

(iv) It is also known that goods costing £1,200 were sent to a customer on a sale or return basis. Of these, the customer has marked part of the consignment up by 25% and sold it for £850 on 25 April, and returned the rest to Avon's stock on 3 May.

(v) It is discovered that the stock has been valued using LIFO principles, whereas the firm usually uses the first in first out method. The difference is £1,450 at a time when the prices of similar stocks are rising.

Required

(a) A detailed calculation of the closing stock value for the final accounts. (11 marks)

(b) An explanation of your treatment of items ii)a), iii) and iv). (6 marks)

(c) A discussion of the advantages a computerised system of invoicing, purchase orders and stock records could bring to the firm. (6 marks)

(Total 23 marks)
(OXFORD)

2   The following information relates to three employees; Arnold, Brown and Carter.

		Workers	
	Arnold	Brown	Carter
Actual hours worked	37	41	35
Hourly pay rate (£)	3.20	2.75	4.10
Output (units); product S	50	–	174
product T	93	70	–
product U	99	75	225

The standard time for each item is product S 5 minutes; product T 10 minutes; product U 12 minutes. For piece rate purposes, each minute is valued at £0.05.

You are required to calculate the weekly pay for each of the three workers using:

(a) guaranteed hourly rates only (basic pay); (3 marks)

(b) piece work, with earnings guaranteed at 80 per cent of basic pay; (6 marks)

(c) premium bonus, where the employee receives half of the time saved in additional pay. (6 marks)

(Total 15 marks)
(LONDON)

3   (a) Distinguish between wages systems based upon i) time rates and ii) piece rates, and give *two* examples of the relevant use of each method. (7 marks)

(b) It is sometimes stated that wage systems based upon time rates offer no incentives to employees to improve output. Use i) high day rates and ii) measured day work methods to show how this may be a misconception. (6 marks)

(c) Show the benefits to a company, of paying high wages. (7 marks)

(Total 20 marks)
(LONDON)

4   (a) Why might the piece rate system not be an appropriate payment system for staff engaged in research and development? (3 marks)

(b) Using the information given below, calculate the remuneration of each employee according to the following methods:

(i)   hourly rate;

(ii) basic piece rate;

(iii) individual bonus scheme, where the employee receives a bonus calculated as:

$$\frac{\text{Time saved}}{\text{Time allowed}} \times \text{Weekly wages as per hourly rate}$$

Employee	Alice	Brenda
Units produced	420	360
Time allowed (minutes/unit)	5	10
Time taken (hours)	28	54
Rate per hour (£)	6.25	7.50
Rate per unit (£)	0.45	1.25

(12 marks)

(Total 15 marks)
(LONDON)

5   Andy Pandy deals in only one product. Opening stocks on 1 May, 1991, comprised 40 items which had cost a total of £1,600. Purchases and sales for May 1991 were as follows:

Purchases			Sales		
May 1	150 @ £41		May 6	110 @ £50	
8	60 @ £42		10	80 @ £52	
15	130 @ £43		18	120 @ £53	
22	140 @ £45		23	170 @ £54	
29	60 @ £47		31	50 @ £55	

(a) Calculate the profit for the month when closing stock is valued on a periodic basis using:
   (i)   First in, first out (FIFO);
   (ii) Last in, first out (LIFO);
   (iii) Weighted average cost (AVCO).   (9 marks)

(b) Which of the three methods would you recommend and why?   (6 marks)

(Total 15 marks)
(LONDON)

6   Islay Ltd is a wholesale business that prepares its annual accounts on 30 June every year. The company has suffered serious employee problems which caused the annual stocktaking to be delayed and then carried out three weeks late on 21 July 1992. The stocktake was not performed with its usual efficiency.

At the conclusion of the stocktake the closing stock figure was £23,790. The outcome of using this figure produced the following results at 30 June 1992:

	£
Gross profit	157,000
Net profit	31,560
Net current assets	24,540

The management felt it was important that the correct closing stock figure should be determined, so a firm of expert stocktakers was engaged.

After a thorough investigation of the stock and related records the following matters were revealed:

(1) Some stock was found to be obsolete and was scrapped. This stock cost £700 when purchased in January 1985;

(2) On 10 June 1992 goods costing £450 had been sent to Joan Bramley on a sale or return basis. The customer had bought some of these goods immediately at an invoice price of £180. (All goods have a mark-up of 20%.) No goods on a sale or return basis had been included in the closing stock;

(3) Unused advertising material worth £1,120 had been incorrectly included in the stock of goods valuation;

(4) Carriage inwards relating to unsold stock amounting to £120 had been incorrectly debited to carriage outwards;

(5) After checking the individual stock sheets it was found that two were undercast by £100 and £40 respectively and one was overcast by £60;

(6) The trading transactions that took place between 30 June 1992 and 21 July 1992 were:

	£
Sales	2,970
Sales returns	480
Purchases	4,200
Purchase returns	340

These figures were used in the stock calculations at 21 July 1992 but otherwise were correctly entered in the accounts as transactions relating to the year 1992/93.

Required

(a) A computation of the correct stock value at 30 June 1992.   (8 marks)

(b) Statements to show the correct gross and net profits for the year ended 30 June 1992 and the correct net current assets at that date.   (6 marks)

(c) What are the main elements in maintaining accurate stock valuation?   (5 marks)

(Total 19 marks)
(AEB)

7   P L Gallon manufactures chemicals from a liquid stock which is stored in bulk containers before being issued to manufacturing processes. The following is an extract of the information contained on the relevant bin card for the month of February.

Date	Receipts (purchases) litres	Issues (to production) litres	Balance litres	Purchase price per litre
Feb 1			100	£30.00
Feb 3	300		400	£31.50
Feb 8		80	320	
Feb 12		140	180	
Feb 15	150		330	£33.50
Feb 22		130	200	
Feb 26		110	90	
Feb 28	150		240	£35.00

Required

(a) set out a statement showing the pricing of each issue and the value of stock remaining after each issue under each of FIFO and LIFO.   (11 marks)

(b) compare and contrast the FIFO and LIFO methods of pricing stocks.   (4 marks)

(Total 15 marks)

(NI)

8   Your company sells, for £275 each unit, a product which it purchases from several different manufacturers, all charging different prices. The manufacturers deliver at the beginning of each week throughout each month. The following details relate to the month of February.

		Qty.	Cost each £	Sales (units)
Opening stock		10	145	
Deliveries	Week 1	20	150	15
	Week 2	34	165	33
	Week 3	50	145	35
	Week 4	30	175	39

From the above data you are required to

(a) prepare stock records detailing quantity and values using the following pricing techniques:
   (i)   last in, first out (LIFO),
   (ii) first in, first out (FIFO),
   (iii) weighted average calculated monthly,

(Calculations should be taken to one decimal place.)   (11 marks)

(b) prepare Trading Accounts using each of the stockpricing methods in a) above and showing the gross profit for each method,   (3 marks)

(c) compare the results of your calculations and state the advantages and disadvantages of FIFO and LIFO pricing methods in times of inflation.   (6 marks)

(Total 20 marks)

(JMB)

9   On 1 January 1987, Sharon commenced business trading in rugby shirts. She used a machine, purchased for £3,000 to print individual club designs on the shirts. She planned to use the machine for five years, and expected to sell it for £504 at the end of that time.

During the five years, her purchases and sales of shirts were as follows:

Year to:	Purchased	Sold
31 December 1987	1,000 @ £8	800 @ £12
31 December 1988	1,000 @ £10	800 @ £14
31 December 1989	1,000 @£12	800 @ £16
31 December 1990	1,000 @ £14	1,200 @ £17
31 December 1991	–	400 @ £18

Each year other expenses of £1,000 were incurred. On 31 December 1991 Sharon ceased trading and sold her machine for £504.

Required

(a) compute gross profit and net profit for each of the five years to 31 December 1991 assuming use of 'Last in First Out' (LIFO) stock valuation and reducing balance depreciation at a rate of 30%; (8 marks)

(b) compute gross profit and net profit for each of the five years to 31 December 1991 assuming use of 'First in First Out' (FIFO) stock valuation and straight line depreciation; (8 marks)

(c) explain the relative merits of straight line and reducing balance depreciation, and advise which approach you consider most appropriate for Sharon's situation; (8 marks)

(d) explain the relative merits of FIFO and LIFO stock valuation, and advise which approach you consider most appropriate for Sharon's situation; (10 marks)

(e) explain the going concern concept, and discuss its relevance to Sharon's situation. (6 marks)

(Total 40 marks)
(JMB)

10 W. Scarlett commenced in business on 1 October 1990 as a garage door fitting specialist. During the first six months his transactions were:

	Purchases of garage doors	Sales of fitted doors
October	7 @ £160 each	3 @ £350 each
November	8 @ £162 each	9 @ £360 each
December	6 @ £164 each	6 @ £365 each
January	6 @ £165 each	5 @ £375 each
February	8 @ £167 each	11 @ £378 each
March	14 @ £172 each	9 @ £383 each

During this time his expenses were £2,780.

All transaction were on a cash basis.

Required

(a) Calculate his net profit for the six months ending 31 March 1991 under the FIFO, LIFO and AVCO methods of stock valuation (periodic). (13 marks)

(b) Explain the advantages of each method of stock valuation. (5 marks)

(c) According to SSAP 9 explain how stock should be valued in the final accounts. Why is stock valuation important in the final accounts? (5 marks)

(Total 23 marks)
(OXFORD)

11 Airwaves Ltd. are retailers who sell mobile telephones. During January to March 1993 they decided to concentrate their selling activities on the "Meteor" model, which experienced several cost price fluctuations during the period. The company found that because of this it had to adjust its own selling price.

During the period the following transactions took place.

(1) 1 Jan An opening stock of 50 telephones was obtained at a total cost of £8250.

(2) 10 Jan Initial sales were good so extra telephones had to be obtained from abroad; 200 telephones were purchased at a cost of £135 each but in addition there was a freight charge of £3 each, as well as a customs import duty of £5 each.

(3) 31 Jan During the month 180 telephones were sold at a price of £175 each.

(4) 1 Feb A new batch of 120 telephones was purchased at a cost of £170 each.

(5) 28 Feb The sales for February were 120 at a selling price of £215 each.

(6) 2 Mar A further 220 telephones were purchased at a cost of £240 each and these were subject to a trade discount of 12.5% each.

(7) 31 Mar 250 telephones were sold during March at a price of £230 each.

All purchases were received on the dates stated.

The accountant of Airwaves Ltd. decided he would apply First In, First Out (FIFO) and Weighted Average (AVCO) methods of stock valuation in order that the results could be compared.

Required

(a) Calculate the stock value at 31 March 1993 using each of the methods indicated (if necessary calculate to one decimal place).   (16 marks)

(b) Prepare the trading accounts using each of the above methods for the period January/March 1993.   (8 marks)

(c) What considerations should an accountant bear in mind in deciding on a basis of stock valuation? Reference should be made to relevant accounting concepts.   (20 marks)

(Total 44 marks)

(AEB)

18 Absorption or total costing

Chapter objectives

Questions on absorption or total costing require:

☐ an understanding of the concept of absorption accounting
☐ ability to prepare an absorption cost statement
☐ ability to apportion overheads to cost centres
☐ ability to calculate machine hour and direct labour hour rates
☐ an understanding of over- and under- recovery of overheads

18.1 Some costing terms defined

Direct Costs. Those costs which are directly attributable to a product or service i.e direct materials, direct labour and other direct expenses.

Direct Labour. The cost of employing those workers who are actually engaged in the production of goods or providing services i.e the wages etc. of the 'operatives' as distinct from non-productive workers such as supervisors, foremen etc.

Direct Materials. The cost of materials which actually form part of the goods being produced e.g. wood used in the construction of a desk, brass used for the desk drawer handles, but not, hopefully, the lubricating oil for the machinery! (This last would be an example of an indirect expense)

Direct Expenses. Other expenses directly connected with the goods produced or services provided e.g. royalties payable to an inventor or patentee for the right to produce certain goods.

Prime cost = direct labour + direct materials + direct expenses

Indirect Expenses. Any expenses other than direct expenses: indirect labour (foremen, store-keepers, factory canteen staff etc.); indirect materials (lubricating oil for machines, cotton waste for cleaning machines etc.); indirect expenses (rent of factory, depreciation of machinery etc.).

Overhead Cost. The total of all the indirect expenses.

18.2 Absorption costing (also known as total costing)

Absorption costing bases the cost of production on total costs i.e. direct cost plus overhead cost. All overheads are 'absorbed' into the cost of production (or total factory cost).

Example of absorption cost statement for the month of May 19-5

Production for the month of May 19-5: 1,000 units

	£
Direct labour	55,000
Direct materials	27,000
Direct expenses (royalties)	2,000
PRIME COST	84,000
Indirect labour	8,500
Indirect materials	12,500
Depreciation	4,000
Carried forward	109,000

	£
Brought forward	109,000
Other indirect expenses	
(including rent of factory, heat and light etc.)	9,000
Total cost of production	118,000
Selling expenses (all fixed)	22,000
Administration expenses (all fixed)	35,000
Total cost	175,000

On an absorption cost basis each unit has cost $£\frac{175,000}{1,000} = £175$.

If 1,001 items had been produced, the total cost for the month would have been increased by 1/1,000th of the variable costs, i.e. by direct labour, £55; by direct materials, £27; by direct expenses, £2 i.e. by a total of £84. Fixed costs would not have been affected.

On an absorption cost basis, then, each unit would have cost £175,084/1,001 = £174.909

If 1,010 units had been produced the cost of each unit on this basis of calculation would have been £175,840/1,010 = £174.099

The reason for the different answers to the question 'What has each unit cost' lies in the fact that the fixed costs are being spread over ('absorbed' by) different quantities of items produced in the month.

Uses of Absorption Costs

Calculation of profit/loss when selling price is fixed, or calculation of selling price to achieve a predetermined level of profit.

18.2.1 Example

Given the data in 18.2 for the production of 1,000 items calculate:

(a) the profit if the unit selling price is £220

(b) the selling price if a net profit of 20% on sales is required.

Answer

(a)
Sales = 1,000 × £220	£220,000
Total cost	£175,000
Net profit	£45,000

(b) Net profit on sales of 20% = 25% of cost of sales; 25% of £175,000 = £43,750; therefore selling price to achieve 20% on sales must be £218,750/1,000   =   £218.75 per unit

18.2.2 Exercise: to prepare an absorption cost statement

Bigthings Ltd. owns a freehold factory which it bought for £900,000, plant and machinery which cost £1,200,000 and a fleet of delivery vans which cost £60,000.

The annual budget for 19-2 includes the following:

	£
Factory overheads (not including depreciation)	510,000
Salaries of sales staff	50,000
Wages of delivery van drivers	34,000
Motor van running costs (excluding depreciation)	48,000
Office rent	33,000
Other administration costs	252,000

It is Bigthings Ltd.'s policy to provide for depreciation on a straight line basis as follows:

Freehold factory	2% on cost
Plant and machinery	20% on cost
Delivery vans	25% on cost

Bigthings Ltd. manufactures Whoppers, its only product, and it has a budgeted output for 19-2 of 24,000 Whoppers. Production is spread evenly over the months of the year.

The raw materials for each Whopper cost £15. Direct labour costs are £26 per Whopper.

Required

An absorption cost statement for Bigthings Ltd. for the month of March 19-2 showing:

(a) the total profit or loss for the month if the selling price of each Whopper is £100.

(b) the selling price per Whopper if a profit of 40% of total cost is to be achieved in March 19-2.

18.3 Overhead absorption

Overheads are added to the direct, or prime, cost to arrive at the total cost of production; the overheads are said to be 'absorbed' by production. The example in 18.2 is a very simple illustration of the principle involved based upon historic data. Seldom, if ever, are things so simple in real life:

1. Most businesses make more than one product
2. Probably a number of different departments are involved in the manufacturing process, and each department incurs its own overheads
3. The involvement of each department in the manufacture of each product varies according to the product.
4. Calculation of the amount of overheads to be absorbed by individual products must be made for future periods to enable selling prices to be fixed.

The difficulties arising from the first three points may be illustrated as follows:

Deal Ltd makes two products, A and B. Both products pass through the assembly department. In March, it makes 1,000 of A and 1,000 of B. The assembly department overheads for the month were:

	£
Indirect wages	6,000
Rent	12,000
Light and heat	4,000
Insurance of premises	2,000
Machinery depreciation	3,000
Total overheads for the month	27,000

If the overheads are divided by the total number of units produced, the overheads to be added to each unit of A and each unit of B should be $\dfrac{£27,000}{£2,000}$ = £13.50.

If product A requires twice the amount of time to assemble as product B, it is reasonable to argue that it incurs twice the amount of overheads as product B. One unit of product A should have £18 overheads added to cost, and each unit of product B should have only £9 added. $(1,000 \times £18 + 1,000 \times £9 = £27,000)$

Matters become more complicated if the products pass through other departments which have different total overheads and the relative times required for each product vary in each department.

It should be understood that it is virtually impossible to calculate the amount of overheads to be added to a single unit of production accurately. Even if it were possible, the cost of doing so would probably be prohibitive and would not be justified. It would simply add even more to the overheads.

The aim is to calculate the overheads to be added to units of production as equitably as possible; that is, the overheads attributable to each unit should be fair and reasonable.

The process involves two stages:

1. Allocation or apportionment of overheads to cost centres (see 18.4 and 18.5).
2. Calculation of overhead absorption rates for cost units (see 18.6).

18.4 Allocation or apportionment of overheads to cost centres

Cost centres

A cost centre is an entity to which costs may be attributed.

In a manufacturing business, the cost centres may be:

Foundry	Packing department
Machine shop	Stores
Finishing department	Warehouse
Paint shop	Canteen
Assembly department	Accounts office
	etc., etc.

A cost centre may even be a particular machine or person.

Allocation and apportionment

Expenditure is allocated to a cost centre when it was made specifically for that centre. Examples of expenditure which can be allocated are:

Expenditure	Cost centre
Pig iron	Foundry
Lubricating oil	Machine shop
Repairs to racking	Stores
Food	Canteen

Expenditure which is made for the benefit of the business generally cannot be allocated; it is apportioned on some equitable basis. Such expenditure is rent, rates, insurance, heating and lighting etc.

The following diagram should make the treatment of expenses clear

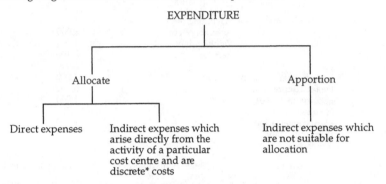

* *discrete* means separate or individually distinct.

18.4.1 Bases of apportionment

Apportionment of indirect expenses to cost centres must be made on fair and reasonable bases. Different types of expense require different bases according to their individual characteristics.

The basis adopted for each expense should take account of the nature of the expense and the impact of each cost centre on the amount of expense incurred or the relative benefit enjoyed by the cost centre. Bases of apportionment of the following overheads to cost centres are usually as shown:

Overhead	Basis of apportionment to cost centres
Buildings: rent, rates maintenance, depreciation insurance	On floor area of each cost centre
Heating, lighting	Either on volume of space occupied by cost centre, but may be on floor area
Plant, machinery and equipment – depreciation	On cost or book value of plant etc. in cost centre
Plant, machinery and equipment – insurance	On cost or replacement value of plant etc. in cost centre
Costs of storekeeping	On number or value of stores requisitions raised by each cost centre
Costs of canteen, personnel dept administration	On number of personnel in each cost centre.

18.4.2 Example: involving production departments only

Cruet Ltd is a manufacturing company with four production departments: machining, assembly, painting, and packing. The following data relates to the four departments:

	Machining	Assembly	Painting	Packing
Floor area (Metres^2)	2,000	1,500	1,000	500
Plant etc cost (£000's)	90	30	20	10
Plant etc replacement cost (£000's)	120	50	30	20
No. of stores requisitions	300	200	250	50

During the three months to March 31, Cruet Ltd incurred the following expenditure:

		£
Production materials	– Machining dept.	130,000
	Assembly dept.	24,000
	Painting dept.	34,000
	Packing dept.	17,000
Direct labour	– Machining dept.	36,000
	Assembly dept.	12,000
	Painting dept.	15,000
	Packing dept.	12,000
Indirect labour	– Machining dept.	4,100
	Assembly dept.	5,000
	Painting dept.	4,700
	Packing dept.	3,400
Factory rent		15,000
Factory repairs and maintenance		7,500
Factory depreciation		3,000
Factory insurance		1,000
Heating		2,500
Plant depreciation		9,000
Plant insurance		1,320
Storekeeping costs		6,400

Cost	Basis of charge	Total	Machining	Assembly	Painting	Packing
		£	£	£	£	£
Direct materials	Allocation	205,000	130,000	24,000	34,000	17,000
Direct labour	Allocation	75,000	36,000	12,000	15,000	12,000
Indirect labour	Allocation	17,200	4,100	5,000	4,700	3,400
Allocated costs		297,200	170,100	41,000	53,700	32,400
Apportioned costs						
Factory rent	Floor area	15,000	6,000	4,500	3,000	1,500
Factory repairs and maintenance	Floor area	7,500	3,000	2,250	1,500	750
Factory depreciation	Floor area	3,000	1,200	900	600	300
Factory insurance	Floor area	1,000	400	300	200	100
Heating	Floor area	2,500	1,000	750	500	250
Plant depreciation	Cost of plant	9,000	5,400	1,800	1,200	600
Plant insurance	Replacement value	1,320	720	300	180	120
Storekeeping	No. of requisitions	6,400	2,400	1,600	2,000	400
		342,920	190,220	53,400	62,880	36,420

18.4.3 Exercise: in apportionment of overheads

Rainbow Cloths Ltd manufactures fabrics for the soft furnishings industry. Three processes are involved in the manufacture: spinning, weaving and dyeing which are carried out in separate departments of the factory. The following data is available for the three departments:

Department	Floor area (metres^2)	Plant & machinery at cost	Plant & machinery replacement cost	No. of stores requisitions (3 months)
		£'000	£'000	
Spinning	1,260	100	130	240
Weaving	1,890	150	210	90
Dyeing	1,050	50	80	120
	4,200	300	420	450

Rainbow Cloths Ltd's overheads for a three months period are as follows:

Factory –	amortisation of lease	£20,000
	insurance	£2,000
	repairs and maintenance	£4,500

Plant & machinery – insurance		£3,150
	repairs and maintenance	£9,000
	depreciation	£7,500
Stores –	overheads	£13,500

Required

Using appropriate bases of apportionment, prepare a table showing the apportionment of Rainbow Cloths Ltd's overheads to the three departments and indicate the bases used for each overhead.

18.5 Shared costs of service departments

Service departments such as the stores, buildings maintenance and canteen are not directly involved in production; their overheads must be re-apportioned to the production departments according to the use they make of the service departments. This has already been shown in the example of Cruet Ltd above, in which the cost of the stores has been apportioned to the production departments in proportion to the number of requisitions raised by each department.

Reciprocal services

If two or more service departments are involved, and the service departments provide services for each other as well as for the production departments, the service departments are said to provide reciprocal services for each other. These require special consideration in the apportionment of overheads.

The continuous allotment method

The first (primary) attempt to apportion overheads results in an increase in the overheads of the other service departments. As a result secondary, and possibly tertiary and more, apportionments may be necessary, until the amount remaining to be apportioned is insignificant.

18.5.1 Example

Reciprocal Services Ltd has three production departments: machining, assembly and paintshop. In addition, there are two service departments: stores and premises maintenance. The premises maintenance department uses materials which it draws from the stores; the stores, in turn, uses the services of the premises maintenance department.

Stores overheads are apportioned to the other departments on the basis of the number of stores requisitions raised by each department. Charges for premises maintenance are based on the floor area of each department.

The numbers of stores requisitions raised in March were:

Machining dept.	600
Assembly dept	500
Paintshop	400
Premises maintenance	100

The floor areas of the departments are:

Machine dept.	2,400m^2
Assembly dept.	2,000m^2
Paintshop	1,200m^2
Stores	1,400m^2
Premises maintenance	600m^2

The allocated and apportioned costs in total for each department in March were:

	£
Machine dept.	96,000
Assembly dept.	41,000
Paintshop	26,000
Stores	8,000
Premises maintenance	14,000

	Machine dept	Assembly dept	Paintshop	Stores	Premises maintenance
	£	£	£	£	£
Costs	96,000	41,000	26,000	8,000	14,000
First apportionment (Stores)	3,000	2,500	2,000	(8,000)	500
					14,500
Second apportionment (Premises maintenance)	4,971	4,143	2,486	2,900	(14,500)
				2,900	
Third apportionment (Stores)	1,088	906	725	(2,900)	181
					181
Fourth apportionment (Premises maintenance)	62	52	31	36	(181)
				36	
Final apportionment*	14	12	10	(36)*	
	105,135	48,613	31,252	–	–

* The residual amount in the final apportionment is considered insignificant and is apportioned to the production departments only.

Stores overheads have been apportioned on the basis of the number of requisitions raised by each department; premises maintenance overheads have been apportioned on the basis of floor areas.

18.5.2 Exercise: in apportionment of overheads involving departments offering reciprocal services using the continuous allotment method

The Speedy Transport Company has three operating departments as follows:

1. Local collections and deliveries
2. Long distance trunk services
3. Contract hire.

The company also has two service departments:

1. Engineering services, which maintains and repairs the company's vehicles, including those of the building maintenance department
2. Building maintenance, which maintains the premises at the company's depots and those accommodating the engineering services.

The overheads of the company for the coming year are estimated to be £1,035,500 and are being apportioned as follows:

	£
Local collections and deliveries:	400,000
Long distance trunk services:	300,000
Contract hire:	100,000
Engineering services:	144,000
Building maintenance:	91,500

The following additional information is available:

	Average no. of vehicles in year	No. of Building maintenance orders in the year (based on previous year)
Local collections and deliveries	180	300
Long distance trunk services	30	210
Contract hire	20	30
Engineering services	7	70
Building maintenance	10	–

Required

Show how the service departments' overheads should be apportioned to the operating departments and the resulting total overheads of the operating departments

18.5.3 Apportionment of overheads using the elimination method

The elimination method is simpler than the continuous allotment method. The overheads of one of the service departments are apportioned over the other departments in the normal way. That department is then eliminated from the reckoning in the subsequent apportionment of the other service department.

Using the elimination methods the overheads of Reciprocal Services Ltd. (18.5.1) would be apportioned as follows.

	Machine dept	Assembly dept	Paintshop	Stores	Premises maintenance
	£	£	£	£	£
Costs	96,000	41,000	26,000	8,000	14,000
First apportionment (Stores)	3,000	2,500	2,000	(8,000)	500
					14,500
Second apportionment (Premises maintenance)	6,214	5,179	3,107		(14,500)
	105,214	48,679	31,107	–	–

The criticism levelled at the elimination method is that it is illogical because it ignores the proportion of Premises maintenance overheads which should be borne by the Stores, and is therefore not as accurate as the continuous allotment method. It may be argued, however, that any method used to apportion overheads is only one of several conventions and strict accuracy is not claimed for any of them. Probably, in most cases, the difference will not be significant.

18.5.4 Exercise: in apportionment of overheads using the elimination method

Using the data given in 18.5.2, apportion the overheads for The Speedy Transport Company using the elimination method.

18.5.5 Apportionment of overheads using simultaneous equations

A third method of apportioning overheads when two departments offer reciprocal services employs the use of simultaneous equations. The method is demonstrated using the data for Reciprocal Services Ltd in 18.5.1.

Stores overheads are apportioned on the basis of requisitions

Premises Maintenance department accounts for $\frac{1}{16}$ of stores requisitions.

Premises Maintenance overheads are apportioned on the basis of floor areas.

Stores department occupies $\frac{1,400}{7,000}$ or $\frac{1}{5}$ of the floor area attributable to the departments over which Stores overheads have to be apportioned.

Let a = the total overheads of the Premises Maintenance dept. after the Stores overheads have been apportioned.

And let b = the total overheads of the Stores after Premises Maintenance overheads have been apportioned.

Then $\quad a = £14,000 + \frac{1}{16} b$

and $\quad b = £8,000 + \frac{1}{5} a$

Rearrange the equations so that the monetary amounts are the only terms on the right in each case. (This involves moving the fractional amounts of a and b to the other side and changing the sign in each case.) :

$$a - \frac{1}{16} b = £14,000$$

$$b - \frac{1}{5} a = £8,000$$

The next step is to eliminate either a or b from the equations; a can be eliminated if the second equation is multiplied by 5 and added to the first equation:

$$a - \frac{1}{16} b = £14,000$$

$$5b - a = £40,000$$

Therefore $(5 - \frac{1}{16})\,b$, or $4\frac{15}{16}\,b = £54,000$

and $b = £10,937$

Now substitute £10,937 for b in one of the equations:

$$£10,937 - \tfrac{1}{5}a = £8,000$$

Deduct £10,937 from both sides and change the signs:

$$\tfrac{1}{5}a = £10,937 - £8,000$$

$$= £2,937$$

Therefore $a = £14,685$

Finally, the service department overheads are apportioned over the production departments:

	Machine dept £	Assembly dept. £	Paintshop £	Stores £	Premises maintenance £
Costs	96,000	41,000	26,000	8,000	14,000
Stores	4,100	3,418	2,734	(10,937)	685
Premises maintenance	5,035	4,196	2,517	2,937	(14,685)
	105,135	48,614	31,251	–	–

18.5.6 Exercise: in apportionment of overheads using simultaneous equations

Wellhouse Ltd processes a certain material which passes through three workshops, A,B and C. In addition to a general stores, there is a factory canteen. The following information is available for each department:

		Apportioned overheads £	No. of stores requisitions	No. of staff
Workshop	A	120,000	300	40
	B	108,000	250	30
	C	210,000	150	25
Stores		45,000	–	5
Canteen		15,000	50	4

Required

Choosing suitable bases for apportionment, use simultaneous equations to calculate the apportionment of the service department overheads to the workshops.

18.6 Calculation of overhead absorption rates (OAR) for cost units

When overheads have been apportioned to cost centres, the next stage is to calculate the amount of overhead to be added to each cost unit passing through the cost centres.

Cost units

A cost unit is a unit of production. What constitutes a cost unit depends upon the nature of the business concerned. Examples of cost units are:

Industry	Cost unit
Television set manufacturer	A television set
Umbrella manufacturer	An umbrella
Brick manufacturer	A pallet of bricks*
Breakfast cereal manufacturer	A thousand packets
Passenger transport	A passenger-mile
Freight transport	A tonne-mile
Electricity generation	A kilowatt-hour

* A pallet is a wooden platform on which bricks are stacked to enable them to be transported. A standard pallet load might consist of, say, 5,000 bricks.

Items such as bricks or packets of breakfast cereal which are produced in extremely large quantities and are themselves of small value are too trivial to count as single cost units.

The amount of a cost centre's overheads to be added to (or 'absorbed by') each unit of production passing through the cost centre is determined by an overhead absorption rate (OAR).

Overhead absorption rates (OAR)

Overhead absorption rates are predetermined and applied over a given period. The calculation of OARs is based on budgeted production and overhead expenditure.

Six possible bases for calculating overhead absorption rates are now considered.

1. Machine hour OAR

This is an appropriate basis when the means of production are capital intensive and the production processes are predominantly mechanised. Machine costs such as repairs, maintenance and depreciation will form a substantial proportion of the overheads. Overhead absorption rates will take account of the number of machine hours required to produce each unit of output.

18.6.1 Example

Macour Ltd makes two products, A and B. Its budgeted output for March is as follows:

	Units	Machine hours per unit
Product A	1,000	3
Product B	2,000	2

Budgeted overheads for March are £49,000

The budgeted overhead absorption rates will be:

$$\text{Total machine hours} = 3,000 + 4,000 = 7,000$$

$$\text{Machine hour OAR} = \frac{£49,000}{7,000} = £7$$

Overhead absorption rate: each unit of A = £7 × 3 = £21

each unit of B = £7 × 2 = £14.

If the budgets are met, the total overheads will be absorbed as follows:

	£
1,000 units of A (1,000 × £21)	21,000
2,000 units of B (2,000 × £14)	28,000
Total	49,000

18.6.2 Exercise: in calculation of machine hour rates

Anbin Ltd manufactures two products, Ancrum and Bino. Each unit of Ancrum requires $2\frac{1}{2}$ hours of machine time to make, while Bino requires $1\frac{1}{2}$ hours of machine time.

Anbin Ltd uses 10 machines in the manufacture of Ancrum and Bino. Each machine is used for 50 hours per week. In a period of 8 weeks, it is planned to manufacture 1,000 units of Ancrum and 1,000 units of Bino. Total overheads are expected to be £82,000 for the period.

Required

Calculate the overhead recovery rates for Ancrum and Bino and prepare a statement showing how the total overheads will be absorbed by production.

2. Direct labour hour OAR

If processes are labour intensive so that machine involvement is small and machine costs low but labour costs relatively high, OAR may be calculated on the basis of man hours required to make each unit of production.

18.6.3 Example

Dilabour Ltd manufactures two products, X and Y. The budget for March is as follows:

	Units	Direct labour hours per unit
Product X	4,000	0.5
Product Y	6,000	1.5

Budgeted overheads for month: £55,000

Total budgeted direct labour hours for March: 2,000 + 9,000 = 11,000

Direct labour hour OAR = $\frac{£55,000}{11,000}$ = £5

The overhead absorption rate per unit: X = 0.5 × £5 = £2.50

                                                Y = 1.5 × £5 = £7.50

If the budgets are met, the total overheads will be absorbed as follows:

	£
4,000 units of X (4,000 × £2.50)	10,000
6,000 units of Y (6,000 × £7.50)	45,000
Total	55,000

18.6.4 Exercise in calculation of direct labour hour rates

Belshaze Ltd manufactures chairs. The chairs are of two designs called Wessex and Cumbria. The chairs are largely made by hand and a Wessex requires 8 hours labour while a Cumbria takes 10 hours to make.

The company employs 35 men to make the chairs and they each work 40 hours a week. In the 12 weeks to 30 June, factory overheads are estimated to be £54,600. It is planned to make 800 Wessex chairs and the balance of production hours will be utilised in manufacturing Cumbria chairs.

Required

Calculate the overhead recovery rate for each chair and state the number of Cumbria chairs which it is planned to make in the twelve weeks to 30 June. Prepare a statement showing how the overheads will be recovered in the period.

3.   Direct wages OAR

A simple method of calculating an absorption rate is to express overheads as a proportion of direct wages. The weakness of this method lies in the fact that, although overheads may generally accrue on a time basis, direct wages may not be directly related to time taken in production. This may be the result of differential rates paid to different workers, overtime and shift working premiums, and piecework and bonus systems.

4.   Direct material OAR

An absorption rate based on the cost of direct materials ignores the possibility that a product with a high material cost may take less time to make than one with a low material cost. The former would have an unjustifiably higher OAR than the latter in spite of the fact that the time required to manufacture it clearly indicates that it should be loaded with less overheads and not more.

5.   Prime cost OAR

This method combines the weaknesses of the direct wages OAR and the direct materials OAR.

6.   Cost unit OAR

Attributing the same OAR to all units of production is only sensible if only one product is involved and every unit is produced by a similar process.

18.6.5 Calculation of overhead absorption rates where more than one product and more than one cost centre are involved

Where two or more cost centres are involved in production, a separate OAR should be prepared for each. This may well require different bases of calculating the OARs. Separate overhead recovery calculations should also be made for each product.

Example

Plurioars Ltd manufactures two products known as H and J. Both products require processing in departments I and II of the company. The following budgeted information is available for the month of March:

Products		H	J
Budgeted production		2,000 units	1,000 units
Direct materials per unit		£8	£10
Direct wages per unit		£40	£40
Machine hours per unit:	Dept.I	4	2
	Dept.II		1
Direct labour hours per unit:	Dept.I	2	3
	Dept.II	3	2
Cost centres		Dept I	Dept II
Budgeted overheads		£40,000	£30,000
Budgeted machine hours		10,000	1,000
Budgeted direct labour hours		7,000	8,000

Budgeted overhead recovery rates:

Dept.I (using machine hour rate) $\dfrac{£40,000}{10,000}$ = £4 per machine hour

Dept. II using direct labour hour rate $\dfrac{£30,000}{8,000}$ = £3.75 per direct labour hour

	Dept I	Dept II
Product H	(£4 × 4) £16	(£3.75 × 3) £11.25
Product J	(£4 × 2) £8	(£3.75 × 2) £7.50

Total overhead recovery

		Dept I £		Dept II £
Product H	(2,000 × £16)	32,000	(2,000 × £11.25)	22,500
Product J	(1,000 × £8)	8,000	(1,000 × £7.50)	7,500
Total overhead recovery (per budget)		40,000		30,000

Total (absorption) cost statement for March

	Product H			Product J	
	Per unit £	2,000 units £		Per unit £	1,000 units £
Direct materials	8.00	16,000		10.00	10,000
Direct wages	40.00	80,000		40.00	40,000
Prime cost	48.00	96,000		50.00	50,000
Production o'heads					
£(16 + 11.25)	27.25	54,500	£(8 + 7.50)	15.50	15,500
Total cost	75.25	150,500		65.50	65,500

18.6.6 Exercise

Alcansted Ltd processes two substances called Eon and Pysin. Both products pass through two stages of electrolysis and filtration. Budgeted overheads for the month of April are as follows:

	£
Electrolysis dept.	17,340
Filtration dept.	19,800

Planned production for April is 900 units of Eon and 1,200 units of Pysin.

Other data is as follows:

Machine hours required per unit:	Eon	Pysin
Electrolysis	3	2
Filtration	1	3
Direct labour hours required per unit		
Electrolysis	1	2
Filtration	4	3

Budgeted hours for April are	Machine	Direct labour
Electrolysis	5,100	3,300
Filtration	4,500	7,200

Direct costs for each unit of production are as follows:

	Eon £	Pysin £
Direct materials	2	5
Direct labour	20	20

Alcansted Ltd recover Electrolysis dept. overheads on a machine hour basis, and Filtration dept. overheads on a direct labour hour basis.

Required

(i)   Calculate the overhead recovery rates for Eon and Pysin in each of the departments.

(ii) Prepare a statement showing how the total overheads are recovered by production

(iii) Prepare a total cost statement for each of the two products.

18.7 Over/under recovery of overheads

Overhead absorption rates are based upon budgeted overhead expenditure and budgeted levels of activity. It follows that if actual expenditure and activity are equal to budget, the overheads will be recovered exactly. If actual out-turn does not correspond to budget, an over or under recovery of overheads will result.

18.7.1 Examples

Sherlock Ltd budgets for overhead expenditure of £16,000 in June, and for an output of 4,000 units. The overhead absorption rate is £4 per unit.

(i)   Actual output for June was 4,060 units; actual expenditure equalled budget. Over recovery was $60 \times £4 = £240$

(ii) Actual output for June was 3,970 units; actual expenditure equalled budget. Under recovery was $30 \times £4 = £120$

(iii) Actual expenditure was £17,000; actual output equalled budget. Under recovery was £1,000

(iv) Actual expenditure was £15,980; actual output equalled budget. Under recovery was £20.

Over/under recovered overheads will be credited/debited in the cost profit and loss account.

18.8 Advantages and disadvantages of total costs

Advantages

1.   It is necessary to know the total cost of a product in order to fix a selling price.

2.   Total costs are necessary for long term planning as revenue must cover overheads as well as direct costs.

Disadvantages

1.   Overhead absorption rates must be kept under constant review and adjusted for changes in overhead expenditure, levels of activity and operational changes.

2.   Information provided by total costs is inadequate for much management decision making.

Key points to remember

1.   Overhead expenditure is allocated when it is made for one specific cost centre. All other expenditure is apportioned to cost centres on equitable bases.

2.   Reciprocal services offered between cost centres require overhead expenditure to be re-apportioned over all cost centres in stages until the unapportioned residue is not significant. The elimination method or simultaneous equations may be used.

3.   The overheads of cost centres are attributed to cost units in accordance with calculated overhead absorption rates.

4.   Overhead absorption rates are based on machine hours if the operation is capital intensive, or on direct labour hours if the operation is labour intensive.

5.   Higher than budgeted production and/or lower than expected overhead expenditure leads to over-recovery of overheads. Lower than budgeted production and/or higher than expected overhead expenditure leads to under-recovery of overheads.

6.   Ascertainment of total cost is essential for price fixing and long term planning. It does not provide information vital for many management decisions.

> ### Common errors
> 1. Choice of unsuitable bases for apportionment of overheads and calculation of OARs.
> 2. Arithmetical errors in calculations of apportionments and OARs.

Questions

Multiple choice questions

1   Rent expense is usually apportioned to cost centres on the basis of
   A   areas of cost centres
   B   number of employees per cost centre
   C   revenue earned by each cost centre
   D   space occupied by machinery in each cost centre

2   Stores overheads are usually apportioned to production departments on the basis of
   A   areas occupied by production centres
   B   number of employees in each production centre
   C   number or values of requisitions raised by each production centre
   D   quantities of finished goods produced by each cost centre.

3   Overhead absorption rates (OARs) are used to determine the
   A   amount which will be spent on overheads
   B   apportionment of service department overheads to production departments
   C   prime cost of a product
   D   total cost of a product

4   It is not necessary to calculate overhead absorption rates when
   A   all types of products are processed through all the company's production departments
   B   only one standard type of product is made
   C   the amount which will actually be spent on overheads is not known
   D   there is only one production department

Further examination questions

1   R. E. Lee Ltd is a company that manufactures building equipment. It has three production departments and a service department and has produced the following budgeted cost of production for the year ended 31 March 1992:

		£	£
Production cost	Direct materials	240,000	
	Carriage inwards	10,000	
	Direct wages	200,000	450,000
Indirect wages	Dept. X	8,000	
	Dept. Y	12,000	
	Dept. Z	18,300	
	General Service Dept.	6,700	45,000
Other costs	Consumable stores	32,000	
	Rent	21,000	
	Light and heat	14,000	
	Power	36,000	
	Depreciation	80,000	
	Insurance – machinery	2,000	185,000
			680,000

The following is a set of data relating to the physical and performance aspects of the company:

Department	Area m²	Book Value of Plant	Stores Requisitions	Effective Horse Power	Direct Labour Hours	Direct Labour Cost	Machine Hours
		£				£	
X	15,000	140,000	180	80	100,000	50,000	70,000
Y	22,500	180,000	120	100	80,000	60,000	90,000
Z	20,000	10,000	100	5	220,000	90,000	10,000
Service	12,500	70,000	–	15	–	–	–

The general service department is apportioned to the production departments on the basis of direct labour cost.

Required

(a) An overhead analysis sheet for the departments, showing clearly the basis of apportionment.
(13 marks)

(b) A computation (correct to three decimal places) of hourly cost rates of overhead absorption for each production department using the performance data given. (6 marks)

(c) A critical assessment of the methods used in b) above. (6 marks)

(Total 25 marks)
(AEB)

2 Kalmo Ltd offers a subcontracting service in assembly, painting and packing. Components are supplied by customers to the company, the required operations are then carried out, and the completed work returned to the customer. The company is labour intensive, with only a relatively small amount of materials purchased.

Currently, one factory overhead recovery rate is used which is a percentage of total direct labour costs. This is calculated from the following budgeted costs.

Department	Direct Labour Costs	Direct Labour Hours	Machine Hours	Factory Overheads
	£			£
Assembly	450,000	150,000	6,000	180,000
Painting	500,000	140,625	–	225,000
Packing	250,000	100,000	8,000	75,000

The cost sheet for Job 131190 shows the following information:

Department	Direct Labour Costs	Direct Labour Hours	Machine Hours	Direct Material Costs
	£			£
Assembly	2,500	1,000	120	100
Painting	2,200	900	–	400
Packing	4,800	960	80	500

General Administration expenses of 20% are added to the total factory costs, and then a further 25% of the total cost is added as profit, to arrive at the selling price.

Although the company has been using the blanket factory overhead recovery rate for a number of years, one of the directors has questioned this method, and asks if it would be possible to apply overhead recovery rates for each department.

Required

(a) Calculate the current factory overhead recovery rate, and apply this to arrive at the selling price for Job 131190. (4 marks)

(b) In line with the director's comments, calculate overhead recovery rates for each department, using two alternative methods, and apply both to arrive at new selling prices for Job 131190. (10 marks)

(c) Briefly evaluate the methods you have used for the recovery of factory overheads, justifying which one you consider to be most appropriate. (6 marks)

(d) Outline how an unsatisfactory method of overhead absorption can affect the profits of a business. (3 marks)

(Total 23 marks)
(OXFORD)

3 (a) "The apportionment of overheads to departments is based upon estimates and accounting conventions."

Briefly explain this statement. (4 marks)

(b) Retro Ltd uses the continuous apportionment method to apportion overheads between its two service sections.

Service Sections	Technical Services	Administration
Overheads (£)	30,000	20,000
Apportionment (%):		
Administration	10	–
Technical Services	–	5

For each service section, calculate the amount of overheads to be apportioned to production. (7 marks)

(c) Explain two other methods that Retro Ltd could have used to apportion the service departments' overheads between Technical Services and Administration. (4 marks)

(Total 15 marks)
(LONDON)

4 A company's overhead cost items for a year are illustrated by the following graphs.

State a) which graph relates to the following overheads and b) give reasons for your answer.

(i) Factory rent of £50,000 per year.

(ii) Cost of a service: £2 per unit produced up to a maximum of £5,000 per year.

(iii) Maintenance in the form of a standing charge of £2,500, plus a charge of £5 per unit produced to a maximum of £10,000 per year.

(iv) Depreciation charged on the basis of a cost per unit.

(v) Supervisors' salaries:

under 500	units produced – one supervisor
501-1,000	units produced – two supervisors
1,001-1,500	units produced – three supervisors

(15 marks)

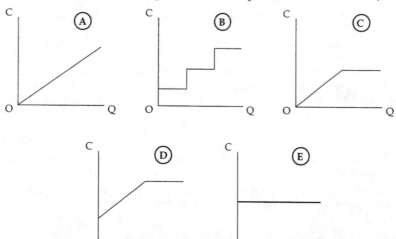

Note: in each case OQ represents output and OC represents cost.

(LONDON)

5 (a) Explain the difference between the terms *overhead allotment, overhead apportionment,* and *overhead absorption*. (5 marks)

(b) Why are estimated figures used in calculating overhead absorption rates? (2 marks)

(c) The following information relates to the Flyby Knight plc for the six months ended 31 December, 1991:

	Production Departments			Service Departments	
	A	B	C	X	Y
Overheads (£)	14,000	12,000	8,000	4,000	3,000
Overheads to be apportioned:					
Dept (X) (%)	35	30	20	–	15
Dept (Y) (%)	30	40	25	5	–

(i) Use the continuous apportionment (repeated distribution) method to apportion the service departments' overheads between each other.

(ii) Apportion the service departments' overheads calculated in i) to the production departments.

(iii) Show how the overheads apportioned to the production departments would have differed if the elimination method had been used for the service departments.

(iv) State how far it is true to say that the elimination method produces an inaccurate answer, and is therefore not to be recommended. (18 marks)
(LONDON)

6 The Whacky Engineering Co plc is organised into five departments. Departments A, B and C are production departments; and X and Y are service departments. Department X's overheads are to be apportioned on the basis of floor areas; department Y's overheads are to be apportioned on the basis of staff numbers.

Details are shown below for the six months ending 30 September 1992.

Department	Floor area	Estimated Number of staff	Estimated Overheads
	m		£
A	450.0	14	50,000
B	337.5	10	40,000
C	225.0	6	30,000
X	–	10	20,000
Y	112.5	–	10,000

(a) Calculate:
   (i) the proportion of department X's overheads which are to be apportioned to A, B, C and Y;
   (ii) the proportion of Y's overheads which are to be apportioned to A, B, C and X. (4 marks)

(b) Use the simultaneous equation (algebraic) method to apportion X's overheads to Y and Y's overheads to X. (8 marks)

(c) Apportion X's and Y's overheads to the production departments. (6 marks)

(d) For what reasons might a company recover more in overheads for a particular period than it incurs in that period? How are such differences dealt with in the accounts? (7 marks)

(Total 25 marks)
(LONDON)

7 (a) Why might it be incorrect to describe any method of apportioning overheads as being more accurate than another? (4 marks)

(b) Use the repeated distribution method (continuous apportionment method) to apportion the overheads between the two service departments shown below:

	Service Departments	
	Maintenance	Administration
Indirect costs (£)	120,000	86,000
Apportionment: Maintenance %	–	5
Administration %	10	–

(6 marks)

(c) Identify **five** methods which may be used to divide overheads between departments of a business. In each case give an example demonstrating the circumstances most appropriate to its use. (5 marks)

(Total 15 marks)
(LONDON)

8   Krupp Industries plc operates a factory with four Departments. Two of the Departments – the Machine Shop and the Assembly Shop – are production departments, whereas the Maintenance Department and the Power House provide a service. For the coming year the budgeted costs are as follows:

	Machine Shop £	Assembly Shop £	Maintenance Department £	Power House £	Total £
Indirect costs					
Indirect materials	1,491	2,414	665	760	5,330
Indirect labour	3,534	4,581	11,410	3,365	22,890
Rent and rates					7,130
Supervision					3,300
Plant depreciation					8,250
					46,900

You ascertain the following information:

	Machine Shop	Assembly Shop	Maintenance Department	Power House
Number of employees	20	40	10	5
Area (sq. metres)	1,500	2,500	500	100
Plant valuation (£000s)	6,500	2,500	1,200	800
Direct labour hours	1,600	2,400		
Machine hours	5,540	1,160		
Maintenance hours	900	300	–	–
Units of power used	2,100	600	300	–

Required

(a) Analyse the above Indirect costs between the four Departments showing the bases of apportionment you have used. (9 marks)

(b) Re-apportion the costs of the Service Departments over the two Production Departments using appropriate bases. (6 marks)

(c) Calculate an overhead absorption rate for the Machine Shop based on machine hours and an overhead absorption rate for the Assembly Shop based on direct labour hours. (6 marks)

(d) Explain the meaning of the terms:
   (i)   'overhead absorption';
   (ii) 'overhead under-absorption';
   (iii) 'overhead over-absorption';

   illustrating you answer by reference to the Machine Shop. (4 marks)

(Total 25 marks)
(CAMBRIDGE)

9   Downpike Ltd is a manufacturing company that utilises a large number of different machines in its production process and uses machine hour rates to absorb the production overheads in job costs.

The following details are available for machine XR 8.

(1) The cost of the machine is £24,000; estimated life is 8 years. The straight line method of depreciation is applied.

(2) Machine department overheads per annum are:

	£
Heat and light	7000
Supervision	6000

The area of this department is 8750 square metres of which machine XR 8 occupies 250 square metres. The number of machines in the department is 20.

(3) The annual cost of repair equipment for XR 8 is £110.

(4) Machine running time is 2500 hours per annum (2300 hours production and 200 hours setting up).

(5) The power cost is 5p per hour for both setting up and production.

(6) The labour rate for machinists is £4.80 per hour. When machines are being set up, full time attention is needed from the machinists but once machines are in production then one machinist can control three machines.

(7) The company has arranged insurance coverage for the machines for an annual premium of £8000 (total cost of all machines is £768 000).

A typical job carried out by this machine is coded Z22. This job involves using 15 kilos of material costing £2.50 per kilo, 12 machine hours and 3 hours assembly work using labour paid £3.60 per hour.

Required

(a) Prepare a statement showing the machine hour rate for XR 8 (correct to two decimal places).   (14 marks)

(b) Calculate the job cost of Z22.   (8 marks)

(c) Identify the possible reasons for Downpike Ltd's use of machine hour rates in its costing.   (8 marks)

Total 30 marks
(AEB)

10 Togfell Ltd has decided to abandon its present costing system and change to one using absorption costing techniques. The company manufactures three products – Tog A Tog B and Tog C. Each product has to pass through two production departments before it is completed. These departments are identified as the Cutting Department and the Machining and Finishing Department. Both departments are labour intensive so it has been decided to use a direct labour hour rate of overhead absorption. Only overheads primarily involved with production will be used. The budgeted overhead costs for the coming year are:

	£
Factory power	59,500
Sales commission	30,000
Light and heat (factory)	46,200
Depreciation of equipment	62,500
Repairs to factory equipment	17,500
Delivery charges to customers' premises	21,700
Advertising	15,000
Supervisory staff costs (factory)	54,600
Canteen expenses (used by all factory staff)	39,360

The following is data upon which an appropriate basis of apportionment can be determined:

	Cutting Dept.	Machining and Finishing Dept.	Administration and Selling Dept.
Labour force (excluding supervisory)	20	50	20
Floor space (sq. metres)	4,000	5,000	2,000
Book value of equipment (£000)	80	420	–
Equipment (kilo-watt hours (000))	25	75	–
Supervisory staff	1	5	–
Production time per product (hours)			
Tog A	0.6	3.5	
Tog B	0.5	2.9	
Tog C	0.4	2.4	

The total hours worked by the factory labour force per person is expected to be 1800.

Required

(a) Calculate, to two decimal places, the selected overhead absorption rate for each department (Cutting; and Machining and Finishing) stating the apportionment basis used.   (24 marks)

(b) Calculate, to two decimal places, the total unit overhead cost per product.   (12 marks)

(c) A report to the managing director briefly describing **three** methods of overhead absorption and in each case stating why each may or may not be adopted.   (10 marks)

Total 46 marks
(AEB)

11 Easigear plc manufacture and market a wide range of leather products. Recently a large chain store has approached Easigear for a quotation to supply them with a bulk order of 'Adonis' leather jackets.

The standard specifications for 12 leather jackets are as follows:

Materials	Standard quantity	Total standard price
Leather hide	12	£192.00
Zips	72	£34.56
Buttons	96	£24.00
Thread	72 metres	£0.36
Hangers	12	£9.36

Labour	Standard time	Standard rate
Cutters	10 hours	£6.00 per hr
Sewers	3 hours	£6.00 per hr
Packers	30 mins	£4.00 per hr

Annual overheads	
Cutting room	£17,870
Sewing dept.	£14,960
Packing dept.	£20,070

Budget activity level:

Easigear plc employs 3 cutters, 3 sewers, 2 packers. All workers work a 37.5 hour week for 48 weeks of the year.

It is company policy to allocate all departmental overheads on the basis of direct labour hours in that particular department.

Required

(a) Calculate the selling price of a batch of 12 leather jackets if a gross profit of 50% on selling price is to be achieved.   (35 marks)

(b) Define the term "overhead expenses".   (5 marks)

(c) Critically examine the difficulties encountered in allocating overhead expenses to a range of products being produced by a single manufacturer.   (10 marks)

Total 50 marks
(AEB)

12 Horden Products Ltd manufactures goods which could involve any or all of three production departments. These departments are simply entitled **A**, **B** and **C**. A direct wages cost percentage absorption rate for the recovery of production overheads is applied to individual job costs.

Details from the company's budgets for the year ended 31 March 1995 are as follows:

	Dept.A	Dept.B	Dept.C
Indirect materials	£23,000	£35,000	£57,000
Indirect wages	£21,000	£34,000	£55,000
Direct wages	£140,000	£200,000	£125,000
Direct labour hours	25,000	50,000	60,000
Machine hours	100,000	40,000	10,000

The following information is also available for the production departments.

	Dept.A	Dept.B	Dept.C
Area (square metres)	30,000	20,000	10,000
Cost of machinery	£220,000	£160,000	£20,000
Horse power of machinery	55	30	15

Other budgeted figures are:	£
Power	120,000
Rent, rates, light , heat	90,000
Insurance (machinery)	20,000
Depreciation	80,000

Machinery is depreciated on the basis of 20% on cost.

Job No. 347 passed through all three departments and incurred the following actual direct costs and times.

	Direct Material £	Direct Wages £	Direct Labour Hours	Machine Hours
Dept.A	152	88	35	60
Dept.B	85	192	90	30
Dept.C	52	105	45	10

A sum amounting to 30% of the production cost is added to every job to enable a selling price to be quoted.

Required

(a) A statement to show the total production overheads per department and calculate the absorption rate which the company has adopted. (28 marks)

(b) Calculate the selling price to be quoted for Job No. 347 (8 marks)

(c) Using the available data, calculate absorption rates when based on:
    (i) direct labour hour rate; (3 marks)
    (ii) machine hour rate. (3 marks)

(d) Explain clearly the meaning of the following terms relating to overheads:
    (i) allotment; (3 marks)
    (ii) allocation; (3 marks)
    (iii) apportionment. (2 marks)

Total 50 marks
(AEB)

19 Job, batch, contract and process costing

19.1 Specific order costing and continuous operation costing

Total absorption costing principles can be applied to the operations of every business. The method of application depends upon the type of business in question. In general, the operations of businesses fall into two categories:

1. Specific order
2. Continuous operation

Specific order operations are those in which the work consists of separate jobs, batches or contracts, each of which is carried out as a result of a special order or contract.

Examples are:

Job   – Installing double glazing or central heating in a house

Batch   – Making doors and window frames to the specific specifications of a builder who is building a new housing estate

Contract – Constructing an office block, factory, oil rig etc.

Continuous operations are those where goods or services are produced as a result of a sequence of continuous or repetitive operations or processes. Examples are:

Process   – Oil refining, manufacture of chemicals, soap, paint etc.

Service   – Passenger or freight transport, health services.

19.1.1 Job costing

A job is work which is carried out by a firm when a customer places an order for the work to be done. Usually, the customer requires the firm to quote for the work before the order is placed. This gives the customer an opportunity to compare quotes from different firms to determine which firm will do the job for the best price. This is not necessarily the cheapest price because quality of materials used and workmanship must be taken into account with other factors in determining which quote will be accepted.

Quoting for a job

When a firm is asked to quote for a job, it must estimate the quantities of each of the materials to be used, and the number of hours required to be spent on the job by various grades of labour. The materials and labour must be priced and an appropriate amount added for overheads. If the firm has no shortage of work, it will decide what profit margin it expects to make on the job, and add this to arrive at the amount of the quotation. In some circumstances, the firm may want the order regardless of the profit margin. This will be the case when the firm is short of work and is prepared to accept orders which will help to cover the firm's overheads even if the profit is small or non-existent. Firms may also accept work at very low prices in times of temporary slackness in business in order to avoid making skilled and loyal staff redundant; the firm will need these workers when business revives.

Every job is allocated a job number and the quotation will be prepared on a job cost sheet which will also provide for the actual costs to be entered on the sheet when the job is completed.

19.1.2 Example: job costing

A Harvey (Builders) Ltd is asked to quote for the construction of a conservatory at the private residence of Mr T Lee, 3, The Drive, Pulchrington, Buckshire. The company allocates Job no. 123

to the job and estimates that the materials will cost £1,500. Two men will be required for the job for two weeks of 35 hours each week. The men are paid £14 an hour. The company recovers overheads on the basis of direct labour hours at a rate of £12 an hour. A profit margin of 20% is added to cost.

The Job Cost Sheet will be completed as in Table 1.

Mr Lee accepts the quotation of £6,168 and the company carries out the construction of the conservatory. When the job is finished the actual costs are found to be as follows:

Direct materials £1,640; Direct labour 154 hours at £14 an hour.

The Job Cost Sheet will be completed as in Table 2.

Job no.123 Mr T Lee, 3, The Drive, Pulchrington, Buckshire Construction of conservatory to customer's own design and specification			
Item	Estimate	Actual	Variance
	£	£	£
Direct materials	1,500		
Direct labour 140 hours at £14 p.h.	1,960		
Overheads 140 direct labour hours at £12 p.h.	1,680		
Total cost	5,140		
Profit margin 20% of cost	1,028		
Price	6,168		

Table 1

Job no.123 Mr T Lee, 3, The Drive, Pulchrington, Buckshire Construction of conservatory to customer's own design and specification			
Item	Estimate	Actual	Variance
	£	£	£
Direct materials	1,500	1,640	(140)
Direct labour 140 hours at £14 p.h.	1,960	2,156	(196)
Overheads 140 direct labour hours at £12 p.h.	1,680	1,848	(168)
Total cost	5,140	5,644	(504)
Profit margin 20% of cost	1,028	524	(504)
Price	6,168	6,168	–

Table 2

Adverse variances, those which result in reduced profit, are placed within brackets. If any variances are favourable, that is, they increase profit, they are not enclosed in brackets.

The Job Cost Sheet serves two useful purposes:

1. It identifies causes for the actual profit being different from the estimated profit in the quotation
2. The information contained on the sheet will be an important guide when estimates are made in the future for similar jobs.

19.1.3 Exercise: preparation of a job cost sheet

Alan Pannell is a commercial photographer. Job no. 59 is for the production of a video to promote the sales of Bona Fido Dog Foods. Alan estimates that the video will require materials costing £800 and will require 18 hours of his time, which he charges for at £80 an hour, and 12 hours of an assistant's time, at £20 an hour. Overheads are recovered on the basis of £30 per direct labour hour. Although Alan normally expects a profit margin of 25% on cost, he knows that a competitor is quoting for the job; as Alan wants to secure the job for prestige purposes, he estimates that if he quotes £3,750, he will undercut the competitor and get the contract.

Alan gains the contract and, on its completion, calculates actual costs as follows: materials £640; direct labour hours: Alan 20, assistant 15.

Required

Prepare the Job Cost Sheet for Job 59, showing the estimated and actual costs and profit.

19.2 Batch costing

When a 'job' consists of the production of a number or batch of identical units for a customer, batch costing is used. It is similar to job costing and the cost of one unit of production is calculated by dividing the total costs of the batch by the number of units produced.

Key points to remember

1. A job is work which is carried out by a firm when a customer places an order for the work to be done.
2. A job cost sheet forms the basis for a quotation for a job
3. When actual costs are inserted on a job cost sheet, differences in the cost elements between estimates made for a quotation and actual costs indicate the reasons for actual profit being different from the expected profit.
4. Job cost sheets are useful guides when similar jobs are tendered for in future.
5. Batch costing is similar to job costing, except that it is used when a customer places an order for the production of a number or batch of identical units.

Common errors

1. arithmetical errors in calculating the elements of cost.

19.3 Contract costing

Contract costing is similar in many respects to job costing but recognises the factors that make contracts different from jobs.

19.3.1 Contracts

A contract differs from a job in the following respects:

(i) It is of longer duration than a job

(ii) The amount of money involved is considerably greater than for jobs.

(iii) The customer and contractor sign a formal contract for the work.

Examples of contracts are those entered into by the building industry, civil engineering firms, shipbuilders etc.

Long term contracts

SSAP 9 defines a long term contract as one:

(i) entered into for the design, manufacture or construction of a single substantial asset or the provision of a service *

(ii) where the time taken substantially to complete the contract is such that the contract activity falls into different accounting periods

(iii) it will usually extend for a period exceeding one year.†

* this includes a combination of assets or services which constitute a single project.

† duration exceeding one year is not an essential feature of a long term contract.

19.3.2 Special considerations to be taken into account in contract costing

When contracts span two or more accounting periods, two accounting concepts in particular demand attention: the concepts of matching and of prudence.

Concept of matching. It is important that costs and profits and losses are recognised in the correct accounting periods.

Concept of prudence. No profit may be taken in the accounts of the contractor before the profitable outcome of the contract can be assessed with reasonable accuracy. Losses estimated to arise over the duration of a contract must be provided for as soon as they are recognised.

19.3.3 Special accounting features of a contract

Because, almost by definition, contracts are usually performed on their own sites, most expenditure which would be indirect in other activities, can be classed as direct expenditure on contracts. For example, supervisory salaries in a factory are an indirect expense; but supervision on a contract site is a direct expense. Electricity and telephones on site are direct expenses. Head office administration charges are debited to contract accounts periodically.

A contract usually provides for the customer to make progress payments during the term of the contract e.g. for the construction of a building, progress payments may be required when the foundations have been laid, on completion of building to first floor level and so on. Payments will be made when an architect certifies that an appropriate stage of the building work has been completed. The customer is usually allowed to deduct from each payment a percentage, probably 10%, called retention money. The retention money is the customer's guarantee that the contractor will perform the contract satisfactorily. It will be paid to the contractor some time after the completion of the contract when it is apparent that the work has been completed satisfactorily, or that the contractor has remedied any defects in the work at his own expense.

19.3.4 Contract accounts

A contract account is opened in the contractor's books for each contract. Postings to the account are:

Debit	Credit
Cost of materials sent to site	Materials removed from site
Net book values of plant and machinery sent to site	Net book value of plant and machinery transferred from site
Other site expenses	Value of work certified*
Apportioned head office costs	

* The value of work certified will be debited to cost of sales in the Profit and loss account. (A Trading account is not appropriate)

At the end of a financial period, if the contract has not been completed, the following debit balances will be carried down on the account:

(a) the cost of materials still on site

(b) the net book value of plant and machinery still on site

(c) work in progress (balancing figure)

When the contractor receives an architect's certificate at the completion of a stage of the contract, the contractor invoices the customer for the progress payment. The following entries will be made in the contractor's books:

Debit Customer account   *Credit* Work Certified account

At the end of the financial period, the balance on the Work Certified account will be transferred to the profit and loss account.

19.3.5 Example

CLP Construction plc is involved in a project, Contract 111. The contract commenced on 1 January 19-3 when materials costing £400,000, and plant and machinery with a net book value at that date of £384,000 were delivered to the site. During the year to 31 December 19-3, materials returned to head office were valued at £72,000, and plant and machinery with a net book value of £76,000 was transferred to another site. Other site expenses amounted to £212,000 and head office expenses charged to the contract were £97,000

At 31 December 19-3, materials on site were valued at £34,000 and plant on site had a net book value of £280,000. Work certified during the year amounted to £327,000. CLP Construction plc invoiced the customer for a progress payment in the sum of £380,000 on 30 September 19-3.

The relevant accounts in CLP Construction plc's books will appear as follows:

Contract 111

19-3		£	19-3		£
Jan 1	Materials	400,000	Dec 31	Materials returned	72,000
	Plant and machinery	384,000		Plant transferred	76,000
Dec 31	Site expenses	212,000		Cost of sales (P&L)	327,000
	Head office expenses	97,000		Materials c/d	34,000
				Plant & machinery c/d	280,000
				Work in progress	
				(balancing fig.)c/d	304,000
		1,093,000			1,093,000
19-4		£			
Jan 1	Materials b/d	34,000			
	Plant and machinery b/d	280,000			
	Work in progress b/d	304,000			

Work Certified

19-3		£	19-3		£
Dec 31	P & L a/c	380,000	Sep 30	Customer	380,000

Customer

19-3		£	19-3		£
Sep 30	Work certified	380,000			

19.3.6 Exercise in the preparation of a contract account

Lladnar Ltd commenced work on contract 2354 for Biggleswick District Council on 1 April 19-2. At 31 December 19-2, the materials on site were valued at £65,000, plant and machinery on site had a net book value of £170,000 and work in progress was valued at £102,000.

In the year to 31 December 19-3, the following transactions took place:

	£
Materials sent to site	360,000
Proceeds of materials sold on site	14,000
Plant sent to site	84,000
Plant and machinery transferred to other sites	38,000
Expenses incurred on site	91,000
Head office expenses charged to contract	75,000
Work certified during the year	460,000
At 31 December 19-3: Materials on site at cost	32,000
Plant and machinery on site at net book value	180,000

During the year, Lladnar Ltd invoiced Biggleswick District Council in the sum of £580,000.

Required

Prepare the accounts required to record the above transactions relating to contract no. 2354 in the books of Lladnar Ltd.

19.3.7 Treatment of profits and losses on contracts

Profit

If a contractor waited until the completion of a contract before recognising any profit on it in his accounts, his annual profit and loss accounts could give distorted impressions of the profitability of his business. For example, a contractor enters into a contract in 19-1 which will not be completed until 19-3. The contract price is £5,000,000. The contractor incurs the following costs on the contract:

	£
19-1	£800,000
19-2	£2,300,000
19-3	£700,000

If this is the only work the contractor has in those years and he does not recognise profit before the contract is completed , his profit and loss account will show the following results:

	£
19-1 loss	(800,000)
19-2 loss	(2,300,000)
19-3 profit	4,300,000

Clearly this is an unsatisfactory position, especially if this is a limited company whose share price depends upon its annual published results and whose shareholders are not content with waiting for three years before they can expect a dividend.

SSAP 9 (Stocks and Long-term Contracts) recognises that the profit on a contract may be earned over the period of the contract. It refers to attributable profit.

Attributable profit is that part of the total profit on a contract that fairly reflects the profit attributable to that part of the work performed at an accounting date. Calculation of the total profit must allow for increases in cost not recoverable under the contract and the contractor's liability for remedial and maintenance costs. (The contractor will normally be responsible for remedying at his own expense any faulty work discovered after completion of the contract.)

In the example given above, using the information given, calculation of profit at 31 December 19-2 would be as follows:

	£	£
Contract price		5,000,000
less Costs incurred to date	3,100,000	
Estimated further costs to completion	700,000	
Estimated remedial work	–	
Total estimated costs		3,800,000
Estimated profit		1,200,000

Attributable profit and the concept of prudence

In the early stages of a contract it is difficult to be certain that the contract will be profitable, and therefore no profit will be anticipated in the contractor's accounts. A contract which is less than 35% complete, i.e. less than 35% of the estimated contract cost has been incurred, will fall into this category.

If a contract is, say 35% to 85% complete, it is normally the practice to take only $\frac{2}{3}$ or $\frac{3}{4}$ of the profit calculated as the value of work certified, less the cost of the work certified. This is further modified, where the customer withholds retention money, by applying the fraction

$$\frac{\text{cash received on account}}{\text{value of work certified}}$$

In the example above, if the value of work certified at 31 December 19-2 was £3,000,000, the cost of the work certified was £2,356,000, and the customer had paid £2,700,000, the attributable profit would be calculated as follows:

$$\frac{2}{3} \times £(3,000,000 - 2,356,000) \times \frac{2,700,000}{3,000,000} = £386,400 \text{ or, alternatively,}$$

$$\frac{3}{4} \times £(3,000,000 - 2,356,000) \times \frac{2,700,000}{3,000,000} = £434,700$$

If the contract is more than, say, 85% complete, the profit on the contract can be estimated with a fair degree of certainty and attributable profit may be calculated in one of four ways: (For the purpose of these examples, we shall assume that the contract is considered near completion although it is slightly less than 85% complete)

(i) $\dfrac{\text{value of work certified}}{\text{contract price}} \times \text{estimated total profit} = \dfrac{3,000,000}{5,000,000} \times £1,200,000$

$$= £720,000$$

(ii) $\dfrac{\text{cash received to date}}{\text{contract price}} \times \text{estimated total profit} = \dfrac{2,700,000}{5,000,000} \times £1,200,000$

$$= £648,000$$

(iii) $\dfrac{\text{cost of work done}}{\text{estimated total cost of contract}} \times \text{estimated total profit} = \dfrac{3,100,000}{3,800,000} \times £1,200,000$

$$= £978,947$$

(iv) $\text{work certified to date less cost of work certified} = £3,000,000 - £3,100,000$

$$= £100,000 \text{ (loss)}$$

The methods should be compared to evaluate the respective degrees of prudence shown by each. Methods (i) and (ii) are probably the preferred ones.

The profit to be taken in any year, therefore, will be:

Attributable profit to date less profit already taken in previous years.

Therefore, if attributable profit has been calculated as in (ii) above, and up to the end of the previous year, credit had been taken for £360,000, the profit to be taken in the current year is £(648,000 − 360,000) = £288,000.

Losses

If, at the end of an accounting period, the costs to date on a contract plus the estimated further costs to completion exceed the contract price, the result is an estimated total loss. This must be provided for in the accounting period. The loss will be credited to the contract account and debited to Profit and Loss account.

19.3.8 Exercise: to calculate attributable profit

It is the policy of Collinson Construction plc to calculate the profit to be taken on contracts for its financial year on the following bases:

In the case of contracts less than 85% complete, by the formula $\frac{2}{3}$ of the profit (profit calculated as the difference between the work certified to date and the cost of that work) $\times$ $\dfrac{\text{cash received on account}}{\text{value of work certified}}$.

Profit on contracts more than 85% complete is calculated by the formula: estimated total profit from contract $\times$ $\dfrac{\text{cash received to date}}{\text{contract price}}$

At 31 December 19-3, Collinson Construction plc had the following contracts outstanding:

	Contract A £'000	Contract B £'000	Contract C £'000	Contract D £'000
Contract price	3,000	100	1,000	900
Cost to date	850	65	85	700
Estimated further costs to completion	1,100	48	800	20
Work certified to date	600	25	–	650
Cost of work certified	420			
Payments received on account	540	20	–	585
Profit already taken into accounts up to 31 December 19-2	50	–	–	70

Required

Calculate the profit or loss to be taken into Collinson Construction plc's accounts for the year to 31 December 19-3.

Key points to remember

1. Long term contracts span different accounting periods and usually extend for a period exceeding one year.

2. The problems associated with long term contracts are associated with the concepts of matching and prudence.

3. Contract costs must be matched in the contract account to the period in which they are incurred. Costs of materials and the net book value of plant still on site at the end of a period, and work in progress must be carried down as debit balances on the contract account.

4. Profit on a contract should be spread over the term of the contract by an appropriate method.

5. Prudence must be exercised in the recognition of profit. No profit should be assumed on contracts which have not progressed sufficiently for the ultimate profit to be estimated. A loss on a contract should be provided for as soon as it is recognised.

Common errors

1. taking credit for profit on contracts which have not progressed sufficiently to enable ultimate profitability to be predicted.

2. failure to recognise an impending loss on a contract and to take appropriate accounting action

3. arithmetical errors made in calculating attributable profit

19.4 Process costing

Process costing is used when goods or services are produced in a series of continuous or repetitive operations or processes. The units of each product are identical, produced in some volume and of low value. Costs are attributed to the processes, or cost centres . Unit costs are found by dividing the total costs of a cost centre for a period by the number of cost units produced in that period . Hence the need for the products to be identical. If the units are of high value, they would be more suitably costed individually.

Process costing is appropriate for an industry such as the manufacture of household detergents; it would not be practicable to cost each packet of detergent individually. Other applications are the food industry, textile manufacture, chemical manufacture, etc.

19.4.1 Cost units

Typical cost units for process costing are: cans (of peas), metres (of materials), tonnes (of chemicals) etc.

19.4.2 Process costs

The following diagram illustrates the build up of costs when products pass through a series of processes.

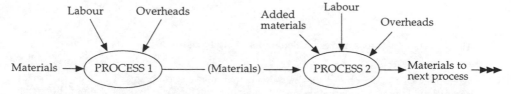

The output of process 1 consisting of the cost of materials, labour and overheads, becomes the material cost of process 2. In process 2, further materials may be added together with further labour costs and overheads. If the product then has to go through a further process, the output of process 2 is the cost of material in process 3, and so on.

19.4.2 Example: simple process accounts

Pascal Ltd manufactures a certain product involving three processes. In one month, 25,000 units of the product were made and the costs for that month were as follows:

	Process 1 £	Process 2 £	Process 3 £
Direct materials	36,000	12,000	24,000
Direct labour	28,000	22,000	34,000
Production overheads	16,000	17,000	11,000

There were no stocks of work in progress either at the beginning or the end of the month.

The cost ledger accounts for the three processes will be as follows:

Process 1

	£		£
Direct materials	36,000	Balance carried to process 2	80,000
Direct labour	28,000		
Production overheads	16,000		
	80,000		80,000

Process 2

	£		£
Materials from process 1	80,000	Balance carried to process 3	131,000
Added materials	12,000		
Direct labour	22,000		
Production overheads	17,000		
	131,000		131,000

Process 3

	£		£
Materials from process 2	131,000	Balance to finished goods	200,000
Added materials	24,000		
Direct labour	34,000		
Production overheads	11,000		
	200,000		200,000

The cost of producing one unit = $\dfrac{£200,000}{25,000}$ = £8

19.4.2 Exercise: on simple process accounts

Bon Bon Ltd manufactures Christmas crackers. In August 19-3, 10,000 boxes of crackers were produced. Three processes are involved in manufacture and the costs of each process in August 19-3 were as follows:

	Process 1 £	Process 2 £	Process 3 £
Direct materials	3,000	1,500	1,000
Direct labour	5,000	1,000	500
Production overheads	14,000	8,000	6,000

Required

Prepare the accounts for the three processes and calculate the unit cost of a box of Christmas crackers.

19.4.3 Work in progress and equivalent units of production

Work in progress

Example 19.4.1 and Exercise 19.4.2 assumed that all work commenced in the month was completed in the same month. It is more usual in real life for some of units of production to be incomplete at the end of an accounting period; this is work in progress. If any of the units in 19.4.1. had not been completed by the end of the month, the total costs would have related to both finished and unfinished units. Therefore, the costs for the month could not be divided by the total of finished units to calculate unit cost. The cost of the work in progress must be taken into account.

Equivalent units of production

The method of valuing work in progress at cost is to express the unfinished units in terms of their equivalent in finished goods. For example, 100 half completed units are equivalent to 50 complete units; 150 units $\frac{2}{3}$ complete are equivalent to 100 complete units.

In reality, the material content may not be in the same proportion as labour content in work in progress. It is likely that all or most of the materials are added to work in progress at the start of a process and that most of the labour involved is expended after the materials have been added. Therefore, work in progress could be 100% complete as to materials, but only, say, 50% complete as to labour.

19.4.4 Example: calculation of value of equivalent units of production

Fretwork Ltd manufactures book shelves. The cost of making one bookshelf is as follows:

	£
Wood	6
Direct labour (3 hours at £8 an hour)	24
Production overhead (£10 per direct labour hour)	30
Cost per bookshelf	£60

At 30 June 19-3, work in progress consisted of 10 bookshelves 100% complete as to direct material and 75% complete as to labour. A further 12 bookshelves were 75% complete as to direct material and 50% complete as to labour.

Work in progress is valued as follows:

	£
10 [£6 + 75% of £(24 + 30)]	465
plus 12 [75% of £6 + 50% of £(24 + 30)]	378
Total value of work in progress	£843

19.4.5 Exercise: calculation of value of work in progress

Plough Ltd manufactures a product which requires two processes. The unit cost of each process is as follows:

	Process 1	Process 2
	£	£
Materials added in process	20	8
Direct labour (8 hours at £10 an hour)	80	
(4 hours at £8 an hour)		32
Production overhead (£15 per direct labour hour)	120	60

At the 31 December 19-3, the work in progress in each Process was as follows:

Process 1	20 units	100% complete as to materials and 80% complete as to direct labour
	40 units	80% complete as to materials and 50% complete as to labour.
Process 2	15 units	100% complete as to materials and 25% complete as to labour.

Required

Calculate the value of work in progress at 31 December 19-3.

Treatment of work in progress

The value of work in progress is carried down as a debit balance on the process account at the end of an accounting period.

19.4.6 Joint products and by-products

Joint products

Two or more different products may result from one process. They are not recognisable as different products until they emerge at the point of separation. If the products each have a significant sales value, either at the point of separation or after further processing, they are known as joint products.

Examples of joint products are:

Coal gas production: (i) coal gas   (ii) coke

Wood tar distillation: (i) creosote   (ii) carbolic acid

Oil refining: (i) petrol   (ii) diesel oil   (iii) lubricants   (iv) paraffin

By-products

A by-product is produced in a similar manner to a joint product, but it has a low sales value compared to the sales value(s) of the other (main) product(s) resulting from the process.

Examples of by-products are:

    Joinery: offcuts of wood and sawdust

    Garment manufacture: remnants of material (can be sold for various uses.)

    Foundries: slag (used in construction industries)

The following illustrates the emergence of joint products and by-products at their separation points:

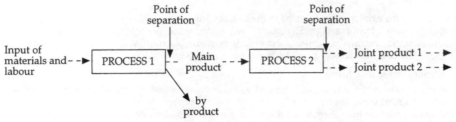

Diagrammatic representation of points of separation of joint products and by-products

19.4.7 Joint product costing

Up to the point of separation, the joint products have shared the processing costs although no one product can be identified with a specific share of the costs. Once the products have become separately identifiable at the point of separation, each will be charged with any further costs to be incurred in putting it into a saleable condition. The joint costs up to the point of separation may be apportioned to the products on one of two arbitrary bases:

(i) If the products are measured in similar terms, (tonnes, or litres or cubic metres), the joint costs may be apportioned between them in the proportions in which they are produced.

Example

Joint products are A and B. As a result of a process, 10,000 litres of A and 2,000 litres of B are produced. Total joint processing costs = £36,000. Costs will be apportioned as follows:

    Product A 10,000/12,000 × £36,000 = £30,000

    Product B 2,000/12,000 × £36,000 = £6,000

(ii) If the products are measurable in different terms, e.g. one product in kilograms, another in litres, joint costs may be apportioned in their respective sales value.

Example

Joint products are P and Q. P sells at £50 per kilo, Q sells at £3.75 per litre. As the result of a process, 500 kilos of P and 4,000 litres of Q are produced. The joint processing costs are £5,000. The costs will be apportioned as follows:

Total sales revenue from production:

		£
Product P	500 × £50	25,000
Product Q	4,000 × £3.75	15,000
		40,000

Apportionment of joint costs: Product A 25,000/40,000 × £5,000 = £3,125

                                         Product B 15,000/40,000 × £5,000 = £1,875

19.4.8 Exercise: to apportion joint costs.

Baldock Ltd processes a material, X. Process 1 results in the production of 500 litres of product A and 1,600 kilos of product B. Both products are then subjected to further processing. The further processing costs of Product A amount to £50.

Product B is subjected to process 2 which results in the production of 300 kilos of Product B_1 and 900 kilos of Product B_2.

Process 1 costs are £27,500 and the additional costs of Process 2 are £2,000.

On completion of Process 1, Product A can be sold at £18 per litre. and Product B for £15 per kilo.

Required

Calculate the cost per litre of Product A and the costs per kilo of Products B_1 and B_2.

19.4.9 Normal losses and abnormal losses and gains

Normal loss

Some loss of material may be expected in the course of processing. This may result from spoilage, evaporation or other wastage. Experience will show what percentage of wastage may be expected under normal conditions and this is regarded as normal wastage inherent in the process. The cost of such waste will be borne by good production.

Abnormal losses and gains

Any wastage in excess of normal is treated as abnormal loss and written off to Profit and Loss account via Abnormal Loss account.

If wastage is less than normal, the difference between actual wastage and normal is treated as an abnormal gain and is credited to an Abnormal Gain account.

Numerical example

1500 kilos of material are issued to production. Normal loss is expected to be 3%.

(a) Actual production was 1,420 kilos.

(b) Actual production was 1,475 kilos.

	(a) Kilos	(b) Kilos
Materials issued to production	1,500	1,500
Normal loss (3%)	(45)	(45)
	1,455	1,455
Actual production	1,420	1,475
Abnormal gain/(loss)	(35)	20

The accounting entries for normal and abnormal losses are:

Normal loss	Dr Scrap a/c *With scrap value of normal loss*	Cr Process a/c
Abnormal loss	Dr Abnormal Loss a/c *With abnormal loss (balance on process a/c)*	Cr Process a/c
	Dr Scrap a/c *With scrap value of abnormal loss*	Cr Abnormal Loss a/c
	Dr Profit and loss a/c *With balance on Abnormal Loss a/c*	Cr Abnormal Loss a/c
Abnormal gain	Dr Process a/c *With abnormal gain (balance on process a/c)*	Cr Abnormal Gain a/c
	Dr Abnormal Gain a/c *With loss of scrap revenue due to abnormal gain* (Note: this entry has the effect of reducing the debit to Scrap account for normal loss – see above)	Cr Scrap a/c
	Dr Abnormal Gain a/c *With balance on Abnormal Gain a/c*	Cr Profit and loss a/c
Sale of scrap	Dr Cash/Bank *With proceeds of sale.*	Cr Scrap a/c

19.4.10 Example: normal losses and abnormal losses and gains

Shotton Ltd manufactures beldonium which involves two processes. The processing costs for March are as follows:

	Process 1 £	Process 2 £
Direct materials (1,000 units)	5,000	
Added direct materials (275 units)		2,500
Direct labour	6,300	8,460
Production overheads	7,750	10,500
Output transferred to process 2	925 units	
Output transferred to finished goods		1,180

Normal loss in each process is 5%. Scrapped units sell for £1 each.

Process 1 (see note 1)

	units	£		units	£
Direct materials	1,000	5,000	Scrap (normal loss)	50	50
Direct labour		6,300	Process 2 (Note 1)	925	18,500
Production overheads		7,750	Abnormal loss	25	500
	1,000	19,050		1,000	19,050

Process 2 (see note 2)

	units	£		units	£
Direct materials from Process 1	925	18,500	Scrap (normal loss)	60	60
Added materials	275	2,500	Finished gds (Note 2)	1,180	41,300
Direct labour		8,460			
Production overhead		10,500			
	1,200	39,960			
Abnormal gain	40	1,400			
	1,240	41,360		1,240	41,360

Abnormal Loss

	£		£
Process 1	500	Scrap (25 units @ £1)	25
		Profit and Loss a/c	475
	500		500

Abnormal Gain

	£		£
Scrap (loss of scrap sales due to abnormal gain, 40 units @ £1)	40	Process 2	1,400
Profit and Loss	1,360		
	1,400		1,400

Scrap

	£		£
Scrap value of normal losses		Bank – sale proceeds	
Process 1(50 × £1)	50	Loss in Process 1 (75 units)	75
Process 2(60 × £1)	60	Process 2 (20 units)	20
Abnormal loss – Process 1	25	Abnormal gain	40
	135		135

Note 1 Cost per unit for output and abnormal loss $\dfrac{£(19,050 - 50)}{95\% \text{ of } 1,000} = \dfrac{£19,000}{950} = £20$

Note 2 Cost per unit for output and abnormal gain $\dfrac{£(39,960 - 60)}{95\% \text{ of } 1,200} = \dfrac{£39,900}{1,140} = £35$

19.4.11 Exercise

Sandybeds Ltd produces Neitshurtz, a product requiring two processes. Normal loss in each process is 10%. The following information relates to Period 2:

	Process 1 £	Process 2 £
Direct materials (4,000 units)	32,400	
Added direct materials (1,200 units)		6,480
Direct labour	18,640	20,000
Production overheads	24,000	33,000
Output transferred to Process 2	3,800 units	
Output transferred to finished goods		4,250 units

Scrapped units are sold for £4 each

Required

Prepare the accounts for Processes 1 and 2, and the accounts to record abnormal losses and gains.

19.4.12 By-product costing

There are various methods of dealing with the cost of by-products. A suitable and convenient method is to deduct sales revenue received from by-products from the total of processing costs before apportioning them to joint products.

Key points to remember

1. Process costing is used when goods are produced in a series of continuous or repetitive operations or processes.
2. The units of each product are identical, produced in some volume, and of relatively low value.
3. The output of one process is transferred as direct material input to the next process.
4. Work in progress is valued in terms of equivalent units of production
5. Joint products have significant sales values. Joint costs are apportioned to joint products either in proportion to volumes of production or in proportion to their relative sales revenues.
6. By-products have low sales values compared to those of the main products. By-product sales revenue is deducted from total process costs before the costs are apportioned to joint products.
7. Normal loss is the loss expected to arise in a process. Abnormal losses result from the normal losses being exceeded. An abnormal gain arises when actual loss is less than normal loss.

Common errors

1. Errors in calculating equivalent units of production
2. Failure to apportion joint costs correctly
3. Incorrect calculations of abnormal losses and gains.

Questions

Multiple choice questions

1 A machine is hired for use on one job only.
   A The rental will be charged to the job as a direct expense.
   B The rental will be charged to the job as an indirect expense
   C The rental and depreciation of the machine will be charged to the job as direct expenses
   D The rental and depreciation of the machine will be charged to the job as indirect expenses.

2   A material passes through two processes in the course of production. At the beginning of a month there was no opening stock of material in either process. During the month the cost of material input to Process 1 was £1,600 and the labour cost was £4,000. Overhead absorbed on procsess 1 during the month totalled £2,400. Work in progress at the end of the month was valued at £400. The material input to process 2 from process 1 during the month was valued at

A   £1,200

B   £1,600

C   £7,600

D   £8,000

Further examination questions

1   (a) What is meant by 'specific order costing'?   (3 marks)

   (b) In what ways does specific order costing differ from process costing?   (6 marks)

   (c) The Acme Shelving Co Ltd manufactures shelving brackets in batches of 300. During May, Batch No. 23 was machined at a rate of 15 per hour. Sixty of the brackets failed to pass inspection, but of these, 40 were thought to be rectifiable. The remaining 20 were scrapped, and the scrap value was credited to the batch cost account. Rectification work took nine hours.

Batch No. 23

	£
Raw materials per bracket	1.60
Scrap value per bracket	0.86
Machinists' hourly rate	4.20
Machine hour overhead rate (running time only)	3.60
Setting up of machine: normal machining	21.00
rectification	18.00

Calculate:

   (i)   the cost of Batch No. 23 in total and per unit, if all units pass inspection;

   (ii) the actual cost of Batch No. 23, in total and per unit, after crediting the recovery value of the scrapped components, and including the rectification costs;

   (iii) the loss incurred because of defective work.   (16 marks)

                                                                        (Total 25 marks)
                                                                            (LONDON)

2   (a) Define the term *equivalent production* and state when the principle is used.   (4 marks)

   (b) During May 1991, M. Wurzel & Co. Limited's output was 4,000 finished items plus 600 partly finished items. There was no work in progress on 1 May 1991.

      The details for the month were:

	Materials	Labour	Overheads	Total
Total cost (£)	8,172	7,120	5,196	20,488
WIP degree of completion %	90	75	55	–

      Calculate for the month of May 1991:

      (i)   the total equivalent production for each cost element;

      (ii) the cost per complete unit;

      (iii) the value of the Work in Progress.   (11 marks)

                                                                        (Total 15 marks)
                                                                          (LONDON 1991)

3   Beeford Manufacturing Limited makes lifts to customers' requirements. The company operates a job costing system which charges the cost of manufacture and installation to each lift. The following activity report gives details of production and installation costs during the past month.

Job Number	Position at beginning of month	Costs at beginning of month	Costs of input requisitioned for use on jobs during month		Position at end of month
			Direct Materials	Direct Labour	
		£	£	£	
Job 76	Finished	260,000	–	–	Sold
Job 77	In progress	172,000	28,000	75,000	Sold
Job 78	In progress	58,000	57,000	135,000	Finished
Job 79			60,000	99,000	Sold
Job 80			32,000	68,000	In Progress
Job 81			28,000	41,000	In Progress

Additional information:

1. The 'position' columns in the above report indicate whether a lift is being made and installed (In progress) or completed but still to be accepted by the customer (Finished) or completed, installed and awaiting payment (Sold).

2. General production overhead expenses are allocated to all jobs on the basis of 30% on the cost of Direct labour.

3. At the beginning of the month raw materials in stock and valued at cost totalled £87,000.

4. During the month the following actual costs were incurred:

	£
Purchase of raw materials	212,000
Direct labour wages	420,000
Actual production overhead expenses	127,000

Required

(a) Prepare the following ledger accounts for the month
  (i) Raw materials (4 marks)
  (ii) Direct labour (4 marks)
  (iii) Production overhead expenses (4 marks)
  (iv) Jobs in progress (4 marks)
  (v) Finished Goods. (5 marks)

(b) A brief indication of the advantages of Job Costing in this type of company. (4 marks)

(Total 25 marks)
(CAMBRIDGE)

4 Barley Construction plc are the contractors for the building of a replacement high technology factory for a multinational company. The total value of the contract is £8,500,000 over a three year period. The contract commenced on 1 March 1990, and the following details are available as at 28 February 1991.

	£
Materials purchased	765,000
Material transfers in from another site	23,000
Material transfers out to another site	8,000
Materials on site, not yet used	38,000
Direct labour	448,000
Direct labour accrued	19,500
Indirect labour	63,000
Indirect labour accrued	2,400
Plant delivered to site	120,000
Hire of equipment	57,000
Hire charges owing	3,200
Head office charges	48,000
Cost of work not yet certified	86,000

Barley Construction plc have received payment of £1,555,500 which represents work certified as completed by the architects as at 28 February 1991, less a 15% retention. The company takes credit for two thirds of the profit on work certified (less retention).

The plant is estimated to last the life of the contract, and no residual value is expected.

Required

(a) The Contract Account for the year ended 28 February 1991, together with a calculation of the value of work in progress as at that date. (15 marks)

(b) Briefly explain the accounting concept involved in the calculation of profit to be credited to the accounts for the year ended 28 February 1991.

In the event of a loss being made, how would this be dealt with? (3 marks)

(c) It is intended that the new factory be fully automated with the consequence of a number of redundancies amongst existing employees. From the social responsibility viewpoint, what factors should the company consider, and what assistance could it give to employees who will eventually be made redundant at the site (the majority of whom it is anticipated will be taking early retirement)? (5 marks)

(Total 23 marks)
(OXFORD)

5 BHI Ltd is a firm of civil engineering contractors. At its last balance sheet date work was proceeding on three uncompleted long-term contracts to which the following details relate.

	Contract No.		
	41	42	43
	£	£	£
Contract price (Sales value of contracts)	150,000	600,000	350,000
Costs incurred to date	20,000	375,000	240,000
Estimate of further costs to completion	100,000	125,000	160,000

Required

(a) explain the main principles of stock valuation as outlined in SSAP 9. (4 marks)

(b) illustrate how BHI Ltd should value its long-term contract work in progress to include an explanation of how it resolves the accruals/prudence conceptual conflict. (8 marks)

(c) draft the accounting policy of BHI Ltd in regard to long-term contract work in progress as it might disclose it in a note to its published accounts. (3 marks)

(Total 15 marks)
(NI)

6 (a) How and why do companies account for profit on uncompleted contracts? (8 marks)

(b) From the following information prepare a contract account for the year ending 31 December 1990. Show clearly the amount of profit that may prudently be taken.

Paddy Quick Construction Co
Contract No. 1234 (Start date 1 January 1990)

	£
Contract price	850,000
Materials issued to site during 1990	120,480
Materials returned to stores	1,460
Materials on site, 31 December, 1990	15,340
Direct wages	134,200
Wages owing at 31 December, 1990	5,220
Plant issued to contract (at cost)	82,600
Plant value at 31 December, 1990	63,200
Sub-contractors' charges	27,560
Head office expenses charged to contract	71,430
Direct expenses (site expenses)	42,570
Direct expenses owing at 31 December, 1990	2,840
Work certified by architect	500,000
Cost of work not yet certified	27,350

The money received from the client (£425,000) was equivalent to the value of work certified less the agreed 15 per cent retention. Paddy Quick uses the fraction $\frac{2}{3}$ in calculating the profits on uncompleted contracts.

(17 marks)

(Total 25 marks)
(LONDON)

7 'Milk is separated into cream and skim. Skim, once treated as a waste product is now commonly classified as a by-product, because of the demand for powdered products. The growing demand for skimmed milk created by the 'slimming industry' may raise skim to the status of a joint product in the near future.'

K Slater and C Wootton 'A Study of Joint and By-Product Costing in the UK' CIMA 1984.

(a) In process costing how do the stages of waste product, by-product, and joint product represent changes in a product's importance to a manufacturer?   (8 marks)

(b) Examine three methods of apportioning joint costs to joint products, bringing out the advantages and disadvantages of each.   (12 marks)

(Total 20 marks)
(LONDON)

8 Belfast Chemicals Ltd manufactures an adhesive which passes through two processes, Y and Z.

Details of the second process, Process Z, for the month of May were as follows:

Opening work in progress	Nil
Materials transferred from Process Y	5,000 kilos at £23,000
Labour costs	500 hours at £4.40 per hour
Overheads	60% of labour cost
Output transferred to finished goods	4,000 kilos
Closing work in progress	400 kilos
Normal loss	10% of input (scrap value £1 per kilo)

Closing work in progress is 100% complete for material content and 75% complete for both labour and other overheads.

Required

(a) prepare

(i) Process Z account for the month of May showing clearly the value of the transfer to finished stock account and also the valuation of work in progress; and   (9 marks)

(ii) abnormal gain/loss account.   (3 marks)

(b) explain in relation to process costing the concept of 'equivalent units'.   (3 marks)

(Total 15 marks)
(NI)

20 Marginal costing

Chapter objectives

Questions on marginal costing require:

- ability to compare and contrast absorption and marginal costing, either descriptively or by using quantified data to produce comparative statements.
- recognition of the uses and limitations of absorption and marginal costing
- an understanding of how marginal costing can be used by management for decision making
- ability to calculate and use contribution/sales ratio
- ability to calculate profits/losses using marginal costing
- calculation of break even points and margins of safety
- construction and interpretation of break-even charts, contribution charts and profit charts

20.1 The difference between fixed and variable costs

Variable costs are those costs which vary with the level of activity of a business. Examples are direct materials, direct labour (if remunerated on a piece work basis and not a time basis), royalties payable on units produced and commissions based on turnover. The essential characteristic of a variable cost is that it increases proportionately with the level of production or turnover.

Fixed costs are those which do not vary with the level of activity; they are time based. Examples of fixed costs are indirect labour, rent payable, heating and lighting, and fixed asset depreciation based on straight line or reducing balance methods. These costs are described as 'fixed' because they remain constant, at least within given limits. Beyond those limits, they may vary. For example, a manufacturing business may have to acquire additional premises and plant and machinery if it is to increase output beyond a given level. The result will be an increase in rent payable or depreciation of premises, and increased plant depreciation.

20.2 The need for marginal costing in management decision making

Total cost is an inadequate basis on which to make many day-to-day management decisions. Consider the following summarised statement of costs of a manufacturing company:

Production costs for the month of April (output 10,000 units)

	£
Variable costs	150,000
Fixed costs	200,000
Total cost of production	350,000

Cost per unit: £35.

The cost per unit has been found by dividing the total cost of production by the number of units produced. However, if 10,100 units are produced, the total production cost will not be £35 × 10,100, or £353,500, as the following statement for the production of 10,100 units shows:

	£
Variable costs (increased by $\frac{10,100}{10,000}$)	151,500
Fixed costs (unchanged)	200,000
Total cost of production	351,500

If the cost of production is now divided by output, the unit cost of production is $\frac{£351,500}{10,100}$ = £34.80. The difference between the unit costs calculated from these two statements arises from the same amount of fixed costs being divided by different volumes of output.

It is clear that total cost calculations are inadequate bases for making many management decisions where it is essential to know the cost of a unit of production with some certainty. Marginal costing isolates fixed costs from variable costs, and is a useful tool for much decision making.

MARGINAL COST is the total of the variable costs incurred in producing one unit of a good or in the provision of a service. All fixed costs i.e. those related to time and not to volume, are ignored for the purpose of ascertaining marginal cost. Marginal cost is often defined as the cost of producing one additional item.

Illustration:

Marginal Products Ltd. produces variable grommets under licence and its budget for the month of September 19-3 is as follows:

Production: 1,000 variable grommets.

	£	£
Direct materials		56,000
Direct labour		84,000
Royalties		10,000
Prime cost		150,000
Other production costs:		
Variable	12,000	
Fixed	30,000	42,000
Selling and distribution costs:		
Variable	10,000	
Fixed	25,000	35,000
Administration expenses (all fixed)		55,000
Total cost		282,000
Budgeted net profit		148,000
Budgeted sales		430,000

The above could be redrafted as a marginal cost statement as follows:

	Total cost/1000 units	Marginal cost/unit
Variable costs:	£	£
Direct materials	56,000	56
Direct labour	84,000	84
Direct expenses – royalties	10,000	10
Production costs – variable	12,000	12
Selling and distribution		
costs – variable	10,000	10
MARGINAL COST	172,000	172
CONTRIBUTION	258,000	258
Sales (selling price)	430,000	430

Fixed costs have been omitted.

CONTRIBUTION is the difference between the marginal cost and the selling price; it represents the contribution each unit of production makes towards:

(i) covering the fixed expenses

(ii) the profit

in that order.

20.3 Contribution and the C/S Ratio

CONTRIBUTION/SALES RATIO – C/S Ratio (often misnamed the profit/volume ratio or p/v ratio): contribution is expressed as a percentage of sales. In the above illustration the C/S ratio is:

$$\frac{258}{430} \times 100 = 60\%$$

The C/S ratio is very useful for calculating profit at various levels of activity:

To find profit if sales of variable grommets reached (a) £300,000 (b) £600,000

		£'000
(a)		
	Contribution = 60% of £300,000	180
	less fixed overheads: (30,000 + 25,000 + 55,000)	110
	Net profit	70

		£'000
(b)		
	Contribution = 60% of £600,000	360
	less fixed overheads	110
	Net profit	250

20.4 Break-even

BREAK-EVEN POINT: The level of activity at which the business makes neither profit nor loss i.e. total contribution = total fixed costs.

Calculation of break-even point: divide total fixed costs by the contribution per unit.

Break-even point for variable grommets (above) is:

$$\frac{£110,000}{£258} = 426.36 \text{ grommets}$$

As Marginal Products Ltd. can hardly sell 0.36 of a grommet, it will not have completely covered its fixed costs until it has sold the 427th. grommet.

When the break-even point is to be calculated in terms of sales revenue multiply the number of units by the unit price:

$$426.36 \times £430 = £183,334.80$$

alternatively:

Divide the total fixed costs by the contribution per £ of revenue:

C/S ratio of variable grommets = 60%, or 60p per £1 of revenue.

$$\frac{£110,000}{0,60} = £183,333 \text{ (the difference is in roundings)}$$

BREAK-EVEN CHARTS show sales revenue plotted against total cost and provide, within limits, useful information about various aspects of a product or service (exhibit 1).

1. Break-even occurs where the sales line intersects the total cost line; the sales at that point is denoted by the vertical scale and the number of units by the horizontal scale.

2. **Profit** at any particular level of activity to the **right of break-even point** is represented by the **vertical distance** between the sales revenue line and the total cost line at that point.

3. **Loss** at any particular level of activity to the **left of the break-even point** is represented by the vertical distance between the total cost line and the sales revenue line.

4. **Margin of safety** is the distance between break-even point and expected level of activity. It depicts the amount by which actual activity can fall short of expected activity before a loss is incurred. It is a measure of risk.

Calculate margin of safety as follows:

$$\frac{\text{Profit}}{\text{C/S ratio}} \times 100$$

e.g. if budgeted sales of variable grommets is £430,000

$$\text{margin of safety} = \frac{£148,000}{60} \times 100$$

$$= £246,666 \text{ (or sales – b/e}$$

$$= £430,000 – £183,334) \text{ i.e. 57\% of budgeted sales.}$$

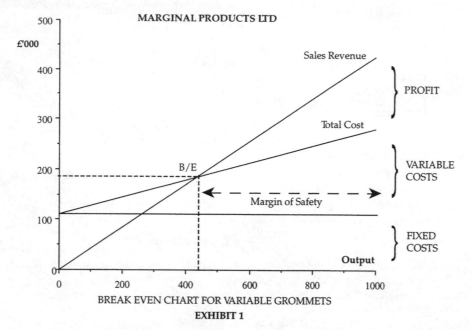

MARGINAL PRODUCTS LTD

BREAK EVEN CHART FOR VARIABLE GROMMETS

EXHIBIT 1

5. The closer the break-even point is to the left of the chart, the earlier break-even is reached and the greater the margin of safety is likely to be. (The lower the risk for the product) Conversely, a break even-point nearer to the right of the chart indicates greater risk.

6. The position of the break-even point is decided by the slope of the sales line compared with that of the total cost line; the greater the angle between the two lines, the sooner break even point is reached. (Exhibit 2)

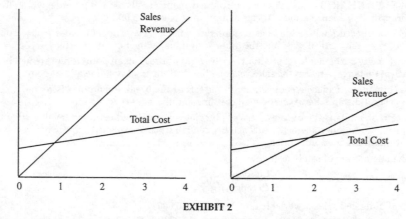

EXHIBIT 2

7. The wider the angle between the sales line and the total cost line, the greater will be the rate of increase in profits after break even point has been reached; but by the same token, the rate at which losses are incurred will also accelerate the more activity falls short of the break even point.

8. High fixed costs relatively to total cost will result in a high break even point (exhibit 3); low fixed costs relatively to total cost will result in a low break even point (exhibit 4):

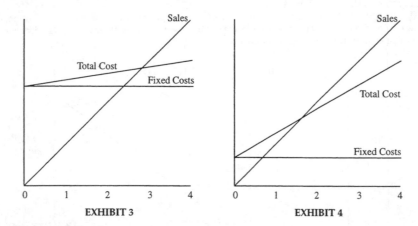

EXHIBIT 3   EXHIBIT 4

CONTRIBUTION CHART. The fixed cost line is plotted above the variable cost line to give total cost line (Exhibit 5).

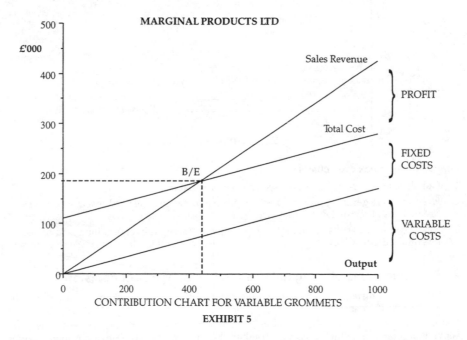

CONTRIBUTION CHART FOR VARIABLE GROMMETS

EXHIBIT 5

The vertical distance between the variable cost line and the sales line up to the break even point shows the amount of 'contribution' towards the fixed costs at a particular level of activity. Beyond the break even point, the vertical distance between the sales line and the total cost line shows how the unit contributions have now become clear profit.

PROFIT CHART (Contribution/sales chart): Sales revenue is plotted along the horizontal axis and profit/ loss are plotted on the vertical axis (exhibit 6). The maximum loss occurs at zero sales and is equal to the total of fixed costs.

The budgeted profit at a particular level of sales is plotted and the two plots joined by a straight line which represents the cumulative contributions. The profit or loss for any intervening level of sales may then be read from the chart.

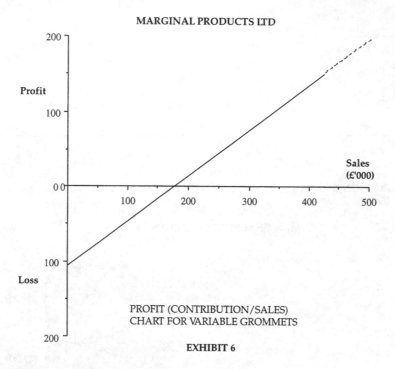

MARGINAL PRODUCTS LTD

PROFIT (CONTRIBUTION/SALES)
CHART FOR VARIABLE GROMMETS

EXHIBIT 6

Limitations of break even charts

1. Not all costs can be easily categorised as fixed or variable.
2. Fixed costs are generally only fixed within given parameters. The fixed cost line may need to rise in steps at certain levels of activity.
3. Sales revenue and costs can rarely be represented by straight lines; e.g. increased discounts given in order to achieve higher levels of turnover will tend to 'flatten out' the sales curve.

20.5 Applications of marginal costing in management decisions

(a) Pricing: circumstances may require a reduction in the selling price of a product e.g. the emergence of competition.

The product price may be reduced provided it is not set below the marginal cost. Any price above marginal cost will produce a contribution towards fixed costs. (However, there may be other factors to be taken into account to arrive at a decision.)

(b) Acceptance of order below normal selling price.
(c) 'Make or buy' decision as to whether to make own product or buy it in from an outside source.
(d) Optimum use of scarce resources;.

20.5.1 (a) Pricing decision

Example: Proposed reduction in selling price

Peters Ltd. manufactures a special kind of shoe for buskers which sells at £40. The monthly turnover is 200 pairs of shoes and the company is anxious to increase its share of the market.

The Sales Director considers that if the price of the shoes was reduced to £39 a pair the sales would rise to 400 pairs a month; the production manager is quite sure that if the price were further reduced to £38 a pair, the turnover would rise to 600 pairs a month.

The monthly budget for the production of 200 pairs of the shoes is:

Direct materials £3,000; direct labour £4,000; selling and distribution expenses (variable) £400. Fixed overheads are £500 per month.

Answer

	£
Total of variable expenses:	
Direct materials	3,000
Direct labour	4,000
Selling and distribution	400
Marginal cost	7,400

	£
Marginal cost per pair of shoes	37
Contribution per pair of shoes	3
Selling price	40

Total contribution from 200 pairs of shoes sold at £40	=	£600
If price reduced to £39 per pair, total contribution on 400 pairs of shoes will be 400 × £(3-1)	=	£800
If price reduced to £38 per pair, total contribution on 600 pairs of shoes will be 600 × £(3-2)	=	£600

The best option will be to sell 400 pairs of shoes at £39 per pair.

20.5.1 (b) Acceptance of order below normal selling price

Circumstances may sometimes justify selling goods below the normal selling price:

(a) To combat competitors who are selling similar goods at a lower price.

(b) Acceptance of an order to produce and sell goods at a special price if this will increase profit or help to cover overheads.

(c) To maintain production in temporarily difficult trading conditions so that a skilled workforce may be retained.

(d) To dispose of obsolescent or perishable goods.

(e) To promote a new product.

It is important to remember the risks of price cutting; other businesses may follow suit and cut prices even more. If this becomes a permanent situation the industry itself may be harmed.

Example 2: for basic data see page 374 Marginal Products Ltd., 20.2

Floggitt and Company approach Marginal Products Ltd. with a proposal for a contract that will require an additional production of 300 variable grommets per month. Floggitt and Company would be prepared to pay £390 for each of the additional variable grommets produced.

At the same time, Baggett & Sons Ltd. require Marginal Products to produce an additional 200 variable grommets per month for which they will be prepared to pay £160 per grommet.

Required

A statement showing the effect on profit of each of the potential orders from Floggitt and Company and Baggett & Sons Ltd., and your opinion as to whether or not Marginal Products should accept either or both of the orders.

Answer	Floggitt	Baggett
	£	£
Marginal cost of grommets	172	172
Price offered	390	160
Contribution	218	(12)
Additional profit on 300 grommets	£65,400	
Reduction of profit on 200 grommets		£2,400

Marginal Products Ltd. should accept the order from Floggitt and Company provided the supply to that company on terms far more favourable than those offered to their other customers will not have an adverse effect upon trading relationships with those other customers.

The order from Baggett & Sons Ltd. should be refused.

20.5.1 (c) 'Make or buy' decision

Firms may manufacture their own products for various reasons such as:

(a) The product is unique, is not produced by anybody else, and there is a demand for it.

(b) The firm wants to supply its own brand of a particular product.

(c) The firm does not want to be dependent upon outside suppliers who may be unreliable regarding delivery and price.

(d) The firm believes it can manufacture its products more cheaply than it can buy them from outside. (Hence profit on manufacture in a manufacturing account – see Chapter 16 §2)

With regard to (d), the marginal cost of production must be compared with the cost of ready made goods bought from outside (which is the 'alternative' marginal cost.)

Example 3 Jayesh Ltd. manufactures uggle boxes

The budget for March 19-4 is as follows:

	£
Direct materials	10,000
Direct labour	15,000
Factory overheads: variable	5,000
fixed	7,000
Selling and distribution expenses:	
variable	4,000
fixed	9,000
Administration expenses – fixed	32,000

Planned output for March: 2,000 Uggle Boxes

Each uggle box is sold for £45.

Jayesh Ltd. can buy uggle boxes from Devram's Super Box Manufacturing Co. Ltd. at a cost of £14 per box.

Required

(a) A financial statement for March 19-4 to show whether Jayesh Ltd. should continue to manufacture uggle boxes or should cease production of the boxes and retail those made by Devram's Super Box Manufacturing Co. Ltd.

(b) A calculation of the profit for March 19-4

   (i) if Jayesh Ltd. continues to make and sell uggle boxes

   (ii) if Jayesh Ltd. discontinues production and retails those made by Devram's Super Box Manufacturing Company Ltd.

Answer

(a)

Marginal cost of own boxes:	£
Per box: Direct materials	5
Direct labour	7.50
Factory overheads – variable	2.50
Marginal cost of production	15

As this is more than the boxes can be bought from outside, Jayesh Ltd. should discontinue production and 'buy-in' boxes from Devram's Super Box Manufacturing Co. Ltd. at £14 per box.

(Variable selling and distribution expenses are ignored as these will presumably still be incurred anyway.)

(b) (i)   Contribution if own boxes are made and sold:

£(selling price per unit – marginal cost per unit) × no. sold

Variable selling and distribution expenses must be included in the calculation of marginal cost of sales

= £(45 – 17) × 2,000 = £56,000.

Net profit = total contribution less fixed overheads

	£
Total contribution	56,000
less Fixed overheads £(7,000 + 9,000 + 32,000)	48,000
Net profit	8,000

(ii)   Increase in total contribution if boxes bought from Devram's Super Box Manufacturing Co. Ltd

£(15 – 14) × 2,000 = £2,000; therefore net profit would be £10,000

20.5.1 (d) Optimum use of scarce resources

LIMITING FACTOR or KEY FACTOR: Any factor which places a limit on the level of activity; e.g. a shortage of raw materials, or of suitable labour.

Application: Where two or more products use the same raw material which is in short supply; or the number of man hours or machine hours available for the manufacture of two or more products is insufficient to meet the total demand.

Rank each product in the order of the contribution yielded per unit of the scarce resource.

Example 4

Kelly Ltd. manufactures three products: Aonyx, Bionyx and Cronyx. Planned production for the three months to 31 March 19-1 is: Aonyx 10,000 units, Bionyx 7,000 units, Cronyx 4,000 units.

The following information about production costs for each of the products is available:

Per unit	Aonyx	Bionyx	Cronyx
Raw materials: Onyxium	5 kilos	6 kilos	4 kilos
Man hours (at £8 per hour)	10	8	12
Other variable expenses	£115	£144	£78
Selling price	£800	£880	£670

Onyxium costs £100 per kilo. and it has now been ascertained that while 108,000 kilos are needed to produce budgeted output, only 96,000 kilos will be available in the three months to 31 March 19-1.

Fixed overheads amount to £300,000 per month.

Required

A revised production budget which will produce the maximum net profit for the three months to 31 March 19-1.

Answer

Cost of producing each unit:	Aonyx	Bionyx	Cronyx
	£	£	£
Direct materials	500	600	400
Direct labour	80	64	96
Other variable expenses	115	144	78
Marginal cost	695	808	574
Selling price	800	880	670
Contribution	105	72	96
Contribution per kilo of onyxium:	$\frac{105}{6}$	$\frac{72}{6}$	$\frac{96}{4}$
	= £21	= £12	= £24
Ranking order	(2)	(3)	(1)

Revised production budget:

	kilos of Onyxium			Total contribution £
	Available	96,000		
4,000	units Cronyx	(16,000)	4,000 × £96	384,000
		80,000		
10,000	units Aonyx	(50,000)	10,000 × £105	1,050,000
		30,000		1,434,000
5,000	units Bionyx	(30,000)	5,000 × £72	360,000
				1,794,000
Less fixed overheads (3 × £300,000)				900,000
Net profit				894,000

Example 5

Data as in exercise 4, but although adequate supplies of onyxium will be available to meet budgeted production, there is a shortage of skilled labour and it is estimated that the maximum number of man hours worked will be 180,000.

	Aonyx	Bionyx	Cronyx
Contribution per unit (as above)	£105	£72	£96
Contribution per man hour	$\frac{£105}{10}$	$\frac{£72}{8}$	$\frac{£96}{12}$
	= £10.50	= £9	= £8
Ranking order	(1)	(2)	(3)

Revised production budget:

	Man Hours			Total contribution £
	Available	180,000		
10,000	units of Aonyx	(100,000)	10,000 × £105	1,050,000
		80,000		
7,000	units of Bionyx	(56,000)	7,000 × £72	504,000
		24,000		
2,000	units of Cronyx	24,000	2,000 × £96	192,000
				1,746,000
Less fixed overheads				900,000
Net profit				846,000

20.5.2 Exercise 1: calculation of break even point and margin of safety

D Brown Ltd. manufactures bicycles under licence; it sells the bicycles for £260. Planned production for the six months to 30 June 19-6 is for 5,000 bicycles and the budget for that period is as follows:

		£
Direct materials		300,000
Direct labour		400,000
Royalties under licence		50,000
Selling and distribution expenses:	variable	20,000
	fixed	200,000
Administration costs:	variable	10,000
	fixed	220,960

Required

Calculate (i) the break even point and (ii) the margin of safety from the data given above.

Exercise 2: calculation of 'best price'

Mei Ling Ltd. manufactures decorative lanterns. Each lantern requires materials costing £8 and requires 2 hours of labour at £6 an hour.

The lanterns are sold at £25 each and current output is 400 lanterns a week.

Fixed expenses amount to £700 a week.

If the price of the lanterns were reduced to £23 each, sales would rise to 600 lanterns a week.

A further reduction in price to £22 would increase sales to 1,100 a week. An increase in production above 1,000 lanterns, however, would require extra resources which would add 15% to fixed expenses.

Required

Calculations to show price Mei Ling Ltd. should charge for the lanterns in order to make most profit.

Exercise 3: acceptance of order below normal selling price

T.Lambrou Ltd. manufactures an electronic accessory for the motor trade. Each accessory requires components costing £25 and requires 4 hours of labour at £9 an hour.

Other variable costs, per accessory, include selling and distribution £4 and administration £2.

Monthly fixed overheads are: selling and distribution £15,000, administration £18,000.

The list price charged by T. Lambrou Ltd. for the accessory is £80.

Manjeet Motors, specialists in custom built cars, has approached T. Lambrou Ltd. with the following proposals:

1. That T. Lambrou Ltd. produce an additional 1,000 units per month as a special order for Manjeet Motors, the latter to be allowed a special trade discount of 10% on the catalogue price.
2. That the special order be increased to 2,000 units per month provided the trade discount is increased to 20%.

Required

Prepare a report to the directors of T. Lambrou Ltd. explaining why they should accept or reject the offers made by Manjeet Motors. Your report should quantify the effect on T. Lambrou Ltd.'s profit of each proposal.

Exercise 4: 'Make or buy'

Ninasim & Son Ltd. makes three products: Ninabits, Simlabits and Sonybits.

The monthly budgets for the three products are as follows:

		Ninabits	Simlabits	Sonybits
No. of units of production		1,000	1,000	500
		£	£	£
Direct materials		18,000	7,000	4,500
Direct labour		25,000	21,000	13,000
Selling and distribution:	variable	5,000	4,000	–
	fixed	21,000	10,000	10,000
Administration:	fixed	9,000	9,000	9,000

Ninasim & Son Ltd. have the opportunity to purchase each of the three products from Husseyin & Husseyin and Co. Ltd. at the following prices:

Ninabits	£50 each
Simlabits	£30 each
Sonybits	£33 each

Required

A recommendation as to which product or products, if any, Ninasim & Son Ltd. should continue to manufacture, and which should be 'bought in' from Husseyin & Husseyin and Co. Ltd.

Exercise 5: maximising profit when there are limiting factors

C. Yiannakou manufactures three products: Boxydons, Doxydons and Moxydons. Planned production for 19-4 is as follows:

Boxydons	10,000 units
Doxydons	9,000 units
Moxydons	11,000 units

Production details per unit are as follows:

	Boxydons	Doxydons	Moxydons
3/8" Boxium alloy sheeting	3 sq.metres	6 sq.metres	4 sq.metres
Labour (man hours)	4	5	5
Selling price per unit	£50	£64	£60

$\frac{3}{8}$" Boxium alloy sheeting costs £2 per sq. metre. All labour is remunerated at the standard rate of £8 an hour. All other costs of C Yiannakou are fixed.

Only one Boxium mine is known to exist in the world, and that has recently been put out of action by a geological fault and production of the mineral is not expected to resume until 19-5. C Yiannakou has, however, stockpiled $\frac{3}{8}$" Boxium sheeting and has presently got 92,000 sq. metres available for use.

Required

A revised production schedule for C. Yiannakou in order to produce the maximum profit for the year 19-4.

20.6 Sensitivity analysis

Forecasts of the profitability of a product are based upon estimates of future revenues and costs. The profit will be dependent on the accuracy of the forecast information; this is another way of saying that it will be sensitive to inaccuracies in the estimates of revenue and costs.

Example 20.6.1

The planned sales of a product are 16,000 units at £25 per unit. The marginal cost per unit is £8. Fixed costs are estimated to be £200,000.

A profit statement based on this information is as follows:

	£	£
Sales (16,000 units at £25)		400,000
Variable cost (16,000 × £8)	128,000	
Fixed cost	200,000	328,000
Planned profit		72,000

The break even point indicates the level of activity below which sales of the product will result in a loss:

$$\frac{\text{Total fixed cost}}{\text{contribution per unit}} = \frac{200,000}{25-8} = 11,765 \text{ units}$$

To produce a loss, sales volume will therefore have to fall short of planned volume by (16,000 – 11,765) = 4,235 units,

$$\text{or} \quad \frac{4,235}{16,000} \times 100 = 26.5\%$$

The planned profit will be at risk if actual sales are 26.5% less than planned sales.

A loss may result if the price per unit is reduced. If revenue from the sale of 16,000 units does not equal the total cost of £328,000, there will be a loss. The reduction in revenue would therefore have to be £(400,000 – 328,000), or £72,000. This would represent a reduction of £72,000/£400,000 × 100 or 18% in the price.

The planned profit would therefore be at risk if the unit selling price were reduced by 18% to (£25 × 82%) = £20.50p

The planned profit will be eliminated if the variable costs increase by £72,000, or $\frac{72,000}{128,000} \times 100$ = 56.25%

Similarly, there will be no profit if fixed costs increase by £72,000 or $\frac{72,000}{200,000} \times 100 = 36\%$

This analysis is, of course, oversimplified. It assumes that only one aspect of the sales or costs will differ from plan. In practice, most if not all aspects will vary from plan and sensitivity analysis then becomes more complex.

Exercise 20.6.2

Planned output is for 25,000 units at a selling price of £14 per unit. Marginal cost is £10 per unit and fixed costs are estimated to be £80,000.

Required

Calculate the sensitivity of the planned profit to variations in sales volume, price, marginal cost and fixed costs.

Key points to remember

1. Absorption cost has limited uses; it is not suitable for most decision making as absorption of fixed overheads per unit depends upon the number of units produced.
2. Marginal cost includes only those costs which vary with the level of activity.
3. Contribution is the difference between selling price and marginal cost.
4. Break-even point is found by dividing total fixed costs by unit contribution.
5. Margin of safety is the amount by which expected or budgeted output exceeds break-even point.
6. Marginal costing may be used to aid management decision making, particularly:
    'make or buy',
    acceptance of orders below normal selling price
    maximising profit when resources are scarce.
7. SSAP 9 recommends absorption cost to be used for valuation of closing stock in published financial accounts as it recognises costs in the same period as related revenue arises, thus complying with the 'matching' concept. Either marginal or absorption costs may be used by management for their own use.
8. Marginal costing questions may be recognised by references in them to fixed and variable costs, 'break-even', limiting factors etc.
9. Draw break-even charts carefully and neatly to enable readings to be taken from them with an acceptable degree of accuracy.
10. Give clear, concise headings to break-even charts and indicate the total cost and sales revenue lines and break even point clearly.

Common errors

1. failure to recognise marginal costing questions.
2. failure to use the contribution/sales ratio as a quick method of calculation.
3. poor presentation of marginal cost statements (omission of heading etc.)
4. badly drawn, untidy and inaccurate break even charts often without appropriate headings or keys.

Questions

Fully worked examination question

(i) Explain the meaning of
 (a) absorption costing,
 (b) marginal costing,
 (c) contribution. (6 marks)

(ii) A firm which uses cost plus (full cost) pricing makes 100 each of a range of products each month. The unit costs of the whole range are:

	J	K	L	M	N
	£	£	£	£	£
Direct materials	10	12	13	16	19
Direct labour	8	9	10	13	13
Variable overhead	4	5	7	9	10
	22	26	30	38	42
Fixed overhead	3	4	5	7	8
	25	30	35	45	50
Profit (20%)	5	6	7	9	10
	30	36	42	54	60

Market conditions have moved against the firm and competitors are charging the following prices for the whole range, beginning with J: £21; £34; £38; £51; £40.

Show how the firm can still compete at the new prices, and earn itself an overall profit of £200 per month by producing K,L and M. Explain fully how this can be so. (6 marks)

(iii) Why is the marginal costing approach not suitable for analysing long-term decisions?

(3 marks)

(Total 15 marks)
(LONDON)

Answer

(i) Absorption costing: this is also known as total costing because the cost of a unit of production or of a service, includes all costs, direct and indirect, variable and fixed. The overheads are said to be 'absorbed', or added into, the total cost of cost units. Overhead absorption rates are used to calculate the amount of overhead to be absorbed by each cost unit.

Marginal costing is concerned with the variable costs of a product or service as a means of aiding management decisions. It calculates 'marginal cost of production', or the total of the variable costs associated with the production only of a product, and marginal cost of sales, which includes all variable costs.

Contribution is the difference between marginal cost of sales and selling price. It is the contribution made by units of production towards covering fixed costs. When the contributions are sufficient to cover the fixed costs, any additional contributions make up the profit.

(ii) Contribution statement:

	K	L	M
	£	£	£
Marginal cost per question	26	30	38
Selling price	34	38	51
Contribution	8	8	13

Total contributions from 100 units of K L and M:	£
(100 × (8+8+13))	2,900
Total fixed overheads (100 × (3+4+5+7+8))	2,700
Contribution	200

(iii) The marginal costing approach is concerned with the amount by which selling price exceeds marginal cost i.e contribution. Provided selling price exceeds marginal cost, the product makes a contribution to the fixed costs of the business. Decisions concerning the viability of a product, the fixing of a selling price, the acceptance of an order below the normal selling price, make or buy decisions and the optimum use of scarce resources are short term decisions and may be made on marginal cost.

On the other hand, long term decisions must be based on the need to cover total fixed costs over the longer term. In addition, corporate plans usually require a specified rate of return on capital. Therefore long term decisions must be based on total cost and profit.

Multiple choice questions

1   The marginal cost of a product is the
    A   cost of production
    B   cost of production plus selling costs
    C   prime cost
    D   total of the variable costs

2   Break even point is found by dividing
    A   total fixed costs by total contributions
    B   total fixed costs by contribution per unit
    C   total contributions by fixed cost per unit
    D   fixed cost per unit by contribution per unit

3   Contribution per unit of production is the difference between its
    A   selling price and cost of production
    B   selling price and marginal cost
    C   selling price and prime cost
    D   selling price and total cost

4   The C/S ratio shows the
    A   contribution as a percentage of selling price
    B   difference between break even point and planned sales
    C   profit from each £ of sales
    D   revenue at which a business breaks even.

5   Study the following break even chart

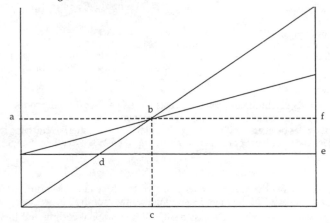

    The margin of safety is represented by the line
    A   a – b
    B   b – c
    C   b – f
    D   d – e

6   A company makes four products, P,Q,R and S. The relevant unit costs are as follows:

	P	Q	R	S
	£	£	£	£
Variable production cost	17	13	15	12
Fixed production cost	8	9	6	10
Cost of production c/f	25	22	21	22

	£	£	£	£
Cost of production b/f	25	22	21	22
Other variable costs	2	3	1	1
Other fixed costs	4	2	3	2
Total cost	31	27	25	25

The prices at which the products can be obtained from other suppliers are

P	Q	R	S
£20	£15	£14	£24

The company can increase its profit if it ceases production of the following product and buys it from another supplier:

A   product P

B   product Q

C   product R

D   product S

7   A company makes four products which all require the same raw material. The material is in short supply and the company cannot obtain sufficient of it to meet its budgeted production of each product. In order to maximise profit, the products should be ranked in order of

A   contribution per unit of the product

B   contribution per unit of the scarce material

C   profit per unit

D   quantity of material required per unit of the product

Further examination questions

1   Reed Ltd manufactures three products A, B and C. Budgeted costs and selling prices for the three months ending 30 September 1992 are as follows:

	A	B	C
Sales (units per month)	6,000	8,000	5,000
	£	£	£
Selling price per unit	45	44	37
Unit costs			
Direct labour	6	9	6
Direct materials	20	24	16
Variable overhead	4	3	2
Fixed overhead	5	5	6

Labour costs are £3 per hour, and material costs are £4 per kilo for all products. The total fixed costs are of a general factory nature, and are unavoidable.

The company has been advised by its supplier that due to a material shortage, its material requirement for the month of September will be reduced by 15%. No other changes are anticipated.

Required

(a) A statement to show the maximum net profit for the three months ending 30 September 1992, taking into account the material shortage for the month of September.   (15 marks)

(b) Explain how the fixed cost element is dealt with in marginal costing and in absorption costing. Briefly explain how this affects any closing stock valuation.   (8 marks)

(Total 23 marks)
(OXFORD)

2   (a) What are the main differences between final accounts prepared under the principles of (i) absorption costing and (ii) marginal costing?   (4 marks)

(b) Thorpe Products has previously used absorption costing in calculating profits. The firm's managers wish to know what profits would have been in 1991 and 1992 had marginal costing been used.

From the following information calculate the profits for each year under (i) absorption costing and (ii) marginal costing.

Thorpe Products

	1991	1992
Sales (units)	3,200	3,500
Price/unit (£)	60	65
Production (units)	3,400	3,600
Direct labour (£/unit)	9	10
Direct materials (£/unit)	23	25
Direct expenses (£/unit)	4	6
Fixed overheads (£)	23,800	25,200

For the purposes of calculation assume no opening stocks at January, 1991. The firm values closing stock on the First in, First out (FIFO) method. (16 marks)

(c) For 1992, prepare a statement reconciling the profit shown under the absorption costing method with that which might have arisen under the marginal costing method. (5 marks)

(Total 25 marks)
(LONDON)

3 Derek Lowe decided to commence business as a manufacturer making a single product. As a matter of business policy he set the following conditions for his first two years of operation:

Year I To at least break-even, but also if possible to achieve a return on his capital employed of 5% per annum.

Year II Through increased efficiency to lower the break-even point and to achieve a return on his capital employed of 15% per annum.

His forecast average net capital employed is:

	£
Year I	100,000
Year II	500,000

Additional information:

(1) His projected costs per unit produced are:

	Year I	Year II
	£	£
Direct materials	10	11
Direct labour	8	7
Variable production overheads	5	4.5
Variable sales overheads	4	3.5

(2) He expected that his fixed costs would remain constant throughout the two years at £60,000 per annum.

(3) His forecast sales are:

	Price per unit	Unit volume
	£	000s
Year I	34	10
Year II	36	13

(4) It can be assumed that all expense and revenue relationships will be unchanged except where identified.

(5) All output produced will be sold.

Required

(a) A detailed profit and loss statement showing his projected profit for year I. (4 marks)

(b) A calculation of the number of sales units necessary to break-even for each year. (4 marks)

(c) A graph showing break-even charts for each year. Indicate the break-even points on the graph. (7 marks)

(d) A calculation of the number of sales units necessary to achieve the target return on capital employed for each of the first two years of operation.
Comment on your results. (7 marks)

(e) If Lowe decided to aim to maintain his Year II target return on capital employed at an output of 14,000 units, what is the minimum selling price he should charge? (3 marks)

(Total 25 marks)
(AEB)

4   Arbalat Ltd manufacture and sell a single product. An accounting clerk prepared the
    following summarised information for the year ended 31 May 1991.

	Budget £	Actual Results £
Sales (Budgeted selling price £50 per unit)	300,000	319,000
Fixed manufacturing overhead	24,000	28,000
Direct materials	120,000	116,000
Variable sales overhead	21,000	23,500
Direct labour	40,000	46,000
Variable manufacturing overhead	19,000	21,000
Other fixed costs	35,000	33,000

Additional information:

(1) The actual results did not include direct wages in arrears of £11,000 at 31 May 1991.

(2) On 31 May 1991 a batch of goods (50 units) had been returned damaged. The goods had
    been sold for £55 per unit, but no adjustment had been made to the sales figure above.
    The goods had a nil scrap value.

(3) Arbalat Ltd had prepared the budget on the basis that 6,000 units would be produced
    and sold. The final total of the number of units actually sold during the year was 5,750
    units i.e. when the damaged units in 2) above are ignored.

(4) There was no work in progress and no stocks of finished goods were held at the
    beginning or end of the period.

(5) You may assume that all other expenses and revenue relationships remain unchanged.

Required

(a) A detailed revenue statement showing the budgeted and actual net profits for the year
    ended 31 May 1991.   (6 marks)

(b) Calculate the sales variance for 1990/91 distinguishing between the sales volume
    variance and the sales price variance.

    Comment on the sales variances.   (8 marks)

(c) Prepare a break-even graph using the budgeted figures and the actual figures for
    1990/91. Show on the graph
    (i)   the budgeted break-even point;
    (ii) the actual break-even point;
    (iii) the actual margin of safety.   (6 marks)

(d) Use figures derived from a) above to calculate the volume of sales units necessary to
    break-even for both budgeted and actual costs.   (5 marks)

                                                                        (Total 25 marks)
                                                                             (AEB)

5   Jason Ltd manufactures a product called Dufton. The normal annual output of this product
    is 200,000 units.

    The following is a cost statement relating to the production of a Dufton:

		£	£
Materials			5.00
Wages			7.00
Factory overheads:	fixed	4.50	
	variable	1.00	5.50
Administration overheads:	fixed		2.00
Selling overheads:	fixed	3.50	
	variable	3.00	6.50
			26.00

The selling price of a Dufton is £36.

During the year the company received enquiries about two possible special orders each
involving the production of 2,000 units. One enquiry related to the production of a Super
Dufton (Ref. no. 610) and the other to a Premier Dufton (Ref. no. 620). Due to normal
production commitments only one of these possible orders could be handled in the factory.

The conditions of order (Ref. no. 610) are that the variable costs will increase by 25% but the selling price cannot exceed £25.00 per unit. The conditions relating to order (Ref. no. 620) are that variable costs will decrease by 25% but the selling price will be £19.00 per unit.

Required

(a) A computation of the break-even point of normal trading in terms of:
    (i) sales revenue;
    (ii) units produced;
    (iii) percentage of normal capacity (assume all units sold).   (11 marks)

(b) What profit would be earned in normal trading if:
    (i) the selling price was increased to £40 per unit and output restricted to 160,000 units;
    (ii) the selling price was reduced to £28 per unit and output increased to 260,000 units?
                                                                                      (8 marks)

(c) Advise the Board as to which of the two special orders should be accepted. Computations must be shown and a reason given for the choice made.   (6 marks)

                                                                          (Total 25 marks)
                                                                                    (AEB)

6   Marlon Plc is a company operating a department store and the management are conducting an analysis of all departments. In department ZR products have been classified into three broad categories and the profit/volume graph below has been compiled for the year ended 31 January 19-9.

Additional information:

The average selling prices of each product category in department ZR is as follows:

Product Category	Selling price each £
A	4.00
B	2.50
C	1.50

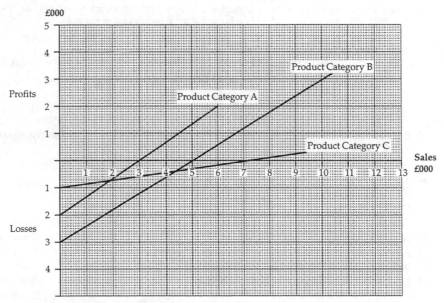

Required

(a) Using the profit/volume graph and the information given, prepare a total profit statement for department ZR for the year ended 31 January 19-9.   (5 marks)

(b) Calculate the break-even point for each category of product and express your answer in sales units.   (3 marks)

(c) Using the total figures in the statement you prepared in (a) above, prepare a break-even graph for the department. Reading from the graph you prepare, at what income did the department break even? (5 marks)

(d) By means of an accountancy equation utilising the total figures in your statement prepared in (a) above, calculate the *actual* income at which the department began to move into profit. (3 marks)

(Total 25 marks)
(AEB)

7 Polemic Ltd manufacture and sell a single product. The following information is available for three financial years ending 30 September.

	Price per Unit £	Unit Volume 000s
Sales		
Actual 1991	130	50
Forecast 1992	129	52
Forecast 1993	128.5	53

Costs per unit produced	Actual 1991 £	Forecast 1992 £	Forecast 1993 £
Direct materials	50	55	55
Direct labour	30	31.5	33
Variable production overhead	10	11	12
Direct expenses	5	5	6
Variable sales overhead	15	16	16
Other costs for the year	£ 000s	£ 000s	£ 000s
Fixed production overhead	50	55	55
Other fixed overhead	200	220	220

Additional information:

(1) When the management of Polemic prepared its direct labour forecast unit cost for 1992 and 1993, direct wages were increased only by the forecast rate of inflation.

(2) The trade union representative of the production workers wished to press for a greater wage increase. They suggested that:
  (i) Direct wages be increased at twice the rate of inflation. The effect of this would be to increase direct labour costs per unit as follows:

	1992 £	1993 £
Direct labour	33.0	35.0

  (ii) Unit selling prices be increased in order to cover the increased labour costs.

(3) It is to be assumed that all expense and revenue relationships will be unchanged except where indicated.

Required

(a) A schedule for 1991, 1992 and 1993 for Polemic Ltd showing:
  (i) the break-even points;
  (ii) the net profit for each year.
  Base your calculations on the original labour costs. (8 marks)

(b) A graph showing a break-even point for 1992. (5 marks)

(c) Advise Polemic Ltd's management as to their response to the trade union's claim for higher wages. Include relevant financial analysis. (7 marks)

(d) Explain the limitation of break-even analysis. (5 marks)

(Total 25 marks)
(AEB)

8 (a) Prepare a break-even chart to accompany the following profit graph if the selling price for the product is £1.50 per unit. (Graph paper is not required.) (5 marks)

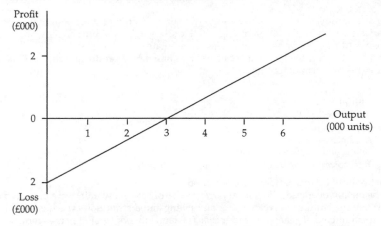

(b) Using your answer to part a), discuss five limitations of the break-even chart as a management tool. (10 marks)

(Total 15 marks)
(LONDON)

9 Solamo Ltd manufactures three types of domestic tubular chairs. These are designated Alpha, Beta and Delta. All three types are made exclusively from the same basic metal. The metal costs £2.50 per square metre.

The following is a unit cost statement for each type.

		Alpha £	Beta £	Delta £
Direct material		2.25	2.00	1.75
Direct labour –	cutting	1.20	1.40	0.60
	finishing	1.00	1.18	1.15
Direct expenses		0.35	0.52	0.75
		4.80	5.10	4.25
Selling price per unit		5.60	5.80	4.90

Sales for December 1994 in normal circumstances would be:

Alpha	1 600 chairs
Beta	2 000 chairs
Delta	1 200 chairs

Due to a shortage of the metal used, the suppliers have stated that they can only deliver 2100 square metres to cover the production during December. This means that the management will have to amend production schedules which in turn will influence the level of sales of the various types of chair. All chairs produced in each month are sold.

Required

(a) Calculate the most profitable production pattern to follow due to the shortage of the metal. (Calculations to the nearest penny.) In these circumstances state the number of chairs of each type that can be manufactured. (24 marks)

(b) Briefly indicate the matters the management should consider when confronted with such a shortage. (10 marks)

(c) State the arguments for using a marginal costing approach in routine accounting. (12 marks)

(Total 46 marks)
(AEB)

10 Mark Taylor commenced business on 1 April 1993 assembling and selling a single product: a petrol driven electrical generator. The business is the major employer in Mellerby, a rural village in the North of England.

Mark employs 23 people who assemble the components which are bought in from several factories throughout the North of England. He also employs 2 supervisors who work in the factory, 5 administrative staff and a sales representative.

He had forecast the following costs per unit based on a production run of 12 000 generators in his first year of trading.

	£	£
Components	38	
Direct labour	36	
Other direct costs	6	80
Factory overheads	51	
Administration expenses	14	
Selling and distribution expenses	6	71
Total costs per unit based on an output of 12 000 units		151

In fact only 10 000 generators were produced.

The factory overheads did not vary irrespective of how many units were produced or sold.

50% of the administrative expenses and selling and distribution expenses varied directly with the numbers of generators produced. The remainder of these expenses remained fixed.

The selling price of a generator was £170.

Mark has seen in his trade association journal that an overseas supplier is able to sell a generator with identical performance specifications for £155. "Fortunately my costs only amount to £151 per generator," says Mark, "but perhaps I should still consider buying them, rather than making them myself. I would not be much worse off and I would have fewer business worries."

All units produced are sold immediately.

Required

(a) Calculate
  (i) the number of generators Mark needs to sell in order to break-even;   (12 marks)
  (ii) the sales revenue Mark needs to generate in order to break-even.   (4 marks)

(b) A definition of "margin of safety".   (4 marks)

(c) Calculate Mark's "margin of safety" in units produced   (4 marks)

(d) Advise Mark Taylor whether, on the basis of information given, he should continue to assemble and sell the electrical generator. Give reasons for your advice.   (8 marks)

(e) Discuss other factors that Mark may need to take into account if he decides to close the assembly line.   (18 marks)

(Total 50 marks)
(AEB)

11 (a) How far is it true to state that a company's break-even point occurs where the contribution just equals the fixed costs?   (5 marks)

(b) A company's detailed information of costs and sales has been destroyed because of a computer malfunction. The following data has, however, been gleaned from various sources:

Sales volume (units)	10,000	12,000
Costs (£)		
direct materials	30,000	36,000
direct labour	28,000	33,000
overheads	20,500	24,100

Selling price per unit at all volumes of output is £12.30.

Calculate:
(i) the cost of an additional 2 000 units of output;
(ii) the variable costs of 10 000 units of output
(iii) the fixed element – if any – of each component cost;
(iv) the break-even point.   (10 marks)

(Total 15 marks)
(LONDON)

21 Budgets and budgetary control

Chapter objectives

Questions on this topic require:

- ❏ an ability to define and explain budgeting terms
- ❏ a knowledge of the uses and benefits of budgets
- ❏ an understanding of the control function of budgets
- ❏ ability to prepare operational and master budgets from given data

21.1 Definitions

Forecast

A prediction of the result of carrying on business over a future period of time, and of the position of the business at the end of that time if present and, as far as they are known, future conditions and trends are allowed to continue without management intervention.

Budget

A statement in money terms of management's plans for operating a business over a future period of time and their plans for the position of the business at the end of that time.

Budget centre

A budget centre is any part of an organisation for which a budget is prepared. What constitutes a budget centre depends upon the nature of the business, its operations and functions, and its organisational structure. A budget centre must be under the control of a manager who is responsible for its revenue and/or expenditure. Budget centres may be

revenue centres (earning revenue)	e.g. sales budget
cost centres (incurring costs but not earning revenue)	e.g. production departments
profit centres (earning revenue and incurring costs)	e.g a branch of the business, or a department of a store.

Operating Budgets (Functional Budgets)

Budgets prepared for each individual department, function etc. of a business showing the budget-responsibility of each manager.

Master Budget

A profit and loss account and balance sheet based upon the operating budgets. (Often referred to in examination questions as 'forecast' profit and loss accounts and balance sheets.)

Budget Periods

The period for which a budget is prepared, commonly for one year, but it will depend upon the particular business.

Budgetary Control

The use of budgets to monitor the performance of managers against their functional budgets. The system allows for the continuous comparison of actual with budgeted results at frequent intervals so that corrective action may be taken when necessary. Budget periods are broken down into control periods of, say, months or 4-weekly accounting periods

Illustration:

Budget for 4 weeks to 28 January 19-1

	Budget	Actual	Better/ (Worse)
	£'000	£'000	£'000
Staff costs	240	250	(10)
Property costs	105	98	7

Principal budget factor (Limiting factor, Key factor)

Anything which restricts the budgeted level of activity of a business. It is often the volume of sales which is restricted by the demand of the market, but it may be a shortage of materials, or of available labour hours or machine capacity.

Management By Exception (Exception reporting)

The focussing by management of its attention upon those items, processes etc. which are deviating from budget, on the principle that matters conforming to budget need no management intervention. Computers may be programmed to print out 'exception reports' of items deviating from budget.

Top Down Budgeting

Budgets are prepared for lower management by top management with, or without, discussion. (The concept would usually imply little or no discussion.) Lower management tend to feel little commitment to this type of budget.

Bottom Up Budgeting

Lower management prepare their own functional budgets and submit them to higher management for approval and incorporation into the master budget. Lower management tends to set its targets low in order to reduce the risk of not meeting budget, or to appear to merit credit when actual performance is seen to be better than budget.

Budget Committee

A committee of senior management to co-ordinate the preparation of budgets.

Budget Manager (Or budget controller or officer)

Usually the accountant who gives assistance to managers in the compilation of their budgets, and to the Budget committee.

Budget Manual

Contents: Statement of objectives and procedures; the budget organisation structure (showing functional responsibilities); timetable for preparing budget; report format; frequency and distribution of reports.

Zero Based Budgeting

Budget preparation based on the principle that each item of expenditure and the amount thereof must be justified by the benefit which will accrue from it before it is included in the budget. This contrasts with the alternative method of starting with the previous year's budget and 'updating' it, including adding some percentage points for inflation. This latter method has the defect of perpetuating previous inaccuracies and inefficiencies.

Flexible Budget

A budget that recognises the different behaviours of fixed and variable costs at different levels of activity.

21.2 Objectives, plans and budgets

Small businesses

The owner of a small business will probably have one or more objectives in mind for the business. It may be to expand the business and to obtain larger premises; or it may be to introduce new lines of merchandise to sell. Quite commonly the objective will be to make the business more profitable or to increase its cash flow. If the owner does not want to do any of these things, but simply to allow the business to continue in the future without change, the objective is to do nothing new.

Whatever the objectives, the owner must plan how they are to be achieved. The plans may be prepared in a formal way and written down on paper; or they may be less formal and not recorded at all but sinply remain in the mind of the owner.

Larger businesses

Larger businesses, especially companies, will have objectives for longer terms than sole traders. The objectives may be set for many years ahead, typically for 10, 20, 30 or more years. The objectives may involve expenditure of very considerable amounts of money running into many millions of pounds. Examples are the construction of factories, ocean-going vessels, and aircraft. Whatever the objectives, management must plan the means by which it is going to achieve them. The plans will be long term. Companies usually have 'rolling' plans for, say, five years. As each year passes, another year is added on so that the plans remain ones for five years ahead.

Budgets are management plans expressed, usually in money terms. They are prepared initially in quantitative terms such as sales volume, quantities of materials, numbers of man- and machine- hours required for production. Prices, rates of pay etc. are then applied to the budgeted quantities to turn the budgets into financial statements.

Long term plans will generally be broken down into periods of twelve months. A budget period will then be that of one year. The year will be broken down into monthly or four weekly periods so that actual income and expenditure may be compared with budget at frequent intervals during the year. If 'actuals' are found to differ significantly from budget during the year, action can be taken promptly to correct the trend.

Factors to be considered in budgeting

(i) Long term objectives of business (Corporate, strategic planning)

(ii) Principal budget, or limiting, factors

(iii) Internal factors   (behavioural aspects of management when preparing budgets – the tendency of some managers to produce budgets that are easy to meet; number of each grade of employee; staff training and morale; available finance etc.)

(iv) External factors (International, political, economic, environmental etc.)

Uses and benefits of budgets

(a) Budgets formalise management plans

(b) Budget preparation ensures that all functions of a business are properly co-ordinated.

(c) Budgets may indicate possible future shortages of resources so that remedial action may be taken in good time, or other functional budgets modified (e.g. A cash budget may give prior warning of a shortage of liquidity and the need to re-phase expenditure, arrange a bank overdraft, loan etc. in good time.)

(d) Participation by management at all levels in budget preparation induces a sense of commitment by all of them to the budget.

(e) The preparation of budgets for individual departments, functions etc. is a form of responsibilty accounting. The manager in charge of a department or function is responsible for earning the budgeted revenue or keeping within his budgeted expenditure. Budgets should present managers with a challenge to meet them, but should be achievable.

(f) Budgets provide information for on-going control of business activities.

Flexible budgets

Although a budget may be prepared on the basis of a pre-determined level of activity, management may anticipate the actual level of activity being greater or less than budget. The budget may therefore be 'flexed', that is, prepared for various levels of activity to enable realistic comparisons of actual with budget possible.

21.3 Budget preparation

Budgeting starts with the preparation of a budget for each budget centre, often a department, branch, or function of the business. These are usually referred to as operating or functional budgets.

The budgets must be co-ordinated. For example, the production budget must match the sales budget and be based upon the volume of goods which can be sold. Otherwise insufficient goods may be produced to meet demand, or goods will be produced which cannot be sold. Similarly, the materials purchasing budget must be geared to the requirements of the production budget.

The budgets will be governed by the principal budget factor. This is usually the volume of goods for which the sales department forecasts a demand. The principal budget factor may be the availability of a resource such as materials, or productive man hours or machine capacity. The principal budget factor will therefore decide which budget must be prepared first. As the principal budget factor is usually the demand for the goods, the sales budget will normally be prepared first.

21.4 Sales budget

As already explained, the sales budget is based upon the forecast demand for the goods. The forecast will be based upon market research, salesmens' reports and other trade information sources, and be expressed in sales volumes i.e. in numbers of units.

The pricing policy will have a bearing upon the demand for the goods. When the volumes have been forecast, the budgeted units of sale can be multiplied by the price to give the sales revenue.

Sales are frequently the key factor in a business and the sales budget will then largely determine the shape of the other budgets.

A simple sales budget will record quantities and prices and total revenue:

Sales budget for Product A for six months to 30 June 19-1

Month	Quantity £	Price £	Revenue
Jan	5,000	1.50	7,500
Feb	6,000	1.50	9,000
Mar	8,000	1.50	12,000
Apr	7,000	1.60	11,200
May	7,500	1.60	12,000
Jun	8,000	1.60	12,800
	41,500		64,500

Additional columns will be used when more than one product is involved; a total column will then be necessary as well.

Further columns may be added to allow sales to be analysed over regions, departments. Alternatively, separate budgets may be prepared for each region or department and these combined into a summary statement.

21.4.1 Example: sales budget for a single product

Naveed sells a single product, Deevan Beds, at a price of £160 each. During the three months to 31 December 19-1, he sold 1,500 beds; turnover was constant per month. He expects the volume of sales to remain unchanged for January 19-2, but to increase by 5% in February, and by a further 20% in April. The price of the beds will be increased by 10% in January and by a further 5% in June.

Required

Prepare a sales budget for Deevan Beds for the six months to 30 June 19-2.

Answer

Deevan Beds
Sales budget for the six months to 30 June 19-2

19-2	Quantity	Price	Amount
	£	£	£
January	500	176	88,000
February	525	176	92,400
March	525	176	92,400
April	630	176	110,880
May	630	176	110,880
June	630	184.8	116,424
	3,440		610,984

21.4.2 Exercise: preparation of a sales budget

M. Cohen markets two products, A and B. The sales of Product A averaged 1,000 per month in 19-3 and in the same year an average of 500 of Product B were sold per month.

M. Cohen estimates that in 19-4, sales of Product A will increase by 5 per cent in March and by a further 8 per cent in August. Sales of Product B will increase by 6 per cent in February, by a further 10 per cent in June and then to increase to 600 a month by August with a further increase of 4 per cent by October.

Product A has been selling for £100 each and Product B for £120. The price of Product A will increase by 10 per cent in March 19-4 and by a further 5 per cent in the following September. The price of Product B will be increased by 5 per cent in May and again by a further $33\frac{1}{3}$ per cent in October.

Required

M.Cohen's sales budget for the year to 31 December 19-4.

21.5 Production budget

This is a budget for the production of finished goods

Even Production Budget

This type of budget is required by a firm employing skilled labour which cannot readily be hired, made redundant and then re-hired to meet seasonal fluctuations of business. Continuous employment of a stable, skilled workforce with an even flow of production, even if it results in seasonal stockpiling is preferable to a skilled labour shortage just when it is needed, or the costly training of new unskilled staff.

Uneven Production Budget

This could be required by a firm with a highly seasonal type of business in a product which it is not feasible to stockpile, e.g. ice cream, and which can be produced by unskilled labour which can be hired and released as occasion demands, e.g. students seeking holiday jobs.

Method

(i)   Read question through carefully to ascertain its requirements e.g. the exact period to be covered by the budget, whether even or uneven production is required, sales, opening stocks, minimum stocks, etc.

(ii) Prepare a column for each month, quarter or other period required.

(iii) Prepare rows for opening stocks of goods, units produced, sales and closing stocks.

21.5.1 Example 1: even production

Sital Ltd. manufactures codgetts of which it produces 750 a month. Sales for the four months May to August are expected to be as follows: May 600; June 800; July 1,000; August 600.

At 30 April, Sital Ltd. will have 800 codgetts in stock.

Required

Sital Ltd.'s production budget for the four months May to August.

Answer

Sital Ltd.
Production Budget 4 months to 31 August

	May	June	July	August
Opening Stock	800	950	900	650
Production	750	750	750	750
	1550	1700	1650	1400
Sales	600	800	1000	600
Closing stock	950	900	650	800

Example 2: even production with minimum stock level

Hocus plc manufactures gas pokers with a regular monthly production of 1,000 pokers. Sales for the four months September to December are expected to be: September 900; October 1,000; November 1,300; December 900. Hocus Ltd. maintains a minimum stock of 600 pokers.

Required

Hocus plc's production budget for the four months to 31 December.

Answer

Tutorial note: No opening stock is given. Begin by preparing the budget, inserting monthly opening and closing stocks in pencil. (Insert 'negative' balances at this stage.) Find the month which has the biggest shortfall compared with minimum stock; the shortfall will be the required opening stock.

Hocus plc
Production Budget – 4 months to 31 December

	Sept	Oct	Nov	Dec
Opening stock b/f	?	*100	*100	*(200)
Production	1000	1000	1000	1000
	1000	1100	1100	800
Sales	900	1000	1300	900
Closing stock c/f	*100	*100	*(200)	*(100)

* = balances 'pencilled in' at this stage

November has the greatest shortfall from minimum stock: 600 + 200= 800.

Enter 800 as the opening stock in September and substitute new balances for the ones pencilled in for opening and closing stocks for the other months:

	Sept	Oct	Nov	Dec
Opening stock b/f	800	900	900	600
Production	1000	1000	1000	1000
	1800	1900	1900	1600
Sales	900	1000	1300	900
Closing balance c/f	900	900	600	700

Example 3: uneven production

Okalas Ltd. produces Iyesan, a chemical product which they have patented. The stock of Iyesan at 1 January 19-1 was 1,200 kilos.

Sales for the four quarters of 19-1 are budgeted to be: Qtr. to 31 March 3,000 kilos; Qtr. to 30 June 5,000 kilos; Qtr. to 30 September 7,000 kilos; Qtr. to 31 December 4,000 kilos.

Closing stocks are required to be as follows: 31 March 1,500 kilos; 30 June 1,800 kilos; September 1600 kilos; December 1,300 kilos.

Required

Okalas Ltd.'s quarterly production budget for the year to 31 December 1996.

Tutorial note: Production = sales + closing stock – opening stock. Therefore production for three months to 31 March = 3,000 + 1,500 – 1,200 = 3,300 kilos etc.

Answer

Okalas Ltd.
Production budget for the year to 31 December 1996

Quarters ending	March 31	June 30	Sept 30	Dec 31
	kilos.	kilos.	kilos.	kilos
Opening stock	(1,200)	(1,500)	(1,800)	(1,600)
Sales	3,000	5,000	7,000	4,000
Closing stock	1,500	1,800	1,600	1,300
Production	3,300	5,300	6,800	3,700

21.5.2 Exercise 1: budget for even production

Murude plc manufactures beauty care packs and has a fixed production of 15,000 packs a month. The stock of beauty care packs at 1 January 19-2 was 16,000. Budgeted sales for 19-2 are as follows:

three months to	31 March	42,000 packs
	30 June	52,000 packs
	30 September	55,000 packs
	31 December	32,000 packs

Required

Murude plc's production budget for the four quarters of 19-2.

Exercise 2: even production and minimum stock level

Shwish Ltd. produces cans of fizzy drink. 100,000 cans are produced each month and sales for 19-3 are budgeted to be as follows:

three months to	March 31	250,000 cans
	June 30	350,000 cans
	September 30	500,000 cans
	December 31	400,000 cans

The minimum stock at any time is to be 300,000 cans.

Required

Shwish Ltd's production budget for the four quarters of 19-3.

Exercise 3: uneven production

The Aaisha Company produces fashion packs for home made garments. Budgeted sales and closing stocks are as follows:

	Sales (packs)	Closing stocks (packs)
December	7,000	1,000
January	6,000	2,000
February	8,000	4,000
March	7,000	5,000
April	8,000	4,000

Required

The Aaisha Company's production budget for the four months to 30 April 19-5.

21.6 Materials purchasing budget

Budgets for the purchases of supplies of materials used for production will be compiled from production budgets. The procedure is similar to that followed for production budgets.

Stock purchasing budgets may be produced either in units purchased or cost of purchases.

21.6.1 Example

Maranah Med Ltd. manufactures a product each unit of which requires two kilos of a material called prudice. Production for the months of September 1996 to January 1997 is budgeted as follows:

1996	No. of units produced
September	1,000
October	3,000
November	4,000
December	2,000
1997	
January	3,000

The stock of prudice at 1 September 1996 is 2,000 kilos. It is expected that this material will become difficult to obtain in 1997 and that the price will increase. It has therefore been decided that the stock of this material will be increased by 1,000 kilos each month to the end of 1996. Prudice costs £2 per kilo. at present but the price is expected to rise to £3 in November.

Required

The raw materials purchasing budget for Maranah Med Ltd. for the four months to 31 December 1996.

Answer

Maranah Med Ltd.
Raw Materials purchasing budget for the four months to December 1996

(Kilos)	Sept	Oct	Nov	Dec
Opening stock	(2,000)	(3,000)	(4,000)	(5,000)
Issues	2,000	6,000	8,000	4,000
Closing stock	3,000	4,000	5,000	6,000
Purchases	3,000	7,000	9,000	5,000
Price	£2	£2	£3	£3
Cost of material	£6,000	£14,000	£27,000	£15,000

21.6.2 Exercise: budget for purchase of raw materials at cost price

Pi Manufacturers Ltd. make product X. Each unit of product X requires 3 kilos of mucronium. Product X is made in the month prior to sale and the raw materials are purchased one month before production. Since 1 January 19-1, mucronium had cost £1.50 per kilo but the price was increased to £2 from 1 June 19-1. The FIFO basis is used for charging mucronium to production.

Budgeted sales of product X are as follows:

19-1	units
March	500
April	600
May	800
June	1,000
July	900
August	600

The stock of mucronium at 28 February 19-1 was equal to the production requirement for March.

Required

The budget for the purchase of mucronium by Pi Manufacturers Ltd. for the period March to June 19-1.

21.7 An extended example of budgeting

The examples given in this chapter so far have shown sales, production and materials purchasing budgets which are not related to each other. A company will produce, in addition to those already mentioned, materials stock budgets, finished goods budgets, labour budgets, machine utilisation budgets, capital expenditure budgets, cash budgets, and perhaps other budgets. Each budget must be made to fit with all the others. It could be disastrous for a budget to be prepared for the production of 2,000 items a month if the sales budget showed that only 1,000 items could be sold each month. It would be equally bad if the production budget allowed for only 500 items to be made.

Examination questions sometimes require candidates to prepare two or more related budgets which must be made to fit with each other.

Example 21.7.1

A company makes garden chairs from moulded plastic. 80% of the chairs are made in the month before sale. Each chair requires 2 kilos of plastic material. The raw plastic material is purchased one month before it is required for production and suppliers allow the company one month's credit. 50% of sales are for cash and the remainder are on one month's credit.

Sales for eight months December 1996 to July 1997 are forecast as follows:

		No. of chairs	Price £
1996	December	2,300	4
1997	January	2,000	4
	February	2,500	4
	March	3,500	5
	April	5,000	6
	May	7,000	6
	June	9,000	6
	July	8,000	6

The raw material presently costs £1.30 per kilo., but a 10% price increase is expected in February.

Prepare the following budgets:
Sales
Production
Materials purchase
Cash (extract)

Sales budget

	Jan	Feb	Mar	Apr
No. of chairs	2,000	2,500	3,500	5,000
Price per chair (£)	4	4	5	6
Sales revenue (£)	8,000	10,000	17,500	30,000

Production budget

	Jan	Feb	Mar	Apr
Chairs required to meet				
current month's sales (a)	2,000	2,500	3,500	5,000
next month's sales (b)	2,500	3,500	5,000	7,000
Production required				
20% of (a)	400	500	700	1,000
80% of (b)	2,000	2,800	4,000	5,600
Total production	2,400	3,300	4,700	6,600

Materials Purchase budget

	Jan	Feb	Mar	Apr
Next month's production	3,300	4,700	6,600	8,600*
Material required				
2 kilos per chair	6,600	9,400	13,200	17,200
Price per kilo (£)	1.30	1.43	1.43	1.43
Cost	£8,580	£13,442	£18,876	£24,596

Cash budget (extract)

	Jan £	Feb £	Mar £	Apr £
Receipts: Cash sales	4,000	5,000	8,750	15,000
Debtors	4,600*	4,000	5,000	8,750
	8,600	9,000	13,750	23,750
* December debtors:				
50% of (2,300 × £4) = £4,600				
Payments: Suppliers	3,120*	8,580	13,442	18,876

* Materials for January production purchased in December

Exercise 21.7.2

The forecast sales of product x are

	Units	Price per unit
		£
April	5,000	2
May	7,000	2
June	8,000	4
July	10,000	4
August	11,000	4

All sales are for cash.

Each unit of x requires 5 litres of material at a cost of 25p per litre. The raw material is purchased one month before production. Payment for the materials is made one month after purchase.

Units of x are manufactured one month before sale.

2,000 units of x are in stock at 1 April. It has been decided to increase stocks of x by 800 units each month in anticipation of a big demand later in the year.

Required: Prepare the sales, production, materials purchase budgets and an extract of the cash budget for the months of April, May and June.

21.8 Cash budget

Method

(i) Examiners expect cash budgets to be prepared in a template similar to the following:

Periods	1	2	3	4	5	6 etc.
	£	£	£	£	£	£
Receipts (details)						
Payments (details)						
Net receipts/(payments)						
Balance b/f						
Balance c/f						

(ii) Read the question very carefully at least twice before preparing the outline template, noting the nature of receipts and payments. Enter these in the template, leaving a few lines to allow for the insertion of additional items later which may have been overlooked.

(iii) Once the outline template has been prepared, it is usually not too difficult to fill in the figures, but careful reading of the question, a little common sense and great care in performing calculations are essential.

(iv) Sales and purchases on credit. Take care to enter receipts and payments in the period in which the money is expected to be received or paid. If some sales are for cash and others on credit, the receipts will be split between cash sales and the balance, received in a later period, as receipts from debtors.

Credit transactions require information for the period prior to the budget period to be given; do not be confused by this.

(v) Other expenses may be paid currently or one period later than that in which they are incurred.

(vi) Depreciation is a non-cash item and must be ignored.

(vii) Receipts and expenditure occurring before the period covered by the budget must be adjusted, if necessary, in the opening balance of cash brought forward and not shown as transactions in the first month, week etc.

(viii) Cash budgets are prepared on a cash and not an accruals basis. Any item, revenue or capital in nature, which should appear in the cash book in the period in question should be included in the budget; but all other items should be ignored.

21.8.1 Example: preparation of cash budget from supplied data

Niblick supplies golf equipment. Ten per cent of his sales are for cash; the remainder is on one month's credit. He receives one month's credit on all purchases. Sales and purchases are as follows:

	Sales £	Purchases £
December 19-1	30,000	16,000
January 19-2	25,000	14,000
February	18,000	20,000
March	22,000	25,000
April	28,000	30,000

Niblick pays wages of £2,000 per month. He pays rent of £10,000 per annum.; he paid one year's rent in advance on 1 January 19-2. Other expenses, £1,500 per month are paid currently.

On 6 February 19-2, Niblick plans to sell a van for £2,300 and to buy a new one for £6,000 on 15 March 19-2.

Niblick draws £1,000 a month for living expenses.

At 31 December 19-1, Niblick's bank balance was £7,000 (in hand). His father will lend the business £4,000 on 1 April 19-2.

Required

Niblick's cash budget for the four months to 30 April 19-2.

Answer

Niblick
Cash budget for 4 months to 30 April 19-2

	Jan £	Feb £	Mar £	Apr £
Receipts				
Cash sales	2,500	1,800	2,200	2,800
Receipts from debtors	27,000	22,500	16,200	19,800
Sale of van		2,300		
Loan from father				4,000
	29,500	26,600	18,400	26,600
Payments				
Creditors for supplies	16,000	14,000	20,000	25,000
Wages	2,000	2,000	2,000	2,000
Rent	10,000			
Other expenses	1,500	1,500	1,500	1,500
Purchase of van			6,000	
Drawings	1,000	1,000	1,000	1,000
	30,500	18,500	30,500	29,500
Net receipts/(payments)	(1,000)	8,100	(12,100)	(2,900)
Balance brought forward	7,000	6,000	14,100	2,000
Balance carried forward	6,000	14,100	2,000	(900)

21.8.2 Exercise: preparation of a cash budget

Kadriye commenced business on 1 January 19-2 trading as 'Kadriye's Kitchen Kabinets', selling 3-K kitchen furniture. She had opened a business bank account on 15 December 19-1, paying £25,000 into it as her opening capital. On 21 December 19-1, she rented premises, paying the first quarter's rent, due on 25 December 19-1, £1,200. Other expenditure in the same month was for the purchase of fixed assets for cash, £8,000, and stock £20,000 which was bought on one month's credit.

Kadriye estimates that her other purchases and the sales for the year to 31 December 19-2 will be as follows:

3 months to	Purchases £	Sales £
March 31	12,000	15,000
June 30	18,000	24,000
September 30	21,000	30,000
December 31	15,000	36,000

All purchases and sales will be on one month's credit.

Other expenditure in 19-2 will be as follows:

January 5 Purchase of motor van for cash £5,000; the van is to be depreciated annually at the rate of 20% on cost.

Wages £2,000 per month paid currently.

Kadriye will draw £500 per month for living expenses. She plans to sell her private car in June for £3,500 and to pay the proceeds into the business as additional capital. A friend has also promised to lend the business £6,000 in September 19-2.

Kadriye's bank has agreed to allow overdraft facilities if they are required with interest at 10 per cent per annum. Interest will be debited in the bank statements on the last day of each half year and will be calculated on the average overdraft, if any, for the half year. For this purpose, the overdraft on the last day of the immediately preceding quarter is to be taken as the average for the half year.

Required

Kadriye's cash budget for the year to 31 December 19-2.

21.9 Master budgets

The functional (or operational) budgets are summarised in the master budget which takes the form of a forecast profit and loss account and balance sheet.

In examinations, the preparation of a master budget is often required in conjunction with the preparation of a cash budget.

It is essential to remember the differences between a cash budget and a forecast profit and loss account:

– a cash budget is compiled on a 'cash' basis and includes all receipts and payments, capital as well as revenue. It does not include non-monetary items such as depreciation.

– a forecast profit and loss account is prepared on an accruals basis and includes revenue receipts and payments only. It includes non-monetary items such as depreciation, profits and losses on sales of fixed assets and provisions for bad debts.

21.9.1 Example: cash budget and master budget

P. Blowers balance sheet at 30 June 19-3 was as follows:

Fixed assets	Cost	Depn	Net
	£	£	£
Equipment	5,000	3,000	2,000
Motor vehicles	8,000	5,000	3,000
	13,000	8,000	5,000
Current assets			
Stock		4,800	
Trade debtors		6,800	
Cash at bank		10,000	
		21,600	
Less **Current liabilities**			
Trade creditors		3,100	
Net working capital			18,500
			23,500
Financed by Capital account: balance at 1 July 19–2			20,000
add profit for the year			8,500
			28,500
less Drawings			5,000
			23,500

P.Blowers estimates that his purchases and sales for the year to 30 June 19–4 will be as follows:

		Purchases	Sales
		£	£
19-3	July – September	18,000	33,000
	October – December	24,000	51,000
19-4	January – March	21,000	42,000
	April – June	24,000	48,000

P.Blowers receives one month's credit on all purchases and allows one month's credit on all sales.

The following expenses will be incurred in the year to 30 June 19-4:

Rent £800 per quarter payable in advance on 1 January, 1 April, 1 July, 1 October.

Wages £1,800 per month payable currently

On 1 July 19-3 P.Blowers will pay an insurance premium in the sum of £1,500 up to 30 September 19-4.

Other expenses will amount to £2,000 per month

P.Blowers will purchase additional equipment on 1 October 19-3 for £3,000.

A van which cost £4,000 and has a written down value at 30 June19-3 of £1,500 will be sold for £1,100 on 1 January 19-4.

A new van will be purchased on 1 October 19-3 for £8,000.

Motor vans are depreciated at $12\frac{1}{2}$% per annum on cost.

Equipment is depreciated by 10% per annum on cost.

P.Blowers will draw £1,000 per month for living expenses.

Stock of goods at 30 June 19-4 will be £7,300.

Required

(a) P.Blowers cash budget for the year to 30 June 19-4 and

(b) A forecast trading and profit and loss account for the year to 30 June 19-4 and a balance sheet as at that date.

Answer

(a)

P.Blowers
Cash budget for the year to 30 June 19-4

	19-3		19-4	
	Jul-Sep	Oct-Dec	Jan-Mar	Apr-Jun
	£	£	£	£
Receipts				
Receipts from debtors	28,800	45,000	45,000	46,000
Proceeds of sale of van			1,100	
	28,800	45,000	46,100	46,000
Payments				
Suppliers	15,100	22,000	22,000	23,000
Rent	800	800	800	800
Wages	5,400	5,400	5,400	5,400
Insurance	1,500			
Other expenses	6,000	6,000	6,000	6,000
Purchase of equipment		3,000		
Purchase of motor van		8,000		
Drawings	3,000	3,000	3,000	3,000
	31,800	48,200	37,200	38,200
Net receipts/(payments)	(3,000)	(3,200)	8,900	7,800
Balance b/f	10,000	7,000	3,800	12,700
Balance c/f	7,000	3,800	12,700	20,500

(b)

**Forecast trading and profit and loss account
for the year ending 30 June 19–4**

	£	£
Sales		174,000
Less Cost of sales: Stock at 1.7.–3	4,800	
Purchases	87,000	
	91,800	
less Stock at 30.6.–4	7,300	84,500
Gross profit		89,500
less		
Wages	21,600	
Rent	3,200	
Insurance	1,200	
Other expenses	24,000	
Loss on sale of motor van	150	

Depreciation: equipment	725		
motor vehicles	1,500	2,225	52,375
Net profit			37,125

Forecast Balance Sheet as at 30 June 19–4

Fixed assets	Cost	Depn	Net
	£	£	£
Equipment	8,000	3,725	4,275
Motor vehicles	12,000	3,750	8,250
	20,000	7,475	12,525
Current assets			
Stock		7,300	
Trade debtors		16,000	
Prepayment (insurance)		300	
Cash at bank		20,500	
		44,100	
Less **Current liabilities**			
Trade creditors		8,000	36,100
			48,625
Capital account: Balance at 1.7.–3			23,500
Profit for year			37,125
			60,625
less drawings			12,000
			48,625

Tutorial notes

1. Cash budget:

   (a) Receipts in July 19-3 will include trade debtors shown in balance sheet at 30 June 19-3.

   (b) One third of the sales in each quarter will be received in the following quarter. (Make a note of the receipts outstanding for the June sales for inclusion as trade debtors in the balance sheet.)

   (c) Payments for purchases in July 19-3 will be to trade creditors shown in the balance sheet at 30 June 19-3.

   (d) One third of purchases in each quarter will be paid for in the following quarter. (Make a note of the outstanding amount for June purchases for inclusion as trade creditors in the June balance sheet.)

   (e) Make a note that £300 insurance paid in July 19-3 is to be shown as a prepayment in the balance sheet.

2. Profit and loss account:

   (a) Loss on sale of motor van: Net book value at 30 June 19-3 = £1,500; further depreciation for 6 months = £250 making net book value £1,250 at date of sale.

   (b) Depreciation of equipment includes depreciation on new equipment for 9 months.

   (c) Depreciation of motor vehicles includes depreciation on motor van sold as above plus depreciation on new motor van for 9 months.

21.9.2 Exercise: preparation of cash budget, forecast profit and loss account and balance sheet for a limited company

Courante Ltd.'s balance sheet at 31 December 19-1 is as follows:

Fixed assets	Cost	Depn	Net
	£	£	£
Freehold premises	20,000	4,000	16,000
Plant and machinery	15,000	9,000	6,000
	35,000	13,000	22,000
Current assets			
Stock		12,000	
Trade debtors		17,000	
Cash at bank		9,500	
Administration expenses prepaid		2,400	
		40,900	
less **Current liabilities**			
Trade creditors	9,000		
Selling and distribution expenses accrued	1,200	10,200	30,700
			52,700
less Long term liabilities: 12 per cent debentures			10,000
			42,700
Share capital and reserves			
Ordinary shares of £1			25,000
General reserve			15,000
Retained profit			2,700
			42,700

Sales and purchases for the four months to 30 April 19–2 are as follows:

	Jan	Feb	Mar	Apr
	£	£	£	£
Sales	25,000	28,000	30,000	33,000
Purchases	10,000	8,000	12,000	15,000

It is expected that 40 per cent of sales will be for cash; one month's credit is allowed to debtors. One month's credit is allowed on all purchases.

Additional information:

1. Selling and distribution expenses: 10 per cent of sales, payable in following month.

2. Administration expenses: £8,000 per month. Prepaid administration expenses at 30 April 19-2: £1,300.

3. Stock at 30 April 19-2: £9,000.

4. Additional machinery will be purchased on 1 March 19-2 at a cost of £24,000

5. Provision is made yearly for depreciation as follows: freehold premises: 3 per cent on cost; plant and machinery 20 per cent on cost. 50 per cent of all depreciation is charged to selling and distribution expenses and the balance to administration expenses.

6. Debenture interest is payable on 30 June and 31 December.

7. Payment of an interim dividend of 10p a share will be made in April 19-2.

8. It is planned to transfer a further £10,000 to general reserve at 30 April 19-2.

Required

(a) A cash budget for Courante Ltd. for the four months to 30 April 19-2.

(b) A forecast profit and loss account for the four months to 30 April 19-2 and a forecast balance sheet as at that date.

Key points to remember

1. Budgets need present little difficulty if
   (i) The question is read carefully
   (ii) All instructions are followed (tick them as you do them)
   (iii) All calculations are made accurately.
2. Learn the appropriate template to use for each type of budget. Prepare the outline as soon as you have read the question. Leave a few lines so that you can insert additional items at a later stage if you have overlooked any at the start.
3. SHOW ALL WORKINGS. This applies to all answers in examinations.
4. Give every budget a proper heading. This applies to all examination answers.
5. Cash budgets should be summaries of the entries which will be expected to appear in the cash book in the budget period. No other items (e.g.depreciation) should appear.
6. If asked how the liquidity of a business can be improved, make sensible suggestions based on the cash budget. e.g. capital expenditure may be deferred, or assets purchased on credit, or on hire purchase, or leased. Some suggestions may need qualification, e.g. getting debtors to pay more promptly may involve a cost (discounts allowed), or loss of custom. Delaying payment of creditors may result in loss of discounts receivable, stopping of supplies or a requirement to 'pay cash with order' in future. Do not make any suggestions that would be against the public interest or would result in penalties e.g. delaying payment of tax.
7. Forecast profit and loss accounts are compiled in the same way as such statements for past periods but remember the essential differences between a cash budget and a profit and loss account.

Common errors

1. inclusion of depreciation in cash budgets.
2. failure to make any necessary adjustments to the opening bank balance for items occurring before the budget period. (Generally applicable to new business starting up.)
3. failure to account for opening debtors, creditors, accruals and prepayments in cash budget.

Questions

Fully worked examination question

Herbert Limited make a single product, whose unit budget details are as follows:

	£	£
Selling price		30
Less costs		
Direct material	9	
Direct labour	4	
Direct production expenses	6	
Variable selling expenses	4	23
Contribution		7

Additional information:

(1) Unit sales are expected to be :

	June	July	August	September	October
	1,000	800	400	600	900

(2) Credit sales will account for 60% of total sales. Debtors are expected to pay in the month following sale for which there will be a cash discount of 2%

(3) Stock levels will be arranged so that production in one month will meet the next month's sales demand.

(4) The purchases of direct materials in one month will just meet the next month's production requirements.

(5) Suppliers of direct materials will be paid in the month following purchase.

(6) Labour costs will be paid in the month in which they are incurred. All other expenses will be paid in the month following that in which they are incurred.

(7) Fixed expenses are £2,000 per month and include £180 for depreciation.

(8) The bank balance at 1 July 19-9 is £3,900 favourable to the business.

Required

(a) A cash budget for Herbert Limited for the three month period ending on 30 September 19-9 showing the balance of cash at the end of each month. (16 marks)

(b) List and explain **three** ways in which the preparation of a cash flow budget could be of advantage to the management of Herbert Limited. (6 marks)

(Total 22 marks)
(AEB)

Answer

(a)

Tutorial notes

Herbert Limited   1.
Cash budget for the three months ending 30 September 19-9

	July £	August £	September £	
Receipts				2.
Cash sales	9,600	4,800	7,200	
Receipts from debtors	17,640	14,112	7,056	
	27,240	18,912	14,256	
Payments				
Creditors for materials	3,600	5,400	8,100	3.
Direct labour	1,600	2,400	3,600	
Direct production expenses	4,800	2,400	3,600	
Variable selling expenses	4,000	3,200	1,600	
Fixed expenses	1,820	1,820	1,820	
	15,820	15,220	18,720	
Net receipts/(payments)	11,420	3,692	(4,464)	
Balance b/f	3,900	15,320	19,012	
Balance c/f	15,320	19,012	14,548	4.

(b) Answers should include: 5.

(i) Cash budgets are essential for proper management of funds

(ii) They indicate likely requirements for additional finance

(iii) They show *when* additional finance will be required

(iv) They show whether additional funds are required temporarily or for longer term.

(v) They indicate possible future surpluses of funds so that suitable arrangements may be made in advance for investing them.

(vi) Cash budgets play an important part in coordinating the operational budgets of a business.

(vii) If a business has to approach a bank for a loan or overdraft facilities, the bank will certainly expect to see a cash budget. Failure to produce one will convince the bank that the business is not being properly managed and will not encourage the bank to provide finance.

(Only three advantages are required by the question)

Tutorial notes

1. Proper title including Herbert Ltd is important

2. The form of layout of a cash budget is important. Examiners expect to see it set out as in this model answer.

3. Payments to creditors: §(3) (4) and (5) in the question must be read together. Goods to be sold in July will be made in June; the materials for those goods will be bought in May and paid for in June. Therefore the payment to creditors in July will be for the materials to make the goods to be sold in August (400 × £9 = £3,600)

4. The question must be read just as carefully as any other type of question, especially to ascertain the times when payments are expected from debtors and payments must be made to creditors and for other expenses etc.

5. Part (b) This part carries 6 marks only, but the comments made in note 7 for question 3 above are equally applicable to this question.

Multiple choice questions

1   A   principal budget factor is
    A   anything which acts as a constraint on the level of activity
    B   the amount by which current prices must be increased to take account of inflation
    C   the biggest item of expenditure in a budget
    D   the required profit

2   The basis on which a sales budget is prepared is
    A   the expected volume of sales
    B   the previous year's sales revenue
    C   the previous year's sales revenue plus an addition for anticipated price increases
    D   the sales necessary to produce the forecast profit.

3   The sales revenue budget for 5 months to May is as follows:

Jan	Feb	Mar	Apr	May
£50,000	£70,000	£80,000	£120,000	£90,000

Cost of materials is 60% of sales. Materials are purchased one month before they are processed and finished goods are sold two months after production. 50% of raw materials are paid for in the month of purchase; the remainder are paid for in the following month. Payments to suppliers in February will be

    A   £27,000
    B   £54,000
    C   £60,000
    D   £63,000

4   If sales revenue is £3,000 above budget, cost of materials is £4,000 below budget, wages are £1,000 above budget and overheads £2,000 above budget, net profit will be
    A   £2,000 less than budget
    B   £4,000 less than budget
    C   £4,000 more than baudget
    D   the same as budget

5   A company expects to buy a new motor lorry for £25,000. It has agreed with the seller to part exchange one of its existing lorries for the new lorry. The existing lorry has a net book value of £8,000 and the part exchange will result in a loss of £2,800 on its disposal. The company will pay the balance due on the new lorry by cheque. The entries to record the deal in the company's cash budget will be

A   payment for new lorry £17,000

B   payment for new lorry £17,000, cash receivable from disposal of old lorry £5,200

C   payment for new lorry £19,800

D   payment for new lorry £25,000, cash receivable from sale of old lorry £5,800

6   A company allows its customers one month's credit. Budgeted sales revenue for five quarters to December 1997 is

		£
1996	3 months to December	39,000
1997	3 months to March	42,000
	3 months to June	45,000
	3 months to September	54,000
	3 months to December	48,000

The entries in the cash and master budgets for the year to 31 December 1997 will be

	Cash budget		Forecast Trading account for the year to 31 12.97		Forecast Balance Sheet at 31.12.95
	£		£		£
A	Sales	180,000	Sales	186,000	Trade debtors	16,000
B	Sales	186,000	Sales	189,000	Trade debtors	16,000
C	Sales	186,000	Sales	189,000	Trade debtors	32,000
D	Sales	189,000	Sales	189,000	Trade debtors	48,000

Further examination questions

1   The procedures and terminology of budgeting and budgetary control can be very confusing to non-accountants. You are required to explain, in writing, to a group of people with no accounting background, each of the following.

(a) The term 'Limiting Factor' and its influence in the creation of a budget.   (5 marks)

(b) How budgets are set.   (5 marks)

(c) The participation required of management to implement a sound system of responsibility accounting.   (5 marks)

(d) How 'Budgetary Control' can increase the efficiency of an organisation.   (5 marks)

(Total 20 marks)

(JMB)

2   A company's estimated pattern of costs and revenues for the first four months of 19-7 is as follows:

Costs And Revenues: January – April 19-7
(£'000)

Month	Sales	Materials	Wages	Overheads
JANUARY	410.4	81.6	16.2	273.6
FEBRUARY	423.6	84.8	16.8	282.4
MARCH	460.8	93.6	18.3	306.7
APRIL	456.3	91.2	18.6	304.5

1.   One quarter of the materials are paid for in the month of production and the remainder two months later: deliveries received in November 19-6 were £78,600, and in December 19-6 £74,800.

2.   Customers are expected to pay one-third of their debts a month after the sale and the remainder after two months: sales expected for November 19-6 are £398,400, and for December 19-6, £402,600.

413

3. Old factory equipment is to be sold in February 19-7 for £9,600. Receipt of the money is expected in April 19-7. New equipment will be installed at a cost of £38,000. One half of the amount is payable in March 19-7 and the remainder in August 19-7.

4. Two-thirds of the wages are payable in the month they fall due, and one-third a month later: wages for December 19-6 are estimated at £15,900.

5. £50,000 of total monthly overheads are payable in the month they occur, and the remainder one month later: total overheads for December 19-6 are expected to be £265,200.

6. The opening bank balance at 1 January 19-7 is expected to be an overdraft of £10,600

   (a) Using the information above, prepare the firm's cash budget for the period January-April, 19-7.   (16 marks)

   (b) Provide a statement to show those items in part (a) which would appear in a budgeted balance sheet as at 30 April 19-7.   (9 marks)

                                                                        (Total 25 marks)
                                                                        (LONDON)

3 The following is a summary of the balance sheet for G. White Ltd as at 31 May 1991.

	£	£
Fixed Assets at cost		65,000
Less depreciation to date		14,000
		51,000
Current Assets		
Stock	60,000	
Trade Debtors	35,000	
Bank	14,300	
	109,300	
Current Liabilities		
Trade Creditors	30,000	
		79,300
		130,300
Capital and Reserves		130,300

The company is in the process of preparing budgets for the three months ending 31 August 1991, and the following information is available.

(i) Budgeted sales (which provide a gross profit of 25% on cost) are:

	£
May	70,000
June	75,000
July	65,000
August	100,000
September	90,000

Half the sales are paid for in the month in which the sales are made and attract a 2% cash discount. The remainder are paid net the following month.

(ii) It has been company policy since January 1991 to arrange purchases, such that stock at the end of each month exactly covers sales for the following month. Half of the purchases are paid in the month received and the company have negotiated a $2\frac{1}{2}$% discount for prompt payment, the remainder are paid net the following month.

(iii) Expenses (excluding depreciation) are £8,400 per month, payable in the month they are incurred.

(iv) The company will be purchasing additional fixed assets costing £17,000 on 1 June 1991, with 50% payable in July and the balance payable in October 1991. Depreciation on all fixed assets is at the rate of 10% p.a. on cost (rates being charged from the date of purchase).

Required

(a) A cash budget for the three months ending 31 August 1991.   (13 marks)

(b) A budgeted trading and profit and loss account for the three months ending 31 August 1991, together with a balance sheet as at that date. (12 marks)

(c) Outline the main differences between a cash budget and a budgeted trading and profit and loss account. (6 marks)

(Total 31 marks)

(OXFORD)

4 Pankake Ltd provided the following summarised financial information for the year ended 30 April 1990:

Trading and profit and loss account for the year ended 30 April 1990

	£000s	£000s
Sales		2,000
less Cost of goods sold		1,449
Gross profit		551
Administrative expenses	180	
Selling and distributive expenses	130	
Depreciation of fixed assets	60	370
Net profit		181

Balance Sheet as at 30 April 1990

	£000s	£000s
50p ordinary shares fully paid		300
Retained earnings		175
		475
Fixed assets: at cost	500	
Less aggregate depreciation	180	320
Current assets		
Stocks	250	
Trade debtors	190	
Cash	20	
	460	
less current liabilities		
Trade creditors	110	
Accrued expenses	15	
Bank overdraft	180	
	305	155
		475

The company accountant provided the following additional information which will be used as the basis of the company's budget for the year ending 30 April 1991:

(1) The stock at 1 May 1989 was £164,000.

(2) Sales values are expected to be 30% higher than the year ended 30 April 1990. 40% of all sales will be for cash. The remainder will be on credit and occur at a uniform monthly rate. Credit customers will be allowed 3 months credit. The forecast gross profit margin on sales will be 30%.

(3) The average rate of stock turnover will be the same as the year ended 30 April 1990.

(4) Selling and distributive expenses will be 6% of all sales.

(5) Administrative expenses will increase by £20,000.

(6) Depreciation will continue to be provided at 10% of cost per annum. On 1 May 1990 further expenditure of £150,000 will be incurred on fixed assets. There will be no fixed asset disposals.

(7) Other forecast balances as at 30 April 1991:

	£000
Cash	20
Trade creditors	130
Accrued expenses	20
Bank overdraft	101

(8) No dividend will be declared for 1990/91. However there will be a bonus issue of one share for every share currently held. The issue will be made on 30 April 1991.

Required

(a) A forecast budget trading and profit and loss account for the year ending 30 April 1991.
(5 marks)

(b) A forecast budget balance sheet as at 30 April 1991. (9 marks)

(c) Explain why the preparation of forecast budget final accounts is regarded as a necessary part of the managerial control of a business. (8 marks)

(Total 22 marks)

(AEB)

5   Mtoto Ltd operate as wholesale 'cash and carry' stores and in addition to its main store have two other depots.

The company's summarised balance sheet as at 31 August 1991 was as follows.

	£	£		£	£
Fixed assets		549,600	Authorised and Issued Capital		
(at net book value)			450,000 £1 Ordinary shares.		
Current assets			Fully paid		450,000
Stock	399,900		Retained earnings at		
			1 Sept 1990	300,000	
Trade debtors	21,000	420,900	Less current year ended		
			31 Aug 1991 loss.	130,000	170,000
			Current liabilities		
			Trade (and other) creditors	110,500	
			Bank overdraft	240,000	350,500
		970,500			970,500

Over the past year the company has experienced increased competition and as a consequence reported a net trading loss for the year ended 31 August 1991.

The company has decided that in the new financial year tighter control must be exercised over cash resources.

The following information is available:

(1) All goods are purchased by the main store.

Purchases 1991

Actual		Forecast			
JUL	AUG	SEPT	OCT	NOV	DEC
£	£	£	£	£	£
55,800	61,200	64,300	41,000	46,000	41,800

Mtoto Ltd pays suppliers two months after the month of purchase.

Forecast purchases are being reduced since the managing director regarded current stock levels as too high.

In addition, shop-soiled stock which cost £20,000 is to be sold for cash in October. It is anticipated that this stock will be sold for £17,000. This sale is not included in the sales of note 2) below.

(2) All sales are on a cash basis only except for several important customers who trade only with Mtoto's main store.

Sales 1991

	Actual		Forecast			
	JUL	AUG	SEP	OCT	NOV	DEC
	£	£	£	£	£	£
Mainstore						
Cash sales	21,500	21,600	18,000	26,300	19,200	24,700
Credit sales	24,000	21,000	32,500	26,000	25,400	27,800
Depot 1	15,500	17,400	19,700	18,000	17,600	17,900
Depot 2	21,000	24,000	26,300	19,700	21,000	19,100

(3) Mtoto Ltd pays £9,500 fixed overhead costs per month.

(4) Wages and salaries are paid each month through a centralised payroll system.

Wages and salaries 1991

Actual			Forecast	
AUG	SEP	OCT	NOV	DEC
£	£	£	£	£
16,000	17,000	19,000	13,000	12,000

In October 10 staff were made redundant and are to receive their redundancy compensation of £12,000 in December. This amount is not included in the above figures.

(5) Other variable overhead charges are paid by Mtoto Ltd in the month following the month they are incurred.

Variable overhead charges 1991

AUG	SEP	OCT	NOV	DEC
£	£	£	£	£
5,600	6,800	6,100	7,400	6,900

(6) Plant surplus to requirement is to be sold in September for £26,500 cash. The plant cost £55,000 and depreciation to date is £20,000.

Required

(a) A detailed cash budget, on a month by month basis, for the first four months of the financial year ending 31 August 1992 for Mtoto Ltd. (13 marks)

(b) A report commenting on:
   (i) the current and forecast liquidity position. (7 marks)
   (ii) the action that Mtoto Ltd could take to attempt a return to a profit situation.
(5 marks)
(Total 25 marks)
(AEB)

6   Springtime Ltd own a retail store that sells clothes.

The company's summarised balance sheet as at 31 March 1992 was as follows.

	£000
Called-up capital	
200,000 £1 Ordinary shares fully paid	200
General reserve	150
Retained earnings	250
Current liabilities	90
	690
Fixed assets less depreciation	458
Current assets	
Stock and debtors	120
Balance at bank	112
	690

The company decided to open a branch store in a neighbouring town. The branch is to be opened on 1 May 1992 in newly acquired freehold premises which cost £100,000. Half of this cost will be paid on 1 May 1992, and the remainder on 1 July 1992. The refurbishment of these premises will cost £20,000, and this amount is due to be paid on 1 July 1992. All these amounts are paid by the company's main store.

Additional information:

(1) **1992**

	ACTUAL SALES			FORECAST SALES		
	FEB	MAR	APR	MAY	JUN	JUL
	£	£	£	£	£	£
Main store	160,000	150,500	153,000	149,500	158,000	161,000
Branch	–	–	–	8,000	19,000	24,000

Main store: cash from sales is received two months after the month of sale.

Branch: cash from sales is received one month after the month of sale.

The branch will operate its own bank current account and receipts from debtors will be banked each day. The account was opened on 1 April 1992 with an initial balance of £20,000.

(2) The following fixed costs are paid:

Main store £15,000 every month.
Branch £1,000 every month, except April.

As a cost transfer the company allocates £2,500 of the main store fixed costs every month (except April) to the branch.

(3) The company pays variable costs as follows:

	MAR	APR	MAY	JUN	JUL
	£	£	£	£	£
Main store	25,000	30,000	33,000	31,000	29,000
Branch	–	–	2,500	2,700	1,900

All variable costs are paid one month in arrears except that in May the branch is required to pay them in that month.

(4) The main store will be required to pay £5,000 legal costs on 1 July 1992 in respect of the new freehold premises.

(5) Staff salaries paid:

Main store £12,000 every month.
Branch £1,000 every month, except April.

(6) Springtime Ltd are due to pay an interim ordinary share dividend of 5% on 1 July 1992.

(7) All goods for re-sale are bought by the main store and are charged to the branch store at cost price.

	FEB	MAR	APR	MAY	JUN	JUL
	£	£	£	£	£	£
Goods purchased by Main store	61,000	58,000	153,000	48,000	49,500	152,000
Goods received at Branch store	–	–	8,000	12,000	23,000	24,000

Springtime Ltd receives two months credit on all of its clothing purchases. The branch remits payment for its goods to the main store by credit transfer at the end of the month of receipt.

(8) In order to fund further business development Springtime Ltd plan to issue £100,000 of 11% debentures at par on 1 July 1992. The issue is expected to be fully subscribed and the cash will be received on the same date.

(9) The branch store is scheduled to earn a 50% mark-up on cost.

Required

(a) Separate monthly cash budgets for each store for the four months ending 31 July 1992.
(15 marks)

(b) For the forecast period ending 31 July 1992:
  (i) A profit and loss statement for the branch;
  (ii) A report giving an assessment of the branch's expected profitability during this period.
(10 marks)
(Total 25 marks)
(AEB)

7   The following is the balance sheet of Lenn Steel at 31 December 1989:

		£	£
TANGIBLE FIXED ASSETS			
Premises		300,000	
Equipment		150,000	
Motor vehicles		12,350	
			462,350
Investments			21,000
CURRENT ASSETS			
Stocks:	Finished goods (500 units)	4,250	
	Raw materials	6,000	
Debtors		18,000	
Short-term investments		22,000	
		50,250	
CURRENT LIABILITIES			
Creditors:	Raw materials		
	(Nov £10,000 Dec £13,000)	23,000	
	Fixed expenses	900	
Bank overdraft		26,200	
		50,100	
WORKING CAPITAL			150
			483,500
CAPITAL		476,000	
LONG-TERM LOAN		7,500	
			483,500

The budgeted figures for the six months ending 30 June 1990 are as follows:

(i) Budgeted production in units:

	Jan	Feb	March	April	May	June
	4,000	5,000	4,500	3,500	4,000	4,500

(ii) Budgeted sales in units:

3,500	4,000	4,500	5,000	4,000	3,500

(iii) The selling price of all units is expected to be £10 per unit.

(iv) The variable cost of each unit is expected to be raw materials £6; overheads £2. The variable costs other than raw materials are paid in the month that they are incurred.

(v) Raw material purchases are expected to be:

	Jan	Feb	March	April	May	June
	£28,500	£40,500	£36,300	£28,650	£31,500	£37,500

Purchases are all on credit and are paid for in the second month after the month of purchase.

(vi) Fifty per cent of all sales are expected to be for cash. The remainder of the customers are expected to pay during the month following the month of sale.

(vii) The fixed expenses are £26,400 per year; they are spread evenly over the year and are always paid in the month following the month in which incurred.

(viii) Dividends of £2,100 are expected to be received from the investments in May.

Required

(a) prepare a cash budget of Lenn Steel's business for the six months ended 30 June 1990.

(10 marks)

(b) prepare a budgeted trading and profit and loss account for Lenn Steel for the six months ended 30 June 1990. (6 marks)

(c) comment on the action that management might take in the light of the cash budget that you have prepared under a) above. (4 marks)

(Total 20 marks)

(NI)

8 Chan Heng is about to purchase a furniture shop owned presently by John Robertson. He will acquire all the assets and liabilities of Robertson's business with the exception of cash and bank balances. He will commence trading on 1 July 1995.

Robertson has given Chan an estimate of his working capital as at 30 June 1995. The estimate is as follows:

	£
Current Assets	
Stock	4,000
Debtors	6,000
	10,000
Current liabilities	
Creditors	3,000
	£7,000

After purchasing the business, Chan will invest £8000 in the business. He intends to withdraw this money from a private building society account.

Chan's opening debtors are expected to settle their debts in July. Subsequently debtors are expected to settle their accounts in the month following the sale. All purchases and sales will be on credit. The opening creditors will be paid in July. Chan intends to pay his creditors two months after purchasing his stocks of furniture.

The selling price of all furniture will be a uniform cost plus 25%.

Chan will purchase a computer for the business in July 1995 for £1400; he will pay cash on 9 July. He believes he will use this computer for 2 years and will then trade it in for a larger model. The trade-in price should be £200.

All expenses will be paid in the month after they have been incurred.

The estimated pattern of costs and revenues is:

Month	Purchases	Sales	Expenses
	£	£	£
July	6,000	10,000	7,000
August	10,000	11,250	5,000
September	11,000	12,500	4,000
October	14,000	20,000	4,000

Required

(a) Prepare the following budgets for each of the four months ending 31 October 1995:
  (i) cash budget; (7 marks)
  (ii) stock budget; (8 marks)
  (iii) debtors' budget. (7 marks)

(b) Prepare Chan Heng's forecast trading and profit and loss account for the four months ending 31 October 1995. (10 marks)

(c) Prepare an extract of the balance sheet as at 31 October 1995 which clearly shows in detail the forecast working capital. (6 marks)

(d) Explain briefly why business budgets may be prepared. (6 marks)

(e) Using liquidity ratios, comment on the forecasted liquidity of Chan Heng's business on 31 October 1995. (6 marks)

(Total 50 marks)

(AEB)

9 The following information is available from the books of Abbington Ltd. for the financial year ended 31 October 1993.

Trading and Profit and Loss Account for the year ended 31 October 1993

	£000		£000
Cost of goods sold	910	Sales	1,300
Gross profit	390		
	1,300		1,300

Administration costs	70	Gross profit	390
Selling and distribution costs	40		
Financial charges	10		
Depreciation of fixed assets	30		
Net profit	240		
	390		390

Balance sheet as at 31 October 1993

	£000	£000	£000		£000	£000
Fixed assets				Issued capital		
at cost			1,100	50p ordinary shares,		
less aggregate				fully paid		400
depreciation			230	11% £1 preference shares,		
			870	fully paid		50
						450
				Share premium		200
				Retained earnings		700
Current assets				Current liabilities		
Stock		120		Trade creditors	100	
Trade debtors	100			Accrued expenses	20	120
less provision for						
doubtful debts	10	90				
Balance at bank		390	600			
			1,470			1,470

The newly appointed managing director decided that in order to increase profits it is absolutely necessary to control costs. Thus he decided to introduce budgetary control.

The following forecast information is available for the year ending 31 October 1994.

(1) The sales are forecast to increase to £1.6m for the year.

(2) A more efficient buying programme is expected to increase the gross profit/sales ratio to 32%.

(3) In order to finance further expansion as the recession recedes, a rights issue of one new ordinary share for each two shares currently held is to be made on 1 August 1994. It is expected that the issue will be fully subscribed and the issue will also be underwritten.

The issue price is 65p per share, fully paid.

(4) Despite inflationery pressures the managing director is determined to reduce costs. The forecast level of costs is:

Administration costs will be 5% of forecast sales. Selling and distribution costs will be $3\frac{1}{2}$% of forecast sales. There will be no change in financial charges as compared to 1992/3.

(5) Owing to the recession bad debts are expected to rise substantially and thus the provision for doubtful debts is to be increased to 15% of debtors. Forecast trade debts as at 31 October 1994 are £150,000.

(6) A general reserve will be created on 31 December 1994 of £300 000.

(7) Land and buildings which cost £350,000 (Nil depreciation as at 31 October 1993) are to be written down to £200,000 due to falling prices in the property market.

(8) Dividends during 1993/94 will be restricted to paying:
(i) the preference dividend for the year;
(ii) a final ordinary dividend of 3p per share, but only on the shares issued before 1 August 1994.
The dividends would be paid on 1 January 1995.

(9) All fixed assets other than land and buildings will be depreciated at 10% pere annum based on the cost of the assets held at the end of the financial year. There are to be no additions or disposals of fixed assets during 1993/94.

(10) Other forecast balances as at 31 October 1994.

	£000
Expense creditors	17.00
Trade creditors	97.00
Stock	290.00
Balance at bank	760.50

Required

(a) A budgeted trading, profit and loss and appropriation account for the year ending 31 October 1994
             (18 marks)

(b) A budgeted balance sheet as at 31 October 1994.
             (16 marks)

(c) Identify ways in which profits could be increased by making better use of forecast current assets.
             (16 marks)

             (Total 50 marks)

             (AEB)

22 Standard cost and variance analysis

Chapter objectives

Questions on standard costs and variance analysis cover:-
- ☐ explanation of the concept of standard costing
- ☐ advantages of standard costing
- ☐ flexing budgets
- ☐ calculating sales, direct labour, direct materials and overhead variances
- ☐ explanations for variances and possible relationships between different kinds of variances

Standard costs

Definitions

Standard Costs

Predetermined calculations of the components which contribute to the costs of a business under given conditions.

Standard Costing

The use of standard costs, principally in the preparation of budgets for the purpose of controlling operations and functions of a business through variance analysis. Standard costs are also used in the production of estimates, quotations, etc.

Standard Time

The time, in minutes or hours, in which a given quantity of work should be completed. In addition to the basic time required for completing the work, allowance is included in the standard for contingencies and permitted relaxation. Standard time is, paradoxically, a measure of work, not of time. Standard hours produced = SHP

Overhead Absorption Rate (OAR)

Overheads are 'absorbed' into total costs by the application of an Overhead Absorption Rate. The rate is calculated by dividing period budgeted overheads by the Standard Hours (or by some other measurement of activity such as units or weights produced) for the period.

Variance

The difference between actual revenue or costs and budgeted (or planned or standard) revenue or costs.

Variance Analysis

The examination of variances using calculations to discover the factors which have contributed to the variances, and the magnitude and nature of those contributions. Variances are described as 'favourable' (F) if they contribute to the profitability of a business. If they diminish the profitability, they are described as 'adverse' (A). These are the usual descriptions, but others may be used in practice.

Flexible Budget

An indispensible tool for variance analysis; flexible budgets recognise the different behaviours of fixed and variable costs at varying levels of activity.

22.1 Standard costs

One way of assessing how well or badly a business is managed is in financial terms. Managers are judged, depending upon what their responsibilities are, by revenue earned, control of costs or profit made. This is known as responsibility accounting. Budgets are set for revenue centres, cost centres and profit centres. A good manager may be judged by the way he operates within his budget. This has been described in the previous chapter as *responsibility accounting*.

Budgets should be statements of expected revenue, costs and profit for future periods based on efficient operations. Budgets can be prepared using pre-determined standards for revenue and costs. The standards act as 'benchmarks' against which actual revenue earned and costs incurred may be compared.

Standards are set for costs using appropriate methods. Standard costs for materials are based upon current prices, amended if necessary to take account of future price increases and discounts for bulk purchases. It is also necessary to decide the quantity of each material which should be used in each unit of production.

Standard costs for labour will be based upon the hourly or weekly rates of pay for each grade (unskilled, semi-skilled or skilled) of labour. Account should also be taken of any foreseen pay increases. The amount of time taken to perform tasks is measured (work measurement) and, where possible, more efficient methods introduced (method study).

Three types of standard are possible:

1 Ideal standards. These are based upon 'ideal' conditions in which there is no wastage of materials, all workers work at maximum efficiency and no idle time occurs while machines are being serviced, or production lines are being set up. These assumptions are not realistic. Such standards are not likely to be met and do not, as a result, motivate people.

   Ideal standards can be useful, however, to reveal the extent to which present performance falls short of the ideal; management may be encouraged to examine areas of present performance to see where some improvement may be possible.

2 Current standards are based on existing levels of performance and do not offer any inducement to improve present levels of efficiency. Current standards may be the only ones to use when present conditions make it virtually impossible to improve labour efficiency or material usage.

3 Attainable standards are those which make allowances for normal wastage of materials and normal idle time, but still present management and employees with a reasonable challenge to meet the standards. These standards motivate workers in the efficient use of time and materials and economic purchasing.

Budgetary control and standard costing are very closely linked in a well organised company; the former cannot function well without the latter. Nevertheless, it should be appreciated that while budgetary control applies to departments or other types of cost centres, standard costing is a technique which focuses on products, processes and operations.

Advantages of a standard costing system

1. Budgets are easier to prepare and are more realistic if they are prepared in conjunction with a system of standard costing.

2. The reasons for differences between actual expenditure and budgeted expenditure are easier to trace with a system of standard costing and variance analysis (which will be explained later in this chapter.)

3. Standard costing is an essential aspect of reponsibility accounting.

4. A knowledge of the standard costs of a business for materials and operations makes the preparation of estimates of costs of new products and quotations for orders easier and more reliable.

22.2 Flexing the budget

Comparison of actual performance with budget requires comparison of 'like with like'. If actual activity differs from budgeted activity, the budget must be 'flexed' to produce one for the actual level of activity.

22.2.1 Example 1: flexing a simple budget

A budget has been prepared for the production of 1,000 units of X in March. The actual output for March was 1,100 units.

Using the budget given below for the production of 1,000 units you are required to flex the budget for 1,100 units of X.

		Budget for 1,000 units £	Budget for 1,100 units. £
Direct materials		6,000	6,600
Direct labour		15,000	16,500
Production overheads	– variable	9,000	9,900
	– fixed	22,000	22,000
Selling and distribution expenses	– variable	10,000	11,000
	– fixed	20,000	20,000
Administration costs			
	– fixed	8,000	8,000
		90,000	94,000

Example 2: a slightly more difficult example

A budget was prepared for the production of Bantam Bits at output levels of 1,000 and 2,000 Bits respectively, as shown below. Actual production was 1,800 Bits.

You are required to prepare a budget for the production of 1,800 Bantam Bits.

Answer	Budget (1,000) £	Budget (2,000) £	Budget (1,800) £
Direct materials	21,000	42,000	37,800
Direct labour	35,000	70,000	63,000
Production overheads	60,000	80,000	76,000
Selling and distribution	45,000	60,000	57,000
Administration	29,000	29,000	29,000
	190,000	281,000	262,800

Tutorial note: Production overheads and selling and distribution expenses do not vary proportionately to production. The increases in these costs for an additional 1,000 units are: Production costs £20,000; selling and distribution £15,000. These are the variable elements in these costs per 1,000 units. The balances of £40,000 of Production overheads and £30,000 of selling and distribution expenses are fixed costs.

Therefore: Production costs for 1,800 Bantam Bits = £40,000 + (1.8 × £20,000) = £76,000

Selling and distribution = £30,000 + (1.8 × £15,000) = £57,000

22.2.2 Exercise 1: flexing a budget

The budget for the production of 200,000 packets of 'Brekkinuts' was as follows:

		£'000
Direct materials		10
Direct labour		12
Production overheads	– variable	5
	– fixed	6
Selling and distribution		11
Administration		8
		52

10% of the Selling and distribution expenses are variable; all Administration costs are fixed.

The actual production of 'Brekkinuts' was 190,000 packets.

You are required to prepare a budget for the production of 190,000 packets of 'Brekkinuts'.

22.3 Sales variances

The variances are:

Volume variance: Master budget sales – Flexible budget sales (MBS – FBS)

Price variance: Flexible budget sales – actual sales (FBS – AS)

22.3.1 Example: a budget for the sales of Product 'Q' was as follows:

1,000 units of Product 'Q' at £12 per unit: £12,000

1,300 units were sold for total revenue of £15,200.

Find the volume and price variances for the actual sales.

Answer

Flexed budget: 1,300 units at £12 each = £15,600

Volume variance

	£	
MBS	12,000	
FBS	15,600	
	3,600	(F)

Price variance

	£	
FBS	15,600	
AS	15,200	
	400	(A)

Summary:

	£	
Volume variance	3,600	(F)
Price variance	400	(A)
Total variance (MBS – AS)	3,200	(F)

22.3.2 Exercise 1: calculation of sales variances

Reflections Ltd. produce 'Car Shine' polish. The budgeted sales for 19-2 were 150,000 tins at £3 a tin.

Actual sales of 'Car Shine' polish for 19-2 were 148,600 tins which produced total revenue of £448,950.

Required

Calculations of the sales variances for the sales of 'Car Shine' polish for the year 19-2.

22.4 Total variances – costs

TOTAL COST VARIANCE: Total costs per Master Budget (MBTC)
                      less Actual total costs (ATC)

The total cost variance will be explained in broad terms by the following variances, which will in turn be explained by sub-variances.

QUANTITY VARIANCE: Total costs per master budget (MBTC)
                      less Total costs per flexible budget (FBTC)

Once the total cost and quantity variances have been calculated, all the other variances will be calculated using the flexed budget. There will be no further use for the master budget as far as the calculations are concerned.

In all the calculations of variances that follow, deduct 'actual' from 'budget'; a positive remainder will indicate a favourable variance, and a negative remainder will indicate an adverse variance.

TOTAL DIRECT LABOUR VARIANCE:

                      Direct labour per flexed budget (FBDL)
                      less Actual direct labour (ADL)

TOTAL DIRECT MATERIALS VARIANCE:

Direct materials per flexed budget (FBDM)
less Actual direct materials (ADM)

* TOTAL OVERHEAD VARIANCE:

Total overheads per flexed budget (FBTO)
less Actual total overheads (ATO)

* This variance may be split between fixed overhead variance (FBTFO–ATFO) and variable overhead variance (FBTVO – ATVO)

TOTAL COST VARIANCE =   Quantity variance (F) or (A)
plus or minus Total Labour variance (F) or (A)
plus or minus Total Direct Materials variance (F) or (A)
plus or minus Total Overhead variance(s) (F) or (A)

22.4.1 Example

Meniss Ltd. manufactures skateboards. The budget for March19-3 for the production of 4,000 skateboards was as follows:

	£
Direct materials	5,000
Direct labour	12,000
Overheads – variable	6,000
fixed	8,000
	31,000

4,400 skateboards were produced in March 19–3 and the actual expenditure was as follows:

	£
Direct materials	5,590
Direct labour	13,120
Overheads – variable	6,800
fixed	7,750
	33,260

You are required to calculate the main variances for March 19–3.

Answer

Flexed budget for 4,400 skateboards:

	£
Direct materials	5,500
Direct labour	13,200
Overheads –variable	6,600
fixed	8,000
	33,300

Total cost variance (MBTC – ATC) = £(31,000 – 33,260) =	£2,260	(A)
Quantity variance (MBTC – FBTC) = £(31,000 – 33,300) =	£2,300	(A)
Total direct materials variance = (FBDM – ADM) = £(5,500 – 5,590) =	£90	(A)
Total direct labour variance = (FBDL – ADL) = £(13,200 – 13,120) =	£80	(F)
Total variable overheads variance = (FBTVO – ATVO) = £(6,600 – 6,800) =	£200	(A)
Total fixed overheads variance = (FBTFO – ATFO) = £(8,000 – 7,750) =	£250	(F)
	£2,260	(A)

22.4.2 Exercise: calculation of total variances

Laser, Digit and Co. produce compact disc players. Their budget for April 19–4 and the actual outturn were as follows:

	Budgeted production	
	1,500 players	Actual 1,800 players
	£	£
Direct materials	90,000	110,000
Direct labour	45,000	52,500
Overheads – variable	42,000	55,000
fixed	72,000	70,000
	249,000	287,500

Required

An analysis of the total cost variance for the production of CD players in April 19-4.

22.5 Materials and labour sub-variances

The total variances for material and labour may be analysed into sub-variances. These sub-variances provide further information about the underlying causes of the total variances. For example, a material variance may arise because (i) the quantity of material used was more or less than the budgeted quantity, and/or (ii) the actual price paid for the material differed from the budgeted price. Similarly, the actual cost of direct wages may differ from the flexed budget because (i) the work force was more or less efficient than expected and took more or less than the budgeted hours for the level of output achieved, and/or (ii) the wage rate actually paid differed from the budgeted rate.

The total direct material variance may therefore be analysed into usage and price variances, and the total direct wage variance may be analysed into efficiency and rate variances.

Variance analysis is a form of 'responsibility' accounting because it directs attention to the departments and managers responsible for the variances. This is a point to be borne in mind because it not only explains the purpose of calculating the variances, but it will help in calculating variances correctly.

A variance which increases profit, because actual cost is less than budgeted cost, is a favourable variance. If actual cost is more than budget, profit is reduced and the variance is adverse. As with total variances, deduct 'actuals' from budget in every case; when 'actual' is less than budget the remainder will be positive and indicate that the variance is favourable (F); conversely, an 'actual' which is greater than budget will produce a negative remainder, indicating that the variance is adverse (A).

The sub variances will be explained using the information already given for Meniss Ltd. in example 22.3.1 with further detail added.

The budget for direct materials and direct labour for March for the production of 4,000 skateboards was as follows:

	£
Direct materials (4,000 kilos at £1.25 per kilo)	5,000
Direct labour (1,500 hours at £8 per hour)	12,000
	17,000

4,400 skateboards were produced in March and the actual expenditure was as follows:

	£
Direct materials (4,300 kilos at £1.30 per kilo)	5,590
Direct labour (1,600 hours at £8.20 per hour)	13,120
	18,710

The flexed budget for 4,400 skateboards is

	£
Direct materials (4,400 kilos at £1.25 per kilo)	5,500
Direct labour (1,650 hours at £8 per hour)	13,200
	18,700

Direct materials usage and price variances

Direct material usage variance. This shows the effect on profit of using more or less material than should be expected for the level of output achieved.

The formula used for this variance is (SM – AM)SP
    where SM = standard quantity of materials
        AM = actual quantity of materials used,
    and SP = standard price

	kilos	
Standard materials (SM)	4,400	
Actual materials (AM)	4,300	
Variance (favourable)	100	(F)
Standard price per kilo (SP)	£1.25	
Direct material usage variance (100 × £1.25)	£125	(F)

The standard price is used for this variance. The production (or works) manager is responsible for ensuring that material is used economically, but is not responsible for the price paid for the material; that is the responsibility of the Buying Dept.

    Direct materials price variance. This shows the effect on profit of paying more or less for material than the price used in the budget

The formula used for this variance is (SP – AP)AM
    where SP = standard price
        AP = actual price paid,
        AM = actual quantity of materials used,

	£	
Standard price (SP) per kilo	1.25	
Actual price (AP) per kilo	1.30	
Variance (adverse) per kilo	0.05	(A)
Actual materials (AM)	4,300	kilos
Direct materials price variance (£0.05 × 4,300)	£215	(A)

The usage and price variances = the total materials variance:

	£	
Usage variance	125	(F)
Price variance	215	(A)
Total materials variance	£90	(A)

Direct labour efficiency and rate variances

Direct labour efficiency variance. This shows the effect on profit of the actual hours worked and paid for being different from the standard hours

The formula used is (SH – AH)SR
    Where SH = standard hours
        AH = actual hours worked
    and SR = standard rate of pay

	Hours	
Standard hours (SH)	1,650	
Actual hours (AH)	1,600	
Variance (favourable)	50	(F)
Standard rate per hour (SR)	£8.00	
Direct labour efficiency variance (50 × £8.00)	= £400	(F)

The standard rate (SR) is used to calculate the efficiency variance because the production (or works) manager is responsible for the hours worked (efficiency) but he is not responsible for the hourly rate actually paid; that is the responsibility of the Personnel Dept.

    Direct labour rate variance. This shows the effect on profit of a difference between the actual hourly rate paid and the standard rate.

The formula is: (SR – AR)AH
    Where SR = standard rate of pay
        AR = actual rate paid
    and AH = actual hours worked.

	£	
Standard rate (SR) per hour	8.00	
Actual rate (AR) per hour	8.20	
Variance (adverse) per hour	0.20	(A)
Actual hours (AH)	1,600	
Direct labour rate variance (£0.20 × 1,600)	£320	(A)

The efficiency and rate variances = the total material variance:

	£	
Efficiency variance	400	(F)
Rate variance	320	(A)
Total labour variance	80	(F)

22.6 Overhead sub-variances

Variances may be calculated separately for variable overheads and fixed overheads. Alternatively, variances may be calculated for total overheads. Since the latter are more likely to be required than the former, they will be dealt with first. Even if detailed calculations are not required, the causes of overhead variances should be understood.

It is important to remember that overheads are absorbed into total cost by the application of overhead absorption rates (OARs) as explained in chapter 18.

Standard hours (or minutes) of production

The budgeted level of activity is usually stated in standard hours of production (SHP). A 'standard hour' (or a standard minute) is not a unit of time but the quantity of work achievable at standard performance, expressed in terms of a standard unit of work in-a standard period of time.

Total overhead variances

Total overhead variances are calculated for the combined fixed and variable overheads.

Total overhead total variance

Calculation: actual total overhead
          less   actual SHP × OAR

The total overhead total variance may be analysed into expenditure, volume and efficiency variances.

Overhead expenditure variance

This variance is the difference between the overhead actually incurred and the overhead that should have been incurred.

Calculation: actual total overheads
          less   flexed budgeted total overhead*

* It must be remembered that while fixed overheads do not, in theory, vary with the level of activity, variable overheads do vary. The budgeted overhead must therefore be flexed.

Overhead volume variance

This variance is the difference between the flexed budgeted overhead and the overhead recovered in the hours worked.

Calculation: flexed budgeted total overhead
          less   actual labour hours × OAR

Overhead efficiency variance

This variance is the difference between the overhead recovered in the hours actually worked and the overhead recovery for the quantity of work done in the time.

Calculation: actual labour hours × OAR
          less   actual SHP × OAR

Example

Kite Ltd.'s budgeted and actual overhead and levels of activity for March are as follows:

	Budget	Actual
Fixed overheads	£68,600	£70,340
Variable overheads	£23,100	£24,340
Labour hours	2,800*	2,780
Standard hours of production (SHP)	2,800*	2,840

* these will normally be the same for budget purposes.

It is first necessary to flex the budget for the variable overheads.

The fixed overhead absorption rate is $\dfrac{£68,600}{2,800}$ = £24.50

The variable overhead absorption rate is $\dfrac{£23,100}{2,800}$ = £8.25.

Therefore the total overhead absorption rate is £(24.50 + 8.25) = £32.75

Variable overhead flexed for the actual hours worked is £8.25 × 2,780 = £22,935

The flexed budget for overheads is £(68,600 + 22,935) = £91,535.

Actual total overheads = actual variable overheads (as above) £24,340 + actual fixed overheads (as above) £70,340 = £94,680;

Overhead total variance

			£	
Calculation:		actual total overheads	94,680	
	less	actual SHP × OAR (2840 × £32.75)	93,010	
			1,670	(A)

Overhead expenditure variance

			£	
Calculation:		actual total overheads	94,680	
	less	budgeted total overheads	91,535	
			3,145	(A)

Overhead volume variance

			£	
Calculation:		budgeted total overheads	91,535	
	less	actual labour hours × OAR		
		(2,780 × £32.75)	91,045	
			490	(A)

Overhead efficiency variance

			£	
Calculation:		actual labour hours × OAR	91,045	
	less	actual SHP × OAR (2840 × £32.75)	93,010	
			1,965	(F)

The overhead expenditure, volume and efficiencey variances = the total overhead variance:

	£	
Expenditure variance	3,145	(A)
Volume variance	490	(A)
Efficiency variance	1,965	(F)
Total variance	1,670	(A)

Variable overhead variances

The total variable overhead variance may be analysed into expenditure and efficiency variances. Using the data for Kite Ltd. (VOAR = variable overhead absorption rate as calculated above.)

Total Variable Overhead Variance

			£	
Calculation:		actual variable overheads	24,340	
	−	actual SHP × VOAR (2,840 × £8.25)	23,430	
			910	(A)

Variable Overhead Expenditure Variance

			£	
Calculation:		actual variable overheads	24,340	
	−	actual labour hours × VOAR (2,780 × £8.25)	22,935	
			1,405	(A)

Variable overhead efficiency variance

		£	
Calculation:	actual labour hours × VOAR (as above)	22,935	
−	actual SHP × VOAR (2,840 × £8.25)	23,430	
		495	(F)

Fixed overhead variances

The total fixed overhead variance may be analysed into
> fixed overhead expenditure variance, and
> fixed overhead volume variance *

* the fixed overhead volume variance may be further analysed into:
> fixed overhead capacity variance
and   fixed overhead efficiency variance

Using the data for Kite Ltd. (FOAR = fixed overhead absorption rate as calculated above.)

Total fixed overhead variance

		£	
Calculation:	actual expenditure	70,340	
less	actual SHP × FOAR (2,840 × £24.50)	69,580	
		760	(A)

Fixed overhead expenditure variance

		£	
Calculation:	actual expenditure	70,340	
less	budgeted expenditure	68,600	
		1,740	(A)

Fixed overhead capacity variance

		£	
Calculation:	budgeted expenditure	68,600	
less	actual labour hours × FOAR		
	(2,780 × £24.50)	68,110	
		490	(A)

Fixed overhead efficiency variance

		£	
Calculation:	actual labour hours × FOAR (as above)	68,110	
less	actual SHP × FOAR (2,840 × £24.50)	69,580	
		1,470	(F)

22.7 Explanations for variances

When required to suggest causes of variances in examination questions, make sure your suggestions are reasonable and avoid making assertions which cannot be substantiated from information supplied in the questions. Variance analysis, particularly at the stage required at this level of study, only indicates areas where management should direct their further attention in order to decide what corrective action needs to be taken.

It is important to realise the possible inter-relationships between different variances.

A common cause of variances unfortunately lies in the fact that all too often there are inherent errors in the budget preparation.A favourable labour rate variance may arise because of the employment of a lower grade of labour than that embodied in the budget; but that may be more than offset by adverse labour efficiency and materials usage variances.

A favourable materials price variance may indicate that materials have been purchased 'on the cheap'; the materials in question may prove to be sub-standard as a result, which may reflect in a substantial adverse materials usage variance and an adverse labour efficiency variance.

An adverse labour rate variance may be the result of a wage award which was not foreseen when the budget was prepared. This is most unlikely to be reflected in the workers' performance and would be unlikely, in itself, to reflect in other variances. But if the adverse variance is caused by the employment of more highly skilled workers than those envisaged in the budget, their improved performance may be expected to show in other favourable variances (e.g. usage, efficiency).

A little imagination is helpful when commenting on variances, but the comments must stand up to reason, in the context of the facts, or absence of facts, in the question.

It is important that management be informed about variances as soon as possible after the event in order that they can take necessary remedial action without delay.

'Management by crisis' applies to managers who spend their time 'fighting fires' instead of 'preventing fires'. They are unaware of approaching difficulties until they are hit by crises, and then have to spend all their time and energy getting out of the difficulties; by which time the business has suffered.

Management by exception;. Too much detailed information given to managers may be counter productive. They need not know specially about items that are favourable compared with budget; but they do need to know about those that are adversely deviating from budget so that they can concentrate on the important matters that require their particular expertise. It may be desirable, in fact, not to report any variance which is not really significant.

Permanent, significant changes in factors upon which a budget is based may require that the budget be revised; an out-of-date budget is of no use to management.

22.8 Activity, capacity and efficiency ratios

Variances are calculated in absolute terms, that is, in unqualified numbers which have been calculated without any attempt to relate them to other relevant aspects of the business.

Ratios serve to show relationships which exist between aspects of a business which share some characteristics in common, for example, budgeted labour hours and actual labour hours worked.

The ratios explained below are, in fact, expressed as percentages to make them easier to comprehend.

Activity ratio expresses actual standard hours of production as a percentage of budgeted labour hours. (Bear in mind that budgeted labour hours are normally the same as budgeted standard hours of production.)

Calculation: $\dfrac{\text{Actual standard hours produced}}{\text{budgeted labour hours}} \times 100$

Capacity ratio expresses actual labour hours worked as a percentage of budgeted labour hours

Calculation: $\dfrac{\text{Actual labour hours worked}}{\text{budgeted labour hours}} \times 100$

Efficiency ratio expresses actual standard hours produced as a percentage of actual labour hours worked.

Calculation: $\dfrac{\text{Actual standard hours produced}}{\text{budgeted labour hours worked}} \times 100$

Example

The relevant data extracted from the example of Kite Ltd. is:

Budgeted labour hours	2,800
Actual labour hours worked	2,780
Standard hours actually produced	2,840

Activity ratio

$\dfrac{\text{Actual standard hours produced}}{\text{budgeted labour hours}} \times 100 = \dfrac{2,840}{2,800} \times 100 = 101.43\%$

Capacity ratio

$\dfrac{\text{Actual hours worked}}{\text{budgeted labour hours}} \times 100 = \dfrac{2,780}{2,800} \times 100 = 99.29\%$

Efficiency ratio

$\dfrac{\text{Actual standard hours produced}}{\text{actual labour hours worked}} \times 100 = \dfrac{2,840}{2,780} \times 100 = 102.16\%$

Point to note

Activity ratio = capacity ratio × efficiency ratio: 101.4

Key points to remember

1. Standard costs are predetermined costs which are possible of attainment under conditions of an acceptable degree of efficiency.

2. Standard costs are used in the preparation of budgets and in preparing quotations for contracts.

3. Flexible budgets recognise the different behaviours of fixed and variable costs as activity levels vary, and in that way, allow actual performance to be compared with budget at various levels of activity and meaningful variances to be calculated.

4. It may be necessary to flex the budget in examination questions.

5. Memorise all the variances covered in this chapter and the method of calculating each one.

6. Be prepared, not only to suggest reasons for variances, but also to say how they may relate to each other.

7. Variances indicate to management areas where further enquiry may be necessary before any decision can be made about remedial action to be taken.

Common errors

1. failure to flex budgets

2. inability to calculate variances

3. inadequate, poorly expressed explanations as to possible causes of variances and lack of appreciation of the relationships between variances.

Questions

Fully worked examination questions

1. (a) Examine three different levels of activity which may be used when setting activity levels for standard costing. Identify the strengths and weaknesses of each   (7 marks)

   (b) Calculate material and labour variances from the following:

	Standard	Actual
Price of material (£ tonne)	6.40	6.30
Usage of material (tonnes)	570	610
Wage rate (£ per hour)	3.42	3.22
Direct labour hours	120	140

   (4 marks)

   (c) State with reasons those variances in (b) above which the production manager may be able to control.   (4 marks)

   (Total 15 marks)
   (LONDON)

   Answer

   (a) See 22.1

   (b) Material price variance £(6.40 − 6.30) × 610   =   £61   (F)
   Material usage variance (570 − 610) × £6.40   =   £256   (A)
   Wage rate variance £(3.42 − 3.22) × 140   =   £28   (F)
   Direct labour efficiency variance (120 − 140) × £3.42

   =   £68.40   (A)

(c) Production manager should be able to control material usage variances and direct labour efficiency variances because he is responsible for economy in material usage and efficient working of production staff. He is not responsible for material price variances (for which Buying dept. is responsible) nor for wage rate variances (Personnel Dept. negotiates wages agreements).

2. (a) Brunswick Products uses a system of standard costing. The following details relate to December 19-8:

Department

	Blasting	Painting
Direct labour hours worked	3,400	9,200
Direct wages earned	£12,648	£38,272
Units produced	900	2,400
Standard hours per unit	4	3
Standard hourly wage rate	£3.70	£4.00

For each department, you are required to calculate:
(i) the standard direct labour cost per unit;
(ii) the direct wages (direct labour) variance;
(iii) the direct wages **rate** variance;
(iv) the direct wages **efficiency** variance. (8 marks)

(b) What do the answers to (a) above indicate to the production manager of Brunswick Products about the performance of the two departments and why? (7 marks)

(Total 15 marks)
(LONDON)

Answer

Workings

Actual rate paid:	Blasting £12,648/3400 = £3.72
	Painting £38,272/9,200 = £4.16
Standard hours produced:	Blasting 900 × 4 = 3,600
	Painting 2,400 × 3 = 7,200
Standard wages:	Blasting 900 × 4 × £3.70 = £13,320
	Painting 2,400 × 3 × £4 = £28,800

Department

	Blasting	Painting
(i) Standard direct labour cost p.u		
(4 × £3.70)	£14.80	
(3 × £4)		£12
(ii) Direct labour variance £(13,320 – 12,648)	£672 (F)	
£(28,800 – 38,272)		£9,472 (A)
(iii) Direct wages rate variance		
£(3.70 – 3.72) × 3,400	£68 (A)	
£(4.00 – 4.16) × 9,200		£1,472 (A)
(iv) Direct wages efficiency variance		
(3,600 – 3,400) × £3.70	£740 (F)	
(7,200 – 9,200) × £4		£8,000 (A)

(b) Blasting dept. is producing results better than budget (£672 F). Although the wage rate variance is worse than budget (£68A) it is more than offset by the efficiency variance (£740F). This may indicate either (i) the labour force is more highly skilled than the budgeted labour force, but is more than compensating for the increased cost by more efficient performance, or (ii) a larger than expected wage award has resulted in a more highly motivated workforce and productivity has improved as a result.

The Painting dept. is performing worse than expected (£9,472A). Both the direct labour rate variance and the efficiency variance are worse than budget. Perhaps the rate variance suggests that a wage award has been made but it was less than the workers had expected, their morale is still not very high and it is affecting their efficiency. Perhaps there are other factors such as working conditions which are adversely affecting staff morale.

Further examination questions

1 J. Wilkinson Limited uses a system of standard costing. The following information relates to the week ending 4 January 1992, when standard output was achieved:

	Standard	Actual
Price of materials (litre)	£1.50	£1.60
Usage of materials (litre)	220	200
Labour hours worked	45	48
Wage rate/hour	£5.30	£5.00

(a) From the figures above calculate the following. In each case state clearly whether the variance is adverse or favourable.
  (i)   the total labour variance;
  (ii) the wage rate variance;
  (iii) the labour efficiency variance;
  (iv) the total materials variance;
  (v)   the materials price variance;
  (vi) the materials usage variance.   (6 marks)

(b) In what circumstances is
  (i) a favourable labour variance; and
  (ii) a favourable materials variance not always desirable?   (9 marks)

(Total 15 marks)
(LONDON)

2 (a) What is meant by the terms:
  (i)   a fixed budget;
  (ii) a flexible budget;
  (iii) flexing a budget?   (7 marks)

(b) **Blending Department**
Manufacturing Overheads Budget: January – June 1993

	Weekly production (000's litres)			
	3	4	5	6
Variable overheads £000	6.5	7.0	7.7	8.6
Fixed overheads £000	3.5	3.5	3.5	3.5
Hours worked/week	200	250	300	350

Calculate:
  (i) the overhead rates per hour for each level of production;
  (ii) the cost of 100 litres of product produced in *week* 1 when 3,000 litres were produced, and in *week* 2 when 5,000 litres were produced. On each occasion, the labour costs were £575, and the material costs were £1,245. Assume that during each week, the 100 litres took 10 hours to produce.   (8 marks)

(Total 15 marks)
(LONDON)

3 The Duke Manufacturing Company had decided to implement a system of standard costing as from the beginning of its new financial year, beginning on 1 March 1992. It now has the actual results of its operation for the first month to compare with its standard figures.

Standard costs:

Materials per unit	5 kg at £4 per kg
Labour per unit	2 hours at £6 per hour
Variable overheads	2 hours at £3 per hour
Fixed overheads	2 hours at £2 per hour
Production and Sales per month	2,000 units.

The standard selling price allows for a standard profit margin of 20%.

Actual results for the month have been:

Production	2,200 units
Sales	2,100 units at £55 each
Materials	£49,950 for 11,100 kg
Labour	£30,100 for 4,300 hours
Variable overheads	£12,200
Fixed overheads	£8,400

Stocks are valued at standard costs.

Required

(a) Calculate variances for materials, labour, variable overheads, fixed overheads and sales in as much detail as the above information permits. (14 marks)

(b) A Trading Account showing actual profit for the month, together with a reconciliation statement of budgeted and actual profit for the month. (6 marks)

(c) Suggest possible explanations for the material and labour variances. (3 marks)

(Total 23 marks)

(OXFORD)

4   Pensive Products Ltd manufacture and sell a single product. The company use a standard cost system for the control of direct materials and direct labour. The following information was available for the month of May 1990:

Direct labour:
　　Budget 11,300 hours at £6 per hour
　　Actual 11,840 hours at £6.20 per hour
Direct material usage:
　　Budget 9,400 kgs at £2.40 per kg
　　Actual 9,650 kgs at £2.10 per kg

Other costs:	£
Repairs: plant and machinery	1,250
Factory supervisory staff salaries	8,500
Factory heating and lighting	2,400
Factory rent and rates	3,500
Depreciation of plant and machinery	4,800
General factory expenses	8,400

Additional information:

(1) The company transfer finished products to the warehouse at a transfer price of 150% of prime cost.

(2) Ignore work-in-progress.

(3) During the month of May the target production levels were achieved.

Required

(a) A manufacturing account for the month of May 1990 showing clearly the appropriate classification of costs and the manufacturing profit. (6 marks)

(b) A calculation of the following cost variances for the month of May 1990:
　(i) Direct labour: rate and efficiency
　(ii) Direct materials: price and usage. (6 marks)

(c) Comment on the direct labour cost variances and give possible reasons for the variances. (5 marks)

(d) If the direct labour and direct material total cost variances had been 50% above standard cost, explain what significance this ought to have for the management of Pensive Products Ltd. (5 marks)

(Total 22 marks)

(AEB)

5   Borrico Ltd manufacture a single product and they had recently introduced a system of budgeting and variance analysis.

The following information is available for the month of July 1991:

(1)

	Budget £	Actual £
Direct materials	200,000	201,285
Direct labour	313,625	337,500
Variable manufacturing overhead	141,400	143,000
Fixed manufacturing overhead	64,400	69,500
Variable sales overhead	75,000	71,000
Administration costs	150,000	148,650

(2) Standard costs were:

    Direct labour 48,250 hours at £6.50 per hour.
    Direct materials 20,000 kilograms at £10 a kilogram.

(3) Actual manufacturing costs were:

    Direct labour 50,000 hours at £6.75 per hour.
    Direct materials 18,900 kilograms at £10.65 a kilogram.

(4) Budgeted sales were 20,000 units at £50 a unit.

Actual sales were

    15,000 units at £52 a unit
    5,200 units at £56 a unit

(5) There was no work-in-progress or stock of finished goods.

Required

(a) An accounting statement showing the budgeted and actual gross and net profits or losses for July 1991. (6 marks)

(b) The following variances for July 1991.
    (i) Direct material cost variance, direct material price variance and direct material usage variance.
    (ii) Direct labour cost variance, direct labour rate variance and direct labour efficiency variance. (6 marks)

(c) What use can the management of Borrico Ltd make of the variances calculated in b) above? (3 marks)

                                            (Total 15 marks)
                                                   (AEB)

6   The company for which you are the accountant manufactures three related, but different, products. These are dishwashers, washing machines and refrigerators.

Each product had a standard time per unit of production. These are

    dishwashers   10 hours
    washing machines   12 hours
    refrigerators   14 hours

In the month of March the actual production was

    dishwashers   150
    washing machines   100
    refrigerators   90

and the labour details were

    actual hours worked   4,100
    standard hourly rate of pay   £4
    actual wages incurred   £18,450

Required

(a) explain the term 'standard hour', (2 marks)

(b) calculate the standard hours produced in the month of March, (2 marks)

(c) calculate the following variances, using the above data:
    (i) total direct labour variance,
    (ii) direct labour rate variance,
    (iii) direct labour efficiency variance, (12 marks)

(d) give **two** possible causes for each of the labour rate and efficiency variances in c). (4 marks)

                                            (Total 20 marks)
                                                   (JMB)

7 (a) What is meant by
   (i) management by exception and
   (ii) management by crisis? (8 marks)

(b) Discuss how far standard costing might be viewed as
   (i) management by exception and
   (ii) management by crisis. (12 marks)

(Total 20 marks)
(LONDON)

8 (a) In a standard costing system, what information is required when setting material cost standards for a product? How is such information obtained? (7 marks)

(b) The Harlton Manufacturing Company produces a uniform product and operates a standard costing system.
   The standard costs for the first quarter of 1996 are as follows. It is planned to produce 50 units from each ton of raw material. The standard price per ton is £250. The company employs 30 people at a standard wage rate of £5.00 per hour. The standard working week is $37\frac{1}{2}$ hours, and during the first quarter of the year, the company will operate for 12 weeks. The standard performance for the whole factory is 240 units per hour. Budgeted production overhead for the three months is £324 000. Budgeted output for the period is 108 000 units.
   During the first week in January 1996, production was 9 180 units, consumption of raw material was 190 tons at an actual price of £230 per ton. Four employees were paid at £6.50 per hour and two at £5.50 per hour; the remainder were paid at the standard rate. Actual production overhead incurred was £26 000 and actual hours worked was $37\frac{1}{2}$.

Calculate the following variances:
   (i) direct material cost;
   (ii) direct material price;
   (iii) direct material usage
   (iv) direct wages cost;
   (v) direct wages rate;
   (vi) direct labour efficiency;
   (vii) production overhead cost;
   (viii) production overhead expenditure
   (ix) production overhead volume. (18 marks)
(LONDON)

23 Capital expenditure appraisal

Chapter objectives

Questions on this topic require:

☐ an appreciation of the particular nature of capital expenditure and the importance of basing capital expenditure decisions on as much information as possible

☐ an understanding of profitability, risk and the time-value of money in relation to capital expenditure

☐ ability to calculate accounting rate of return (ARR), payback period, net present value (NPV) and Internal Rate of Return (IRR)

☐ critical analysis of the various appraisal methods used – recognition of the non-financial factors which may affect capital expenditure decisions

23.1 Capital expenditure

(i) Capital expenditure is expenditure on fixed assets (including additions to fixed assets) which is intended to benefit future periods.

(ii) It usually involves very large sums of money.

(iii) In the case of the construction of very large assets such as factories, ships, bridges, oil rigs, etc., the expenditure may be committed for 20, 50 or more years ahead.

(iv) Capital expenditure may well decide the 'shape' (i.e. the location, size, pattern of operations, efficiency, ability to compete in the market, etc.) of a business for a very long time.

(v) Errors of judgement made in capital expenditure decisions cannot easily be reversed, and may indeed be irreversible. The expenditure may be irretrievably lost.

(vi) It is therefore particularly important that as much information as possible should be available to management to enable it to make prudent capital expenditure decisions.

(vii) Some pieces of information provided for management may contradict other information because the different methods used to provide the information assess the proposed expenditure from different viewpoints. It is then that management judgement is required to decide how much weight should be given to each piece of information.

(viii) Management often have to take non-financial information into account. Capital expenditure may be necessary even if it will not in itself be profitable; this will be true when the expenditure is required simply to preserve the business. For instance, a factory which is polluting the atmosphere with obnoxious fumes, or a river with effluent, risks being closed down by environmental authorities unless it spends money on abating the nuisance. Health and Safety at Work legislation may force a firm to spend money on making its premises and machinery safe if it is not to be threatened with closure by Government Inspectors. Profitability is not a prime consideration in these cases.

23.2 Incremental revenue and expenditure

Capital expenditure appraisal is concerned with incremental revenue and expenditure, that is, the additional revenue and expenditure that arises from a project. Existing revenue and expenditure cannot normally have any bearing upon a project which has not yet been undertaken. (But see opportunity cost below.)

A *sunk cost* is expenditure which has already been incurred prior to a project. For example, Lladnar Ltd intends to introduce a new product into its range. To make the new product, the company will need to use two machines which it bought a few years ago at a cost of £50,000 each and are not presently being used, plus a new machine which will have to be purchased for £20,000. Only the additional cost of £20,000 will be considered for appraisal purposes.

An *opportunity cost* is the value of a benefit which must be sacrificed if a new project is undertaken. For example, Lladnar Ltd intends to introduce a new product, to make which it will need the exclusive use of an existing machine. The machine is currently earning £25,000 revenue for Lladnar Ltd each year. This revenue will be lost if the new product is introduced using the machine. The £25,000 lost revenue is an opportunity cost which must be recognised in appraising the new project.

23.2 Accounting rate of return (ARR)

Accounting Rate of Return calculates average annual profit as a percentage of average capital employed. Average capital is calculated as one half of the capital outlay on the project based on the assumption that the fixed assets will be completely depreciated by the end of the project.

It must be emphasised that profit for this purpose is the additional profit that will be earned by the business, and the capital expenditure is the additional capital required for the project.

The return on capital from the project will be compared with the return being earned on the capital already invested in the business. For example, if a business is earning a profit of 20% on its capital, it will not be particularly interested in a new product which will earn a profit of only 15% on the capital required to produce the new product, because the new product will dilute present profitability.

23.2.1 Example: a calculation of the accounting rate of return

Venture Ltd. presently earns a return on its capital of 18%.

It proposes to manufacture and market a new product, Truveen.

The manufacture of Truveen will require the purchase of a new machine at a cost of £100,000 and additional working capital of £40,000.

Sales of Truveen are expected to be £66,000 per annum. The cost of manufacture will be £25,000 per annum. Selling and distribution costs will amount to £3,000 per annum. There will be no additional administration expenses.

Venture Ltd. depreciates its machinery at the rate of 10 % on cost each year.

Required

(a) Calculate the accounting rate of return expected from Truveen.

(b) State, with your reasons, whether or not Venture Ltd. should proceed to make and market Truveen.

(c) Your views on the advantages and disadvantages of using the accounting rate of return to assess capital expenditure.

Answer

(a)

Venture Ltd. – Statement of profitability of Truveen (annual)

	£	£
Sales		66,000
less Cost of manufacture	25,000	
Selling and distribution	3,000	
Depreciation	10,000	38,000
Net profit		28,000
Additional capital employed:	£	
Machinery	100,000	
Additional working capital	40,000	
	140,000	

Average capital employed = £($\frac{1}{2}$ of 100,000) + £40,000 = £90,000

Accounting rate of return: $\dfrac{28,000}{90,000} \times 100 = 31\%$

(b) Venture Ltd. may proceed to produce and market Truveen as the accounting rate of return at 31% is greater than its present rate of return on capital employed of 18%. This is subject to any other factors which are not discoverable from the question.

(c) Advantages:

1. Management can compare the expected profitability of a project with the present profitability of the business.

2. ARR is easy to calculate

Disadvantages:

1. ARR is based on 'average annual profit' which may not be typical of any year.

2. The timing of cash inflows and outflows is ignored. (Obviously, the earlier cash comes in, and the later cash goes out, the better.)

3. ARR does not show whether, or how soon, the net receipts will cover the initial outlay; it ignores the risk factor.

4. ARR ignores the time-value of money.

5. 'Profit' cannot be defined objectively. Depreciation, provisions for bad debts etc. are subjective judgements. Profit may be before or after tax. The timing of cash flows is more objective.

6. There is no commonly accepted method of calculating capital employed. It may or may not include additional working capital. It may be based upon the initial expenditure on the project, or it may be the average capital employed.

7. ARR takes no account of the duration of the project.

23.2.2 Exercise: use of ARR to compare projects

A company is considering whether to invest in project A, project B, or project C. It will be unable to invest in more than one of those projects. (i.e. the projects are mutually exclusive). Each project will entail an initial outlay of £150,000.

Forecast profits:		Project A	Project B	Project C
		£	£	£
Year	1	15,000	8,000	8,000
	2	15,000	12,000	12,000
	3	15,000	20,000	15,000
	4	15,000	30,000	20,000

The company is presently earning a return of 10% on capital.

Required

Calculate the Accounting Rate of Return for each project and comment on which project you consider the company should adopt.

Note: If it is anticipated that the assets purchased with the initial outlay will have a saleable value at the end of the project, the expected proceeds of such sale must be added to the cost of the assets to calculate the average capital employed for the purpose of finding the ARR.

Example. The initial outlay on a project involves the purchase of a machine costing £100,000. At the end of the project the machine will be sold for £12,000. The average capital employed for the purpose of calculating ARR is $\frac{1}{2}(100,000 + 12,000) = £56,000$.

23.3 Payback period

Risk is an important factor to be considered in capital expenditure decisions. The sooner the outlay on a project is covered by the inflow of cash, the better; this is the payback period. A long payback period increases the risk that the outlay will not be recouped.

The payback period is measured in years. Only cash paid or received enters into the calculations; non-cash items such as depreciation and accruals and prepayments are ignored.

23.3.1 Example: comparison of the payback periods of two projects

	Project 1 Cash inflow/ (outflow)	Balance	Project 2 Cash inflow/ (outflow)	Balance
Years	£	£	£	£
0	(100,000)	(100,000)	(100,000)	(100,000)
1	20,000	(80,000)	15,000	(85,000)
2	40,000	(40,000)	20,000	(65,000)
3	40,000	–	25,000	(40,000)
4			30,000	(10,000)
5			30,000	20,000

Required

(a) Calculate the payback periods for projects 1 and 2 and state which project would be the better one to choose.

(b) Comment on the advantages and disadvantages of the payback period as an aid to making investment decisions.

Tutorial note: By convention, initial investment is shown as taking place on the last day of year 0, the first year's receipts occur on the last day of year 1, and so on.

Answer

(a) Payback periods:

Project 1, the original outlay of £100,000 is paid back after 3 years.

Project 2. At the end of year 4, £10,000 still remains to be paid back. Assume that net receipts accrue evenly throughout the year; the initial outlay will be recouped 1/3 of the way into the fifth year. Payback period = 4 years 4 months.

Project 1 would appear to be the better of the two projects as the period of risk is less than that of Project 2. However, much more information would be necessary in order to make a balanced decision between the two options, such as the life expectancies and comparative profitability of the two projects.

Non financial factors, if any, must be considered.

(b) Advantages:

1. Payback periods are relatively simple to calculate.
2. Calculation of net cash flows is more objective than calculation of profitability.
3. Payback indicates the project which is at risk for the least time before the initial outlay has been recouped.
4. Short payback periods benefit a firm's liquidity and facilitate faster growth.

Disadvantages:

1. Payback ignores the life expectancy of a project. In the example above, Project 1 may produce no further cash receipts after year 3, whereas Project 2 may continue to generate cash for 10 years.
2. Two projects may have the same payback period although they have different patterns of cash inflows; one may make a more immediate improvement in the firm's liquidity position than the other.
3. Payback takes no account of the time-value of money.

23.3.2 Exercise: calculation and interpretation of payback periods

Flexi-Budgets Ltd. plans to market packaged systems for companies to use when evaluating capital expenditure proposals.

The choice is between three packages: Uniflex, Duoflex and Triflex. Each system will involve an initial outlay of £10,000.

The net receipts for each package are as follows:

	Uniflex	Duoflex	Triflex
	£	£	£
Year 1	2,000	4,000	2,000
Year 2	3,000	4,000	2,000
Year 3	5,000	2,000	2,000
Year 4	4,000	3,000	3,000
Year 5	4,000	3,000	3,000
Year 6	4,000	3,000	4,000

Required

Calculate the payback period for each package and state which package you consider Flexi-Budgets Ltd. should market. Give your reasons.

23.4 Net present value (NPV) and discounted cash flow (DCF)

Accounting Rate of Return and Payback period have been criticised for not taking account of the time value of money.

The time value of money recognises that £1 received now is worth more than £1 received in one year's time. For example, £1 received now, if invested at 10% per annum at compound interest will amount to £1.10 in one year's time and to £1.21 in two years time and so on. If £0.909 were invested now at 10% compound interest, it would amount to £1 in one year's time. If £0.826 were invested now at 10% per annum compound interest, it would amount to £1 in two year's time. Therefore using a discounting rate of 10%, £1 received in one year's time is equivalent to having 90.9p now, and £1 received in two year's time is equivalent to having 82.6p now.

If meaningful comparisons are to be made, they must be made 'like with like'. If future receipts are to be compared with present outlay, they should be discounted to present day values. The Net Present Value of a project is calculated by discounting the cash flows (DCF).

A positive net present value suggests that the project concerned is worthy of further consideration; the larger the amount of the NPV the better. A negative NPV indicates that the project should not be considered.

The discounting factors required for DCF may be calculated, but are available from tables (Present value of £1). A table of discounting factors is provided on page 452.

When the net receipts for a project are a constant amount for several years, save time in discounting them by using the appropriate factor from Present Value Annuity tables if one is available. Otherwise total the factors for those years from the Present Value of £1 tables; this usually achieves almost the same result. (There may be a small difference due to roundings.)

e.g. Net receipts for each of years 1,2 and 3 are £20,000.

Discounting rate being used: 10%

Year 1	£20,000 × 0.909	=	£18,180
Year 2	£20,000 × 0.826	=	£16,520
Year 3	£20,000 × 0.751	=	£15,020
	2.486		£49,720

Using a Present Value Annuity table:

Year 3	£20,000 × 2.487	=	£49,740

Cost of capital

The cost of capital will usually be stated in examination questions. Sometimes candidates are required to calculate the cost of capital to be applied in the question.

If a project is being financed out of capital subscribed entirely by the ordinary shareholders who expect dividends of 6%, the cost of capital is clearly 6%. If the finance comes from the issue of 8% preference shares, the cost of that capital is 8%. It is rarely possible to identify a single source of capital which finances a project. The finance comes from the general pool of funds available to the company and the funds may have been contributed in various proportions by ordinary shareholders, preference shareholders and debenture holders, each class being entitled to different rates of reward. It is therefore necessary to calculate a weighted average cost of capital.

Example 23.4.1

A company's sources of finance are as follows:

	£
Ordinary share capital	1,800,000
9% preference shares	900,000
10% debentures	300,000

The ordinary shareholders expect dividend payments of 6% p.a.

Debenture interest is an allowable expense for corporation tax purposes. Therefore, in paying debenture interest, a company reduces its tax bill and this reduction must be allowed for in calculating the cost of capital supplied by the debentures. This is done by multiplying the rate of debenture interest by (1 – the rate of corporation tax)

If the rate of corporation tax is 30% (0.3), the cost of capital provided by the debentures is $10\%(1 – 0.3) = 10\% \times 0.7 = 7\%$

The weighted cost of capital is:

	Cost %	Amount £000	Weight*	Cost × weight
Ordinary shares	6	1,800	60	360
Preference shares	9	900	30	270
Debentures	7	300	10	70
		3,000	100	700

* individual amounts expressed as a percentage of total amount, £3,000,000

Weighted average cost of capital = $\dfrac{700}{100} = 7\%$

Exercise 23.4.2

The following information is extracted from the balance sheet of a company:

	£
8% Debentures	80,000
Ordinary shares	600,000
6% Preference shares	120,000

The ordinary shareholders have received a dividend of 5% for some years past.

The rate of Corporation Tax is 30%

Calculate the weighted average cost of capital.

A project which will not produce any additional revenue may be considered on the grounds that it is expected to reduce costs. Reduction in costs should be treated in an appraisal as though it were additional revenue. Additional revenue and a reduction in costs have the same effect on the bank balance.

23.4.3 Example: selection of an option by finding the net present value of each available option

Discount (Factors) Ltd. are considering marketing a new product, but they have to choose between two possibilities: Product M and Product Q.

Either product will require the purchase of a new machine costing £110,000.

The estimated receipts for the two products are as follows:

	Product M £	Product Q £
Year 1	40,000	20,000
Year 2	35,000	25,000
Year 3	30,000	30,000
Year 4	25,000	35,000
Year 5	20,000	40,000

Discount (Factors) Ltd. cost of capital is 12%

Required

(a) Calculations to show which of the two products Discount (Factors) Ltd. should market, with reasons.

(b) The advantages and disadvantages of using the Discounted Cash Flow technique for making decisions about capital expenditure.

Answer

Year	Product Discounting Factor at 12%	M £	NPV £	Q £	NPV £
0	1	(110,000)	(110,000)	(110,000)	(110,000)
1	0.893	40,000	35,720	20,000	17,860
2	0.797	35,000	27,895	25,000	19,925
3	0.712	30,000	21,360	30,000	21,360
4	0.636	25,000	15,900	35,000	22,260
5	0.567	20,000	11,340	40,000	22,680
Net Present Values			2,215		(5,915)

(a) Discount (Factors) Ltd. should market Product M as it has a positive Net Present Value of £2,215 showing that future net receipts at present day value exceed the initial cost of the outlay.

Product Q should not be considered as it has a negative NPV, indicating that Discount (Factors) Ltd. might do better to invest £110,000 at 12% compound interest rather than use the capital for this product.

Note: Both products will produce (undiscounted) net receipts of £150,000, but they arise earlier in Product M than in Product Q.

(b) Advantage: The method recognises the time-value of money and produces more meaningful results than the simple Payback method. DCF can be applied to the Payback method, however.

Disadvantage: It is more complicated than ARR and Payback and in practice can require a large volume of complicated calculations to be made. This does not have to be a problem if a computer with a suitable program is available.

23.4.4 Exercise: the comparison of two projects using DCF

Wyezed Ltd. is contemplating the purchase of a new machine and must choose between two models: 'Goliath', which costs £80,000 and is capable of producing 12,000 units per year, and 'Cyclops' which costs £120,000 and is capable of producing 14,000 units per year.

The costs of production are: 'Goliath' £6 per unit; 'Cyclops' £5 per unit.

All units produced by either machine can be sold at £8 each.

All purchases and sales are on a cash basis.

Both machines have an estimated useful life of 5 years and will be depreciated at the rate of 20% per annum on cost.

Required

Calulate the net present values for the two machines, using a rate of 15%, and state which of the two machines Wyezed Ltd. should consider purchasing and why.

23.5 Internal rate of return (IRR)

The net present value of a project is calculated by discounting net receipts at a rate equivalent to the cost of capital. This shows whether or not future net receipts, when discounted, will be at least equal to the initial outlay in terms of the present value of money.

If a company is to make a profit, it must earn a higher rate of return on an investment than the cost of its capital. Management needs to know what rate of return an investment will yield. The expected yield can be compared with the rate earned on its other capital. The rate is found by calculating the Internal Rate of Return.

The Internal Rate of Return is the discounting rate which equates the discounted net receipts from a project to its cost, i.e., the rate which produces a nil NPV.

The IRR is found by

(i) discounting the cash flows using two different rates sufficiently far apart to give one positive and one negative NPV

(ii) interpolating the NPVs to arrive at the IRR

23.5.1 Example: finding the internal rate of return for a project

A project involves an initial outlay of £100,000. The annual net receipts for each of the first five years are estimated to be £28,000

Calculation (using the rates of 10% and 14%)

		£	10%	NPV £	14%	NPV £
Year 0	Outlay	(100,000)		(100,000)		(100,000)
1	Net receipts	28,000	0.909	25,452	0.877	24,556
2		28,000	0.826	23,128	0.769	21,532
3		28,000	0.751	21,028	0.675	18,900
4		28,000	0.683	19,124	0.592	16,576
5		28,000	0.621	17,388	0.519	14,532
	Net present values			£6,120		£(3,904)

One way of interpolating the results is to draw a chart

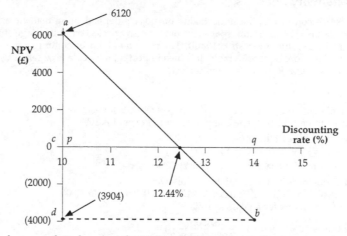

Net present values are plotted against the vertical axis ad. Discounting rates are plotted along the horizontal axis pq. Point a is plotted where the NPV is £6,120 at 10%; point b is plotted where the NPV is £(£3,904) at 14%. The line joining points a and b intersects the axis pq where the NPV is zero. The intersection occurs at 12.44% which is the Internal Rate of Return.

It will be observed that the relationship between the net present values and the discounting rates is represented by a straight line. This linear relationship means that the IRR can be calculated using formula:

$$\text{IRR} = X + pq \times \frac{ac}{ad}$$

where   X = the rate giving the positive NPV

         pq = the distance between the two rates used to give the NPVs

         ac = the positive NPV

and   ad = the positive + the negative NPVs.

therefore:

$$\text{IRR} = 10\% + (4\% \times \frac{6,120}{6,120 + 3,904}) = 12.44\%$$

The Internal Rate of Return of 12.44% can be compared with the required rate (rate presently earned on existing investment) to help decide whether or not the project is acceptable

NPV and IRR compared

(i) NPV is easier to calculate than IRR

(ii) NPV is a better method for ranking projects in order of priority.

(iii) Normally NPV and IRR agree on the acceptability or non-acceptability of a project

(iv) IRR is frequently used in business in spite of its limitations

23.5.2 Exercise: calculation of IRR

Abednego can borrow £20,000 at 12% per annum. He is considering a particular venture which involves an initial outlay of £20,000.

The venture will produce net receipts of £6,000 per annum for five years.

Required

Calculate the Internal Rate of Return for the venture and advise Abednego whether or not he should go ahead with it.

23.6 Sensitivity analysis

Good decisions concerning the undertaking of projects depend upon realistic assessments of costs and receipts. The long time spans covered by many projects and the large sums of money involved make reliable forecasts difficult. The risks involved in committing expenditure to projects may therefore be considerable. It is then important to decide how sensitive the outcome of a project is to variations in costs and receipts.

Example 23.6.1

A project will involve an initial outlay of £1m. Net receipts for each of the five years of the project are estimated to be £300,000. The company's cost of capital is 10%.

The net present value of the project is
£[(300,000 × 3.791*) − 1,000,000] = £137,300

* 3.791 is the sum of the factors for 5 years at 10%

The internal rate of return is calculated as follows:
Net present value at 18% = £[(300,000 X 3,127*) − 1,000,000] = £(61,900)
* the sum of the factors for 5 years at 18%

Therefore IRR is 10% + (8% × $\dfrac{137,300}{137,300 + 61,900}$) = 15.5%

If the cost of capital is 10% the project should not be considered if the net present value is negative. Such a situation will result if

the net present value of the initial outlay exceeds the proposed outlay by £137,300, i.e by

$\dfrac{137,300}{1,000,000}$ × 100 = 13.73%

or the net present value of the net receipts fall short of expectation by £137,300 i.e. $\dfrac{137,300}{1,137,300}$ × 100 = 12.07%

or the cost of capital increases to 15.5% i.e. and increase of 55% on the present cost.

A more detailed sensitivity analysis of net receipts has been covered in chapter 20 (20.6)

It should be appreciated that sensitivity analysis is more complex in practice because more than one aspect of a project may vary from forecast.

Exercise 23.6.2

A project requires an initial outlay of £400,000. Annual net receipts are estimated to be £110,000 for five years. The cost of capital is 8%.

Show how the acceptability of the project is sensitive to changes in initial outlay, net receipts and cost of capital.

Key points to remember

1. Capital expenditure decisions are especially important because of the large amounts of money often involved and the long term effects on the business. Bad decisions are usually not easily reversed.

2. Management needs as much information as possible to enable it to make capital expenditure decisions. Some of the information may be of a non-financial nature. See 23.1 above and Chapter 27.

3. Each method of appraisal has advantages and disadvantages. Be prepared to discuss these in an examination.

4. Whichever method of appraisal is used, the results depend upon the accuracy of the profit forecasts and estimates of future receipts and payments.

5. The longer the period covered by a forecast, the less accurate it is likely to be.

6. Risk and the time-value of money are two important factors in capital appraisal.

7. Payback period, DCF and IRR are concerned only with cash inflows and outflows; depreciation is not relevant in these calculations, but it must be included for ARR purposes.

8. Questions which incorporate extracts of Net Present Value tables require DCF calculations to be made (a fact not readily recognised by some examinees!)

9. A SUNK COST is expenditure which has already been incurred; it is represented by assets which may continue to be used to serve their present purpose but have little or no resale value for any other purpose. Sunk costs should be ignored in capital expenditure appraisal calculations.

10. Ignore book values of assets in capital expenditure calculations.

11. OPPORTUNITY COST is the value of a benefit foregone, or the value of the next best alternative course of action which is eliminated by the chosen project.

Common errors

1. inclusion of depreciation in Payback period, DCF and IRR calculations.

2. discounting annual revenue and expenditure separately instead of calculating net receipts before discounting.

3. omitting to include the proceeds of sale or scrap of an asset as a receipt in the DCF calculation in the final year.

Questions

Concentric Ltd, a manufacturing company, has recently appointed a new managing director.

After completing a review of the company's machinery he reported to the Board of Directors that the present machinery was out-of-date and incapable of sustaining high production levels without frequent breakdowns, and that the quality of the present production was poor.

The managing director proposed that the company should change to robotic machines.

The following information was available on the robots being considered for purchase.

(1)

	Robot A £M	Robot B £M	Robot C £M
Purchase cost of machines	10.0	9.0	15.5
Estimated net cash inflows			
Year 1	3	3	3
Year 2	3.5	3	5
Year 3	4	3.5	6
Year 4	4	4	6

(2) The company's cost of capital is 12%.

(3) Owing to their productive efficiency the robots would make the following number of manufacturing workers redundant:

	Robot A Number of workers	Robot B Number of workers	Robot C Number of workers
At end of Year 1	50	50	50
At end of Year 2	60	60	80

(4) The manufacturing workers' unions were opposed to the implementation of robotics, but in negotiations they had indicated that they would agree to the following: Redundant workers should each receive

(i) an amount equal to half a year's wages at the end of the year in which they were made redundant, and

(ii) an additional flat rate terminal payment of £2,000 per worker

Note: The average annual wage is £6,000.

(5) All estimated net cash inflows arise at the end of the relevant year.

The net cash inflows in (1) above do not take account of the redundancy payments.

Required

(a) (i) Appropriate computations using the net present value method for each of the robots being considered. (12 marks)

(ii) A report to the Board of Directors of Concentric Ltd advising them as to which robot should be purchased, based on your results in (i) above. (4 marks)

(b) (i) Give **five** factors which the directors should consider before reaching their final decision. (5 marks)

(ii) Briefly outline the aspects of social accounting that the company needs to consider before making a final decision (4 marks)

(Total 25 marks)
(AEB)

Answer

Concentric Ltd

(i) Workings: The redundancy payments arising in respect of each Robot in year 1 will be 50(£3,000 + £2,000) = £250,000

In year 2, the redundancy payments will be: for Robots A and B, 60(£3,000 + £2,000) = £300,000.

For Robot C it will be 80(£3,000 + £2,000) = £400,000

The adjusted estimated net cash inflows will be:

	Robot A	Robot B	Robot C
	£m	£m	£m
Year 1	2.75	2.75	2.75
Year 2	3.20	2.70	4.60
Year 3	4.00	3.50	6.00
Year 4	4.00	4.00	6.00

Calculation of net present values

Year	Discounting factor at 12%	Robot A		Robot B		Robot C	
		Net cash flow	NPV	Net cash flow	NPV	Net cash flow	NPV
		£m	£m	£m	£m	£m	£m
0	1	(10.00)	(10.0000)	(9.00)	(9.0000)	(15.50)	(15.5000)
1	0.893	2.75	2.4558	2.75	2.4558	2.75	2.4558
2	0.797	3.20	2.5504	2.70	2.1519	4.60	3.6662
3	0.712	4.00	2.8480	3.50	2.4920	6.00	4.2720
4	0.636	4.00	2.5440	4.00	2.5440	6.00	3.8160
	Net present values		0.3982		0.6437		(1.2900)

(ii) To: The Directors of Concentric Ltd
From: Accountant
Subject: Choice of Robots to replace existing machinery.

I have examined the financial implications of purchasing each of the Robots A, B and C. I have to report as follows:

1. I have discounted the net receipts for each Robot for each of the first four years so as to relate them to the present value (NPV) of the initial outlay.

2. Robot C produces a substantial negative NPV (£1.29m) and should not therefore be considered. The other Robots produce positive NPVs. Robot B produces a larger NPV (£0.644k) compared with that of Robot A (£398k).

3. The net receipts for each Robot have been discounted at the company's cost of capital, 12%

4. The initial outlay on Robot B will be £1m. less than that on Robot A.

5 Subject to other aspects of the project which the Board has to consider, I would advise that Robot B should be considered for purchase.

(Sgd.)   Date

(b) (i) Five factors which the directors should consider:

    1. Accounting rate of return.
    2. Payback period.
    3. Availability of finance. Can machines be leased or hire-purchased?

    4. Costs etc. of training workers to use new machine.
    5. Costs of maintaining Robots; manufacturer's guarantees given for free maintenance for a period after purchase; fall back arrangements in case of lengthy period of breakdown?
    6. Effect of depreciation on profit.
    7. Life expectancy of products.
    8. Reliability of each machine.
    9. Will quality of product be maintained?

(Only 5 factors required)

(ii) Social accounting:
1. Effect of redundancy on morale of workers, including those not being made redundant.
2. Possibility of finding alternative employment for those being made redundant; retraining or placing them elsewhere in the organisation.
3. Effect of redundancy on local population; possible adverse publicity and loss of goodwill.

14

Tutorial notes

1. Title is essential

2. All workings should be shown clearly. This is an important examination requirement.

3. The form of presentation is important. Adhere to the form shown here.

4. Calculations must be accurate and to at least as many decimal places as in the discounting factors.

5. The question asks for a report; note the form used here. Address the report to the person(s) concerned and show who has prepared it.

6. State subject of report

7. Short introductory sentence.

8. Be factual and concise

9. Give advice or conclusion clearly and with reasons.

10. Recognise that there may be non-financial factors to be considered.

11. Report should be signed and dated.

12. Only five factors are required

13. Use a little (but not fanciful) imagination. Imagine this is a decision you have to make for your own business. What factors would you consider important?

14. A little sensible imagination is required here, too. Examiners are not expecting a thesis for a sociology degree, but for some recognition of the social accounting aspects.

Further examination questions

Present Value of £1

Years	10%	11%	12%	13%	14%	15%	16%	17%	18%	19%	20%
1	0.909	0.901	0.893	0.885	0.877	0.870	0.862	0.855	0.847	0.840	0.833
2	0.826	0.812	0.797	0.783	0.769	0.756	0.743	0.731	0.718	0.706	0.694
3	0.751	0.731	0.712	0.693	0.675	0.658	0.641	0.624	0.609	0.593	0.579
4	0.683	0.659	0.636	0.613	0.592	0.572	0.552	0.534	0.516	0.499	0.482
5	0.621	0.593	0.567	0.543	0.519	0.497	0.476	0.456	0.437	0.419	0.402
6	0.564	0.535	0.507	0.480	0.456	0.432	0.410	0.390	0.370	0.352	0.335
7	0.513	0.482	0.452	0.425	0.400	0.376	0.354	0.333	0.314	0.296	0.279
8	0.467	0.434	0.404	0.376	0.351	0.327	0.305	0.285	0.266	0.249	0.233
9	0.424	0.391	0.361	0.333	0.308	0.284	0.263	0.243	0.225	0.209	0.194
10	0.386	0.352	0.322	0.295	0.270	0.247	0.227	0.208	0.191	0.176	0.162

1 Vernon Chemicals plc were considering the installation of a new processing plant.

The two plants under consideration were:

Plant A The capital cost of this plant was £5M. The plant had a proven track record for operating efficiency, but its method of processing tended to be costly.

Plant B This newly designed plant cost £10M.

One of Vernon's directors was very enthusiastic about this plant since in operations elsewhere it had proved relatively profitable. However, it was known that the plant did tend to have some pollutive effect on the environment and the atmosphere.

Forecast information for each of the plants was produced as follows:

	PLANT A		PLANT B	
	Revenue Receipts £M	Operating Payments £M	Revenue Receipts £M	Operating Payments £m
YEAR 1	3.8	2.0	6.5	2.9
YEAR 2	5.1	2.6	7.2	3.1
YEAR 3	6.4	3.9	9.3	4.8
YEAR 4	6.9	4.7	9.9	5.2
YEAR 5	8.1	5.2	11.4	5.8

Additional information:

(1) A modification to Plant B to treat the pollution would need an extra capital cost of £1.5M. In addition, operating payments would increase in each year by £200,000.

The director was convinced that this modification would eliminate the pollution.

(2) The Chief Environmental Health Officer of the region consulted a team of government scientists about the pollutive effect. The scientists agreed that the plant modifications would reduce the level of pollution but they could give no precise figures to support the company's claim that it would be eliminated.

(3) The company's cost of capital is 10% per annum.

(4) The following extract is from the present value table for £1 at 10% per annum.

YEAR 1	£0.909
YEAR 2	£0.826
YEAR 3	£0.751
YEAR 4	£0.683
YEAR 5	£0.621

(5) It should be assumed that all operating payments and revenue receipts occur at the end of each year.

Required

(a) Net present value calculations for each of Plants A and B for the five year period.

For Plant B provide computations for the plant in its basic form and also with the modification to treat pollution. (11 marks)

(b) Write a report advising Vernon Chemicals plc which plant should be purchased.

Give careful consideration to:
(i) any factors about which you may have reservations.
(ii) the social accounting aspects of the project. (14 marks)

(Total 25 marks)
(AEB)

2 Street-Wise Boutiques are considering re-equiping one of their city-centre stores at a cost of £35,000. It is estimated that the new fittings and equipment will have a life of five years, after which they may be sold for £2,000.

The company estimates that the new appearance of Street-Wise will increase net cash inflows by £10,500 per annum.

(a) Calculate the Net Present Value (NPV) of the investment if the company expects a 20 per cent rate of return on their investment. Assume that the capital expenditure occurs at the beginning of Year 1, and that all cash inflows occur at the end of the respective years. (4 marks)

(b) Show the maximum interest that Street-Wise should pay if it needs to borrow money to finance the project. (4 marks)

(c) Calculate the Payback period. (2 marks)

(d) Using your answers, advise Street-Wise upon their planned investment. (5 marks)

(Total 15 marks)
(LONDON)

3   Ukec plc, a company of diverse interests, was considering the purchase of a factory on the European mainland in order to take advantage of the greater market opportunities that the changes in European Community regulations in 1992 would bring.

The following information was available on the factories under consideration:

(1)

	Factory A £m	Factory B £m	Factory C £m
Purchase cost	50	100	90
Estimated net cash inflows			
1991	3	10	15
1992	6	15	19
1993	14	30	26
1994	16	45	40
1995	20	60	45

(2) Factory A was still only 70% complete and it was estimated that a further £25m of capital expenditure was necessary in order to complete the factory and be ready for production in 1991.

(3) The company's estimated cost of capital is 10%.

(4) The following extract is from the present value table for £1.

	10%
Year 1	0.909
Year 2	0.826
Year 3	0.751
Year 4	0.683
Year 5	0.621

(5) Subsequent to the preparation of the forecast information in 1) above, the company's economic research department had provided the following additional information:

(i) The EC country in which Factory B was located would have to devalue their currency against the £ by 15% on 1 January 1994. It was estimated that the currency/volume effect on the estimated net cash inflows of Factory B would be to reduce them subsequently by 5%.

(ii) Accelerating wage inflation in the EC country where Factory C was located would probably reduce estimated net cash inflows of Factory C by the following amounts:

	£m
1992	2
1993	3
1994	4
1995	6

(6) It is to be assumed that

(i) the estimated net cash inflows arise at the end of the relevant year

(ii) the factory purchase plus the work necessary to finish Factory A would have been completed by the end of 1990.

Required

(a) A detailed table of computations using the net present value method for each of the factories being considered.   (11 marks)

(b) A report advising the managing director of Ukec plc as to which factory should be purchased. Your report should pay particular attention to analysing the factor of risk.   (6 marks)

(c) Define the payback method of project appraisal.   (2 marks)

(d) A calculation of the payback period for each of the factories under consideration by Ukec plc.   (3 marks)

(e) Compare the results obtained by using the net present value method with the results obtained by using payback.   (3 marks)

         (Total 25 marks)

         (AEB)

4 The Hereford Production Company is expanding, and has the opportunity to undertake a new project starting on 1 January 1991.

The chief accountant has provided cost and revenue figures for each of two technically possible schemes, with their capital costs, each of which would involve a different product for which there is an adequate and increasing demand.

The company has neither the space nor the funds to undertake both projects, and the directors must shortly make a decision as to whether to go ahead with one project or neither.

(i)

	Estimated demand in units	Estimated demand in units	Estimated selling price £ per unit	Estimated selling price £ per unit
	X	Y	X	Y
1991	10,000	9,000	9.60	10.50
1992	12,000	12,000	10.00	10.90
1993	13,000	15,000	10.50	11.30
1994	14,000	18,000	11.10	11.70
1995	14,000	21,000	11.20	12.30

(ii)

	Estimated variable cost £ per unit	Estimated variable cost £ per unit	Fixed cost of project excluding depreciation £ per annum	Fixed cost of project excluding depreciation £ per annum
	X	Y	X	Y
1991	5.20	5.80	25,000	30,000
1992	5.40	6.00	26,000	34,000
1993	5.80	6.20	27,000	38,000
1994	6.30	6.40	28,000	42,000
1995	6.90	6.60	36,000	42,000

(iii) Capital cost of project 1 January 1991:

X	£90,000
Y	£120,000

(iv) Scrap value 31 December 1995:

X	NIL
Y	£20,000

(v) Assume that all costs are paid and revenues received on 31 December each year.

(vi) The cost of capital is 12%.

Extract from Present value tables of £1 at 12%:

Year 1	0.893
2	0.797
3	0.712
4	0.636
5	0.567

Required

(a) Calculate the annual cash flows and the pay back period for each of the two projects.

(11 marks)

(b) Calculate the net present value of each project at 31 December 1995. (6 marks)

(c) State which, if either, of the two projects you think the directors should authorise, giving reasons for your recommendation and any reservations you may have. (6 marks)

(Total 23 marks)
(OXFORD)

5   Two years ago Sandstone Ltd conducted market research at a cost of £16,000 to investigate the potential market for new products. They are now considering two new product developments, only one of which will be undertaken. The anticipated profitabilities of these two separate projects A and B are given below.

	Project A		Project B	
	£	£	£	£
Annual sales		80,000		100,000
Cost of sales	40,000		50,000	
Administration costs	15,000		10,000	
Depreciation	5,000		10,000	
		60,000		70,000
Net profit		20,000		30,000

It is expected that the above will continue for each year of each project's forecast life. The Capital cost for Project A is £45,000 and for Project B £53,000.

The expected economic lives are

Project A   8 years

Project B   5 years

Depreciation has been calculated on a straight line basis, and assumes estimated scrap values of £5,000 for Project A at the end of Year 8, and £3,000 for Project B at the end of Year 5.

All costs and revenue take place at the end of each year.

The cost of capital is 12%

Extract from Present Value Tables of £1 @ 12%

Year 1	0.893	Year 5	0.567
Year 2	0.797	Year 6	0.507
Year 3	0.712	Year 7	0.452
Year 4	0.636	Year 8	0.404

Required

(a) Calculate the payback period and net present value of each project.   (14 marks)

(b) State, with reasoning, which of the two projects you would recommend.   (3 marks)

(c) Briefly explain why net present value is considered a more meaningful technique compared to payback when making capital expenditure decisions   (4 marks)

(d) Explain how you have treated the original market research costs in relation to the evaluation of the projects.   (2 marks)

(Total 23 marks)
(OXFORD)

6   Kimrab Ltd employs five sales representatives who currently use their own vehicles and are paid 30p per mile for company business, which is 25,000 miles per year for each representative. The company is considering two alternatives, either purchasing outright or leasing vehicles. Whichever is chosen it is estimated that the vehicles will be replaced in three years.
    Under the leasing agreement all costs, with the exception of petrol, will be met by the leasing company and the agreement calls for three annual payments of £6,500 per vehicle, payable in arrears.
    If purchased the original price will be £12,500 each and the vehicles will have a residual value of £500 each.

The following annual costs, per vehicle, are estimated.

	£
Petrol	2,000
Insurance	150
Repairs	1,500
Depreciation	4,000

The company's cost of capital is 20%.

Assuming that all cash flows occur at the year end you are required to identify which of the three alternatives is more financially attractive to Kimrab Ltd. Your workings must be shown.

Extract from Discount Tables:

Year	Present Value Factors for 20%
1	0.833
2	0.694
3	0.579

(20 marks)
(JMB)

7   A proposed capital expenditure project will cost £1 million pounds and will have a five year life span after it becomes fully operational in year 3. The timing of costs and other data relating to the project are as follows:

	£
Costs incurred at the end of year 1	350,000
Costs incurred at the end of year 2	480,000
Costs incurred at the end of year 3	170,000
Annual cash inflow from years 3-7 inclusive	
(assumed to be received at the end of each year)	300,000
Scrap/residual value	NIL

Required

(a) prepare a discounted cash flow (DCF) statement using a discount rate of 15% to ascertain whether or not the project is acceptable. (Note the discount factors below)   (8 marks)

(b) explain how the DCF rate of return (internal rate of return) for a project of this nature is calculated.   (4 marks)

(c) list THREE separate factors not taken into consideration under investment appraisal methods, which may determine whether a project will go ahead.   (3 marks)

(Total 15 marks)

15% Discount Factors

Year (n)	Present Value of £1 due n years hence
1	0.870
2	0.756
3	0.658
4	0.572
5	0.497
6	0.432
7	0.372

(NI)

8   Eastinteg plc, a major chemical company, had been invited to set up a plant in Eastern Europe in order to provide work in a region of high unemployment. The regional government also hoped that plant modernisation may be possible as well.

Eastinteg have the choice of two alternative plants:

(i) Plant A. A modern complex from Japan; highly efficient but expensive. Its capital cost is £85m.

Its expected annual output is:

1993	1994	1995	1996
Tons	Tons	Tons	Tons
30,000	36,000	41,500	80,000

This plant produces a high quality output and fetches the following prices on the open market.

	1993	1994	1995	1996
	£	£	£	£
Price per ton	1,000	1,100	950	1,150

(ii) Plant B. This plant is manufactured locally in Eastern Europe and is relatively unsophisticated and inefficient. Many experts have reported that it pollutes the environment.

The plant will cost £45m, but since many regional government officials were keen to have locally provided plant, there would be a government grant for the initial capital cost of £20m.

In addition an annual subsidy would also be paid for the first 4 years of £5m per year. This is to offset some of the plant's running costs.

The expected annual output is:

	1993	1994	1995	1996
	Tons	Tone	Tons	Tons
	26,000	28,000	27,000	60,000

The output quality of Plant B is relatively inferior to Plant A and is expected to fetch the following lower prices.

	1993	1994	1995	1996
	£	£	£	£
Price per ton	600	650	570	750

Additional information:

(1) The forecast operating payments for the plants are as follows:

Payments per ton of output			
	1993	1994	1995	1996
	£	£	£	£
Plant A	400	450	460	500
Plant B	450	500	500	550

(2) Both plants have an expected life of 10 years, but it is known that Plant B becomes even less operationally efficient after 6 years.

(3) Whilst the East European regional government is aware of the pollutive effect of Plant B, it feels that pollution is so common in the region that the additional amount caused by this plant can be ignored.

(4) The company's cost of capital is 12% per annum.

(5) It should be assumed that all costs are paid and all revenues received at the end of each year.

(6) The following is an extract from the present value table for £1:

	11%	12%	13%	14%
Year 1	£0.901	£0.893	£0.885	£0.877
Year 2	£0.812	£0.797	£0.783	£0.770
Year 3	£0.731	£0.712	£0.693	£0.675
Year 4	£0.659	£0.636	£0.613	£0.592

Required

(a) The forecast revenue statements for each of the years 1993-1996 and for each of the plants being considered. Show the expected yearly net cash flows. (8 marks)

(b) Appropriate computations using the net present value method for each of the Plants A and B, for the first four years. (6 marks)

(c) A report providing a recommendation to the management of Eastinteg plc as to which plant should be purchased. Your report should include:
  (i) a critical evaluation of the method used to assess the capital project;
  (ii) a social accounting assessment of the effects of chemical pollution. (11 marks)

(Total 25 marks)
(AEB)

9   Trenton Ltd is a small manufacturing company situated in the market town of Wexfield. The company currently employs 250 people. The company has recently gone through a difficult period and there is now a need to re-develop its activities. Part of this re- development involves investment in one of the three possible capital expenditure projects which it is hoped would return the company to prosperity.

One of these possible projects, called Alpha, has already been examined. It was felt that the other two projects, called Beta and Delta, should be considered. The following table provides the data for these projects.

Project name		**Alpha**	**Beta**	**Delta**
Expected life of the project		6 years	5 years	4 years
Cost of capital		14%	14%	14%
Initial cost		£820,000	£700,000	£630,000
Projected cash inflow	Year 1	£315,000	£210,000	£210,000
	Year 2	£245,000	£280,000	£230,000
	Year 3	£190,000	£245,000	£330,000
	Year 4	£175,000	£228,000	£300,000
	Year 5	£165,000	£192,000	–
	Year 6	£140,000	–	–
Payback period		3 years 5 months	?	?
Net present value		+£25,985	?	?

Whatever project is undertaken will mean that some employees will be made redundant.

The discount factors are

	14%
Year 1	0.877
Year 2	0.769
Year 3	0.675
Year 4	0.592
Year 5	0.519

Required

(a) Calculate the payback period for **each** project.   (6 marks)

(b) Calculate the net present value for **each** project   (17 marks)

(c) Outline the relative advantages of **each** of the three projects and state which project should be accepted.   (12 marks)

(d) A report to the directors of Trenton Ltd indicating the possible consequences to the staff, the company and the locality when redundancies occur.   (15 marks)

(Total 50 marks)
(AEB)

24 Interpretation of accounts

Chapter objectives

Questions on accounting ratios require:

☐ an understanding of the use of ratios

☐ calculation of specified ratios

☐ selection of appropriate ratios to demonstrate aspects of a business

☐ trend analysis and inter-firm comparison

☐ an appreciation of possible relationships between ratios

☐ comments on ratios, the information they convey about a business and suggested factors which may underlie the ratios.

☐ an understanding of, and ability to comment critically upon, the gearing of a company

☐ limitations of ratios

24.1 Ratios

The purpose of accounting is to convey information, but 'absolute' numbers in isolation are generally meaningless. A profit of £10,000 could be very satisfactory or most unsatisfactory. It may be very good for a small business with a capital of £25,000 for it would represent a return of 40% on capital. The same profit in a larger business with a capital of £1,000,000 would represent of return of 1% which would be a poor result indeed. It is only possible make a judgement about profit if it can be related to some other figure such as the amount of money invested in the business. It would be difficult to find an alternative investment which would give a return of more than 40%, but an investor in a company which yields a return of only 1% should have little difficulty in finding a more profitable investment.The small business above appears to be managed more efficiently than the larger one. However, further enquiry might reveal the following:

	Small business £		Larger business £	
Year before last	50,000	(profit)	(20,000)	(loss)
Last year (as above)	10,000	(profit)	10,000	(profit)
Next year (forecast)	(20,000)	(loss)	100,000	(profit)

Clearly, the small business appears to be in decline whilst the larger one is becoming more successful. One year's results do not reveal these trends;, but the results of several years have given a new and important perspective to the relative results.

From the above, the following basic points emerge which must be continually borne in mind when appraising any business by its accounts:

1. Figures in isolation are meaningless; they need to be related to other figures (ratios) to put them in perspective.

2. Trends in the same business over a number of years will show whether it is progressing or deteriorating.

3. Results in one business may be compared with the results of other businesses (inter-firm comparison) to see if it is performing as well as it should, provided:

   (i) they are in the same line of business (it would not be sensible to compare the accounts of a fish shop with the accounts of an iron foundry.) and

   (ii) the structures of the businesses are similar (it would not be realistic to compare a sole trader with a large company because they are two different kinds of entity.)

4. The ratio of profit to capital has not explained why the businesses have been performing differently, or why one is in decline and the other growing. There are other ratios which will further analyse the operations of a business and show how they have contributed to a particular rate of return on capital;. They will not explain the operations; but they will assist management by indicating areas where the operations of the business need to be investigated and corrective action taken. It is very important to bear this last point in mind when commenting upon a business. Examination questions generally do not give sufficient information to allow for identification of precise causes for the results or state of a business.

24.2 A summary of ratios

The ratios covered in this chapter are represented in the following 'diagram, which shows their inter-relationship.

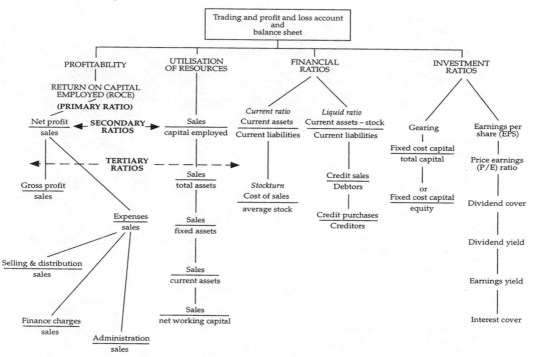

Diagrammatic representation of accounting ratios

Ratios are calculated to be used; to be useful they must be meaningful. To be meaningful, there must be a direct relationship between the constituent parts of each ratio.

24.3 Users of ratios

1. Management,
   (a) to analyse past results
   (b) to plan for the future (e.g preparation of budgets)
   (c) to control their business.

2. Investors, to compare their investments with alternative forms of investment.
3. Bankers and Finance Houses, to assess the credit worthiness of businesses.
4. Financial analysts working for the financial press, trade associations, trade unions etc.
5. Government statisticians, to compile tables of national statistics.

24.4 Ratio analysis

THE HORATIO COMPANY PLC
Trading and Profit and Loss Account for the years ended 31 December

	19-1 £'000	19-1 £'000	19-2 £'000	19-2 £'000
Sales (all on credit)		1,000		1,220
less Cost of Sales:				
Opening stock	60		68	
Purchases (all on credit)	710		812	
	770		880	
less closing stock	68		72	
		702		808
Gross Profit		298		412
less				
Selling and distribution	60		78	
Administration	105		134	
		165		212
Operating profit		133		200
Interest payable		5		15
Profit before tax		128		185
Taxation		47		57
Profit after tax		81		128
Preference dividend	4		4	
Ordinary dividend	25	29	50	54
		52		74
Transfer to General Reserve		30		50
Balance of profit for the year		22		24
Balance brought forward from 19–0		4		26
Retained profit carried forward		26		50

Balance Sheet as at 31 December

	19–1 £'000	19–1 £'000	19–2 £'000	19–2 £'000
Fixed Assets (net book value)		316		520
Current assets				
Stock	68		72	
Trade Debtors	83		112	
Balance at Bank	85		77	
	236		261	
less Current Liabilities				
Trade Creditors	80		120	
Taxation	47		57	
Preference and ordinary dividends	29	156	54	231
Net working capital		80		30
		396		550
less 12½% Debentures		40		120
		356		430
Share capital and reserves				
Ordinary shares of £1		250		250
8% Preference shares		50		50
General reserve		30		80
Retained profit		26		50
		356		430

The ratios that follow are grouped according to their characteristics, i.e. profitability ratios, liquidity ratios, utilisation of resources etc. For each ratio the model is given, followed by the calculation of the ratio, using The Horatio Company plc., and appropriate comments. Each of these is important in examination answers on ratio analysis.

24.5 Profitability ratios

Return on capital employed (R.O.C.E.)

This is sometimes called return on net assets although the calculation may also be made using gross assets.

R.O.C.E. is the PRIMARY RATIO as it is considered to be the most important of the ratios and the one that forms the starting point in ratio analysis. It is expressed as a percentage.

Model:

$$\frac{\text{Profit before interest}}{\text{capital employed}} \times 100$$

19-1	19-2
$\dfrac{133}{396} \times 100 = 33.59\%$	$\dfrac{200}{550} \times 100 = 36.36\%$

ROCE relates profit to the resources employed in earning the profit. It shows how much profit has been earned per £100 of long term capital. In the case of this company, £33.59p profit was earned for every £100 of the long term capital in 19-1. In 19-2, the profit increased to £36.36p for every £100 of capital employed showing that there had been an improvement in profitability.

This ratio is important because:

1. A low percentage is indicative of a profit which could quickly be turned into a loss with a reversal of the company's fortunes.

2. Additional borrowings will have an adverse effect upon profitability if the cost of borrowing is higher than the percentage return on capital.

3. It serves as a 'benchmark' against which to measure the accounting rate of return when assessing a new project, the purchase of a new business etc.

4. If the ratio is available for separate parts or activities etc. of a business, any part or activity with a percentage return below the average for the business as a whole may be considered for disposal, closure or cessation, if the return on capital cannot be improved.

5. Investors use this ratio when considering alternative forms of investment.

When comparing ROCE for different firms it is important to ensure that they are all in the same line of business and their operations are similar. A firm which produces bicycles, making all the parts itself, will be more capital intensive than another firm which merely assembles bought-in parts.

For examinations, unless required to do otherwise by the question, use profit before interest. In practice, accountants may use different profit figures for this ratio, e.g. profit after tax. The use of profit before tax recognises that tax liabilities largely depend upon the annual budgets of the Chancellor of the Exchequer and regard taxation as a factor over which directors have little control. The use of profit after tax affixes the directors with the responsibility for managing company affairs in such a way as to reduce the tax liability. Capital employed should be taken to mean:

Issued share capital + reserves + long term loan capital (unless otherwise stated in the question.)

Capital employed may be calculated as:

Net assets: Total assets less short term liabilities, as above. This is the usual interpretation, but it is sometimes interpreted as:

Equity (Issued ordinary capital plus reserves)

or   Total assets (The total of fixed and current assets)

Return on equity

Model: $\dfrac{\text{Profit before tax but after preference dividends}}{\text{ordinary share capital plus reserves}}$

19-1	**19-2**
$\dfrac{128\text{-}4}{250+30+26} \times 100 = 40.52\%$	$\dfrac{185\text{-}4}{250+80+50} \times 100 = 47.63\%$

Alternatively, profit after tax and preference dividends may be used.

Return on equity is a measure of the return earned on the finance provided by the ordinary shareholders.

Return on total capital employed (i.e. on total fixed and current assets)

Model: $\dfrac{\text{Profit before interest and tax}}{\text{share capital + reserves + long term and current liabilities}}$

19-1	**19-2**
$\dfrac{133}{356 + 40 + 156} \times 100 = 24.09\%$	$\dfrac{200}{430 + 120 + 231} \times 100 = 25.61\%$

Return on total capital employed recognises short term creditors as suppliers of finance to the business.

Return on Capital further considered

Strictly speaking, in calculating return on capital, the average capital employed during the period should be used. Additions to capital in the period should be included in the calculation. Such additions will include profit earned which is usually deemed to accrue evenly throughout the period. Average capital is then calculated by taking half of the sum of the opening and closing capitals. If the opening capital is not given, the return is calculated on closing capital as in the calculations above. Some accountants calculate the return on opening capital.

Net Profit Percentage

This is known as one of the secondary ratios as, with the other secondary ratio, $\dfrac{\text{Sales}}{\text{Capital employed}}$, (see below), it helps to explain ROCE. The net profit percentage expresses the net profit as a percentage of sales or turnover. (Turnover= net sales or sales less sales returns.)

Model: $\dfrac{\text{Profit before interest and tax}}{\text{sales}} \times 100.$

HORATIO:

19-1	**19-2**
$\dfrac{133}{1,000} \times 100 = 13.3\%$	$\dfrac{200}{1220} \times 100 = 16.39\%$

This shows that in 19-1, out of every £100 of sales, £13.30 was left as profit after deducting the cost of sales and all operating expenses. This had improved to £16.39 per £100 of sales in 19-2. This could have happened if Horatio had increased its selling prices without increasing its costs proportionately; or it could have reduced its costs; or there could have been a combination of both factors.

When comparing the net profit percentage of different firms, it is important to ensure that they are in the same line of business. A retail grocery chain needs to sell its stock quickly while it is fresh and to ensure this, will operate on a narrower profit margin than firms which sell electrical equipment. Profit margins, which will be studied below, together with the overheads of the business, will decide the net profit percentage. The next five ratios will help to explain the net profit percentage.

Gross Profit Percentage

The gross profit percentage shows the margin which is being earned on sales.

Model: $\dfrac{\text{Gross profit}}{\text{sales}} \times 100$

HORATIO:

19-1	**19-2**
$\dfrac{298}{1,000} \times 100 = 29.8\%$	$\dfrac{412}{1220} \times 100 = 33.77\%$

This shows that the margin (gross profit) on every £100 of sales made by Horatio in 19-1 was £29.80p; in 19-2, the margin had improved to £33.77p.

The gross profit percentage will vary with the type of business; a business which needs to turn its stock over quickly (e.g. fish shop) will work on a low gross profit percentage to encourage sales. A shop which sells television sets will have a lower rate of stock turnover and will expect a higher profit percentage.

The gross profit achieved on sales can be compared with the expected gross profit, using the mark-up/ margin relationship where necessary. (See Chapter 4.3). A lower than expected gross profit percentage may be explained by:

1. An increase in the cost of goods sold has not been passed on to customers.
2. In order to dispose of old or slow moving stocks, the selling price has been reduced e.g. 'winter sales'.
3. The business has adopted a policy of giving bulk discounts to major customers.
4. A 'price-cutting' policy has been adopted in the face of local competition.
5. 'Shop soiled' or damaged stock has been sold below the normal price.
6. Stock which has been stolen but not identified as such has been included in cost of sales. (Where stock losses have been identified, the value of the goods should be taken out of the cost of sales by crediting purchases and debiting profit and loss account so as not to distort the gross profit percentage.)
7. Gross profit margin may be lower than expected if the sales mix differs from the expected mix. Sales mix is the term used to define the proportions in which the sales of various products make up total sales. When the products have different profit margins it is crucial that the mix of products actually sold should correspond to the budgeted mix if the planned overall gross profit margin is to be achieved. If actual turnover is made up of an unplanned preponderance of low margin products, the gross profit margin will be depressed.

Operating Expenses/Sales

Total operating expenses are related to the sales.

Model $\quad \dfrac{\text{Total operating expenses}}{\text{sales}} \times 100$

HORATIO

19-1	**19-2**
$\dfrac{165}{1000} \times 100 = 16.5\%$	$\dfrac{212}{1220} \times 100 = 17.38\%$

In 19-1 Horatio spent £16.50 on overheads for every £100 of sales; this had increased to £17.38 in 19-2. There may be good reasons for this, but the next three ratios will help the management understand why the increase has taken place.

Selling and Distribution Expenses/Sales

Selling and distribution expenses are related to sales. These expenses are expected to vary with sales, not necessarily proportionately, but it is important to compare the rate of change with the rate of change in turnover.

Model $\quad \dfrac{\text{Selling and distribution expenses}}{\text{sales}} \times 100$

HORATIO

19-1	**19-2**
$\dfrac{60}{1000} \times 100 = 6\%$	$\dfrac{78}{1220} \times 100 = 6.39\%$

Horatio's selling and distribution costs show an increase of 0.39% in 19-2 which suggests slightly less efficiency in this aspect of the business. It may be explained by the increase in turnover being attributable to sales to a number of small customers resulting in higher distribution costs per sale.

Administration/Sales

Administration overheads are related to sales.

Model $\dfrac{\text{Administration expenses}}{\text{sales}} \times 100$

HORATIO

19-1	**19-2**
$\dfrac{105}{1000} \times 100 = 10.5\%$	$\dfrac{134}{1220} \times 100 = 10.98\%$

Whereas in 19-1 Horatio spent £10.50 on administration overheads for every £100 received from sales, this expenditure had risen to £10.98 percent in 19-2. Administration overheads may normally be expected to consist mainly of fixed costs and should not increase in line with turnover. The expenditure for 19-2 could have been expected to be nearer the 19-1 expenditure of £105,000 after making allowance for inflation, etc. How much of the increase, if any, can be justified will only be ascertained by an examination of Horatio's expenditure on administration.

Finance charges/sales

Borrowed money will normally be expected to generate revenue. This ratio relates the cost of borrowing money to sales.

Model: $\dfrac{\text{Interest on borrowed money}}{\text{sales}} \times 100$

Calculation

19-1	**19-2**
$\dfrac{5}{1000} \times 100 = 0.5\%$	$\dfrac{15}{1220} \times 100 = 1.23\%$

The ratio has deteriorated in 19-2. The increased interest payable is due to a 200% increase in the debentures issued at the beginning of 19-2. The new issue of debentures was necessary to finance the increase in fixed assets. It is likely that the additional assets did not 'come on stream' i.e. start to earn revenue, until later in the year. (See utilisation of capital employed below.) A fairer assessment of the efficient use of the additional loan capital may be possible when this ratio is calculated in 19-3.

24.6 Utilisation of resources ratios

These ratios are used to measure the efficiency with which the resources (fixed assets etc.) have been used. The method is to calculate the amount of sales that have been generated per £100 of resources.

Utilisation of Capital Employed

This ratio is used to show how effectively the capital employed has been used to generate sales. It is one of the secondary ratios.

Model $\dfrac{\text{Sales}}{\text{capital employed}}$

HORATIO

19-1	**19-2**
$\dfrac{1000}{396} = 2.53$ times	$\dfrac{1220}{550} = 2.22$ times

The capital employed in 19-1 produced 2.53 times the amount in sales, i.e. each £100 of capital produced £253 sales. In 19-2 the ratio had fallen to 2.22. The higher the ratio, the more effectively the capital is being employed. The capital employed in Horatio has increased by £154,000 [£(550,000 − 396,000)]. £80,000 of the increase is accounted for by the issue of £80,000 debentures which were evidently required to help finance the purchase of additional fixed assets (£204,000). The interest debited in the profit and loss account (£15,000) in 19-2 indicates that the debentures were issued at the beginning of that year, but the assets acquired may not have started to earn revenue until later in the year. There would not in that case be a full year's incremental revenue as a return on the additional capital employed.

Strictly, the capital employed should be the average capital employed during the year and this would take account of the time for which additional share capital, debentures and other long term loans had been enjoyed by the business; it would also include a proportion of the profit earned in that year.

Relationship between the Primary and Secondary Ratios

The product of the secondary ratios = the primary ratio i.e. Net profit percentage × utilisation of capital = ROCE

HORATIO

19-1:   13.3% × 2.5252512 =   33.585852%

19-2:   16.39344% × 2.2181818 =   36.363636%

(More exact figures than those previously calculated have been used to demonstrate conclusively the relationship between the secondary and primary ratios)

A business dealing in goods with a low profit margin must turn its stock over more quickly than a business earning a high profit margin in order to achieve the same net profit percentage.

The utilisation of capital employed can be further analysed in the following ways:

Utilisation of total assets

Model: $\dfrac{\text{Sales}}{\text{total fixed assets} + \text{total current assets}}$

Calculation	**19-1**	**19-2**
	$\dfrac{1000}{316+236} = 1.81$ times	$\dfrac{1220}{520+261} = 1.56$ times

The constituent parts of this ratio are the utilisation of total assets and the utilisation of current assets:

Utilisation of fixed assets

Model $\dfrac{\text{Sales}}{\text{fixed assets}}$

Calculation	**19-1**	**19-2**
	$\dfrac{1000}{316} = 3.16$ times	$\dfrac{1220}{520} = 2.35$ times

Utilisation of current assets

Model $\dfrac{\text{Sales}}{\text{current assets}}$

Calculation	**19-1**	**19-2**
	$\dfrac{1000}{236} = 4.24$ times	$\dfrac{1220}{261} = 4.67$ times

Utilisation of net working capital

Model $\dfrac{\text{Sales}}{\text{net working capital}}$

Calculation

19-1	**19-2**
$\dfrac{1000}{80} \times 100 = 1250\%$	$\dfrac{1220}{30} \times 100 = 4066.67\%$

24.7 Financial ratios

Working capital is the amount by which total current assets exceed total current liabilities. The ratios test the ability of a business to pay those creditors who are due to be paid within twelve months (usually within two or three months).

Current Ratio (Sometimes called the working capital ratio)

This ratio shows how many times current liabilities are covered by current assets; it is usually expressed as a true ratio. The right hand term of ratios (in this case, current liabilities) should always be expressed as unity.

Model   Current assets: current liabilities

HORATIO

19-1	**19-2**
236:156 = 1.51:1	261:231 = 1.13:1

A ratio of between 1.5:1 and 2:1 may generally be considered reasonable. Therefore Horatio's working capital seems barely satisfactory in 19-1 and has fallen to a very low level in 19-2. A current ratio in excess of 2:1 may indicate poor management of resources with capital tied up in stocks, debtors or lying idle in the bank instead of being put to work to earn profit.

Various factors must be considered when commenting on this ratio:

1. The nature of the business. The business may require large stocks to be carried; or one in which sales are mainly on credit can be expected to have substantial debtors. These two factors will increase the current ratio.

2. The working capital of a seasonal business will fluctuate more than a non-seasonal business which has a steady working capital.

3. The component parts of working capital need to be examined in order to see how sound the working capital is. Slow moving stocks and slow paying debtors may give a favourable appearance to the current ratio but will be little help in paying creditors already due for payment.

Liquid Ratio (Also known as the 'Quick' ratio or the 'acid test')

Liquid assets are those which are in the form of cash and those which can readily be converted into cash. The least liquid form of current asset is stock whether of materials, work in progress or finished goods. The liquid ratio tests the ability of the current assets other than stock to meet the current liabilities.

Model   Current assets less stock: current liabilities

HORATIO

19-1	**19-2**
168:156 = 1.08:1	189:231 = 0.82:1

A liquid ratio of 1:1 is generally considered satisfactory but it may be allowed to fall to 0.9:1 if the debtors pay promptly and there is a regular inflow of cash from them. A business which sells almost wholly for cash but enjoys normal credit terms for its purchases may well have a liquid ratio of 0.5:1 or even less. A supermarket would be a good example of this. Horatio's liquid ratio was satisfactory in 19-1 but has fallen to a level at 31 December 19-2 which would be dangerously low for many businesses, but without knowing more about this particular company, no definite judgement can be made.

Three ratios are commonly used to test the various components of working capital:

Stockturn

Model $\dfrac{\text{Cost of sales}}{\text{average stocks}}$

Stock turn indicates how many times during a year stock is turned over.

(For examination purposes, average stock = $\dfrac{\text{opening stock+closing stock}}{2}$.)

HORATIO

Average stocks: 19-1: $\dfrac{60{,}000 + 68{,}000}{2} =$ 64,000

19-2: $\dfrac{68{,}000 + 72{,}000}{2} =$ 70,000

	19-1	**19-2**
Stockturn	$\dfrac{702}{64} = 10.97$ times	$\dfrac{808}{70} = 11.54$ times

The rate of stock turnover has improved slightly in 19-2.

The more quickly stock is turned over, the sooner the profits are earned on it and the more times the profit can be earned.

A shop selling fresh food will have a much quicker stockturn than one selling high class jewellery; but the jeweller will make a much larger profit margin on his sales.

Debtors' Ratio

This may be expressed as sales/debtors but is more usually expressed as the average period of credit taken by customers.

Model $\dfrac{\text{Debtors}}{\text{credit sales}} \times 365 = \text{average days credit}$

HORATIO

	19-1	**19-2**
	$\dfrac{83}{1000} \times 365 = 30.3$ days	$\dfrac{112}{1220} \times 365 = 33.5$ days

It would appear that on average, the debtors were taking 3 days longer to pay their invoices in 19-2 than in 19-1.

The period of credit being taken must be compared with the period normally allowed by Horatio.

A period of credit may appear to be unduly long simply because a large volume of credit sales has taken place in the last week of the year and the debtors were given four weeks credit.

One factor that must be borne in mind is that the older a debt is allowed to become before it is collected, the greater the risk that it will not be collected at all. There is then a potential risk that the real working capital is less than it appears on the balance sheet.

Creditors Ratio

This may be expressed as credit purchases/trade creditors, but is more usually used to calculate the period of credit being taken from suppliers.

Model $\dfrac{\text{Trade creditors}}{\text{credit purchases}} \times 365 = \text{days credit taken}$

HORATIO

	19-1	**19-2**
	$\dfrac{80}{710} \times 365 = 41.1$ days	$\dfrac{120}{812} \times 365 = 53.9$ days

Horatio has taken 13 days longer in 19-2 to pay creditors than in 19-1. Whether this is good or bad depends upon the time allowed for payment by suppliers. Extended credit benefits Horatio's cash flow but it may be at the expense of the goodwill of the suppliers.

24.8 Investment ratios

The holders of the ordinary shares of a company (its 'equity') are interested in the return on their investment and the value of their shares. Their interest, however, takes third place to the interests of the providers of long term loans (usually debenture holders) and the preference shareholders. Debenture holders are entitled to interest on their loans whether a company makes a profit or not; the preference shareholders' entitlement to dividends has priority over the rights of ordinary shareholders. The interests of ordinary shareholders may therefore be at risk if their company's long term capital is provided substantially by holders of debentures and/or preference shares. The degree of risk may be measured by:

(i) the gearing ratio

(ii) the debt/equity ratio

Gearing

$$\frac{\text{Fixed cost capital}}{\text{total capital}} \times 100$$

(Fixed cost capital = long term loans + preference shares, if any; total capital = fixed cost capital + equity. Equity = issued ordinary share capital + reserves.)

HORATIO

	19-1		19-2
$\dfrac{40 + 50}{306 + 40 + 50} \times 100$		$\dfrac{120 + 50}{380 + 120 + 50} \times 100$	
$= \dfrac{90}{396} \times 100 =$	22.7%	$= \dfrac{170}{550} \times 100 =$	30.9%

Debt/equity ratio

$$\frac{\text{Fixed cost capital}}{\text{equity}} \times 100$$

HORATIO

	19-1		19-2
$\dfrac{40 + 50}{306} \times 100 =$	29.4%	$\dfrac{120 + 50}{380} \times 100 =$	44.7%

The gearing of a company's capital is assessed as follows:

	Debt/total capital	Debt/equity
High gearing	more than 50%	more than 100%
Neutral gearing	50%	100%
Low gearing	less than 50%	less than 100%

The effect of gearing on the holders of a company's equity:

	Company A (Low gearing)	Company B (High gearing)
	£'000	£'000
Ordinary shares	80	20
10% debentures	20	80
	100	100
If profits before interest are	10	10
deduct debenture interest	2	8
profits available for ordinary shareholders	8	2
representing return on equity of	10%	10%

If profits double:	20	20
deduct debenture interest	2	8
profits available for ordinary shareholders	18	12
representing return on equity of	22.5%	60%
or, an increase in return of	225%	600%

From this it will be seen that in a situation when profits are increasing, the rate of increase in the profits available for the equity shareholders in a highly geared company is greater than in a low geared company. It follows that a drop in profits in a high geared company affects the ordinary shareholders more severely than in a low geared company.

It follows that investment in the ordinary shares of a highly geared company may present a greater risk than investment in a low geared company.

A bank may be reluctant to provide a loan to a highly geared company on the grounds that the ordinary shareholders ought to be prepared to put more of their own money into the company. They should not expect a bank to take a risk which they themselves appear to be unwilling to take.

Earnings per Share (EPS)

Earnings are profits after tax and preference dividends.

Model $\dfrac{\text{Earnings (in pence)}}{\text{no. of ordinary shares}}$

HORATIO

19-1	19-2

$$\frac{8,100,000 - 400,000}{250,000} = \quad 30.8p$$

$$\frac{12,800,000 - 400,000}{250,000} = \qquad\qquad 49.6p$$

The earnings per share have increased by 18.8p in 19-2.

Investors regard Earnings per Share as a convenient measure of the success of a company.

Price Earnings Ratio (PER)

The P/E ratio relates the market price of a share to the earnings per share.

Model $\dfrac{\text{Market price of share}}{\text{earnings per share}}$

HORATIO

(Assume that the market price of The Horatio Company's ordinary shares was as follows: at 31 December 19-1 was £2.50 and at 31 December 19-2 was £4.50)

19-1	19-2
$\dfrac{250}{30.8} = 8.1$	$\dfrac{450}{49.6} = 9.1$

The Price Earnings Ratio may be regarded as the number of years' earnings that investors are prepared to pay for in the purchase price of the company's shares. The higher the PER, the greater the confidence of investors in the future of the company.

Dividend cover

Directors' dividend policy and the potential ability of a company to be able to maintain dividends in the future may be examined by calculation of dividend cover.

Model: $\dfrac{\text{Profit available to pay ordinary dividend}}{\text{ordinary dividend paid}}$

Calculation

	19-1	19-2
Profit after tax less preference dividend	£77,000	£124,000
	$\dfrac{77}{25} = 3.08$	$\dfrac{124}{50} = 2.48$

This is the same as dividing the earnings per share by the dividend paid per share.

A high dividend cover may be indicative of a conservative dividend policy; but it also suggests that the company should be able to maintain the present level of dividend to the ordinary shareholders even if profits should decline temporarily. Low dividend cover indicates that a relatively small reduction in profit may put the ordinary dividend at risk.

Dividend yield

Dividends are declared either as a percentage of the nominal value of a share or as an amount in pence per share. Yield expresses the dividend as a percentage of the market price of the share.

Model:

$$\text{Declared rate of dividend} \times \frac{\text{nominal value of share}}{\text{market price of share}}$$

(Strictly speaking, the dividend per share should be grossed up by the amount of the tax credit, and the share price should be ex div.)

Calculation

[Rate of dividend: 19-1: $25/250 \times 100 = 10\%$ 19-2: $50/250 \times 100 = 20\%$]

$10\% \times 100/250 = 4\%$ $20\% \times 100/450 = 4.44\%$

Earnings yield

Different companies have different dividend policies which makes it difficult to compare them on the basis of dividends paid. Another way is to examine the comparative earnings yields of companies.

The earnings of the company are expressed as a percentage of the market price of its shares.

Model: Dividend yield × dividend cover

or $$\frac{\text{Earnings}}{\text{market price per share} \times \text{number of shares}}$$

Calculations

	19-1		19-2	
	$4\% \times 3.08$	$= 12.32\%$	4.44×2.48	$= 11.01\%$ *
or	$77,000/(2.50 \times 250,000)$	$= 12.32\%$	$124,000/4.50 \times 250,000$	$= 11.02\%$ *

* small difference on roundings.

Interest cover

The ability of a company to pay for the cost of its long term borrowing out of profit is measured by its interest cover.

Model: $$\frac{\text{Profit before interest and tax}}{\text{interest charges}}$$

Calculation   19-1   19-2

$$\frac{133}{5} = 26.6 \text{ times}$$ $$\frac{200}{15} = 13.3 \text{ times}$$

It is usually accepted that interest should be covered by profit before interest and tax at least 3 times.

A low interest cover is a warning to ordinary shareholders that their dividend may be endangered if profits are not maintained.

Note: Ratios calculated on historic costs can be misleading. The effects of inflation are ignored. Trends over previous years may be false indicators if inflation is not taken into account.

24.9 Value added statements

Some companies supplement their annual accounts with value added statements. These statements show how much value the company has added to its bought in goods, materials and services to generate its sales. They show how much of the added value is due to the company's employees and providers of capital, appropriated to government taxation or retained in the company for the maintenance of assets and expansion of the business.

Value added statements present information under the following headings:

Turnover

Cost of sales and services

Employees wages, salaries and benefits

Payments to providers of capital (dividends and interest)

Taxation

Maintenance of assets and expansion of the business.

A value added statement is a restatement of the information contained in a company's profit and loss account but in a form which highlights the value added to its products or services by the company and how each group has contributed to and benefited from the result.

Example

Value added statements for the Horatio company plc for the years ended 31 December 19-1 and 19-2.

In addition to the profit and loss accounts for Horatio plc in 24.4, the following information is available:

		Years to 31 December	
		19-1	**19-2**
		£'000	£'000
Total costs:	Cost of sales	702	808
	Selling & distribution	60	78
	Administration	105	134
		867	1,020
The costs are made up as follows:			
Wages, salaries etc.		334	384
Depreciation		102	132
All other costs		431	504
Average no. of employees		120	130

The Horatio Company plc
Value Added Statements for the years to 31 December

	£'000	19-1 £'000	£'000	19- 2 £'000
Turnover		1,000		1,220
Bought-in materials and services		431		504
Value added		569		716
Applied as follows				
To pay employees wages, salaries		334		384
To pay providers of capital				
Interest on loans	5		15	
Dividends to shareholders	29	34	54	69
To pay government				
Corporation tax		47		57
To provide for maintenance of assets and expansion of business				
Depreciation	102		132	
Increase in general reserve	30		50	
Retained profits	22	154	24	206
Value added		569		716

Ratios which may be derived from Value added statements

Wages per employee

Horatio   (19-1) £2,783.33   (19-2) £2,953.85

Employees' wages and salaries as a percentage of added value

Horatio   (19-1) 58.7%   (19-2) 53.7%

The employee's share of the added value has decreased in 19-2

Sales per employee

Horatio   (19-1) £8,333.33   (19-2) £9,384.62

Sales per employee have increased by 12.62%. No allowance has been made in this calculation for any effect of inflation.

Value added per employee

Horatio   (19-1) £4,741.67   (19-2) £5,507.69

Value added per employee has increased by 16.16%. This has improved more than sales per employee but no allowance has been made in the calculation for inflation.

Provision for maintenance of assets and expansion of business per employee:

        (19-1) £1,283.33   (19-2) £1,584.62

This suggests an improvement in the maintenance and future of the business upon which the employee's jobs depend.

Value added statements may be presented in the form of pie charts, especially when the information is presented for employees. Such visual aids assist people without financial or accountancy training to understand the facts about a business.

24.10 Limitations of ratios

1. Ratios only show the results of carrying on business; they do not indicate the causes of poor ratios. Further investigation is required.
2. The accuracy of ratios depends upon the quality of the information from which they are calculated; the required information is not always disclosed in accounting statements and account headings may be misleading.
3. Ratios can only be used to compare 'like-with-like'.
4. Ratios tend to ignore the time factor in seasonal businesses e.g. widely fluctuating stock levels and debtor levels.
5. They can be misleading if accounts are not adjusted for inflation.

24.11 Ratios in examinations

1. Calculations of ratios. Name the ratio, show the model and all workings.
2. Selection of ratios. Choose ratios that are relevant to the question whether it be about profitability, liquidity or some other aspect of a business.
3. Comments. These should be concise and relevant. Avoid making assumptions which are not in the question unless your answer makes it clear that it is based on assumptions.
4. Comparison of the financial statements of two different businesses, or of the same business for different years, may require adjustments to be made to one or both sets of statements to place them on the same basis. The usual adjustments are for a management salary in the profit and loss account of a sole trader when comparing it with that of a limited company; or the inclusion of a 'notional' rent in a business which owns its own premises when the comparison is with another business which rents its premises.

24.11.1 Example 1: calculation of profitability and liquidity ratios

The trading and profit and loss accounts and balance sheets of Laurel, a sole trader, and Hardy Ltd. at 30 June 19-1 were as follows:

Trading and profit and loss accounts

	Laurel £	Laurel £	Hardy Ltd. £	Hardy Ltd. £
Sales		100,000		200,000
less Cost of sales				
Opening stock	6,000		29,000	
Purchases	44,000		94,000	
Carried forward	50,000	100,000	123,000	200,000

	£	£	£	£
Brought forward	50,000	100,000	123,000	200,000
Closing stock	5,000		31,000	
		45,000		92,000
Gross profit		55,000		108,000
Operating expenses		25,000		58,000
Net profit		30,000		50,000

Balance sheets

	Laurel		Hardy Ltd.	
	£	£	£	£
Fixed assets		80,000		145,000
Current assets				
Stock	5,000		31,000	
Debtors	4,000		25,000	
Bank balance	6,000		18,000	
	15,000		74,000	
less				
Current liabilities				
Creditors	9,000		51,000	
		6,000		23,000
		86,000		168,000
Capital		86,000		
Ordinary shares of £1				125,000
Retained profit				43,000
				168,000

Both Laurel and Hardy Ltd. are in the same line of business. All purchases and sales of both businesses are on credit.

Laurel has been offered a position with another company at a salary of £15,000 per annum. He manages his own business and if he were to employ somebody to manage it for him, he estimates he would have to pay the manager £10,000 per annum. If Laurel sold his business he could reinvest his capital at 15 per cent per annum.

Required

(a) Three ratios to compare the profitability of the two businesses.

(b) Three ratios to compare the liquidity of the two businesses.

(c) Comment on the businesses, using the ratios prepared for(a) and (b) above.

(d) Advise Laurel on the best way of maximising his income in the future.

Answer

Adjustment of Laurel's net profit:

	£
Profit per profit and loss account	30,000
less: Notional management salary	10,000
Adjusted profit	20,000

(a)

	Laurel	Hardy Ltd

(i) Return on capital employed

$$\frac{\text{Net profit}}{\text{capital employed}} \times 100$$

$$\frac{20,000}{86,000} \times 100 \qquad\qquad 26.26\%$$

$$\frac{50,000}{168,000} \times 100 \qquad\qquad\qquad\qquad 29.76\%$$

	Laurel	Hardy Ltd

(ii) Net profit percentage

$$\frac{\text{Net profit}}{\text{sales}} \times 100$$

$$\frac{20,000}{100,000} \times 100 \qquad\qquad 20\%$$

$$\frac{50,000}{200,000} \times 100 \qquad\qquad\qquad\qquad 25\%$$

(iii) Gross profit percentage

$$\frac{55,000}{100,000} \times 100 \qquad\qquad 55\%$$

$$\frac{108,000}{200,000} \times 100 \qquad\qquad\qquad\qquad 54\%$$

(b) (i) Current ratio
Current assets: current liabilities

15,000:9,000   1.67:1

74,000:51,000   1.45:1

(ii) Liquid ratio
Current assets – stock:current liabilities

10,000:9,000   1.11:1

43,000:51,000   0.84:1

(iii) Debtors ratio

$$\frac{\text{Debtors}}{\text{sales}} \times 365$$

$$\frac{4,000}{100,000} \times 365 \qquad\qquad 14.6 \text{ days}$$

$$\frac{25,000}{200,000} \times 365 \qquad\qquad\qquad\qquad 45.6 \text{ days}$$

(c) After adjusting Laurel's profit for a notional management salary of £10,000 his net profit has been reduced by $33\frac{1}{3}\%$. The remaining profit of £20,000 more truly represents the return he is getting on his capital.

Laurel's return on capital is 26.26% compared with a better return of 29.76% for Hardy Ltd. This is explained partly by the fact that Laurel's net profit percentage, allowing for his notional management salary, is only 20% against that of 25% for Hardy Ltd. A comparison of the gross profit percentage, however, shows that Laurel's is a little better at 55% as against 54%. This indicates that Laurel appears to be managing the overheads of his business less efficiently than Hardy Ltd.

His overheads (including management salary) are 35% of turnover as compared with 29% in Hardy Ltd's.

Laurel's utilisation of capital ratio is $\frac{100,000}{86,000}$ or 1.16 compared with 1.19 ($\frac{200,000}{168,000}$) for Hardy; there is little difference between them.

The current ratio for Laurel's business (1.67:1) is slightly better than Hardy Ltd's (1.45:1). Without any information about the nature of the business being carried on by the two concerns, the adequacy of these ratios is difficult to judge: normally a current ratio between 1.5:1 and 2:1 is considered to be satisfactory. The liquid ratio of Laurel's business is 1.11:1 which may be considered satisfactory, but Hardy Ltd.'s liquid ratio is 0.84:1 which seems very low. A noticeable feature of the two businesses is the disparity between their respective stock turnovers:

Laurel: $\frac{45,000}{5,500}$ = 8.2 times; Hardy Ltd: $\frac{92,000}{30,000}$ = 3.1 times.

The information in the question does not reveal the likely cause of this difference but the substantial difference between Hardy Ltd's current and liquid ratios, combined with its stockturn suggests very strongly that Hardy Ltd. may be carrying unduly high stocks.

Another noticeable disparity between the two businesses is the surprising difference between their debtors' ratios. The average period of credit taken by Laurel's customers is only 14.6 days, while that taken by Hardy Ltd. is 45.6 days. The difference between the two credit periods is one month, and that is itself a normal time allowed for credit. It would appear that Laurel may be too strict in his allowance of credit to customers whilst Hardy Ltd. suggests a lax control over credit.

It is not surprising, given the above information, that Hardy Ltd is taking extended credit from its suppliers; the surprise is the extent of the creditors ratio, which is $\frac{94,000}{51,000} \times 365 = 184$ days which must surely mean impending trouble for Hardy Ltd. from its creditors.

Hardy Ltd. is clearly suffering from the effects of overtrading i.e. expanding its business with inadequate working capital to support the expansion. This seems to be borne out by stockpiling, substantial debtors, and creditors nearly three times the amount of the liquid funds available.

(d) Laurel has three options:

1. To employ a manager for his business at a salary of £10,000 per year, reducing his annual profit to £20,000 per annum. He could then accept the offer of employment with another company at a salary of £15,000 per annum, giving a total income of £35,000 per annum.

2. To accept employment with another company at a salary of £15,000, sell his own business for £86,000 and invest the capital at 15 percent per annum giving him further income of £12,900, making a total income of £27,900.

3. To continue to run and manage his own business on his existing income of £30,000 per annum.

Option 1. would give Laurel the largest income, but he should seek a suitable contract of employment from his prospective employer before committing himself. He may possibly prefer the freedom of self-employment to an additional income of £5,000 per annum.

Example 2: reconstruction of trading and profit and loss accounts and balance sheet from given accounting ratios

Redvers was in business and at 31 December 19-4 his capital was £40,000. All his sales and purchases were on credit.

The following information is available for the year to 31 December 19-5:

At 31 December 19-5 stock was valued at £19,000, which was £5,000 less than at the end of the previous year.

Rate of stockturn: 6 times.
Mark up 25%.
Selling and distribution expenses: 8% of sales.
Other overheads ?
Net profit percentage 10%.
Sales/fixed assets: 5 times.
Sales/current assets: 4 times.
Average period of credit taken by debtors: 30 days.
The only current assets are stock, debtors and balance at bank.
Average time taken to pay creditors 60 days.
Bank at 31 December 19-5?

Required

Prepare the trading and profit and loss account for the year to 31 December 19-5 and a balance sheet as at that date.(Make all calculations to the nearest £)

Answer

Workings:

Opening stock	£(19,000 + 5,000) = £24,000
Average stock	£24,000 + 19,000/2 = £21,500
Cost of sales:	£21,500 × 6 = £129,000

Sales: $$£129{,}000 \times \frac{125}{100} = £161{,}250$$

Purchases: (Cost of sales + closing stock − opening stock) = £(129,000 + 19,000 − 24,000)
$$= £124{,}000$$

Selling and distribution: 8% of £161,250 = £12,900

Net profit: 10% of £161,250 = £16,125

Fixed assets: $$\frac{£161{,}250}{5} = £32{,}250$$

Debtors: $$\frac{£161{,}250}{365} \times 30 = £13{,}253$$

Total current assets $$\frac{£161{,}250}{4} = £40{,}313$$

Creditors: $$\frac{£124{,}000}{365} \times 60 = £20{,}384$$

Redvers
Trading and profit and loss account for the year to 31 December 19-5

	£	£
Sales		161,250
Less Cost of sales		
Opening stock	24,000	
Purchases	124,000	
	148,000	
less closing stock	19,000	129,000
Gross profit (20% of £161,250)		32,250
Selling and distribution	12,900	
Other expenses (balancing figure)	3,225	16,125
Net profit (10% of sales)		16,125

Balance sheet as at 31 December 19–5

	£	£
Fixed assets		32,250
Current assets		
Stock	19,000	
Debtors	13,253	
Bank (balancing figure)	8,060	
	40,313	
less Current liabilities – Creditors	20,384	19,929
		52,179
Capital at 1 January 19–4		40,000
Net profit for the year		16,125
		56,125
Drawings (balancing figure)		3,946
		52,179

24.11.2 Exercise 1: calculation of accounting ratios

Anita and Leila are partners in business. Their Trading and profit and loss accounts for the years ended 31 December 19-2 and 19-3, and the balance sheets of their business at 31 December 19-2 and 19-3 respectively are as follows:

Trading and profit and loss accounts for the years ended 31 December

	19-2 £	19-2 £	19-3 £	19-3 £
Sales		125,000		150,000
Less Cost of sales				
Opening stock	8,500		11,500	
Purchases	88,000		95,125	
	96,500		106,625	
less Closing stock	11,500	85,000	12,125	94,500
Gross profit		40,000		55,500
Wages	17,125		21,400	
Rent and rates	5,600		5,600	
Sundry expenses	4,025		4,500	
Depreciation	2,000		3,000	
		28,750		34,500
Net profit		11,250		21,000

Balance sheets as at 31 December

	19–2 £	19–2 £	19–2 £	19–3 £	19–3 £
Fixed assets (NBV)					
Premises	–			25,000	
Equipment	24,000			20,000	
Motor vehicles	12,000			15,000	
Office furniture	2,250			3,270	
		38,250			63,270
Current assets					
Stock	11,500			12,125	
Debtors	9,590			14,380	
Bank balance	2,010			–	
	23,100			26,505	
less					
Current liabilities					
Creditors	10,800		10,425		
Bank overdraft	–		4,600		
		12,300		15,025	11,480
		50,550			74,750
Capital accounts					
Anita	25,000			35,000	
Leila	25,000	50,000		35,000	70,000
Current accounts					
Anita	1,000			2,000	
Leila	(450)	550		2,750	4,750
		50,550			74,750

Required

Calculate the following ratios for Anita and Leila:

(i)   Return on capital employed;

(ii) Gross profit percentage;

(iii) Net profit percentage;

(iv) Current ratio;

(v) Liquid ratio;

(vi) Stockturn;

(vii) Debtors ratio;

(viii) Creditors ratio.

Exercise 2: preparation of trading and profit and loss account and balance sheet using given ratios

John Kelworthy is considering purchasing the business of Ken Porter and is looking into the financial aspects of the business. Kelworthy is waiting for a copy of the accounts for the past year, to 30 June 19-3, from Porter but in the meantime he is trying to reconstruct the accounts from statistical information which Porter has already given him.

The information is as follows:

All sales and purchases are on credit.

Net book value of fixed assets at 30 June 19-3 (i.e. after depreciation has been provided for the year): £42,000

Porter has charged depreciation on his fixed assets on the reducing balance method using a rate of 20% per annum. There were no purchases or sales of fixed assets during the year to 30 June 19-3.

Other information for the year to 30 June 19-3:

Sales:fixed assets ratio 5.5:1.

Mark-up 100%

Stock turn 15 times. The average stock maintained by Porter during the year to 30 June 19-3 was £7,700. At the end of the financial year, the closing stock was 50 per cent higher than the stock at the beginning of the year.)

Net profit percentage: $12\frac{1}{2}\%$

Average period of credit taken by debtors: 28 days.

Average time taken to pay creditors: 35 days.

Current ratio at 30 June 19-3: 2:1.

The only current assets are stock and debtors. The bank account is overdrawn.

Porter has drawn £100 per week for living expenses.

Required

Prepare a Trading and profit and loss account for Ken Porter for the year to 30 June 19-3 and a balance sheet as at that date. (Calculations should be to the nearest £).

Key points to remember

1. Answers involving the calculation of ratios should always give the names of the ratios, the model in each case and show the workings. (If the calculation is arithmetically incorrect, the model may still earn a mark.)

2. Make sure the ratios are always relevant to the question.

3. Learn the form in which each ratio is normally shown e.g. percentage, no. of times, days, or as true ratios.

4. When required to select ratios, choose the more common or obvious ones for the purpose; avoid the temptation to select unusual ratios just for the sake of being seen to be clever or different from other students.

5. Take care to calculate ratios accurately. It is not necessary to take answers to too many places of decimals; use discretion. It would be quite unnecessary to express the debtors' average period of credit as 28.645 days; 28.6 will do.

6. When commenting on ratios, express the answer clearly, noting any relationships between the ratios concerned. Avoid being 'dogmatic' about causes of adverse ratios as the question will almost certainly not give sufficient information for a definitive answer.

> ### Common errors
> 1. selecting wrong amounts from accounts; eg. taking the figure of net current assets when gross current assets are required for the current ratio.
> 2. failure to reduce the right hand term of a ratio to 1 e.g. 3.5:2 instead of 1.75:1.
> 3. 'inventing' ratios by selecting items between which there is no real relationship.

Questions

Fully worked examination question

The following summarised financial information is available on two companies for the year ended 31 December 19-8.

	Amigo plc £million	Barres plc £million
Sales	50	10
Administration charges	1.5	0.4
Selling and distribution charges	2.5	0.8
Gross profit percentage	25%	50%
Other balances at 31 December 19-8	£million	£million
Fixed assets at cost less aggregate depreciation	21	2.9
Net current assets	16	3.23
Balances as at 1 January 19-8 Issued capital		
£1 ordinary shares fully paid	15	2
Share premium	5	Nil
Retained earnings	8	3
10% Debentures	5	Nil

The balances at 1 January 19-8 had remained unchanged throughout the year.

Additional information:

(1) Both companies had declared and paid a final dividend as follows:

   Amigo plc 10%
   Barres plc 50%

(2) The directors of Amigo plc were considering buying shares in Barres plc as an investment. On 31 December 19-8 Barres plc ordinary shares were quoted on the Stock Exchange at £4 per share.

Required

(a) For the year ended 31 December 19-8:
   (i) summarised revenue statements
   (ii) profit and loss appropriation accounts for each of the companies.   (8 marks)

(b) Calculate three suitable ratios to illustrate the profitability of each of the companies. Comment on the profitability of each company.   (7 marks)

(c) What is the minimum amount that Amigo plc must invest in the equity of Barres plc in order to achieve a controlling interest? (Note: use the share price quoted on 31 December 1988.)   (3 marks)

(d) Write a brief report giving reasons why Amigo plc may see Barres plc as a suitable investment.   (5 marks)

(e) Prepare a balance sheet extract to show how Amigo plc would record its investment in Barres plc on the assumption that 1.1 million shares were purchased on 1 January 19-9.   (2 marks)

(Total 25 marks)
(AEB)

Answer

(a) (i)

Amigo plc and Barres plc
Profit and loss accounts for the year ended 31 December 19-8

	Amigo plc £ million	Barres plc £ million	Tutorial notes
Sales	50.0	10.0	
less Cost of sales	37.5	5.0	1.
Gross profit	12.5	5.0	2.
Administrative charges	(1.5)	(0.4)	
Selling and distribution charges	(2.5)	(0.8)	
Profit before interest	8.5	3.8	
Debenture interest	(0.5)	–	3.
Net profit	8.0	3.8	

(ii)

Net profit	8.0	3.8	
Final dividend on ordinary shares	(1.5)	(1.0)	4.
Retained profit for the year	6.5	2.8	
Retained profit brought forward	8.0	3.0	
Retained profit carried forward	14.5	5.8	

(b)

Net profit percentage	17.0%	38%	5.
Return on capital employed	25.76%	76.0%	
Earnings per share	53.33p	190p	6.

(c) Minimum investment by Amigo plc in Barres plc to achieve control £4,000,004. 7.

(d) Report should contain following points:

   (i) Dividend yield on Barres plc shares is 12.5% compared with its present ROCE of 22.8%. Amigo plc may wish to acquire control of Barres plc for other than directly financial reasons: 8.

   (ii) Earnings per share in Barres plc is good at 190p and dividend is covered 3.8 times.

   (iii) Control over Barres plc may give Amigo plc control over – source of supply of goods or materials
   – outlet for own goods
   – a competitor

(e) Amigo plc

Balance sheet extract as at 1 January 19-9

	£million	
Fixed assets		
Investment: Shares in a group company at cost	4.4	9.

Note to balance sheet: 10.

Investment: Shares in a quoted company, stated at cost.

Tutorial notes

1. Cost of sales is balancing figure
2. Gross profit must be 25% and 50% respectively per question
3. Show this separately (10% of £5m)
4. Based on 10% and 50% of issued capital respectively
5. Gross profit percentage would not be acceptable; it has been given in the question
6. Profit after debenture interest divided by number of issued shares
7. Control requires acquisition of 50% of issued ordinary shares + 1; 1,000,001 at £4 per share
8. The question requires recognition of relevant financial and non-financial factors.
9. The Companies Act 1985 requires the investment in Barres plc to be shown in the balance sheet as a fixed asset at cost.
10. The note is required by the Companies Act.

1   Solac Ltd, a manufacturing company, has recently appointed a managing director who has been supplied with the following information for the company.

Summarised Revenue Statement for the year ended 31 December 1990

	£000	£000
Sales		1,000
Less cost of sales		700
Gross profit		300
Variable expenses	200	
Fixed expenses	50	250
Net profit		50

The return on capital employed for 1990 was estimated at 3% per annum.

The managing director was also informed that:

(i)   50% of the cost of sales were manufacturing direct labour costs.

(ii) the company had been operating without adequate financial controls.

(iii) the company had relied on workers' loyalty since all the manufacturing direct labour had accepted low wage increases in order that the company could survive.

The managing director argued that if the company was to survive during the very rapid changes taking place both in Eastern and Western Europe, machine and labour rationalisation would have to take place. It was necessary to raise the return on capital employed.

He wanted a significant increase in productivity and this would involve substantial labour redundancies.

He proposed that all machine staff over the age of 55 should be made redundant.

Required

(a) Explain briefly why the managing director may be concerned about a low return on capital employed.   (8 marks)

(b) Explain why machine and labour rationalisation may be very important in raising company profits.
What other financial factors should the managing director consider?   (8 marks)

(c) The managing director thinks that all machine workers over the age of 55 should be made redundant.
Comment critically on this view, including social accounting implications.   (7 marks)

(Total 23 marks)
(AEB)

2   The following information is available for Mount Manufacturing over the past two years.

Trading Results

	1990 £'000	1990	1991 £'000	1991
Sales		1,600		1,780
Materials	720		800	
Wages	460		330	
Factory overhead	90		250	
Cost of Sales		1,270		1,380
Gross Profit		330		400
General Administration		260		315
Net profit		70		85
Balance Sheets				
Fixed Assets				
Premises		90		90
Plant and Machinery		110		236
Motor Vehicles		20		25
Carried forward		220		351

	£'000	£000	£'000	£000
Brought forward		220		351
Current Assets				
Stock	150		180	
Debtors	200		260	
Cash at Bank and in hand	40		2	
	390		442	
Current Liabilities				
Creditors	147		153	
Bank	–		130	
		243		159
		463		510
Capital and Reserves				
Ordinary shares of 25p each		300		300
General Reserve		120		180
Profit and Loss		43		30
		463		510

Note: Opening stock at the start of the 1990 period was £132,000.

Required

(a) By means of appropriate accounting ratios, analyse the information given, with particular reference to:
(i) profitability including expense analysis and utilisation of resources;
(ii) liquidity. (14 marks)

(b) From your analysis comment on the change in performance over the two year period.
(12 marks)

(c) In addition to the published annual report an increasing number of companies prepare special reports for employees. Outline the merits of this trend together with any disadvantages. (5 marks)

(Total 31 marks)
(OXFORD)

3 The summarised final accounts of Black and Green, two companies selling similar goods, for the last complete financial year are given below (ignoring Corporation Tax).

Trading and Profit and Loss Accounts

	Black		Green	
	£	£	£	£
Turnover		330,000		870,000
Opening stock	32,000		60,000	
Purchases	211,000		531,000	
Closing stock	(26,000)		(52,000)	
Cost of sales		217,000		539,000
Gross profit		113,000		331,000
Expenses		66,000		284,000
Net profit		47,000		47,000

Balance Sheets

	Black		Green	
	£	£	£	£
Fixed Assets (net)		210,000		220,000
Current Assets				
Stock	26,000		52,000	
Debtors	28,000		51,000	
Bank	5,000		–	
	59,000		103,000	
Current Liabilities				
Creditors	29,000		67,000	
Bank overdraft	–		16,000	
		30,000		20,000
		240,000		240,000
Capital and reserves		240,000		240,000

Required

(a) A calculation of at least six ratios to compare profitability and liquidity of Black and Green. (12 marks)

(b) Referring to your calculations in part A, comment on the relative performances of Black and Green. (8 marks)

(c) Outline the limitations of ratio analysis. (3 marks)

(Total 23 marks)
(OXFORD)

4 Alban Speaks is an ordinary shareholder of BZT plc. He purchased 10,000 ordinary shares of 50p each on 1 January 1988 at £1.50 per share. The market value of each share on 1 January 1991 was £2.60 per share.

Recently he had received a document from BZT plc regarding a proposed rights issue. The company planned to issue a one for two ordinary share rights issue on 1 January 1991 at £2.30 per share.

Speaks was undecided as to whether he should take up the rights issue.

Additional information:

(1) The issued share capital of BZT plc as at 31 December 1990 was:

		£
1,000,000	50p ordinary shares	500,000
400,000	£1 13% cumulative preference shares	400,000

(2) Other balances as at 31 December 1990

	£
Share premium	300,000
Short term creditors	186,000
General reserve	400,000
Long term loan	750,000
Retained earnings	850,000

(3) BZT plc paid an ordinary share dividend for the financial year ended 31 December 1990 of 40%.

It is forecast that the ordinary dividend for the financial year ending 31 December 1991 will fall to 30%, but this dividend will be paid on all ordinary share capital including the rights issue.

(4) It is to be assumed that the market price of BZT plc ordinary shares will remain constant throughout 1991 at £2.60 per share.

(5) As an alternative to the rights issue Speaks was also considering an investment of an equivalent amount of cash in a banking institution at the rate of 6% interest per annum.

Required

(a) (i) For an investment in ordinary shares, define 'dividend yield'.
(ii) Calculate Speak's historical dividend yield for 1990 based on the cost of his investment.
(iii) Calculate Speak's forecast dividend yield for 1991 based on the market value of his investment assuming he subscribes to the rights issue. (6 marks)

(b) Briefly explain the relative merits of ordinary shares and preference shares as an investment. (5 marks)

(c) What is meant by shareholders' total funds?

Give a detailed calculation of BZT's shareholders' total funds as at 1 January 1991 after the rights issue. (6 marks)

(d) Prepare a brief report advising Speaks on whether he should take up the rights issue; consider both the short term and long term situations. (8 marks)

(Ignore taxation in this question) (Total 25 marks)
(AEB)

5   The management of Trends Ltd pays particular attention to the ratios and percentages which they calculate from their annual accounts. For the year ended 31 December 1990, they have calculated the following figures, which they are comparing with those of another company, Attractive Figures Ltd, shown alongside.

	Trends	Attractive Figures
Gross Profit percentage	60%	5%
Net Profits percentage	20%	2%
Debtors' Collection period	30 days	5 days
Working capital ratio	2:1	0.4:1
Gearing percentage	20%	70%

One of the two companies is a manufacturing company; the other is a food retailer, with an expanding number of shops.

(a) Which of the two companies is more likely to be the food retailer? Give two reasons for your choice.   (4 marks)

(b) Assuming that the total cost of sales of Trends Ltd was £200,000 in 1990, the closing cash and bank balances were £11,005, sales and purchases accrue evenly over the year, and the closing stock for 1990 was £40,000, calculate:
  (i) the total of debtors at 31 December 1990, assuming all sales were on credit terms;
  (ii) the total of current liabilities at 31 December 1990.   (6 marks)

(c) Assuming you are an ordinary shareholder of Attractive Figures Ltd, what is the significance to you of the company's gearing percentage?   (5 marks)

          (Total 15 marks)
          (LONDON)

6   (a) The two companies A Brown Ltd and C Dawes Ltd have the following capital structures:

	AB	CD
	£000	£000
Ordinary £1 shares fully paid	2,000	800
Preference shares (14%)	1,100	500
Debentures (12%)	900	2,700

Debenture interest is an allowable expense against corporation tax, which for 1989 and 1990 stands at 45 per cent. For both companies, the return on total capital employed during 1989 was 25 per cent and during 1990 it was 10 per cent. All profits remaining after the payment of debenture interest, corporation tax, and preference dividend are paid to holders of the ordinary shares.

Calculate the percentage return on the ordinary shares for each company for 1989 and 1990.   (18 marks)

(b) Use your answer to (a) above to illustrate:
  (i) the value of incorporating some gearing into a company's capital structure, and
  (ii) the factors which may limit the proportion of debt capital to equity within a company's capital structure.
Be careful to define your terms.   (7 marks)

          (Total 25 marks)
          (LONDON)

7   The following ratios are given for Gargery Auto Products PLC for the past three years, together with average ratios for comparable companies in 1991:

	Gargery Auto Products			Average for Comparable Companies
	1989	1990	1991	1991
(i) Gross Profit as a percentage of Sales	30%	26%	25%	30%
(ii) Expenses as a percentage of Sales	15%	35%	8%	15%
(iii) Rate of stock turnover (times)	7	7	10	8
(iv) Current Ratio	2:1	1:1	0.7:1	1.5:1
(v) Acid Test	1.5:1	0.6:1	0.4:1	1:1

(a) Analyse the above information and comment on each of the five ratios listed. (15 marks)

(b) State, with reasons, TWO other ratios which you would find useful for inter-firm comparisons. (4 marks)

(c) Suggest one use and one limitation of inter-firm comparisons. (6 marks)

(Total 25 marks)
(LONDON)

8 The following are the summarised revenue statements of Gupta Ltd for the years ended 31 May.

	1992		1993		1994	
	£000	£000	£000	£000	£000	£000
Sales		1,200		1,400		1,500
Cost of sales		780		840		750
Gross profit		420		560		750
Less expenses						
Distribution	200		210		230	
Administration	150	350	152	362	156	386
Net profit		70		198		364
Balance b/fwd		110		60		118
		180		258		482
Less proposed dividends:						
Ordinary shares	80		100		150	
Preference shares	40	120	40	140	40	190
Balance c/fwd		60		118		292
Market price of ordinary shares per share		£2.00		£3.25		£4.50

Gupta Ltd Balance Sheet as at 31 May 1992

	£000
Fixed assets	1,800
Net current assets	560
	2,360
9% debentures	800
	1,560
Issued capital	
1,000,000 ordinary shares £1 each	1,000
2,500,000 8% preference shares 20p each	500
Retained earnings	60
	1,560

Notes

(1) During the three years under review, there were no further issues of shares or debentures.

(2) Sales for the year ended 31 May:

	1992	1993	1994
	£000	£000	£000
Fridges/freezers	400	450	500
Microwave ovens	100	200	250
Televisions	700	750	750

Required

(a) Show by means of suitable diagrams
   (i) the turnover by product for 1994 (5 marks)
   (ii) the trend in total turnover for the **three** years 1992, 1993, 1994; (5 marks)
   (iii) the net profits for the **three** years 1992, 1993, 1994. (5 marks)

(b) Explain why the annual report of a public limited company may show certain statistics in diagrammatic form. (5 marks)

(c) For **each** of the three years ended 31 May 1992, 1993, 1994, calculate, showing the formulae used
   (i) the return on capital employed; (4 marks)
   (ii) the gearing ratio; (4 marks)
   (iii) the dividend yield per share. (4 marks)
   (*Note*: calculations should be correct to 1 decimal place.)

(d) Comment on the trends of the capital gearing structure of the company. (10 marks)

(e) "A highly geared company is a high risk company." Explain what is meant by this statement. (8 marks)

(Total 50 marks)
(AEB)

9 Captain Haddock is a wealthy investor, who is considering the purchase of 10% of the ordinary shares of a public limited company. He has asked for a report from a friend who is knowledgeable on financial matters. Unfortunately, Captain Haddock says the report contains too much accountancy jargon, and as he cannot decide whether to buy the shares, he passes on the first page of the two page report for your comment.

The page contains the following observations:

"The acid test in 1993 has dropped from 0.8:1 to 0.6:1, but the current ratio has improved from 1.5:1 to 1.9:1. Gearing remains very high, but this should be a benefit if interest rates drop. Profitability remains a problem, with Return on Capital Employed at only 2%, compared with 5% last year. The product mix may have changed, as the gross margin has dropped from 65% to 35%.

"The managing director seems too powerful. He needs a good team of fellow directors, but there are only two others, who are retired politicians.

"The company is considering an expansion programme, which may prove risky for many reasons."

The second page contained the friend's recommendations to the captain as to whether he should buy the shares.

(a) Explain briefly the meaning of the following terms used in the report:
    (i)   acid test;
    (ii) current ratio;
    (iii) gearing;
    (iv) return on capital employed;
    (v)   product mix;
    (vi) gross margin. (12 marks)

(b) Write your own reasoned recommendation to Captain Haddock regarding whether he should purchase the shares. (13 marks)

(Total 25 marks)
(LONDON)

25 **The management
of working capital and
short-term finance;
long-term finance**

Chapter objectives

Questions concerned with these topics require:

☐ an appreciation of the importance of working capital and its vital role in business

☐ an understanding of the circulating nature of current assets

☐ recognition of the necessity for adequate liquidity

☐ ability to explain ways in which working capital may be controlled so as to maintain liquidity

☐ discussion of sources of short-term and long-term finance

25.1 Working capital

Exhibit 1 is a diagrammatic representation of the flow of funds into a business and the way they circulate internally.

Some of the funds are used to purchase fixed assets which are required for retention in the business for the purpose of providing goods or services; fixed assets are not acquired with the intention of reselling them in the normal course of trading.

When fixed assets are of no further use to the business, they are disposed of, and any proceeds provide another source of funds for the business.

The operation of fixed assets needs to be supported with an adequate supply of WORKING CAPITAL. For example, manufacturing machinery requires:

raw materials,

labour to operate and maintain the machines,

overhead expenditure, such as rent of the factory,

power to drive the machinery etc.

Raw materials, while being worked on become work in progress; work in progress becomes finished goods. The finished goods may be sold for cash which becomes another source of funds for the business. If the goods are sold on credit the asset of finished goods is replaced by another asset: debtors. When the debtors pay for the goods they provide more funds for the business.

Meanwhile cash has had to be paid to the suppliers of the raw materials (creditors), the workforce and for the business overheads; more raw materials have had to be purchased for future production.

The way in which cash circulates around the working capital system of a business in various guises as stocks of raw materials, work in progress, finished goods, debtors, and returns as cash again may clearly be seen in Exhibit 1 (on the following page).

It is easy to appreciate why current assets are known as the CIRCULATING CAPITAL of a business.

As with any circulatory system, whether it be in the human body or in a machine, the health or efficiency of the whole entity depends upon the efficiency of the circulatory system. For this very reason, the analysis of business performance uses ratios to test the state of working capital and its constituent parts.It should also be remembered that a business is expected to generate funds internally by its operations and not to depend on external sources except when a major expansion is being considered. No doubt the study of Cash flow Statements will have made this point apparent already. (Chapter 14).

Examination questions are usually based upon:

(a) The distinction between profitability and liquidity

(b) The role of profitability in the generation of funds

(c) The effect of the generation of funds on the working capital

(d) Analysis and assessment of working capital

(e) Management of working capital

(f) Methods of raising additional short-term and long-term funds.

Items (a) - (c) have already been dealt with in Chapters 14 and 24; this chapter will now deal with (d),(e) and (f).

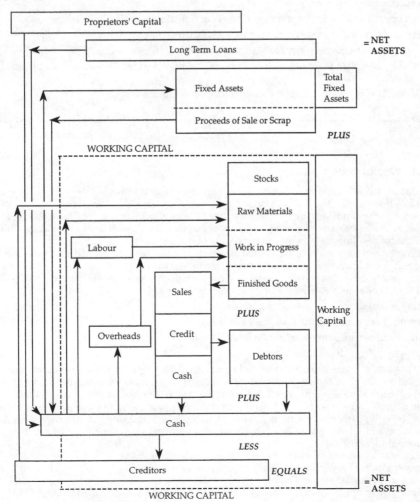

Exhibit 1

25.2 Analysis and assessment of working capital

Every business needs to recover, with as little delay as possible, cash from sales to replace the cash it has to pay to its suppliers for its stock. The CASH OPERATING CYCLE measures the time it takes for 'cash' to circulate around the working capital system.

The cash operating cycle for a trader will be found as follows:

	Days
Stock turnover	X
plus Average period of credit taken by customers	X
	X
Average period of credit taken from suppliers	(X)
Cash operating cycle	X

The cash operating cycle for a manufacturing company takes into account the turnover periods for raw materials, work in progress, and finished stocks. These periods are calculated as follows:

Raw materials:

$$\frac{\text{Average stock of raw materials}}{\text{Cost of raw materials used}} \times 365 = x \text{ days}$$

Work in progress:

$$\frac{\text{Average stock of work in progress}}{\text{Cost of goods manufactured}} \times 365 = x \text{ days}$$

Finished goods:

$$\frac{\text{Average stock of finished goods}}{\text{Cost of goods sold}} \times 365 = x \text{ days}$$

If the cash operating cycle is too long, the cause should be apparent from the ratios used in the calculation; further investigation of the causes will lead to the taking of corrective action.

25.2.1 Example: calculation of cash operating cycle for a sole trader

The following is the trading account for B. Ingo Ltd. for the year to 31 December 19-5:

	£	£
Sales (all on credit)		45,000
Less: Cost of sales		
Opening stock	3,100	
Purchases (all on credit)	28,000	
	31,100	
Closing stock	3,310	27,790
Gross profit		17,210

Other information:

	At 31 December 19-5
Debtors	£5,918
Creditors	£4,600

Required

A calculation of the cash operating cycle for B.Ingo Ltd.

Answer

Stock turnover:

$$\text{Average stock} = \frac{3,100 + 3,310}{2} = 3,205$$

Days

$$\text{No. of days} = \frac{3,205}{27,790} \times 365 = \qquad 42$$

$$\text{Debtors period of credit } \frac{5,918}{45,000} \times 365 = \qquad 48$$

Carried forward 90

	Days
Brought forward	90
Time taken to pay creditors	

$$\frac{4,600}{28,000} \times 365 =$$ (60)

| Cash operating cycle | 30 |

25.2.2 Exercise: calculation of cash operating cycle for a manufacturing company

The following information is available for The Batwing Manufacturing Company for the year to 31 December 19-3:

	£
Direct materials used:	99,985
Cost of goods produced:	151,072
Cost of sales:	181,100
Sales (all on credit)	211,970
Purchases of raw materials (all on credit)	95,900
Raw materials:	
Stock at 1 January 19-3	6,500
Stock at 31 December 19-3	8,840
Work in progress:	
Stock at 1 January 19-3	7,800
Stock at 31 December 19-3	7,100
Finished goods:	
Stock at 1 January 19-3	15,000
Stock at 31 December 19-3	16,754
Debtors at 31 December 19-3	18,000
Creditors at 31 December 19-3	15,764

Required

Calculate the cash operating cycle for The Batwing Manufacturing Company.

25.3 Management of working capital and short-term finance

A satisfactory cash operating cycle requires good management of working capital. The cycle will be lengthened by excessive stock levels, inadequate control over the period of credit taken by customers or by failure to take full advantage of the period of credit allowed by suppliers.

Management of Stock

Stockturn should be compared with the rate which might be expected in an efficiently run business in the same trade. Too high stock levels are costly:

1. Capital 'locked up' in the stocks is idle money which is not earning profits.
2. Storage of stock is costly and should be kept to a minimum consistent with efficient storage. The costs include rent, heating and lighting and maintenance of stores or warehouse, wages of staff, handling costs etc.
3. Stock may be lost through deterioration, evaporation etc.
4. Stock may become obsolete.

On the other hand, stock levels which are too low may lead to:

1. 'Stockouts' which may interrupt production or result in a failure to meet orders.
2. Excessive purchasing department costs resulting from the large volume of small orders.
3. Loss of quantity discounts obtainable for bulk orders.

Maximum and minimum levels should be fixed for each item of stock and re-order levels should take account of the minimum permitted stock level, the rate of usage and the lead-time required for the receipt of stock after placing the order.

Excessive stock levels may be reduced by:

1. Delaying re-ordering until the stock has been reduced to the desired level. This will gradually decrease the stock level and increase the liquidity of the business. The current ratio

should not be affected (in theory), but the liquidity ratio should gradually improve. The cash operating cycle will be shortened.

2. Disposal of surplus stock by sale; the current ratio should not, in theory, be affected but there should be an immediate improvement in the liquidity ratio and in the cash operating cycle.

Management of Debtors

Capital is sometimes referred to as being 'locked up' in debtors. In reality, such cash is financing other peoples' businesses instead of the one for which it was intended.

Granting credit to customers is an essential part of business, especially if trade is to be encouraged. However it requires, on the part of the creditor, credit control and credit management.

Credit Control

It is implicit in credit transactions that the customer agrees to pay on or before an agreed date. Failure on the part of the customer to pay as agreed constitutes the breaking of the agreement by the customer. The creditor should take such action as is possible to obtain payment without further delay. Further credit allowed to defaulting debtors before they have paid overdue debts will only worsen the working capital position of the creditor. Debts become more difficult to collect the older they are allowed to become and the rate at which they become bad debts increases rapidly once they pass the due date. No further credit should be extended to such debtors until they have paid the overdue debts; until then further dealings should require 'cash with order'.

Credit Management

An efficient system of credit management will minimise credit control problems. Credit management involves enquiring into prospective customers' credit-worthiness and their past payments records with other suppliers before allowing them credit terms. Special agencies exist to supply such information to businesses.

Discounts for Prompt Payment

Debtors may be encouraged to pay promptly by the offer of cash discounts if they pay within a stipulated time. On no account should they be permitted to take the discount if they do not pay within the time allowed.

Debt Factoring

This is the sale of book debts to a Factoring Company which exists to buy other peoples' book debts at a discount. The selling company receives the money for the debts, less the discount, at once. The Factoring Company collects the debts; its profit comes from the discount. If the factoring is 'without recourse', the Factoring Company has to bear the loss if any of the debts prove to be bad. If the factoring is 'with recourse', the selling company must compensate the Factoring Company for bad debts.

A company which factors its debts may improve its cash operating cycle quite considerably but its current and liquid ratios remain virtually unchanged, being only slightly worsened by the discount allowed to the factor.

Management of Cash

This is done by the preparation of cash budgets. Annual cash budgets must be broken down into monthly cash budgets and prior to the commencement of each month the monthly budget should be further broken down into weekly budgets. If the cash situation is critical, the weekly budget will be further broken down into daily forecasts. It should be remembered that cash budgets show the expected cash position on the last day of the budget period but the incidence of cash inflows and outflows may produce quite unexpected and critical positions within the period.

Where the cash situation is seen to become critical it may be necessary to take steps to expedite the collection of debts or to delay some payments. Capital expenditure may be deferred, or alternative ways of acquiring the assets considered, such as:

1. Purchase on credit terms. Payment of the capital outlay is delayed for a limited period. This has the effect of worsening the working capital ratios because creditors will be increased by the amount of the outlay. However, the liquidity of the company will not be depleted until the debt becomes due.

2. Hire purchase;. Payment is made by instalments over a period of time. Each instalment consists of part of the cash price of the asset and an element of interest. The asset will be shown at its full cash price in the fixed assets on the balance sheet with a corresponding amount as a creditor in the current liabilities. This will result in a worsening of the working capital ratios but cash will be reduced only by the amounts of the instalments instead of by the full cash price.

3. Leasing;. The assets are leased or hired. Working capital is reduced only by the periodic leasing payments.

4. Sell/lease back;. Assets are sold to a finance company which then leases them back to the user. This is similar to leasing (above) except that the assets have already been purchased by the user. The sale of the assets to a finance company produces cash for the business without the loss of the use of the assets.

    The importance of making arrangements in good time for anticipated requirements for bank overdrafts or loans by an early approach to the bank manager with a competently prepared budget cannot be emphasised too strongly.

Off Balance Sheet Financing

This term describes sources of finance which do not appear on the face of the balance sheet such as factoring trade debts and leasing fixed assets.

Management of Surplus Funds

Too much liquidity in a business can be harmful inasmuch as money is lying idle in a bank account instead of being used to earn revenue. If it is surplus to immediate requirements it should be invested. The following are some of the opportunities available:

1. Loans to other companies in the group, if any.
2. Bank deposit account.
3. Purchase of Treasury Bills.
4. Loans to Finance Houses, Merchant Banks overnight or for longer periods.
5. Loans to Local Authorities for 7 days or longer periods.

(Options 4 and 5 are only possible where substantial sums of money are surplus to requirements, usually in excess of £10,000 in the case of 4. and £50,000 in the case of 5.)

Any of the above investments would appear as working capital in the balance sheet.

Management of Creditors

It is important to recognise the risks of delaying payment of creditors when trying to overcome liquidity problems:

1. Loss of discounts.
2. Loss of credit facilities
3. Risk of losing suppliers
4. Risk of legal action
5. Reputation of poor credit rating in the trade.

25.4 Overtrading

Overtrading occurs when a business expands too quickly without adequate working capital to support the expansion.

In order to meet the expansion, stocks are built up; as sales increase so do the book debts. Because of the increase in stock, creditors also increase. The liquidity of the business is inadequate to meet the situation. The cash operating cycle is too extended and there is insufficient cash in the system. When the creditors press for payment the business defaults on payment and collapses.

25.5 Long-term sources of finance

1. ADDITIONAL SHARES ISSUED FOR CASH

   Advantages

   (i) If existing shares in issue are popular with investors, there may be little difficulty in raising additional capital by increasing the shares in issue.

   (ii) If existing shares are exchanging hands above their par value, the additional shares may be issued at a premium, increasing the inflow of cash to the company.

   (iii) The shares may be issued as redeemable shares to avoid permanent dilution of the share capital.

   (iv) Unless the shares are redeemable, there is no requirement to repay the capital at some future date when it may be inconvenient.

   (v) Unlike loans, on which interest has to be paid whether profits are being made or not, dividends are only paid on shares if profits are available.

   Disadvantages

   (i) The high cost of making a new issue of shares.

   (ii) Unless there is an immediate increase in profit, the dividend cover, and therefore dividends, may be diluted.

   (iii) The voting rights of existing shareholders may be affected unless the shares form a rights issue.

2. LONG-TERM LOANS: DEBENTURES

   Advantages

   (i) Debentures can be redeemed at a future date.

   (ii) Debenture holders are not normally entitled to voting rights.

   (iii) Debentures do not interfere with the benefits accruing to equity shareholders in periods of increasing profitability.

   Disadvantages

   (i) Debenture interest must be paid whether or not the company has made a profit.

   (ii) The debentures will have to be redeemed at some future date which may cause liquidity problems.

   (iii) Possible adverse effect on 'gearing'.

   (iv) Debenture holders are entitled to repayment of their loan in priority to the repayment of capital to shareholders in a winding up.

25.6 Other sources of finance

GOVERNMENT GRANTS aimed at attracting industry to development areas. The grants may be towards operating costs (e.g. labour costs) or capital expenditure (e.g. towards cost of construction of a factory.)

25.7 Capital structure generally

Any consideration of the capital structure of a business takes into account the proportion of the total assets which should be financed by long-term capital and how much by short-term sources of finance (i.e. current liabilities). Furthermore, the proportion of long-term borrowing to proprietors' capital (i.e.gearing or leverage;) needs to be considered.

Obviously, it is impossible to make hard and fast rules to decide the proper capital structure for any business. However, the following are some of the matters relevant to this topic.

Long-term investment (i.e.fixed assets) should be financed by long-term capital. If it were financed by short-term sources of finance the assets may have to be sold in order to repay the short-term indebtedness; that could eventually lead to there being no business left to continue.

If it is accepted that a particular current ratio is appropriate for any business in question, that will suggest the proportion of current assets which may be financed by short-term creditors. For instance, a current ratio of 1.5:1 indicates that about $66\frac{2}{3}$% of the current assets may be financed by the creditors and the remainder by long-term capital.

From the above, it may be argued that long-term capital should therefore equal the total of the fixed assets plus at least one third of the current assets. It must again be emphasised that no hard and fast rule can be laid down.

The next consideration is how much of the long-term capital should be subscribed by the proprietors (equity shareholders) and how much by fixed cost capital (debentures, preference shares). This will be decided by the required gearing, neutral gearing being equal contributions to the long-term capital by the ordinary shareholders on the one hand and the debenture/preference share holders on the other.

25.7.1 Example: the diagrammatic representation of the capital structure of a company

The following is the abbreviated balance sheet of Snodix Ltd. at 31 December 19-2:

	£'000	£'000
Fixed assets		850
Current assets	300	
less Current liabilities	150	150
		1,000
less Long-term liabilities:		
Debentures		100
		900
Ordinary share capital and reserves		900

Required

(a) Prepare a suitable diagram, using the information in the balance sheet, to show as at 31 Dec 19-2,

   (i) the various sources of finance

   (ii) the spread of the total funds over the various categories of assets.

(b) Comment briefly on the capital structure and the working capital of Snodix Ltd. as at 31 December 19-2.

Answer

(a)

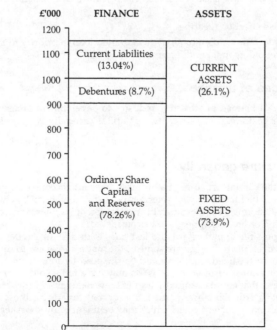

Diagram to show the sources of finance and spread of total funds

Tutorial note: The finance and asset columns should be equal in height and width, giving them equal areas. Show the scale in £'000s and calculate the percentages of the components of finance.

(b) The current ratio of Snodix Ltd. at 31 December 19-2 was $\frac{300}{150}$ = 2:1 which may be considered to be satisfactory for most businesses.

As 50% of the current assets are financed by the current liabilities, the remaining 50% (£150,000) plus the fixed assets are financed by the long-term capital.

Snodix Ltd. is a low geared company as only 10% of long-term finance is supplied by the debentures.

$(\frac{100,000}{900,000 + 100,000} \times 100)$.

25.7.2 Exercise: to compare the capital structure of two companies

Apex Ltd. and Base Ltd. both have financial years ending on 31 March. Their balance sheets as at 31 March 19-1 were as follows:

	Apex Ltd.		Base Ltd.	
	£'000	£'000	£'000	£'000
Fixed assets		1,200		1,400
Current assets	800		700	
less				
Current liabilities	500	300	420	280
		1,500		1,680
less 10% Debentures		300		–
		1,200		1,680
Share capital and reserves:				
Ordinary shares of £1		800		800
8% Preference shares of £1		–		500
Profit and loss account		400		380
		1,200		1,680

Both companies made a profit of £60,000 before interest in the year to 31 March 19–1

Required

(a) For each of the two companies Apex Ltd. and Base Ltd. prepare diagrams to represent their various sources of finance and the spread of their total funds over the various categories of their assets.

(b) Make brief comments on their working capital ratios, capital structure, and earnings. (Ignore tax.)

Key points to remember

1. Adequacy of working capital must be related to various factors such as the industry concerned, the nature of the business and its trading pattern e.g. giving credit etc.

2. Overtrading should be recognised as a dangerous situation.

3. The cash operating cycle shows how long, on average, the outlay on stocks of goods or raw materials is recovered in sales.

4. Management of the cash operating cycle involves management of the individual components of working capital; stock, debtors etc.

> ### Common errors
>
> 1. failure to identify ways in which liquidity can be improved by generating cash from stock and debtors.
> 2. failure to understand how various actions affect working capital, the bank balance or the cash operating cycle.
> 3. failure to make appropriate recommendations for improving liquidity e.g. delaying capital expenditure or alternatives to outright purchase. Delaying payment of tax is not a good suggestion, it being against public policy.

Questions

Fully worked examination question

Extracts for the last two available balance sheets of Dee Ltd., whose financial year ends on 30 September.

	19-8		19-9	
	£000	£000	£000	£000
Current assets				
Stocks	24,000		35,000	
Trade debtors	16,000		18,000	
Prepayments	2,000		1,500	
Balance at bank	4,000	46,000	–	54,500
Creditors due in less than one year				
Trade creditors	20,950		39,000	
Dividends proposed	3,500		4,700	
Corporation Tax	4,300		5,100	
Balance at bank	–	(28,750)	19,325	(68,125)
Net current assets (liabilities)		17,250		(13,625)
Creditors, due in more than one year		36,600		31,700

Required

(a) Define and calculate two ratios relating to the liquidity of Dee Ltd. for each of the two years.

(4 marks)

(b) From the information given explain the possible causes of the change in the liquid position of Dee Ltd. over the two years.

(6 marks)

(c) Advise the management of Dee Ltd. how the liquid position of the company could be improved.

(4 marks)

(Total 14 marks)

(AEB)

Answer

19-8   19-9

(a) Current ratio (46,000/28,750)   1.6:1   (54,500/68,125)   0.8:1
    Acid test (22,000/28,750)   0.76:1   (19,500/68,125)   0.29:1

(b) Bank balance change   £23,325 (worse)

Causes:	£
Redemption of debentures	4,900
Increase in stock	11,000
Increase in debtors	2,000
Dividends paid	3,500
Corporation tax paid	4,300
Reduction in prepayments	(500)
Increase in trade creditors	(18,050)
Net outgoings on fixed assets	16,175
	23,325

(c) The liquid position of the company may be improved by:

  (i) reduction of stock by:

    (i) not replacing stock which has been sold until the stock level has fallen

    (ii) encouraging sales by price reduction, discounts, advertising.

  (ii) reduction of debtors by:

    (i) tighter credit control,

    (ii) factoring debts

    (iii) encouraging cash sales

    (iv) accepting credit/debit cards

  (iii) an alternative policy regarding purchase of fixed assets e.g. purchase on credit terms, hire purchase, leasing, sale/lease back.

Further examination questions

1   Selangor Manufacturers Ltd are reviewing their working capital requirements for the next twelve months. An extract from their balance sheet at today's date is shown below.

Current Assets:		£
Stock		280,000
Debtors		400,000
Cash and Bank		100,000
		780,000
Creditors due for payment within one year:		
Trade creditors	120,000	
Taxation	60,000	
Dividend	40,000	
		220,000
Current assets less current liabilities		560,000

The directors estimate that they will need a minimum of £620,000 for working capital throughout the next twelve months, and are considering the following *alternative* possibilities.

(1) Increase stock levels by £60,000, to be paid for by selling fixed assets.

(2) Increase credit sales, so that debtors will average £460,000 during the next year.

(3) Borrow £60,000 from the company's bank, on a long-term loan.

(4) Delay paying the taxation liability.

(5) Sell ordinary shares for £60,000 to existing shareholders.

Required

For each of the five alternative possibilities, give two arguments (for or against), for following that particular course of action, and state whether the aim of increasing working capital will be achieved in each case.

(15 marks)
(LONDON)

2 Bryant supplies materials to the building trade and has sold to customers on a cash and credit basis for several years. He is reviewing his sales policy owing to a sharp increase in bad debts over the last two years. The following figures refer to the last two financial years.

	Year ended 31 October 1989	Year ended 31 October 1990
	£	£
Cash sales	85,000	110,000
Credit sales	24,000	30,000
Closing debtors	10,000	14,000

During this period on average gross profit of 15% on selling price has been earned and debtors have on average been taking six months to settle their accounts.

A provision for doubtful debts of 5% of debtors has been maintained throughout the period and on 1 November 1988 the balance on the account was £250.

Bad debts written off in the last two years have been:

Year ended	£
31 October 1989	2,000
31 October 1990	4,800

Over the last two years interest rates have averaged 20%.

Faced with the increase in bad debts Bryant is considering selling on a cash only basis. He estimates that if he reduces his average gross profit to 10% on selling price, cash sales over the next two years will be £105,000 and £120,000 respectively.

Required

(a) The bad debts account and the provision for doubtful debts account for the years ended 31 October 1989 and 31 October 1990. (7 marks)

(b) A statement showing the effect on the profits of the business over the next two years if the decision not to sell on credit is implemented. State any necessary assumptions. (6 marks)

(c) Advise Bryant whether he should continue to sell on credit. (6 marks)

(d) State and explain two accounting concepts that necessitate the creation of a provision for doubtful debts at the end of an accounting period. (6 marks)

(Total 25 marks)
(AEB)

3 Channel Ltd, a manufacturer of confectionery, is considering expanding its production to commence exporting into Europe. To achieve this the company will need to invest £3,000,000 in fixed assets and an additional £2,000,000 is required to fund an increase in working capital.

It is company policy to depreciate fixed assets at the rate of 15% per annum on cost. Two alternative methods of financing the necessary investment are being considered.

Alternative 1

To issue 5,000,000 of its 50p ordinary shares at £1 per share. The directors expect the annual dividend payable to ordinary shareholders to remain at 20%.

Alternative 2

To purchase the fixed assets on credit. The terms of the credit agreement provide for four annual instalments of £1,000,000 commencing at the end of the first year. Assume that interest accrues evenly over the period of the loan. To finance the working capital requirement, the company will be able to negotiate a bank overdraft facility for two years. The overdraft is expected to average £1,500,000 in the first year and £500,000 in the second year. The bank will charge interest at the rate of 20% per annum on the overdraft.

Required

(a) The entries which would appear in the revenue accounts at the end of the first year for both alternatives, showing clearly the section of the revenue accounts which would be affected. (5 marks)

(b) The relevant extracts from the balance sheet at the end of the first year for both alternatives. (6 marks)

(c) Discuss the financial implications of both proposals for an existing shareholder in Channel Ltd.

(6 marks)

(Total 17 marks)

(AEB)

4   The following are the 1988 and 1989 balance sheets of Erne Ltd together with the abridged profit and loss account for 1989.

Balance Sheets at 31 December 1988 and 1989

	1988		1989	
	£000	£000	£000	£000
FIXED ASSETS				
Land and buildings		183		200
Plant and vehicles		129		155
Investments		76		90
		388		445
CURRENT ASSETS				
Stocks	267		440	
Debtors	224		391	
Cash balances	18		2	
	509		833	
CREDITORS: amounts falling due within one year				
Trade creditors and accruals	222		432	
Taxation	16		25	
Bank overdraft	33		117	
	271		574	
NET CURRENT ASSETS		238		259
TOTAL ASSETS LESS CURRENT LIABILITIES		626		704
CREDITORS: amounts falling due after more than one year				
12% Debentures 1992/93	200		200	
Long-term bank loan	179	379	138	338
		247		366
CAPITAL AND RESERVES				
Called up share capital		80		110
Share premium account		10		55
Revaluation reserve		9		29
General reserve		94		109
Profit and loss account		54		63
		247		366

Abridged Profit and Loss Account for 1989

	£000
OPERATING PROFIT	59
Income from fixed asset investments	11
PROFIT BEFORE TAX	70
Tax	25
PROFIT AFTER TAX	45
Dividends	21
RETAINED PROFIT	24

Notes:

(i) The operating profit is stated after charging:

	£000
Depreciation	39
Loan interest	48
Directors' fees	3
Directors' other emoluments	56
Auditor's remuneration	8

(ii) The fixed assets are shown at net book value; the land and buildings were revalued during 1989 increasing their value by £20,000.

(iii) During 1989 £62,000 was spent on new plant and vehicles; the only other acquisition of fixed assets was investments which are shown in the balance sheets at cost and there were no disposals of fixed assets.

(iv) On 31 December 1989 £15,000 was transferred from profit and loss account to general reserve.

Required

You are required to report to the board of directors of Erne Ltd explaining why the liquidity of the company has fallen by £100,000 despite the fact that the company has made a satisfactory return on its capital in 1989.

(You should include in your report whatever accounting statement(s) you consider necessary to support your explanation.) (20 marks)

(NI)

26 Computers in accounting

Chapter objectives

Questions on computers in accounting require:-

❑ an acquaintance with some basic computing terms

❑ some knowledge of computer hardware

❑ a general understanding of computer software – ability to explain how computers can be used in accounting

❑ discussion of the advantages of computer systems and some of the problems associated with them

26.1 Some computer terminology

Hardware

The computer itself and its associated peripheral equipment. The computer, or Central Processing Unit, consists of:

Internal storage facility for data being processed,

An arithmetic and logic unit to operate on data

A control unit to manage the processing of data.

The associated peripheral equipment consists of:

A data inputting device (e.g. keyboard, optical character recognition scanners etc.)

External backing storage to hold data until it is required for processing (e.g. hard or floppy disks.)

Output devices (e.g. laser printers, print wheel printers.)

Software

The name given to the programs or packages that control computer functions. Examples of programs are those written to maintain sales ledger or purchases ledger accounts; general ledger accounts; preparing payrolls, stock records,or final accounts from the financial records. The appropriate program must be loaded into the Central Processing Unit before data processing can begin.

File

This may be likened to the files in any office filing system; a computer system file is a collection of related records (e.g. clock cards for a payroll) kept on disk. The file, and any record in it can be 'accessed' through the appropriate 'key' data field.

Batch Processing

Refers to the method of processing batches of similar data in the same run; e.g. all sales invoices for a week may be processed together in a single weekly run in much the same way as an accounts clerk might set time aside each week to post the invoices to the sales ledger.

On-Line Processing

The input of data takes place at the point of origin. e.g. where the Central Processing Unit is situated at Head Office, data may be input from remote terminals at branches.

Time Sharing

An arrangement that allows on-line users to access different files and programs simultaneously.

Real-Time

A further development of 'on-line' processing. Data originating at a branch office may be input to the Head Office computer, processed, and the results transmitted back to the branch immediately. Examples of this may be seen in travel offices where they are used for booking air tickets etc.

26.2 Examples of computer applications in accounting

Financial accounting:

(i)   Sales ledger

(ii) Purchases ledger

(iii) General ledger

(iv) Payroll records

(v)   Stock records

(vi) Trading and profit and loss accounts

(vii) Balance sheets.

Management and cost accounting:

(i)   Costing calculations and costing records.

(ii) Forecasting/budgeting

(iii) Estimating job costs

(iv) Project appraisal

(v)   Credit control

26.3 Database systems

Data stored in these systems has to be input only once; it is then accessible for any process for which it is required. For example, data concerning the sale of an item of stock, once input to the database, will be used to create an invoice, make appropriate entries in the Sales ledger and General ledger accounts, update the stock record and be used for management accounts, costing purposes and statistical returns.

Each of the applications in the paragraph above would require data to be recopied each time with the risk of errors if done manually. Provided data is input correctly to the database in the first instance, it will be copied accurately to every other record in which it is required. On the other hand, if data is input to the system incorrectly, the error will be perpetuated in all the accounting and statistical operations carried out by the computer.

It should be apparent that database systems are of immense use in accounting and statistical work.

26.4 Spreadsheets

A spreadsheet is a computer program which provides the user with a template of rows and columns via the screen. By using the rows and columns of the template, the user can build financial and statistical models. Where the entries in some of the positions in the template derive from arithmetical operations performed on data entered elsewhere in the template, the program can be designed to calculate and make the entries automatically with a speed and accuracy greatly in excess of that to be expected from the user.

There are many spreadsheet applications; the following are but a few:

(a) Operational or functional budgets

(b) Master budgets (forecast profit and loss accounts and balance sheets)

(c) Cash flow charts

(d) Capital expenditure appraisals (NPV and IRR)

(e) Estimates for jobs and contracts

(f) Stock records

(g) Financial and statistical projections of sales

(h) Profit projections (e.g. marginal costing applications)

Some of the more important facilities offered by spreadsheet software are:

1. The ability to manipulate data in the spreadsheet to discover the effect upon the model. This is very useful for what are known as 'what if' calculations. For example, in budgeting, it is important to know the effect a reduction of, say, 5% on sales would make to the final result. As the level of sales is varied on the spreadsheet, the program will recalculate other items in the spreadsheet to show, apart from other things, the effect on gross and net profit etc.

2. The ability to print spreadsheets or any part(s) of them. The print facility includes the ability to print 'graphics' (diagrams, charts etc.)

26.5 Word processing

The combined use of word processing with computers enables the production of financial reports for management, sales catalogue information for mailing to customers etc.

Credit control is a particularly important application of word processing as individual letters can be produced for debtors whose accounts are overdue, incorporating the balance on their accounts extracted from the database.

26.6 Advantages of computers in accounting

1. They process data at phenomenally faster speeds than is possible by manual methods.

2. They are capable of handling vast quantities of data which could only be processed by a large number of clerks if done manually.

3. They are extremely accurate. Nearly every reported 'computer error' is, in fact, a user error.

4. They make the provision of financial and statistical information available which would otherwise be too difficult or expensive to produce within the required time-scale.

5. They enable 'exception reports;' to be produced easily. These are reports of any item which does not conform to specified limits of acceptability. These reports facilitate 'management by exception'.

26.7 Disadvantages of computers

1. Installation costs are high. This is often compensated for later by a reduction in staff costs.

2. Operating and user staff need special training.

3. 'Garbage in, garbage out' means that if data input to a computer is faulty, the computer will produce faulty results. Computers cannot think for themselves; they will only do what they are programmed to do with the input data..

4. Once a computer system has been designed and installed, it may be very difficult and expensive to change if modification is required. It may take some time to modify it. This contrasts with manual systems in which clerks can change the system instantly once they have received the necessary instruction to do so.

26.8 Exercises

(You will need to visit dealers and exhibitions to answer the following exercises.)

1. How many makes and models of microcomputers can you find which would be suitable to perform the accounting function in a small business?

2. How much does the most expensive microcomputer in your list for Exercise 1 cost? How much does the cheapest one cost.

What additional capabilities does the most expensive microcomputer have over the cheapest?

3. What peripheral equipment is available for each of the computers you have listed in Exercise 1? To what extent are the computers compatible with each other? (i.e. can they be linked in any way? Can they use common software? Can they use peripheral equipment produced by another manufacturer?)

Key points to remember

1. Advanced level accounting papers do not require an in-depth knowledge of computer systems; that is reserved for advanced level computer studies papers. However, a good understanding of the uses of computers in accounting is expected and students should take every opportunity to obtain some 'hands on' experience and to visit computer exhibitions.

2. Show some practical knowledge of the subject in your answers if you can, and be prepared to discuss the disadvantages as well as the advantages of computers.

Questions

Examination questions

1 What is a posting run in a computer accounting system? Give two examples of such runs and explain what information is being posted.   (8 marks)
                                                                                              (OXFORD)

2 Name and explain four types of accounting information that you would expect to obtain from a computer by using **either** a sales ledger or a stock control package.   (8 marks)
                                                                                              (OXFORD)

3 Since the Second World War, technological changes and similar factors have brought about many changes in the environment in which accounting systems operate.

   Explain what you consider to be the most important of these changes and factors, and explain their effects upon the development and use of accounting systems.   (18 marks)
                                                                                              (WJEC)

4 Explain 'Management by exception' and state what accounting systems are available to enable managers to apply this principle in their work.   (8 marks)
                                                                                              (OXFORD)

27 Social accounting

Chapter objectives

Questions on social accounting require:

- ❏ an understanding of the limitations of financial statements as bases for management decision making
- ❏ a recognition of factors, other than financial ones, which must be taken into account in the management of a business

27.1 The limitations of financial statements as bases for management decisions

The concept of money measurement results in the limitation of entries in financial records to those transactions which can be expressed in money terms. As a result there are many factors affecting business which must be omitted from financial statements. Examples are:

(i)   Staff morale

(ii)   The quality of staff (its degree of skill, training etc.)

(iii)   The quality of the management of the business

(iv)   The attitude of the public towards the business

(v)   The effect of the business upon the local community

(vi)   The contribution, for good or ill, of the business to the environment (e.g 'green' issues.)

(vii) Where the business stands on political issues e.g. trading with countries with which there are trading sanctions; trading in arms etc.

At this point it should be mentioned that attempts have been made to place values on many 'social' factors, but these are economists' values rather than accountants' values and, whatever their validity as economic concepts, are not generally recognised by accountants as complying with the accounting concept of money measurement.

There are situations in which profitability alone should not be the sole or main determinant of policy.

For ease of memory, and as a guide to the approach to social accounting aspects in examination questions, the non financial factors to be considered are summarised under the broad headings of THE FOUR P's:

PEOPLE

PLACES

PRODUCTS

POLITICS.

It will often be found that there is a close relationship between these four factors. For example, people are involved because of a threat to the environment (place) or because some political issue is at stake.

27.2 People

People may be affected by the conduct of a business in varying degrees of involvement. One way of ranking peoples' involvement could be: first in order, the employees and the proprietors; next the customers; people living in the immediate locality and the local authority; more remotely, the general public and government. The degree of involvement will obviously depend upon the situation in question and it is easy to think of a situation in which government is more concerned about the conduct of a business than are people living in the vicinity.

Employees

These may be affected by:

- redundancy;, particularly in rural areas, inner cities or other regions where unemployment may be high.
- introduction of advanced technology;.
- the use of dangerous materials
- inadequate Health and Safety at Work protection.
- psychological factors relating to premature retirement.
- lack of consultation or information about changes which affect them
- being expected to contribute to economies of cost in a business while management make no contribution at all. (e.g. wages being cut at the same time as the managing director gets a big pay-rise.)

Some points to bear in mind:

(a) Is a trade union involved?

(b) If a grievance is not removed, what consequences may result? Disaffection of the employees? Industrial action? What will be the effect upon the business and its profitability, goodwill, even its continued existence?

(c) Costs of redundancy.

(d) Is there any alternative to making workers redundant? Can they be retrained for other jobs or re-located elsewhere within the organisation?

(e) Is any action contemplated or possible to soften the blow to workers being made redundant

(f) It may be easy to recruit unskilled labour, but if skilled labour is made redundant, will it be as easy to re-employ or replace them later if the need arises?

The Local Population

Consider the effect on the local population if a business:

- has a poor reputation as an employer
- causes a nuisance because of noise, fumes, use of large or heavy lorries to transport materials, goods etc.

Some points to bear in mind:

(a) effect on trade of business.

(b) the business's dependence upon the local population for staff recruitment.

The Local Authority

The local authority will be concerned with local amenities, environmental issues, Health and Safety at Work conditions, trading standards etc. It may become involved because of complaints received from local residents.

It has powers to enforce abatement of nuisances, enactment of statutory requirements regarding working conditions, trading standards etc. It may take legal action which could have unfortunate consequences e.g. heavy fines etc.

The General Public

A business which infringes the law, causes a nuisance or conducts its business in an ecologically unacceptable manner risks unwelcome publicity in the Press, on Radio or Television.

This could adversely affect its trade.

Government

Government is concerned with political implications such as illegal trading in arms, drugs etc., trading with countries subject to embargoes. Government is also concerned with the collection of taxes and duties. Taxpayers are entitled to conduct their affairs with a view to minimising their liability to tax (tax avoidance); it is illegal for them to evade payment of their proper tax liability e.g. by supplying the Inland Revenue with false information, (tax evasion).

27.3 Places

Ecology, or the care of the environment, is a popular issue today and is a favourite topic with examiners. It features prominently daily in the media.

'Places' should be interpreted widely to include, as appropriate, the rain forests, the ozone layer etc.

Typically, questions are based on businesses which seem unable to afford necessary modifications to their buildings or plant to make them ecologically acceptable. A careful examination of the facts in the question may show that there is a financial aspect as well as a social one:

A division of a large manufacturing concern has a factory in a rural area. The factory is annoying the local community by emitting obnoxious fumes into the atmosphere and the local inhabitants are complaining that the fumes are affecting their health.

The latest accounts for the factory show the following results for the past year:

	£m
Gross receipts	100
Operating expenses	(65)
Fixed overheads	(45)
Loss for year	(10)

Fixed overheads include an annual charge of £25m from the Head Office of the undertaking.

The capital cost of modifying the production process so as to abate the nuisance caused by the fumes would be £5m and the directors have stated that the company cannot afford the cost of modification.

In this example, the factory is making a profit of £15m before taking Head Office fixed costs into account. If the Local Authority were to use its powers to close the factory because it failed to abate the nuisance, Head Office would lose that contribution to its fixed costs which would have to be shared by the remaining part of the organisation. The directors' contention that the factory cannot afford the additional expenditure can not be supported.

The social aspects to be mentioned are the effect of the nuisance on the local population; the factory's reputation; the risk of compulsory closure of the factory if the nuisance is not abated, probably with heavy fines imposed as well; unwelcome bad publicity in the national Press, etc.

27.4 Products

Consideration of these must include:

- their compliance with trading standards
- the use of rare or scarce materials
- the use of dangerous materials (link with people, place) - ethical or social acceptability (tobacco, publication of a book which might be offensive racially or religiously etc.)
- unethical advertising

27.5 Politics

This heading should be interpreted widely to include any matter which appertains to government, but not party politics in the narrower sense.

Government is concerned with trading:

- in illegal commodities (e.g.drugs, arms, etc.)
- in markets on which there is a trade embargo.

Government is also concerned with fiscal policies and taxation; and with legislation affecting the whole of the industrial, commercial and service industry environment.

Businesses should be conducted in such a manner as to comply with all legal requirements at all times.

Key points to remember

1. Financial considerations are important, but by no means the only matters to be taken into account in the management of a business.

2. Financial statements are limited in the amount of information they convey; they cannot convey information about anything which cannot be quantified in money terms.

3. Businesses should be managed in a socially responsible manner as well as a financially prudent manner.

4. Any statement of business objectives which fails to take account of social implications may be setting the wrong objectives. For instance, an objective to maximise profit may be counterproductive if it fails to recognise the need to appear to be socially responsible. The attempt to achieve a big profit (at all costs!!) may alienate its market.

5. It is worthwhile to keep abreast of social issues as they affect business by reading a good newspaper regularly.

6. The purpose of this chapter has been to stimulate thought. Many students do not know how to approach social aspects of accounting in examinations or what is expected by the examiner.

7. Do not, on any account, express your own political views or views on social matters, in the examination. The examiner may not agree with your views and is entitled to have his own thoughts on these matters. An examination is not the occasion to win support for your views. The examiner is only interested to find out if you can recognise social accounting topics and offer some objective comments on them. Social accounting usually forms part only of a question and may only have 4 or 5 marks allocated to it. It is not, for that reason, to be left unattempted. 5 marks can make a difference of two grades to the examination result in some circumstances. On the other hand, 5 marks does not warrant a thesis for a degree!

Questions

Further examination questions

1 The following profit statement relates to a division of Citizen plc:

Profit statement for the year ended 31 October 19-8

	£	£
Sales		300,000
Less Expenses		
Direct production expenses		
Material	110,000	
Labour	75,000	
Overhead	30,000	
Indirect production expenses		
Depreciation of machinery	30,000	
Fixed	15,000	
Administration and selling expenses		
Variable	6,000	
Fixed	18,000	284,000
Profit		16,000

Additional Information:

(1) The division's machinery had a net book value at 31 October 19-7 of £90,000 and is being depreciated at £30,000 per annum.

(2) Citizen plc is actively considering a proposal to close the division at the end of a financial year on or before 31 October 19-1.

The Management has estimated the resale values of the machinery as follows:

	£
at 31 October 19-8	70,000
31 October 19-9	50,000
31 October 19-0	36,000
31 October 19-1	Nil

(3) Certain costs have been estimated to increase in each of the following three years as follows:

	£
Direct labour	5,000
Direct material	9,000
Indirect fixed production expenses	2,000
Fixed selling expenses	2,000

(4) (i) Sales – sales volume will not change but selling prices will increase by 10% on 1 November 19-8 and not increase thereafter.

(ii) Direct production overheads – are expected to remain at the same percentage of direct labour as in the year ended 31 October 19-8.

(iii) Variable selling expenses – as a percentage of sales value are expected to remain constant.

Required

(a) (i) Forecast profit statements, in columnar format, for each of the three years to 31 October 19-1 assuming that the division continues until that date. (9 marks)

(ii) An accounting statement showing the financially optimum date for the closure of the division. (4 marks)

(b) A brief outline of the non-financial relevant factors to be borne in mind when considering the future of the division. (5 marks)

(Total 18 marks)

(AEB)

2   The following financial information was available on Yeso Ltd. as at 31 March 19-8.

	£		£
Current assets	70,000	Retained earnings at 31 March 19-7	32,000
Fixed assets (at net book value)	126,000	General reserve	15,000
Current liabilities	45,000	Share premium	18,000
Net profit for the year		Ordinary share capital	
ended 31 March 19-8	6,000	£1 shares fully paid	80,000

Additional information:

(1) No interim dividend had been paid, but the directors decided to recommend a final dividend of 10% and to transfer £10,000 to general reserve.

(2) The recently appointed managing director wishes to improve the profitability of the business and he issued a policy statement that all new capital investment must show a minimum return on capital employed of 15% per annum.

(3) Adam, a sole proprietor about to retire, offered to sell his business to Yeso Ltd.
(i) The recent financial history of the business is as follows:

	19-4	19-5	19-6	19-7
	£	£	£	£
Net assets employed	35,000	40,000	39,000	46,000
Net profit for year	7,000	7,700	8,100	8,600

The price Adam has set for his business is the 19-7 net assets valuation plus £5,000 for goodwill.

(ii) An examination of Adam's books, by the managing director of Yeso Ltd. revealed that the net assets included an unused derelict building with book value of £5,000. The market valuation of the site was £20,000.

Required

(a) The profit and loss appropriation account of Yeso Ltd. for the year ended 31 March 19-8.

(5 marks)

(b) Calculate the return on capital employed for Yeso Ltd. for the year ended 31 March 19-8 using two definitions of capital employed. (4 marks)

(c) Prepare a brief report advising whether Yeso Ltd. should purchase Adam's business. Your report should include appropriate calculations to support your argument. (6 marks)

(d) Identify ways, through appropriate action, in which the company may be able to raise the return on capital employed of Yeso Ltd. (5 marks)

(e) If a company continues to earn a persistently low return on capital employed, what are the implications for:
(i) the financial position of the company
(ii) the social accounting aspects relating to the employees? (5 marks)

(Total 25 marks)

(AEB)

28 Inflation accounting

28.1 Historic cost accounting

It is the practice in accounting to record transactions at cost. This is known as the cost concept. It is described as an objective method of recording the purchase of assets and services, and the sale of goods because there can be general agreement about the monetary values attributed to the transactions. The amounts can be supported by evidence such as invoices, receipts etc. Any other basis for recording transactions would be subjective; the amount in which a transaction would be recorded would be dependent upon individual points of view. For example, if an asset were to be recorded in a ledger account at its estimated value to the business, it is probable that different people would have quite different opinions about the value of the asset. A company car provided for the use of a sales representative may have different values placed upon it by different people. The sales representative values his car highly; he justifies it as an indispensable part of his job, saving valuable time when he visits customers and increases his status in their eyes. He asserts that the car repays its cost many times over. A clerk in the company's sales ledger department is not supplied with a company car and the prospect of ever being given one seems remote. He places a much lower value on the sales representative' s car on the grounds that the representative could just as easily use public transport to visit customers; he sees the car as nothing more than a salesman's perk. Clearly, the same asset is being valued very differently by different persons. These are controversial, subjective valuations. The only amount on which both the representative and the ledger clerk can agree is the actual cost of the car which can be proved by reference to an invoice

28.2 Advantage of historic cost accounting

Transactions are recorded objectively at amounts which can be proved; there will not usually be any argument about the cost of assets purchased from outside the business. (There may, however, be differences of views about the cost of assets made by a business for its own use.)

28.3 Disadvantages of historic cost accounting

The validity of historic cost accounting rests on the assumption that the currency in which transactions are recorded remains stable ; that is, its purchasing power remains unchanged, or very nearly so, from one year to another. This has patently not been the case within living memory. A Ford motor car could be bought for just £97 in 1939. Now, nearly 60 years later, the cheapest car costs about 100 times as much. In 1939, a new house could be bought for £500; a similar house would cost more than 200 times as much now. £1 now buys much less than it did in 1939; it has been devalued by the process known as inflation which increases the prices of goods. Inflation in 1979 was at the rate of 17.5%; at the time of writing this chapter it is down to 1.3%, the lowest for 30 years.

The effect of the changing value of money on the recording of transactions at historic cost may be seen from the following examples.

Example 1: the revenue earning capacity of assets

Lladnar Ltd purchased a machine on 1 January 19X1 at a cost of £10,000. It was capable of producing 2,000 units of output each year, and each unit was sold for £10. In the year to 31 December 19X1, it earned £20,000, or twice its cost.

The same machine has been maintained in a proper state of repair and in 19X5 earns revenue of £36,000, or 3.6 times its original cost. It has apparently become more productive and therefore more profitable. However, the price of each unit has risen in line with inflation to £18. The machine has therefore produced 2,000 units, the same as in 19X1. The apparent improvement in performance is illusory because income in £s of 19X5 value are being compared with the cost of the machine in £s of 19X1 value. To get the right perspective, the cost of the machine must be adjusted by the same rate of inflation as the price of the goods, i.e. 80%. The adjusted cost will be £10,000 × $\frac{180}{100}$ = £18,000. On this basis, the machine has earned an income of twice its adjusted cost, the same as in 19X 1.

Example 2: comparison of income of different periods

The turnover of Lladnar Ltd in each of three years has been as follows:

19X1	£1,000,000
19X2	£1,150,000
19X3	£1,200,000

The directors of the company are pleased to see that the company's turnover is growing steadily. However, given that the average price index in 19X1 was 100, and the average indices for 19X2 and 19X3 were 117 and 125 respectively, the turnover for each of the years, on an inflation adjusted basis, was as follows:

19X1	£1,000,000 × $\frac{125}{100}$	= £1,250,000
19X2	£1,150,000 × $\frac{125}{117}$	= £1,228,632
19X3	£1,200,000 × $\frac{125}{125}$	= £1,200,000

In real terms, using inflation adjusted figures for all years, the company's turnover is declining.

Example 3: depreciation of fixed assets calculated on historic costs

The purpose of depreciation is to charge the cost of an asset against revenue over the term of its useful economic life. The effect is intended to reduce the amount of profit available for distribution to shareholders, or available as drawings for a sole trader. In theory, cash is retained in the business to replace the asset when it is worn out. In practice, the money may have been spent on other things before the asset is replaced. At least, it should not have been drawn out of the business by the owners.

Given the intention underlying the provision of depreciation on fixed assets, depreciation based upon the historic cost of assets is found to be inadequate in times of inflation.

Lladnar Ltd purchased a machine on 1 January 19X1 for £40,000. The machine was estimated to have a life of 4 years at the end of which time it would have no residual value. At 31 December 19X3, the replacement cost of the machine with an identical model has risen to £46,000. To fulfil the purpose which underlies the provision for depreciation on fixed assets, depreciation should be calculated on the replacement cost of the asset. An additional depreciation charge in addition to the normal one should be provided. The normal depreciation charge on the straight line basis and the additional depreciation charge for 19X3 would be calculated as follows:

Normal charge on the straight line basis $\frac{£40,000}{4}$ = £10,000.

	£ 19X3
Depreciation based on replacement cost (25% of £46,000)	11,500
Normal charge	10,000
Additional depreciation	1,500

Example 4: holding gains

Historic cost accounting does not recognise that profit may accrue from inflationary tendencies in the period during which goods are held before they are sold.

Lladnar Ltd purchases goods for £1,000 in 19X1 when they could be sold for £1,200. The stock remains unsold until 19X2, by which time the selling price has risen to £1,350. Historic cost accounting records a profit on the sale in 19X2 of £350. If the goods had been sold in 19X1, historic cost accounting would have recognised a profit of £200. The extra £150 has arisen not from the sale, but from inflation which occurred before the sale; it is a 'holding gain' which has resulted not from selling stock, but from holding it.

Example 5: balance sheet presentation of similar assets purchased at different times

The balance sheet of a business shows the total of the historical costs of all assets in each category. The assets in a category may all be similar but purchased at different times at different prices. Price differences are not recognised in the balance sheet.

Lladnar Ltd purchased a machine for £10,000 on 1 January 19X1 when the index of prices was 100. It purchased a second similar machine on 1 January 19X3 when the index of prices was 115 and paid £11,500. It purchased a third similar machine on 1 January 19X4 when the price index was 125, and paid £12,500. The three machines are recorded in the machine at cost account in the sum of £34,000 and this amount is shown in the balance sheet. If the machines are depreciated on the straight line method at 10% on cost each year, the total depreciation provided at 31 December 19X4 will be £[(40% of 10,000) + (20% of £11,500) + (10% of £12,500)] = £7,550. The machines are identical but, on the historical cost basis, are recorded at different costs simply by accident of being bought at different times. The annual depreciation charges are anomalous as well. The annual depreciation on the machine purchased in 19X1 is £1,000, while the annual depreciation charges on the other two are £1,150 and £1,250.

If the costs are adjusted, the machines and the related depreciation will be recorded in the balance sheet at 31 December 19X4 as follows:

Machines	Cost £	Adjustment	Balance sheet £
Machine purchased 1.1.X1	10,000	$\frac{125}{100}$	12,500
Machine purchased 1.1.X3	11,500	$\frac{125}{115}$	12,500
Machine purchased 1.1.X4	12,500	$\frac{125}{125}$	12,500
			37,500

Depreciation			£
4 × 10% of £10,000	4,000	$\frac{125}{100}$	5,000
2 × 10% of £11,500	2,300	$\frac{125}{115}$	2,500
1 × 10% of £12,500	1,250	$\frac{125}{125}$	1,250
			£8,750

The machines, which are identical, will be shown in the balance sheet at identical values and the related depreciation has been adjusted accordingly.

28.4 SSAP 16 (withdrawn in 1988)

In the 1970's, the Accounting profession became convinced that where historic cost accounts are materially affected by changing prices, information about the effects of changing prices was necessary for an appreciation of a company's results and financial position. Current Purchasing Power (CPP) accounting was favoured at this stage. This is explained below.

After much deliberation and consultation, Statement of Standard Accounting Practice (SSAP) 16 was issued requiring companies to provide Current Cost Accounts either as an addition to their statutory historic cost accounts, or as the main statutory accounts. Current Cost Accounting, CCA, is explained below. The SSAP was initially introduced for a period of three years, after which time its operation would be reviewed. It proved to be a controversial standard and subject to much criticism. The Statement was suspended in 1985 and withdrawn in 1988.

Nevertheless, the Accounting Standards Committee reaffirmed its belief in current cost accounting as an acceptable method of accounting for the effects of changing prices and issued a handbook 'Accounting for the effects of changing prices' in 1986. Although the Companies Act 1985 assumes that accounts will be based on historical costs, it does allow for the use of Current Cost Accounting as an alternative basis.

28.5 Current purchasing power accounting (CPP)

CPP requires the retail price index (RPI) to be used to convert historical cost accounts to Current Purchasing Power accounts. It measures income after allowing for maintenance of the purchasing power of the shareholders' capital. Money itself has no intrinsic value, but it is a medium of exchange. It seems reasonable that what the shareholders' capital will buy at the end of a year should be related to what it could have bought at the beginning of the year.

It is easy to convert profit and loss accounts and balance sheets of previous years to current purchasing power to aid comparison with the latest financial statements.

The distinction between gains or losses on trading, and gains or losses on monetary assets and liabilities is shown clearly. Monetary assets and liabilities consist of cash, debtors, creditors, loan capital and preference share capital. These items in the balance sheet do not require adjustment to reflect changes in price levels. If Lladnar Ltd borrows £100,000 in 19X1 and repays the loan in 19X5, it repays only £100,000 regardless of any rise in the price index in the meantime. If the value of the £ in 19X1 has fallen from 100 pence in to 80 pence in 19X5, Lladnar Ltd's repayment is worth only £80,000 in terms of the £s that it borrowed. There is a gain of £20,000 which belongs to the ordinary shareholders.

Gains on monetary items may give a quite misleading impression in the CPP accounts of a highly geared company. Large gains may be recorded on long term loans at the same time as the company has a deficiency of working capital.

Another objection to CPP is the fact that it uses the RPI which may reflect the purchasing power of the shareholders' money, but probably bears little relationship to the company's own costs. Rent of premises may not increase from one year to another in spite of in creases in the RPI. In the year in which the rental agreement provides for a review, the rent increase may then far exceed any increase in the RPI. Labour costs have often exceeded the rise in the cost of living. Raw materials imported from abroad may have little direct connection with the RPI.

CPP is not concerned to show the economic value of a company's assets. It revalues the money spent in acquiring assets rather than the assets themselves. Historic cost is the base on which revaluation rests and CPP therefore shares the same limitations as historic cost accounting.

28.6 Current cost accounting (CCA)

CCA values assets in the balance sheet at their value to the business whether that be replacement cost, net realisable value or economic value. Specific price indices may be used to calculate current costs. It differs in this respect from CPP which uses the RPI.

Only operating gains are recognised in the profit and loss account from which holding gains, as described earlier, are excluded.

CCA attempts to maintain the real value of assets whereas CPP's objective is to maintain the purchasing power of the shareholders' capital.

Four adjustments are required to be made to historic cost accounts under CCA:

1. Depreciation adjustment (as demonstrated earlier.)

2. Cost of sales adjustment (COSA) by which opening and closing stocks are adjusted to the average current cost for the year to allow for price changes when calculating cost of sales

3. Monetary working capital adjustment (MWCA) which represents the increase or decrease in finance needed for monetary working capital as a result of changes in the input prices of goods and services used and financed by the business.

4. Gearing adjustment to take account of gains or losses accruing to the equity shareholders as a result of debt financing.

Current cost reserve. This reserve does not appear in a balance sheet prepared on historic cost but does feature in a current cost balance sheet. It is credited with surpluses on the revaluation of fixed assets and stocks, the working capital adjustment and the gearing adjustment. It is also known, appropriately, as the capital maintenance reserve.

28.7 Measurement of profit

Sir John Hicks, an eminent economist, defined income in personal terms as 'the maximum value which a man can consume during a week and still expect to be as well off at the end of the week as he was at the beginning.' Although Sir John was referring to personal income, the same holds true if it is applied to the profit of a business.

A government committee, known as the Sandilands Committee after the name of its chairman, published a report on inflation accounting in 1975 in which it rephrased Hick's definition of income to define company income. It read as follows: 'A company's profit for the year is the maximum value which a company can distribute during the year and still expect to be as well off at the end of the year as it was at the beginning.' The principle involved is precisely the one involved when the profit or loss of a business is calculated by comparing its net assets (capital) at the end of the year with its net assets at the beginning of the year. (See Incomplete records, Chapter 4 §4.1).

It is generally accepted that if the owner of a business has withdrawn the same amount of money during the year as he has made in profit, his capital at the end of the year will be the same in money terms as it was at the beginning. However, this begs the question as to whether real profit can be measured by comparing the historic cost of the net assets at the beginning of the year with the cost of the net assets at the end of the year in times of changing price levels. Clearly, the net asset value of the business at the end of a year only equals the value of the net assets at the beginning of the year if the real value of the assets has been maintained. The net assets at the beginning of the year should be adjusted to take account of inflation. Current cost accounting is the method required to calculate this adjustment.

Key points to remember

1. Historic Cost accounting maintains the monetary amount of shareholders' equity

2. Current Purchasing Power accounting maintains the current purchasing power of shareholders' equity

3. Current Cost Accounting maintains the net operating assets which are financed by the shareholders

4. Current Purchasing Power uses the Retail Price Index which is based upon consumers' purchasing power rather than business costs.

5. Current Cost Accounting uses replacement cost, net realisable value, economic value or indices which are specific to assets.

Questions

Further examination questions

1   On 1 November 1990, John Smith commenced business as a dealer in Landmaster farm tractors with a capital of £40,000 which was used immediately to purchase four Landmasters at £10,000 each from the manufacturers.

On 1 February 1991, the manufacturers increased the price of the Landmaster farm tractor to £11,500 and subsequently during the year ended 31 October 1991 John Smith sold, for £16,000 each, all four of the tractors he bought; two on 1 May 1991 and two on 1 August 1991. On 31 October 1991, John Smith bought a further four Landmasters at £11,500 each.

John Smith's business expenses during the year ended 31 October 1991 amounted to £1,650; it can be assumed that this expenditure was incurred on 1 May 1991.

All transactions during the year ended 31 October 1991 were on a cash, non-credit, basis.

The following are appropriate general price indices:

1 November 1990	100
1 May 1991	110
1 August 1991	120
31 October 1991	130

Required

(a) Trading and profit and loss accounts for the year ended 31 October 1991 and balance sheets as at that date on each of the following bases:
 (i) historical cost accounting;
 (ii) current cost accounting;
 (iii) current purchasing power. (19 marks)

(b) Identify the circumstances for which i) current cost accounting and ii) current purchasing power accounting may be appropriate. (6 marks)

(Total 25 marks)
(CAMBRIDGE)

2 On a Caribbean island where the local currency is Carib dollars(C$) Tom and Marlene set up on 1 May 1991 as directors of Island Products Incorporated (IPI) which they formed to deal in a local commodity called Shugapine.

All IPI's transactions in the year to 30 April 1992 were for cash, as follows:

	C$
1 May 1991 Share Capital subscribed	180,000
Bought 18,000 tons of Shugapine at C$5 per ton	90,000
At average dates around 1 November 1991:	
Sold 16,200 tons of Shugapine at C$9 per ton	145,800
Bought 30,000 tons of Shugapine at C$6 per ton	180,000
Paid handling expenses	45,000

There were no other expenses and IPI's bank balance at 30 April 1992 was C$10,800.

At 30 April 1992 Tom calculated IPI's profit for the year as C$19,800 having used the historical cost basis (HC) of accounting with stock values arrived at by the FIFO method. The directors referred their calculations to their Cambridge accountants for advice because local prices had been changing through the year as follows:

For dates around	Island retail price index	Index of buying prices for Shugapine
1 May 1991	90	50
1 November 1991	100	60
30 April 1992	120	70

The reply from the Cambridge accountants was damaged in the fax machine but enough of their letter survived for Tom and Marlene to piece together the following information:

1. Tom's historic cost profit figure was confirmed as correctly calculated.

2. The Cambridge accountants had also calculated profits and asset values by two other methods which they described as:
 (i) The Current Purchasing Power method (CPP) which adjusted the historic cost accounts by reference to the Island's retail price index expressed in Carib dollars at 30 April 1992, and
 (ii) The Current Cost Accounting method (CCA) which charged Shugapine at replacement cost at the date of sale and valued stock in hand in the balance sheet at replacement cost at 30 April 1992.

3. From the damaged letter only the figures given below could be positively identified.

	C$ HC	C$ CPP	C$ CCA
Sales	–	174,960	145,800
Cost of sales	–	108,000	97,200
Stock 30 April 1992	–	228,000	222,600
Total assets	199,800	–	233,400
Share capital	–	240,000	180,000

Required

(a) Prepare for the company for the year ended 30 April 1992 a profit and loss account and a balance sheet at the year end:
  (i) using the historic cost (HC) basis;
  (ii) using the current purchasing power (CPP) basis;and
  (iii) using the current cost accounting (CCA) basis.   (19 marks)

(b) A brief explanation of the C$53,400 difference under the current cost accounting basis between total assets and the subscribed share capital.   (6 marks)

(Total 25 marks)
(CAMBRIDGE)

3   The following extracts have been taken from the published accounts of Utility PLC.

Profit and Loss accounts	Under the Historical Cost convention		Under the Current Cost convention	
	1991	1990	1991	1990
	£m HC		£m CC	
Turnover	7,980	7,520	7,980	7,520
Cost of sales	(4,040)	(3,820)	(4,110)	(3,860)
Gross Profit	3,940	3,700	3,870	3,660
Distribution costs	(1,700)	(1,545)	(1,855)	(1,750)
Administration expenses	(870)	(730)	(920)	(790)
Operating profit	1,370	1,425	1,095	1,120
Gearing adjustment	–	–	30	25
Net interest	(75)	(90)	(75)	(90)
	1,295	1,335	1,050	1,055
Taxation	(370)	(435)	(370)	(435)
Profit after taxation	925	900	680	620
Dividends	(445)	(380)	(445)	(380)
Profit retained	480	520	235	240
Earnings per share	21.7p	21.2p	16.0p	14.6p

Balance Sheets	1991	1990	1991	1990
	£m HC		£m CC	
Tangible Fixed Assets	8,735	7,960	20,500	18,800
Stocks	340	330	340	330
Debtors	2,370	1,875	2,370	1,875
Investments	620	1,215	620	1,215
Cash at banks	30	50	30	50
	3,360	3,470	3,360	3,470
Less Creditors (due within one year)	(3,200)	(3,090)	(3,200)	(3,090)
Net Current Assets	160	380	160	380
Total assets less current liabilities	8,895	8,340	20,660	19,180
Less Creditors				
(due after more than one year)	(1,160)	(1,080)	(1,160)	(1,080)
	7,735	7,260	19,500	18,100
Called up share capital	1,065	1,065	1,065	1,065
Current cost reserve	–	–	16,245	15,075
Other reserves	6,670	6,195	2,190	1,960
	7,735	7,260	19,500	18,100

Note: the par value of the shares is 25p each.

Required

(a) Explain the main reasons for the differences in gross and operating profits between the historic cost and the current cost bases of accounting.   (8 marks)

(b) Explain the items:
  (i) Gearing adjustment
  (ii) Current cost reserve.   (8 marks)

(c) Calculate for 1991 only, the interest cover and the dividend cover under both the historic cost and the current cost conventions.   (4 marks)

(d) Show for 1991 only how the figure for 'Earnings per share' has been calculated under both conventions. (2 marks)

(e) Calculate for 1991 only the return on total capital employed under both conventions. Total capital employed may be taken to be total assets less current liabilities. (3 marks)

(Total 25 marks)
(CAMBRIDGE)

4   (a) Give **three** reasons why historical cost accounting may not be entirely valid as a measure of a management's performance. (12 marks)

(b) Give **brief** details of **two** alternatives to historical cost accounting that may be used for decision-making purposes. (6 marks)

(Total 18 marks)
(WJEC)

5   (a) Why is historic cost accounting of less value in decision-making when an economy is subject to relatively high inflation? (6 marks)

(b) **Briefly** outline how a management accountant may assist his firm to maintain its profitability if inflation persists. (8 marks)

(c) State why a firm may find it beneficial to make use of loan capital during a period of inflation. (4 marks)

(Total 18 marks)
(WJEC)

6   A company was formed with share capital of £2,000 and immediately invested £1,000 in fixed assets and purchased stock costing £1,000. In the period which followed it turned its stock over twice suffering a price rise of £50 on each occasion that it replenished its stock. At the end of the period the fixed assets would have cost £1,200 to replace. During the period the rise in the retail price index was 8%.

The following are the company's final accounts for the period prepared under three alternative conventions.

Profit and Loss Accounts

	Historical cost	Current cost	Current purchasing power
	£	£	£CPP
Sales	2,450	2,450	2,496
Cost of sales	(2,050)	(2,050)	(2,170)
Overheads	(50)	(50)	(50)
Depreciation at 10%	(100)	(100)	(108)
Net profit	250	250	
Cost of sales adjustment		(100)	
Depreciation adjustment		(20)	
Loss on holding of monetary assets			(6)
Profit	250	130	162

Closing Balance Sheets

	£	£	£CPP
Fixed assets at net book value	900	1,080	972
Stock	1,100	1,100	1,100
Cash	250	250	250
	2,250	2,430	2,322
Share capital	2,000	2,000	2,000
Current cost reserve		300	
Capital maintenance reserve			160
Undistributed profits	250	130	162
	2,250	2,430	2,322

Required

(a) discuss the reason for adjusting accounts to reflect the effects of changing prices. (5 marks)

(b) comment on the differences thrown up by the three sets of accounts and explain the conceptual differences between them. (7 marks)

(c) identify the users of accounts who would be attracted to the different conventions. (3 marks)

(Total 15 marks)

(NI)

7 "The calculation of profit is related to the concept of capital maintenance."

Required

(a) set out a generally accepted definition of profit. (6 marks)

(b) discuss the basis of calculating charges made in the profit and loss account for capital maintenance under each of the following accounting conventions:
   (i)   historical cost; (3 marks)
   (ii) current purchasing power; (3 marks)
   (iii) current cost. (3 marks)

(Total 15 marks)

(NI)

Appendix – Answers to exercises

Keys to Multiple Choice Questions

Chapter 1

1 C; 2 B; 3 C; 4 C; 5 D; 6 C; 7 A; 8 B; 9 A; 10 B; 11 B; 12 B.

Chapter 2

1 B; 2 C; 3 A.

Chapter 3

1 A; 2 B; 3 C; 4 B; 5 C.

Chapter 4

1 B; 2 B; 3 C; 4 D; 5 D; 6 B.

Chapter 5

1 A; 2 C; 3 C; 4 B.

Chapter 6

1 C; 2 C; 3 B; 4 B; 5 D.

Chapter 7

1 A; 2 A; 3 C; 4 B.

Chapter 9

1 D; 2 D; 3 A; 4 A; 5 C; 6 C; 7 B; 8 B; 9 B; 10 B; 11 A; 12 C; 13 C; 14 D.

Chapter 16

1 B; 2 C; 3 B; 4 A; 5 C; 6 B.

Chapter 17

1 A; 2 A; 3 C; 4 C.

Chapter 18

1 A; 2 C; 3 D; 4 B.

Chapter 19

1 A; 2 C.

Chapter 20

1 D; 2 B; 3 B; 4 A; 5 B; 6 C; 7 B.

Chapter 21

1 A; 2 A; 3 D; 4 C; 5 C; 6 B.

Answers to exercises

Chapter 1

1.3.2

Colombo
Trial balance as at 31 December 19–9

	Dr £	Cr £
Premises	80,000	
Plant and machinery	65,000	
Office furniture	15,000	
Provision for depreciation: plant and machinery		35,000
Provision for depreciation: office furniture		10,000
Stock at 1.1.–9	6,000	
Debtors	5,500	
Creditors		2,700
Purchases	47,000	
Carriage inwards	1,200	
Carriage outwards	2,100	
Sales		90,000
Returns inwards	2,600	
Returns outwards		1,400
Provision for doubtful debts		500
Selling and distribution expenses	20,800	
Administration expenses	15,400	
Discounts receivable		2,000
Discounts allowed	1,800	
Drawings	12,600	
Capital		133,400
	275,000	275,000

Note: Closing stock does not appear in the books at all until the trading account is prepared.

Chapter 2

2.1.2

Total Controls Ltd.
Sales ledger control account for the month of September 19–0

19–0		£	19–0		£
Sept 1	Balance b/f	5,000	Sept 1	Balance b/f	76
30	Sales for the month	21,790	30	Sales returns	1,760
	Bad debt recovered	70		Discounts allowed	580
	Cash book–				
	dishonoured cheques	826		Cash book – cash received	
	Interest debited to accounts	36		from debtors	20,450
	Balance c/d	150		Cash book– bad debt	
				recovered	70
				Bad debts w/o	424
				Contras–Purchases ledger	1,200
				Balance c/d	3,312
		27,872			27,872
Oct 1	Balance b/d	3,312	Oct 1	Balance b/d	150

Purchases ledger control account
for the month of September 19–0

19–0		£	19–0		£
Sept 1	Balance b/d	124	Sept 1	Balance b/d	3,600
30	Purchases returns	440	30	Purchases for the month	14,500
	Discounts received	276		Balance c/d	80
	Cash paid	11,120			
	Contras – sales ledger	1,200			
	Balance c/d	5,020			
		18,180			18,180
Oct 1	Balance b/d	80	Oct 1	Balance b/d	5,020

Tutorial notes:

1. Cash sales and cash purchases are irrelevant as far as control accounts are concerned and so are ignored in this exercise.

2. The provision for doubtful debts is irrelevant and is also ignored.

2.2.2

Dodgson

Purchases ledger total account for the three months ended
30 June 19–3

19–3		£	19–3		£
Apr 1	Balance b/d	625	Apr 1	Balance b/d	32,000
30	Purchases returns	3,200	30	Purchases	120,000
	Bank	100,200		Balance c/d	410
	Discounts	2,500			
	Balance c/d	45,885			
		152,410			152,410
May 1	Balance b/d	410	May 1	Balance b/d	45,885
31	Purchases returns	4,800	31	Purchases	160,000
	Bank	148,000		Balance c/d	570
	Discounts	3,800			
	Balance c/d	49,445			
		206,455			206,455
Jun 1	Balance b/d	570	Jun 1	Balance b/d	49,445
30	Purchases returns	4,000	30	Purchases	144,000
	Bank	130,000		Balance c/d	220
	Discounts	2,700			
	Balance c/d	56,395			
		193,665			193,665
Jul 1	Balance b/d	220	Jul 1	Balance b/d	56,395

2.3.2 (a)

Datchett

Purchases Ledger Control Account (corrected)
for the month of January 19–9

19–9		£	19–9		£
Jan 31	Balance b/d	540	Jan 31	Balance b/d	
	Discounts received	1,026		(balancing figure)	10,915
	Balance c/d (see (b) below)	13,960		Correction of casting	
				error in P.D.B.	1,250
				Correction of cash posting	
				for month	1,800
				Cancellation of discounts	
				allowed posted in error	1,321
				Balance c/d (see (b) below)	240
		15,526			15,526
Feb 1	Balance b/d	240	Feb 1	Balance b/d	13,960

(b)

Calculation of the corrected totals of the debit and credit
balances in the Purchases ledger as at 31 January 19–9

	Dr	Cr
	£	£
Purchases ledger balances as included in the trial balance	540	15,240
Correction of posting error to Sawyer's account		(600)
Cancellation of credit note erroneously posted to W. Lynne's account	(300)	100
Credit note now posted to L.Wynne's account		(400)
Transfer to James' account from sales ledger		(380)
	240	13,960

Chapter 3

3.2.2

(a)

G.Sobers
Suspense account

19–3		£	19–3		£
	Sales	180	Jun 30	* Difference on trial balance	35
				Lloyd	45
				Bad debt w/o	100
		180			180

* In this type of question, when the difference on the trial balance is not given, the difference is found by calculating the amount required to make the suspense account balance.

(b)   Journal

			Dr	Cr
			£	£
2.	Machinery at cost		750	
	Machinery repairs			750
	Profit and loss		75	
	*Provision for depreciation of machinery			75
4.	Purchases		300	
	F Engineer			300

* Additional depreciation must be calculated and provided on machinery as the calculation of depreciation in the draft accounts would not have taken account of the improvement.

(c)   **Statement of corrected profit for the year to 30 June 19–3**

	Decrease	Increase	
	£	£	£
Profit per draft accounts			7,550
Reduction in machinery repairs		750	
Increase in provision for depreciation of machinery	75		
Increase in sales		180	
Increase in purchases	300		
Increase in bad debts w/o	100		
	475	930	
		475	
Net increase in profit			455
Revised net profit			8,005

3.2.3

P.Hendrie

(a)   **Journal**

		Dr	Cr
		£	£
1.	Repairs to motor cars	2,780	
	Suspense	90	
	Motor cars at cost		2,870

(Cancellation of amount debited in error to Motor cars at cost and posting of cost of repair work to Repairs to motor cars; consequent reduction to 'difference on trial balance' in Suspense account.)

2.	Suspense	500	
	Sales		500

(Sales understated by £500 because of omission of Boon's invoice from Sales Day Book. Consequent reduction to 'difference on trial balance' in Suspense a/c.)

3.	Suspense	3,600	–

(Opening stock figure overstated by £3,600 in trial balance, causing a trial balance difference, but double entry not affected.)

4.	Stock		1,300		
	Cost of sales			1,300	

(Closing stock understated by omission of stock sheet)

5.	Suspense		320	–

(Credit balance of £160 in sales ledger extracted as debit balance causing a trial balance difference of double that amount but not affecting the double entry)

(b)

Suspense account

19–2		£	19–2		£
Mar 31	Motor car at cost	90	Mar 31	Difference on trial balance	4,510
	Sales	500			
	Adjustment of stock at				
	1 Apr 19–1	3,600			
	Adjustment of trade debtors	320			
		4,510			4,510

(c)

Calculation of adjusted net profit for the year ended 31 March 19–2

	Decrease £	Increase £	£
Net loss per draft profit and loss account			(2,300)
Increase in motor repairs	2,780		
Increase in sales		500	
Reduction in cost of sales (decrease in opening stock)		3,600	
Reduction in cost of sales (increase in closing stock)		1,300	
	2,780	5,400	
		2,780	
Net reduction in loss			2,620
Adjusted net profit			320

Chapter 4

4.1.2 **Mr. Blower**

Statement of Affairs as at

		1 July 19–2 £		30 June 19–3 £
Fixed assets:				
Premises at valuation		8,000		8,000
Motor van		4,000		3,200
Motor car		–		5,500
Plant and equipment		900		1,000
		12,900		17,700
Current assets:				
Stock of materials	100		175	
Debtors for work done	1,250		640	
Balance at bank	2,400		120	
	3,750		935	
less Current liabilities:				
Owing to suppliers	(975)		(1,800)	
Rates owing	–		(400)	
Telephone owing	(15)		(40)	
		2,760		(1,305)
		15,660		16,395
Less long term liability:				
Loan from father		–		(2,000)
Capital		15,660		14,395
less capital at 1 July 19–2				(15,660)
				(1,265)
Add Drawings during year (52 × £80)				4,160
				2,895
Deduct capital introduced during year (motor car)				(5,500)
Net loss for the year to 30 June 19–3				(2,605)

4.2.2

A Smith Purchases total account

19–4		£	19–3		£
Mar 31	Cheques	168,000	Apr 30	Creditors b/f	14,640
	Discounts	6,400	19–4		
	Creditors c/f	16,100	Mar 31	Purchases (bal.fig.)	175,860
		190,500			190,500

Sales total account

19–3		£	19–4		£
Apr 30	Debtors b/f	19,730	Mar 31	Cash	199,700
	Sales (bal.fig.)	205,940		Discounts	4,820
				Debtors c/f	21,150
		225,670			225,670

4.3.2

Mr. Peters

Trading account for the year to 30 September 19–5

	£	£
Sales		260,000
less Cost of sales Stock at 1 Oct 19–4	11,000	
Purchases	211,000	
	222,000	
Stock at 30 September 19–5	14,000	208,000
Gross profit (20% of sales)		52,000

4.5.2

J.T.Forster

Profit and loss account for the year to 31 December 19–3

	£	£
Work done (40,764 – 3,000 + 6,000)		43,764
less cost of materials (9,000 + 2,000		
2,600 + 4,250 – 2,700 – 3,500)		11,650
		32,114
Wages (6,000 + 1,800)	7,800	
Rates (1,000 + 400 – 500)	900	
Electricity (800 – 200 + 280)	880	
Advertising (700 + 120 – 340)	480	
Motor expenses (2,100 – 900)	1,200	
Loss on sale of motor lorry	2,200	
Depreciation of motor lorries	1,800	
Depreciation of plant and equipment	1,400	16,660
Net profit		15,454

Balance sheet as at 31 December 19–3

				£
Fixed assets:	Premises			45,000
	Motor lorry (10,000 – 1,000)			9,000
	Plant and equipment			11,000
Current assets:	Stock		3,500	
	Debtors		6,000	
	Prepayments:	rates	500	
		advertising	340	
	Cash at bank		3,540	
	in hand		450	
			14,330	
less Current liabilities:				
	Creditors	4,250		
	Accrual – electricity	280		
	Mrs. Forster	2,500	7,030	7,300
				72,300
Represented by				
Capital at 1 Jan 19–3				66,896
Net profit				15,454
				82,350
Drawings (10,000 + 50*)				10,050
				72,300

* cash shortage.

| Depreciation of motor lorries: | 20% of £8,000 for six months |
| | 20% of £10,000 for six months) |

Loss on sale of motor lorry:

CWT100R at 1 Jan 19–3		£8,000
less depreciation as above		800
		7,200
less sale proceeds		5,000
		2,200

4.6.2.

Conn, Flagge, Ray & Son
Calculation of claim for stock lost in fire on 5 November 19–1

Proforma trading account for the period 1 Jul 19–1 to 5 November 19–1:

			£
Sales (17,220 + 61,000 + 18,780 – 16,000)			81,000
Less			
Stock at 1 July 19–1		23,750	
Purchases (59,630 + 14,210 – 11,520)		62,320	
		86,070	
Stock at 5 November destroyed	26,070*		
salvaged	6,000	32,070	54,000
Gross profit (33 1/3% of £81,000)			27,000

* Stock destroyed: £26,070 (balancing figure)

Chapter 5

5.2.2

Diplock, Pibworth and Parkland Sports and Social Club
Bar Trading Account for the year ended 31 December 19–1

	£	£
Bar takings		4,100
Bar stocks at 1 Jan	800	
Purchases (2,050 + 430 – 350)	2,130	
	2,930	
Bar stocks at 31 Dec	600	2,330
		1,770
Barman's wages		750
Bar profit carried to Income and Expenditure Account		1,020

Income and Expenditure Account for the year to 31 December 19–1

Income	£	£	£
Members' subscriptions			
(2,100 – 60 + 180+ 130 – 110)			2,240
Profit on bar			1,020
Annual dinner/dance: Sale of tickets		2,400	
less expenses:			
catering	1,440		
dance band	300	1,740	660
Sale of raffle tickets		180	
less cost of prizes		60	120
			4,040
Expenditure			
Subscriptions written off		140	
Hire of hall (1,500 + 100 – 150)		1,450	
Printing and postage		200	
Lighting and heating (581 – 105 + 140)		616	
Hon. Secretary's expenses		122	
Affiliation fees		100	
Repairs to equipment		300	
Depreciation of equipment (2,500 + 800 – 2,800)		500	3,428
Excess of income over expenditure			612

Balance sheet as at 31 December 19–1

Fixed assets:	Equipment. Balance at 1.1. –			£ 2,500
	Additions during year			800
				3,300
	less depreciation			500
				2,800
			£	
Current assets:	Bar stocks		600	
	Subscriptions in arrear		180	
	Balance at bank		1,300	
			2,080	
less				
Current liabilities:	Subscriptions in advance	110		
	Creditors for bar stocks	430		
	Accrued expenses (140 + 100)	240	780	1,300
				4,100
Accumulated fund: Balance at 1 1.–1				3,488
Excess of income over expenditure				612
				4,100

Chapter 6

6.2.2 Exercise 1

Gray and Green
Profit and loss appropriation account
for the year ended 31 March 19–0

		£	£
Net profit b/d (8,000 – 500*)			7,500
Partners' current accounts:	Gray	3,750	
	Green	3,750	7,500

Note: In the absence of a partnership agreement, Gray is entitled to interest at 5% on his loan, such interest being debited in the profit and loss account, and the partners are entitled to equal shares of the profit.

Balance sheet extract as at 31 March 19–0

			£	£
Capitals:	Gray		20,000	
	Green		14,000	34,000
Current accounts:		Gray	Green	
		£	£	
Balances b/f		7,000	2,000	
Interest on loan		500	–	
Share of profit		3,750	3,750	
		11,250	5,750	
Drawings		(4,000)	(3,000)	
		7,250	2,750	10,000
				44,000
Long term liability: Gray – Loan				10,000
				54,000

Exercise 2

(a)

Palmer and Green
Profit and loss account for the year ended 31 December 19–0

	£	£
Gross profit b/d		80,000
Selling and distribution (23,500 + 1,500)	25,000	
Administration (16,400 – 800)	15,600	
Interest on loan – Palmer	800	
Depreciation: Premises	4,000	
Motor cars	3,200	48,600
Net profit (carried forward)		31,400

	£	£
Net profit (brought forward)		31,400
Interest on drawings: Palmer	700	
Green	800	1,500
		32,900
Interest on capitals: Palmer	3,500	
Green	2,000	5,500
		27,400
Salary: Green		8,000
		19,400
Share of profits: Palmer ($\frac{3}{5}$)	11,640	
Green ($\frac{2}{5}$)	7,760	19,400

Partners' Current accounts for the year ended 31 December 19–0

		Palmer £	Green £			Palmer £	Green £
19–0				19–0			
Jan 1	Balance b/d		3,000	Jan 1	Balance b/d	4,000	
Dec 31	Interest onDrawings	700	800	Dec 31	Interest on loan	800	
	Drawings	7,000	8,000		Int. on Caps.	3,500	2,000
	Balances c/d	12,240	5,960		Salary		8,000
					Profit	11,640	7,760
		19,940	17,760			19,940	17,760
				19–1			
				Jan 1	Balance b/d	12,240	5,960

Balance sheet as at 31 December 19–0

	Cost £	Depn £	Net £
Fixed assets			
Premises	100,000	29,000	71,000
Motor cars	16,000	11,200	4,800
	116,000	40,200	75,800
Current assets			
Stock		12,000	
Debtors		36,000	
Prepayment		800	
		48,800	
less			
Current liabilities			
Creditors	8,300		
Bank overdraft	3,600		
Accrued expense	1,500	13,400	35,400
			111,200
Deduct long term liabilities: Bank loan		30,000	
Palmer		8,000	38,000
			73,200

Represented by

	Capitals £	Current accounts £	Total £
Palmer	35,000	12,240	47,240
Green	20,000	5,960	25,960
	55,000	18,200	73,200

Exercise 3

Doyle, Lee and Carter
Appropriation account for the year ended 31 December 19–3

			£	£
Net profit b/d				7,000
less Interest on Capitals	Doyle		2,500	
	Lee		1,700	
	Carter		600	4,800
				2,200
less Guaranteed share of profit: Carter				5,000
				(2,800)
Share of loss:	Doyle ($\frac{5}{8}$)		(1,750)	
	Lee ($\frac{3}{8}$)		(1,050)	(2,800)

Exercise 4

(a)

Bath and Wells
Forecast trading and profit and loss account for the year to 31 December 19–1

		£	£
Sales (70,000 + 10,000 + 120,000)			200,000
less Cost of sales (balancing figure)			132,000
Gross profit (40% of £80,000) + (30% of £120,000)			68,000
less			
Salaries and wages (10,000 + 4,000)		14,000	
Rent and rates		3,600	
Insurance		800	
Entertainment		1,000	
Car expenses (2,600 × 2)		5,200	
Advertising		3,300	
Sundry expenses		1,000	
Depreciation: Motor cars (25% of (3,000 + 5,000)		2,000	
Fixtures and fittings		600	31,500
Net profit			36,500
Interest on capital:	Bath	680	
	Wells	1,000	
		1,680	
Salary: Wells		8,000	9,680
Share of profit:	Bath ($\frac{3}{5}$)	16,092	26,820
	Wells ($\frac{2}{5}$)	10,728	26,820

Forecast balance sheet as at 31 December 19–1

	£	£
Fixed assets		
Motor cars (3,000 + 5,000)	8,000	
less depreciation	2,000	6,000
Fixtures and fittings	3,000	
less depreciation	600	2,400
		8,400
Current assets		
Stock (2,200 + 8,000)	10,200	
Debtors	9,000	
Bank (balancing figure)	29,500	
	48,700	
Less Current liabilities		
Creditors	3,800	44,900
		53,300

			£	£
Represented by				
Capitals	Bath		6,800	
	Wells		10,000	16,800

	Bath	Wells	
Current accounts			
Interest on capital	680	1,000	
Salary		8,000	
Share of profit	16,092	10,728	
	16,772	19,728	36,500
			53,300

(b) Bath should consider taking wells into partnership for the following reasons:

(i) His share of the profit will give him a greater income than he can expect as a sole trader as the question states that his profit in recent years has remained static at around £6,800 p.a.

(ii) The liquidity of the business, which is beginning to cause Bath concern, will greatly improve if Wells is admitted as a partner. The bank overdraft of £2,500 will be repaid and replaced by a satisfactory balance at the bank.

Chapter 7

7.1.2 Exercise 1

Toll, Puddle and Martyn
Trading and profit and loss account
for the year to 31 December 19–2

	£	£
Sales		74,000
less Cost of sales		38,000
		36,000
less		
Wages	8,000	
General expenses	3,000	
Depreciation	1,000	12,000
Net profit c/d		24,000

	1 Jan–30 Jun £	1 Jul–31 Dec £	Total £
Net profit b/d	12,000	12,000	24,000
Salary – Toll ($\frac{6}{12} \times$ 3,000)		(1,500)	(1,500)
	12,000	10,500	22,500
Share of profit			
Toll ($\frac{3}{6}$)	6,000	($\frac{1}{3}$) 3,500	9,500
Puddle ($\frac{2}{6}$)	4,000	($\frac{1}{3}$) 3,500	7,500
Martyn ($\frac{1}{3}$)	2,000	($\frac{1}{3}$) 3,500	5,500
	12,000	10,500	22,500

Exercise 2

Crook, Shank and Spindle
Trading and profit and loss account
for the year to 31 March 19–2

	£
Sales	190,000
less Cost of sales	100,000
Gross profit c/d	90,000

	1 Apr–30 Sep		1 Oct–31 Mar		Total	
		£		£		£
Gross profit b/d		30,000		60,000		90,000
less						
Wages & salaries	10,500		10,500		21,000	
Rent and rates	3,000		3,000		6,000	
Lighting and heating	2,000		2,000		4,000	
General expenses	1,100		1,300		2,400	
Carried forward	16,600	30,000	16,800	60,000	33,400	90,000

	£	£	£	£	£	£
Brought forward	16,600	30,000	16,800	60,000	33,400	90,000
Loan interest						
Crook			600		600	
Depreciation:						
Motor cars	2,000		2,800		4,800	
Provision for						
doubtful debts	(20)	18,580	80	20,280	60	38,860
Net profit		11,420		39,720		51,140

		£	£	£
Interest on capitals				
Crook		2,000		
Shank		1,500		
Spindle		1,400		
		4,900		
Salary – Spindle		2,000	6,900	6,900
	11,420		32,820	44,240
Shares of profit				
Crook	6,852	13,128	19,980	
Shank	4,568	13,128	17,696	
Spindle	–	11,420	6,564	32,820	6,564	44,240

7.2.2

(a)

Legge and Spinner
Journal

	Dr. £	Cr. £
Premises	30,000	
Revaluation a/c		30,000
Revaluation a/c	5,000	
Plant and machinery		5,000
Revaluation a/c	8,000	
Motor van		8,000
Revaluation a/c	6,000	
Stock		6,000
[i.e.£(7,000 – 3,000) + 2,000]		
Revaluation a/c	400	
Provision for doubtful debts		400

(b)

Revaluation account

19–2			£	19–2		£
Dec 31	Plant & machinery		5,000	Dec 31 Premises		30,000
	Motor van		8,000			
	Stock		6,000			
	Sundry debtors		2,000			
	Provision for doubtful debts		400			
	Capital: Legge	4,300				
	Spindle	4,300	8,600			
			30,000			30,000

(c)

Legge and Spinner; Capital accounts

		Legge £	Spinner £			Legge £	Spinner £
19–2				19–2			
Dec 31	Bal. c/d	44,300	44,300	Dec 31	Bal b/f	40,000	40,000
					Profit on Reval.	4,300	4,300
		44,300	44,300			44,300	44,300
				19–3			
				Jan 1	Bal b/f	44,300	44,300

7.3.2 (a)

Carey and Street
Journal

	Dr £	Cr £
Revaluation a/c	1,000	
Provision for depreciation of plant and equipment	9,000	
Plant and equipment		10,000
Revaluation a/c	700	
Provision for depreciation of motor vans	8,300	
Motor vans		9,000
Provision for depreciation of office machinery	2,800	
Office machinery		1,000
Revaluation a/c		1,800
Revaluation a/c	940	
Sundry debtors		800
Provision for doubtful debts		
[(5% of £5,200) – 120]		140

(b)

Carey and Street
Revaluation account

19–2		£	19–2		£
June 30	Plant and equipment	1,000	June 30	Office machinery	1,800
	Motor vans	700			
	Sundry debtors	940		Capitals	
				Carey	504
				Street	336
		2,640			2,640

Plant and Equipment

19–2		£	19–2		£
Jun 30	Balance b/f	14,000	Jun 30	Revaluation	10,000
				Balance c/d	4,000
		14,000			14,000
Jul 1	Balance b/d	4,000			

Provision for depreciation of plant and equipment

19–2		£	19–2		£
Jun 30	Revaluation	9,000	Jun 30	Balance b/d	9,000

Motor Van

19–2		£	19–2		£
Jun 30	Balance b/d	11,000		Revaluation	9,000
				Balance c/d	2,000
		11,000			11,000
Jul 1	Balance b/d	2,000			

Provision for depreciation of motor van

19–2		£	19–2		£
Jun 30	Revaluation	8,300	Jun 30	Balance b/d	8,300

Office Machinery

19–2		£	19–2		£
Jun 30	Balance b/d	5,000	Jun 30	Revaluation	1,000
				Balance c/d	4,000
		5,000			5,000
Jul 1	Balance b/d	4,000			

Provision for depreciation of Office Machinery

19–2		£	19–2		£
Jun 30	Revaluation	2,800	Jun 30	Balance b/d	2,800

Sundry debtors

19–2		£	19–2		£
Jun 30	Balance b/d	6,000	Jun 30	Revaluation	800
				Balance c/d	5,200
		6,000			6,000
Jul 1	Balance b/d	5,200			

Provision for doubtful debts

19–2		£	19–2		£
Jun 30	Balance c/d	260	Jun 30	Balance b/d	120
				Revaluation	140
		260			260
			Jul 1	Balance b/d	260

7.5.2

(a)

Parchment, Deedes and Tape
Journal

	Dr.	Cr.
	£	£
Freehold premises	30,000	
Revaluation		30,000
Revaluation	5,000	
Motor cars		5,000
Revaluation	5,000	
Office furniture and equipment		5,000
Revaluation	2,400	
Provision for unpaid costs		2,400

(b)

Partners' Capital accounts

19–4		Parchment £	Deedes £	Tape £	19–3		Parchment £	Deedes £	Tape £
Jan 1	Goodwill			10,000	Dec 31	Balance b/f	100,000	100,000	
	Balance c/d	113,800	113,800	52,000		Revaluation	8,800	8,800	
						Bank			50,000
						Car			12,000
					Jan 1	Goodwill	5,000	5,000	
		113,800	113,800	62,000			113,800	113,800	62,000
					Jan 1	Balance b/d	113,800	113,800	52,000

Note: Goodwill

	Old firm	New firm	Adjustment to Capital accounts	
	£	£	£	
Parchment	25,000	20,000	5,000	Cr
Deedes	25,000	20,000	5,000	Cr
Tape		10,000	10,000	Dr
	50,000	50,000		

(c)   **Parchment, Deedes and Tape Balance Sheet as at 1 January 19–4**

	£	£
Fixed assets:		
Freehold premises		130,000
Motor cars (35,000 + 12,000)		47,000
Office furniture and equipment		1,000
		178,000
Current assets		
Stock	20,000	
Debtors (48,000 – 2,400)	45,600	
Bank (12,000 + 50,000)	62,000	
Carried forward	127,600	178,000

	£	£
Brought forward	127,600	178,000
less		
Current liabilities – creditors	8,000	119,600
		297,600

Represented by	Capitals	Current Accounts	
	£	£	£
Parchment	113,800	12,000	125,800
Deedes	113,800	6,000	119,800
Tape	52,000		52,000
	279,600	18,000	297,600

7.6.2

(a) and (b)

Johanne, Sebastian and Bach
Trading and profit and loss accounts for
(a) six months to 31 December 19–2 and
(b) six months to 30 June 19–3

	£	£
Sales		96,000
less cost of sales		
Stock at 1 Jul 19–2	8,000	
Purchases	29,000	
	37,000	
Stock at 30 Jun 19–3	4,000	33,000
Gross profit c/d		63,000

	1 Jul – 31 Dec 19–2		1 Jan – 30 Jun 19–3		Total	
	£	£	£	£	£	£
Gross profit b/d		31,500		31,500		63,000
Selling expenses	3,600		3,600		7,200	
Distribution expenses	2,400		2,400		4,800	
Wages and salaries	10,000		10,000		20,000	
General expenses	1,600		1,600		3,200	
Depreciation:						
Freehold premises	500		750		1,250	
Motor cars	2,000		600		2,600	
Office machinery	2,250		500		2,750	
Interest on loan			1,500		1,500	
		22,350		20,950		43,300
Net profit		9,150		10,550		19,700
Interest on drawings						
Johanne	200					
Sebastian	300					
Bach	250	750				750
		9,900		10,550		20,450
Salary Johanne	5,000				5,000	
Sebastian			3,500		3,500	
Bach			1,500		1,500	
Interest on capitals						
Johanne	1,500				1,500	
Sebastian	750				750	
Bach	750				750	
		8,000		5,000		13,000
		1,900		5,550		7,450
Share of profit						
Johanne ($\frac{1}{2}$)	950				950	
Sebastian ($\frac{1}{4}$)	475		($\frac{1}{2}$) 2,775		3,250	
Bach ($\frac{1}{4}$)	475	1,900	($\frac{1}{2}$) 2,775	5,550	3,250	7,450

(c)

Sebastian and Bach
Balance Sheet as at 30 June 19–3

Fixed assets	At valuation	Depn.	Net
	£	£	£
Freehold premises	60,000	750	59,250
Motor cars	6,000	600	5,400
Office machinery	4,000	500	3,500
	70,000	1,850	68,150
Current assets			
Stock		4,000	
Debtors		5,000	
Bank		15,100	
		24,100	68,150
Less Current liabilities			
Creditors	7,000		
Accrued expenses	2,200		
Interest on loan	1,500	10,700	13,400
			81,550
Less long term liability: Loan from Johanne			30,000
			51,550

Represented by	Capital	Current a/c	Total
	£	£	£
Sebastian	25,000	2,275	27,275
Bach	25,000	(725)	24,275
	50,000	1,550	51,550

(d)

Partners' Capital accounts

	Johanne	Sebastian	Bach			Johanne	Sebastian	Bach
19–2	£	£	£	19–2		£	£	£
Dec 31 Current a/cs		2,075	10,025	Jul 1 Balance b/d		30,000	15,000	15,000
Goodwill		5,000	5,000	Dec 31 Current a/c		8,250		
Motor car	4,000			Goodwill		10,000		
Loss on dis-				Revaluation		16,175	8,088	8,087
posal of car	800	400	400	Bank			9,387	17,338
Transfer–loan	30,000							
Bank	29,625							
19–3								
Jun 30 Balances c/d		25,000	25,000					
	64,425	32,475	40,425			64,425	32,475	40,425
				19–3 Balance b/d			25,000	25,000

Partners' Current accounts

	Johanne	Sebastian	Bach			Johanne	Sebastian	Bach
19–2	£	£	£	19–2		£	£	£
Jul 1 Balance b/f			6,000	Jul 1 Balance b/f		5,000	3,000	
Dec 31 Interest				Dec 31 Salary		5,000		
on drawings	200	300	250	Interest on				
Drawings	4,000	6,000	5,000	capitals		1,500	750	750
Capital a/c	8,250			Share of profit		950	475	475
				Capital a/cs			2,075	10,025
	12,450	6,300	11,250			12,450	6,300	11,250
19–3				19–3				
Jun 30 Drawings		4,000	5,000	Jun 30 Salaries			3,500	1,500
Balances c/f		2,275		Share of profit			2,775	2,775
				Balance c/d				725
		6,275	5,000				6,275	5,000
Jul 1 Balance b/d			725	Jul 1 Balance b/d			2,275	

Chapter 8

8.1.2.

(a)

Fortnum, Marks & Co.
Revaluation accounts

	Fortnum & Mason £	Marks & Spencer £
Fixtures	400	
Freehold property	4,000	
Creditors	320	280
Stock	(400)	(1,000)
Vehicles	(400)	(400)
Debtors	(800)	(1,000)
Profit/(loss) on revaluation	3,120	(2,120)
Capital accounts: Fortnum	(1,664)	
Mason	(1,456)	
Marks		1,272
Spencer		848

(b)

Partners' Capital Accounts – old firms

	Fortnum £	Mason £	Marks £	Spencer £		Fortnum £	Mason £	Marks £	Spencer £
Revaluation loss			1,272	848	Balances b/f	24,000	21,000	22,000	15,600
Realisation loss	320	280			Current a/cs	2,000	1,200		
Investments	2,400				Goodwill	8,000	7,000	6,000	4,000
Balance c/d	32,944	30,376	31,048	21,632	Revaluation profit	1,664	1,456		
					Realisation profit			4,320	2,880
	35,664	30,656	32,320	22,480		35,664	30,656	32,320	22,480

(c)

Partners' Capital accounts – new firms

	Fortnum £	Mason £	Marks £	Spencer £		Fortnum £	Mason £	Marks £	Spencer £
Goodwill	7,500	6,250	6,250	5,000	Balances b/d	32,944	30,376	31,048	21,632
Balance c/f	30,000	25,000	25,000	20,000	Cash	4,556	874	202	3,368
	37,500	31,250	31,250	25,000		37,500	31,250	31,250	25,000
					Balance b/d	30,000	25,000	25,000	20,000

(d)

Fortnum Marks & Co. Cash account

	£	£		£
Balance b/f			Balance c/f	43,600
Fortnum & Mason	8,400			
Marks & Spencer	26,200	34,600		
Partners' capital a/cs				
Fortnum		4,556		
Mason		874		
Marks		202		
Spencer		3,368		
		43,600		43,600
Balance b/f		43,600		

(e)

Fortnum Marks & Co.
Balance Sheet as at 1 September 19–1

		£	£
Fixed assets	Freehold property		19,000
	Fixtures		4,000
	Vehicles		7,600
			30,600
Current assets	Stock	23,800	
	Debtors	25,400	
	Bank balance	43,600	
		92,800	
less Creditors		23,400	69,400
			100,000

		£	£
Capital accounts	Fortnum		30,000
	Mason		25,000
	Marks		25,000
	Spencer		20,000
			100,000

Workings:

Realisation Accounts

	Fortnum & Mason	Marks & Spencer
	£	£
Cash book – proceeds		20,000
Capital account – Fortnum (Investments taken over at valuation)	2,400	
Freehold property		(10,000)
Fixtures		(2,800)
Investments (at cost)	(3,000)	
Profit/(loss) on disposals	(600)	7,200
Capital accounts: Fortnum	320	
Mason	280	
Marks		(4,320)
Spencer		(2,880)

8.2.2

(a)

Penn, Punch and Staple
Realisation account

19–0		£	19–0			£
Jun 30	Leasehold premises	5,000	Jun 30	Penn – Capital		2,500
	Delivery vans	2,000		Staple – Capital		6,000
	Fixtures and Fittings	2,000		Bank		11,500
	Stocks	12,000		Capitals –		
	Debtors – diff.	175		Penn	470	
				Punch	470	
				Staple	235	1,175
		21,175				21,175

(b)

Bank

19–0		£	19–0		£
Jun 30	Realisation	11,500	Jun 30	Balance b/f	900
	Sundry debtors	3,225		Sundry creditors	3,900
	Staple – capital	2,535		Loan – Quire	3,000
				Penn – capital	5,430
				Punch – capital	4,030
		17,260			17,260

(c)

Partners' capital accounts

	Penn	Punch	Staple		Penn	Punch	Staple
	£	£	£		£	£	£
Realisation a/c				Balances b/f	5,000	2,000	2,000
– van	2,500			Current a/cs	3,400	2,500	1,700
– stock			6,000	Bank			2,535
– loss on realisation	470	470	235				
Bank	5,430	4,030					
	8,400	4,500	6,235		8,400	4,500	6,235

8.3.2 (a)

Bent, Bold and Broke
Realisation account

19–2		£	19–2		£
Jan 1	Fixed assets	22,000	Jan 1	Bank	20,000
	Stock	18,000		Capitals (loss)	
	Debtors – diff.	1,000		Bent ($\frac{3}{6}$)	10,500
				Bold ($\frac{2}{6}$)	7,000
				Broke ($\frac{1}{6}$)	3,500
		41,000			41,000

(b)

Bank

19–2		£	19–2		£
Jan 1	Balance b/f	3,000	Jan 1	Sundry creditors	6,000
	Realisation	20,000		Capitals –	
	Debtors	4,000		Bent	10,750
				Bold	10,250
		27,000			27,000

(c)

Partners' capital accounts

		Bent	Bold	Broke			Bent	Bold	Broke
19–2		£	£	£	19–2		£	£	£
Jan 1	Current accounts		2,000	3,000	Jan 1	Balances b/f	20,000	20,000	5,000
	Loss on realisation	10,500	7,000	3,500		Current account	2,000		
	Broke – debit					Transfer to			
	balance on capital					Capital a/s Bent			
	(20:20)	750	750			and Bold			1,500
	Bank	10,750	10,250						
		£22,000	£20,000	£6,500			£22,000	£20,000	£6,500

8.4.2

(a)

Dee, Emma and Fay
Realisation account

19–5		£	19–5		£
Mar 31	Sundry fixed and		Mar 31	Enterprise Ltd.	90,000
	current assets	75,000			
	Capitals – Dee	5,000			
	Emma	5,000			
	Fay	5,000			
		90,000			90,000

(b)

Enterprise Ltd.

19–5		£	19–5		£
Mar 31	Realisation a/c	90,000	Mar 31	10% Debenture stock	4,000
				Ordinary shares	
				– Enterprise Ltd	60,000
				Bank	26,000
		90,000			90,000

10% Debentures in Enterprise Ltd.

19–5		£	19–5		£
Mar 31	Enterprise Ltd.	4,000	Mar 31	Dee – capital	4,000

Ordinary shares in Enterprise Ltd.

19–5		£	19–5		£
Mar 31	Enterprise Ltd	60,000	Mar 31	Capitals – Dee	20,000
				Emma	20,000
				Fay	20,000
		60,000			60,000

Bank

19–5		£	19–5		£
Mar 31	Enterprise Ltd.	26,000	Mar 31	Capitals – Dee	16,000
				– Emma	10,000
		26,000			26,000

Dee – Loan

19–5		£	19–5		£
Mar 31	Capital	5,000	Mar 31	Balance b/f	5,000

(c)

	Dee £	Emma £	Fay £			Dee £	Emma £	Fay £
19–5					19–5			
Mar 31 10% debentures in Enterprise Ltd.	4,000				Mar 31 Balances b/f	30,000	25,000	15,000
Ordinary shares					Loan	5,000		
in Enterprise Ltd.	20,000	20,000	20,000		Realisation a/c	5,000	5,000	5,000
Bank	16,000	10,000						
	40,000	30,000	20,000			40,000	30,000	20,000

Partners' Capital accounts

Note: Allocation of shares:

Capital/profit sharing ratio	**Dee**	**Emma**	**Fay**
Capitals	£30,000	£25,000	£15,000
Profit sharing ratio	1	1	1

Fay has lowest capital/psr; her capital account will be satisfied in full by allocation of shares, which will then be divided between the partners in profit sharing ratio.

Chapter 9

9.4.2

Chance Ltd.

(i) If 10% preference shares are non–cumulative

	19–1 £	19–2 £	19–3 £	19–4 £	19–5 £
Profit	22,000	6,000	11,000	7,000	10,000
10% Pref. share dividend	8,000	6,000	8,000	7,000	8,000
Profit available for ordinary dividend	14,000	–	3,000	–	2,000
Pref. div. %	10	7.5	10	8.75	10
Ord. div.%	11.7	–	2.5	–	1.7

(ii) If 10% preference shares are cumulative

	19–1 £	19–2 £	19–3 £	19–4 £	19–5 £
Profit	22,000	6,000	11,000	7,000	10,000
10% Pref. share dividend	8,000	6,000	8,000 +2,000	7,000	8,000 +1,000
Profit available for ordinary dividend	14,000	–	1,000	–	1,000
Pref. div %	10	7.5	(10+2.5)	8.75	(10+1.25)
Ord. div.	11.7	–	0.8	–	0.8

9.5.2

The Goodbuy Co. plc
Application & allotment

	£		£
Bank (monies returned)	11,750	Bank (on application)	186,750
Ordinary share capital	225,000	Bank (on allotment)	125,000
Share premium	75,000		
	311,750		311,750

Bank

	£		£
Application and allotment	186,750	Application and allotment	11,750
do.	125,000		
Call	75,000	Balance c/d	375,000
	386,750		386,750
Balance b/d	375,000		

Ordinary share capital

	£		£
Balance c/d	300,000	Application and allotment	225,000
		Call	75,000
	300,000		300,000
		Balance b/d	300,000

Share premium

	£		£
		Application and allotment	75,000
		Call	
	£		£
Ordinary share capital	75,000	Bank	75,000

9.6.2

Jollysticks Ltd.
Application and allotment
Ordinary share capital

	£		£
Balance c/d	30,000	Application & Allotment	30,000
		Balance b/d	30,000

Bank

	£		£
Application & Allotment	21,300	Application & Allotment	3,300
Application & Allotment	15,903	Balance c/d	34,343
Investment: Own Shares	440		
	37,643		37,643
Balance b/d	34,343		

Share Premium

	£		£
Balance c/d	4,343	Application & Allotment	4,200
		Investment: Own Shares	143
	4,343		4,343
		Balance b/d	4,343

Application and Allotment

	£		£
Bank (returned money)	3,300	Bank (application money)	21,300
Ordinary share capital	30,000	Bank (allotment money)	15,903
Share premium	4,200	Investment: Own Shares	297
	37,500		37,500

Investment: Own Shares

	£		£
Application & Allotment	297	Bank	440
Share Premium	143		
	440		440

9.7.2

Jill Ltd.

		£
(i)	Valuation of an ordinary share:	
	based on balance sheet values:	
	Total of net assets	147,000
	Deduct Preference share capital	25,000
	Ordinary share capital and reserves	122,000

Value of one ordinary share: $\dfrac{£122,000}{75,000}$ = £1.63

		£
(ii)	Valuation based on realisable values of net assets:	
	Fixed assets at realisable values	86,000
	Current assets at realisable values	48,000
		134,000
	less creditors	9,000
	Net asset value	125,000
Value of one ordinary share:		
	Net asset value	125,000
	less Preference share capital	25,000
		100,000

$\dfrac{£100,000}{75,000}$ = £1.33

9.8.2

Splendiferous plc

	£	£
The retained profit		10,000
less:		
Debenture interest	600	
Preference share dividend	160	760
Profit available for ordinary dividend		9,240
But:		£
Balance at bank		8,000
less debenture interest and preference dividend as above		760
Maximum cash available for ordinary dividend		7,240

Note: The cash position may be different when the dividend becomes payable. Also the General reserve may be available to increase the profit available for dividend if, in the opinion of the directors, that reserve is in excess of the company's requirement.

Chapter 10

10.4.2

The Wooden Box Co. Ltd

Note to the accounts – Tangible fixed assets.

	Freehold Land & Buildings	Leasehold property	Plant & Machinery	Motor Vehicles	Total
	£	£	£	£	£
Balance at 1.1. 19–2	400,000	–	396,000	130,000	926,000
Increase on revaluation	600,000				600,000
Disposals			(106,000)	(20,000)	(126,000)
Additions		100,000	110,000	32,000	242,000
	1,000,000	100,000	400,000	142,000	1,642,000
DEPRECIATION					
Provisions at					
1.1. 19–2	–	–	(127,200)	(42,500)	(169,700)
Provisions on disposals			52,100	11,250	63,350
Charge for year	(40,000)	(5,000)	(69,000)	(33,500)	(147,500)
	(40,000)	(5,000)	(144,100)	(64,750)	(253,850)
Balance sheet	960,000	95,000	255,900	77,250	1,388,150

TANGIBLE FIXED ASSETS

Freehold land and buildings have been revalued by Messrs. Coffyn, Paul, Bayer and Stone, Chartered Surveyors on 1 July 19–2 at £1m., of which £200,000 relates to the value of the land.

Depreciation is calculated to write off the cost of the fixed assets on a straight line basis over the expected useful lives of the assets concerned.

The annual rates used for this year are:

Freehold buildings	5%
Leasehold property	5%
Plant and machinery	20%
Motor vehicles	25%

The rates shown above are consistent with those used in the previous year. Freehold buildings are being depreciated for the first time this year at 5%, based upon the revalued amount and the expected remaining useful economic life of 20 years. The additional annual charge resulting from the revaluation amounts to £40,000. Freehold land is not depreciated.

The leasehold property is being amortised over the period of the lease, which is 20 years. The additional annual charge resulting from this is £5,000.

Chapter 12

12.1.3

Pinewood plc

Working

	Balance sheet 31.1.–3	Bonus issue	Rights issue	Revised balance sheet
	£	£	£	£
Ord. share cap.	200,000	700,000	300,000	1,200,000
Share premium	53,000	(53,000)	30,000	30,000
General reserve	600,000	(600,000)		
Profit & loss	185,000	(47,000)		138,000
				1,368,000

Answer

Revised balance sheet as at 1 February 19–3

	£'000	£'000
Fixed assets		852
Current assets (377,000 + 330,000)	707	
less Current liabilities	191	516
		1,368
Financed by		
Share capital and reserves		
1,200,000 ordinary shares of £1 fully paid		1,200
Share premium		30
Profit and loss account		138
		1,368

12.2.2

(a)

Pinewood Ltd.

Capital Reduction account

	£		£
Profit and loss	44,000	Ordinary share cap.	50,000
Provision for depn. of fixed assets	5,000		
Provision for bad debts	1,000		
	50,000		50,000

(b)

Re–drafted balance sheet

	£	£	£
Fixed assets (45,000 – 5,000)			40,000
Current assets (28,000 – 1,000)		27,000	
less Current liabilities Creditors	12,000		
Bank overdraft	5,000	17,000	10,000
			50,000
100,000 Ordinary shares of 50p fully paid			50,000

12.3.2 Exercise 1

Penguin Beakers Ltd.

Working

	Before redemption	New issue	Redemption of pref. shares	New bal. sheet
	£'000	£'000	£'000	£'000
Net assets	101	12.5	(12)	101.5
Ord. shares	75	10		85
Red. pref. shares	10		(10)	–
Share premium	6	2.5	(2)	6.5
Retained profits	10			10
	101			101.5

Answer

Revised balance sheet

	£'000
Net assets	101.5
Capital and reserves	
85,000 ordinary shares of £1 fully paid	85.0
Share premium	6.5
Retained profit	10.0
	101.5

Exercise 2

Flamingo plc

Working	Before redemption	Create CRR	Redeem Pref. shares	New bal. sheet
	£'000	£'000	£'000	£'000
Net assets	1,250		(110)	1,140
Ord. shares	750			750
Pref. shares	100		(100)	–
Cap. Red. Res.		100		100
Share premium	40			40
Revenue reserves	360	(100)	(10)	250
	1,250			1,140

Answer   **Balance sheet after redemption of preference shares**

	£'000
Net assets	1,140
Capital and reserves	
750,000 ordinary shares of £1 fully paid	750
Capital redemption reserve	100
Share premium	40
Revenue reserves	250
	1,140

Exercise 3

Ostrich Ltd.
Balance sheet as at 30 September 19–2

	£
Net assets (13,000 – 4,000)	9,000
Capital and reserves	
6,000 ordinary shares of £1	6,000
Capital redemption reserve	3,000
	9,000

Note: The Companies' Act 1985 permits a private limited company to use capital reserves to create a capital redemption reserve if the revenue reserves are insufficient for the purpose provided the revenue reserves are exhausted for this purpose first. It further allows such a company to create a capital redemption reserve less than the amount of the shares being redeemed if all the reserves, revenue and capital, are insufficient.

Chapter 13

13.1.2   **Merger (19–1) Ltd.**

Working: Calculation of goodwill.

	Gerald Menswear	Mercer Fashions	Combined
	£'000	£'000	£'000
Freehold premises	75	25	100
Delivery vans	8	5	13
Fixtures & fittings	4	11	15
Office equipment	3	1	4
Stock	38	55	93
Debtors	4	60	64
	132	157	289
less creditors	(48)	(98)	
Net assets	84	59	
Purchase consideration	100	60	
Goodwill	16	1 Total	17

Calculation of share premium.	£
Total consideration	160,000
Cash payments	40,000
Consideration payable in shares	120,000
Number of shares to be allotted	100,000

Each share is therefore valued at £1.20 i.e. at a premium of 20p

Answer

Merger (19–1) Ltd.
Balance sheet as at 1 July 19–1

		£'000	£'000
Fixed assets			
Intangible: Goodwill			17
Tangible			
Freehold premises		100	
Delivery vans		13	
Fixtures and fittings		15	
Office equipment		4	132
			149
Current assets			
Stock		93	
Debtors		64	
Bank (100 – 16 – 22 – 40)		22	
		179	
Current liabilities: Creditors(32+76)		108	71
			220
Capital and reserves			
200,000 Ordinary shares of £1			200
Share premium			20
			220

13.3.2

Exercise 1

Doulla Ltd. and subsidiaries
Consolidated balance sheet as at 31 December 19–1

		£'000	£'000
Fixed assets			
Intangible:	Goodwill (see below)		11
Tangible:	Freehold land and buildings	100	
	Plant and equipment	185	
	Motor vehicles	105	
	Office machinery	65	455
			466
Current assets			
	Stock	164	
	Debtors	113	
	Bank	117	
		394	
Amounts due for settlement within one year:			
	Creditors	120	274
			740
Share capital and reserves			
Ordinary shares of £1			600
Reserves			140
			740

		£'000	
Goodwill			
Rosalia Ltd.	Purchase consideration	200	
	Net asset value acquired	182	
	Goodwill	18	
Tracey Ltd.	Purchase consideration	150	
	Net asset value acquired	157	
	Negative goodwill	(7)	
Goodwill (18 – 7)		11	

13.4.2

Exercise 2

Hon Wai Ltd. and subsidiaries
Consolidated balance sheet as at 30 April 19–4

	£'000	£'000
Intangible Fixed Assets		
Goodwill (see below)		13
Tangible Fixed Assets		
Freehold property	180	
Plant and machinery	219	
Motor vehicles	103	502
		515
Current assets		
Stock (153 – 8)	145	
Debtors (99 – 5)	94	
Bank	48	
	287	
Less amounts due to be paid within one year		
Creditors (76 – 5)	71	216
		731
Share capital and reserves		
Ordinary shares of £1		700
Reserves		31
		731

Goodwill	Mei Yiu Ltd	Sing Yiu Ltd
	£'000	£'000
Cost of acquisition	195	150
Value of ordinary		
shares and reserves	177	155
	18	(5) Net 13

Exercise 3

Buckle Ltd. and subsidiaries
Consolidated Balance Sheet as at 1 January 19–0

	£'000	£'000
Intangible Fixed Assets		
Goodwill (see below)		10
Tangible Fixed Assets		
Freehold premises	40	
Motor vehicles	135	
Equipment	75	250
		260
Current assets		
Stock	106	
Debtors	92	
Bank	24	
	222	
Amounts due to be paid within one year		
Creditors	60	162
		422
Capital and reserves		
Ordinary shares of £1		300
Retained profit		46
		346
Minority interests (see below)		76
		422

Goodwill		Lace Ltd.		Pin Ltd.
		£'000		£'000
Cost of acquisition		100		70
Value of shares & reserves acquired	(80% of 110)	88	(75% of 96)	72
Goodwill		12		(2)

		£'000		£'000
Net goodwill			10	
Minority interests	(20% of 110)	22	(25% of 96)	24
Add Preference shareholders		30		
		52		24
Total			76	

Exercise 4

Wader Ltd. and subsidiaries
Consolidated Balance Sheet as at 1 May 19–5

	£'000	£'000
Intangible Fixed Assets		
Goodwill (see below)		31
Tangible Fixed Assets		
Freehold property	384	
Plant and machinery	277	
Motor vehicles	88	749
Current Assets		
Stock (140 – 6)	134	
Debtors (134 – 7)	127	
Bank	85	
	346	
Amounts due for payment within one year		
Creditors (111 – 7)	104	242
		1,022
Amounts due for settlement after more than one year		
Debentures (60 – 20)		40
		982
Share capital and reserves		
Ordinary shares of £1		800
Retained profits		101
		901
Minority Interests (see below)		81
		982

Goodwill		Swan Ltd.		Heron Ltd.	
	£'000	£'000	£'000	£'000	
Cost of acquisition		180		75	
Share capital and reserves	205		120		
less preference shares	25				
	180				
less minority interest (20%)	36	144	($\frac{1}{3}$) 40	80	
Goodwill		36		(5)	= 31

Minority Interests	£'000
Ordinary shares in Swan Ltd. (as above)	36
Ordinary shares in Heron Ltd.(as above)	40
Preference shares in Swan Ltd. (20%)	5
	81

13.5.2

Exercise 1

Box Ltd. and its subsidiary
Consolidated Profit and Loss Account
for the year to 31 March 19–1

	£'000	£'000	Note
Turnover		162	1
Cost of sales		95	2
Gross profit		67	
Distribution costs	13		
Administration expenses	35	48	
Profit on ordinary activities before taxation		19	
Taxation on profit on ordinary activities		7	
Profit on ordinary activities after taxation (carried forward)		12	

	£'000	£'000	Note
Profit on ordinary activities after taxation (brought forward)		12	
Extraordinary profits net of tax		7	
Profit for the financial year		19	
Retained profit brought forward		20	
		39	
Proposed dividend	8		
Transfer to reserve	18	26	
Retained profit carried forward		13	

Note 1. Combined turnover less inter–company sales of £18,000

Note 2. Combined cost of sales less inter–company sale as above and deletion of unrealised profit £3,000 on unsold stock.

Exercise 2
Bat Ltd. and its subsidiary
Consolidated Profit and Loss Account
for the year ended 30 September 19–3

	£'000	£'000	Note
Turnover		1,726	1
Cost of sales		1,193	2
Gross profit		533	
Distribution costs	54		
Administrative expenses	120	174	
Profit on ordinary activities before taxation		359	
Taxation on profit on ordinary activities		117	
		242	
Minority interests		64	3
		178	
Extraordinary profit net of taxation		39	4
Profit for the financial year		217	
Retained profit from the previous year		176	5
		393	
Proposed dividends	120		
Transfer to reserves	104	224	6
Retained profit carried forward		169	

Note 1. Turnover 1,000 + 750 – 24

2. Cost of sales 684 + 525 –24 + 8 (unrealised profit)

3. Minority interests: Pref. div. $\frac{1}{3} \times 42 =$ 14
   Ord.shareholders
   $\frac{1}{4} \times 242 - 42$ (pref.div.)
   $= \frac{1}{4} \times 200$ 50   64

4. Extraordinary profit $24 + \frac{3}{4} \times 20 = 39$

5. Retained profit from previous year $116 + \frac{3}{4} \times 80 = 176$

6. Transfer to reserves $80 + \frac{3}{4} \times 32 = 104$

Chapter 14

14.3.2
(a)
Mary
Cash flow statement for the year to 31 March 19–4

	£	£
Net cash inflow from operating activities		23,320
Returns on investments and servicing of finance Interest paid	(400)	
Drawings	(14,440)	
Net cash outflow from returns on investments and servicing finance		(14,840)
Taxation (not applicable)		
Investing activities		
Payments to acquire fixed assets – equipment	(9,000)	
Receipts from sale of fixed assets	200	
Net cash outflow from investing activities		(8,800)
Net cash outflow before financing		(320)
Financing		
Repayment of loan	(2,000)	
Net cash inflow from financing		(2,000)

	£	£
Decrease in cash		(2,320)

Reconciliation of operating profit to net cash inflow from operating activities

	£	£
Net profit before interest (18,940+400)	19,340	
Depreciation (including amortisation of lease) (2,000+1,400+1,600+400)	5,400	
Increase in stock	(3,000)	
Increase in debtors	(1,000)	
Increase in creditors	2,580	23,320

Analysis of changes in cash during the year

	£
Balance at 1 April 19–3	7,160
Net cash outflow	(2,320)
Balance at 31 March 19–4	4,840)

(b) Dear Mary,

Your normal business operations produced sufficient cash to cover the normal requirements of your business including £9,000 required for new fixed assets, interest payments and your drawings of £14,440. Your bank balance would have been reduced by only £320 if you had not repaid £2,000 to your father on account of his loan. It was this repayment that accounted for almost the whole of the reduction in your bank balance

14.4.2

Andrew and Demetriou plc
Calculation of net profit before tax

	£'000
Retained profit for the year (85–110)	(25)
Increase in General Reserve (230–200)	30
Increase in asset replacement reserve (185–160)	25
Proposed dividends	600
Provision for taxation on current year's profit	540
Debenture interest	100
Net profit for the year before tax	1,270

14.5.2

Pondayne plc

Workings

Freehold premises at valuation

19–4		£000	19–4		£000
Jan 1	Balance b/f	900	Dec 31	Balance c/f	1,200
Dec 31	Property revaluation	300			
		1,200			1,200

Plant and machinery at cost

19–4		£000	19–4		£000
Jan 1	Balance b/f	450	Dec 31	Disposal	80
Dec31	Purchases (bal.fig)	320		Balance c/f	690
		770			770

Provision for depreciation of plant and machinery

19–4		£000	19–4		£000
Dec31	Disposals	64	Jan	Balance b/f	376
	Balance c/f	520	Dec	P & L (bal. fig.)	208
		584			584

Disposal of plant and machinery

19–4		£000	19–4		£000
Dec 31	Plant & machinery	80	Dec 31	Prov. for depn.	64
				Cash	8
				P & L (bal. fig.)	8
		80			80

Fixtures and Fittings at cost

19–4		£000	19–4		£000
Jan 1	Balance b/f	60	Dec 31	Disposals	40
Dec 31	Purchased (bal. fig.)	20		Balance c/f	40
		80			80

Provision for depreciation of fixtures and fittings

19–4		£000	19–4		£000
Dec 31	Disposals	38	Jan 1	Balance b/f	54
	Balance c/f	30	Dec 31	P & L (bal.fig.)	14
		68			68

Disposal of fixtures and fittings

19–4		£000	19–4		£000
Dec 31	Fixtures & fittings	40	Dec 31	Prov.for depn.	38
				Cash	5
	P&L (bal.fig.)	3			
		43			43

(a) Non–cash items:

Revaluation of premises	£300,000 (not shown in cash flow statement)
Depreciation for year:	
Plant and machinery	£208,000
Fixtures & fittings	£14,000
Loss on disposal of Plant and machinery	£8,000
Profit on disposal of Fixtures and fittings	£3,000

(b) Payment of cash for purchase of tangible fixed assets:

Plant and machinery	£320,000
Fixtures and fittings	£20,000

14.8.2

The Vortex Puzzle Co. Ltd.

Taxation

19–6		£000	19–5		£000
Jun 30	Provision (19–6) c/f	201	Jul 1	Provision (19–5) b/f 19–6	157
	Paid (bal.fig)	166	Jun 30	P&L	210
		367			367

Tax paid in the year to 30 June 19–6: £166,000

14.9.2

Portable Grummitts plc

19–4		£000	19–3		£000
May 31	Paid in year (bal fig)	330	Jun 1	Proposed div. b/f 19–4	300
	Proposed div.c/f	250	May 31	P&L	280
		580			580

Dividends paid in the year to 31 May 19–4: £330,000

14.10.2

The Ovid Egg Products Ltd.

Cash flow statement for the year to 31 December 19–1

	£'000	£'000
Net cash inflow from operating activities		99.6
Returns on investments and servicing of finance		
Interest paid	(9.6)	
Dividends paid	(45.0)	
Net cash outflow from returns on investments and servicing of finance		(54.6)
Taxation		
Corporation tax paid	(49.0)	
Tax paid		(49.0)
Investing activities		
Payments to acquire fixed assets	(118.0)	
Receipts from sales of fixed assets	45.0	
Net cash outflow from investing activities		(73.0)
Net cash outflow before financing		(77.0)
Financing		
Issue of ordinary share capital (note 3)	60.0	
Increase in debenture loans	30.0	
Net cash inflow from financing		90.0
Increase in cash		13.0
Reconciliation of operating profit to net cash inflow from operating activities		
Net profit before tax and interest (note 1)	106.6	
Depreciation	63.0	

	£'000	£'000
Net loss on disposal of fixed assets (note 2)	9.0	
Increase in stock	(40.0)	
Increase in debtors	(26.0)	
Decrease in creditors	(13.0)	99.6

Analysis in changes of cash during the year

	£'000
Balance at 1 January 19–1	24.0
Net cash inflow	13.0
Balance at 31 December 19–1	37.0

Analysis in changes in Financing during the year

	Share capital (including premium)	12% Debentures
	£'000	£'000
Balance at 1 January 19–1	215	50
Cash inflows from financing	60	30
Balance at 31 December 19–1	275	80

Note 1. Profit before tax and interest:

	£'000	£'000
Retained profit at 31 December 19–1	52.0	
Retained profit at 1 January 19–1	(100.0)	
Reduction in retained profit	(48.0)	
Increase in General reserve	50.0	
Dividends – interim		
(5p on 200k ordinary shares)	10.0	
proposed final	30.0	40.0
Taxation debited in profit & loss account		55.0
Debenture interest (12% on £80k)		9.6
		106.6

Note 2. Net loss on disposal of fixed assets:

	£'000	£'000
Freehold premises – cost	49	
Sale proceeds	37	
Loss on disposal		12
Plant – net book value (20 – 18)	2	
Sale proceeds	3	
Profit on disposal		(1)
Motor vehicles – net book value (23 – 20)	3	
Sale proceeds	5	
Profit on disposal		(2)
Net loss on disposal of fixed assets		9

Note 3. Cash inflow from issue of 50,000 ordinary shares includes premium (£10,000)

Chapter 15

15.1.4

Harwoods Stores Ltd.
Trading and profit and loss accounts for the year to 30 June 19–3

	Hardware			Kitchen furniture			Total	
	£	£	£	£	£	£	£	£
Sales		490,000			310,000		800,000	
Less cost of sales								
Opening stock		120,000			45,000		165,000	
Purchases	350,000			250,000		600,000		
Carriage inwards	2,800			2,000		4,800		
		352,800			252,000		604,800	
		472,800			297,000		769,800	
Closing stock		132,000			65,000		197,000	
			340,800			232,000		572,800
Gross profit			149,200			78,000		227,200

	£	£	£	£	£	£	£	£	£
Discounts received			7,000			5,000			12,000
			156,200			83,000			239,200
Wages		25,000			20,000			45,000	
Rent		20,000			10,000			30,000	
Heating & lighting		1,600			800			2,400	
Discouts allowed		1,470			930			2,400	
Carriage outwards		3,675			2,325			6,000	
Depreciation of fixtures & fittings		6,000			1,500			7,500	
		57,745			35,555			93,300	
Net profit		98,455			47,445			145,900	

15.2.3

Firtree Limited
Branch Stock

19–2		Selling price £	£	19–2		Selling price £	£
Oct 1	Balance b/f	24,000	18,000	Oct 31	Goods sent to branch	800	600
31	Branch stock	72,000	54,000		Sales: cash	25,000	25,000
	Branch debtors	1,200	1,200		credit	42,000	42,000
	Branch debtors		200		Stock c/d	28,800	21,600
	Profit & loss		15,800		Stock loss	600	
		97,200	89,200			97,200	89,200
Nov 1	Balance b/d	28,800	21,600				

Goods Sent to Branch

19–2		£	19–2		£
Oct 31	Branch Stock	600	Oct 31	Branch Stock	54,000
	Branch debtors	600			
	Balance to trading a/c	52,800			
		54,000			54,000

Branch Debtors

19–2			£	19–2			£
Oct 1	Balance	b/f	1,200	Oct 31	Branch Stock		1,200
31	Branch stock		42,000		Goods Sent to Branch		600
					Branch Stock		200
					Bank		39,400
					Balance	c/d	1,800
			43,200				43,200
Nov 1	Balance	b/d	1,800				

15.2.6

Firtree Limited
Branch stock (at selling price)

19X2			£	19X2			£
Oct 1	Balance	b/f	24,000	Oct 31	Goods sent to branch		800
31	Goods sent to branch		72,000		Sales – cash		25,000
	Branch debtors		1,200		– credit		42,000
					Branch stock adjustment (loss)		600
					Stock	c/d	28,800
			97,200				97,200
Nov 1	Balance	b/d	28,800				

Goods sent to branch

19X2		£	19X2		£
Oct 31	Branch stock	600	Oct 31	Branch stock	54,000
	Branch debtors	600			
	Trading account	52,800			
		54,000			54,000

Branch stock adjustment

19X2			£	19X2				£
Oct 31	Branch stock (returns)		200	Oct1	Balance	b/f		6,000
	Branch debtors (returns)		200	31	Branch stock			18,000
	Branch stock (loss)		600					
	Balance	c/d	7,200					
	Profit & loss		15,800					
			24,000					24,000
				Nov 1	Balance	b/d		7,200

Branch Debtors

19X2			£	19X2			£
Oct 1	Balance	b/f	1,200	Oct 31	Branch stock (rets.)		1,200
31	Branch stock		42,000		Goods sent to branch		600
					Branch stock adjust.		200
					Bank		39,400
					Balance	c/d	1,800
			43,200				43,200
Nov 1	Balance	b/d	1,800				

15.2.9 Ofra Ltd.

(a) In head office books

Hexham Branch Current account

19–3			£	19–3			£
Oct 1	Bank – freehold premises		150,000	Oct 7	Bank – cash remitted by branch		4,000
	Bank – fixtures and fittings		18,000		Balance	c/d	219,000
2	Bank – branch cash float		5,000				
3	Kopak Ltd. – stock		40,000				
	Goods sent to branch		10,000				
			223,000				223,000
Oct 8	Balance	b/d	219,000				

(b) In Hexham branch books

Head Office Current account

19–3			£	19–3			£
Oct 7	Bank – remitted to Head Office		4,000	Oct 1	Freehold premises		150,000
	Balance	c/d	219,000		Fixtures and fittings		18,000
				2	Bank		5,000
				3	Goods from Head office		40,000
					Goods from Head Office		10,000
			£223,000				£223,000
				Oct 8	Balance	b/d	219,000

Bank

19–3			£	19–3			£
Oct 2	Head office current account		5,000	Oct 5	Purchases		3,000
	Sales		7,000	6	Wages		900
				7	Head Office current account		4,000
					Balance	c/d	4,100
			£12,000				£12,000
Oct 8	Balance	b/d	4,100				

Freehold premises

19–3		£	19–3	£
Oct 1	Head Office current account	150,000		

Fixtures and fittings

19–3		£	19–3	£
Oct 1	Head Office current account	18,000		

Goods from Head Office

19–3		£	19–3	£
Oct 3	Head Office current account	40,000		
	Head Office current account	10,000		

Purchases

19–3		£	19–3		£
Oct 5	Bank	5,000			

Sales

19–3		£	19–3		£
			Oct 7	Bank	7,000

15.2.12

Trunk Limited

Trading and profit and loss accounts for the year ended 31 October 19X2

	Head office £	Branch £	Combined £
Sales	490,000	301,000	791,000
Goods sent to branch	232,400		
	722,400	301,000	791,000
Opening stock (W1)	21,000	12,600	31,500
Purchases	315,000	–	315,000
Goods received from head office		215,600	
	336,000	228,200	346,500
Less closing stock (W2)	(28,000)	(33,600)	70,000
Cost of sales	308,000	194,600	276,500
Gross profit	414,400	106,400	514,500
Increase in provision for unrealised profit	(6,300)		
Administrative expenses	(189,000)	(12,600)	(201,600)
Distribution costs	(42,000)	(16,800)	(58,800)
Net profit for the year	177,100	77,000	254,100
Branch profit transferred through current accounts	77,000	(77,000)	
Profit brought forward	39,200		39,200
Profit carried forward	293,300		293,300

Trunk Limited

Balance sheets as at 31 October 19X2

	Head office £	Branch £	Combined £
Fixed assets at net book value	536,200	53,200	589,400
Current assets			
Stocks	28,000	33,600	56,000
Goods in transit	14,000		14,000
Debtors	21,000	28,000	49,000
Branch current account	105,000		
Cash at bank and in hand	26,600	2,800	29,400
Cash in transit	14,000		14,000
	208,600	64,400	162,400
Creditors: amounts falling due within one year			
Creditors	31,500	7,000	38,500
Head office current account		110,600	
	31,500	117,600	38,500
Net current assets	177,100	(53,200)	123,900
Total assets less current liabilities	713,300		713,300
Capital and reserves			
Called up share capital	420,000		420,000
Profit and loss account	293,300		293,300
	713,300		713,300

Trunk Limited Workings

W 1	Opening stock	£	£
	Head office		21,000
	Branch (at cost to branch)	12,600	
	less unrealised profit $\frac{1}{6}$	2,100	10,500
	Combined		31,500

W 2	Closing stock		£	£
	Head office			28,000
	Branch		33,600	
	less unrealised profit $\frac{1}{6}$		5,600	28,000
	add goods in transit at cost to branch		16,800	
	less unrealised profit $\frac{1}{6}$		2,800	14,000
	Combined			70,000

W 3	Provision required for unrealised profit	£
	On goods at branch (W2)	5,600
	On goods in transit (W2)	2,800
		8,400
	less provision brought forward 1.10.91	2,100
	Increase required	6,300

W 4 Reconciliation of current accounts

Branch current account

		£			£
Balance	b/f	64,400	Goods in transit	c/d	16,800
Net profit		77,000	Cash in transit	c/d	14,000
			Balance	c/d	10,600
		141,400			141,400
Goods in transit	b/d	16,800			
Cash in transit	b/d	14,000			
Balance	b/d	110,600*			

* This must be reduced by the unrealised profit on goods in stock at the branch in the head office balance sheet: £(110,600 – 5,600) = £105,000

Head office current account

		£			£
Balance c/d		110,600	Balance	b/d	33,600
			Net profit		77,000
		110,600			110,600
			Balance	b/d	110,600

15.2.16 (a)

	Chiswick branch		Richmond branch
	£		£
Sales	100,000		60,000
Cost of sales	40,000		24,000
Gross profit	60,000		36,000
less branch expenses	39,000	(12,000+8,000+4,000+6,000)	30,000
(15,000+10,000+6,000+8,000)			
Contributions	21,000		6,000

(b) The Chiswick branch has made a contribution towards head office overheads of £21,000. Richmond branch, which made a net loss of £1,000, actually makes a contribution of £6,000 to head office overheads. It is questionable whether the apportionment of head office overheads is fair. Richmond branch appears to be smaller than Chiswick branch but they have been debited with equal proportions of head office overheads. It may be fairer to apportion the overheads on the basis of relative turnovers to reflect the differences in size; the charges would then be: Chiswick £8750, Richmond £5,250 and the net profits would be: Chiswick £12,250, Richmond £750.

15.3.9
Zeta Limited
Machine Hire Purchase Loan

19–2			£	19–2		£
Oct 1	Bank		8,000	Oct 1	Machine at cost	75,000
19–3				19–3		
Mar 31	Bank		20,000	Mar 31	Interest payable	5,200
	Balance	c/d	52,200			
			80,200			80,200

19–3			£	19–3			£
Sep 30	Bank		20,000	Apr 30	Balance	b/d	52,200
19–4				19–4			
Mar 31	Bank		20,000	Mar 31	Interest payable		6,500
	Balance	c/d	18,700				
			58,700				58,700
19–5				19–5			
Mar 31	Bank		20,000	Apr 30	Balance	b/d	18,700
				19–5			
				Mar 31	Interest payable		1,300
			20,000				20,000

Hire Purchase Interest

19–3		£	19–3		£
Mar 31	Machine HP loan	5,200	Mar 31	P & L	5,200
19–4			19–4		
Mar 31	Machine HP loan	6,500	Mar 31	P & L	6,500
19–5			19–5		
Mar 31	Machine HP loan	1,300	Mar 31	P & L	1,300

Zeta Limited
Balance sheet (extract) as at 31 December

	19–3	19–4	19–5
	£	£	£
Tangible fixed assets			
Machine at cost	75,000	75,000	75,000
less provision for depreciation	3,500	10,500	17,500
Net book value	71,500	64,500	57,500
Creditors: amounts payable within one year			
Obligation under hire purchase contract	33,500	18,700	
Creditors: amounts falling due after more than one year			
Obligation under hire purchase contract	18,700		

Chapter 16

16.1.2

1.

The Jobbitt Co. Ltd.
Manufacturing, trading, profit and loss account for the year ended 30 September 19–8

	£	£
Raw materials	115,000	
less stock at 30 Sep 19–8	13,000	102,000
Direct labour		200,000
PRIME COST		302,000
Add factory overheads		
Indirect materials	10,000	
Indirect labour	25,000	
Rent and rates	35,000	
Electricity	8,000	
Salaries	20,000	
Depreciation: machinery	12,000	110,000
		412,000
Less Work in progress at 30 Sep 19–8		9,500
COST OF GOODS PRODUCED		402,500
Sales		700,000
Less cost of goods sold		
Cost of goods produced	402,500	
less stock of finished goods		
at 30 Sep 19–8	2,800	399,700
GROSS PROFIT		300,300
Less Salaries	40,000	
Rent and rates	15,000	
Electricity	2,000	
Sundry expenses	2,000	
Depreciation: office equipment	1,000	60,000
NET PROFIT		240,300

Balance sheet extract:

		£	£
Current assets:	Raw materials	13,000	
	Work in progress	9,500	
	Finished goods	2,800	25,300

2.

Collette Fabrications Ltd.
Manufacturing, trading, profit and loss account
for the year ended 30 April 19–9

		£	£
Raw materials:	Stock at 1 May 19–8	15,000	
	Purchases	176,000	
	Carriage inwards	15,340	
		191,340	
	Stock at 30 April 19–9	(17,500)	188,840
Direct wages			195,000
PRIME COST			383,840
Factory overheads			
Indirect wages		26,000	
Rent and rates (75% of 51,000)		38,250	
Heating and lighting (2/3 of 60,000)		40,000	
Insurance (9/10 of 3,000)		2,700	
Motor van expenses (50% of 8,000)		4,000	
Depreciation:	Loose tools (5,000+9,000–4,000)	10,000	
	Factory building	4,000	
	Machinery	14,000	
	Motor vans (50%)	5,000	143,950
			527,790
Work in progress at	1 May 19–8	24,000	
	30 April 19–9	(21,000)	3,000
Cost of goods produced			530,790
Sales			800,000
Cost of sales	Stock at 1 May 19–8	36,000	
	Cost of goods produced	530,790	
		566,790	
	Stock at 30 April 19–9	32,000	534,790
Gross profit			265,210
Discounts receivable			4,125
			269,335
Office salaries		68,600	
Rent and rates (25% of 51,000)		12,750	
Heating and lighting ($\frac{1}{3}$ of 60,000)		20,000	
Insurance ($\frac{1}{10}$ of 3,000)		300	
Carriage outwards		3,360	
Motor van expenses (50% of 8,000)		4,000	
Depreciation:	Motor vans	5,000	
	office machinery and equipment	5,000	119,010
Net profit			150,325

16.2.2

Exercise 1

Bonnie and Clyde
Manufacturing, trading, profit and loss account
for the year ended 31 March 19–7

		£'000	£'000
Raw materials	Stock at 1 April 19–6	7	
	Purchases	96	
		103	
	Stock at 31 March 19–7	13	90
Direct labour			124
Prime cost carried forward			214

	£'000	£'000
Prime cost brought forward		214
Factory overheads	85	
Depreciation: Factory	8	93
		307
Work in progress at 1 April 19–6	8	
31 March 19–7	(15)	(7)
Cost of production		300
Factory profit		50
Transfer to trading account		350
Sales		400
Cost of sales Stock of finished goods 1 April 19–6	14	
Goods transferred from factory	350	
	364	
Stock of finished goods 31 March 19–7	24	340
Gross profit		60
Rent receivable		20
		80
Office overheads	64	
Depreciation: Offices	2	66
Net profit on trading		14
Factory profit		50
Overall Net profit		64

Exercise 2

Kontakki Ltd.
Manufacturing, trading, profit and loss account
for the year ended 30 June 19–8

	£'000	£'000
Raw materials Stock at 1 July 19–7	40	
Purchases	110	
	150	
Stock at 30 June 19–8	55	95
Direct wages		85
Prime cost		180
Rent and rates (75% of 40,000)	30	
Heating and lighting (75% of 16,000)	12	
Repairs to factory	20	
Depreciation: machinery	30	92
		272
Work in progress at 1 July 19–7	16	
30 June 19–8	(14)	2
Factory cost of goods produced		274
Factory loss		(24)
Goods transferred to trading account		250
Sales		300
Cost of sales Stock of finished goods at 1 July 19–7	32	
Cost of goods manufactured	250	
Purchases of finished goods	60	
	342	
Stock of finished goods at 30 June 19–8	30	312
Gross loss		(12)
Office salaries	28	
Rent and rates (25% of 40,000)	10	
Heating and lighting (25% of 16,000)	4	
Redecoration of offices	15	
Depreciation: Salesmens' cars	15	(72)
Net loss on trading		(84)
Add factory loss		(24)
Overall Net loss		(108)

16.3.2

Exercise 1

Dorritt and Dombie Ltd.
Manufacturing, trading, profit and loss account
for the year to 31 March 19–2

		£'000	£'000
Raw materials	Stock at 1 April 19–1	28	
	Purchases	300	
		328	
	Stock at 31 March 19–1	32	296
Direct wages			360
Licence fees			104
Prime cost			760
Indirect wages		88	
Property expenses ($\frac{4}{5} \times 90$)		72	
Canteen expenses ($\frac{4}{5} \times 40$)		32	
Depreciation: machinery		36	
canteen equipment ($\frac{4}{5} \times 10$)		8	236
			996
Work in progress	1 April 19–1	58	
	31 March 19–2	(54)	4
Factory cost of goods produced			1,000
Factory profit (10% of £1,000,000)			100
Transfer to trading account			1,100
Sales			1,800
Cost of sales	Stock at 1 April 19–1	33	
	Transferred from factory	1,100	
	Purchases	58	
		1,191	
	Stock at 31 March 19–2	66	1,125
Gross profit			675
Office salaries		50	
Property expenses ($\frac{1}{5} \times 90$)		18	
Canteen expenses ($\frac{1}{5} \times 40$)		8	
Selling and distribution		40	
Other administration		45	
Depreciation: office machinery		5	
canteen equipment		2	168
Net profit on trading			507
Add factory profit		100	
Less increase in provision for unrealised profit		(3)	97
Overall Net profit			604

(b) Balance sheet extract at 31 March 19–2:

			£'000	£'000
Current assets				
Stocks	Raw materials			32
	Work in progress			54
	Finished goods		66	
	less provision for unrealised profit		6	60
				146

(c) Calculation of absorption cost of each unit completed in the year to 31 March 19–2:

	units
Sales	4,500
Increase in stock	132
less 'bought in'	(232)
Manufactured	4,400

Absorption cost per unit: $\dfrac{£1,000,000}{4,400} = £227.27$

Exercise 2

The Premier Manufacturing Co. Ltd.
Manufacturing, trading, profit and loss account
for the year to 31 December 19–8

		£	£	£
Raw materials	Stock at 1 Jan 19–8		18,000	
	Purchases	245,500		
	Carriage inwards	1,350	246,850	
			264,850	
	Stock at 31 Dec 19–8		22,000	242,850
Direct wages				351,000
Prime cost				593,850
Factory overheads				
Indirect wages			22,900	
Rent and rates			58,000	
Electricity			27,000	
Repairs and maintenance			10,000	
Insurance			10,200	
Motor vehicle expenses (50%)			8,800	
Cost of loose tools (15,000+13,650–13,400)			15,250	
Depreciation:	Freehold premises		7,200	
	Plant and machinery		43,000	
	Motor vehicles		10,500	212,850
				806,700
Work in progress at	1 Jan 19–8		27,800	
	31 Dec 19–8		(24,500)	3,300
				810,000
Factory profit on completed goods				90,000
Finished goods transferred to trading account				900,000
Sales				1,200,000
Cost of sales	Stock at 1 Jan 19–8		42,500	
	Goods transferred from factory		900,000	
			942,500	
Stock at 31 Dec 19–8			67,500	875,000
Gross profit				325,000
Discounts received				1,760
				326,760
Administration			74,000	
Selling and distribution			55,190	
Rent and rates			30,000	
Electricity			13,500	
Repairs and maintenance to offices			8,200	
Insurance			3,400	
Motor vehicle expenses (50%)			8,800	
Discounts allowed			2,140	
Debenture interest (800 + 800)			1,600	
Depreciation:	Freehold premises		2,400	
	Motor vehicles		10,500	
	Office machinery		5,200	
				214,930
Net profit on trading				111,830
Factory profit			90,000	
less increase in provision for unrealised profit			2,750	87,250
Net profit				199,080

Balance sheet as at 31 December 19–8

	Cost £	Depn £	Net £
Fixed assets			
Freehold property	240,000	105,600	134,400
Plant and machinery	215,000	168,000	47,000
Motor vehicles	84,000	63,000	21,000
Office machinery and equipment	26,000	23,200	2,800
Carried forward	565,000	359,800	205,200

		£	£	£
Brought forward				205,200
Current assets				
Stocks	Raw materials		22,000	
	Work in progress		24,500	
	Finished goods	67,500		
	less provision for unrealised profit	6,750	60,750	
	Loose tools		13,400	
			120,650	
Debtors			114,640	
Bank			54,260	
Prepayments (1,800 + 600 + 1,000 + 800)			4,200	
			293,750	
Amounts due to be settled within one year				
Creditors		23,540		
Accrued expenses (6,000+1,900+				
5,000+2,800+3,000+800)		19,500	43,040	250,710
				455,910
Amounts due to be settled after more than one year				
8% Debentures				20,000
				435,910
Share capital and reserves				
150,000 ordinary shares of £1				150,000
Retained profits (86,830 + 199,080)				285,910
				435,910

(b) Answer should include reference to:

(i) Accruals or matching concept: expenditure has been matched to revenue included in the accounts, and to period of time covered by the manufacturing, trading, profit and loss account. e.g. rent, wages, selling and distribution expenses have been adjusted for accrued expenditure; rates and insurance have been adjusted on a time basis for amounts prepaid.

(ii) Cost concept: All expenses and fixed assets have been recorded in the books at their cost to the company rather than at some other value. The net book value of the fixed assets represents the amount of the original cost of those assets being carried forward to be set against the revenue which those assets will earn in future periods. (Another example of the matching concept)

(iii) Going concern concept: The business has been regarded as likely to continue its operations in their present form for the foreseeable future. If there had been any likelihood of the present operations being discontinued or curtailed in the foreseeable future, fixed assets should have been shown in the balance sheet at their likely realisable values. Stocks of raw materials, work in progress and finished goods should have been valued on the basis of worth in an enforced sale instead of at cost.

Note: The question specifically requires you to comment on the concepts in relation to your answer to Part (a). A general discussion of the concepts unrelated to Part (a), no matter how good, would not be regarded as an answer to the question as set.

Chapter 17

17.2.2

The Beta Manufacturing Co. Ltd.
Manufacturing accounts for the three months to 31 May 19–2

	FIFO	LIFO	AVCO
	£	£	£
Direct materials Purchases	10,150	10,150	10,150
less closing stock	(2,210)	(2,070)	(2,163)
Direct wages	16,500	16,500	16,500
Prime cost	24,440	24,580	24,487
Variable overheads	4,000	4,000	4,000
Fixed overheads	11,200	11,200	11.200
Depreciation	3,180	3,180	3,180
Factory cost	42,820	42,960	42,867

Chapter 18

18.2.2

Bigthings Ltd.
Absorption cost statement for the month of March 19–2
Number of units: 2,000

	Unit cost	£
	£	
Direct materials	15	30,000
Direct labour	26	52,000
Prime cost	41	82,000
Factory overheads	($\frac{1}{12}$)	42,500
Depreciation: factory		1,500
plant and machinery		20,000
Factory cost		146,000
Salaries: sales staff		4,167
Wages: delivery van drivers		2,833
Motor van running costs		4,000
Depreciation of motor vans		1,250
Office rent		2,750
Other administration costs		21,000
Total cost		182,000

(a) If selling price is £100 per Whopper
sales will be £200,000;
Net profit will be £18,000

(b) Total profit of 40% of total cost = £72,800
Selling price = £254,800 ÷ 2,000 = £127.40

18.4.3

Rainbow Cloths Ltd.
Table of apportionment of overheads for a period of three months

Overhead expense	Basis of apportionment	Total	Spinning	Weaving	Dyeing
		£	£	£	£
Factory					
– amortisation of lease	Floor area	20,000	6,000	9,000	5,000
repairs & maintenance	Floor area	4,500	1,350	2,025	1,125
insurance	Floor area	2,000	600	900	500
Plant and machinery					
– depreciation	Cost	7,500	2,500	3,750	1,250
repairs & maintenance	Cost	9,000	3,000	4,500	1,500
insurance	Replacement cost	3,150	975	1,575	600
Stores – overhead costs	no. of requisitions	13,500	7,200	2,700	3,600
		59,650	21,625	24,450	13,575

18.5.2

The Speedy Transport Company

	Local C & D	Trunk services	Contract	Engineering	Building maintenance
	£	£	£	£	£
First apportionment	400,000	300,000	100,000	144,000	91,500
Second apportionment	108,000	18,000	12,000	(144,000)	6,000
Third apportionment	47,951	33,566	4,795	11,188	(97,500)
Fourth apportionment	8,391	1,399	932	(11,188)	466
Fifth apportionment	229	160	23	54	(466)
Sixth apportionment	41	7	6	(54)	
	564,612	353,132	117,756	–	–

18.5.4

The Speedy Transport Company

	Local C & D	Trunk services	Contract	Engineering	Building maintenance
	£	£	£	£	£
First apportionment	400,000	300,000	100,000	144,000	91,500
Second apportionment	108,000	18,000	12,000	(144,000)	6,000
Third apportionment	54,167	37,917	5,416	–	(97,500)
	562,167	355,917	117,416	–	–

18.5.6 **Wellhouse Ltd.**

(calculations are rounded)

Let a = total overheads of stores after apportionment of canteen overheads

and b = total overheads of canteen after apportionment of stores overheads

$a = £45,000 + (\frac{1}{20})b;$

$b = £15,000 + (\frac{1}{15})a$

$a - (\frac{1}{20})b = £45,000$

$b - (\frac{1}{15})a = £15,000$

$20a - b = £900,000$

$b - (\frac{1}{15})a = £\ 15,000$

$19(\frac{14}{15})a = £915,000; a = £45,903; b = £18,060$

	Apportionment				
	Workshop A	Workshop B	Workshop C	Stores	Canteen
	£	£	£	£	£
Apportioned	120,000	108,000	210,000	45,000	15,000
Stores	18,361	15,301	9,181	(45,903)	3,060
Canteen	7,224	5,418	4,515	903	(18,060)
	145,585	128,719	223,696	–	–

18.6.2 Anbin Ltd.

The total number of machine hours in period of 8 weeks is

$10 \times 50 \times 8 = 4,000$

Machine hour rate = $\dfrac{£82,000}{4,000}$ = £20.50

OAR for Ancrum = £20.50 × 2 $(\frac{1}{2})$ = £51.25

OAR for Bino = £20.50 × 1 $(\frac{1}{2})$ = £30.75

Overhead recovery in period of 8 weeks	£
Ancrum: 1,000 × £51.25	51,250
Bino: 1,000 × £30.75	30,750
Total overhead recovery	82,000

18.6.4 Belshaze Ltd.

OAR = $\dfrac{£54,600}{35 \times 40 \times 12}$ = $\dfrac{£54,600}{16,800}$ = £3.25

OAR per Wessex chair = 8 × £3.25 = £26

OAR per Cumbria chair = 10 × £3.25 = £32.50

	£
Total overheads in 12 week period	54,600
Overhead recovery from 800 Wessex chairs (800 × £26)	20,800
Balance of overheads to be recovered from Cumbria chairs	33,800

No. of Cumbria chairs = £33,800/32.50 = 1,040

18.6.6 Alcansted Ltd.

(i)   OAR: Electrolysis dept.(machine hour) $\dfrac{£17,340}{5,100}$ = £3.40

Filtration dept. (direct labour hour) $\dfrac{£19,800}{7,200}$ = £2.75

Eon Electrolysis (3 × £3.40) = £10.20 Filtration (4 × £2.75) = £11

Pysin   Electrolysis (2 × £3.40) = £6.80 Filtration (3 × £2.75) = £8.25

(ii)

Total overhead recovery		Electrolysis		Filtration
		£		£
Eon	(900 × £10.20)	9,180	(900 × £11)	9,900
Pysin	(1,200 × £6.80)	8,160	(1,200 × £8.25)	9,900
		17,340		19,800

(iii) Total cost statement

	Eon Per unit £	Eon 900 units £	Pysin Per unit £	Pysin 1,200 units £
Direct materials	2.00	1,800	5.00	6,000
Direct wages	20.00	18,000	20.00	24,000
Prime cost	22.00	19,800	25.00	30,000
Production o'heads	21.20	19,080		
(10.20 + 11.00)				
(6.80 + 8.25)			15.05	18,060
Total cost	43.20	38,880	40.05	48,060

Chapter 19

19.1.3

Alan Pannell

Job no.59			Video film Bona Fido Dog Foods		
Item			Estimate	Actual	Variance
			£	£	£
Direct materials			800	640	160
Direct labour					
Self –	18 hrs at £80	£1,440			
Assistant –	12 hrs at £20	240	1,680	1,900	(220)
Overheads 30 direct labour hours at £30 p.h.			900	1,050	(150)
Total cost			3,380	3,590	(210)
Profit margin			370	160	(210)
Price			£3,750	£3,750	–

19.3.6

Lladnar Ltd.
Contract 2354

19–3			£	19–3			£
Jan 1	Materials	b/d	65,000	Dec 31	Materials sold on site		14,000
	Plant and machinery	b/d	170,000		Plant transferred		38,000
	Work in progress	b/d	102,000		Work certified		460,000
Dec 31	Materials sent to site		360,000		Materials	c/d	32,000
	Plant sent to site		84,000		Plant and machinery	c/d	180,000
	Site expenses		91,000		Work in Progress	c/d	223,000
	Head office expenses		75,000				
			947,000				947,000
19–4							
Jan 1	Materials b/d		32,000				
	Plant and machinery	b/d	180,000				
	Work in progress	b/d	223,000				

Work Certified

19–3		£	19–3		£
Dec 31	Profit and loss account	580,000	Dec 31	Biggleswick Dist.Council	580,000

Biggleswick District Council

19–3		£	19–3	£
Dec 3	Work certified	580,000		

19.3.8

Collinson Construction plc

	Contract A	Contract B	Contract C	Contract D
Percentage complete	44	57.5	8.5	97
	£'000	£'000	£'000	£'000
Work certified to date	600			
Cost of work certified	(420)			
Notional profit	180			
Contract price		100		900
Costs to date		(65)		(700)
Estimated further costs		(48)		(20)
Profit/(Loss)		(13)		180

	£'000	£'000	£'000	£'000
£180K × 540/600	108			
£180K × 585/900				117
less taken into accounts up to				
31 December 19–2	50			70
Profit/(loss) for year to				
31 December 19–3	58	(13)		47

19.4.2

Bon Bon Ltd.

Process 1

19–3		£	19–3		£
Mar 31	Direct materials	3,000	Mar 31	Output transferred to Process 2	22,000
	Direct labour	5,000			
	Production overheads	14,000			
		22,000			22,000

Process 2

19–3		£	19–3		£
Mar 31	Materials from process 1	22,000	Mar 31	Output transferred to Process 3	32,500
	Added materials	1,500			
	Direct labour	1,000			
	Production overheads	8,000			
		32,500			32,500

Process 3

19–3		£	19–3		£
Mar 31	Materials from process 2	32,500	Mar 31	Transfer to finished goods	40,000
	Added materials	1,000			
	Direct labour	500			
	Production overheads	6,000			
		40,000			40,000

Cost of single box of Christmas crackers: £4

19.4.5

Plough Ltd.

Process 1

20 units		£	£
	Materials (20 × £20)	400	
	Direct labour (20 × 80% of £80)	1,280	
	Production overhead (20 × 80% of £120)	1,920	3,600
40 units			
	Materials (40 × 80% of £20)	640	
	Direct labour (40 × 50% of £80)	1,600	
	Production overheads (40 × 50% of £120)	2,400	4,640

Process 2

15 units			
	Materials transferred from Process 1 (all)		
	15 × £(20 + 80 + 120)	3,300	
	Added materials (15 × 25% of £8)	30	
	Direct labour (15 × 25% of £32)	120	
	Production overhead (15 × 25% of £60)	225	3,675
	Total value of work in progress		11,915

19.4.8

Baldock Ltd.

Process 1

Products A and B are not measurable in similar units and joint processing costs are apportioned according to sales value.

		£
Sales values:	Product A: 500 litres @ £18	9,000
	Product B: 1,600 kilos @ £15	24,000
		33,000
Apportionment of Process 1 costs (£27,500)		£
	Product A: 9,000/33,000 × £27,500	7,500
	Product B: 24,000/33,000 × £27,500	20,000
		27,500

Process 2

Both products B1 and B2 are measurable in kilos, so joint costs are apportioned on basis of quantities produced (Product B1, 300 kilos, product B2, 900 kilos, total 1,200 kilos)

Apportionment of Process 2 costs (£20,000 from 1 and £2,000 further costs in 2 = £22,000)

		£
Product B1	300/1,200 × £22,000	5,500
Product B2	900/1,200 × £22,000	16,500
		22,000
Unit costs:	Product A £(7,500 + £50)/500	= £15.10
	Product B1 £5,500/300	= £18.33
	Product B2 £16,500/900	= £18.33

19.4.11 Sandybeds Ltd.

Process 1

	units	£		units	£
Direct materials	4,000	32,400	Normal loss	400	1,600
Direct labour		18,640	Process 2	3,800	77,520
Production overheads		24,000			
	4,000	75,040			
Abnormal gain	200	4,080			
	4,200	79,120		4,200	79,120

Process 2

	units	£		units	£
Direct materials from process 1	3,800	77,520	Normal loss	500	2,000
Added direct materials	1,200	6,480	Finished goods	4,250	127,500
Direct wages		20,000	Abnormal loss	250	7,500
Production overheads		33,000			
	5,000	137,000		5,000	137,000

Abnormal Gain

	£		£
Scrap (200 × £4)	800	Process 1	4,080
Profit and loss	3,280		
	4,080		4,080

Abnormal Loss

	£		£
Process 2	7,500	Scrap (250 × £4)	1,000
		Profit and loss	6,500
	7,500		7,500

Scrap

	£		£
Normal loss			
Process 1 (400 × £4)	1,600	Bank – Process 1 (200 × £4)	800
Process 2 (500 × £4)	2,000	Process 2 (750 × £4)	3,000
Abnormal loss	1,000	Abnormal gain	800
	4,600		4,600

Workings:

Process 1

Cost per unit of output and abnormal gain:

$$\frac{£(75,040 - 1,600)}{90\% \text{ of } 4,000} = \frac{£73,440}{3,600} = £20.40$$

Process 2

Cost per unit of output and abnormal loss:

$$\frac{£(137,000 - 2,000)}{90\% \text{ of } 5,000} = \frac{£135,000}{4,500} = £30$$

Chapter 20

20.5.2 **D.Brown Ltd.**

Marginal cost of 5,000 bicycles:

		£
Direct expenses:	Materials	300,000
	Labour	400,000
	Royalties	50,000
Other variable costs:		
	Selling and distribution	20,000
	Administration	10,000
		780,000

Marginal cost per bicycle £156
Selling price per bicycle £260
Contribution per bicycle £104

Total fixed costs:	£
Selling and distribution	200,000
Administration	220,960
	420,960

(i) Break even point: 420,960/104 = 4,047.69
or 4,048 bicycles
or sales total of £1,052,399.40

(ii) Margin of safety: (5,000 – 4,048) = 952 or 19.04%

Exercise 2 **Mei Ling Ltd.**

Marginal cost of each lantern:

	£	£	£
Direct material	8		
Direct labour	12	20	
Unit selling price	£25	£23	£22
Unit contribution	£5	£3	£2
No. sold	400	600	1,100
Sales	£10,000	£13,800	£24,200
C/s ratio	20%	13.04%	9.09%
Total contribution	£2,000	£1,799	£2,199.78
Fixed costs per week	£700	£700	£805
Profit	£1,300	£1,099	£1,394.78

Provided there is a demand for 1,100 lanterns per week, Mei Ling Ltd. should reduce the unit price of lanterns to £22.

Exercise 3 **T.Lambrou Ltd.**

The answer, which should be in good report form, should contain the following information.

Calculation of contribution per unit of accessory

	£
Components	25
Labour (4 × £9)	36
Other variable costs	6
Marginal cost	67
Contribution	13
List selling price	80

Proposal 1.

Selling price will be reduced by 10% to £72. This is £5 in excess of the marginal cost and will produce a unit contribution. The proposal may therefore be acceptable. Profit would be increased by 1,000 × £5 (£5,000)

Proposal 2.

Selling price will be reduced by 20% to £64. This is £3 below marginal cost and is therefore unacceptable. Acceptance of the proposal would affect profit adversely by 2,000 × £3 (£6,000)

Exercise 4   Ninasim & Son Ltd.

The 'bought in' price of each product should be compared with the marginal cost of its production. Ignore variable selling and distribution costs as these will be incurred whether the products are manufactured by Ninasim or Husseyin & Husseyin.

Marginal cost per unit of production:

	Ninabits	Simlabits	Sonybits
	£	£	£
Direct materials	18	7	9
Direct labour	25	21	26
Marginal cost	43	28	35
'Bought in' price	50	30	33

Ninasim & Son Ltd. should continue to manufacture Ninabits and Simlabits as they can do so more cheaply than they can buy the items from outside.

It would appear that Sonybits should be bought from Husseyin & Husseyin and Co. Ltd. but this might be subject to other considerations such as the cost of discontinuing production, costs of making workers redundant, the possibility of using the freed resources profitably for other purposes etc. etc.

Exercise 5   C.Yiannakou

This is a question concerning limiting factors and is solved by finding the contribution per unit of limiting factor for each product.

	Boxydon	Doxydon	Moxydon
	£	£	£
Unit cost			
Material	6	12	8
Labour	32	40	40
Marginal cost	38	52	48
Selling price	50	64	60
Contribution	12	12	12
Contribution per			
sq. metre of Boxium	4	2	3
Rank as follows:	1	3	2

Revised production schedule:

Item	Production in units	Usage Sq. metres	Balance Sq. metres	Contribution £
Boxydons	10,000	30,000	62,000	120,000
Moxydons	11,000	44,000	18,000	132,000
Doxydons	3,000	18,000	–	36,000
				288,000

20.6.2

Profit statement:		£	£
Sales (25,000 × £14)			350,000
Variable cost (25,000 × £10)		250,000	
Fixed cost		80,000	330,000
Profit			20,000

B/e point = $\dfrac{£80,000}{£4}$ = 20,000 units

Volume sensitivity: $\dfrac{5,000}{25,000}$ × 100 = 20%

Price sensitivity: Price to break even = $\dfrac{£330,000}{25,000}$ = £13.20p per unit, or a reduction of £0.80 or 5.7%

Sensitivity to variable cost = $\dfrac{£20,000}{£250,000}$ × 100 = 8%

Sensitivity to fixed cost = $\dfrac{£20,000}{£80,000}$ × 100 = 25%

Chapter 21
21.4
M.Cohen
Sales Budget for the year to 31 December 19–4

19–4	Product A			Product B			
	Volume	Price	Amount	Volume	Price	Amount	Total
		£	£		£	£	£
Jan	1,000	100	100,000	500	120	60,000	160,000
Feb	1,000	100	100,000	530	120	63,600	163,600
Mar	1,050	110	115,500	530	120	63,600	179,100
Apr	1,050	110	115,500	530	120	63,600	179,100
May	1,050	110	115,500	530	126	66,780	182,280
Jun	1,050	110	115,500	583	126	73,458	188,958
Jul	1,050	110	115,500	583	126	73,458	188,958
Aug	1,134	110	124,740	600	126	75,600	200,340
Sep	1,134	115.5	130,977	600	126	75,600	206,577
Oct	1,134	115.5	130,977	624	168	104,832	235,809
Nov	1,134	115.5	130,977	624	168	104,832	235,809
Dec	1,134	115.5	130,977	624	168	104,832	235,809
	12,920		1,426,148	6,858		930,192	2,356,340

21.5.2

Exercise 1
Murude plc
Production Budget for the year to 31 December 19–2

Quarter to	Mar 31	Jun 30	Sep 30	Dec 31
Balance b/f	16,000	19,000	12,000	2,000
Production*	45,000	45,000	45,000	45,000
	61,000	64,000	57,000	47,000
Sales	42,000	52,000	55,000	32,000
Balance c/f	19,000	12,000	2,000	15,000

* monthly production × 3

Exercise 2
Shwish Ltd.
Production Budget for the year to 31 December 19–3

Quarter to	Mar 31	Jun 30	Sep 30	Dec 31
Balance b/f	600,000	650,000	600,000	400,000
Production*	300,000	300,000	300,000	300,000
	900,000	950,000	900,000	700,000
Sales	250,000	350,000	500,000	400,000
Balance c/f	650,000	600,000	400,000	300,000

* monthly production × 3

Exercise 3
The Aaisha Company
Production Budget for the four months to 30 April 19–5

Month	January	February	March	April
Balance b/f	1,000	2,000	4,000	5,000
Production	7,000	10,000	8,000	7,000
	8,000	12,000	12,000	12,000
Sales	6,000	8,000	7,000	8,000
Balance c/f	2,000	4,000	5,000	4,000

21.6.2
Pi Manufacturers Ltd.
Purchasing budget for four months to 30 June 19–1

	March	April	May	June
Kilos purchased	2,400	3,000	2,700	1,800
Price per kilo	£1.50	£1.50	£1.50	£2
Cost of purchases	£3,600	£4,500	£4,050	£3,600

Note: Purchases in March will be in respect of the material forming the product to be sold in May (3 kilos per unit sold), and so on.

21.7.2

Sales budget

	April	May	June
Units	5,000	7,000	8,000
Price	£2	£4	£4
Revenue	£10,000	£28,000	£32,000

Production budget

	April	May	June
Next month's sales	7,000	8,000	10,000
Closing stock	2,800	3,600	4,400
Opening stock	(2,000)	(2,800)	(3,600)
Production	7,800	8,800	10,800

Materials purchase budget

	April	May	June
Next month's production (units)	8,800	10,800	11,800*
× 5 litres per unit	44,000	54,000	59,000
Cost at 25p per unit	£11,000	£13,500	£14,750

* July production: August sales 11,000 plus increase in stock 800

Cash budget

	April £	May £	June £
Receipts			
Cash sales	10,000	28,000	32,000
Payments	9,750*	11,000	13,500

* March purchases for April production, 7,000 units plus increase in stock, 800 units. 7,800 X 5 litres at 25p = £9,750.

21.8.2

Kadriye
Cash budget for the year to 31 December 19–2

Quarter to	March 31 £	June 30 £	Sept. 30 £	Dec. 31 £
Receipts				
Cash received from debtors	10,000	21,000	28,000	34,000
Sale of car		3,500		
Loan			6,000	
	10,000	24,500	34,000	34,000
Payments				
Creditors	28,000	16,000	20,000	17,000
Purchase of motor van	5,000			
Wages	6,000	6,000	6,000	6,000
Rent	1,200	1,200	1,200	1,200
Drawings	1,500	1,500	1,500	1,500
Bank interest		795		580
	41,700	25,495	28,700	26,280
Net receipts/(payments)	(31,700)	(995)	5,300	7,720
Balance b/f	15,800	(15,900)	(16,895)	(11,595)
Balance c/f	(15,900)	(16,895)	(11,595)	(3,875)

21.9.2

(a)

Courante Ltd.
Cash budget for four months to 30 April 19–2

	January £	February £	March £	April £
Receipts				
Sales – cash	10,000	11,200	12,000	13,200
Debtors	17,000	15,000	16,800	18,000
	27,000	26,200	28,800	31,200

	£	£	£	£
Payments				
Creditors	9,000	10,000	8,000	12,000
Selling and distribution	1,200	2,500	2,800	3,000
Administration	8,000	8,000	8,000	8,000
Interim dividend				2,500
Plant & machinery			24,000	
	18,200	20,500	42,800	25,500
Net receipts/(payments)	8,800	5,700	(14,000)	5,700
Balance b/f	9,500	18,300	24,000	10,000
Balance c/f	18,300	24,000	10,000	15,700

(b)

Forecast profit and loss account for the four months to 30 April 19–2

	£	£
Sales		116,000
Cost of sales:		
Stock at 1 Jan 19–2	12,000	
Purchases	45,000	
	57,000	
Stock at 30 Apr 19–2	9,000	48,000
Gross profit		68,000
Selling and distribution	12,600	
Administration	34,100	46,700
		21,300
Interest on debentures		400
		20,900
Interim dividend		2,500
		18,400
Transfer to general reserve		10,000
Retained profit for the year		8,400
Retained profit brought forward		2,700
Retained profit carried forward		11,100

Forecast balance sheet as at 30 April 19–2

	Cost	Depn	Net
	£	£	£
Fixed assets			
Freehold premises	20,000	4,200	15,800
Plant and machinery	39,000	10,800	28,200
	59,000	15,000	44,000
Current assets			
Stock		9,000	
Trade debtors		19,800	
Prepaid expenses		1,300	
Bank		15,700	
		45,800	
Amounts due to be paid within one year			
Trade creditors	15,000		
Selling and distribution	3,300		
Debenture interest	400	18,700	27,100
			71,100
12% Debentures			10,000
			61,100
Share capital and reserves			
Ordinary shares of £1			25,000
General reserve			25,000
Retained profit			11,100
			61,100

Chapter 22

22.2.2

Brekkinuts
Flexed budget for 190,000 packets.

		£
Direct materials		9,500
Direct labour		11,400
Variable overheads		
Production		4,750
Selling & distribution		1,045
		26,695
Fixed overheads		
Production	6,000	
Selling & distribution	9,900	
Administration	8,000	23,900
		50,595

22.3.2

Reflections Ltd

Total sales variance £(450,000 – 448,950) = £1,050 (A)

	£	
Master budget sales: 150,000 tins @ £3 =	450,000	
Flexed budget sales: 148,600 tins @ £3 =	445,800	
Volume variance	4,200	(A)

	£	
Flexed budget sales	445,800	
Actual sales	448,950	
Price variance	3,150	(F)

22.4.2

Laser, Digit and Co.

Total cost variance (MBTC – ATC)= £(249,000 – 287,500) = £38,500 (A)

Quantity variance (MBTC – FBTC) = £(249,000 – 284,400) = £35,400 (A)

	Flexed budget 1,800 players	Actual	Total variances	
	£	£	£	
Direct materials	108,000	110,000	2,000	(A)
Direct labour	54,000	52,500	1,500	(F)
Variable overheads	50,400	55,000	4,600	(A)
Fixed overheads	72,000	70,000	2,000	(F)
	284,400	287,500	3,100	(A)

22.5.2

Exercise 1

P.A.M. Sportsgear Ltd.

		Master budget	Flexed budget	Actual
		£	£	£
Direct materials		50,400	54,600	63,992.50
Direct labour		36,000	39,000	39,077.50
Production overheads–				
	variable	5,400	5,850	6,000.00
	fixed	16,200	16,200	16,000.00
		108,000	115,650	125,070.00

Total variances

	£	
Total budget variance	17,070	(A)
Quantity variance	7,850	(A)
Total materials variance	9,392.50	(A)
Total labour variance	77.50	(A)
Total overhead variance	50	(F)

Sub–variances

	£	
Materials usage variance (9,100 – 8,950)kilos × £6	900.00	(F)
Materials price variance £(6 – 7.15) × 8950	10,292.50	(A)
	9,392.50	(A)
Labour efficiency variance (3,900 – 3,850)hrs × £10	500.00	(F)

	£	
Labour rate variance £(10 – 10.15) × 3,850	577.50	(A)
	77.50	(A)
Overhead variances – Variable	150	(A)
Fixed	200	(F)
	50	(F)

Exercise 2

	£	
Actual overheads £(25,200 + 39,250) =	64,450	
Total budgeted overheads £(24,640 + 38,080) =	62,720	
Overhead expenditure variance	1,730	(A)
Total budgeted overheads	62,720	
Actual hours × OAR (6,600 × 9.8)	64,680	
Overhead volume variance	1,960	(F)
Actual hours × OAR	64,680	
Standard hours produced × OAR (6,800 × 9,80)	66,640	
Overhead efficiency variance	1,960	(F)

Chapter 23

23.2.2

	Project A	Project B	Project C
	£	£	£
Total profits (4 years)	60,000	70,000	55,000
Average profits p.a.	15,000	17,500	13,750
ARR (on £75,000)	20%	23.34%	18.32%

Whilst B would seem to be the more attractive project, the ARR on B is only slightly better than the ARR on A. If, for this purpose, the funds generated by the operations can be roughly equated with cash inflows, A has the better profile in the earlier years.

There is insufficient information to make a proper judgement between the three projects as the question gives no indication of the their life expectancies. Furthermore, ARR does not take account of the time–value of money.

The judgement is being made on estimated figures of profit which may, with time, prove to be materially inaccurate.

23.3.2   Flexi–Budgets Ltd.

Uniflex and Duoflex both have pay–back periods of 3 years. Duoflex would appear to entail less risk than Uniflex because the cash inflow is greater in years 1 and 2. It would therefore be preferred to Uniflex although the cash inflow of Uniflex is expected to be better in the later years than would be the case with Duoflex.

Triflex would not be considered as the payback period is over 4 years.

23.4.2

Effective rate of debenture interest: 8% × 0.7 = 5.6%

	Cost	Amount	Weight*	Cost × weight
	%	£000		
Ordinary shares	5	600	75	375
Preference shares	6	120	15	90
Debentures	5.6	80	10	56
		800	100	521

Weighted average cost of capital: $\dfrac{521}{100}$ = 5.21%

23.4.3   Wyezed Ltd.

Year	Discounting	Goliath		Cyclops	
	factor	Net receipts	NPV	Net receipts	NPV
	15%	£	£	£	£
0	1	(80,000)	(80,000)	(120,000)	(120,000)
1	0.870	24,000	20,880	42,000	36,540
2	0.756	24,000	18,144	42,000	31,752

		£	£	£	£
3	0.658	24,000	15,792	42,000	27,636
4	0.572	24,000	13,728	42,000	24,024
5	0.497	24,000	11,928	42,000	20,874
	Net present values		472		20,826

Both machines have positive net present values when the net receipts are discounted at 15% although the NPV for Goliath is very small and could become negative given the uncertainties connected with forecasting.

As Cyclops has the much larger NPV, Wyezed Ltd. should consider purchasing that machine.

23.5.2   Abednego

Net receipts of £6,000 for 5 years discounted at 14% produce NPV of £20,592; less initial outlay of £20,000 = £592

Discounted at 16%, NPV = (£356)

Therefore IRR = 14% + 2% $\times \dfrac{592}{592 + 356}$ = 15.25%

23.6.2

NPV of project at 8% = £39,230. IRR = 11.7%

Increase in NPV of outlay: $\dfrac{39,230}{400,000} \times 100$ = 9.8%

Decrease in NPV of net receipts: $\dfrac{39,230}{439,230} \times 100$ = 8.9%

Increase in cost of capital: $\dfrac{3.7}{8} \times 100$ = 46.25%

Chapter 24

24.11.2

Exercise 1		**Anita and Leila**	**19–2**	**19–3**
(i)	R.O.C.E net profit/capital employed			
	$\dfrac{11,250}{50,550}$		22.26%	
	$\dfrac{21,000}{74,750}$			28.09%
(ii)	Gross profit percentage gross profit/turnover			
	$\dfrac{40,000}{125,000}$		32%	
	$\dfrac{55,500}{150,000}$			37%
(iii)	Net profit percentage net profit/turnover			
	$\dfrac{11,250}{125,000}$		9%	
	$\dfrac{21,000}{150,000}$			14%
(iv)	Current ratio Current assets:current liabilities			
	23,100:10,800		2.14:1	
	26,505:15,025			1.76:1

	19–2	19–3

(v) Liquid ratio
Current assets less stock:current liabilities

	19–2	19–3
11,600:10,800	1.07:1	
14,380:15,025		0.96:1

(vi) Stockturn
cost of sales/average stock

$$\frac{85,000}{10,000}$$ 8.5 times

$$\frac{94,500}{11,812.5}$$ 8 times

(vii) Debtors' ratio
debtors/turnover × 365

$$\frac{9,590}{125,000} \times 365$$ 28 days

$$\frac{14,380}{150,000} \times 365$$ 35 days

(viii) Creditors' ratio
creditors/purchases × 365

$$\frac{10,800}{88,000} \times 365$$ 44.8 days

$$\frac{10,425}{95,125} \times 365$$ 40 days

Exercise 2

John Kelworthy
Ken Porter
Trading, profit and loss account for the year to 30 June 19–3

	£	£
Sales		231,000
Cost of sales		
Opening stock	6,160	
Purchases	118,580	
	124,740	
Closing stock	9,240	115,500
Gross profit		115,500
Expenses other than depreciation	76,125	
Depreciation	10,500	86,625
Net profit		28,875

Balance sheet as at 30 June 19–3

		£	£
Fixed assets			42,000
Current assets			
Stock		9,240	
Debtors		17,721	
		26,961	
Current liabilities			
Creditors	11,371		
Bank overdraft	2,110	13,481	13,480
			55,480
Capital at 1 July 19–2 (balancing figure)			31,805
Net profit			28,875
			60,680
Less drawings			5,200
			55,480

Chapter 25

25.2.2   **The Batwing Manufacturing Company**
                                      Cash operating cycle

                                                                    Days

Raw materials turnover
Average stock = $\frac{1}{2}$ (6,500 + 8,840) = 7,670

$$\frac{7,670}{99,985} \times 365$$ 28

Work in progress turnover
Average work in progress = $\frac{1}{2}$ (7,800 + 7,100) = 7,450

$$\frac{7,450}{151,072} \times 365$$ 18

Finished goods turnover
Average stock of finished goods
$\frac{1}{2}$ (15,000 + 16,754) = 15,877

$$\frac{15,877}{181,100} \times 365$$ $\underline{32}$

Debtors ratio

$$\frac{18,000}{211,970} \times 365$$ $\underline{31}$

                                                                    109

Creditors ratio

$$\frac{15,764}{95,900} \times 365$$ $\underline{60}$

Cash operating cycle $\underline{49}$

25.7.2   **Apex Ltd. and Base Ltd.**

(a)

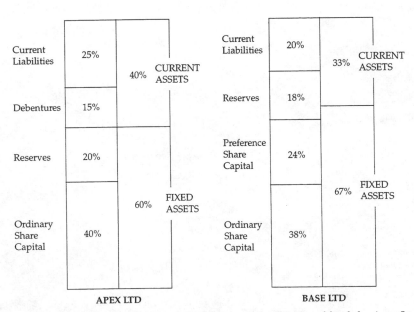

Diagrammatic representation of the sources of finance and utilisation of funds by Apex Ltd. and Base Ltd as at 31 March 19–1.

(b) Answer should include reference to:

	Apex Ltd.	Base Ltd.
Current ratios	1.6:1	1.67:1
Capital structure: gearing	$\dfrac{300}{800 + 400 + 300}$ 20%	$\dfrac{500}{800 + 380 + 500}$ 29.76%
Earnings (after interest/preference dividend)	£30,000	£20,000
Earnings per share	3.75p	2.5p

Index